HISTORY OF
INDIAN NATIONAL MOVEMENT

By the Same Author

- International Law
- International Politics
- International Relations

HISTORY OF
THE INDIAN NATIONAL MOVEMENT

PRAKASH CHANDRA
Retd. Head, Deptt. of Political Science
B.S.M. (P.G.) College, Roorkee

VIKAS PUBLISHING HOUSE PVT LTD

VIKAS PUBLISHING HOUSE PVT LTD

576, Masjid Road, Jangpura, New Delhi-110 014 Ph. 4615313, 4615570
Email: chawlap @ giasdl01. vsnl.net.in, Fax: 91-11-3276593

First Floor, N.S. Bhawan, 4th Cross 4th Main
Gandhi Nagar, Bangalore-560 009 Ph. 2204639

Distributors:

UBS PUBLISHERS' DISTRIBUTORS LTD

- 5, Ansari Road, **New Delhi**-110002 Ph. 3273601, 3266646
- Apeejay Chambers, 5 Wallace St., **Mumbai**-400001 Ph. 2070827, 2076971
- 10, First Main Road, Gandhi Nagar, **Bangalore**-560009 Ph. 2263901
- 6, Sivaganga Road, Nungambakkam, **Chennai**-600034 Ph. 8276355
- 8/1-B, Chowringhee Lane, **Calcutta**-700016 Ph. 2441821, 2442910
- 5-A, Rajendra Nagar, **Patna**-800016 Ph. 652856, 656169
- 80, Noronha Road, Cantonment, **Kanpur**-208004 Ph. 369124, 362665

Copyright © P. Chandra, 1997

First Edition, 1997

Laser-Typeset at PROMPT COMPUTER SYSTEMS, Jangpura, New Delhi-14
Printed at Vishal Printers, Delhi - 110032

Dedicated
to
Our Freedom Fighters
In the Golden Jubilee Year
of Independence

CONTENTS

PREFACE

Today, as India approaches the celebration of its fifty years of independence, it appears that country seems to have lost its sense of direction and purpose. There has been a massive erosion of values and a rapid decline in the country's political and social institutions. Criminalisation of civil society and the political process, communalisation of the political landscape and corruption pose a severe threat to the country's polity. The challenge faced by India at the moment is grave indeed. It calls for introspection. In the opinion of the author, the remedy lies in reforging our links with the legacy of the Indian freedom struggle. This book seeks to do just this.

This book is organised in three parts. The first part covers in detail the events of the Indian Freedom Movement that occurred from 1857 to 1947. Besides the landmark events, this part of the book highlights the contributions of the leading luminaries of the freedom movement who through their thoughts, actions and dare-devilries provided the saga of our freedom struggle an epical dimension.

The second part deals in depth with the phenomenon of communalism in modern India which, the author is of the view, was mainly responsible for the tragic denouncement of the Indian freedom struggle.

The third part of the study presents a systematic portrayal of the efforts made by the Indian political leaders. The Hindu revivalists and spiritual nationalists, the Moderates and the Extremists, the Liberals, the revolutionaries and the leftists for emancipating their motherland. It also makes an analytical study of their social, economic and political ideas having strong bearings on the Indian Freedom Movement.

The author is indebted to all those who have helped him in various ways in the writing of this book. He is particularly grateful to those authors whose writings he has quoted profusely. Here, special mention may be made of A.R. Desai's 'Social Background of Indian Nationalism'; J.P. Suda's 'Indian Constitutional Development And National Movement;

Bipin Chandra's 'India's Struggle for Independence' and 'Communalism
In Modern India'; Anita Inder Singh's 'Origins of the Partition of India';
S.R. Mehrotra's 'Towards India's Freedom and Partition'; Ayesha Jalal's
'The Sole Spokesman'; K.K. Aziz's 'History of the Partition of India'
(IV Vols.); V.P. Verma's 'Modern Indian Political Thought' and Vishnu
Bhagwan's 'Indian Political Thinkers'.

P. Chandra

PART-I

HISTORY OF THE INDIAN FREEDOM MOVEMENT (1857-1947)

Chapter 1

FEATURES OF THE INDIAN FREEDOM MOVEMENT

15th August 1947 marked the end of a colonial era and the realisation of the cherished dream of self-rule for which generations of Indians had fought for about a century. But tragically enough, the birth of a free nation was accompanied by its simultaneous breakup too. The result was a tragic bloodbath. History will never forget that the Indian state was born out of the pyres of one of the biggest communal holocausts in recorded history. In its ferocity, in its unexpectedness, in its scale of carnage, and in the scars it left behind, the partition of India has no other parallel. Regrettably, India achieved her freedom in the midst of one of the most shameful and terrifying interludes of savagery in human history. Admittedly, this climactic finale soured the fruits of freedom. There was a mixed feeling of ecstasy and agony all around. Not surprisingly, while all other leaders were basking in the glow of the dawn of freedom, Gandhi, painfully aware of the terrible tragedy, refused to celebrate the birth of free India and Pakistan. It was a personal trauma for Gandhi to see the undoing of his life time's work (Hindu-Muslim unity), and be a helpless witness to a horrible holocaust. Indeed, the partition and the communal carnage which accompanied it were a sad commentary on a movement which had prided itself on secularism and nonviolence under the leadership of the Mahatma.

SPECIAL FEATURES OF THE INDIAN FREEDOM MOVEMENT

The Indian freedom movement had some distinctive character and unique features: Undoubtedly, the Indian national movement was the biggest and the most wide-spread anti-imperialist movement in world history. It was the pioneer of liberation movements in Asia and Africa. Its national leadership always thought of national freedom in the context of international politics. Since the days of Raja Ram Mohan Roy, the Indian leaders had developed a broad international outlook. They maintained close link with the progressive, anti-colonial and anti-imperialist forces of the world. As early as 1930 the Congress proposed to call a convention of Asian nations to prepare a blue-print for Pan-Asiatic Federation in India. Even earlier, C.R. Das had projected for the first time the idea of an Asiatic Federation or a Union of Asian States at the Gaya Congress in 1922. To illustrate, China was greeted for attaining full and complete freedom and nationhood, and so were the people of Egypt, Syria and Iraq. The Congress sent a representative to the Second Congress of the League Against Imperialism. When Japan unleashed a new wave of aggression on China, the Indian National Congress denounced this aggression and boycotted Japanese goods. Also as a mark of sympathy and solidarity it sent a medical mission to China. Nehru visited China on the eve of the Second World War. In August 1942, the Quit India Resolution also stated "the freedom of India must be the symbol and prelude to the freedom of all other Asian nations." When independence was still in the offing, an unofficial Asian Relations Conference was convened in March 1947 to discuss common political, economic and cultural problems. In January 1949, the official Asian Conference was called to devise suitable means to counter Dutch aggression against Indonesia.

Another dominant characteristic that marks it out from other great revolutions in history was its tremendous sweep. The Indian National Movement was undoubtedly the biggest mass movement modern society has ever seen. It was all inclusive, comprising all patriotic elements drawn from diverse regions of the subcontinent and covering all religious communities, urban and rural segments. The Indian National Congress, which provided its leadership, included within its fold, individuals and groups which subscribed to widely divergent political and ideological perspectives. It was a popular, multi-class movement. It is incorrect to characterise it as a movement led or controlled by the bourgeoisie, as interpreted by some leftists. From the initial stage the movement adopted a pro-poor orientation, which was further strengthened with the advent of Gandhi and the rise of the leftists who struggled to make the movement adopt a socialist outlook.

Besides, the Indian national movement brought out not a few but a galaxy of glittering personalities, some of whom were living legends. Probably no other nation has been endowed with such an array of towering titans in one period for such a long time.

One more peculiarity of the Indian national movement was that neither its pioneers nor subsequent leaders evolved or accepted a materialist philosophy. All leaders of Indian nationalism in the philosophical, political or cultural field such as Raja Ram Mohan Roy, S.N. Bannerjea, Gokhale, Tilak, B.C. Pal, Aurobindo Ghosh, Lala Lajpat Rai, Tagore, Gandhi, Azad, Iqbal, J.C. Bose and others stood, in different ways and varying degrees, for a revision or restoration of traditional religions. None of them challenged or repudiated religion, or subscribed to the philosophy of materialism, in the formative phase of the movement. "This was in contrast to the period of rising and growing nationalism in Europe, which held a number of philosophers and scientists like Holbach, Diderot, Haechel, Feuerbach and Marx, who were thorough-going materialists. In addition to them, this period projected agnostic philosophers like Kant and Herbert Spencer and sceptical thinkers like David Hume.[1] Unfortunately, the history of the Indian national movement does not record the name of a single outstanding materialist, agnostic or sceptical philosopher who could give a really secular (non-religious) direction to Indian nationalism as in Europe. The only notable exception was M.N. Roy. No doubt, Roy was an outstanding and thorough-going materialist thinker but he could not make a dent in the nationalist movement, as he had no popular base. Ofcourse, rationalist and materialist philosophy and ideas slowly began to spread in India after 1930, but those political groups who subscribed to Marxism as their philosophy, did not play more than a peripheral part in the Indian National Movement.

As such, the Indian freedom movement, which was wholly nationalistic and fully committed to secularism from its early days, was overlaid with religiosity. The Hindu leaders in their writings and speeches instinctively used the imagery and idiom of Hinduism. Of course, this did help them in establishing an immediate rapport with the bulk of the Indian masses for whom Hindu symbols and metaphors were the warp and woof of their socio-religious consciousness. But unfortunately, this compromised the secular credentials of the Indian National Congress and, no wonder, majority of the Muslims came to look upon it as a Hindu organisation. "The strong Hindu tinge in much of the nationalist thought, propaganda and agitation and their permeation through ideas associated with Hindu religion inspite of the basically secular approach and programme of the Congress tended to repel and alienate Muslims instinctively". The Muslim perception was neatly stated by Maulana Mohd. Ali: "Whatever may be the inspiration of Hinduism as a religious creed, the educated Hindus made it a rallying symbol for political unity. Past history was ransacked for new political formulae and by a natural and inevitable process nationality and patriotism began to be associated with Hinduism."[2]

Another feature of the Indian national movement was that it was the first non-violent freedom movement. The Indian National Congress, which provided its mainstream leadership, at no stage subscribed to violent methods to achieve its goal. The stress on non-violence or Satyagraha as the means of securing national freedom and the emphasis on spiritualisation of politics from Raja Ram Mohan Roy to M.N. Roy is the hallmark of our freedom movement. "History does not record any other instance in which a subject people have achieved freedom from foreign bondage without shedding the blood of their opponents on a large scale. Revolutions in the world history have always been associated in the past with violence and bloodshed. But India has demonstrated to the world for the first time that a great and mighty revolution can be brought by non-violence and peaceful means. Remarkably, the Indian freedom struggle was essentially a peaceful movement with marks of few blood spots. In this movement, history witnessed the discovery of a new technique of political revolution which produced something like a miracle.[3] It is remarkable that when the masters and the slaves parted (1947) they did so not as foes but as friends. To win freedom from a nation is a great thing but to win the same nation in the process of struggle is something much greater and this is what our national movement achieved.[4]

Finally, although "the Congress was the mainstream but not the only stream of our national movement: the pre-Congress peasant and tribal movements, the Revolutionistsm, the Ghadr and Home-Rule Movement, the Akali and Temple Reform Movements of the 1920s, the peasant and working class struggles, the state peoples' movement etc. were other streams[5]. Thus there were a number of persons and movements outside the Congress-fold who played a notable role in this history. Here special mention may be made of revolutionaries like Sachindra Nath Sanyal, Bhagat Singh, Chandra Shekhar Azad, Surya Sen, Rash Behari Bose of the I.N.A., led by the S.C. Bose of the RIN Revolt, the socialists who kept alive the spirit of struggle after the 1942 repression, the liberals, communists, Royists, and other activists who worked incessantly among the peasants, labour and the student's organisations. All of these played a crucial role in spreading political consciousness and in mobilising the masses and the youth. They all became an integral part of the Indian National Movement.

Notes

1. Desai, A.R., *Social Background of Indian Nationalism*, Popular Prakashan, Bombay, 1989, p.296

2. Quoted in Gill, S.S., *Religion And Politics in India*, Indian Express, 3 Feb., 1987,

3. Suda, J.P., Indian Constitutional Development and National Movement, Jai Prakash Nath Co. Educational Publishers Meerut, 1956, p.382

4. Prasad, Bimal, 'Gandhi, Nehru & JP-Studies in Leadership' Chanakya Publishers N. Delhi 1985, p. 175

5. Chandra, Bipan, (ed.) 'India's Struggle' For Independence', Viking, New Delhi, 1988, p.27

Chapter 2

BIRTH AND GROWTH OF INDIAN NATIONALISM

It is not always easy to trace the origin of a social phenomenon and this is more so with Indian nationalism. It is known, that there can be no nationalism without a nation. Hence a question which sometimes is posed is whether India is a notion or a nation. In some quarters it is still thought that India is a nation in becoming and not in being and that India is not one but ought to be one. This question was first posed by Sir John Strachey in 1884. His observation was : "The first and the most essential thing to learn about India is that there is not and never was an India." Endorsing Strachey's view point John Seeley also denied that India was a nation and described it as 'geographical expression." It is generally acknowledged that even before the British conquest, India was not a nation but a country of continental dimension, composed of various tribes, castes and classes differing in language, race, religion, customs and culture. However, it is conceded that common intellectual heritage, tradition and social life did create the idea of nationality but one which perhaps was far from being strong and well permeated. It is true that in India there was, before the advent of Islam, one culture, one religion and philosophy, the same scriptures and Varna ashrama, the same manners and customs, common civic institutions and social laws and a common historical tradition. Taking these facts into consideration a few scholars of Indian history hold the view that nationalism was always a phenomenon of Indian life. Even a Western authority on nationalism, Hans Kohn, observed: "A truer basis of unity — the modern national sentiments was to be found in a common intellectual heritage persisting through an unbroken tradition and moulding and permeating India's whole social life".

K.M. Panikkar also maintains that a sense of unity did exist before the advent of Islam and that it was based on the universal culture of the Hinduism. Similarly, Nehru also held that India had been throughout her history haunted by a dream, the dream of unity and some kind of unity occupied the mind of Indians since the dawn of its civilisation. But disagreeing with Nehru, Arvind N. Das says that Nehru, in fact, invented rather than 'discovered India', while presenting his theory of the existence of durable entity on the basis of culture. In the opinion of Prof. A.R. Desai, a concept of unity of India existed and flourished in pre-British India but this unity was conceived as a geographical unity of the country and the religio-cultural unity of the Hindus. India was "both a geographical and cultural continuum."[1] That means India had only a territorial identity or some sort of cultural identity but not a national identity.

But a nation can not be defined alone as a geographical entity or understood only in territorial terms. Correctly understood, a nation is a community of people whose members are bound together by a sense of solidarity, a common culture and national consciousness. Given this meaning to the term 'nation' it is hard to accept that there ever existed sufficient quantum of basic unity in any period of Indian history earlier than the British Rule. Hence it may have to be admitted that in pre-British India there was neither a sense of national identity nor national pride. Prof. Gyanendra Pande observed in his 'Construction of Communalism': "No such things as India, Indian civilisation or Indian nationalism were given from the start, from the dawn of history as it were. All these were constructed." Honestly speaking, "what to say of the past, even today our concept of nationhood continues to be amorphous, an almost intangible, near philosophical subconscious acceptance rooted in a mythical past."[2] Not long ago Dr. Ambedkar's observation was: "In believing that we are a nation we are cherishing a great illusion. We can only attempt to become a nation-state." In the opinion of Arvind N. Das, "India has to be reinvented on the basis of shared commitment to equity, participation and plurality."[3]

Alvin Toffler in his 'The Third Wave' states: "Nations are not 'spiritual unities' (Spenglar) or 'mental communities or imagined communities' (Benedict Anderson), 'social souls,' nor a rich heritage of memories (Renan) or a shared image of the future (Ortega Gasset). In fact, it is a second wave phenomenon marked by a single integrated political authority super-imposed on a single unified economy." Like all social phenomena, nationalism is a historical category. It emerges at a certain stage when conditions, both objective and subjective, attain maturity. In other words, a nation is a product of a concrete historical process. E.H. Carr is of the opinion that 'nation' in the modern sense of the word did not emerge until the close of the Middle Ages." In fact, nationalism appeared during the sixteenth century when nation-states were born on the ruins of the Holy Roman Empire. Thus "it is only from the 16th century onwards that national community in different stages of national consolidation have appeared in the amphitheatre of human history."[4] However, this stage came in India not earlier than the middle of the nineteenth century. Dr. Tara Chand also agrees that until the end of the eighteenth century, no entity existed which socially, politically or even geographically corresponded to the name 'India'. In fact, before the foreigners had given the name 'Hind' to our country there was no term in subcontinent to designate it."

To quote A.R. Desai again, "Indian nationalism is a modern phenomenon it came into being during the British period as a result of the action and interaction of numerous subjective and objective forces and factors which developed within the Indian society under the conditions of the British rule and the impact of world forces.[5]"

However, the process of the growth of the Indian nationalism has been vary complex and many-sided. This is due to a number of reasons: The pre-British Indian society had a social structure quite unique and perhaps without a parallel in history. India was a vast country inhabited by a huge population speaking many languages and professing different religions. It was a subcontinent with many ethnic regions and many languages, many religions and cultures but none of them constituted a nation in the nineteenth century European sense. Each of them had its own heritage and past and, in the opinion of Renan, the forgetting of such a past constitutes one of the elements in the formation of a nation. Even the Hindus, who comprised two-thirds of the population, were socially almost atomised in various castes and sub-castes, a phenomenon peculiar to the Hindu society. Again, Hinduism itself was not a homogeneous religion but a conglomeration of religions a theological supermarket, so to say, which divided the Hindu people into a number of sects.

But despite the apparent diversity of language, race and religion, Prof. S.R. Mehrotra maintains that "India, from the Indus to the Brahmputra and from the Himalayas to Cape Camorin, possessed a certain underlying uniformity of life which distinguished it from the rest of the world. The sense of belonging to an all Indian community cut across regional and linguistic loyalties. Nevertheless, there was nothing like a nation in India until the middle of the nineteenth century."[6]

To conclude, the concept of India as a nation was a gift of British imperial power. For the first time in history India was united and integrated politically for administrative and security considerations under the British crown. The British created India as a unified political entity with a central government, common law, continental communication facilities, standard public services, common educational principles, and English as the common language and, above all, they also created an integrated army. Further, the advanced British nation, for its own purpose, radically changed the economic structure of the Indian society, established a centralised state and introduced modern education, modern means of communication and other institutions. This resulted in the growth of new social forces which by their very nature came into conflict with British imperialism and became the basis of and provided motive force for the rise and development of Indian nationalism. Thus, common subjection, common laws and institutions began to shape the people of India in a common mould. To quote S.R. Mehrotra, "a common yoke imposed common disabilities and occasioned common grievances which, in their turn, created common interests and sympathies."[7] In addition, travelling facilities over one's country now available under the British rule was a great education in patriotism. It heightened people's consciousness of the geography, history and culture of their motherland.

Admittedly, pre-colonial India did have some elements of common existence and common consciousness. She was not entirely lacking in some of basic elements which are essential for the making of any nation. Some of these favourable circumstances were provided by the British rule. The colonisation of the Indian economy, society and polity strengthened the elements of unification.

However, this process of India developing into a unified people was quickened by the middle of the nineteenth century. Growth of internal and external trade and concept of an all-India market, introduction of modern trade, industries, banking and means of communication on all-India scale and a uniform system of law and administration increasingly unified the country and created a single economic, administrative and political entity. But actually "it was during the freedom movement that Indian people acquired the necessary collective consciousness and identity. In India's case, the formation of the nation and the struggle for its emancipation are simultaneous."[8]. Thus it has to be acknowledged that "nationalism in India drew its first breath and grew in the cradle of the British Raj."

FACTORS RESPONSIBLE FOR THE
GROWTH OF INDIAN NATIONALISM

The process of growth of Indian nationalism, however, has been very complex and many sided. As in any other country, the national consciousness in India was the cumulative effect of the operation of a number of factors and elements over a long period of time. Some of these factors are religious awakening, Western education, the rapid improvement of means of communication, the rise of the Indian press and certain events which took place in the seventies of the nineteenth century both internal and external.

RELIGIOUS REFORM MOVEMENTS

"The contradictions between the old religious outlook, practices and organisation, on the one hand, and the new social economic reality on the other, gave rise to various religious reform movements in the country."[9] It is notable that the first phase of national awakening expressed itself in the form of a series of religious reform movements. In other words, the growth of Indian nationalism started with religious renaissance. To quote Dr. Zacharias "the Indian national movement was a part of the Indian Renaissance of India which manifested in the form of a general reform movement and produced striking religious and social reforms long before it issued in a movement for political emancipation."[10] Some of these movements aimed at revising the traditional religions in the spirit of the principles of liberalism. Others, however, aimed at restoring in the pure form in which it existed in earlier times. Further, the religious reform movements were national in content but religious in form. It was only in the later stages that the national awakening deepened and broadened and found increasingly secular forums.

The first in the line of reformers was Raja Ram Mohan Roy (1772-1833). Ram Mohan Roy was the pioneer of Indian awakening and is rightly called the father of the Indian Renaissance. To quote Tagore, "he inaugurated the modern age in India." His name is associated with two great social reforms: the abolition of evil practices like sati, enforced widowhood, girl infanticide, early marriage, untouchability and rigid caste system and the introduction of western learning in India. In his religious philosophy and social outlook Ram Mohan Roy was deeply influenced by monotheism and anti-idolatory of Islam, Deism of Sufism, the ethical teachings of Christianity and the liberal, rationalist doctrine of the West. He was essentially a democrat and a humanist. He was a great rationalist who denounced age old rituals and practices. Avowedly a monotheist, he was against Avatarvad and idol worship. Though proud of India's past heritage and culture, he wanted the Indians to benefit from Western science, technology and political institutions.

To bring about awakening among the masses Ram Mohan Roy founded Brahmo Samaj (1828). He believed that religious renovation was the vital condition for revising the decadent social structure. The Brahmo

Samaj was the pioneer of the reform movements. It aimed at liberating the individual from the dead weight of an authoritarian religion. Roy wanted regeneration of old values not for is own sake only but to revive self-confidence in the people who had lost cultural roots. At the same time he advocated religious tolerance and stood for blending of the best of the indigenous and the Western culture. He valued the modern Western culture, and organised educational institutions in the country for its spread among the people. However, the Renaissance Movement was not confined to Bengal only. Its repercussion reverberated all over the country.

In Poona, the reform movement assumed the name of Prarthna Samaj, founded in 1867 under the leadership of M.G. Ranade and Sarvjanik Sabha under Rao Bahadur Krishnaji. The Prarthana Samaj had a programme of religious and social reforms on the same line as those of the Brahmo Samaj.

In Punjab and U.P., the same was accomplished by Arya Samaj, founded in 1875 under Swami Dayanand. The Arya Samaj worked for the removal of untouchability, the caste system and enforced widowhood. The Arya Samaj, though echoing the same national feeling as the Brahmo Samaj, had a more revivalist character. Dayanand stood for the superiority of the Vedic culture and emphasised that the Vedas were the source of all knowledge. He declared the Vedas as infallible and an inexhaustible reservoir of all knowledge of the cosmos, past, present and future. By postulating the infallibility of the Vedas the Samaj did not permit individual judgement to override the divine text. The nationalist-chauvinist claims of the Arya Samaj arose out of its ignorance that all-knowledge is historically conditioned, and that, though growing, it is finite at a given moment and its depth and extent depend upon the level of social development which a people has reached.

Nevertheless, its slogan 'Back to Vedas' was inspired with the urge to bring about national unity and to kindle national pride and consciousness. The Samaj did create strong patriotism among Hindus. In fact, Dayanand was the first Indian to declare 'India for Indians'. In the earlier phase of Indian nationalism, the Samaj did play a progressive role but subsequently it became a hindrance to its growth by creating a belligerent religio-communal atmosphere because of its Shudhi and Sangathan programmes in order to counteract the proselyting activities of Islam, Christianity and Sikhism. By retaining its narrow Hindu basis, the national unity it proclaimed could not attract the non-Hindu communities to its fold.

Likewise, Swami Ram Krishna Paramhansa (1821-86) also played a significant role in Hindu Renaissance. He revived the cult of the Upanishad and proclaimed the virtue of renunciation, self sacrifice and social service. His great disciple, Swami Vivekanand (1863-1902) 'the patriot saint of India' also contributed a great deal towards the revival of Hinduism. More than any other reformer, he made Indians feel proud of their ancient heritage. He founded the Ram Krishna Mission on the pattern of Western missionary societies. He undertook extensive tours of Europe and the USA, and in 1893 he attended the World Congress of Religions at Chicago. Indeed, it was Vivekanand who put Hinduism on the map of the Western world.

The Ram Krishna Mission aimed at protecting India from the materialist influence of the Western civilisation. It idealised Hinduism, lauding its practice of idol worship and polytheism. It aimed at the spiritual conquest of the Western world for revived Hinduism. Vivekanand told Indians that the East was deep in wisdom and rich in spiritual virtues, and exhorted them to conquer the West, which he said was spiritually hollow. By his teachings, he created among the people a sense of confidence and self-reliance.

The work of the Theosophical Society was another reform movement in the South. Theosophy was introduced in India by Madam Balavatsky and Henry Steel Olcoltt in 1879, and was mainly popularised by Annie Besant. Annie Besant was an Irish lady who adopted Hinduism and proclaimed the superiority of the whole Hindu system to the civilisation of the West. She reminded Hindus that they possessed "the key to superior wisdom and that their philosophy and morality were on a higher plane than the West has ever reached." Theosophy subscribed to the spiritual philosophy of ancient Hinduism and recognised its doctrine of the transmigration of soul. However, Theosophy failed to strike deep roots in the country.

Somewhat similar was the effect of the work done by European and Indian scholars like Cole Brook, Wilson, Max Mueller, R.L. Mitra and Dr. Pandu Sen, who were full of praise for the ancient culture and civilisation of India.

In addition to these national religious reforms and religious-revivalist movements, individuals of outstanding capacity and political pre-eminence, such as B.C. Pal, Aurobindo Ghosh, Tilak and Gandhi, etc. also contributed to the work of religious reform.

The work of national rejuvenation, however, was not confined to the Hindus alone. The Muslims under able leadership also began to shake off lethargy and depression that had overtaken them after the disruption of the Mughal Empire. As a consequence of anti-Muslim policy adopted by the British, the entire community was overtaken by a sense of frustration, despondency and decay. Those who once held the highest positions and honour were reduced to the position of "hewers of wood and drawers of water". Thus revivalism among the Muslims was the need of the hour and this was provided by the Wahabi Movement on the one side and the by the personality of Sir Sayd Ahmed Khan on the other. The Wahabi Movement was started in Arabia by Ibn Abdul Wahab (1691-1787) emphasizing the virtues of Islam and the oneness of God. This movement was brought to India by Sayed Ahmed of Rai Bareli (UP) after his return from Mecca in 1823. He established all over India branches to restore Islam to its pristine purity and denounced unislamic practices which had crept into the community. Incidentally, the Wahabies were the primemovers in the uprising of 1857.

A work similar to that of Ram Mohan Roy was undertaken by Sir Syed Ahmed Khan for the Muslims. During his visit to England in 1869 he was immensely inspired by Western liberal ideas. Like Ram Mohan Roy, he firmly believed that only in the adoption of Western learning and literature lay the future of his community. He deftly defied orthodox hostility. After retirement, Aligarh became the centre of his activity. He founded MAO College in 1875. The college developed into the Aligarh Muslim University in 1890. Thus began reawakening of the Muslims of India, a task carried forward by poets and authors such as Altaf Hussain Hali, Zakaullah, Nazir Ahmed, Mohd. Shibli Numani etc.

These movements breathed new life into the degenerated Hindu and Muslim communities. On the one hand, they attacked social and religious evils and brought about many reforms, on the other, they unfolded before them the picture of their glorious past, ancient civilisation and hoary culture. With self confidence came the sense of self-respect which, in its turn, brought dissatisfaction against the British rule. They preached love for India and Indian things. Undoubtedly, the work of these religious and social reformers and the influence of the religious awakening they brought about were among the most potent causes of the growth of Indian nationalism.

Further, the religious foundation of our national movement impressed upon it the character which distinguishes it from national movements in other lands, mainly its spiritual basis.

SIGNIFICANCE OF THESE RELIGIOUS MOVEMENTS

Before the advent of the religious movements, Indian cultural and national life had touched a very low ebb culturally. India stood stupefied against the superior civilisation of the Western conqueror. The process of internal disruption because of loss of political power was accelerated by the efforts of Western education. To these disturbing influences were added the preachings of the Christian missionaries who poured ridicule on Hindu religious beliefs and practices. The citadel of Hinduism was badly shaken. Therefore, before any national awakening could be possible the influence of contact with a virile and apparently superior civilisation had first to be countered and the faith of the people in themselves and their glorious heritages revived. Without these religious seers and savants India could have been lost. Hence, to quote Prof. R.S. Sharma, "there was some excuse for conjuring up a glorious past to compensate for a shaky present in the colonial days and thus nurse the wounded national ego back to health."

Again, these religious reform movements were the first expression of national awakening. They represented attempts to revise the old religion in the spirit of the new principles of nationalism and democracy which were the conditions for the development of the new society. The new society demanded, as the very condition of its development, the abolition of privileges based on birth and sex. The early religious reformers strove to extend the principles of individual liberty to the sphere of religion. In fact, the reform movements were in different degrees endeavours to recast the old religion into a new form suited to meet the needs of the new society. They were progressive in the sense that they were the expression of the first national awakening of the Indian people. By and large, national progress became the main objective of their reconstructed religions.

Another characteristic of these movements was that their programme was not restricted to the task of mainly reforming religion but extended to that of reconstructing social institutions and social relations. These movements thus had an all embracing scope. This was due to the fact that in India religion and social structure were organically interwoven. For instance, caste hierarchy, gender inequality, untouchability and social taboos flourished because of the sanction of religious scriptures. Social reforms therefore constituted a platform of all religio-reform movements.

DRAWBACKS OF RELIGIOUS REFORM MOVEMENTS

However, it should be noted that the religo-reform movements in the earlier phases of Indian nationalism, when it was just growing, was immature and restricted to a small social section, were the forms in which the national awakening found expression and even further developed for some time. In phases, however, when new classes and communities came into existence and developed national, class or group consciousness, and further, when national movement acquired a broader, multiclass and multicommunal basis, most of these even became anti-national disruptive forces retarding the process of a united national movement for freedom. The reversal of their role was mainly due to their transformation from national religo-reform movements into religio-communal movements. This became particularly manifest from 1918 onwards. They weakened the steadily growing national unity of the Indian people and the economic and political unity of the poor strata of various communities which organised trade union, peasant, and other movements against these vested interests, Further, the religio communal movements subserved the British interests. The introduction of such devices as communal representation and electorates objectively thwarted the growth of national unity by perpetuating communal distinctions. Besides, these religious movements had some unfortunate repercussions on national movement. Hindus went back to their historical past and Muslims to early Islam and the history of Arabia. These reform movements tried to rely on two separate sources of spiritual and intellectual sustenance.

To summarize, "initially these religio-reform movements did play a historically progressive role. They were the first breaches in the fortress of medievalism and the declaration in religious and social reform language that the modern India was born and growing. But subsequently, when the national consciousness extended and the national movement became strong and even militant, such attempts as were made by the radical nationalists like B.C. Paul and Aurobindo Ghosh to build them on the basis of religio-mystical philosophy of ancient Hinduism, in a way, hindered and retarded the extension of its social bases. One of the many reasons why the national movement did not draw within its orbit wide sections of the Muslim community was that even under the leadership of Gandhi, it continued to have a religious tinge"[11] The presence of foreign rule prompted these leaders not only to reject this foreign rule but often also to recoil from the culture of the ruling nation. They instead invoked the obscurantist and mystical parts of the nation's past culture and attempted to base a democratic and progressive contemporary national movement on them. But this introduced confusion and mysticism in the national movement and thereby obstructed the growth of national unity of various socio-religious groups. Thus, the Indian National Movement which began with a religious taint ended in the terrible tragedy of partition largely because of this.

WESTERN LEARNING AND ENGLISH LANGUAGE

Probably the greatest contribution of the British rule to the growth of Indian nationalism lay in the encouragement which it gave to the dissemination of Western education in the country. Perhaps, the Western education was the foremost factor that nourished Indian nationalism. Comparatively speaking, the spread of Western education was more important than the religious awakening as a factor contributing to the emergence of Indian nationalism. Ofcourse, the various religious and social reform movements created the soil for national consciousness by reviving the faith of the people in their own culture and civilisation and making them feel proud of their heritage, but it was Western education that brought them into touch with the works of great European thinkers and writers like Milton, Thomas Paine, Burke, J.S. Mill, Spencer, John Locke, Voltaire, Rousseau, Mazzini and got them imbibed with the ideas of liberty, equality, fraternity, self-determination and national freedom.

The introduction of Western learning brought about a profound intellectual transformation in India. It was under the influence of Western learning that the pioneers of Indian nationalism were moved by the aspirations for self-government, for political power and representative institutions; Soon they began to claim that since India was a nation, it was entitled to national freedom like the United States of America, Canada and Australia. To quote Griffith, "Whatever else of good or ill Britain may have achieved in India she may justly claim to have brought about the great Indian Renaissance." It can be safely said that the cult of nationalism and the call for free homeland and self-government would not have come to us with such force and so quickly, if those responsible for shaping the educational policy of the Company's government in 1833 had decided to promote oriental learning instead of encouraging English education. However, the credit for introducing Western learning goes largely to Ram Mohan Roy who espoused the importance of Western education as against Orientalists. Admittedly, the decision proved rational, for Classical education would have only strengthened traditionalists and reactionaries.

Lord Macaulay who was responsible for determining the British educational policy in India had thought that the importing of Western education would make available to the government a cheap supply of indigenous clerks and babus to man the various offices. He had also thought that Western education would foster among the educated youth of India a sense of loyalty towards English rule. No doubt, some of these educated Indians did begin to adopt everything Western, and acquired a taste for foreign fabrics and fashions. They even lost faith in their heritage, and culture. They gave up their own way of life, began to ape English manners and thereby fulfilled the prophecy of Macaulay who wanted to create "a class of persons Indian in blood and colour but English in taste, opinion, words and intellect." It proved to some extent the validity of Elphinston's comment: "English education would make the Indian people gladly accept the British rule." But it should not be forgotten that the same Macaulay also wrote in 1833; "It would be the proudest day in English history when having become instructed in European knowledge, they shall demand European institutions." Hence it is difficult to pass any categorical judgement on the ulterior motive of Lord Macaulay in introducing modern education in India.

In 1854, Sir Charles Wood, President of the Board of Control of the Company's Government, prepared a new despatch on the Indian education system and in 1858 three Universities were opened in Calcutta, Madras and Bombay, and Western political philosophy, History, Law and Liberty were included in the curriculum and English was made the medium of instruction.

However, the positive side of modern Western education was that it inevitably contributed to the growth of nationalism not only by making the Indian people familiar with the ideas of liberty, democracy, self-government but also indirectly by creating discontentment among the educated class who began to aspire for higher position in the services after getting university degrees. The result was that the Western education rebounded on its chief promoters by creating a middle class wanting to supplant the British rulers. Ironically, what the British had regarded as their main prop turned out to be the chief prod which eventually pushed them out of India.

Besides, the advantages of the knowledge of English language were almost immeasurable. It gave access to modern English literature, one of the richest in the world which produced luminaries like Francis Bacon, known for his scientific and inductive method, Charles Darwin, for his theory of evolution, John Locke, the great individualist, J.S. Mill, the best exponent of individual liberty, Adam Smith, the father of modern economic science, Issac Newton, the brilliant physicist, Thomas Carlyle and John Ruskin, the ruthless critics of injustice. Moreover, the study of English language not only helped to build up a democratic and rational outlook, it also did a great service to the cause of Indian nationalism by providing a medium of communication for the educated Indians throughout India to exchange views on a national scale. It cut across personal barriers and served the purpose of a lingua franca. It was largely through this medium that educated Indians began to meet each other, to discuss common problems and to meet on a common platform to devise plans for the upliftment of their country. Thus, with the help of a common medium of communication the English educated Indians in different provinces came to possess a common stock of ideas and aspirations, thereby creating national outlook.

THE INDIAN PRESS

Besides Western education, the Indian press also played an equally important role in building and developing Indian nationalism. The press is said to be the surrogate of the people. It moulds and mirrors all complex processes of national and international life. It is an agency which silently moulds and shapes public opinion on a much higher scale than education. With its help the Indian nationalist groups were able to popularise the idea of representative government, liberty, democratic institutions, Home Rule, Dominion Status and even complete independence.

The well known newspapers in English were the Crescent, the Times of India, the Statesman, the Pioneer, the Hindu, the Leader, and the Amrit Bazar Patrika. The vernacular popular papers were the Dig Darshan, the Samachar Darpan, the Bombay Samachar and the Jame Jamshed. These papers became a powerful instrument of political education for the middle class and stimulated the growth of national feeling by making public the grievances of the people and also by exposing the failings and deficiencies of alien rule.

In the beginning the government adopted the policy of freedom. of press in conformity with the British tradition, but by 1878 their policy changed and started imposing restrictions. But in spite of these restrictions for a couple of years, the Indian press continued to advocate the cause of the people and agitate for political reforms. Thus, as B.B. Majumdar rightly said, "Western education and the Indian press were the two of the most important agencies destined to infuse into the people of India the spirit of national unity and to inspire them to achieve independence without bloodshed."

ECONOMIC EXPLOITATION OF INDIA

Despite several announcements and declarations by the British rulers that it would be their duty to promote the interests and happiness of the native subjects in preference to their own interests, the economic policy followed by the British government was such that it led directly to the impoverishment of the country. Firstly, the administration was top heavy and too costly. Secondly, systematic attempts were made to destroy the indigenous industries of India to make room for manufactured goods from England. To substantiate, Lancashire was placated in 1877 by dropping the cotton import duty by five percent. Similarly, the policy of free trade had a throttling effect on native industries. The British wanted India to remain an agricultural country for providing English with cheap raw material and to serve as a captive and exclusive market for her finished goods. Obviously, these steps on the part of the British antagonized the commercial class of Western India.

POLITICAL AND ADMINISTRATIVE UNIFICATION OF INDIA

Another factor of far-reaching significance in bringing about national consciousness was the political unification of India under the British rule. The British conquest of India was followed by the establishment of a centralised state which brought about, for the first time in Indian history, a real, basic and durable political and administrative unification. No doubt, a feeble concept of political unity of India did exist in pre-British India. For instance, the ancient Hindu ideal of Chakravarti was that of a monarch who ruled over the entire subcontinent, and this ideal was briefly realised under the Mauryas in the fourth century BC and under the Guptas in the fourth Century AD and later on in the sixteenth century when the entire subcontinent was under one political umbrella of Mughal Emperors. Yet this unity in reality was nothing more than geographical unity of the country or a religio-cultural unity of the Hindus. At best, India could be conceived as "a geographical and cultural continuum." But the concept of political unity of the entire Indian people could not flourish under the pre-British socio-historical circumstances. Since the people were not socially and economically integrated in the absence of a unified national economy and efficient, well ramified, and extensive means of communication, any sort of political integration was out of the question. The British established a state structure in India which was definitely something new and unprecedented. It was highly centralised and ramified in the remotest corner of the country. Such a state structure became necessary to the new type of economy which came into existence in India for the first time only under the British rule.

With a view to establish a single political- administrative system in the country the British evolved in India a colossus administrative apparatus penetrating even the remotest village. The necessity to create and efficiently operate such an apparatus also prompted them to establish and extend railways, to construct modern roads, to establish post and telegraph system. True, these modern means of transport and communication were primarily established to serve the economic, political and military interests of the rulers, but the establishment of a uniform currency system, a uniform reign of law and a uniform system of administration, went a long way to generate and promote the idea of India as one nation.

DENIAL OF HIGHER JOBS TO DULY QUALIFIED AND DESERVING INDIANS.

The Act of 1833 contained a clause which laid down that fitness was to be the criterion of eligibility for jobs. This assurance was later on reiterated by the Queen Victoria's Declaration of 1858. But this policy was not followed in practice. Rather, deliberate attempts were made to short cut Indians for the key posts specially after the 1857 uprising. Systematic attempts were made to keep Indians out of higher services, especially the ICS. To illustrate, S.N. Bannerjea, who had passed the I.C.S. examination in 1869, found his name removed from the list of successful candidates on the flimsy ground of some discrepancy in the records about his age. Even after he was admitted to the ICS cadre on a writ petition to the QBD, he was again removed under a false case. Similarly, Aurobindo Ghosh was disqualified from the ICS simply because he did not know horse riding, The other victims were Lalmohan Ghosh and Manmohan Ghosh. Furthermore, in 1877 the entrance age to ICS was reduced from 21 to 19 just to reduce the prospects of Indian candidates from the Indian Civil Service. This decision led to a countrywide agitation and marked the beginning of the unity of action and solidarity of purpose. All these issues and events generated great resentment among the educated class and to canalise it, S.N. Bannerjea founded the Indian Association in 1876 to become the first platform of all India activities. He also started an all-India campaign for restoring the entrance age of 21 and for simultaneous ICS examination in India, which incidentally, was granted not before 1925.

REPRESSIVE AND REACTIONARY POLICIES OF THE REGIME OF LORD LYTTON

The regime of Lord Lytton as Governor General (1876-80) was full of reactionary measures. To illustrate, Lytton held an Imperial Durbar at Delhi in 1877 to announce Queen Victoria as the Empress of India at a time when a large part of the country was in the grip of a dire famine, Again, Lytton was also responsible for putting on the statute book two most obnoxious measures — the Vernacular Press Act (1878) and the Indian Arms Act (1878). If the object of the Press Act was to strangle the freedom of the vernacular press, the aim of the latter was an attempt to demilitarise Indians, forbidding them to keep and to traffic arms without licence. The Europeans, however, were exempted from such restrictions.

Another discriminatory measure adopted by his regime was the reducing of the import cotton duties by five percent in favour of Lancashire mill-owners. This step antagonised the commercial class, especially of

Western India. His next provocating measure, especially for the educated class, was the lowering of the entrance age to ICS from 21 to 19 in 1878.

These ill-starred, reactionary and patently discriminatory measures brought India under his regime within a measurable distance of a rebellion. To quote William Wedderburn, "The state of things at the end of Lytton's regime was bordering upon revolution." Among other foolish things done by his administration which drove the country into despair was the wanton invasion of Kabul, followed by the Second Afghan War, a costly experiment for establishing a so-called 'scientific frontier'.

EXTERNAL EVENTS LEADING TO NATIONAL CONSCIOUSNESS

The knowledge about certain contemporary events and movements abroad between 1861 and 1884 such as unification of Italy (1861) and Germany (1870); independence movements in Romania, Serbia and Montenegro; the passing of the Second and Third Reform Acts, making the British Monarchy more democratic; the American Civil War (1861-65), abolition of slavery; liberal policy adopted by Alexander-II of Russia, etc. created deep interest among the educated class, who began to nurse hopes that they too should secure for their own country some of these benefits.

ILBERT BILL AGITATION

These events, as described earlier, were quite effective by themselves in stimulating political awakening among the educated and commercial class on a national scale. But none of them was as significant as the organised opposition against the Ilbert Bill.

In 1880, there was a change of government in England bringing into power the Liberal Party, led by Gladstone. Gladstone believed that good government was no substitute for self-government. He therefore wanted to give India the blessings of free institutions. Accordingly, he sent Lord Ripon, his true follower, as Governor General to effect necessary reforms in the structure of the Indian government. The new Governor General proved true to his job. He repealed the Vernacular Press Act and took steps to promote local self-government in big cities and towns.

Lord Ripon also sought to remove the invidious distinctions existing at that time between the European and Indian members of the Judiciary. The Indian Session Judges and Magistrates were not empowered to try European offenders. Ripon thought it to be against the spirit of Rule of Law. The task of removing this highly objectionable anomaly was assigned to Sir Courtney Ilbert, the Law Member of the Viceroy's Executive Council. He introduced a Bill in the Imperial Legislature called the Ilbert Bill, designed to do away with the racial discrimination found in the existing rule. But the Bill ran into rough weather. The Anglo-Indian community along with Europeans rose to a man to offer a tooth and nail fight against the Bill. In order to put up an organised opposition they formed a European Defence Association with branches all over the country and succeeded in collecting one lakh fifty thousand rupees. Even a plot was hatched to put the Viceroy on board a steamer and send him back home. It was a sort of White Mutiny. As a result, Ripon had to buckle before the storm of agitation. Ultimately, a compromise was negotiated according to which the Indian judges could try Europeans on the condition that they were given right to claim a trial by jury of which at least half of whom were to be Europeans.

The whole episode was an eye-opener for Indians. In the first place, it clearly showed that justice was not to be expected when vested interests and privileges of the governing race were involved. In the second place, it demonstrated the value of organised agitation. It began to dawn on the people that in political matters what mattered was not justice of the cause but united and concerted political action. The Indian leaders learnt the lesson that the way to improve their condition was to organise, agitate and press the government into reforms rather than rely on benevolence of the government, whether Liberal or Conservative. Consequently, demands began to arise for a permanent nationwide organisation to ventilate the grievances of the people. It was in answer to the European Defence Association that S.N. Bannerjea took up the idea of calling a national convention in 1883 which was the fore-runner of the Indian National Congress. The idea caught the imagination of thinking persons in presidency towns where new associations came into being to create public opinion upon political, social and cultural matters.

Altogether, "Indian nationalism was the outcome of the new material conditions created in India and the new social forces which emerged as a result of the British conquest. It was the outcome of the objective conflict of interests, the interest of Britain to keep India politically, economically subjected to her and the interest of the Indian people for a free political economic and cultural evolution of the Indian society, which was intruded by the British rule."[12]

Notes

1. Desai, A.R., 'Social Background of Indian Nationalism', op.cit, p.167
2. Singh, Jaswant, Seminar, Nov. 1965.

3. See Das, Arvind N., Inventing India.
4. Desai, A.R., op.cit, page 1.
5. Desai, A.R., op.cit, page 5.
6. Mehrotra, S.R., Towards India's Freedom and Partition, Vikas Publishing House, New Delhi, 1979, p.4.
7. Ibid., p.8
8. Chandra, Bipan, Basis of Indian Nationhood, Mainstream 13 June 1992.
9. Desai, A.R., op.cit., p.281.
10. Zacharies, Renascent, p.15
11. Desai, A.R., op.cit, pp. 297,298
12. Ibid. p.158

Chapter 3

RISE OF
INDIAN NATIONAL MOVEMENT

Though Indian nationalism crystallised as a national movement during the last decades of the nineteenth century, its first sproutings were visible in the beginning of the last century. The rise of the Brahmo Samaj in 1828 was itself a religious expression of the growing national awakening of the advanced Hindu intelligentsia who received the modern education, and who came in contact with the Western democratic ideologies through that education. But secular political organisations such as the British Indian Society, established in 1843 and the British Indian Association which resulted out of the amalgamation of the few existing political groups in the country in 1851 also sprang up during the early period. It had its organisations at Calcutta, Madras and Bombay. However, these early political groups which embodied the first feeble beginnings of the rise of Indian nationalism were composed of a few individuals and lacked a political basis. They could not also exist on an all-India scale, as the whole of India became British territory long after they were formed. Thus, Indian nationalism as an organised and all-India movement came into existence only when proper historical conditions matured for its birth; that is, during the last decades of the second half of the nineteenth century.

But before a survey of the rise and growth of Indian National Movement, a brief reference to a major event of the nineteenth century is appropriate that event was the Revolt of 1857. The uprising of 1857 was the last, though unsuccessful, attempt of the social classes of the old society to drive out the British from India and to revert to the pre-British social and political existence. The Revolt was the result of pent-up indignation and accumulated discontent among the various strata of the old society who suffered from the British conquest, because of the new economic forces and measures brought into operation by that conquest, and the various social innovations introduced into the country by the British government. The principal causes of this Revolt, however, were the annexation policy of the British which brought about the liquidation of a number of feudal states, the new land revenue system, which reduced the Indian peasantry to acute economic misery as well as the large scale ruination of the millions of Indian artisans and handicraft men as a result of the influx of the machine-made goods from Britain in the Indian market.

Although the Revolt began as a military mutiny, it quickly became a well-spread insurrection. In other words, the mutiny was soon converted into a rebellion in many parts of Northern and Central India. Hence it would be wrong to interpret the Revolt of 1857 as a mere Sepoy Mutiny. It had a far broader social base. In fact, it was a rebellion on the part of the vast multitudes beyond the Sepoy against the British supremacy and sovereignty. All the same, the Revolt had a localised or parochial aspect. The rebellion was 'a brief marvel; it lasted hardly four months.

CAUSES OF FAILURE OF THE REVOLT OF 1857

The Revolt failed because of several factors. One, it was without a clear-cut issue, devoid of a master-mind and lacked in superior weapons and organising capacity. Two, it was not a well-planned attack. It lacked a uniform military strategic plan. It also lacked effective leadership. Thus, lack of planning and cooperation among different sections of the revolting elements, want of singleness of purpose and treachery of the princely order, rich merchants, certain trusted officers and loyalty of the Sikhs and Gorkha troops to British regime were some of the factors that brought about the collapse of the revolt. No wonder, the revolt was crushed within months.

However, the revolt of 1857 cannot be regarded as national in the full modern sense of the world. Though the sentiment was anti-foreign, there was no positive national content. Historians like Dr. R.C. Majumdar and Ashok Sen, etc. refuse to regard the revolt as a War of Independence. Majumdar argues that it was not national in character. Firstly, its operation was regional in character, and secondly, when it broke out, there had not yet developed any general idea of either conscious nationalism or true patriotism. M.N. Roy in his 'India in Transition' (1922) also maintains that by no means the revolt could be looked upon as a national movement. It was nothing more than "the last spasm of the dying feudalism." To quote hm, "the revolt of 1857 was nothing but "the last effort of the dethroned potentates to regain their power."[1]

SIGNIFICANCE OF THE REVOLT OF 1857

Although, the Revolt was not motivated by the historically progressive conception of national unification on a democratic basis, its bold challenge to the foreign rule had been a source of patriotic inspiration in subsequent years to a great majority of the Indian people. For some political groups, especially the terrorist, it was a dress rehearsal for the future successful struggle for freedom. Additionally, the Revolt revealed in action, for the first time in history, that a large scale alliance between the Hindus and the Muslims against foreign rule was possible. It created a tradition for a united national movement of the Indian people.

CONSEQUENCES OF THE REVOLT OF 1857

The end of the 'Mutiny' inaugurated a new stage in the history of Indo-British relations. Not only did the Crown assume the direct political control of India in 1858, but the policy of the British rule also underwent a change. Britain abandoned the policy of annexation of the native states. Their new policy aimed at transforming the native rulers into allies. Instead of being a foe of Indian feudalism it became its defender. "In as much as Britain based its rule on reactionary foundation the limited progressive role of the British conquest of India was proportionally diminished."[2] The English became distrustful of the Indians, and began to consider themselves "as a garrison occupying a country which might always break at in a sudden rebellion." In the opinion of Perceval Spear, "The Indian government's honeymoon with progress was over and was to be followed by humdrum process of getting along with a traditionalist partner." The social forces of the old society were vanquished and they lost their former power and status in the crossfire of 1857. They were too exhausted and emasculated to embark upon a fresh enterprise in future. But the new social forces- the intelligentsia and the commercial bourgeoisie, which were to be the pioneers of the first organised national movement had still not matured to begin their historical task." It was only after 1870 with the combination of a number of factors, the country was again permeated with serious political ferment and, the new social forces acquired appreciable political consciousness and economic and numerical strength and began to be politically articulate."[3] By the early eighties Indian resentment and disillusionment with the British masters had had almost reached it nadir.

Notes

1. Roy, M.N., India in Transition, Indian Renaissance Publishers, Calcutta, 1971, p.21

2. Desai, A.R., op.cit, p.313

3. Ibid., p.315

Chapter 4

BIRTH OF INDIAN NATIONAL CONGRESS — THE PREMIER POLITICAL ORGANISATION OF INDIAN PEOPLE

It is a well observed fact that origins are always obscure and more so of a social movement. So is the case with the origin of the Indian National Congress. The resentment which was piling up against the government, as discussed in the last two chapters, began to express itself in the form of various associations in the presidency towns, such as East India Association, Madras Mahajan Sabha, Bombay Presidency Association, the Poona Sarvajanik Sabha, the Deccan Society and the Servants of India Society. But the credit for starting the first all-India Association, the Indian Association, goes to Surendra Nath Bannerjea. This Association was founded in 1876 with Anand Mohan Bose as its Secretary. The Association became the centre of the agitation on all India basis. It brought together a galaxy of nationalist politicians like A.O. Hume, Manmohan Ghosh, W.C. Bannerjea etc. The immediate spark and inspiration for starting of the Indian Association was provided by the European Defence Association whose object was to defeat the well-meant Ilbert Bill. Its organised active political propaganda throughout India awakened the people to a sense of political unity and concerted activity. At the call of the Indian Association, about one hundred persons from various parts of India assembled in the Albert Hall College Square, Calcutta on December 28, 1883 for the national conference. It was clearly for the first time that people from all over India had come together on the same platform. This great assembly was the precursor of the first session of the Indian National Congress held on the same date in 1885.

The country was thus prepared in men as well as material for the constitution of a national organisation. It only required the genius of an expert architect to devise a suitable plan and lay the foundation stone. That architect was an English man- Allan Octavian Hume, a retired ICS.

Hume had been closely following the trend of events particularly during the Viceroyalty of Lord Lytton and had been anxiously watching the clouds that were darkening the Indian horizon and came to the conclusion that the cure for the growing unrest lay in the foundation of a genuine national movement. He was the first to realise that Western education and ideas has let loose forces which unless guided and controlled may lead to consequences which are too disastrous to contemplate. Accordingly, in an Open Letter dated March 1, 1883 he made his famous appeal to the graduates of Calcutta to set up an organisation with a band of fifty youngmen with sufficient power of self sacrifice, sufficient love for and pride in the country, sufficient, genuine and unselfish heartfelt patriotism, who would be willing to devote the rest of their life to the cause of their countrymen. He urged them to organise an association for the mental, social and political regeneration of the people of India. The appeal met with a ready response, and towards the close of 1884, the Indian National Union was formed. In March 1885, this Union decided to hold a meeting of the representatives from all parts of India during the Christmas. In April 1885, a manifesto was issued inviting important persons to meet at Poona and to establish a national organisation. Hume was put in charge of organising it and settling the details. He made full use of his position as an ex-civilian in enlisting official sympathy and support. When all the preliminaries were settled, Hume sailed for England apparently to consult friends and sympathisers in British Parliament and outside, but actually to guard the British public against all possible misapprehension, suspicion and distrust that the proposed organisation was likely to evoke. He returned to India in November 1885 and preparations started at Poona. But the venue of the conference had to be shifted to Bombay, as Poona came under the grip of cholera.

By the morning of December 27, delegates from all parts of the country reached Bombay and the first meeting took place on 28 December 1885 in the Hall of Gokuldas Tejpal Sanskrit College, and the Indian National Congress was born.

It is clear from the preceding account that the INC did not come into being all of a sudden. As a matter of fact it was the natural and logical issue of the awakening that came over India. It was the result of the religious reform movements and the impact of Western education. It was the fulfillment of the forces set into motion by the British rule itself. In short, it was the culmination of a long process wherein the soul of the nation long struggling to find expression did ultimately manage to emerge. Thus, the INC was brought into existence by the joint efforts of both Indian and British democrats.

ROLE OF HUME IN FOUNDING
THE INDIAN NATIONAL CONGRESS

A.O. Hume is generally regarded as the father of the Indian National Congress. Although it is difficult to establish that the Congress was first conceived by Hume, as Gandhiji believed, but there is no doubt at all that it was his authority, energy and organisational skill that accomplished the seemingly impossible. To quote Gokhale, "No Indian could have started the Indian National Congress if the founder had not been a great European and a distinguished ex-official, such was the distrust of political agitation in those days that the authority would have at once thought some way or the other to suppress the movement. If an Indian had come forward to start such a movement embracing all India, the officials in India would not have allowed the .movement to come into existence."[1] Although it is easy to understand why the Indian politicians showed anxiety to establish a national institution for promoting the cause of national interest, but it is not easy to understand as to why a British civilian took such a keen interest in its foundation. Hence it is not strange if some people doubted or suspected Hume's motive in founding the INC. Generally, three motives are imputed to Hume in the establishment of the INC. One explanation comes from Shri Womesh Chandra Bannerjee who presided over the first session of the Congress at Bombay. He is reported to have remarked that the original intention was "to bring together leading Indian politicians once a year to discuss questions of social interest only". That is, in the beginning Hume intended the Congress to be just a social organisation. But the Congress did not remain a social conference, as desired. It became a political body from its very inception. How did this change come about has been explained in various ways. Some writers hold the view that Mr. Hume changed his ideas and turned the Congress into a political body in order to save the British Empire in India from a violent over-throw.

Lala Lajpat Rai was one of the main Congress leaders who subscribed to this view. He believed that the Congress was a product of Lord Dufferin's brain. He wrote in 'Young India' that the Congress was started more with the object of saving the British Empire from danger than that of winning political liberty for India." But his 'Save the Empire' theory does not carry conviction, for at the time of foundation of the INC there was no sign of any imminent danger of violent and revolutionary activities. As a result of tactful handling of the situation by Lord Ripon whatever tendencies in that direction that existed during the repressive regime of Lord Lytton had died down. This theory also fails to explain why the official sympathy offered to the Congress was withdrawn just after three years after its birth if it was created to 'Save the Empire'.

As regards the objective of the early Congress, it is true that the Congress was not started with the object of winning of political freedom; it had a much humbler objective that of securing piecemeal reform, like expansion of the Legislative Council and the inclusion of Indian representatives in them. As a matter of fact, the idea of national freedom was rather premature at that time.

In a similar vein, another hypothesis is advanced by some leftists which is known as the 'safety valve' theory . In fact, 'safety value' is a staple of left-wing opinion. To quote R.P. Dutt, "The establishment of Congress was an attempt to defeat or rather forestall an impending revolt." It is quite possible that Hume might have felt that unless safe constitutional and legitimate outlets were provided for the discharge of growing Indian ferment, it was likely to run into dangerous channels. As an ICS officer, Hume must have been receiving secret reports on political unrest in the 1870s and '80s, and as such had apprehended the repetition of the uprising. Hence he might have thought it advisable to have a national platform, which would eventuallty play the same role as the opposition plays in the House of Commons. Presumably, he might have recommended the 'safety valve' of the Congress to Lord Ripon. Writing in 'Concise History of the Indian National Congress' some recent writers have also observed: "No doubt, Hume was persuaded that by getting hold of the great lower middle class before the development of the reckless demagogues to which the next quarter of the century must give birth and carefully inoculating them with a mild and harmless form of political fever, as Hume argued: We are adopting the only precautionary method against the otherwise inevitable ravages of a violent and epidemic burst of disorder."[2] But Prof. Bipan Chandra refutes the myth that the Congress was inspired by Hume as a 'safety valve' to stem the tide of growing nationalist feeling after 1857. The Congress, according to him, "was the culmination of the process of political awakening that had its beginning in the 1860s and 1870s and took a major leap forward in the 1880s, and, therefore, he is of the opinion that the organisation would have been established even without Hume."[3] In this context a writer has remarked: "If Hume and other Liberals hoped to use Congress as a 'safety valve', the Congress leaders hoped to use Hume as a lightning conductor."

Another hypothesis advanced by Prof. Nand Lal Chaterjee in his article in the issue of Modern Review for October 1950. was that "the Congress was a child of Russo phobia". In his opinion, Hume propounded the idea of establishing the Indian National Congress at a time when an invasion of India by Russia was apprehended and so Hume's motive was to divert Indian agitation into right lines and prevent Russians from fomenting intrigues in this country. According to this thesis, the Congress was meant to become counterpoise to Russian intrigue. This theory may not be very plausible but at least it explains the withdrawal of official sympathy within three years, because as soon as the danger of Russian invasion was over by 1888, the attitude of British rulers also underwent a radical change.

But whatever might have been the hidden motive of A.O. Hume, it cannot be denied that the Indian National Congress owes a great deal to his initiative, efforts and an organising capacity. This is amply borne out by the fact that he not only became its first General Secretary but continued to serve and guide it till his death (1912).

Notes

1. Quoted in Chandra, Bipan (ed.), India's Struggle For Freedom, op.cit., pp.80,81

2. Ibid., p.71.

3. Ibid., p.71

Chapter 5

GROWTH OF INDIAN NATIONAL CONGRESS

Ever since its inception the Indian National Congress had become the centre and focus of national awakening and attracted all patriotic persons to itself. The Congress was the spearhead of freedom struggle and constituted the mainstream of the Indian National Movement. Consequently, its growth almost became synonymous with the growth of the Indian National movement and its success and failure became the success and failure of the Indian National movement, because the leadership of the movement always remained in the hands of the Congress.

CHARACTER AND OBJECTS OF THE CONGRESS

From the very beginning the INC was meant to be a national organisation of an all-India character. Its aim was to represent all Indians without any distinction of community, caste, colour or sex. It could rightly claim to represent all interests, all classes and all communities and religions. To substantiate, "if the Congress was first conceived in an English man's brain (Hume), it was nursed by two great Parsis (Dada Bhai Naoroji and Pheroz Shah Mehta), and from its commencement it had the good wishes of Muslim leaders like Badruddin Tyabji and Bengali Christians like W.C. Bannerjea.[1]" Almost all the leading personages of the country joined the organisation at the time of its birth. Moreover, the persons who conceived it and helped to bring it into existence not only belonged to different communities and came from different provinces, they also had Pan-Indian outlook. This outlook had never left the Congress even for a moment. The fact that its annual sessions rotated from place to place, and further, the fact that whatever the venues of the session, the delegates mustered strong from every nook and corner of the country, enabled it to retain its national character and outlook even to this day. Though initially conceived as an organisation of the middle classes, after some time, it began to attract delegates from the rural areas and the proletariat. The decision to hold its sessions in villages since 1937 helped it to become representative of the millions all over the land.

While its national character has suffered no alteration during its chequered carrier of more than a century, the Congress has undergone many significant changes. Its methods too have changed along with the changes in its goals and leadership. In the beginning, the Congress was characterised by diffidence. During its infancy the Congress lacked the power of assertiveness. "It was not till the rise and dominance of the left wing that it developed self-consciousness and began to demand self-government as a matter of right."[2] Although it declared Swaraj as its goal as early as 1906, it did not make any modification in its method of work. It continued to pin its faith in the sense of justice and fairplay of the British administration and hoped that Britain would establish responsible institutions. It was not till the advent of Gandhi and his disillusionment as a result of the Punjab tragedy that the Congress changed its method of mendicancy and learned to depend on its own strength to enforce its demands. Under Gandhi's leadership the Congress acquired a mass base and became a countrywide organisation and led several mass movements. And at a very late stage (1929) the Congress declared Complete Independence as its goal and used the method of civil disobedience for its achievement. Although, there have been far-reaching changes in the objectives and methods of the Congress from time to time, it has always respected the voice of moderation, liberalism and compromise.

From the point of view of the changes made in its objectives, methods and leadership, the history of Congress can be divided into three distinct phases periods: the Moderate, the Extremist and the Gandhian. These phases are dealt with in the succeeding chapters.

Notes

1. Suda, J.P., op.cit., p.56
2. Ibid., p.58

Chapter 6

THE EARLY CONGRESS-
FIRST PHASE (1885-1905)

FEATURES OF THE EARLY CONGRESS: One of the striking features of the early Congress was that it contained almost all the notable Indians and distinguished figures of this period with the exception of Sir Syed Ahmed Khan, who alone held aloof from the Congress fold. Every community of the country was represented in the organisation and it was truly a national body. The leaders of the early Congress were mostly lawyers, teachers, journalists and administrators. Most of them came from the upper strata and were in most cases the product of Western education. Some of the notable leaders of the early Congress were Dada Bhai Naoroji, Pheroz Shah Mehta, M.G. Ranade, Baddrudin Tyabji, G.K. Gokhale, S.N. Bannerjea, W.C. Bannerjea, Anand Mohan Bose, Subramanyam Iyer, Vijayraghav Chariar and liberal minded Europeans like A.O. Hume, Wadderbern, Yule and Norton. In this respect, the early Congress stands contrasted with the later day Congress, which excluded several distinguished leaders belonging to liberal Federation, Muslim League, Hindu Mahasabha and other revolutionaries. Its delegates were drawn from all communities. Its presidents were selected from all sections by turn. But India being a predominantly Hindu country, it is but natural that the INC would have been largely more Hindu in its composition, but it is worth noting that in its outlook the Congress had no Hindu tinge in its early phase.

The Congress in this period was an organisation of the middle classes. The delegates to its annual sessions generally came from the cities. The land-owing group and the masses were mostly unconcerned with its activities. Thus, in the beginning, the national movement was not a movement of the masses. It represented and claimed to speak only for the intelligentsia of the Indian society.

Another notable thing about the early Congress was that it enjoyed the goodwill and sympathy of the British authority who encouraged and helped in its foundation. But this attitude lasted hardly for three to four years. Thereafter its friendly neutrality gave place to an attitude of suspicion, intolerance and even of positive hostility. The change in the attitude of British authority was but natural. In the first two years of its existence, the Congress contented itself by passing mere paper resolutions, but after being dissatisfied with the attitude of government by 1887, the Congress started a campaign of agitation against the various acts, omissions and commissions of the government by means of public meetings, pamphlets and leaflets. This led the government to reverse its policy towards the Congress.

During its first session the INC required the British government to introduce reforms in Indian administrative system, such as reduction in expenditure on military, abolition of the India Council, holding of the ICS examination in India, expansion of the Legislative Council, set up in 1861. From 1886 to 1905 some more demands were added; for instance, separation of Judiciary from the Executive, establishment of military colleges in India, reduction of salt duty, decrease in land revenue, change in tenancy laws, repeal of cotton excise duty, removal of restrictions on the press, protective tariff for infant industries, repeal of various repressive laws, more power for local bodies, appointment of Indians to higher posts etc. A glance at reforms demanded by he Congress goes to prove that the Congress even in the period of its infancy acted as a spokesman of every interest and section of the populace. If it supported the demands of industrial and capitalist classes, it showed equal concern for the welfare of labourers and peasants, stoppage of economic drain, and the protection of Indian industries. Although theirs may not have been the voices of the masses, yet the leaders of the early Congress did interpret their grievances and offered prudent suggestions for their redressal. Nevertheless, if one looks at the early proceedings of the Congress, he is bound to be struck by the moderate character of its demands. This was so because the Congress was under the influence of Moderate leadership which believed in piecemeal reforms and subscribed to the philosophy of gradualism. In fact, they were practical reformers imbued with the spirit, principles and methods of Victorian liberalism and believed in winning freedom by gradual stages. They, therefore, took scrupulous care not to pitch their demands too high. Even those who cherished full-fledged self-government as their ultimate ideal wanted to work on the lines of least resistance. The Moderates were confirmed believers in the efficacy of the constitutional method. Having no faith in rebellion or passive resistance, they followed the method of prayer, petition, persuasion, representation and deputation in order to convince the government about the justness of their demands. This method was later-on nicknamed as the method of mendicancy, and the Moderates were described as black-coated petitioners by the left-wingers.

Most of the early Congress leaders believed that the British were essentially fair and just. Their presumption was that since the British were themselves lovers of liberty and justice, they would not grudge to concede the same to Indians after they became fit for self-government. They honestly believed that Britishers gave India a progressive civilisation. They regarded the English literature, their educational system, their system of justice and local self-government as invaluable blessings of the British Raj. They looked to Britain for inspiration and guidance in order to overcome their social and cultural backwardness and for training them in the art of representative government. They considered the interest of Britain and India as allied rather than antagonistic. Given this perception about the British rule it is no wonder if the leadership of the early Congress was marked by loyalty to the British rule.

Now looking to the period they belonged to, the method and approach adopted by the early Congress was probably the only practical, sagacious and farsighted. They made a humble but correct beginning. Not only did they plant the sapling of freedom but gave it a proper nourishment so as to make it deep rooted and well founded.

CONTRIBUTIONS OF MODERATES TO INDIAN NATIONAL MOVEMENT

In spite of certain misconceptions on their part, the Indian liberals, who represented mainly the interests of the developing bourgeois society in India, played a progressive role on the whole. They were the architects of the first all-India political organisation. They infused national consciousness among the people, disseminated democratic conceptions among them, popularised the idea of representative institutions. "They were the passionate supporters of the spread of democratic institutions and scientific/rational culture of modern Europe in India, and zealously campaigned against the mediaeval obscurantism and authoritarian social culture inherited from the pre-British period. They stood for democratisation of social relations and economic advance through industrialisation."[1]

Nevertheless, they suffered from certain political misconceptions. They failed to take account of the pitfalls of foreign rule. They could not clearly see that India was an economic colony of British capitalism and the economic development they sought had to be subordinated to the needs of British capital and therefore had to be necessarily retarded. These liberals could not perceive this objectively existing conflict of interest of the rulers and the ruled. It was presumptive on their part to think that

Britain could part with power or grant even administrative reforms of a far reaching character and thereby jeopardise their own economic interests. Essentially, the problem was not ethical but conflicting political and economic interest. The liberals attached too much importance to a subjective factor — the British sense of justice and fair play, and indulged in a good deal of wishful thinking to counteract the sinister implication of their own 'drain theory' of British exploitation. Further, they could not make the qualitative difference between the White colonies like Canada and Australia and non-White colony like India.

Nonetheless, in our retrospective judgement, we have to appreciate their wisdom and admire them for viewing the British connection in proper perspective and for making correct assessment about the revolutionary impact of the British rule and for showing due appreciation of its beneficial effects on the nation. In fact, "they were practical-minded enough to realise that India could not be fit for parliamentary self-government in there own life time. Hence they advocated the gradualist approach."[2]

All told, the early phase of the Congress may be regarded as the most glorious period of the history of Indian National Movement in many respects. The quality of leadership available in this phase could never be excelled. Remarkably, these leaders were not the captives of the past, and they never harked back to a distant and dead past. In the opinion of M.N. Roy, "It was the golden period of modern Indian history". The extraordinary authority enjoyed by the leadership of this period could be seen in the intellectual and moral statures of the founding fathers. Subsequent developments vindicated their farsightedness. Significantly, the political evolution of British India took place almost on the same line in which the Moderates had anticipated it.

Notes

1. Desai, A.R., op. cit., p.322
2. Mehrotra, S.R., op.cit, p.98

Chapter 7

SECOND PHASE OF THE INC- (1906-1919) BIRTH OF EXTREMISM

"The last decade of the nineteenth century saw the beginning of a movement with many facets, the picturesque and often misguided assertiveness of a people's long maimed self-respect- a movement which was to bring about in the ensuing decade the first great wave of unmistakable unrest."[1] The period roughly from 1897 to 1908 saw a growing discontent of the people and stubborn repercussion practised by the British administration, which had its repercussion on the Congress, and it did not take very long for them to experience disillusionment with the British rule.

Some of the events and forces that led to the emergence of extremism in Indian politics in this period are as follows:

First, the Reforms introduced by the Indian Council Act of 1892 were found to be hopelessly inadequate and deeply disappointing. Though the Act marked some advance on the Council Act of 1861 in t hat it increased the number of Indians in the Council, introduced indirect election and allowed the right of asking questions and the right of discussion on budget, the other major demands remained unrealised.

Second, in 1896-97, a severe famine swept over the country resulting in great economic distress. Hot on the heels of the famine there also broke out a virulent bubonic plague which took a heavy toll of life in Bombay Presidency. The relief machinery set up by the government was found utterly inadequate. It was slow moving and badly organised. Consequently, the nation stood watching helplessly while millions were starving and dying because of the famine and epidemic. This negligence on the part of the British rulers shocked the people. B.G. Tilak trenchantly criticised the official measures in his paper, Kesari' and soon after riots broke-out Mr. W.C. Rand (Plague Commissioner) and Lt. Ayerst were shot dead by the Chapekar brother. Tilak was implicated for the crime and was arrested in 1898 and sentenced to 18 months imprisonment, and he was not given even leave to appeal to the Privy Council. His trial and imprisonment and refusal of appeal sent a wave of indignation throughout the length and breadth of the country and won many fresh entrants to the cult of Extremism.

Third, the repressive policy of Lord Curzon (1898-1905) was the most potent cause of political discontent. Curzon was a diehard conservative and seldom paid any heed to political sentiments and demands. The regime of Curzon was full of missions, omissions and commissions. To illustrate, the Durbar held at Delhi (1902), when large part of the country were reeling under famine, was resented as "a pompous pageant to a perishing people" (Lal Mohan Ghosh). Another objectionable Act of his administration was the passing of the Calcutta Corporation Act of 1899. It was a stroke against the local self-government. His other objectionable acts of commission were the Official Secret Act (1904) and the Indian Universities Act, (1904). The latter was an endeavour to officialise the university administration so as to make them as good as department of the state after destroying their autonomy. Besides, his 'frontier policy' and expedition to Lahasa (Tibet) also received trenchant criticism.

Finally, the last official act of Curzon was the partition of Bengal in 1905. It was the worst and most foolish act of his Viceroyalty. Although the partition was made apparently on administrative grounds but its underlying aim was to disrupt the political unity of Bengali people. In fact, "it was a master strategy to destroy the nascent nationalism in Bengal."[2] If other measures of his governor-generalship had fanned into flame the gathering discontent of the people, the partition of Bengal transformed it into a conflagration.

A vigorous agitation started against the contemplated move. Curzon paid no heed to a petition signed by thousands of Indian people. He was not the person to be deterred by the opposition and protest on the part of the people. He was determined to implement the plan of partition, and rode roughshod over the sentiments of the public. The supreme contempt that he showed for the public opinion exasperated the people. The tremendous upsurge in Bengal found expression in the emergence of new slogan, new method of agitation and new leadership. Swadeshi, Boycott and National Education suddenly became the battle cries of a resurgent and embattled nationalism.

Even more galling was Curzon's sweeping charge that Indians were by environment, heritage and upbringing unequal to the responsibility of high offices under the British rule. While addressing the Calcutta University Convocation he observed: "Truth took a high place in the code of the West before it had been similarly honoured in the East, where craftiness and diplomatic wile have always been held in high esteem." This gratis charge against Indian character evoked strong condemnation. Perhaps nothing fed the fires of extremism more than racial arrogance exhibited in these utterances. He also antagonised the Congress by calling it "an unclean thing", and by impertinently declaring (1900): "The Congress is tottering to its fall and one of any great ambitions is to assist it to a peaceful demise." Undoubtedly, his administration was largely responsible for giving birth to extremism in India politics.

Fourth, events occurring outside India also exercised a profound influence on the mind and outlook of the rising generation and materially helped the rise of extremism. To illustrate, the discriminating and humiliating treatment meted out to Indians in British colonies, particularly in Africa, where the Indians were treated as social pariahs, created much resentment in India. Similarly, the defeat of the Italian army by the Abyssinian (Africa) forces in 1896, and defeat of Russia by Japan in 1905 exploded the myth of European supremacy. Lord Curzon himself admitted: "The reverberations of the victory of Japan have gone like a thunderclap through the whispering galleries of the East." These examples were not lost on Indians who began to shed their inferiority complex. During this period those who watched the revolutionary rumbling in Russia, the rise of the Sinn Fein Movement in Ireland, the Egyptian struggle for freedom, the Young Turk Revolt, the adoption of a constitution in Persia, the introduction of representative institutions in the Philippines and the grant of responsible self-government to the Transvaal and Orange River colony could not but be filled with new born aspirations for their country and prompted to more energetic action."[3]

Obviously, these events and forces gave a new turn to Indian politics and were responsible for the emergence of an aggressive, militant nationalism which found expression in three forms:

(1) Formation of Extremist bloc within the Congress.

(2) Growth of terrorism and formation of terrorist groups.

(3) Organised Revolutionary Movement.

EXTREMIST BLOC AND
THE INDIAN NATIONAL MOVEMENT

The Extremists are also known as militant/radical nationalists or left nationalists. The ideologues of militant nationalism, whose godfather was Raj Narain Bose (Maternal grandfather of Aurobindo Ghosh) believed in the spiritual genius of India. The militant nationalists drew inspiration from the India's past, invoked the great episodes of distant and recent history and tried to infuse national pride and self-respect among the people. They revived the memories of the Vedic past of the Hindus, the great glorious achievements of Ashoka and Chandragupta Maurya, the heroic deeds of Rana Pratap and Shivaji, the epic patriotism of Rani Laxmi Bai, the Queen of Jhansi and other leaders of the Revolt of 1857.

The Bengal School of militant nationalism, led by B.C. Pal and Aurobindo Ghosh was influenced by the neo-Vedantic movement of Swam Vivekanand, the Maharashtrian School of radical nationalism, led by B.G. Tilak, while resuscitating the memory of the cultural past of India, roused the population of Maharashtra to acts of heroism and self-sacrifice by reviving the memory of Shivaji's struggle against the Mughal Empire. Tilak even revived and utilised Ganpati festival for political propaganda. However, the new nationalism in Maharashtra was not dressed in a religio-mythical philosophical garb, as in Bengal. Lala Lajpat Rai, the lion of Punjab, did for the Punjab what Pal was dong in Bengal and Tilak in Maharashtra. These men identified Dharma with nationalism in Bengal. Pal revived the Shakti cult and interpreted anew the message of Kali and Durga. For Pal, Kali was the 'Mother of India'. Similarly, according to Lajpat Rai, the key to freedom lay in the new religion (Arya Samaj) advocated by Swami Dayanand.

Henceforth the nationalist movement aiming at political freedom from the British rule became a function of an all-embracing religious movement and nationalism was expressed n religious term and clothed in religio-mythical form.

The Extremist bloc was organised under the leadership of the famous trio Lal-Bal-Pal. The Extremists criticised the Moderates for looking to Britain for the political salvation of India. They came to realise that real interests and not abstract principles determined political practice in colonial regime. They argued that Britain could not permit the free, unfettered and rapid development of the Indian industries, since it would militate against the British industries. Similar was the hitch regarding the Indianisation of services. Was not the national movement itself the product of the conflict of interest of Britain on the one hand and that of India on the other?, they asked. Mere argument and appeals to the democratic conscience and traditions of the Britishers could not remove the objective fact of this conflict of interest. This was inherent in the colonial type of rule. Lajpat Rai maintained that prayers in political matters, where the interests of one nation clashed with those of another, would be useless. Tilak declared that political rights would have to be fought for; and could only be got with strong pressure rather than persuasion. The Extremists denounced their elders' method of work by way of 'prayers, petitions and protests' as mendicancy and their faith in British benevolence as a delusion. They maintained that there was no room for philanthropy in politics. India should no longer be content to be beggars whining for favour, for if they really cared for their country, they would have to strike blow for themselves. Tilak, therefore, thundered: "Swaraj is my birth right and I shall have it."

Having determined the goal of self-rule the militant nationalists disowned the constitutional approach. In place of constitutional method, they substituted what was called 'passive resistance'. They devised a three-fold programme for effective, practical political action. It comprised Boycott, Swadeshi and National Education. Lajpat Rai felt that the logic of losing business was more likely to impress the nation of shopkeepers than any argument based on the ethics of justice. For the Extremists, Swadeshi was an economic, political and spiritual weapon. They ardently believed in Swadeshi movement which would make the Indians self-respecting, self-reliant and self-supporting.

DIFFERENCES BETWEEN MODERATES AND EXTREMISTS

While the Moderates tended to regard the British rule as a beneficial necessity, the Extremists believed that any foreign rule, however just and benevolent, was a curse. For the Moderates loyalty was synonymous with patriotism but the Extremists thought that loyalty to British rule was incompatible with patriotism. The Moderates had an abiding fath in the liberality and sense of justice of the British people. The Extremists dismissed this as a snare and delusion. The Extremists demanded a radical change in the system of government itself. Again, whereas the elder nationalists believed that the continuance of British rule was the indispensable condition of India's progress and prosperity, the Extremists argued that political freedom was the essential preliminary to all national progress. Further, in the latter's view, the British rule had been economically an unmitigated disaster for India. Comparing the two blocs of the Congress, M.N. Roy remarked: "Whereas the Moderates were socially progressive but politically conservative, the Extremists were socially reactionary but politically progressive."

Since the movement for self-rule led by militant nationalists was based on religion and tradition of the Hindu society, it has been criticised for introducing religious obscurantism and Hindu mysticism in politics. It has also been attacked for creating a sense of estrangement among the Muslims, who comprised one third of the Indian population. How could they be inspired by a past which had nothing to do with Islam? "The insistence on orthodox religion as the heart of the national movement, the proclamation of the supposed spiritual superiority of the ancient Hindu civilisation to modern Western civilisation (what modern psychology calls "compensatory delusion") inevitably retarded and weakened the real advance of the national movement and of political consciousness while the emphasis on Hinduism must bear a share of responsibility for the alienation of wide section of Muslim opinion from the national movement"[4] Prof. A.R. Desai also holds the same view when he states: "By identifying national awakening with a revival of Hinduism they (Extremists) not only cut off the Muslim masses from the national movement but also opened the way to the government's astute counter-move as the formation of the Muslim League in 1906."[5]

Apart from Muslims, many nationalists who were not in favour of religion-based nationalism disoriented from it. According to Nehru, "the revival of religious nationalism in 1907 was definitely reactionary." Retrospectively speaking, had the national movement been based on a programme of the secular interests of the people, the entire nation, irrespective of caste and community, would have been brought within its orbit.

Nevertheless, the radical nationalists constituted the first batch of martyrs in the national movement. They were the first to experience imprisonment, deportation, and suffered privation. They were distinguished for the great qualities of immense self-sacrifice and suffering for the cause of national freedom. The radical nationalists not only gave militancy and assertiveness to the Indian National Movement, they also gave it a proud ego and instilled self-reliance into it. Besides, it expanded the movement to the lower middle classes and at places even to masses. K.P. Karunakarn in his 'Gandhiana-Interpretations' enumerates the positive achievements[6] of the Extremists as follows:

(1) They made the concept of Indian nation more precise;

(2) They instilled courage and self-confidence among the people;

(3) Made patriotism of the masses a major factor in Indian politics,

(4) Championed the boycott of foreign goods, which helped the development of Indian industries,

(5) By their sacrifices they helped the cause of freedom and democracy in the country.

But despite able leadership, the Extremists Bloc could not influence the course of national movement in the direction of active political agitation, as the Moderates, who were still a stronger bloc, would not allow them any such orientation. The old guards like Naoroji, S.N. Bannerjea, Gokhale and Mehta were still firmly wedded to the policy of social reform, gradual political development and the remaking of India largely in the image of the West. The Moderates, though themselves disillusioned with the British policy, did not accept the ideology and methods of the militant nationalists. They were reluctant to launch any agitation for the attainment of Swaraj.

SCHISM WITHIN THE INDIAN NATIONAL CONGRESS

Because of these differences- ideological and methodological the two blocs began to move away from each other. Besides ideological and methodological differences, perhaps, "there was also a conflict between palisade age and fiery youth, between an upper class leadership and lower middle class following."[7] But the immediate cause of the cleavage lay in the fact that the Moderates were satisfied with the prepared scheme of reform under Lord Minto but the Extremists found them wholly unacceptable. All this resulted in estrangement between the two groups, which came to surface at the stormy Congress session at Surat (1907). The open split occurred on the question of Presidentship of the Congress. The extremists wanted to capture the leadership of the organisation and they demanded open election when the name of Rash Behari Ghosh was proposed by the Moderates. Since their demand was not conceded, a complete rupture between the two blocs became inevitable; and it was not until 1916 that the two wings were reunited.

Soon after the Surat Split, the Moderates called a convention (1908) and framed the following constitution in order to debar the extremists from the organisation: "The INC has for its ultimate goals the attainment by India self-government similar to that enjoyed by other members of the British Empire. It seeks to advance towards this goal by strictly constitutional means, by bringing about a steady reform of the existing system of the government." As a result of the new constitution adopted by the Congress, the Extremists were practically excluded and in their absence, the Moderates enjoyed undisputed sway till 1914.

STERN REPRESSION AND ECLIPSE OF EXTREMISTS

The British authority viewed with great concern and consternation the growing strength of militant nationalism. Taking advantage of the cleavage in the Congress, the government decided to crack down on the Extremists in order to crush the agitational politics. It passed the Seditious Meeting Act (1907) to curb public meetings and demonstrations. It enacted the News papers Incitement To Offences Act (1908) to throttle the voice of the critical press. The Criminal Law Amendment Act (1908) was also placed on the statute book to provide a special form of trial for the terrorist offences. Many leaders were deported out of India. Early in May 1907, Lajpat Rai and Sardar Ajit Singh were deported to Mandlay without trial for a few months. Tilak was sentenced to rigorous imprisonment at Mandlay on the basis of some writings in the 'Kesari'. In Bengal alone, nine prominent deportations took place. Aurobindo Ghosh was kept in prison for a year and B.N. Dutt, Editor of Yugantar, was given a long sentence. The Yugantar, Sandhya and Bandematram were suppressed.

Notes

1. Mukerjee, H.N., Indian Struggle For Freedom, Calcutta, p.76

2. Majumdar, R.C., History of Freedom Movement, Vol. 2,p.5

3. Mehrotra, S.R., op.cit., p.43

4. Dutt, R.P., India Today, 1940, p.292

5. Desai, A.R., op.cit., p.333

6. Karunakaran, K.P., Gandhiana: Interpretations, Gitanjali Pub. House, N. Delhi, p.45

7. Mehrotra, S.R., op.cit, p.43

Chapter 8

TERRORIST MOVEMENT

The left-wing of the Congress eventually came to be divided into three groups as a result of agitational outburst and governmental repression: (1) The left nationalists-Extremists, (2) the terrorists, and (3) the revolutionaries. However, the emergence of all the three groups ware the result of the same set of circumstances, as already mentioned in the last chapter.

The Extremists constituted the bulk of the left-wing the Congress. They aimed at Swaraj as the panacea for all the ills from which India was suffering,. They advocated passive resistance, non-violent civil disobedience and non-cooperation with the government in all fields of administration. The Extremists were not in favour of use of force because they realised that India was a disarmed nation, but they did not believe in the purity of means either. They also did not regard Indian connection with England to be for the good of the country. But they could not play any significant role until 1916, when they acquired a command over the Indian National Congress and they continued to maintain their sway until the advent of Gandhi on the Indian political scene in 1920.

However, not all Extremists remained satisfied with the programme of Swadeshi and Boycott. Some of them more young and more sensitive and more impassioned - took to the cult of the bomb. Their disillusionment with the ineffective passive resistance together with their knowledge about revolutionary movements of European nations for freedom and the method of conspiratorial terrorism inspired them to build up similar organisations and adopt similar method in India as well.

The terrorists were a small group of youngmen who believed that the British rule was an unmitigated evil. For them, violence was the only method by which the Britishers could be ousted from India. Though they realised that 'Atankvad' could not be 'Sampoorna Kranti, but they believed that 'Kranti' could not succeed without 'Atankvad'. They argued that an ounce of lead can work more wonders than a ton of arguments and moral persuasion."[1]

Their programme comprised political assassination and armed dacoities with a view to secure money for their work. Though they killed and got killed, they could not be called a trigger-happy lot. The main centres of their activities were Bengal, Punjab and Maharashtra. However, Bengal was the main centre of the terrorists movement in its early phase. In a way, it was the offshoot of the anti-partition of Bengal agitation.

The high priests of the terrorist movement were Barindra Kumar Ghosh (younger brother of Aurobindo Ghosh) and Bhupendra Nath Dutt (younger brother of Vivekanand). They openly preached the cult of violence through journals like Yugantar. They organised revolutionary societies modelled upon the Russian and Italian secret societies for planning and executing acts of terrorism. The deportation of Sardar Ajit Singh (uncle of Bhagat Singh) and Lala Lajpat Rai to Mandlay in 1907 prepared the background of the terrorist movement. Their activities commenced in 1907 with an attempt to blow up the train in which the Lt. Governor of Bengal Presidency, Sir Andan Frazer, was travelling. Shortly after, in December 1907, the District Magistrate of Dacca was shot in the back but without fatal results. On April 30, 1908 an attempt was made by Khudi Ram Bose (member of Yugantar group) on the life of Mr. Kingsford, who, as the Chief Presidency Magistrate of Calcutta, had sent many persons accused of political offences to jail; it however resulted in the death of two innocent ladies because of mistaken identity. Significantly, it was the first case of a bomb explosion in India. In 1909, an attempt was made at Ahmedabad to blow off the carriage in which Lord and Lady Minto were driving.

There was some activity of this nature in Maharashtra also. The murder of W.C. Rand (Plague Commissioner of Poona) and his associate, Lt. Ayerst, (which led to Tilak's imprisonment) marked the beginning of terrorist activity in Maharashtra. In subsequent years, Shyamji Krishan Verma, the Chapekar brothers and the Savarkar brothers were the main organisers of terrorist activities in Maharashtra.[2]

Notes

1. Suda, J.P., op.cit., p.72
2. Ibid., p.72

Chapter 9

REVOLUTIONARY MOVEMENT— FIRST PHASE (1907-1910)

Besides the extremists and the terrorists, there was another group that occupied a middle position between the two groups. They were called revolutionaries. The revolutionaries were those persons who believed in overthrowing the British government in India by means of mass uprising against the government. Unlike the terrorists, they disapproved of individual and secret murders, destruction of public property or killing of foreigners. They wanted to organise a rebellion against the foreign government. They advocated even tampering with the loyalty of the army and guerilla warfare for overthrowing the foreign rule. In such a warfare they depended on the supply of arms from foreign countries hostile to Britain. However, their work was not confined to India alone. They were equally active in China, Japan, London, Paris, Berlin and North America.

Some of the most prominent revolutionaries outside India included Shyamji Krishna Verma, V.D. Savarkar, P.M. Bapat, Madam Bhikaji Cama (a Parsee lady who earlier had worked as Secretary to Naoroji, a British M.P.), who was connected with the Paris Indian Society established by S.R. Rana under the inspiration of Shyamji Krishna Verma, and who also unfurled the first tricolour flag at the International Socialist Congress (Germany), designed by Hem Chand Das in 1907), Bhai Parmanand, Mohd. Barkatullah, V.V.S. Iyer, Lala Hardayal, Virendra Chattopadhaya, M.P. T. Acharya, Gyan Chand Verma, Rash Behari Bose, Sardar Sohan Singh, Obeidullah Sindhi (who translated Savarkar's book, Indian War of Independence in Tamil).

REVOLUTIONARY ACTIVITIES ABROAD.

ENGLAND. Revolutionary societies were at work in England where Shyamji Krishna Verma and V.D. Savarkar were responsible for vigorous propaganda. Shyamji Krishna Verma established the Indian Home Rule Society in February 1905 and opened the India House in London. V.D. Savarkar organised Abhinav Bharat and celebrated the fiftieth anniversary of the 1857 Revolt and wrote 'Indian War of Independence 1857' in 1907. It was under their instigation that one Madan Lal Dhingra assassinated Sir William Curzon Wyllie, the ADC of the Secretary of State for India, who was 'the eye and the brain' of India Office. As a result, Dhingra was hanged (17 August, 1909) and Savarkar was given a sentence of transportation for life.

GERMANY. In Berlin, Virendra Chattopadhyaya (brother of Sarojini Naidu), Dr. Avinash Chandra Bhattacharya (cousin of M.N. Roy), Lala Hardayal, Tarak Nath Das, Dr. Abdul Hafiz, Dr. M.G. Prabhakar, Barkatullah, Jitendra Nath Lahiri, Bhupendra Nath Dutt and others set up an Indian committee, known as the Berlin Committee on 13 September, 1914. The Committee forged links with the Ghadar Party in America and the Anushilan and Yugantar Group in India.

NORTH AMERICA. In 1913, the Indian revolutionaries in North America formed the Ghadr Party under the leadership of Lala Har Dayal. The Party sent people to organise uprisings in India. Besides, an Anglo-American National Association was formed in 1907 and Barkatullah and S.L. Joshi together established India House in New York.

AFGHANISTAN. Another valiant effort was made by Raja Mahendra Pratap, the wandering pilgrim for freedom. Mahendra Pratap was the Chief of Hathras in U.P. He had wide intellectual interests, a very perceptive mind and had a great patriotic fervour. He also felt that Indian struggle for freedom would succeed only with outside help. When the First World War broke out, he went to Europe and submitted a note to German Foreign Office in which he stated that the British Government would be overthrown by the people of India provided the Afghan army would invade India. He expressed desire to go to Kabul, the capital of Afghanistan. His proposal was accepted and an Indo-German Mission was sent to Kabul under the leadership of Mahendra Pratap. Meanwhile, he sent his emissary, Harish Chandra, to India to contact Indian revolutionaries in order to inform them of the proposed plan. The Mission on its way met the Sultan of Turkey, and Barkatullah succeeded in procuring a Fatwa from him asking Muslims of India to act in unison with Hindus. After many meetings between the Mission and the Afghan officials, the revolutionaries in Kabul proclaimed a Provisional Government of Free India on December 1915 with Raja Mahendra Pratap as president and Barkatullah as Prime Minister. Mahendra Pratap then went to the Czar of Russia for help to his government, but there was no response. After the Russian revolution Raja visited Russia in 1918. However, after the end of the War in which Germany was defeated, the Indian revolutionaries left Berlin and some of them went to Moscow. Later on, in 1920, the

Soviet authority decided to entrust to M.N. Roy the responsibility of handling Indian affairs, and M.N. Roy accordingly formed an All-India Central Revolutionary Committee. Roy's scheme was to arrange for the invasion of India through Afghanistan. Though his plan had no chance of success, yet Russia's support to Indian cause did give a new orientation to Indian revolutionaries.

JAPAN. After Ghadr Party's plan of an uprising was foiled at Lahore, Rash Behari Bose left India and went to Japan. Even before his arrival in 1915, Barakatullah had gone to Japan in 1910 and carried on anti-British propaganda. Now it was intensified by R.B. Bose, H.L. Gupta and others. However, the Japanese government did not give any active support to the Indian revolutionaries.

As far as the home turf was concerned, the credit for organising revolutionary activities mainly goes to Rash Behari Bose and Sachindra Nath Sanyal in the Northern part of India and Jatin Mukerjea in Bengal. The organisation of revolutionaries in Bengal was called Anushilan Samiti. It had many branches; the group of Barindra Kumar Ghosh was known as Yugantar Group. The work of revolutionaries were carried out in various forms and at different levels, journals like Sandhya, Bandematram and Yugantar started to stir up public opinion. These journals became the mouth piece of revolutionaries. Besides, there were Akharas for physical and moral training, and secret classes were held. In 1907, Aurobindo worked out a plan of revolutionary action and put forth his scheme in a booklet, Bhavani Mandir, His idea was to develop a band of Karma Yogis. Further, Aurobindo and Barindra published 'Vartman Ranniti' (rules of modern warfare), which made a fervent plea for guerilla warfare.

The first bomb blast on 30 April, 1908 by Khudi Ram Bose had shaken the British Empire. Two days later, the Maniktala Gardens were searched by the police and bombs and dynamites were recovered. A charge of conspiracy was brought against Ghosh brothers and their associates. The case was known as Alipore Conspiracy Case. The case created a sensation all over the country. In the Maniktala bomb case almost all the leaders of the different groups of revolutionaries in Bengal were sentenced either to life imprisonment or to long terms of imprisonment. In fact, by 1910 the revolutionary movement had lost all its well-known ideologues. B.B. Upadhyaya had already died during his trial in 1907. Tilak was sentenced to transportation for life in 1908. Lajpat Rai avoided political activity after release from Mandlay and left for the States. Bipin Chandra Pal left India for England in 1909, and after returning to India in 1911 he began to eschew militant politics. In April 1910, Aurobindo \

Ghosh withdrew to Pondichery (a French colony) in order to avoid arrest. The Howarah Sibpur case (1910) marked the end of the first phase of revolutionary movement in India.

REVOLUTIONARY MOVEMENT - SECOND PHASE (1912-15)

The second phase of the revolutionary movement began in 1912-13 and reached its climax in 1915. If in the first phase the revolutionaries wanted to strike terror by political assassinations and to set before the frightened and apathetic countrymen models of courage, dedication and self-sacrifice, in the second phase, the revolutionaries were more concerned with issues of practical nature, and they were encouraged to think in terms of a resurrection. The second phase also saw the emergence of new revolutionares like Jatin Mukerjea and Narendra Nath Bhattacharya. Narendra was a close friend of Jatin whom he met in jail in connection with Howarah Sibpur Gang case (1910). Jatin Mukerjea carried out the arduous task of bringing many young revolutionaries together. He was a man of extraordinary courage and was known as 'Bagha Jatin'. In 1915, all revolutionary groups were brought into a loose federation under Jatin. He and another veteran revolutionary, Jadu Gopal Mukerjee, had chalked out a plan for armed revolt, and for that purpose wanted to bring arms and also money required for powerful organisation and implementation of the plan. They got the message from Dr. Avinash Chandra Bhattacharya (a member of the Berlin Committee) that German help in the form of arms and money would be made available. Jitendra Nath Lahiri, a revolutionary, who was working in the Far East also sent word to the Bengal revolutionaries to send some revolutionaries to coordinate the plan. The choice of Jatin fell on Narendra Nath Bhattacharya (Jatin's second in command) Narendra (later M.N. Roy) was a young, intelligent and fearless revolutionary. Narendra was asked to proceed to Batavia in order to meet the German Officer-in-Command (Helfferich) and to implement the plan of sending arms and money to India. Narendra travelled under the assumed name, Rev. C. A. Martin, and was able to send a large sum of money. It was decided that a ship 'Maverick' would carry the arms but it could not reach the appointed port. Both Jatin and Narendra then chalked out another plan of bringing the arms through the land route. But that too was aborted. On 7th August, 1915 the police raided the headquarters of Jatin Mukerjee at Balasore (Orissa) and Jatin was killed fighting against the police.

The revolutionary movement remained very active in Bengal and the Punjab during 1913-16. About sixteen outrages were committed in Bengal during 1913 and 1914. The number increased still further in 1916. An unfortunate feature of these outrages were that the dacoities sometimes accompanied with murder, were committed and holds up carried out for the purpose of financing the movement. Some of the Punjab revolutionaries were responsible for an attempt (1912) on the life of Lord Hardinge, the Governor General. As a result, the Delhi Conspiracy case was started which culminated in death sentence being passed on Amir Chand, Avadh Behari, Bal Mukund and Basant Kumar Viswas.

LALA HARDAYAL AND THE GHADR MOVEMENT

The Ghadr movement was led by Lala Hardayal. Lala had a distinguished academic career and had studied at Oxford. He was influenced by Shyamji Krishna Verma and joined his Home Rule Movement in 1907. He started a weekly paper, 'Ghadr'. The different associations were brought together and a regular Ghadr Party was formed in 1913 in North America. The aim of the Party was to overthrow the Raj in India and to establish a national republic based on equality and freedom. The measures adopted by the Ghadr movement were[2]: (a) Seduction of Indian troops, (b) Murder of loyal subjects and officials (c) hoisting of the revolutionary flag, (d) breaking of jails, (e) looting of trains and thanas (f) propagation of seditious literature, (g) courting foreign enemies of Britain, (h) procuring of arms, (i) manufacture of bombs, (j) formation of secret societies, (k) destruction of railways and telegraph, and (l) recruitment of youngmen for revolutionary work.

KOMAGATA MARU EPISODE

The anti-British sentiment which the Ghadr Party sought to create was intensified owing to Komagata Maru incident, in which the British massacred a number of Sikhs. The incident arose because of the Indians in Canada who, under the inspiration of Lala Hardyal, decided to challenge the discriminatory immigration law in Canada prohibiting any immigrants after 31 March, 1914 except those who were direct passengers from Calcutta. Baba Gurudit Singh hired a Japanese ship, Komagata Maru and took five hundred Indians, mostly Sikhs, from Calcutta. When the ship reached Vancouver on 22 May 1914 the Canadian authorities refused permission to the passengers to land. The ship stayed in Canadian waters for nearly two months and the passengers suffered great hardships. The Komagata Maru started the return journey, but it was disallowed entry at Hongkong and Singapore. Ultimately, it reached the mouth of Hooghly (Calcutta) on 26 September, 1914. The Ghadr movement got a further fillip because of this incident. Bhagwan Singh, Barkatullah and Ram Chander directed the activities of the Ghadr Party. They wanted to seize the opportunity which had emerged owing to the advent of the War. At a meeting of the Party on 15 August, 1915 it was decided to declare an open warfare against the British rule in India. However, the British government in India took prompt measures and leaders like Sohan Singh Bhakna, Kesar Singh and Jwala Singh were arrested. The leadership thereafter passed on to Vishnu Ganesh, Pingle and Ras Behari Bose.

Rash Behari Bose, Sachindra Nath Sanyal, V.G. Pingle and Kartar Singh prepared a master plan and fixed 21 February, 1915 as the date for starting the revolution. But on 19 February, before the proposed reprisal, the police (already informed by Kirpal Singh who turned out to be a British spy) raided the headquarters of the Ghadr Party at Lahore and arrested a number of leaders. As a result the plan of the uprising collapsed. Pingle and Kartar Singh were arrested and only Rash Behari Bose succeeded in leaving India. The government prosecuted the revolutionaries under the Defence of India Act and set up a Special tribunal for the trial known as the 'Lahore Conspiracy Case'. Both Kartar Singh and Pingle were executed. Thus ended the Ghadr Movement. In the opinion of Prof. V.D. Mahajan, "The Ghadr Movement was the first purely secular movement which aimed at liberating India by the force of arm. It also marked the beginning of the end of the loyalty of the Sikhs to the British Raj."

During the violent activities of the left-wing the Moderates remained calm. They had no sympathy with the terrorists and revolutionaries. Leaders like S.N. Bannerjee and Sir Ashutosh Mukerjee even asked the government to take stern measures to crush their movement. In order to enlist their continued goodwill and support, the British authorities brought forth another measure of constitutional reforms known as Morley-Minto Reforms.

Like the Terrorist Movement, the Revolutionary Movement also fizzled out without achieving its cherished goal. There were several reasons for its failure: Firstly, the revolutionary movement appealed to a very small circle of youngmen and lacked a central organisation which could direct and control it on an all-India basis; secondly, the procurement of arms from Germany proved a fiasco or what M.N. Roy called a 'wild goose chase'; thirdly, the entry of the USA into the First World War marked a turning point in the course of the War; Germany got demoralised and became reluctant to give arms assistance, as promised; fourthly, the dangling of self-government in the form of Montagu's Declaration of August 20, 1917 took the wind out of the revolutionary sail; fifthly, the upper middle class leadership was unsympathetic to it; sixthly, when Gandhiji appeared on the scene and introduced a new technique of revolution — Satyagraha, the revolutionary technique lost much of its appeal.

To sum up, the cult of bomb and violence died not because of repression but because the government opened the path of reconciliation. In addition, the rise of an Indian leadership commanding the confidence of the people also contributed to the decline of underground activities. But it is to be noted that despite the adoption of Gandhian technique by the mainstream leadership, both the terrorist as well as revolutionary activities continued, though sporadically, during the Gandhian era until the end of the Quit India Movement.

REVOLUTIONARY MOVEMENT THIRD PHASE (1922-42)

The absence of Gandhi from the scene due to his arrest (1922-24) led to great unrest and the revolutionary activities were revived. A group of young revolutionaries was formed in India and thus began the third phase of the revolutionary movement.

Sachindra Nath Sanyal (a disciple of Jatin Mukerjea) was one of the leading revolutionaries of 1920s. After having suffered an imprisonment for five years at Andaman on account of the Benares Conspiracy Case, Sanyal was released in 1922 under a general amnesty. In 1922, he met Prof. Jaya Chandra Vidyalankar who was teaching History in National College at Lahore. Sanyal's sacrifice, sincerity, and above all, his revolutionary fervour cast a spell on some students and two of them, Bhagat Singh (nephew of Sardar Ajit Singh) and Bhagvati Charan joined the Hindustan Republican Association, formed by Sachindra Sanyal. Subsequently, Bhagat Singh and Bhagvati Charan decided to build up a cadre of revolutionary youngmen and they started a new organisation, Navjavan Bharat Sabha. At this very juncture, another youngman Chandra Shekhar Azad, decided to devote his energies for building up an organisation for an armed struggle against the British rule. Azad came in contact with Rajendra Lahiri and joined the revolutionary group of Yogesh Chatterjea.

These different groups of revolutionaries were functioning at different places and were preparing for a revolution. All of them believed that India's freedom could be won only through armed struggle. These revolutionaries keenly felt the need for setting up an all-India organisation with its branches in different parts of India. As a first step in this direction Bhagat Singh from Lahore and Chandra Shekhar Azad from Banares met leaders of different groups of revolutionaries and undertook the work of building a well-knit and efficient secret organisation.

KAKORI CONSPIRACY CASE

On 9 August, 1925 a group of revolutionaries with a view to raising funds looted government cash from a train going from Saharanpur to Lucknow near Kakori. This was organised by Sachindra Sanyal, Yogesh Chandra Chatterjea, S.N. Biswas, Bhupendra Sanyal, Manmath Das Gupta and others. In this case, Ram Prasad Bismil, Rajendra Lahiri, Ashfaqullah Khan and Thakur Roshan Singh were sentenced to death and later on were hanged. Yogesh Chandra Chatterjea and Sachindra Sanyal were given transportation for life. Chandra Shekhar Azad, however, escaped and alongwith Bhagat Singh joined hands with other revolutionaries to form the Hindustan Socialist Republican Party in 1928. Bhagat Singh was chosen its President. The aim of this organisation was "to overthrow by force the government in India and to establish a Federated Republican Government instead." Azad was chosen as the Chief of the active wing of the secret organisation called Hindustan Socialist Republican Army. This was for the first time that the young revolutionaries, who were confident that India would be free, also had a dream that free India would be a Socialist Republic. The Hindustan Socialist Republican Association was a secular organisation. Its members were serious students of politics and were watching the political developments carefully.

The death of Lala Lajpat Rai on 17 November, 1928 caused by lathi blows during the demonstration against the Simon Commission infuriated the members of the Hindustan Socialist Republican Army. They met in Lahore and decided to take revenge against Scott and Saunders to whose blows Lala had succumbed. On 15 December, 1928 Lalaji's death was avenged by the death of Saunders, the Dy. S.P. The British officers in Lahore were terribly shaken. The police carried on a vigorous search for arresting those who had killed Saunders. but the revolutionaries had escaped, and within a few days, they again geared up the secret organisation. In February 1929 a centre for making bombs wars set up at Saharanpur under the charge of Dr. Gaya Prasad.

THE PUBLIC SAFETY BILL

In the meanwhile, the British government came to know about the activities of certain trade unionists and also of some youngmen, who had secretly formed the Communist Party in India. In order to deal a deadly blow to all such activities, the British government moved in the Central Assembly, the Public Safety Bill and Trade Disputes Bill. The Bills empowered the government to destroy all civil liberties and to crush the possible uprising of workers in the mills. On 20 March, 1929 many trade unionists and communists were arrested in different parts of India and were hauled up for hatching a conspiracy to overthrow the British government. This case came to be known as the Meerut Conspiracy Case. Since the Bills were opposed by M.R. Jaykar and Moti Lal Nehru and even Vithalbhai Patel, the first Indian President of the Central Assembly, the Viceroy announced that he would use his Special Powers and give assent to them. This declaration by the Viceroy greatly agitated the people and created an atmosphere of unrest all over India. Bhagat Singh with his fine political insight told his colleagues in the H.S.R.A. that an appropriate demonstration against the highhanded and autocratic policy of the British government was the urgent need of the hour, and on his plea it was decided that a violent demonstration against the proposed repressive measures should be made by throwing bombs in the Central Assembly, but with the precaution that no one could be killed. Further, Bhagat Singh and Batukeshwar Dutt were not to run away after throwing the bombs, rather they should allow the police to arrest them. It was also decided that after the explosion of the bomb, Bhagat Singh and Batukeshwar Dutt should throw, from the spectators' gallery, the leaflets containing their statement.

On 8 April, 1929 when V. Patel rose and announced: "I shall now give my verdict on the proposed Bills", there was a deafening noise of a bomb explosion. Bhagat Singh had thrown the bomb. Soon after Dutt also threw the second bomb. Thereafter they also threw red leaflets all over. The leaflets thrown in the Assembly contained a statement which inter alias read" It takes a loud noise to make the deaf hear."[3]

The trial in the Assembly Bomb Case began on 7 May, 1929. Singh and Dutt made a spirited and noble statement before the judge. This historic statement had a tremendous political significance. At the end of the trial, Justice Middleton sentenced Bhagat Singh and Batukeshwar Dutt to transportation for life.

As the police were making frantic searches at different places there was an accidental discovery of a bomb factory at Lahore. Within a few weeks most of the revolutionaries from Pūnjab, UP and Bengal were arrested. Then began the trial of the Lahore Conspiracy Case in which Bhagat Singh and Batukeshwar Dutt were also among the accused along with Raj Guru, Sukhdev and Chandra Shekhar Azad. While in jail the revolutionaries began the heroic hunger strike, which continued for 63 days and one of them, Jatindra Nath Das (a Chemistry student, who knew the method of making bomb) became a martyr after his hunger strike on the 63rd day.

After nine months of trial before the Magistrate, the British government promulgated an ordinance known as the Lahore Conspiracy

Case Ordinance of 1930. According to it, Bhagat Singh and his colleagues were to be tried by a Special Tribunal. The trial continued without the accused, without defence lawyers, without defence witnesses. After this farcical trial which lasted for five months, the Tribunal gave its judgement. Bhagat Singh, Rajguru and Sukhdev were sentenced to death. Seven of the accused including Dutt, were given transportation for life, and others were given long terms of imprisonment.

While the Lahore Conspiracy Case was going on, Chandra Shekhar and his colleagues were not silent. In December, 1929 there was a bomb explosion near Delhi in which the Viceroy Lord Irwin, travelling in his special train, narrowly escaped death. Then followed a series of bomb explosions in which some police officers were killed and many of them injured. The government arrested many others and there was a second Lahore Conspiracy Case. However, Chandra Shekhar again succeeded in giving a slip to the police and escaped arrest.

On 26 February, 1931 Chandra Shekhar Azad held a secret meeting of revolutionaries at Allahabad. According to a plan, Azad went to Alfred Park on 27th morning to meet his three colleagues. An informer, however, spotted him and conveyed the news to the police. For almost 2 minutes, a battle of bullets went on between Azad and the police. Though Azad fought fearlessly the brave revolutionary succumbed to injuries.

LEFTIST REVOLUTIONARY MOVEMENT

It is worth mentioning here that India's revolutionary movement was not an isolated activity. The momentous events in the world and new ideas, which inspired people in different parts of the world, had a profound influence on India's freedom struggle. The success of the Russian Revolution in 1917 and the communist philosophy, which had inspired the leaders of the Russian Revolution, influenced some leaders in India and created in them an awareness of the significance of the part which the working class played in changing the course of history. M.N. Roy, who was a close associate of Lenin, was the first Indian leader to send communist literature to India. The working class in India was becoming politically conscious and the trade union activity assumed a great significance. In 1921, a group of young idealists, who were deeply influenced by the Marxist philosophy and by the Communist Party's method of organising workers and peasants, started their activities in the urban industrial centres, like Bombay, Calcutta, Madras and Kanpur. There were also some efforts in organising the peasantry in Punjab and UP. The Communist Party started functioning secretly in India. It was a part of the International Communist Movement, and took its dictates regarding policy decision from Moscow. However, this movement gathered momentum when Philip Spratt, a member of the British Communist Party, came to India and helped the local communists in organising trade unions and in propagating the idea of socialism.

MEERUT CONSPIRACY CASE

The British government was shaken by the prospect of revolutionary activities on the Russian pattern and decided to crush it. On 20 March 1929, 31 trade unionists and important communist workers in different centres were arrested and brought to Meerut for a trial which came to be known as the Meerut Conspiracy Case. Among the accused were Philip Spratt, S.A. Dange, S.V. Ghate, K.N. Joglekar, R.S. Nimbkar, S.S. Mirajkar, Dr. Gangadhar Adhikari, Muzaffar Ahmed, S.H. Jhabwalla and others. The team of lawyers who formed a defence committee included Moti Lal Nehru, Kailash Nath Katju and Jawahar Lal Nehru. The trial went on for four years. The Session Court delivered severe punishments. Muzaffar Ahmed was given transportation for life; fifteen others, including S.A. Dange, Dr. Adhikari, P.C. Joshi and M.N. Roy (in absentia) were given long terms of imprisonment from five years to twelve years. When an appeal was made to High Court, the sentences were considerably reduced.

CHITTAGONG ARMOURY RAID

Certain cities in India have always been in the forefront of the freedom struggle. Chittagong in East Bengal was one of such cities since the days of partition of Bengal. On 18 April, 1930, a raid known as the Chittagong Armoury Raid under a plan (the Death Programme) was hatched by the President of the Indian Republican Army, Chittagong branch, Surya Sen. After the raid, the police and the army were on the offensive, but the revolutionaries were not cowed down. During the next two and a half years there were in and around Chittagong several bomb explosions. In the Chittagong Armoury Raid Case, Surya Sen and Tarkeshwar Dastidar were given death sentence and were later on executed. Thirteen were given transportation for life and others varying terms of imprisonment.

The last important incident of this violent nature was the assassination of Michael O'Dwyer, the ex-Governor of Punjab. "After the Jallianwala Bagh massacre in 1919, Udham Singh resolved to punish Michael O'Dwyer. Significantly, when he launched on a mission to pursue O'Dwyer, Udham Singh (as a mark of national integration) named himself Ram Mohammed Singh. Udham Singh waited patiently for 20 years and his chance to kill O'Dwyer came only in 1940."[4]

By the early 1930s the revolutionary movement came to an end with the introduction of Provincial Autonomy under the Act of 1935, when the energies were directed to capture of power. The remaining terrorists and revolutionaries either joined the Communist Party or the Hindu Mahasabha. To conclude, the revolutionaries were ardent patriots. They were impatient at the unjust and repressive measures of the government, and gave expression to their wrath through violent action, and as a consequence suffered long terms of imprisonment. Their sacrifices and sufferings stirred even those who did not agree with their violent methods. "These revolutionaries believed in the maximum sacrifice by minimum men and tried to awaken the masses not through preaching but by practising highest penance for freedom."[5] To quote V.P. Verma, "they were men of heroic courage, immense patriotic enthusiasm and noble dedication. They represented the recklessness of youthful idealism."[6] They deserve an important place in the history of freedom struggle. People like Chapekar Brothers, K.R. Bose, Bhagat Singh, Chandra Shekhar Azad, Rash Behari Bose, etc. will occupy a perennial place of honour among Indian freedom fighters. Significantly, at a time when the main stream leaders were thinking in terms of constitutional agitations, they stood for complete independence — two decades earlier than the Congress." It is also significant that the early revolutionists were believers in Hindu spiritual metaphysics and they had faith in Providence and Divine forces. Particularly in the first and second phase of Indian terrorism, the spiritual foundations were very dominant, but after the early twenties a socialist and communist element was sought to be added. The Hindustan Republican Association was not only a secular organisation but was also committed to end economic exploitation. When the old revolutionaries were arrested during the Kakori Conspiracy Case, Bhagat Singh and Chandra Shekhar Azad changed the name of the Hindustan Republican Association into Hindustan Socialist Republican Association. Bhagat Singh in particular had faith in the establishment of the sovereignty of the Proletariat.[7] Thus, their vision was not confined only to the birth of a new nation but it also envisaged an end of the suffocating control of the exploiters, who had the political power in their clutches. They were not just patriots and romantic revolutionaries but men committed to social and economic revolution.

No doubt, the terrorist and the revolutionary movements failed in their main objective — the liberation of the country from the foreign yoke. "But it is not correct to regard their movement as a total failure. Revolutionary Terrorism gave the Congress much of its bargaining strength, since the Congress was a lesser evil in the eyes of the British. Besides, the revolutionaries became evocative symbols in the nationalist movement and provided inspiration to millions of Indians. The sacrifices of these terrorists and revolutionaries form the subject matter of national saga. Some of them were glamourised as national heroes. Their examples continued to influence people for a long time to come. The Quit India Movement (1942) was inspired by the terrorist movement in some of its techniques. Subhash Chandra Bose was closely assisted by Rash Behari Bose, a former revolutionary, in the organisation of the Indian National Army."[8]

In the opinion of Prof. V.P. Verma, "Terrorism generally appeared in the early stages of the movement of national liberation and so long as the national movement does not become mature and broad-based, the historical channel for the release of frustration and for the expression of national rage."[9] The terrorists and revolutionaries may be described as 'misguided patriots' (Gandhi), but their movement formed a necessary stage in the freedom saga.

Notes

1. For details see Pradhan, G.P., 'The Revolutionaries in India and Abroad' (Chapter - 6), India's Freedom Struggle, Popular Prakashan, Bombay, 1990, pp. 43-70.

2. Ibid., pp.61-62.

3. Ibid., pp.115

4. Jain, L.C., 'Indian Political Scene A Sky Without Stars', The Radical Humanist, April 1, 1991 p.8

5. Pradhan, G.P., op.cit., p. 124

6. Verma, V.P., Modern Indian Political Thought, Laxmi Narain Aggarwal Education Publishers, Agra, 1974, p.265

7. Ibid., pp. 266, 268

8. bid., p.268

9. Ibid., p.269

Chapter 10

BIRTH OF MUSLIM SEPARATISM—
BEGINNING OF COMMUNAL POLITICS

Far more vital in its effect on the political life of the nation than the rise of terrorists and revolutionaries activities was the introduction of communal politics.[1] Sadly enough, its pernicious effect persists and pollutes political life even today. The topic of communalism in Indian politics has been dealt with at length in Part-II of this book. But a brief reference to it here too is called for to understand the further political developments.

The Congress was ushered into existence with secret sympathy and official support, and was designed to be a counterpoise to threatened Russian intrigues in the country. But with the disappearance of the Russian danger and the claim of the Congress for self-rule, the policy of the government vis-a-vis the Congress underwent a major metamorphosis. Now it began to think of a counterpoise to the Congress. To counteract the growing challenge of militant nationalists, it began to wean away Muslims, a major community in the country. As such, the traditional anti-Muslim policy of the government since 1857 was now reversed and it became anti-Congress and even anti-Hindu. In fact, the partition of Bengal was clearly a clever move to drive a wedge between Hindus and Muslims. The Policy of what was called 'divide and rule' was intensified after the entry of Extremists in Indian politics.

To keep away Muslims from the national mainstream the services of Sir Syed Ahmed Khan- an acknowledged leader of the Muslim community was enlisted. Under the influence of Mr. Theodore Beck and his successor, Archibald, both principals of M.A.O. College, Sir Syed came to believe that an Anglo-Muslim alliance would be more conducive to the interest of his community than a Hindu-Muslim alliance. The result was the creation of two Muslim Organisations — The Anglo-Muslim Defence Association and the Muslim Educational Conference both under the leadership of Sir Syed Ahmed Khan. Needless to say, both enjoyed

British patronage. Interestingly, just as A.O. Hume was the inspiration behind the Congress movement, Sir Syed Ahmed became the guiding spirit behind the Muslim movement. These organisations marked the beginning of separatism in Indian politics.

BIRTH OF THE MUSLIM LEAGUE

In the year 1906 something happened which coloured the whole subsequent history of the national movement, and had a far-reaching effect on Hindu-Muslim relations. In 1906, Lord Minto had formed a committee to consider the necessity of further constitutional reforms for India. This immediately led to a deputation of seventy five Muslims headed by His Highness, the late Agha Khan, which met Minto at Simla on 10 October, 1906 and claimed separate electorate or communal representation from the Imperial Legislative Council down to the District Boards and weightage to the Muslims. Minto was too eager to agree and readily accepted the principle of communal representation, which found a place in Morley-Minto Reforms and was subsequently institutionalised in the Indian Council Act of 1909. In a way, it was Lord Minto who unconsciously became the real father of Muslim separatism, resulting in the partition of the country. There is a controversy as to whether the deputation was sponsored by the British bureaucracy or depended on the initiative of the Muslim leaders themselves. According to Maulana Mohd. Ali, it was a 'command performance'. But Mr. Coupland maintains: "There is no evidence to suggest that the deputation was in any case engineered by the government." However, it is generally believed that it was Archibald, the principal of M.A.O. College, who wrote to the College Secretary, Nawab Mohsin-ul-Mulk suggesting him to send a Muslim deputation. Subsequently, on December 30, 1906, exactly three months after the Simla Deputation, the Muslim League was founded at Dacca under the Presidentship of Nawab of Dacca, Mushtaq Hussain. The objectives of the Muslim League were defined as follows: "To promote among the Muslims of India feeling of loyalty with the British government, to protect and advance the political rights and interests of the Muslims and respectfully represent their needs and aspirations to the government." Thus was born the first political organisation with a communal bias.

MORLEY-MINTO REFORMS
(INDIAN COUNCIL ACT OF 1909)

According to Coupland, "The Morley-Minto scheme was designed to control and canalise the now fast flowing current of Indian nationalism."[2] If, on the one hand, Moderates were to be satisfied for their continued cooperation, on the other, the growing extremism in the country too had to be stymied. To secure the first, the Legislative Councils were considerably enlarged and their powers increased. For instance, the number of additional members in the Imperial Legislature was enlarged from sixteen to sixty. Besides, the principle of direct election was also recognised for the first time. But the elected members were everywhere kept in a minority to ensure that the official members and the nominated non-officials together outnumbered the elected members, except in Bombay Legislative Council. Thus, only official majority was done away with under the new scheme. In the Imperial Legislature, however, even the official majority was retained. Lord Morley's explicit assertion was that the Act was not designed to introduce any element of responsibility with the government of India. He did not appreciate the idea of self-government for India like that of Canada. To quote him, "The fur coat of Canada was not suitable wear for tropical India." Moreover, the Councils though enlarged, still remained only advisory bodies without any decisive powers. The chief purpose was to include a large number of landlords, industrialists, and loyal Muslims in the Legislative Councils and thereby setting one class or community against the other. Though the Act did recognise the principle of direct election, the communal venom introduced into the body politic through communal electorate poisoned Indian democracy at source. All the same, the Act of 1909 was a conspicuous improvement on the Act of 1892.

Notes

1.   Suda, J.P., op.cit., p.73
2.   Coupland, India A Restatement, p.104.

Chapter 11

FIRST WORLD WAR — ITS IMPACT ON INDIAN POLITICS

Between the inauguration of Morley-Minto Reforms (1910) and the beginning of the First World War in 1914, political life in India was rather at a low key barring stray and sporadic revolutionary activities at different places. The subdued political activity was mainly due to the fact that the leadership of the Congress had passed into the hands of Moderates. In the absence of extreme leaven, the Congress again settled into an uneventful course of constitutionalism. Despite various short-comings in the Indian Council Act, the Moderates were willing to work out the Reforms. Another important reason for the lull in the national movement was that Lord Hardinge, the new Governor General, sought conciliation and pacification. To pacify the Indian temper, he annulled the partition of Bengal and synchronised this step with the visit to India of George V and Queen Mary in December 1911. The capital was also shifted from Calcutta to Delhi, the legendary Capital of Indian history.

In August 1914, the War began in Europe. India being a British dependency automatically found itself a belligerent. It is worth remembering that in this War India joined whole-heartedly on the side of their masters. She helped in the War efforts magnificently with men, money and material. Interestingly, even the Mahatma, the apostle of non-violence, threw himself whole-heartedly in the support of the War efforts. India began to entertain hope that their efforts should be duly rewarded in the form of political advancement, if not emancipation. They felt encouraged by the Allies' Declaration that the War was being fought "to make the world safe for democracy" and by Wilson's (US President) emphasis on the right of self-determination. India found it opportune to advance the cause of self-rule. The reappearance of Extremists on the scene after completing their terms of imprisonment reinforced it. Tilak, who became the undisputed leader of the Indian masses after passing away of Gokhale and Pheroze Shah Mehta, took stock of the political situation and came to realise that the two wings of the Congress should reunite to make the Congress an effective force. He also felt that the Muslim community should be brought within the mainstream so that the campaign for Swaraj and constitutional democracy should be resumed. With these moves, the national movement gathered a new momentum.

LUCKNOW SESSION AND
THE CONGRESS-LEAGUE PACT (1916)

The Lucknow session of 1916 was significant not only in that it brought the two wings of the Congress together, it also led to an entente between the Congress and the Muslim League. Although, the Muslim League had been loyal to the Empire ever since its inception, events were happening in India and outside, which led it to give up its loyalist instance. Internally, the annulment of partition of Bengal jolted the Muslim Leage out of its loyalist rut. Externally, the Muslim community was further disillusioned by the hostile attitude of the British government towards the Sultan of Turkey (the Caliph of Islam), who had been humbled by Italy and the Balkan Powers through the connivance of England. Italy snatched away Tripoli from Turkey, and Serbia, Greece, Bulgaria, Montenegro broke away from the Ottomon Empire. The treatment meted out by the Allied Powers to the Sultan during the War caused tremendous resentment among the Muslims. A few Muslim leaders, such as Maulana Azad and Maulana Mohd. Ali were engaged in bringing home to their brethren that the interests of all the Indian communities were intertwined.

All these developments brought about a change in the attitude of Muslims towards the government, and compelled them to come closer to the Congress. For instance, at the Lucknow Session in 1913, the Muslim League adopted as its objective the attainment, under the aegis of the British Crown, of the system of self-government suitable to India through constitutional means by promoting national unity, by fostering public spirit among the people of India, and by cooperating with other communities in the said purpose. The Congress at its Session at Karachi the same year responded to the hand of friendship extended by the League and warmly appreciated the adoption by the League of the ideal of self-government within the British Empire. Incidentally, M.A. Jinnah, who had just joined the League (1913) was greatly responsible for this change in the League's attitude.

CONGRESS-LEAGUE SCHEME—THE LUCKNOW PACT (1916)

At Lucknow the two main political bodies adopted a joint scheme of reforms known as the Congress-League Scheme. Its adoption was the result of a bargain between them. The scheme was worked out by Jinnah,

Sir Wazir Hassan, Tilak, Moti Lal Nehru and Sir Tej Bahadur Sapru. If the League accepted the long-standing Congress demand for self-government, the Congress on its part accepted the Muslim League's demand for separate communal electorates. Although, the Congress-League entente was held as a signifcant step towards national solidarity, it had a dark side too. The submission to League communalism and a compromise on the fundamental issue of Indian nationality proved disastrous for the country. To quote R.C. Majumdar, "The Congress action in 1916 well and truly laid the foundation of Pakistan thirty years later."[1] The Montford Report also declared that the principle of communal representation was highly dangerous and an obstacle in the way of unity and evolution of one nationalism in India. The Congress naively thought that it was a temporary measure and would be abandoned at a later day. But as the later events showed, their belief turned out to be illusory and fatal. The communal demands once conceded continued to figure in all later constitutional schemes like the Act of 1919, the Communal Award (1932) and the Act of 1935. Perhaps the Lucknow Pact was made without the slightest thought for its fatal consequences. All the same, the Lucknow Pact is regarded a land mark in Indian political history.

The constitutional provisions of the Congress-League Scheme for post-War reforms[2] were as follows :

Firstly, it was proposed that the provinces should be freed from the Central government as far as possible in matters of administration and finance; secondly, four-fifths of the Central as well as Provincial Legislators should be elected on the basis of as wide a franchise as possible. In the Central Legislature, the Muslims were to have one-third of the elected seats, although they constituted one-fourth of the total population; thirdly, one-half of the members of Central as well as Provincial Executive Councils were to be elected members of the respective Legislative Councils; fourthly, both the Central as well as Provincial governments were bound to act according to the resolutions passed by their respective Legislative Councils, unless vetoed by the Governor General or the Governors as the case may be; fifthly, the Central Legislative Council will have no say in military and foreign affairs; and lastly, it proposed that the relation of the Secretary of State should be similar to those of the Colonial Secretary with the governments of Dominions. But these constitutional proposals were 'too radical' to be accepted by the government which was not willing to part with real power. Needless to add, these demands were considered extravagant, and hence were summarily rejected by the authors of the Montford Scheme of Reforms.

HOME RULE MOVEMENT

The First World War (1914-18) was important for India not only in that it witnessed the unity between the Congress and the League on the one side and between the Moderates and the Extremists on the other, it was also significant in that it broke the lull in Indo-British relations and gave a new impetus to the national movement. The involvement of England in the War appeared to the Indian nationalists, particularly the Extremists, a God-sent opportunity, and the latter decided to advance their own cause. This was the opportune time to force Britain to agree to the Indian demand for extracting political concessions out of British difficulties. They were greatly influenced by the emergence of the Irish Home Rule Movement under the leadership of Issac Butt. Realising the British allergy to the word 'Swaraj', Tilak and Annie Besant decided to substitute a new term— 'Home Rule', and by their combined efforts they succeeded 'n establishing the Home Rule League in April 196. While Tiak's Home Rule League confined its operations to Maharashtra and Karnataka, Besant's League worked in the rest of the country. The objective of the Home Rule League was to attain Home Rule or Self-Government within the British Empire by all constitutional means. But the Home Rule Leagues demanded self-government not as a gift but as a right. By their propaganda, preaching, speeches and writings the movement infused among the people the spirit of patriotism, fearlessness, self-respect and sacrifice. The Home Rule Movement acquired an all-India character when action was taken against Annie Besant and Tilak on their refusal to furnish securities and personal bonds. The action caused a storm of opposition and indignation from one end of the country to another.

Regarding the significance of the Home Rule Movement, Prof. S.R. Mehrotra observes, "The Home Rule Leagues created a significant impact on the national movement in India. For the first time an agitation had been aroused on a nation-wide scale and a network of political committees covered much of India."

MONTAGU-CHELMSFORD REFORMS

The continued political agitation in India under the aegis of Home Rule League and the Congress-League entente caused great uneasiness in London. The war situation in Europe had also become grave in the early summer of 1917. The campaign against Turkey was a great military disaster. It exposed the incompetence of the Indian government and the report on this disaster known as 'Mesopotamian Muddle' led to replacement of Austin Chamberlain by Montagu as the Secretary of State for India.

The Report recommended a measure of self-government to enable India help whole heartedly in war efforts.

Soon after the assumption of office, Montagu made the following famous Declaration on 20 August, 1917 in keeping with Declaration on the War aims of the Allies: "The policy of His Majesty's Government, with which the government of India are in complete accord is that of the increasing association of Indians in every branch of the administration and the gradual development of self-governing institutions with a view to progressive realisation of responsible government in India as an integral part of the British Empire." Montagu also made a whirlwind tour of India for six months with Viceroy, Chelmsford. The Montford Report on India's constitutional reforms was published on 8 July, 1918. The Declaration was a bold departure from the old policy. It was for the first time declared that the goal was the introduction of the responsible government. The goal of Dominion status at some future date was also implicit in this scheme.

The Montford Scheme received a mixed reaction in India. To Annie Besant, "the Reforms were unworthy of England to offer and India to accept." The Special Session of the Congress convened by Tilak in August 1918 at Bombay criticised the Montford proposal as "unsatisfactory, inadequate and disappointing." But to Gandhi and the Moderates, the Scheme was a substantial instalment in India's struggle for self-rule. "While the Congress looked the gift horse of dyarchy rather closely in the mouth, moderates prepared to ride it."[3] The Moderates entered into a sort of compact with authorities and stayed away from the Special Session of the Congress held at Bombay in August 1918. Subsequently, they met in November, 1918 at Bombay under the leadership of S.N. Bannerjea and organised a new party- the Liberal Federation. It is worth mentioning here that the Moderates left the Congress and never returned to this fold. The Liberal Federation stood for 'responsive cooperation'. They agreed to work out the Reforms and believed that it would make the realisation of full responsible government easier. They favoured to give it a fair trial.

All the same, the Montford Scheme, though faulty and hedged around by many limitations, makes a progressive stage in the British policy towards India. It offered a substantial dose of responsibility. As it happened, the Report became the basis of the Act of 1919. The main principles on which the Act was based were :

(1) Partial responsibility in Provinces-Dyarchy;

(2) Relaxation of Central control over the Provinces;

(3) Responsible government at the Centre to continue;

(4) Elective majority allowed in the Central Legislature for the first time;

(5) Extension of communal franchise to Sikhs, Europeans and Christians as well;

(6) Relaxation of the control of the Secretary of State and British Parliament over the Indian Government.

Notes

1. Majumdar, R.C., History of Freedom Movement, Vol. 2, p.353
2. Suda, J.P., op.cit, p.81
3. Mehrotra, S.R., op.cit, p.89

Chapter 12

ENTRY OF GANDHI AND BEGINNING OF THIRD PHASE OF THE CONGRESS (1920-47) — CONGRESS MOVES FROM COOPERATION TO NON-COOPERATION

Gandhi came to India in January 1915 under the persuasion of Gokhale. A follower of Gokhale, Gandhi was a Moderate to begin with, and as such offered his full cooperation to the British government during the war, and was even awarded the Kaisar-i-Hind gold medal for his war services. Like the Moderates, he too was willing to work out the Montford Reforms, and it was on his insistent plea that the Amritsar Congress (1918), while declaring the 1919 Act as "inadequate, unsatisfactory and disappointing," agreed to workout the Reforms, although senior leaders like B.C. Pal and C.R. Das stood for its total rejection. But events passed so swiftly and dramatically during the succeeding months that the situation was completely reversed, so much so that at the Special Session of the Congress held at Calcutta in September 1920, Gandhi himself reneged and became a noncooperator. But, as B.R. Nanda observes, "To seek the explanation of Gandhi's transition from loyalist to a rebel only in 1920 is a superficial understanding." According to him, the year 1920 only completed a process which began much earlier with Gandhi's disappointment over the conduct of British Bureaucracy in Champaran and Kheda. Still greater shocks came to Gandhi in the shape of the Rowlett Act followed by Jallianwala Bagh tragedy and the Khilafat wrongs.

Realising that the Defence of India Act (1915), which had armed the government with extraordinary power to deal with the terrorist movement, would lapse, the Viceroy on December 10, 1917 set up a committee headed by Sydney Rowlett (an English Judge) to recommend measures to deal with revolutionary crimes and acts of sedition. The Committee submitted its report in April 1918. On the lines of their recommendations two Bills were drawn up which came to be known as Rowlett Bills. In the face of a fierce countrywide agitation against the Bills, nicknamed the "Black Bills," only one of these Bills was passed on March 17, 1919, known as the Anarchical and Revolutionary Crimes Act. The Act was mainly of three parts: (1) Trial by Special Court for specific offences; (2) Power to direct execution of bonds for good behaviour, and (3) Power of arrest without warrants. In effect the Act permitted no pleader, no argument and no appeal (no Vakil, no daleel and no appeal). Even though the Act was not enforced even in a single case, it became responsible for a couple of tragedies that followed, causing a revolutionary change in the method of the Indian National Congress in conducting agitation.

JALLIANWALA BAGH TRAGEDY

In the wake of strong protests from all quarters and universal opposition to the Act, Gandhi announced to resort to Satyagraha- his unique weapon tried successfully earlier in South Africa. He fixed 6 April, 1919 as the day for a countrywide hartal. But the hartal was actually observed at Delhi on 31 March, 1919 as previously fixed, and led to minor clashes between the public and the authority at places. Gandhi was invited to Delhi to control the situation, but orders were passed by the government refusing his entry in Punjab and Delhi. Since Gandhi disobeyed the order, he was arrested on his way to Delhi on April 8, 1919 and sent back. News of his arrest led to disturbances in several places. The agitation against the Rowlett Act was at its highest in Amritsar (Punjab). The hartal, as such, had passed off peacefully but the city and the province were set ablaze by the arrest and deportation of Dr. Satya Pal and Saifuddin Kitchlew, the two prominent leaders of Punjab, on 10 April, 1919 to some unknown places. This enraged the public, and protests were organised against their arrest. On account of the disturbed atmosphere, the government banned public meetings. The civil authority requisitioned military authority to take up the charge of Amritsar and General Dyer was put in charge. The administration prohibited the public meeting scheduled to be held on 13 April, the Baisakhi day. But the notice banning the meeting was not publicly proclaimed. Hence a public meeting was duly held on 13 April at 4.30 p.m. to denounce the police atrocities and to condole the bereaved families. In the forenoon of the Baisakhi day, Dyer along with 150 troops marched through the main streets. Not fully aware of the possible consequences, about 20,000 (men, women and children) assembled at the Jallianwala Bagh. The Bagh was an open piece of wasteland. It was surrounded by walls and buildings and had only one narrow passage for entry and exit. Dyer and his troops also went in. As soon as the proceedings commenced, Dyer, without warning the people to disperse, ordered the troops to fire till the ammunition exhausted. The people found themselves trapped. Within ten minutes 1650 rounds of 303 were fired resulting in an unprecedented butchery. About 380 persons were killed and about 1500 were wounded. A reign of terror followed. Indiscriminate flogging, firing and bombing followed in its wake. On one of the streets on which an English woman was assassinated, the people were not only flogged but were made to lie flat on their bellies and to crawl. The Punjab Lt. Governor Michael O'Dwyer applauded General's action and the latter was hailed as a valiant hero by the British community, and was presented a purse of £30,000. Apprehending the outbreak of violence, Martial Law was promulgated all over Punjab. The Jallianwala Bagh tragedy was well described by C.F. Andrews as "a cold and calculated massacre, an unspeakable disgrace, undefensible, unpardonable, and unexcusable." This deliberate and unprovoked massacre would remain a dark spot upon the British administration for all times to come. Gandhi's comment on the tragedy was "if Plassey had laid the foundation of the British Empire, Amritsar had shaken it." Indeed, Amritsar became a turning point in the Indo-British relations. Infact, "the events of 1919 burnt themselves deep into the soul of India and remained a symbol to the emotional Indians of all that was worst in the British rule." Echoing the universal feeling of resentment, Tagore renounced the Knighthood and Sir Shankar Nair resigned from the Viceroy's Executive Council as a mark of protest.

Realising the gravity of the situation an Inquiry Committee under Hunter was set up to look into doings of the Punjab government under the Martial Law. General Dyer in his testimony stated: "My object was to shoot well and shoot strong so that I or anybody else should not have to shoot again and I wanted to crush the morale of the people." The Congress set up their own non-official committee comprising Moti Lal Nehru, C.R. Das, Abbas Tyabji, M.R. Jayakar and M.K. Gandhi to hold a parallel enquiry. This Committee held General Dyer responsible for "a cold blooded, calculated massacre unparalleled for its heartlessness and cowardly butchery in modern times." In fact, the Jallianwala Bagh massacre was a premeditated plan. It was hatched in the Government House (Lahore) and its Chief Architect was Michael O'Dwyer. It was designed as a demonstrative deterrence.

THE KHILAFAT MOVEMENT

While the whole of India was outraged at the Jallianwala Bagh tragedy, the Muslim community was seething with discontentment against the British policy towards the Sultan of Turkey, who was also looked as the Khalifa of Islam. Turkey had fought the war on the side of Germany against the Allies. The British Prime Minister, Lloyd George had assured (July 1918) the Indian Muslims that Turkey would be treated fairly after the War. But in October 1918, Turkey was forced to sign the armistice terms, which aimed at dissolving the Turkish Empire. The Indian Muslims got disillusioned at the treatment meted out to the Khalifa. The Ulemas began to incite their community members against Britain.

Like a practical politician, Gandhi perceived in the emerging situation an opportunity to cement the bonds of Hindu-Muslim unity. He therefore, urged the Hindus to give full support to the movement which the Muslims were planning to launch and in return win the sympathy of Muslims for the national movement. The Ali Brothers (Mohd. Ali and Shaukat Ali) who had gone to England to plead the Khilafat cause returned empty handed, and began to take a leading part in the Khilafat movement. On 24 November, 1919, an All India Congress Committee met in Delhi under Gandhi's chairmanship and resolved to withdraw all cooperation with the government until the promises made to the Sultan were redressed.

In May 1920, the terms of the Peace Treaty with Turkey (Treaty of Sevres) were published. Under its terms the Sultan was deprived of all his territories in Europe and Asia. Turkey lost the whole of Thrace to Greece and the richest area of Asia Minor was divided between France and England in the guise of Mandates. Thus the Holy places of Islam passed into non-muslim hands. This arrangement obviously infuriated the Indian Muslims who launched a strong movement in support of the Khalifa, the Head of Islamic World. In this hour of despair for the Muslims, Gandhi advised them to begin a non-cooperation movement. This proposal was readily accepted by the Khilafat Committee.

Another event that provoked the Congress to adopt this course was the publication of the Hunter Committee Report which whitewashed the whole crime and exonerated the culprits of Jallianwala Bagh tragedy. Furthermore, the culprits were protected under the Indemnity Act passed by the Imperial Legislative Council. The Lt. Governor (Michael O'Dwyer), was allowed to go scotfree. As regards General Dyer, he was simply declared unfit for service in future. The Report stated that his conduct was based upon "an honest but mistaken conception of duty and that he exceeded the reasonable requirements of the case due to grave error of judgement." To add insult to the injury, in the House of Lords, Dyer was praised as a "Champion of the British Empire," and the public presented him a Sword of Honour and a purse of £30,000 for his services to the nation. Both these events- the dismemberment of the Turkish Empire and the Hunter Committee Report converted the loyalist Gandhi into a rebel against the British Raj. Gandhi lost all faith in the British sense of justice and liberalism and decided to launch a non-cooperation movement.

A Special Session was held in Calcutta in September 1920 under the Presidentship of Lajpat Rai to consider the programme of non-cooperation which was presented by Gandhi. Gandhi urged the Congress to adopt the policy of progressive non-violent non-cooperation until the wrongs were righted and self rule was established. However, Gandhi's resolution was not supported by Stalwarts like Lajpat Rai, Moti Lal Nehru, C.R. Das. Even then Gandhi carried the day and his resolution was approved by 1886 delegates against 881. It came up again before the annual Congress at Nagpur in December 1920. Interestingly, now C.R. Das himself moved the resolution for non-cooperation and Lajpat Rai seconded it. The Nagpur session is significant in many ways. It was a personal triumph of Gandhi who outmanoeuvered veterans like B.C. Pal, M.M. Malviya, Annie Besant and M.A. Jinnah. It is also significant in that it marked the final breakup of Jinnah with the Congress fold. The Nagpur Session will also remain memorable for making two monumental changes in the constitution of the Congress: Firstly, the goal of the Congress hitherto was the attainment of self-government within the British Empire. But now it was declared to be the attainment of Swaraj within the Empire, if possible and outside, if necessary; secondly, till then the Congress could employ only constitutional means to attain its objectives. But now it was laid down that the Congress could adopt "all peaceful and legitimate means to achieve its ends." Thus, at Nagpur the era of constitutional struggle came to an end and the Gandhian era of direct action began. Henceforth, Gandhi became the undisputed leader of the Congress. He came to acquire this position because of several factors favouring him. His rise to power in Indian politics was greatly aided by the accidents of time and circumstances, such as death of old, established leaders like Gokhale, Mehta and Tilak. Moreover, the Liberals had already left the Congress in 1918 and Extremists were in complete command of the Congress. But with the death of Tilak (31 July, 1920) none else was acceptable to Congress members except Gandhi. Gandhi was acceptable because he alone had the mastery over the technique of Satyagraha that he had successfully tested in South Africa, Champaran and Kheda. Gandhi succeeded in capturing the leadership of the Congress also because "he brought a new message of faith and hope by offering them a new ideology, a new programme of action, which were revolutionary without ceasing to be constitutional."[1] To be sure, young nationalist India needed a new leadership and a new programme and these were provided by M.K. Gandhi.

NON-COOPERATION MOVEMENT (1920-22)

The non-violent non-cooperation movement was started with the dual object of redressing the Punjab and Khilafat wrongs. Its objective was later broadened by the inclusion of 'Swaraj'. The movement captured the hearts of the Indians from the very start and gathered momentum throughout the year 1921. The people were called upon to go through the ordeal, privation and suffering and to make the utmost sacrifices for winning Swaraj, which was promised within one year by Gandhi. There was intense activity and unprecedented cooperation between Hindus and Muslims, and joint political action for securing redress for the Khilafat and the Punjab wrongs. Gandhi and the Ali Brothers undertook whirlwind tours of the country to carry the Nagpur mandate.

HIGHLIGHTS OF THE NON-COOPERATION MOVEMENT

During the movement several distinguished persons like Moti Lal Nehru, C.R. Das, Dr. Jayakar, Rajendra Prasad, V.B. Patel, C. Rajgopalachari gave up heir lucrative practice at the bar and plunged into the movement. Among prominent Muslim leaders who played a notable role were the Ali Brothers, Dr. M.A. Ansari, Maulana Abdul Kalam Azad, etc. Thousands of students boycotted government schools and colleges and joined the newly opened national schools and colleges, such as National Muslim University (Aligarh), Gujarat Vidyapith (Ahmedabad), Bihar Vidyapith (Patna), Kashi Vidyapith (Benares) Tilak Maratha Vidyapith (Poona), the Bengal National University (Calcutta) and the Jamia Millia (Delhi). But it is notable that the boycott of elections under the Montford Reforms in 1920-21 was only a qualified success, because inspite of boycott by the Congress, only few seats (six) remained vacant. In January, 1921, Seth Jamna Lal Bajaj gave up the title of Rai Bahadur and donated Rupees one lakh to the Tilak Swaraj Fund and towards the maintenance of non-cooperation sufferers. Swadeshi got great impetus and hand spinning was revived. Khaddar became the 'Livery of Freedom' and Charkha became the 'Cross'. In February 1921, the visit of the Duke of Connaught (uncle of King George VI), who came to India to inaugurate the reformed legislative councils, as well as the visit of Prince of Wales were boycotted. Besides boycott of foreign goods and use of Swadeshi goods, anti-liquor agitation was also launched. Gandhi himself surrendered his title of Kaisar-i-Hind and many others followed him.

Undoubtedly, there was great ferment and commotion all over the country, and the bureaucracy was deeply shaken. As a measure of suppression of the movement, section 108 or 144 of the Criminal

Procedure Code was promulgated at places. Sedition Meetings Act was also passed and as a result thousands of volunteers were put in jail without trial, hundreds of them were wounded by firing and many were killed. In September 1921, the Ali Brothers were arrested. Thus by the end of 1921 all important leaders except Gandhi were put behind the bars. The total tally of arrested persons came in the neighbourhood of about 25,000. In August 1921, both the Congress and the Khilafat organisations were declared unlawful and public meetings were totally banned.

Some leaders and political organisations sought to bring about a rapprochment between the authorities and the Congress in time for the visit of Prince of Wales, but negotiations broke down as the Congress demand to release Ali Brothers was not acceptable to the authorities. In view of the recalcitrant attitude of the authorities the Congress was left with no alternative but to launch the non-cooperation movement. In a letter dated 22 February 1922, Gandhi informed the Viceroy, Lord Reading, that he would start a civil disobedience movement after seven days, unless repression stopped and the government gave proof of a change of heart by releasing all prisoners, including the Ali Brothers.

But before Gandhiji could start the movement, there was the tragedy of Chauri Chaura (UP) on 5 February 1922. While a Congress procession was passing, a mob pushed 21 constables and one sub-inspector into a police station and set it on fire. Chauri Chaura incident was not the only act of violence committed by the people during the course of the movement, similar tragic events had already taken place at other places like Bombay and Madras. The most terrible acts of violence were committed by the Moplahs of Malabar, who brutally murdered several Hindus at the time of the visit of Prince of Wales at Bombay. Gandhiji was sorely grieved at all these happenings. He felt that the movement was losing its non-violent character. He realised that the country was not yet ready for a non-violent movement, as envisaged by him. On his suggestion, the Congress Working Committee suspended the movement on 12 February 1922. Naturally, the sudden withdrawal came as a shock to many leaders like Lala Lajpat Rai, C.R. Das and the two Nehrus, who took him to task for punishing the whole country, Moti Lal Nehru questioned: "Why should a town at the foot of Himalayas be punished if a village at Cape Camorin failed to observe non-violence?" This action of Gandhiji was bitterly resented by the rank and file of the Congress in general and Muslims in particular. As a matter of fact, Muslims by and large never shared Gandhi's faith in Satyagraha technique in a political struggle. The Ali Brothers attacked Gandhi for switching off the movement in such a fashion and at such a critical stage: "To sound the order of retreat just when public enthusiasm was reaching the boiling point was something short of a national calamity." Even Romain Rolland, an ardent admirer of Gandhiji, wrote: "It is dangerous to assemble all the forces of nation and to hold the nation pointing in a prescribed movement to lite one's arms to give the final command and then at the last moment let one's arms drop and thrice call a halt, just as the formidable machinery has been set in motion." To quote the comment of S.C. Bose, "To have sounded the bugle for retreat at a time when the enemy was on its knees was nothing short of a national disaster.

APPRAISAL OF NON-COOPERATION MOVEMENT

To be sure, the first mass movement led by Gandhiji failed in his main objective. In place of "Swaraj' there was frustration in the country"[2]. Gandhi himself admitted that it was a 'Himalayan blunder' on his part to have launched the movement without adequate ground work and proper training of the masses in the technique of Satyagraha. The promise of 'Swaraj within one year' was unrealistic and even 'childish,' to borrow the comment of S.C. Bose. But for Gandhi, "Freedom was like a birth and all births take place in a moment."

Nevertheless, the movement was not altogether barren of results. It raised the pitch of political agitation to a height never dreamed of before. The programme of organising national educational institutions, of popularising values of Khadi and boycotting the foreign goods, and of setting up panchayats was something that began to eat into the vitals of the British Raj. Further, the Mahatma gave the Congress a new constitution and a nation-wide network of Congress committees. By his organising skill Gandhi converted the Congress, hitherto a disorganised structure, into a firmly cohesive well-knit party with a mass base that lasts even to this day. With his efforts the Congress became a revolutionary body from a 'resolutionary' one. It was transformed from an upper class debating club into a mass organisation. In short, Gandhi gave the country a highly organised political outfit. Moreover, as a main driving force of national will against British colonialism, the Congress was transformed into a mighty national front coalescing many strands: moderates, liberals radicals, terrorists and several dominant interests — class, regional and ideological. To quote Prof. Harbans Mukhia, "Gandhi changed the idiom of the freedom struggle by bringing it much closer to the indigenous ambience, and simultaneously introduced a strong moral and ethical element into the movement so that it did not remain confined to mere political agitations or demands but highlighted the very immorality of the British rule in India." Besides, "the movement greatly helped the cause of nationalism in India: Uniform slogans were repeated everywhere and a uniform policy and ideology gained currency from one end of India to another. The Congress adopted Hindi as the lingua franca for the whole country."[3] The English language lost its importance for the Party's official purposes. Indeed, it was the first truly revolutionary movement in India since the birth of the Congress. Constitutionalism was buried once and for all. The Congress accepted instead the method of direct and self-reliant action.

NEGATIVE SIDE OF THE NON-COOPERATION MOVEMENT

While recounting the positive side of the movement, its negative side should not be lost sight of. The introduction of Khilafat question, admittedly a religious issue, into a movement with a secular objective was unfortunate and proved ultimately counter productive. The appeal to the cause of Khilafat issue led to the rise of Muslim fanaticism, creating a great communal divide between Hindus and Muslims which never existed before and which eventually led to partition of the country. In fact, the Khilafat movement was based on a symbolic myth to preserve the inept ruler of a sick empire. It overlooked the Arab aspiration to seek freedom from Turkish hegemony. What is more, even the Turks, for whose benefits the issue was raised, discarded Khilafat as a medieval jargon. Turkey was declared a secular state under Mustafa Kamal Pasha in 1923 and the Khalifa was exiled in 1924. With the departure of Abdul Majid (who had succeeded Sultan Abdul Hamid after the latter's flight from Turkey) ended the thirteen hundred year-old office of the Caliph of Islam. One therefore wonders why Gandhi failed to see that the Khilafat was a moribund institution and no more than a historical relic. However, Gandhi justified it on tactical grounds. He said "not for a hundred years would such an opportunity recur for Hindu-Muslim unity." But whatever may be the justification that Gandhi offered for supporting the Khilafat movement on humanitarian or tactical grounds, it was like riding a tiger, as future events showed. Far from forging new bonds of communal amity, the end result was a new kind of communal ill-will. In retrospect the disastrous consequences of the movement for Indian nationalism are now being recognised. Instead of cementing communal amity the Khilafat movement provided legitimacy to the most regressive trends in Indian Islam. The movement established the religious under-pinning of Muslim mobilisation. Even the radicals who entered into an understanding with the Congress during non-cooperation movement were later to champion separatism on the ground that secular nationalism no longer offered anything specific for Muslims. Equally significant, the Khilafat movement gave sanctity to latent Pan-Islamic tendencies and legitimised the principle of extra-territoriality. In short, it subverted composite Indian nationalism.

Notes

1. Mehrotra S.R., op.cit., p.52
2. Suda, J.P., op.cit., p.173
3. Bose, S.C., The Indian Struggle, p.104

Chapter 13

SWARAJIST INTERLUDE (1923-26)

The decision of the Mahatma to suspend the Swaraj movement caused a great deal of resentment among the leaders and rank and file of the Congress. Several leaders like Lajpat Rai, C.R. Das, Moti Lal Nehru, Subhash Chandra Bose, B.S. Moonji resented Gandhi's action. They were deeply disappointed when the Movement was withdrawn while at its peak. They began to uncover many short-comings in Gandhi's programme: One, the introduction of Khilafat issue was considered by them unwise, because the Khilafat agitationists left the Congress as soon as the issue became dead and swelled the ranks of the Muslim League. Two, the election boycott (1921) proved counter-productive, Three, instead of the Congress, the Liberals captured legislatures and supported the government. Given their support, the government could demonstrate that the policy of repression had the support of the representatives of the people. C.R. Das and other Bengal leaders therefore evolved a new programme- Non-cooperation within the legislatures. They advocated that the Congress should enter the legislatures in large numbers and should carry on a policy of "uniform, continuous and consistent" opposition to the government.

After the arrest of Gandhi and other leaders in March 1922 the Congress was left leaderless. In view of the new thinking among certain Congress leaders, the authorities released leaders like Moti Lal Nehru, C.R. Das, etc. The AICC met at Lucknow in June 1922 to take stock of the situation and to consider the future line of action. It decided to set up a committee to report on the general psychological climate. When the report came up for discussion before the AICC at Calcutta in November 1922, the schism among Congress leaders became quite manifest. One group led by C.R. Das, Hakim Ajmal Khan, Moti Lal Nehru supported Council entry, but the other group (still in majority) led by C. Rajgopalachari, Dr. M.A. Ansari, K.R. Iyenger opposed this programme. The annual session at Gaya (1922) became a battle ground between the "changers" and "no-changers". However, the session was a victory for no-changers. Consequently, C.R. Das resigned from the Congress and announced the decision to form a new party. Thus the parent organisation suffered a second setback, the first being the exit of the Liberals since the advent of the Mahatma. M.L. Nehru and C.R. Das left Gaya not with a sense of defeat but with a determination to go ahead with their programme. On 1 January, 1923, they announced the formation of another party, known as the Swaraj Party. The Swaraj Party conference met for the first time at the residence of the Nehrus and the constitution of the party was framed. Its outstanding leaders were Vithalbhai Patel, M.L. Nehru, C.R. Das, Ajmal Khan, Dr. M.R. Jayakar, N.C. Kelkar, Srinivas Iyenger, G.B. Pant etc. The immediate objective of the party was proclaimed to be the attainment of Dominion Status. It also decided to contest the elections due in 1923 and after entering the legislature to wreck it from within. The Swarajists considered the capturing of the legislatures as necessary to check them from falling into the clutches of undesirable persons serving as tools of the bureaucracy. According to P.B. Sitaramaya, "Their aim was to carry on non-cooperation in the very aisles and channel of the bureaucratic Church."

The Swarajists fought the elections of 1923 and achieved some success: a majority in Central Province, a dominant position in Bengal and a decisive position in U.P. In the Central Legislature, they won 45 out of 145 seats and did some memorable work with the support of others. In February 1924, they supported the idea of summoning at an early date a Round Table Conference to revise the Act of 1919, as Dyarchy under the Act was proving unworkable. One tangible outcome of their efforts was the appointment of Reform Enquiry Committee (the Muddiman Committee) to report on the working of Dyarchy. They rejected some of the demands for grants asked for and demanded repeal of some obnoxious measures. They succeeded in their demand for the release of Gandhi who fell ill and got him set free on 5 February, 1924.

But gradually the Swarajists began to realise that the obstructionist policy did not bear fruit, and hence replaced it by a policy of reconciliation and construction. In 1924, the General Elections in England brought a change of government and Lord Birkenhead became the new Secretary of State for India, He spoke of the Swaraj Party as the most highly organised political party in India and sought for settlement with the Swarajist leaders. Furthermore, after the death of C.R. Das in 1925, the Party began to swerve from its original policy of undiluted opposition, and its leaders began to accept office. For instance, M.L. Nehru accepted membership of the Skeen Commission, set up on the question of Indianisation of the Army, V.B. Patel became the Chairman of the Central Legislative Assembly, Kelkar and Jayakar began to favour responsive cooperation with the government.

All this led to a gradual dilution of the original policy. The Swaraj Party became the constitutionalist party of the Indian bourgeoisie and began to utilise the legislatures generally to press the programme of that class, embodying demands such as free industrial expansion, development of heavy industries and others.

APPRAISAL OF SWARAJ PARTY

Undoubtedly, the Swaraj Party failed to bring the government machinery to a standstill. To be sure, there was some contradiction in their policy. One may ask why they fought elections when they wanted nothing but obstruction? To quote Dr. Zacharias, "The Swarajists position was that of the people who wanted to eat their cake and have it at the same time."[1] Nevertheless, they served a very useful purpose for some time when the Congress was in disarray in the absence of Gandhi on the political scene. At least the Swaraj Party kept the torch of freedom struggle burning when the nation was plunged into diffidence and despondency. To conclude, the Party was formed at a crucial juncture. "It rendered great and timely service by keeping up the spirit of resistance to the authorities and thereby whipping up the enthusiasm of the people."[2] However, by the end of 1926 none of the Swarajists talked of carrying on the policy of "uniform, continuous and consistent" obstruction against the government. Eventually, an important section of the Party began to advocate the advantages of the policy of responsive cooperation instead of the policy of outright obstruction.

Notes

1.   Zacharias, Renascnet India, p.240
2.   Suda, J.P., op.cit., p.177

Chapter 14

SIMON COMMISSION AND
THE NEHRU REPORT

There is not much to chronicle about the national movement during 1925-27 except that the Hindu-Muslim goodwill slumped sharply. The communal forces came to the surface during this period. If the Muslims started the movement for Tabligh and Tanzeem, the Hindus, not to be left behind, started their Shuddhi and Sangathan movement, the period was marked by unprecedented communal riots. The reactionaries within both the communities exploited the situation and began to create feelings of animosity between them. Both the Muslim League and the Hindu Mahasabha took to belligerent propaganda on a massive scale. Even the efforts by the leaders of the two communities to patch up were not successful. The Mahatma was so concerned with these happenings that he went on a three week fast as a penance for their misdeeds. But side by side this negative development of the late 1920s also witnessed another development of a positive nature. It was the birth and growth of socialist and communist groups and the rise of independent organisations of the working class in the country.

The Council Front experiment having failed, the country again came in the grip of a political slump and depression. In the year 1927, the national movement was at its lowest ebb. At this juncture what provided a splendid opportunity to the leading politicians of both the communities for a countrywide agitation was the appointment of the Simon Commission by the government.

In November 1927, the new Viceroy, Lord Irwin (the successor of Lord Reading since 1926) announced the appointment of the statutory Commission under section 84 (a) of the political situation in India every ten years. In keeping with this stipulation, the Commission should have been appointed in 1929, but Lord Birkenhead decided to predate it by two years. The main reason for advancing the date was that the Tory (Conservative) government did not like to leave its appointment to the likely successor, the Labour government) and wanted to dispose of the Indian question while still in power. They were afraid that the Labour government might make a further concession to the Indian demand for Swaraj. Another reason for advancing the date was that the working of the reform had revealed a number of constitutional defects, and the authorities desired to remove some of them. Offering another viewpoint, Prof. A.B. Keth felt that "appointment was accelerated because of the growth of the youth movement and growing socialist ideas both in India and England." The Commission was to consist of seven members of the British Parliament with Sir John Simon as its Chairman. The most objectionable feature of the Commission from the Indian point of view was its all white composition. Surprisingly, not a single Indian was considered fit to be included in the inquiry. Even Lord Sinha, an M.P., was not included, nor were any of the Indian Liberals who had all along cooperated with the government.

The Commission reached India on 3 February, 1928 but its composition provided a rallying point to all political groups and parties, Mr. Jinnah, who had dubbed the Commission as 'lily white', tried in vain for the inclusion of at least two Indians in the blue ribbon body. The composition as such was taken to be a deliberate insult to the dignity and self-respect of the nation. As such, almost all leaders and groups irrespective of party affiliation decided to carry out the boycott of the Commission. As a mark of protest an All-India hartal was observed on the arrival day. The Commission thus, once again, provided a forum for organised opposition and crystallized country's latent passion and pride. Birkenhead's justification for the all-White composition added insult to injury. He wanted his jury to be without any preconceived prejudice. He held the domestic division also as the reason for the exclusion of Indian leaders exclusion. But to our countrymen, as Mr. Jinnah observed. "If the Jallianwala Bagh was physical butchery the Simon Commission was butchery of our soul."

The Commission was confronted with hartal, demonstration, black flag everywhere it went. Large demonstrations took place in Delhi, Lahore, Madras, Calcutta, Patna and other big towns with resounding slogans of 'Simon go back'. At Lahore Lala Lajpat Rai led a mammoth procession of demonstrators against the Commission. While leading it, he received several lathi blows by the police, which ultimately proved fatal. After this incident, the 'lion of Punjab' roared. "It will prove as nails in the coffin of the British Empire." In U.P. J.L. Nehru and G.B. Pant were similarly molested.

But undeterred by the boycott and the atmosphere of uncompromising hostility, the Commission continued with its assigned work and completed its enquiry. It visited India twice for the purpose and its report was published in May 1930 after a long labour of two years. Surely, the Report bore the mark of great industry. According to Coupland, "It was by far the most complete study of Indian problem that had yet been made and that it added another work of first rate value to the library of Political Science."[1] To quote Griffith, "It was the finest analysis of the Indian conditions in the twentieth century yet written." The Commission recommended in the first place that Dyarchy ("double government") should be scrapped and complete autonomy be given to the Provinces. Each Province should be mistress in her own house subject to the grant of special powers to the governor for the maintenance of peace and security to safeguard the legitimate interests of the minorities. Furthermore, it recommended enlargement of the legislature and extension of franchise with direct election based on separate electorate. But it suggested no substantial change at the Centre — the method of indirect election through the provincial councils for both the Houses of the Central Legislature was kept intact. It also envisaged a federal constitution at a distant future embracing both British India and the Indian states. But the Commission failed to recommend even Dominion Status for India when the Congress had already declared Complete Independence as its goal in 1927. Surely, the wholly irresponsible government at the Centre with indirect election to the Central Legislature were retrograde steps. Its great demerit was that it failed to take note of radical change in Indian thinking. Nevertheless, it is notable that most of its recommendations found place in the Government of India Act of 1935. Indeed, its observations regarding the Federation and future role of the states were prophetic. Despite its several drawbacks and demerits, it can be contended that if the Report had been accepted by the Indian progressive opinion, full responsible governments in the Provinces, that came only in 1937, might have been achieved much earlier.

THE NEHRU REPORT

Lord Birkenhead had a very poor opinion about Indian leadership and held the belief that Indians were incapable of running free democratic institutions. He also thought that the Hindu-Muslim differences were unbridgeable. In 1927, he had almost thrown a challenge to Indian politicians to produce an agreed constitution for India. It was to meet this challenge that an All-party- Conference was called at Delhi on 28 February, 1928, which represented some 29 organisations. On 19 May, 1928 a committee of nine persons (Sir Imam Ali, Shuaib Qureshi, Sardar Mangal Singh, M.S. Aney, M.R. Jayakar, Sir Tej Bahadur Sapru (Liberal), N.N. Joshi (Labour), J.R. Pradhan and S.C. Bose), headed by Moti Lal

Nehru was appointed to draft a constitution for India. The All Party - Conference met again at Lucknow which ratified the constitution drawn by the Sub-Committee.

Main provisions[2] of the Nehru Report were: (1) India should be granted full Dominion Status forthwith; (2) Responsible government should be provided both at the Centre as well as in the Provinces; (3) There should be bicameral legislature at the Centre but not in the Provinces; (4) Direct election both to the Lower House of the Central Legislature as well as to the Provincial Councils with a tenure of five years; (5) The constitution of India should be federal in character with full autonomy to the Provinces and native states; (6) Powers between that Centre and the Provinces were to be divided on a federal basis but residuary powers to remain with the Central government so as to keep the Centre string; (7) The Indian army to be placed under the control of an Indian minister responsible to the Legislature; (9) Separate electorate to be done away with and in its place joint electorate with reservations of seats for Muslims at the Centre and in the Provinces where they were in a minority; (10) Creation of a new province of Sind and North-West Frontier to be made a full fledged province; (11) A Supreme Court to be established as the final court of appeal in India; and (12) Introduction of responsible government in Indian states with a view to weld them into an All-India Federation.

REACTION TO THE NEHRU REPORT

Immediately after its adoption at Lucknow in August 1928, the Report came for consideration of various parties separately. It was approved by the Congress but the socialist and left nationalists criticised the constitutional scheme for abandoning the goal of independence and for conserving the interests of Zamindars regarding their private property. In the light of their protest the annual Congress met at Calcutta in December 1928 and accepted the constitutional scheme on the condition that it be accepted in its entirety by the British Parliament on or before 31 December 1929. The reaction of Indian Muslims to the Report was mixed. While the nationalist Muslims supported it whole-heartedly, the Agha Khan group rejected it on the ground that it had repudiated the Lucknow Pact regarding weightage and separate electorate. The Shafi group adopted a non-positive attitude, a form of refusal. The All Party- Muslim Conference which met at Delhi on 21 December, 1928 rejected the scheme. Both Maulana Mohd. Ali and M.A. Jinnah were opposed to it. On behalf of the Muslim League, Jinnah's fourteen-points were presented as an alternative to the Nehru Report. The Jinnah proposal, because of its advocacy of communal electorate and weak Centre with residuary power vested in the provinces, was too bitter a pill to swallow for the Congress. Thus the efforts to draw up a constitution acceptable to all parties proved abortive and Birkenhead's challenge turned out to be true, for "it was the most noisy demonstration of the inability of Indian leaders to come to a compromise."[3]

Nevertheless, the Nehru Report was an act of constructive statesmanship. To quote Dr. Zacharias," It was a masterly and statesman-like Report." It was quite comprehensive, grappling with every problem from the nationalist point of view. It embodied the frankest attempt yet made to face squarely difficulties of communalism and constitutionalism." In a way, our New constitution of 1949 is an enlarged edition of the Nehru Report.

As regard the Muslim League, it was completely alienated from the Congress. As such, it marked the final parting of the ways between the congress and the Muslim League. In fact, the Congress-League rift became unbridgeable thereafter.

It is worth mentioning here that as things stood, the Nehru Report, like the Simon Commission Report, was consigned to cold storage for the time being. But interestingly, both the Reports found important place in future constitutional schemes- the 1935 Act and the Constitution of Free India respectively.

While the Simon Commission was at its work and the unity conferences were taking place, there were a few other developments both in India and England which merit mention. The political atmosphere in the country had become very tense in the closing months of 1929. To illustrate, a few revolutionaries in Lahore murdered Saunders, an English Dy. S.P., believed to be responsible for Lathi blows on Lala Lajpat Rai to which he succumbed. Besides, Sardar Bhagat Singh and Batukeshwar Dutt threw a bomb each in the Central Assembly. Both were later on arrested along with others and thus started the famous Lahore Conspiracy Case. It aroused great public excitement. One of the prisoners implicated in this case had to resort to hunger strike and died. His martyrdom had a profound impact on the Indian youths. The politics in the country became still more tense. If students were in an agitated mood, there was unrest among workers too. The Bombay strike launched by workers almost paralysed the textile industry. Subsequently, thirty one trade union leaders from all over the country were taken to Meerut for trial lasting four years, known as the Meerut Conspiracy Case. The Congress demand relating to the acceptance of the Nehru Report was receiving no response from the authorities. Gandhi who had again resumed Congress leadership after five years of hibernation, went on a whirlwind tour of the country to prepare the masses for a civil disobedience movement. The peasantry of

Bardoli had already fought a successful battle against the government for periodical settlement of land revenue under the able leadership of Sardar Patel.

In the midst of these upheavals in India, there was a change of government in England. The Labour Party, led by Ramsay Macdonald, came to office and aroused great hopes in the country. The Labour leaders had always been sympathetic towards India's demand of self-government. Moreover, from his election platform Ramsay Macdonald had announced that he was willing to grant Dominion Status to India. He appointed Mr. Wedgewood Benn as the new Secretary of State for India and invited the Viceroy, Lord Irwin, to England for consultation. On coming back to India after three months' sojourn, Irwin made the following announcement on 31 October 1929: "I am authorised on behalf of His Majesty's Government to state clearly that in their judgement it is implicit in the Declaration of 1917 .that the natural issue of India's constitutional progress, as therein contemplated, is the attainment of Dominion Status." The Proclamation was cautiously worded and deliberately vague. It did not pronounce in categorical terms the immediate grant of Dominion Status to India, as the Congress ultimatum had demanded. He also declared that when the Simon Commission Report had been published, a Round Table Conference would be held in London in which His Majesty would meet representatives both of British-India and the native states for the purpose of seeking the greatest possible measure of agreement. By this announcement Irwin wanted not only to soothen the irritated nerves of India but to restore the Indian goodwill towards future proposals.

Within 24 hours of this announcement all the leading personages, excluding the Liberal leaders, met at Delhi and expressed appreciation of the Viceroy's sincerity. However, they sought clarification whether the proposed RTC merely would meet to discuss when the Dominion Status was fully established or to frame a scheme of Dominion Constitution for India. But Irwin expressed his inability to give any promise in categorical terms, because his party, which was only in office but not in power, was trying to wriggle out from the idea of granting Dominion Status as both the Conservatives led by Churchill and Liberals were not in favour of Dominion status at that time. The Labour Party on its part did not like to risk its office on the Indian issue.

THE LAHORE CONGRESS AND THE RESOLUTION FOR COMPLETE INDEPENDENCE.

The Congress leaders, M.L. Nehru and M.K. Gandhi, who made last minute efforts to get an assurance on the issue of Dominion Status before the Lahore Session, returned empty handed. The historic Lahore Session met after the expiry of the date of Congress ultimatum under the Presidentship of young Nehru. Nehru described Benn's Dominion Status as a sop and outdated, and declared that nothing less than Complete Independence should be the goal of the Congress. He proclaimed that the word Swaraj in article one of the Congress Constitution meant Complete Independence. Accordingly, the historic Independence Resolution was adopted and the tricolour flag of Independence was hoisted at midnight on 31 December, 1929 on the banks of the Ravi. Significantly, if at Madras (1927) Independence had been declared as a distant goal, at Lahore it became an immediate goal. The Lahore Congress also decided to observe 26th January as Independence Day everywhere every year. Incidentally, the Constitution of free India appropriately came into force on that very date in 1950 to commemorate the significance of that date in India's national movement. When the first Independence Day was celebrated on 26 January, 1930 great euphoria was visible all over the country. Other factors that contributed to the launching of the civil Disobedience Movement was an unprecedented economic crisis known as the Great Depression (1929-32). India too experienced this acute economic crisis. Moreover, the tremendous success of Bardoli Satyagraha showed an effective way of confronting the government to redress the grievances of the people. Besides, the labour class also was in a restive mood. In short, there was an all-round unrest and turmoil in the country.

Notes

1. Quoted in Suda, J.P., op.cit, p.182
2. Ibid., pp. 184-188
3. Gopal, Ram, 'A Political History of Indian Muslims', Criterion Publication, N. Delhi, 1988, p.221

Chapter 15

CIVIL DISOBEDIENCE MOVEMENT
(1930-32)

Since the country was drifting towards violent revolution Gandhi decided to give it a peaceful direction. Accordingly, the Congress Working Committee Meeting was convened at Sabarmati and Gandhi was vested with full powers to launch a civil disobedience movement at a time and place of his choice. On his part this time Gandhi gave an assurance to his colleagues that the movement would not be stopped because of a sporadic act of violence. Now Gandhi began to grope for a focal point around which the movement would revolve. He noted that at that time there was great resentment and unrest in the country against the Salt Tax just passed (1930). Undoubtedly, salt is the cheapest and commonest article of food. The production of salt was a government monopoly, and in 1930 half the retail price represented tax. Gandhi had learned through experience that to rouse the masses it was necessary to use symbols they could easily recognise. He realised the political potency of common salt and turned it into the gun powder of the freedom struggle. In a stroke of genius he linked the essential need of every Indian to the larger goal of freedom for every Indian. But as his wont, before launching it he made last minute effort to avert it. He appealed to the Viceroy with his 11-point programme to ease the situation, failing which he would start his civil disobedience movement. Instead, Lord Irwin deprecated his contemplated course of action. Thus Gandhi was left with no alternative and the stage was set for the second major struggle.

On 12 March, 1930, Gandhi along with his 79 members of his ashram began a 24 days' march to Dandhi, a sea coast village in Gujarat, to break the salt law, as it was a legal offence to prepare salt even from the sea water. Tremendous enthusiasm was displayed by the villages all along the 200-mile route. The Padyatris of the Dandi March violated the salt law on 6 April 1930 by picking up salt lying on the beach. The March was a symbolic Signal for breaking salt law all over the country.

On the same day salt was made at about 5,000 places throughout India.

The Dandi March was historic. Subhash Chandra Bose compared it Napolean's March on Paris on his return from Elba and to Mussolini's March on Rome.[1] The press gave the widest publicity to this epic. March and salt became the symbol of revolt. But on the other hand, the Anglo-Indian Press equally ridiculated the idea of salt satyagraha saying that "Gandhiji would go on boiling sea water till Dominion Status was attained." Brailsford, an English journalist, described it a 'Kindergarten stage of revolution'. He scoffed at the notion that the "King Emperor can be unseated by boiling sea water in a kettle".[2] To them, it was a futile pantomime.

Soon after Gandhi urged the people to celebrate April 6-13 as the national week and to manufacture contraband salt, picket liquor shops, opium dens, foreign cloth dealers' shops, burn foreign clothes and to leave the government colleges and services. The country responded readily to the call. The Civil Disobedience Movement spread like prairie fire. Huge public meetings took place in big cities. Hundreds left the government jobs, scores of legislators resigned, liquor shops were boycotted, payment of revenue were refused by the peasants. The boycott of foreign cloth was successful beyond calculations. It proved a blessing in disguise to domestic cloth mill owners. Import of foreign cloth was cut down to almost one-fourth. By June 1930 the country appeared to be in full revolt and in many places the writ of the British government almost ceased to run.

The British bureaucracy obviously could not take this movement lying down. It launched a policy of repression. Police firing, lathi charge and arrests became the order of the day. Thousands were put behind the bars. Even women were not spared. The press was also put under restrictions. On 5 May, 1930, Gandhi too was arrested. His arrest added fuel to the fire. There were hartals, mass demonstrations, public meetings and processions. The machinery of repression was in full swing. Jails were filled to capacity. In all, more than sixty thousand people courted arrest. The government resorted to emergency ordinances. Congress was declared unlawful. The struggle continued vigorously for six months more after the arrest of Gandhi. The people revealed remarkable power of organisation, initiative and resourcefulness. Some new institutions like Prabhat Pheris and Vanar Senas came into existence. One of the most remarkable phenomena was the way in which Indian women helped the movement by organising the picketing of liquor and foreign cloth shops. In Delhi alone about 1600 ladies were sent to jail for picketing. However, the Civil Disobedience Movement did not remain non-violent for long. In Midnapore District, a terrorist movement came into being by organising reprisals against officials. But it is worth noting that the bulk of Muslims kept themselves away from this movement and the Muslim League refused to join it.

Notes

1.   S.C. Bose Quoted in Suda, J.P., op.cit, p. 193
2.   Brailsford quoted in Suda, J.P., op.cit, p. 193

Chapter 16

THE ROUND TABLE CONFERENCE

On 12 May, 1930 Lord Irwin announced 12 November, 1930 as the date for the Round Table Conference. On 27 May 1930, the Simon Commission Report was published and the issue of another instalment of constitutional reforms took place. But the political climate of the country was still tense. An attempt was made to persuade the Congress to suspend the movement and attend the proposed RTC through the good offices of George Slocombe but it fall through, for the conditions and demands of the Congress regarding national government along with the right of secession from the Commonwealth were found too high to be accepted even by the Labour government.

The plans for the RTC however went ahead even without the Congress, and 89 distinguished statesmen represented the British political parties, Indian Labour Federation, Muslim League, Hindu Maha Sabha, Depressed Classes and Indian states. Out of 89 persons who gathered in London from 12 November 1930 to 19 January 1931 for the Conference, 57 represented British India, 16 represented the Indian India and 16 represented England. Regarding the choice of Indian delegation Brailsford's apt comment was "In St. James" Palace they did assemble Princes and Untouchables, Sikhs, Muslims, Hindus and Christians and spokesmen of landowners, trade unions and chamber of commerce, but Mother India was not there."

The issues for discussion were: the form of government, Provincial Autonomy and Responsibility at the Centre. Interestingly, the idea of federation was welcomed by all, including the Princes. Without covering much ground, the Conference adjourned sine die, as nothing could be finally adopted without Congress representatives. By the end of the first session of RTC, the points agreed upon were an All-India Federation, Full Responsible Government in the Provinces and Dyarchy at the Centre with Safeguards and Reservations.

In order to seek the cooperation of the Congress with the RTC, Ramsay Macdonald declared that Responsible Government at the Centre would be given after Indian people agreed to Safeguard and Federation, But the Congress described this declaration as too vague to be acceptable. The RTC was a still bigger disappointment to the Muslim League. The League leaders meanwhile met in Allahabad with Dr. Iqbal in the chair, who put forth his plan for a separate state for the Muslims (within India) as a solution to Hindu-Muslim deadlock. He said: "I would like to see the Punjab, NWFP, Sind, and Baluchistan amalgamated into a single state. Dr. Iqbal thus knowingly or unknowingly became the progenitor of Pakistan, a name coined three years later by Chowdhary Rahmat Ali.

GANDHI-IRWIN PACT-TAKING TEA WITH TREASON

The British politicians were anxious to secure the cooperation of Gandhi and other Congress leaders for the success of the Round Table Conference. They were fully aware that no constitutional reforms could materialise unless the mainstream leadership assented to it. Accordingly, Lord Irwin released Gandhi and other members of the Congress Working Committee. Soon after, under the pressure of Sir T.B. Sapru, Dr. Jayakar and V.S. Shastri, Gandhiji met the Viceroy over a cup of tea, and discussed the possibility of a rapprochment with the government. After a long and protracted negotiation for 15 days, an agreement was reached on 5 March 1931 known as the Gandhi-Irwin Pact or the Delhi Pact. On behalf of the Congress, Gandhi agreed to discontinue the movement, to stop the boycott of British commodities and to take part in the second RTC for drafting a constitution on the basis of (a) Federation, (b) Responsibility and (c) Safeguards and Reservations in the interest of Indians for such matter as defene, external affairs, minorities and the financial credit of India. On behalf of the government, the Viceroy agreed to withdraw the emergency ordinances promulgated in connection with the Civil Disobedience Movement, to restore the confiscated property, to permit people to collect or manufacture salt free of duty, to permit peaceful picketing of liquor or opium and foreign cloth shops, and to set free all political prisoners except those who were guilty of violence.

The Delhi Pact however had a mixed reaction. If left-wing Congress felt that Gandhi had unwittingly sold India, the Conservatives in England thought that Irwin had sold Britain. The youth were disappointed with the bargain, for it failed to save Bhagat Singh and his comrades from the death penalty. But the signatories of the Pact had their own reasons for arriving at the compromise. If on the one hand, Gandhi felt that the enthusiasm of the people was on the wane and a campaign might not last for long, on the other hand, the bureaucracy was worried about the failure of law and order. As a matter of fact, "it was a victory of both sides, and "stands as a monument to the good sense and high patriotism of both parties thereto."[2]

The annual session of the Congress at Karachi held on 26-29 March, 1931 endorsed the Pact. The Congress authorised Gandhiji to attend the next RTC as its sole representative, reiterating 'Purna Swaraj' as its goal. Significantly the Karachi Congress outlined for the first time the Fundamental Rights and Duties of the Indian people, which the future constitution should provide. The curtain was thus drawn on the first phase of the Civil Disobedience Movement (1930-31).

BREACH OF THE DELHI PACT

Even before the ink was dry on the Pact, the spirit in which it was signed began to disappear. The government went ahead with the execution of Bhagat Singh, Sukhdev and Rajguru on 23 March 1931 despite pleas from the Congress leaders for mercy. Lord Willingdon, who took over charge as the next Viceroy towards the end of April 1931, began to breach the Pact in several respects.

THE SECOND ROUND TABLE CONFERENCE

Invested with the powers of a plenipotentiary by the Congress, Mahatma Gandhi sailed for England on 29 August, 1931 in order to participate in the Second RTC (which began on 7 September, 1931) and reached London on 12 September, five days late. He was late in another sense also. He arrived at a time when Labour had lost the office and Ramsay Macdonald had formed a new government, national in name but largely conservative in colour and Sir Samuel Hoare had replaced Wedgewood Benn. In all 107 distinguished delegates representing the three British political parties, British-India political parties and Indian states assembled in London to attend the Second Round Table Conference, which continued till 1 December 1931. The main issues for discussion were the future constitutional structure for India and representation of minorities. No agreement could be arrived at on the question of what should be the structure of Indian political system among the Congress, the Muslims League and the Indian Princes. On the question of representation of minorities also there was implacable feud among the delegates. Sadly enough, following the Muslim League, the Depressed Classes also clamoured for separate representation. Dr. B.R. Ambedkar demanded separate constituencies and proper protection for the untouchable millions. Gandhiji, however, vehemently opposed both separate electorates and special safeguards for minorities. Furthermore, Maharaja Dhiraj of Darbhanga and the Raja of Bobhil called for safeguard for the Indian land-holders. Thus the scales were terribly loaded against the Congress at the Conference. To quote Nehru, "In that crowded and gilded hall Gandhiji at a very lonely figures." Subhash Chandra was of the view that Mahatma should have gone to London with a full contingent of notable representatives to counter the mischievous move of the handpicked. Gandhiji found himself alone in the Subcommittee on Minorities. As such, the constitutional problem was overshadowed by the communal problem. The communal claims made by various delegates on behalf of the respective communities were incompatible with each other. For example, it was impossible to reconcile the Muslim claim for absolute majority in the Punjab with the Sikh claim for weightage and the rights of Hindus. The net result of these claims and counterclaims rendered any solution of the communal problem impossible. In the Subcommittee, Gandhiji discovered a diabolic design of British diplomacy in the form of an unholy alliance between Muslim delegates and the reactionary British interest that resulted in the notorious Minorities Pact. The Pact handed over the communal question to Ramsay Macdonald for decision. After the speech of Ramsay Macdonald, Gandhi, while moving a vote of thanks to the Prime Minister, declared that "they had come to the parting of ways and that their ways would hereafter "take different directions". Three days later he left London for India "a saddened, grieved and intrigued man".

STRUGGLE RESUMED-THE SECOND PHASE OF CIVIL DISOBEDIENCE MOVEMENT (1932-34)

By the time Gandhi was back home (28 December, 1931), the Delhi Pact was reduced to shambles. The new government of Willingdon resorted to measures of repression, and repeated attempts were made to cow down the spirit of Indian nationalists. His ordinances put the machinery of repression in full swing. Hence Gandhi was compelled to resume the struggle in 1932. The government declared Congress as unlawful. Within a week almost everybody who was somebody in the Congress was in prison. By April 1932 more than 66,000 persons, including 5,000 women courted arrest. However, Lord Willingdon could not carry out his boast that he would crush the Congress in six months' time. Even when the movement was partially suspended in June 1932 individual Satyagraha continued until 1934.

APPRAISAL OF CIVIL DISOBEDIENCE MOVEMENT

The Civil Disobedience Movement had certain marked features which distinguished it from the Non-Cooperation Movement. This time it was the government which took the initiative and acted with a great swiftness, and was determined to crush the movement. The repression was much more brutal and severe than before. The Movement, however, apparently failed because it came to be stopped without achieving its objective. Further, the support of the Indian business and industrial elites was not as manifest as earlier. The Muslims by and large kept away from this movement. Only Pathans led by Khan Abdul Gaffar Khan actively participated in this Movement. Nevertheless, the spirit of revolt took firm roots in the heart of the people and the fire of patriotism remained smouldering.

THE COMMUNAL AWARD

While the struggle was going on, the British Prime Minister announced on 17 August, 1932 his decision regarding the communal question, known as the Communal Award. In fact, it was an order of the British government imposing a scheme of representation. In this Award separate electorates were allowed not only to Muslims but extended to Sikhs, Indian Christians, Anglo-Indians and Europeans. Besides, Labour, Commerce, Industry, Landlords and Universities were given separate constituencies and fixed seats.. The Europeans were given special weightage. But the most novel feature of the Award was the creation of special constituencies in which the Depressed Classes were entitled to vote. In fact, the Depressed Classes were given two votes — one in a general constituency and the other in special one. Obviously, the Award gave rise to a storm of protest in different quarters, especially Hindus. It was patently partial to the minorities, especially Europeans but unfair to Hindus, the majority community. It was an attempt to perpetuate division based on castes and creeds in India. Further, the Award aimed at the disruption of the Hindu community by giving separate representation to the Depressed Classes, although Dr. Ambedkar, their leader, was not opposed to it. To Gandhi, in particular, the Award was a great jolt, for he had already warned that he would resist with his life, if the British government introduced separate electorate for the Depressed Classes. True to his words, he went on fast unto death on 20 September, 1932. But with a view to save his life, the Hindu leaders met in Poona and concluded an agreement on 25 September, 1932, known as the Poona Pact. The pact recommended joint electorate for the Depressed Classes along with the Hindus. Dr. Ambedkar also became, though reluctantly, a signatory to this pact. The pact provided that the Depressed Classes would forego the separate electorate and in quid pro-quo would have 148 reserved seats in place of 71, as provided in the communal Award. Thus was averted a threat to a permanent split in the Hindu community.

THE THIRD ROUND TABLE CONFERENCE

Undaunted by these developments on the Indian political scene, the British authorities continued to work on the new scheme on constitutional reforms. On 17 November, 1932 the third session of the RTC was held, lasting till 24 December, 1932. This time only 46 delegates, mostly comprising communalists and Liberals, were invited. Even the Labour Party kept away. The participation of the Congress was out of question. This session put together the final features of a concrete plan for a new constitution for India and the same was embodied in a White Paper and presented to the British Parliament in March 1933. A Joint Select Committee (JSC) of both Houses of the British Parliament (sixteen from each) with Lord Linlithgow as Chairman was set up to examine and scrutinise the Plan. The White Paper, however, failed to satisfy any party or group of politicians or any community in India. The JSC consulted some 28 delegates representing the political talent of India. After 18 months of deliberations it published its report on 22 November, 1934 on the basis of which a Bill was drafted. After some amendments the British Parliament passed it on 24 July, 1935 and on 2 August, 1935 it received the Royal assent and became the Act known as the Government of India Act of 1935. The main features of this Act were : (1) An All-India Federation; (2) Statutory division of powers between the Centre and the Units; (3) Dyarchy at the Centre with Safeguards; (4) Provincial Autonomy, and (5) Supremacy of the British Parliament.

Notes

1. Brailsford quoted in Suda, J.P., op.cit, p.196
2. Zacharias, Renascent India. p.274.

Chapter 17

THE DECADE OF DESTINY (1937-47)

The period between 1937 and 1947 is described as the decade of destiny in the history of the Indian freedom movement. Some momentous decisions and monumental declarations were made during this period that determined the course of national movement, the inevitable denouement of which was both triumph and tragedy for the people of the subcontinent.

Nothing sensational happened in the country during 1934-35 except that the Willingdon administration went ahead with its repressive and reactionary policies to supress the lingering Civil Disobedience Movement and revolutionary terrorism. The attention of the Indian leaders during this period was caught by the developments on the world scene. In January 1935, the Fascist rulers of Italy launched aggression on Abyssinia; there were signs of civil war between the army generals led by Francis Franco and the Republican Government in Spain, Hitler, who had stormed to power in Germany (1933), was engaged in a systematic repudiation of the Versailles Treaty of 1919, and the militarists of Japan were poised to attack China after occupying Manchuria in 1932.

On the domestic front the more radical elements inside the Congress formed the Congress Socialist Party (1934) and emphasised the solidarity of the Indian people with the enslaved peoples of the World and urged an unrelenting struggle against British imperialism. The Muslim League was struggling to stage a come-back. After the First RTC M.A. Jinnah had settled in London to practice at the British bar. But in 1934, Raja of Salempore and Liaquat Ali Khan met Jinnah in London and painted a very dismal picture of the League organisation, specially after passing away of Sir Mohd. Shafee, Sir Fazli Hussain, Maulana Mohd. Ali, Hakim Ajmal Khan and others. They succeeded in converting Jinnah from a nationalist Muslim to the Muslim nationalist and called him back to India. In October 1935, Jinnah returned to India and assumed the League leadership and made efforts to revitalise it. In April 1936, he convened a special session of the Muslim League at Bombay, and the decision was taken to fight the election in Provinces under the Act of 1935.

CONGRESS REACTION TO ACT OF 1935

The Act of 1935 received a cold reception in India. To consider this Act the Working Committee of the Congress met at Lucknow (1936) under Nehru's (second) Presidentship. Nehru had already dubbed the Act of 1935 as "the Charter of Slavery". But the Congress Working Committee's majority overruled Nehru and decided to contest the election under this Act. Accordingly, on 23 August 1936, the AICC published its manifesto stating therein that the "Congress would resist British imperialism and work hard to end its various regulations, ordinances and acts, and it would go to legislatures not to cooperate with the Act but to combat it," almost a la Swaraj Party of the mid-1920s. The annual session of the Congress held at Faizpur (Maharashtra) in December 1936 declared that the Congress would have nothing to do with office and the ministry.

In February 1937, elections under the new Act were held for legislatures of eleven provinces. The Congress won 711 out of 1585 general seats came out with a clear majority in six provinces, emerged as the biggest party in three provinces, and had a smaller minority in Punjab and Sind. But the Congress could capture only 26 out of 482 Muslim seats (Muslim League won 108 Muslim seats), though it had fielded 58 candidates. Being the most important and principal party, the question of office acceptance was again confronted the Congress. Many of its leaders, particularly the CSP and Nehru, the President, were opposed to office acceptance. But gradually, the charm of office had its way and the AICC ultimately authorised and permitted the acceptance of office in provinces provided that it was satisfied that the Governor would not use his special powers of interference or set-aside the advice of ministers in regard to constitutional activities. In June 1937, Linlithgow gave the assurance that the Governors would not exercise their special powers arbitrarily. The assurance, however, was the result of a sort of gentleman's agreement between Gandhi and the Viceroy. Except for the fact that there were some differences over the question of release of political prisoners in UP and Bihar, the Governors played their part under provincial autonomy and functioned as constitutional heads in Congress-ruled states. In July 1937, the Congress formed ministries in 7 out of 11 provinces and later on, a Congress Coalition Ministry were formed in Assam as well.

NO COALITION WITH THE MUSLIM LEAGUE

The decision to permit Congressmen to accept office raised a very vital question, namely, whether or not to join other groups to form coalition ministries in Provinces, like Bengal, Assam and the Punjab.

There was also the question of taking in members of the Muslim League as Ministers in Congress majority provinces like UP and Bihar. However, the Congress decided to go against coalition ministries. It was thought that Congress would be stronger if it stood alone. Ofcourse, a joint front against the British authorities was essential. But in a coalition there would have been no binding cement, no common loyalty, and no unified objective, as the Congress leftists like Z.A. Ahmad, Dr. Ashraf and Acharya Narendra Deva etc. argued. With these considerations in mind it is not surprising that no understanding with the Muslim League for coalition government could be arrived at in UP, for the Muslim League was not prepared to dissolve their party as a separate group, a condition that the League was required to fulfil for joining the Ministry. Furthermore, the League was also not prepared to accept joint responsibility. It is said that Nehru rebuffed the overtures of the League for a Congress-League ministry, even as he chided Congressmen who talked in terms of pacts and compromises with Muslim or other religious groups. According to Maulana Azad," the negotiations between the Congress and the League foundered when Nehru, with his theoretical bias, turned down Khaliquzzaman's proposal to include himself and Ismail Khan in the UP Ministry."[1] But Prof. S. Gopal has refuted this contention of Azad and observes that it was Maulana who conducted the negotiations and approved conditions put forth by the Congress. In some quarters, it is also believed that the Congress was willing to accommodate only one member from the League, as there was a good deal of haggling over the other seat.

Constitutionally speaking, the Congress was not obliged to enter into coalition. Nevertheless, "the decision to exclude the Muslim League from the cabinets, however logical and sound technically, had a disastrous consequence. It caused serious disappointment to aspirants like Khaliquzzaman and Ismail Khan for ministership in the UP Government. Not surprisingly, the League drifted more and more from the Congress after this unhappy episode. The communal tension of the following years leading to the demand for Pakistan was thus the direct outcome of the exclusion of Muslim League from the Congress cabinets."[2] Undoubtedly, it was the most fatal decision since the Lucknow Pact (which had accepted the communal electorate)." Jinnah made capital out of this tactical blunder." It can be safely said that this step was the most decisive factor in making the Muslim League fix Pakistan as its goal three years later, for it provided Jinnah a basis to argue that in independent India no sharing of power with the Congress would be possible. K.K.Aziz also holds: "the Congress refusal to share power with the (League) Muslims in 1937 was to crystallize the notion of Pakistan into a definite scheme"[3] Much had been made of the alleged refusal of the Congress to form coalition ministries with the Muslim League, but Anita Inder Singh is of the opinion that "Jinnah's opposition to the negotiations between provincial leaders and the Congress clearly shows that the failure could not have been the reason behind the call for a sovereign Muslim State in March 1940."[4]

WORKING OF PROVINCIAL AUTONOMY UNDER THE CONGRESS MINISTRIES

The working of Provincial Autonomy proved the capacity of the Indian leaders. They showed a high sense of public duty and responsibility. Even the Viceroy paid tributes to their distinguished record of public service. To quote Coupland, "the record of Congress Ministry was in which the Congress could take a reasonable pride."[5] It brought Congress to amass experience in administration and constructive works like elementary education, prohibition, tenancy law, agricultural indebtedness, rural development, cottage industries, removal of untouchability. Besides, the working of Provincial Autonomy advanced the cause of nationalism in India. It increased our eagerness to be free. It proved our capacity to govern overselves. The Congress became a constructive force in the country's politics.

SECOND WORLD WAR AND CONSTITUTIONAL DEADLOCK — BIRTH PANGS OF FREEDOM

In the early 1938, the political situation in Europe began to deteriorate. Hitler seized Austria (March, 1938) and united it with Germany, and began to prepare for the annexation of Czechoslovakia. Hoping that another World War might be averted, England and France concluded a pact at Munich with Germany (September 1930), persuading the Czech government to cede the Sudetenland (predominantly a German-inhabited territory) back to Germany. But instead of appeasing the fascist dictator, it whetted his appetite, who began to lay claims to the Republic of Czechoslovakia. In mid-March 1939 Hitler not only seized the whole of Czechoslovakia but also occupied Lithuania and Romania. In April 1939 Mussolini (another fascist dictator) made Albania a part of the Italian Empire.

In the Far East, Japan's military adventures in the quest of a New Order in East Asia was on the march. Japan occupied Hainan and Spratly islands belonging to China. The US, though consulted, did not come to rescue China against Japan on the plea of 'neutrality'. Since England, France and the USA were not willing to take on the Axis Powers, the inevitable happened. On 1 September, 1939 Germany invaded Poland.

On 3 September, 1939 Britain and France declared war against Germany. On the same day the Viceroy, without consulting or even taking into confidence the Indian leaders, proclaimed India a belligerent nation and began to despatch Indian troops to Singapore and the Middle East. Further, in order to suppress internal disorder the Viceroy also assumed emergency powers under Article 93 of the Act of 1935.

CONGRESS ATTITUDE TOWARDS WAR

A little before War broke out in Europe, the Congress Working Committee affirmed its firm opposition to all types of fascist and Nazi aggression, but at the same time, declared its unwillingness to associate itself with the British government in any way in the prosecution of the War. It said: "India cannot associate itself with such a government or be asked to give her resources for democratic freedom which is denied to her and which is likely to be destroyed." Not once but repeatedly, the Congress made it clear that while it was opposed to Nazism and Fascism and Japanese militarism and all other forms of totalitarianism, but it was equally opposed to give any help in a War which was intended to consolidate and further the interests of British imperialism. It also demanded that India should not be committed to any war without the consent of her people or their representatives.

The Congress Working Committee again met on 14 September, 1939 and asked the British government "to declare in unequivocal terms what their war aims are in regard to democracy and imperialism and the new order that is envisaged, in particular how these aims are going to apply to India and to be given effect to in the present." The resolution further stated that if Britain was fighting "for the maintenance and extension of democracy, then she must necessarily and logically end imperialism in her own possessions and establish full democracy in India." The right of the Indian people to frame their own constitution without external interference was also asserted in the resolution. The Congress contended that only a free and democratic India would have some stake in the victory of fascist powers and that stake alone would goad the Indian people to suffer and sacrifice on behalf of the UK and its allies.

But the British made no clear declaration of War aims except that they had done so to make the world safe for democracy and to uphold the right of all nations to self-determination. The British Prime Minister declared that for the time being his War aim was self-preservation. On 10 October 1939, the AICC met and asked the British government to declare categorically that India would be free after the War and that she would be given immediate control over Indian affairs to the largest possible extent. The Viceroy on his part issued a statement on 7 October 1939: "As regards freedom of India he held out the pledge that Dominion Status was the goal of British policy in India and to that end the Act of 1935 could be reconsidered after the War in the light of Indian views and with due regard for the opinion of the minorities." As to the immediate action, he proposed the establishment of an Advisory Council representing all India, to associate the Indian public opinion with the prosecution of the War.

At this stage it should be remembered that the attitude of the Congress in War-II was in marked contrast to its behaviour during the War-I. Then it had given unconditional help. But since all national leaders were disillusioned by the earlier response of the British government, the Congress this time decided not to be fooled into cooperation. The promise of independence after the War and an effective control over the Indian administration during its pendency were now declared as the conditions prerequisite to any voluntary help in the War efforts.

RESIGNATION OF CONGRESS MINISTRIES

The Declaration of the Governor General fall far short of the Congress demand. In reply to demand for independence after the War, it simply held out a promise of the Dominion Status as a distant goal. A similar statement was made by Lord Zetland, the Secretary of State for India. Both the statements obviously caused great disappointment in different circles of the Congress. In a mood of frustration the Congress Working Committee met on 22 October 1939, which called upon the Congress to resign, and which was done by the end of October in at the eight provinces. In all these provinces the Governors declared the breakdown of the constitution under Article 93 of the Government of India Act of 1935, dissolved the legislatures, and took the entire administration in their own hands. An impasse between the British government and the Congress ensued. The Congress resignation changed the course of history. Retrospectively speaking, this step was another great folly committed by the Congress during the course of freedom struggle. In the opinion of V.P. Menon, "By withdrawing from office at this critical juncture the Congress lost an important bargaining position which it was never able to retrieve." At that time M.N. Roy and Rajaji also questioned the wisdom of this step.

GENESIS OF THE IDEA OF A MUSLIM HOMELAND — MUSLIM LEAGUE DEMANDS PAKISTAN

When and how the idea of Pakistan originated and at what stage became something more than a bargaining counter has not been clearly determined. According to K.K. Aziz, "between 1858 (when muslims of India ceased to be the rulers) and 1940 (when the Muslim League adopted the partition of India as its goal) their appeared some 170 plans and suggestions, ranging from vague hints to carefully drawn up schemes for redistribution, division or partition of India on religious/communal lines. Their authors were the real makers of the idea of Pakistan. However, no serious notice of proposals was taken until 1939-40."[6]

The notion of a Muslim Homeland in North-West and North-East of India was possible, not by the fact that the majority of the Indian Muslims lived in Muslim majority provinces — indeed, more than 60 percent Muslims lived in the Muslim minority provinces — but because of what has been described by Prof. S.R. Mehrotra as an "accident of geography," and "without these Muslim majority areas it becomes inconceiveable that any section of the Muslims would have been able to demand any kind of homeland."[7]

However, the idea of a separate Muslim state is usually ascribed to the great poet, Sir Mohd. Iqbal. At the Allahabad session of the Muslim League held in 1930, Dr. Iqbal spoke; "I have no hesitation in declaring that if the principle that the Indian Muslim is entitled to full and free development on the lines of his own culture and tradition in his Indian Homeland is recognised on the basis of a permanent communal settlement, I would like to seek the Punjab, North-West Frontier Province, Sind and Baluchistan amalgamated into a single state. The formation of a consolidated Western Indian Muslim state appears to me the final destiny of the Muslims at least of North-West India."

The Idea of a separate Muslim Homeland (Pakistan) was again taken up and propagated through a four-page leaflet (Now and Never) by a group led by Chowdhary Rahmat Ali during the Third Round Table Conference. It was in this pamphlet that the acronym forming the word 'Pakistan' was conceptualised. The term 'Pakistan' was coined by Rahmat Ali and stood for Punjab. Afghanistan, Kashmir, Sind and Baluchistan. But it was brushed aside as a chimerical and impractical by the Muslim spokesmen at the RTC. Mr. Jinnah dismissed it as "a student's scheme" and nothing was heard about it for sometime. It was only after 1937 that the idea of partition began to catch the imagination of Muslim leaders.

The year of 1937 was a turning point in the history of the Muslim League. It saw not only the beginning of a definite rupture between it and the Congress but also witnessed the foundation of a new demand and a new theory being laid. The new demand was for a separate nation—Pakistan. Pakistan and the two-nation theory on which it was based germinated and developed between 1937 and 1940.

However, by 1937 the League was not yet a mass party nor was its leader, Mr. Jinnah, considered a mass leader. But in the meantime the Muslim League secured the support of Fazlul Haq of Bengal and Sikander Hayat Khan of Punjab, Thus the idea of partition began to develop and take shape in the minds of Muslim League politicians after the disillusionment in 1937 when the Congress, "flushed with success", ignored the Muslim demand for composite cabinets. This "tactical error of the first magnitude" on the part of the Congress greatly contributed to the adoption of the Pakistan Resolution three-years after. Now the League leadership began to feel that separate electorate, statutory safeguards and even autonomous provinces had proved unsatisfactory, and they began to realise that these artifices would not protect them from the rule of the "Hindu majority" at the Centre in an All-India Federation. They, therefore, began to assert that the Muslims were a separate nation and not only a minority community, and only as a nation they could develop their spiritual, cultural, economic, social and political life to the fullest extent in accordance with their own ideals and according to the genius of their people and enjoy the right of self-determination.

In addition, while the Muslim Community was getting away from the mainstream of Indian nationalism, some sections of the Hindu populace under the leadership of Hindu Maha Sabha and other Hindu wings (RSS) were becoming more and more chauvinistic and militant. For instance, in December 1937, V.D. Savarkar, the President of Hindu Maha Sabha, declared that "the aim of his organisation was maintenance, protection and promotion of the Hindu race, Hindu culture and Hindu civilisation and advancement of the glory of Hindu Rashtra. India cannot be assumed today to be a homogenous nation there are two nations in India in the main the Hindu and Muslim." In a similar vein, Golwalkar of RSS wrote in his book, 'We — Our nation Defined' (1939), "Hindustan is the land of the Hindus and is the terrafirma for the Hindu nation alone to flourish upon... the foreign races in Hindustan must either adopt the Hindu culture and language, must learn to respect and hold in reverence Hindu religion, must entertain no idea but the glorification of the Hindu race and culture; i.e., of the Hindu nation and must lose their separate existence to merge in the Hindu race, or may stay in the country, wholly subordinated to the Hindu nation, claiming nothing, deriving no privileges, facilities or any preferrential treatment not even citizen's right." These utterances and other activities of Hindu Communalists thrust more and more of Muslims into the League fold and led to Hindu-Muslim tension during 1938-39, and several communal riots took place. Consequently, the fear of Hindu domination, real or imaginary, gave an added appeal to the idea of partition.

By 1939 the idea of partition began to acquire a concrete shape. In the summer of 1939, Sir Sikandar Hayat Khan published a scheme for the loosest of federation with regional or zonal legislatures to deal with common subjects. In January 1940, Dr. Abdul Latif of Hyderabad outlined a plan for a minimal federation of homogenous cultural zones. In March 1939, Chaudhary Khaliquzzaman had discussed the possibility of partition with Zetland, the Secretary of state for India. In September 1939, Jinnah had suggested the same to Lord Linlithgow as a political alternative to federation. In February 1940, Aurangzeb Khan, a League leader of NWFP, told Cunningham that the League proposed to press for a Muslim homeland in the North-West and North-East. On 4 March 1940, Jinnah told Edward Benthall (Finance Member) that "Muslims would not be safe without partition," and twelve days later he told the Viceroy that" if the British could not resolve the political deadlock, the League would have no option but to fall back on some form of partition."[8]

The Congress leadership was getting disappointed over the political climate. They felt that the goal of Complete Independence could be attained only if all the people presented a united front. Hence efforts were made to this effect by Subhash, Nehru and Gandhi. But Jinnah's demand was that Congress should recognise the League as the one and only authoritative representative organisation of the Indian Muslims. The Congress, however, was not willing to oblige. Thus during the first half of 1939 the campaign for a separate homeland was built up.

When the War broke out in Europe, Jinnah, too, expressed sympathy for Poland, Britain and France. Taking advantage of British difficulties in the prosecution of War, the Muslim League also, like the Congress, made its cooperation conditional. In October, 1939, it declared "if London wanted to prosecute the War successfully they should take Muslim India into confidence through their accredited organisation — the Muslim League. It told the British government that no assurances must be given as to the constitutional advance nor any new constitution framed without the consent and approval of the League. The Viceroy readily accepted the League claim to speak for the Indian Muslims. Later on, when the Congress governments resigned, Jinnah was so relieved that he declared 22 October, 1939 as the Deliverance Day- a relief from Congress rule meaning thereby Hindu rule. During the months of 1940 the League whipped up its campaign for Pakistan. Finally, on 24 March, 1940 its annual session was held at Lahore which resolved: "It is the considered view of this session of AIML that no constitutional plan would be workable in this country unless it is designed on the following basic principles; viz, that geographically contiguous units are demarcated into zones which should be so constituted, with such territorial adjustment as may be necessary, that the areas in which the Muslims are numerically in a majority as in the North-Western and Eastern zones of India should be grouped to constitute independent states in which the constituent units shall be autonomous and sovereign." In his Presidential address, Jinnah proclaimed that the division of India into autonomous states was the only solution to the Indian problem. The demand for Pakistan began to become stronger in the following years. Thus, the demand for a separate Muslim homeland embodied in the Lahore Resolution was the consequence of the social, cultural religious, educational and economic differences between the two major communities which frustrated the efforts of national leaders to keep India united.

The Indian National Congress was naturally opposed to the idea of Pakistan. Even Muslims outside the League were opposed to it. Despite its emotive appeal, the two-nation idea made no sense to the rank and file of Punjab Unionist Party, Bengal's Krishak Praja Party or the dominant Muslim Party led by Allah Bux in Sind. The schemes was opposed by the Jamaint-ul-Ulema-e-Hind, the Majlis-e-Ahrar, the All India Momin Confernece, the Khudai Khidmatgars of the NWFP, the All-India Shia Political Conference and the Nationalist Muslims. The Sikhs in the Punjab also declared their determination to oppose it tooth and nail. However, the demand for Pakistan began to become firmer as the days passed. On 10 January, 1941 Jinnah declared that if the country were partitioned between them, Hindus and Muslims could regard each other as friendly neighbours and say to the world 'hands off India'. In April 1941, at the Madras session, the League made Pakistan its creed. Jinnah called it a matter of life and death:" Either we achieve Pakistan or we perish." On 6 February, 1943 Jinnah also asserted that the North-Western and the North-Eastern states of Pakistan would be connected by a corridor running along the northern borders of UP and Bihar. Thus, the Muslim League became the third side of the triangle leading to an intractable constitutional deadlock during the War.

While the contending factions in India- the British rulers, the Congress and the Muslim League- were moving further apart from each other, the military situation of the war in Europe was becoming alarming. Having conquered Denmark and Norway, the offensive against Luxembourg, Belgium and Holland was launched by Hitler on 10 May, 1940, followed by invasion of France on 5 June, 1940. The French government surrendered and signed the armistice on 23 June. Even before France capitulated, German bombers inaugurated air raids on British hearths and houses. Now the only country that could have reversed the tide of Hitler's successive victories was the USA, But USA, though sympathetic to the UK and other West-European countries did nothing during the first nine months of the War, as the isolationist sentiment was still very strong among the Americans. Thus, England was left the only opponent of Hitler. Finding themselves in a very tight situation, the British authorities both in England and India made an appeal to the people, princes, politicians and political parties to realise the gravity of the War situation and appealed them to extend all possible support to resist the fascist aggression.

MUSLIM LEAGUE MAKES CONDITIONAL RESPONSE

The Muslim League showed their willingness to cooperate if England sought their cooperation on the condition that no pronouncement or statement and no interim or final scheme of constitution should be made or adopted which militated against the Lahore Resolution. Jinnah suggested that the Viceroy's Council should be enlarged but the representatives of both Muslims and Hindus should be equal in it.

CONGRESS OFFERS CONDITIONAL HELP IN WAR

At the initiative of C. Rajgopalachari, the Congress offered its helping hand to Britain but on some honourable basis. On 1 June, 1940 Gandhi declared: "We do not seek our independence out of British ruin." The CWC met at Poona on 7 July, 1940 and offered to throw its full weight into the efforts for the effective organisation of defence of the country and wholehearted cooperation in men and money. But the Poona offer was made subject to two conditions: one, that India's right to self-government after the War be recognised in clear terms; two, that a provisional national government should be set up forthwith at the Centre consisting of all political parties. This was a toned down and moderate demand and required no over-hauling of constitutional machinery, for earlier at Ramgarh session (1940) the Congress in a formal resolution had reiterated that "nothing short of Complete Independence can be accepted by the people of India and no permanent solution was possible except through the Constituent Assembly."

In the meantime, a ministerial change took place in England. Winston Churchill replaced Chamberlain and Amery took over as Secretary of State from Zetland. The new Prime Minister bluntly stated on 11 May 1940 that "he had not become the premier to preside over the liquidation of the British Empire."

AUGUST OFFER

In response to the Poona Resolution of the Congress Working Committee, the Viceroy, in consultation with Churchill, issued on 8

August 1940 a statement on India and the War, known as the August Offer. The August Offer promised the establishment of full responsible government on the Dominion model after the termination of the War in Europe. This was a great advance on the statement of 17 October 1939 which declared the Dominion Status as the goal of British policy in India. Significantly, it conceded for the first time that the responsibility for framing their constitution was that of Indians themselves; it was to be framed by a body of representative Indians drawn from all the principal elements of national life. To a large extent, it amounted to the acceptance of the Congress demand for a Constituent Assembly. But the Offer was hedged in by two significant provisos: firstly, British obligations in such matters as defence, treaty with the Princes, rights of public services were to be fulfilled; secondly, the interests of the minorities were to be safeguarded. But the most objectionable part of the statement from the Congress point of view lay in the following words: "It goes without saying that they (the British government) could not contemplate the transfer of their personal responsibilities for the peace and welfare of India to any system of government whose authority is directly denied by large and principal elements in India's national life. Nor could they be parties to the coercion of such elements into submission to such a government." As regards the Congress demand for a national government responsible to the legislature, the Viceroy announced that the Executive Council would be enlarged and an War Advisory Council would be established which would comprise representatives of Indian states and of other interests in the national life as a whole. The Viceroy hoped that all parties and communities would join the two Councils and cooperate in the War efforts and thereby pave the way for the attainment by India of a free and equal partnership in the British Commonwealth. It may be noted that for the first time the Viceroy spoke about free and equal partnership of India in the British Commonwealth. This was also an important advance upon the previous attitudes and ideas.

The reaction to this statement was sharp and mixed. It was well received by the Muslim League, the Hindu Maha Sabha and the Liberal Federation. But the Offer fell far short of Congress expectations. It did not come anywhere near the National Government. Moreover, it placed a virtual veto in the hands of the minorities and the princes against further constitutional advancement in India. In effect, it put the majority at the mercy of the minority. The Congress Working Committee considered the statement at Wardha (18-23 August) and rejected it. The Muslim League also rejected the August Offer on the ground that it had not been offered equal partnership at the Centre and in the provinces in return for cooperation with the War effort.

INDIVIDUAL CIVIL DISOBEDIENCE

The Congress, however, could not remain a passive spectator of the deepening crisis. There was no course open to it but to resort to civil disobedience, and it authorised Gandhi to lead it. However, in view of the critical War situation Gandhiji did not like to do anything which could lead to disorder or the cause of the Allied nations. It was merely symbolic in character to draw the attention of world at large to the right of self-determination. In November 1940, the individual Satyagraha was started as a symbolic protest against the attitude of the government. Vinoba Bhave was given the singular honour of being selected as the first individual Satyagrahi. It is estimated that about 25,000 persons courted imprisonment in this movement, including all the top ranking leaders. This novel form of Satyagraha was invented by Gandhiji to give the minimum possible offence to authorities and yet to keep the torch of nationalism burning. While the individual Satyagraha was going on, the Executive Council was expanded and eight out of thirteen were Indians in it, and in October, 1941, was also instituted the War Advisory Council in terms of the August Declaration. The key departments like Home, Finance and Foreign Affairs, however, remained with British members while non-important departments were given to Indian members.

While India was noncooperative, the military situation deteriorated still further. Germans started large scale attack in Britain, the Italian troops struck against Greece and Japan occupied most of Eastern China and launched an attack on South-East Asia on 27 September, 1941. Japan also concluded a tripartite agreement with Germany and Italy and the three aggressors began to talk of a New order in Europe and Greater East Asia. Confronted with such circumstances on the War front the Viceroy declared not to leave the situation go out of hand, and the forces of repression were let loose. The Civil Disobedience by individuals continued during 1940-41 and the leaders including Nehru and Azad were arrested. Not only was the Indian government engaged in suppressing the Congress Compaign, the authorities in London also adopted a more reactionary attitude towards the Congress demand. Mr. Amery (Secretary of State) demanded an agreement among the Indian statesmen belonging to different political groups as a condition precedent to any change at the Centre. The Congress was told that in the absence of an agreement no power could be transferred. To counter the Congress demand, the Muslim League demanded Partition before Independence, a demand described as "divorce before marriage" by Azad.

FOUR FREEDOMS AND THE ATLANTIC CHARTER

The German war machine was in full swing and its bombs were causing considerable damage and havoc to British military targets. London was finding itself unable to withstand the German might. In December 1940, Churchill sent messages to Franklin D. Roosevelt telling him that if the US did not defend the UK, its own security would be jeopardised. These communications created a war hysteria in Washington. On 6 January, 1941 FDR enunciated the doctrine of Four Freedoms- freedom of speech and expression, freedom of worship, freedom from want and freedom from fear. On 14 August 1941, after several meetings in mid-Atlantic Ocean, Roosevelt and Churchill jointly issued a statement of war aims and principles known as the Atlantic Charter and declared inter alia that they respected the right of all peoples to choose the form of government under which they live and they wished to see rights and self-government restored to those who have been forcibly deprived of them. These pronouncements roused some hopes in India and the Congress urged the British to apply them to India. But Churchill interpreted that these principles referred only to European countries. This created deep frustration and disappointment.

EUROPEAN WAR BECOMES GLOBAL

On 22 June, 1941, in utter violation of the Non-Aggression and Neutrality Pact (1939), Germany launched an attack against the Soviet Union. With this attack the War entered into a new phase. The Nazi troops achieved astounding victories on the Soviet territory. This brought upon both London and Washington the realisation that if the Nazis succeeded in overpowering Soviet Russia, the position of both would be greatly imperilled. With this realisation, both Churchill and FDR declared their solidarity with Stalin and began to assist the Soviet Union.

In the Asian theatre also the Allied powers were in sad plight. Japan had penetrated into Indo-China and their thrust was in the South-East Asian region. The negotiations that were started by the Japanese diplomats in Washington in April 1941 to resolve the conflict with the US in a peaceful manners produced no result, and all of a sudden, the Japanese bombers struck at the US navy in Pearl Harbour (Hawaii) on 6 December 1941. The US declared war on Japan on 7 December and her neutrality (qualified) came to an end. Thus the War that started as a European War became a global conflict.

The Japanese armies swept across the South-East Asian region. With the fall of Thailand, Indonesia, Indo-China, Philippines, Malaya and

Singapore, the fall of Burma looked imminent and the invasion of India highly probable. On 8 March, 1942, the Japanese army entered Rangoon. Its occupation of South Burma menaced India itself. Invasion of Eastern India carried within it the danger of the loss of Calcutta and severance of all contact with the National Government of China through Burma. Japan also became a dominant power in the Western Indian Ocean, threatening the British position in the Middle-East.

While Britain and its partners were involved in the War, the Congress was carrying on the Civil Disobedience campaign. Meanwhile, Subhash Chandra Bose had left the country to make "friendship with the enemies of the enemy" and to reinforce the freedom struggle from abroad. As regards the Muslim League, its demand for Pakistan was becoming more and more insistent and its leaders were no longer in a mood to extend cooperation in the War efforts. Now the policy makers in London began to realise that much danger could be done to the cause of war by an unfriendly India, and therefore effort should be made to reconcile differences with the Congress. As a first gesture in that direction the government released many of its leaders, including Azad and Nehru. On the other hand, the failure of British to stop Japanese advance convinced Indian leaders that they must not depend upon the government for the defence of the country. The Congress had no inclination to have the British imperialism replaced by that of Japan. To reciprocate the gesture shown by the government, the Congress suspended the individual Satyagraha. On 16 January 1942, the CWC passed a resolution and offered cooperation in the War efforts. But the offer was subject to the government changing its attitude. The British authority, however, made no appropriate response. On 10 February, 1942, the President of the Republic of China, Chiang Kai Shek and his wife came to India-apparently at the instance of London with the object of rallying Indian opinion against Japan. Chiang impressed upon the Congress leadership the urgency and desirability of an understanding with the British rulers in the face of a common danger from Japan. They also urged the government in a farewell message to win India's full support in the struggle against Japan. Similarly, towards the end of February 1942 FDR instructed the American ambassador in London, Avarall Hariman, to sound Churchill on the possibility of a settlement between the British government and the Indian political leaders and to establish a Dominion government.

CRIPPS MISSION TO INDIA

The attack on Pearl Harbour on 6 December, 1941 inspired the British to consider a fresh political initiative in India to attract a greater measure of popular support for the War effort. Pressures came from India, the USA, China and the UK[9] and Whilehall was confronted with the task of showing its Allies that it was making constitutional moves to end the political deadlock in India. Ultimately, Churchill and his colleagues felt that effort must be made to break the political deadlock, and Sir Stafford Cripps (a Member of War Cabinet and Lord Privy Seal) was sent to India to conduct discussions on the spot with the leaders of all Indian parties and communities. There could be no better choice, for Cripps was a distinguished socialist leader who knew most of the top leaders of the Congress and was a personal friend of Nehru. Earlier also, after the German attack of the Soviet Union, he had been sent on a most delicate mission to Moscow to devise close collaboration. By sending him the British Prime Minister wanted to display that he attached great importance to the solution of India's problem. But the real reason, as subsequent events proved, appeared to be that he wanted to still what he described 'febrile agitation' in order to gain time for the problem to be calmly solved.

CRIPPS PROPOSAL

Cripps arrived in Delhi on 22 March, 1942 and soon after started conferring with leaders of all parties and groups. Having learnt different points of view, he made the following proposal on behalf of the British government, known as the Cripps Proposal: The Proposal was divided into two parts, one dealing with the future and the other with the present. As regards the first part, the objective was stated to be the earliest possible realisation of self-government for India, and to realise this the government contemplated to create a new Indian union which would constitute a Dominion associated with the UK and other Dominions by a common allegiance to the Crown, but equal to them in every respect, in no way subordinate in any respect of its domestic and global affairs. It was proposed (a) that immediately upon the cessation of hostilities steps shall be taken to set up in India an elected body charged with the task of framing a new constitution for India; (b) Provision shall be made for participation of Indian states in the constitution making body; (c) His Majesty's Government undertake to accept and implement forthwith the constitution so framed subject only to (i) The right of any Province of British India that is not prepared to accept the new constitution to retain its present constitutional position, provision being made for its subsequent accession (with such non-acceeding provinces His Majesty's government will be prepared to agree upon a new constitution giving them the same full status of a Dominion), (ii) A treaty will be signed between His Majesty's Government and the Constituent Assembly concerning all matters arising out of complete transfer of responsibility. The Constitution-making body will be elected by the Lower Houses of Provincial Legislatures (as a single electoral college) by the system of proportional representation. This body shall be about one-tenth of the number of electoral college. Indian states shall appoint their representatives which shall be in proportion to their population." No doubt, the proposal dealing with the future marked an appreciable advance on the August Offer.

As regards the other part dealing with the present, the proposal was vague with the only welcome change that it provided that pending the war, the Viceroy's Executive Council would be entirely Indian and would consist of leaders of political parties. But the task of organising to the full the military, moral and material resources of India must be the responsibility of government of India. It was added that during the War period the British government must inevitably have the responsibility for and retain the control and direction of defence of India. But the Congress led by Nehru and Azad wanted that there should be immediately a national government which would function as a constitutional authority. On this point Cripps assured that the Governor General would function as a constitutional head. But this position was taken by Cripps without consultation with the Viceroy and presumably at the suggestion of Col. Louis Johnson, the personal Representative of President Roosevelt in India. Feeling offended, the Governor General sent a despatch against this assurance. Churchill wrote back to Cripps that he would be repudiated if he went too far. He pulled up Cripps for stepping beyond his brief. As such, Cripps had to go back on his assurance to Azad that the Executive Council would have full and unfettered freedom of decision. Thus the Viceroy, by joining hand with Churchill, torpedoed the Cripps Mission. On 11 April, 1942, the CWC adopted a resolution and rejected the Draft Declaration. It restated that "only a free and independent India could undertake the defence of the country on a national basis." Its other major ground for rejection was that the proposal encouraged separatism.

WHY CRIPPS MISSION FAILED

It is worth noting that the Delhi Declaration disappointed all political groups in India and all of them rejected it. The Congress rejected it because the offer did not make the Executive Council responsible to the Legislature. The Muslim League disliked the proposal because the freedom of the Province to opt out of the Union did not concede the demand of Pakistan in clear terms. The depressed classes did not find adequate safeguards for themselves in it. The Liberals also rejected it as "a travesty of self-determination." The only organisation that looked with favour upon the Offer was the Radical Democratic Party led by M.N. Roy, but the

Party was hardly of much consequence in the country. It is interesting to note that the Cripps plan embodied different items palatable to different tastes. To the Congress, it offered full Dominion Status, constituent Assembly and even right to leave the Commonwealth. To the Muslim League, there was the highly comforting provision of any province having the right to join the Union or not. The principle of partition had in fact been incorporated into the Cripps proposal in recognition of the League's demand for Pakistan. H.V. Hodson rightly assessed the inherent dangers in this provision when he wrote in his 'THE GREAT DIVIDE'. "This was a hole in the dyke which Mr Jinnah was determined to widen." The Indian princes were given the right to nominate their own representatives to the Constituent Assembly. But ironically enough, the Plan which intended to please everybody ended in pleasing few. Cripps blamed Gandhi and the Congress leaders for the failure of his mission. Gandhi was, according to him, the real wrecker of the Proposal. "With characteristic frankness Gandhi described the Cripps Offer as "a post-dated cheque" on "a failing bank." He meant by this remark that the offer of Independence was of no value, for the British government would itself fall before the offer could be realised. By "failing bank" (added by J.B. Kriplani) Gandhiji's meaning seems to be that any way British government would have to quit but quitting after the War would mean that the resources of India would be completely depleted."[10] Thus, the onus for the breakdown Cripps Mission was not unjustifiably attached to the Congress and Gandhiji.

The way in which negotiations failed was sufficient to lend some weight to the belief that the proposals were made not with any intention to part with power but to pacify international critics of the British policy in India at that time. The authorities both in England and in India were not prepared to concede power to any national government at that moment. If the Indian government was in the hands of Linlithgow, the English government was in the hands of a person who had stated: "I did not become the Prime Minister of Great Britain so that I could gamble with various parts of the British Empire." To conclude, the Cripps Mission, even though eventually met its doom, yet influenced the course of events that shaped the history of the Indian subcontinent. The Proposals provided a basis for a constitutional advance.[11] They recognised the principle of independence and pronounced the right of framing their own constitution, and both were conceded to the satisfaction of the Congress on the conclusion of the War. Similarly, they recognised the right of Muslim majority provinces to keep out of the Indian Union and the same was conceded to the Muslim League in the form of Pakistan in 1947.

THE QUIT INDIA MOVEMENT (1942)

The failure of the Cripps Mission led to unprecedented disturbances throughout India and a deep sense of frustration grew rapidly. Japan was advancing like a whirlwind. Since the British government was unwilling to part with power and the Congress was equally emphatic that an effective defence against Japan could be organised only by a popular government, there was no meeting ground between the two sides. However, the response of Indian leaders to the developing situation was not uniform. Subhash Chandra Bose, who had been watching from Berlin the march of events in India and on the military front, urged for cooperation with Japan. He broadcasted fiery speeches to incite the Indian public by telling them that "British difficulties were opportunities for them" to attain their freedom. Moreover, there was a strong pro-Japanese sentiment in the country as well. But the Congress High Command did not like that the anti-British feelings among the people to develop into pro-Japanese sentiments, because it was as much opposed to Japanese imperialism as it detested British imperialism. It had no desire "to change masters," as Nehru has put it. Nehru even advocated resistance to Japanese advance. He asserted "If the invading armies sought to take possession of the people's home and field, they must be resisted even into death." The Congress President, Maulana Azad, felt that negotiations could be resumed with Britain and full cooperation to the Allied Powers be extended, if "Britain made absolute promise of Independence after the War and if the US President or the UN guaranteed fulfillment of that promise." It is worth mentioning here that both Nehru and Azad were uncomfortable from the beginning of the War, because by opposing the Allies' war efforts wittingly they were supporting the fascists unwittingly.

Gandhi however, was developing new ideas on the conflict with Britain. Earlier in 1940, he was opposed to any programme of Satyagraha, as it was likely to jeopardise the Allied War efforts. But in the summer of 1942, he became an advocate of mass action to drive the British out of Indian soil with his "get out Britain" slogan. This radical change in his thinking was brought about probably by continued apathy of the British authorities and the unmitigated hardship of the people. Further, the danger of Japanese attack on Calcutta via Burma being imminent, catastrophe and disaster for India appeared inevitable. He began to feel that British might surrender without much resistance, as in Singapore, Malaya and Burma. Like other leaders, he too considered Japanese imperialism worse than the British one, and wanted the country to "oppose Japan to a man". He however, felt that the withdrawal of the British from India could "remove the bait", and the Japanese might not attack and even if they did, he thought free India would be in a better position to deal with the invaders. "Unadulterated cooperation," he wrote, "could then have full sway." He, therefore, thought that the British should be called to quit and leave the country in the hands of God. Brian Lapping in his 'End of Empire' has rightly observed: "The Quit India Movement was a retreat by Gandhiji from complex problems into the impractical."

C. Rajgopalachari, another front rank leader, was equally disturbed by the panic which prevailed among the people and the authorities of Madras in the wake of Japanese bombing of some areas of the province. The Japanese ships were cruising in the Bay of Bengal and the invasion of India was widely feared. In view of all this he began to lose confidence in the efficacy of nonviolent non-cooperation movement, as advocated by Gandhi, and he felt that the League's demand for Pakistan must be complied with in order to establish unity and a solid front against the British. The Congress League combine alone, he felt, would make the country's demand for a national government irresistible. Thus, four different lines of thought as to the future course of action were crystallizing within the top leaders of the Congress.

"The Storm was gathering and India lay," in the words of Nehru, "helpless and inert, bitter and sullen." The danger that the country would become a battle ground for the British and the Japanese forces was increasing. In order to discuss the situation and devise a clear cut policy, the AICC and CWC met at Allahabad towards the end of April 1942. In that session, C. Rajgopalachari moved a resolution that the League demand for Pakistan must be conceded and a joint Congress-League front be presented to the British, but it was lost by a overwhelming majority, eventually leading to his withdrawal from the Congress.

The real tussle, however, took place over the two points of view put forth by Gandhiji and Nehru. The Mahatma suggested the policy of non-violent non-cooperation against the Japanese and the presentation of the demand for withdrawal to the Britishers from India. Nehru too favoured a call to Britain to relinquish its hold over India and recognise India's freedom, but he was not quite enthusiastic about Gandhian policy of dealing with Japanese invaders. Ultimately, a compromise resolution was introduced and adopted. It emphasized three things: (a) That Britain should relinquish its hold over India; (b) That Congress to continue to adhere to the concept of the non-violence non-cooperation; and (c) That the Congress was to oppose the operation of foreign troops in India. The weeks following the Allahabad session were a period of subdued tension within the Congress rank. C. Rajgopalachari was planning to campaign in favour of acceding to the League's demand and in June 1942 he met M.A. Jinnah a number of times, but in vain.

Japan was knocking at the gates of Assam and the danger to India's security was increasing. Bose was inciting the people to welcome the Japanese as "deliverers and helpers." Gandhi was developing the apprehension that if the Congress would not utilise the mass enthusiasm against Britain, the people might passively accept Japanese aggression. At this stage when the country was feeling frustrated and desperate Gandhiji gave a new direction to people's thought and gave shape to their vague ideas. Inaction at that critical stage and submission to all that was happening had become intolerable to him, for it would delay the advent of freedom for a long time. He was thus intent upon devising some plan by which the deadlock could be solved. Thus, he thought of the 'quit India' agitation. Gandhi was also getting convinced that in view of the attitude of the Muslim League no solution of the communal problem could be found as long as the British were on the soil. He felt that the time had come to serve the quit India notice, for in view of the serious threat to India from Japan, Britain could not dare to face the Congress agitation and hence might come to terms with it. All in all Gandhi came to this decision because of several reasons failure of individual Satyagraha and the Cripps Mission, the growing Muslim demand for Pakistan, the presence of American troops in India and the startling Japanese victories.[12] His decision was endorsed by Sardar Patel., Dr. Rajendra Prasad and J.B. Kripalani. He openly talked of action and even revolt if there was no voluntary abdication of power. But Maulana Azad felt otherwise. He was of the opinion that "in that critical stage of War the British would not tolerate any mass movement and put all Congress leaders in jail,"[13] and he proved right. Nehru's feeling was that the Congress cannot and should not stand idly by and allow the country's affairs to be managed by a foreign power. He favoured the view that the British should be called upon to leave India but at the same time he insisted that India should proclaim its willingness to fight the Axis Powers, if given an opportunity to do so honourably and effectively. Gandhiji conferred with Azad and Nehru to persuade them to accept his approach. Finding them unagreeable he even asked them to resign from the Congress Working Committee. But at Sardar Patel's intervention the rift was averted, and a compromise resolution was passed at Wardha on 14 July, 1942. It stated, inter alia, that the abortive cripps proposals showed that there was a change in the British attitude towards India, that the frustration in India over British intransigence had resulted in a rapid and widespread ill-will against Britain and a growing satisfaction at the success of Japanese arms, that Congress desires to build up resistance to any aggression by any foreign power and that the Congress would change illwill against Britain into goodwill, if India feels the glow of freedom." The Congress pleaded that its very reasonable and just proposal be accepted by Britain not only in the interest of India but also that of Britain and of the call of freedom to which the UN proclaims their adherence. But the Congress made it clear that it would resist the Japanese invaders with all the strength at its command, that it would help the Allied Powers' defence operation against aggressive powers and that it had no intention to start any big movement unless forced to do so by British policy. It bears mention here that Gandhiji had sent letters both to Chiang Kai Shek and F.D. Roosevelt before adopting the resolution. Roosevelt forwarded Chiang's message, pleading the Indian cause to Churchill. Churchill was due to meet Roosevelt to discuss the future military strategy in Europe. With a view to save Churchill from the embarrassing demands from American authorities, Cripps declared on 16 June in a statement to the UPI that "we are not going to walk out of India right in the middle of the War, though we have no wish to remain there for imperialist reasons." He observed: "Strategically, India is too vital for our own and our Allies' efforts against the Axis to take any such step without jeopardising the future of Soviet Union, China and the US, to say nothing of India herself." The military and political leaders in the US perhaps took cue from his statement and did not raise the issue of India with Churchill.

On 14 July, 1942 the Congress Working Committee adopted the Quit India Resolution at Wardha. Shortly thereafter the government of Linlithgow proposed to arrest and intern Gandhi, Nehru and the principal members of the CWC. This proposal was endorsed by the War Cabinet, headed by Sir Winston Churchill. But before the Americans could know of this decision, Cripps reminded them of the offer he had made to the Indians four months earlier, denouncing the obduracy of Gandhi and his companions, pinpointing Gandhi's opposition to the stationing of US troops on Indian soil and emphasised the seriousness of Japanese threat to Indian security.

Unmindfull of what was transpiring between New Delhi, London and Washington and full of enthusiasm and hope, the AICC met at Bombay to consider the Quit India Resolution. Late in the evening of 8 August 1942, the Quit India Resolution was endorsed by a overwhelming majority. The Resolution asserted that "the perils of today necessitate the independence of India and the end of British rule. No future promises or guarantees can affect the present situation or meet that peril. They cannot produce the needed psychological effect on the mind of the masses; only the glow of freedom can now release the energy and enthusiasm of millions of people, which will immediately transform the nature of War." The Resolution stressed that the continuance of the British rule in India was good neither for India nor for the success of the cause of the UN and suggested a provisional government of India representing all sections of the people to resist aggression, and resolved in the event of continued British recalcitrance to start a mass struggle on non-violent lines but on the widest scale under the inevitable leadership of the Mahatama. After the Resolution was carried Gandhiji addressed the House for about 70 minutes. He spoke "like a prophet in a moment of inspiration, full of fire, purifying by its flames, full of spirit divine"[14] and exhorted the nation to "do or die." The AICC made still another appeal to Britain and the UN to respond to the call of freedom and justice. Further, it did not decide to launch the Quit India Movement at once. But only after all attempts to bring about an agreement were frustrated by the British. In their concluding speech, Gandhi and Azad declared that they would again approach the Viceroy and the UN Heads for an honourable settlement. A letter was to go to the Viceroy in which Gandhi had written : "I am in your hands. I shall continue to knock as long as the last hope for honourable settlement remains." The AICC decided that on the following morning (9th August) Nehru would explain to the United States and the people of India through the Radio the scope and contents of the Quit India Resolution.

UPHEAVAL OF 1942

Before the Movement could be launched, Churchill and Linlithgow had already decided to crush it and hence in the morning of 9 August 1942 the police swooped and confronted the leaders with warrants of arrest. About 148 leaders were arrested immediately and their internment was followed by the imprisonment of the rank and file all over the country The Congress was declared an unlawful association.

This step worked as a spark that ignited Quite India Movement. In the absence of leaders and a proper direction as to the next line of action the people spontaneously did what they could or what they thought could paralyse the administration and bring an end of the foreign rule. Public resentment took the usual form of hartals, processions and holding of meetings. There was disturbances all over the country. The people of Bombay, Bengal, UP and Bihar took the lead. Communication was disrupted, wires were cut, police stations were raided and burnt, railway carriages were attacked. The students and teachers abstained from schools and colleges and many universities were closed. Workers ceased work in factories. There were mob violence, lawlessness, riots and disorder in certain places. According to official sources, about 250 railway stations were damaged, about 500 post offices were attacked and about 150 police stations were raided. The railway lines in Bihar and Eastern UP went out of order for many weeks and the British administration was uprooted and parallel governments were established in Balia, Basti, Satara and Midnapur.

For the first time since 1857 vast number of people rose to challenge by force the British rule in India. Indeed, it amounted to the biggest threat to British rule in India since the Mutiny. Even Lord Linlithgow described the 1942 movement as "by far the most serious rebellion since that of 1857, the gravity and extent of which we have so far concealed from the world for reasons of military security."[15] In many ways, it was a greater and more genuine revolt than that of 1857.

But an unarmed and leaderless mob could be no match to the leonine violence of a powerful and organised government having unlimited force at its disposal. A veritable reign of terror was let loose by the government. It is officially recorded that the government fired 538 times, killing about 1000 persons and injuring about 1630. A collective fine of one crore was imposed. In all, 26000 persons were arrested. In about three weeks the government was successful in crushing the uprising. The revolutionary leaders went underground for sometime to direct the movement before they were arrested.

REACTION OF DIFFERENT POLITICAL ORGANISATIONS AND LEADERS

The Socialist Party took a glorious part in the Movement. Its leaders like Jai Prakash Narayan, Dr. Ram Manohar Lohia and Mrs. Aruna Asif Ali organised a violent movement to dislodge the British government. J.P. Narayan emerged the hero of this movement. He escaped from the Hazari Bagh jail but was later arrested in dramatic circumstances at Lahore. The Communist Party had declared the World War, when it broke out, as "imperialistic", but when the Soviet Union joined it (June 1941), they began to regard it as a People's War and advocated full support for the government. They also wanted the Congress to start negotiations with the Muslim Leagues on the basis of Pakistan. The Muslim League tried to make capital out of the situation. Jinnah appealed to all Muslims to keep aloof from the Movement and condemned the Movement which, according to him, was "aimed at forcing Congress demand "at the point of bayonet"[16]. He alleged that the Movement aimed at enslaving the Muslims by compelling the government to accept the Congress demand of a free and United India where Muslims would permanently remain under the tyranny of Hindu majority. The Hindu Maha Sabha, led by Savarkar appealed to Hindus not to lend any support to the Congress.

The Sikhs, traditionally loyal to the British, remained aloof from the Movement.

The Movement evoked strong disapproval in certain quarters and outright denunciation in others. For example, M.N. Roy, who advocated unconditional support to the British and Allied forces fighting against the fascist forces, characterised it as "a sabotage movement". Sir Tej Bahadur Sapru, a liberal leader, called the revolution "ill-considered and ill-opportune". C. Rajgopalachari, a Congress dissident, commented: "The Mahatama's proposal is fraught with the greatest mischief. It will leave a legacy of the greatest bitterness behind," and urged a "concerted effort on a collective basis for the settlement of our internal differences." Dr. B.R. Ambedkar, the depressed class leader, described it as "irresponsible and insane," and suggested patience till the termination of War for resolving the deadlock. Jinnah regarded it as "reckless and thoughtless act". Clment Attlee, the British Labour Party leader, and the Deputy Prime Minister, issued a statement appealing to the Indian people that the Congress movement would seriously endanger not merely India's freedom but the freedom of the whole world, and expressed the belief that "the establishment of a free India in the post-War world is secure, is not endangered by any possibility of evasion or procrastination by the British government.

APPRAISAL OF THE QUIT INDIA MOVEMENT

The Movement was an ultimatum to the Britishers to quit India and the last of a series of the Congress led movements for wresting power from foreign rule. Its significance lies in the fact that though it failed in achieving its immediate goal, it unleashed a chain of reactions that culminated with the freedom of India. In fact, it was the '42 Movement, together with subsequent Azad Hind Fauj and the Indian Naval Mutiny that persuaded the British to quit. Agreeing with Bipan Chandra, it can be safely contended that "the Quit India Movement was merely the success story of the Congress drawn out hegemonic struggle waged by the Congress leadership to win the minds and hearts of the Indian people. Certainly, it was a grand success in terms of arousal and mobilisation of the masses in anti-British drive. Of the three large scale extra legal civil movements, the last one was the most intense and vociferous in manifestation because of the nature of the demand — the demand of the national movement was put forward in the most radical terms. Besides, one of the most remarkable features of this Movement was the absence of any communal incident or disorder." To quote, F. Hutchins, "If the aloofness of the Muslim community at large was one of the most notable characteristics of the Movement, the almost complete absence of Hindu aggression against Muslims remains a remarkable fact."[17]

But despite numerous acts of heroism and patriotism performed by the people, the Movement was not entirely a success. According to Frank Moraes, "It was a futile movement." Instead of gaining anything it indirectly aided and abetted the cause of partition. In hindsight, it can be said that if the withdrawal of Congress from ministries in November 1939 was a mistake and the rejection of the Cripps Offer was a blunder, the launching of Quit India Movement was a disaster, during a most critical period. The last one gave a free field for Jinnah and the Muslim League to exploit the situation and make political capital out of it. These steps were mainly responsible for the enhanced status of the League and the growth of the idea of Pakistan. Not only did the Muslim League formed governments in four provinces, Jinnah got an unchallenged opportunity to increase his influence and claim himself as the sole spokesman of the Muslims. The Quit India Movement pushed the Congress into confrontation with the Britishers leaving them little option but to patronise Jinnah and the League. "Jinnah was invested by the British government with a virtual power of veto on Indian political progress." The Viceroy and the India Office wanted to build up Mr. Jinnah as their "crescent card to neutralise the Congress challenge."[18] According to Michael Brecher and R.C. Majumdar "the Quit India Movement paved the way for the creation of Pakistan." According to Wolpert, "Gandhiji's initial response to Lord Linlithgow supporting the War effort as English would have proved a far more politically positive for Congress.[19]" To conclude, while on the one hand, the Quit India Movement was instrumental in loosening the grip of the British and ultimately compelled them to leave India, on the other hand, it also provided an opportunity to the Muslim League to consolidate its position which in turn was exploited to achieve the goal embodied in the Lahore Resolution.[20]

AFTERMATH OF QUIT INDIA MOVEMENT — INTERREGNUM BETWEEN QUIT INDIA MOVEMENT AND QUITTING INDIA

The year 1943 opened with thousands of Congress men, including all the principal leaders, in jail. One more attempt by the Congress to get rid of foreign rule had been foiled. Among the personalities outside India Chiang Kai Shek alone displayed some sympathy for the cause of the Congress and India. He sent protests to Roosevelt over the arrest of the Congress leaders, who forwarded it to Mr. Churchill. The latter, however, resented Chiang's message as intervention in the affairs of the

Empire. Roosevelt put the issue of India's independence on the back burner. In the midst of this phenomenon nothing sensational took place, except some notable events like Gandhi's fast and proclamation of Provisional Government of Free India by S.C. Bose, departure of Linlithgow and arrival of Wavell and reiteration of the Muslim League demand for Pakistan.

The British authorities held the Congress responsible for violence and blood-shed and dubbed Gandhi a pro-Axis. They charged the Congress Working Committee with "duplicity, dishonesty and immorality." Maligning the Congress, the Viceroy charged that though professing nonviolence, its leaders planned to thrust India into an orgy of violence and bloodshed. Gandhi as a mark of protest against these charges and also as a measure of self-purification, decided to undertake a 21-day fast beginning from 10 February, 1943. The government, however, remained unmoved in spite of his failing health during the fast. Distressed by the callous attitude of the government towards Gandhi's deteriorating condition of health, three members, H.P. Modi, M.S. Aney and N.R. Sarkar resigned from the Viceroy's Executive Council, Even the joint appeal of leaders with different affiliations evoked no response from the government. Further, During 1943 all over the world the Allies were making rapid gains and the Axis forces were surrendering and withdrawing. In the Far East, the major offensive was checked. But despite these victories (in reverse direction), the end of the War was still nowhere insight, as both Germany and Italy were still in the occupation of a large part of the World.

FORMATION OF INDIAN NATIONAL ARMY

Another important event of 1943 was the formation of the Indian National Army and the proclamation of Provisional Government of Free India. Subhash Chandra Bose had dramatically escaped from detention in is home in January 1941 and had spent sometime in Germany and Italy. While the freedom fighters in India had been locked up in jail, Subhash Chandra Bose kept the torch of struggle aflame outside India. While in Germany (1942) he had formed what was known as Free India League. This was rechristened as Azad Hind Fauj (INA) when he came to the Far East in 1943. It was composed of a large number of Indian soldiers who had become prisoners of Japan after the conquest of the Malaya peninsula. Its object was to fight the British army in India. Subhash had pinned his hope on a revolution that might break out among the civilians at home and the possible revolt in the army itself fighting under the British flag. His strategy was that if the British government was attacked from both sides it would collapse . Thus, the INA was organised to serve the purpose of a Second Front in India's war of independence. On 21 October, 1943 the Indian Independence League proclaimed the formation of the Provisional Government of Free India at Singapore with Bose as its political-cum-military Head. The INA was its military wing. From February, 1944 onwards it fought in Burma along with the Japanese, but when in late April 1945 the Japanese surrendered to the British, it also had to lay down its arms. On 19 August 1945 Subhash Chandra Bose was killed in a flying accident in Formosa.

1943 also marked the end of seven and a half years of Lord Linlithgow's rule. Linlithgow, being an arch conservative, failed to comprehend the Indian problem in its correct perspective and to advise London on more flexible and liberal lines. He had failed to aapreciate that the spirit of nationalism could not be crushed by force.

On 18 October, 1943, Sir Archibald Wavell took over as the new Viceroy. Wavell was an ex-Commander-in-Chief of India and had a brilliant record as a field Commander. But he hardly had the qualification of a statesman. On leaving England he observed that he was "going with a sense of very great responsibility but also with the vision of a great future in front of India." But because of instructions from the British Government, Wavell could not go beyond the Cripps Offer.

Another event of 1943 was Jinnah's reiteration of the Pakistan demand and that he was willing to meet Gandhi to settle the Congress-League dispute on the basis of Pakistan. During the following months Jinnah continued to consolidate the position of his party.

RELEASE OF GANDHIJI FROM JAIL

In February 1944, the government published a pamphlet under the title "Congress Responsibility For Disturbance' (1942-43) and put the entire blame upon the Congress, particularly Gandhi. While refuting all the charges, Gandhi wrote to Wavell for permission to get into touch with the Congress Working Committee members to seek a solution of the continuing constitutional deadlock. But it could not be granted as Congress was not willing to withdraw the Bombay Resolution of August 1942. On 14 April, 1944 Gandhi fell sick and three weeks later (6 May, 1944) he and a few CWC members were set free in the wake of favourable military situation on the European and Far-Eastern fronts. The decision to release Gandhi might have been also due to invasion of the Indian territory by the INA under the command of Subhash Chandra Bose. Soon after his release Gandhiji took the initiative of opening negotiations with Wavell to break the deadlock. But in his reply on 27 July, 1944, the Viceroy only repeated the Cripps Proposal and pointed out that Indian leaders could be invited to form an interim government only if proper safeguards could be made to protect the interests of the racial and religious minorities, depressed classes and princely states.

THE RAJAJI FORMULA AND THE GANDHI-JINNAH TALKS

Simultaneously, with exchange of letters with the Viceroy, Gandhiji also approached Jinnah to evolve some solutions to the communal tangle. In this attempt C. Rajgopalachari acted as a mediator. He was of the opinion that in view of the League's demand for Pakistan and the sympathy shown to it by the British, it was no longer possible to evade the issue of partition. After his resignation from the Congress before the Quit India Resolution was passed, he had been arguing all through that the creation of Pakistan alone could solve the Hindu-Muslim problem. Accordingly, he evolved a formula known as 'C.R. Formula' which was to form the basis of a Congress-League settlement. The main points of this Formula were : (1) That Muslim League endorse the Indian demand for independence and cooperate with the Congress in the formation of a provisional interim government for the transitional period; (2) After the termination of War a commission be appointed for demarcating contiguous districts in the North-West and East of India wherein the Muslim population was in absolute majority. In areas thus demarcated, a plebiscite of all the inhabitants shall ultimately decide the issue of separation from Hindustan. Such a decision will be given effect to without prejudice to the right of border areas to choose either state; (3) In the event of separation, a mutual agreement shall be entered into for jointly safeguarding defence, commerce, communication, and other essential purposes; (4) Any transfer of population shall only be on an absolutely voluntary basis (5) These terms shall be binding only in case of transfer by Britain of full power and responsibility for the governance of India and Finally, (6) if Gandhi and Jinnah agree to these terms, they will endeavour to get approval of the Congress and the Muslim League respectively for these terms and conditions. Obviously, CR's scheme marked a departure from the earlier position of the Congress.

GANDHI-JINNAH TALKS

During July-August 1944 Gandhiji corresponded with Jinnah on the basis of this formula. But the League President remained non-committal. Gandhiji then sought direct interview with Jinnah and went to Bombay to see Jinnah whom he addressed as 'Quaid-e-Azam'. Between 9 September and 27 September, 1944 both met daily and in all, 14 interviews took place between them. But the talks, though frank and friendly, ultimately broke down on 8 October, 1944. Jinnah insisted that Pakistan must include the whole of six Muslim majority provinces. He was opposed to giving non-Muslims the right of participation in the plebiscite. Further, he wanted only provincewise plebiscite. He was also opposed to joint control of the suggested subjects. In addition, he demanded a corridor to connect the two distant parts of Pakistan. To Jinnah, the CR formula offered "a shadow and a husk, a maimed, mutilated and moth-eaten Pakistan that torpedoed the Muslim-League Resolution of 1940." But it is interesting to note that what he ultimately got under the Mountbatten Plan was no better.

It was as a result of Rajaji's persuasion that Gandhi started believing that 'partition' was merely a slogan and the real aim of Jinnah and the League was to share political power. Gandhiji agreed for a dialogue with Jinnah. and argued forcefully against the two-nation theory. He said, "I find no parallel in history for a body of converts and their descendants for claiming to be a nation apart from the parent stock." He further argued If India was one nation before the advent of Islam, it must remain one in spite of the change of faith of very large body of its children." In short, he maintained that Hindus and Muslims were not two nations and even asserted "those whom God had made one, no man will ever be able to divide." However, all these arguments did not find favour with Mr. Jinnah. In a way, Gandhi's readiness for dialogue on the basis of 'Pakistan' vitiated his proclaimed stand against the vivisection of the country. Moreover, "the talks," in Michael Brecher's view, "placed Jinnah on a footing of virtual equality with Gandhiji."[21]

DESAI-LIAQAT PACT

After the failure of Gandhi-Jinnah Talks, another attempt to reach some kind of accord between the Congress and the League with a view to immediate formation of interim national government was made by Bhola Bhai Desai, the leader of the Congress in Central Assembly, and his counterpart, Nawabzada Liaqat Ali Khan. Desai negotiated with Liaqat, probably with the concurrence of Gandhi and the outcome was the Desai-Liaqat Pact. It contained the following proposals: (1) The Congress and the League agree that they would join in forming an interim government at the Centre, the composition of which would be as follows: Each party (Congress and League) would have 40 percent of the seats and 20 percent would be reserved for the smaller minorities (2) The government thus formed would function within the framework of the Act of 1935 and would be sufficiently independent of the Governor General. But this scheme, too, was not acceptable to Mr. Jinnah.

Meanwhile, from the summer of 1944 onwards, the Allied troops made rapid gains on all battle fronts, and by the end of the year it became certain that Germany would lose the War. Sandwiched by the Anglo American troops in the West and the Red Army in the East, Hitler lost all hopes for further resistance and on 30 April, 1945 he was reported to have committed suicide. On 7 May, 1945, the Germans laid down arms and signed a document of unconditional surrender. On the following day the victory of the Allies in Europe was celebrated.

The War had ended in Europe but the fight with Japan still remained. India's strategic position in the War with Japan once again came to prominence. Now that the hands of the British government were comparatively free, a fresh attempt was made to bring India whole-heartedly into the War. Hence, renewed pressures were put on the Churchill government by the Labour leaders and the Truman administration to take some steps to win over the support of Indian people. It is said that there was also some pressure from the Soviet Union for ending the Indian deadlock.

In the meantime, the Coalition government of the UK had broken down. Churchill had resigned and the General Elections were ordered. While Churchill's achievement in winning the War was lauded, his handling of the Indian problem was severely criticised. Since one Labour member announced to introduce a bill in Parliament advocating the Statute of Westministers to India, Churchill, who did not want to be left behind, called Wavell to London to discuss the next move towards constitutional progress in India. Wavell remained in London from 21 March to 4 June, 1945. On returning to India he announced a new Plan known as the Wavell Plan.

THE WAVELL PLAN

On 14 June, 1945 a White Paper embodying new proposals for the Indianisation of the Viceroy's Executive Council without prejudice to a final settlement of the Indian constitutional problem was issued by Amery, Secretary of State for India, as follows: (1) The Executive Council would be reconstituted and the Viceroy in nominating members would select them from leaders of the Indian political life with balanced representation of the main communities, including parity for Muslims and caste Hindus; (2) The Viceroy would call a conference of leading Indian politicians to invite from it a list of names from which would make recommendations for appointment with unrestricted freedom of choice; (3) The members of the Executive Council would be all Indians with the exception of the Viceroy and the Commander-in-Chief (the latter would retain his position as War member) but external affairs would be in charge of an Indian member; (4) It was also pointed out that the relations of the Crown with Indian states would not be affected; and (5) A British High Commissioner in India would be appointed to look after the British commercial interest. In a broadcast speech on 14 June, 1945 Wavell outlined the new proposal and promised that he would use his veto power sparingly and the interference of the Secretary of State will also be minimised. The Viceroy also issued invitations to Indian leaders to advise him at a conference to open at Simla on 25 June, 1945. This announcement again raised high hopes. To create the necessary atmosphere the Congress leaders were released on 16 June, 1945.

SIMLA CONFERENCE

On 25 June, 1945, the Simla Conference opened, which was attended by all major groups. But at the very outset differences arose between the Congress and the Muslim League on the question of representation. The Congress insisted that being a national organisation it must have Muslims as well as Hindu representatives in its list to which the Muslim League was not agreeable. Jinnah claimed that Muslims could be nominated by the Muslim League alone. Since there could be no agreement on the allocation of seats between the two major parties, the Viceroy announced failure of the Conference on 14 July, 1945. Thus, the whole episode ended in a fiasco and the Wavell Plan was exposed as nothing but 'an election stunt'. Probably the object of this move might have been to bring into prominence the Hindu-Muslim differences in India to make them appear as the real reason for the Indian political deadlock.

CAUSES OF FAILURE OF THE SIMLA CONFERENCE

In the beginning the main political parties had accepted the principle of parity between the caste Hindus (excluding scheduled caste) and the Muslims. But the negotiations broke down, because Jinnah insisted that the League should be recognised as the sole spokesman of the Muslims which was not acceptable to the Congress, the Unionist Party led by Malik Khizr Hayat Khan, the Jamait-ul-Ulema and other nationalist Muslims outside the League, as it amounted to their disfranchisement. The government also cannot be absolved from its responsibility for the failure. One may ask why Wavell allowed one party to exercise veto over all political progress inspite of his earlier assurance to Azad to the contrary. In this connection, H.V. Hodson maintained that "the Viceroy had in effect capitulated to Jinnah. It is arguable that if the Viceroy had been as adamant as Mr. Jinnah, the latter would have been obliged to fall in line."[22] It appears Churchill had agreed to the Simla Conference only because he knew that it was bound to fail and probably, the caretaker government was also no longer keen for settlement after Churchill's Party lost the General Elections. The failure of the Conference revealed that Jinnah was satisfied with nothing less than Pakistan. His comment on the occasion was." Am I a fool to accept this when I am offered Pakistan on a platter".[23] Jinnah felt that the Plan was a suave move to weaken his claim to Pakistan. Thus, Wavell in his anxiety to placate both the Congress and the League finally ended by alienating both. However, the Conference was not altogether devoid of results. The Congress gained in terms of popularity as it was the sufferer for the last three years. Expressing disappointment at the failure V.P. Menon commented. "The Simla Conference afforded a last opportunity to the forces of nationalism to fight a rear-guard action to preserve the integrity of the country and when the battle was lost the waves of communalism quickly engulfed it. Only the Hobson's choice of partition was left."[24]

Meanwhile, two events of far reaching significance took place. One, the General Elections in England brought the Labour Party to power,. Two, the War ended in the Far-East with the surrender of Japan. The Allied powers heaved a sigh of relief and the authorities in London became more sincerely seized of the Indian problem. After the General Elections and the landslide victory of the Labour Party in England, the political complexion of the British government underwent a drastic change. The New Prime Minister, Clement Attlee, invited Wavell to review the whole situation. Wavell returned to India on 18 September, 1945 and on the following day announced that His Majesty's Government was determined to do their utmost to promote the early realisation of full responsible government in India. He also announced that elections to the Central and Provincial Legislatures would soon be held and after which steps would be taken to bring into being an Executive Council which would have the support of the main political parties. The Secretary of State, Pethick Lawrence, also stated that "India should speedily attain her full and rightful position as an independent partner in the British Commonwealth.

The AICC met towards the end of September 1945 and considered the proposals put forward by the Governor General. But it found them "vague, indefinite and unsatisfactory" and reiterated that nothing short of Independence could be acceptable to the Congress and the country. However, it decided to contest the General Elections to the Central and Provincial Legislatures. The Quit India Resolution formed the focal point of their election manifesto, which paid glowing tributes to those who suffered and died in the movement. The results of the general elections in India were quite revealing in many ways. The Congress swept the polls and captured almost all the general seats and even some Muslim seats. The success of the Muslim League was also phenomenal. It captured 446 seats out of 495, polling 75 percent of Muslim votes (as compared to 1937 election results it was spectacular, when it had secured only 108 seats out of 492, polling just 25 percent Muslim votes). In Punjab, the League falsified claims of the Unionists. It failed only in North Western Frontier Province to make any impression. To be sure, the elections convincingly proved that the Muslims of India were now overwhelmingly behind the Muslim League. The Congress secured the absolute majority in seven provinces. In the Frontier Province the Khudai Khidmatgar, an ally of the Congress, came to power. The Muslim League could form government only in two provinces, Sind and Bengal. In Punjab, the Muslim League, the largest single party, could not form the government although it had secured 75 seats out of 88 Muslim seats.

The elections to the Central Legislative Assembly were held as per schedule in the months of November-December 1945. The results showed that out of 102 elected members the Congress had captured 56 seats, the Muslim League 30 and the European group 8, independents 6 and Akali Sikhs 2 seats, the other 40 members of the Central Assembly were nominated — 26 being official and 14 non-official.

After the 1945-46 elections the lines were clearly drawn for claims and counterclaims. The Congress and the Muslim League emerged as the two strongest political contenders to stake claim in power sharing in case of transfer of power. Congress still wanted Independence to come before settling the communal problem, but Jinnah and the League reiterated their demand that the first step must be to accept Pakistan in principle, since the Muslim electorate had given a clear mandate for Pakistan. "Jinnah could now use the League success as an excuse to concentrate upon three cornered game of constitutional higgling which was after all his greatest talent."[25]

While the Indian political parties were engaged in the election campaign, a parliamentary delegation came to New Delhi to learn at first hand the views of the Indian leaders as to the future of India, and on the conclusion of the visit, the leader of the delegation, Robert Richards, admitted: "We are all convinced of the fact that India has at last attained political manhood."

THE CABINET MISSION (MARCH-JULY 1946)

A few days after the return of this delegation Attlee announced in the House of Commons (10 February, 1946) to send to India a special mission of three Cabinet Ministers (Pethick Lawrence, Stafford Cripps, and A.V. Alexander). Again on 15 March, 1946, he stated that "India herself must choose what will be her future government and will be her position in the world hoping that the Indian people may elect to remain in the Commonwealth." The Prime Minister also observed: "Although we are very mindful of the right of minorities but we cannot allow a minority to place a veto on the advance of the majority." Jinnah, however, considered this statement to be deterimental to the demand for Pakistan.

The Cabinet Mission landed in Karachi on 23 March, 1946. Its aim was to find out means for the transfer of power to Indian hands. A chain of meetings and negotiations followed. Every shade of opinion was taken into consideration. After prolonged discussions, a Tripartite Conference was held in New Delhi between the government, the Congress and the Muslim League. As the trio could not arrive at an agreement, the Mission with full approval of the British government announced their own plan for solving the constitutional deadlock. The Plan was divided into two parts the long term plan and the short term plan.

THE LONG-TERM PLAN (16 May, 1946)

The main features of the long term plan were as follows: (a) Rejecting the demand for Pakistan, the Mission recommended a Union of India embracing both British India and the India States, to deal with foreign affairs, defence, communications and financial matters. All subjects other than these and residuary powers were to be vested in the provinces; (b) The Union was to have an Executive and Legislature composed of equal proportions from Hindu majority and Muslim majority provinces, apart from representatives from the princely India. Any question raising a major communal issue would require the support of the majority of the representatives present and voting of each of the two main communities as well as majority of all members present and voting; (c) The constitution-making machinery was to be formed of representatives from provincial Assemblies and the Indian states. Each province would be allowed a total number of seats proportional to its population (roughly in the ratio of one to a million). The total strength of the Constituent Assembly was fixed at 389 (292 from provinces and 93 from States and 4 from Chief Commissioners provinces); (d) In order to give to the minority greater assurance, the Plan divided the country into three groups: Group-A was to include Madras, Bombay, UP, Bihar, CP and Orissa (All Hindu majority provinces), Group-B to comprise the Punjab, Sind, NWFP and British Baluchistan (constituting a Muslim majority area) and Group-C was to include Bengal, and Assam (where Muslims had a small majority over the rest). This grouping was designed to satisfy all legitimate fears of the Muslim League, as in Group-B and C the Muslims would exercise complete autonomy in most of the subjects. Provinces were to be free to form groups with separate executive and legislature and each group would determine the provincial subjects to be taken in common by that group; (e) The constitution of the Union and of the Groups would contain provision whereby any province could by a majority vote of its legislative assembly call for a reconsideration of the term of the constitution after every ten years interval; (f) It would be necessary to negotiate a treaty between the constituent assembly an the United Kingdom to provide for certain matters arising out of the transfer of power. However, India was given the right to go out of the Commonwealth, if so desired, but a hope was expressed that she would not leave the Commonwealth; (g) After the transfer of power it wold not be possible for Britain to retain paramountcy over princely states, nor could paramountcy be transferred to the new government of the British-India, and (h) An interim government having the support of the major political parties would be set up as early as possible.

As regards the Muslim League demand for Pakistan, the Cabinet Mission came to the conclusion that the formation of Pakistan was not desirable for the following reasons: It would not solve the communal problem or the minority problem. The Mission maintained that every argument in favour of Pakistan could be used in favour of the exclusion of non-Muslim areas from Pakistan. After all, the non-Muslims constituted 38 percent in the West zone and 48 percent in the North East zone. Thus there was no justification at all for including non-Muslims with such a high percentage in the Dominion of Pakistan. Moreover, a very large proportion of the inhabitants of these provinces were against the partition of Punjab and Bengal. Moreover, the Muslim League itself was not prepared for a truncated Pakistan; (2) Pakistan was not viable on administrative, economic, and military considerations. Particularly, the break up of the army was against the grain of Auchinlek's (C-in-C) thinking and feeling; and (3) If Pakistan was granted, the two halves of Pakistan would be separated by more than 1,000 miles, which would be "a geographical monstrosity." According to the Mission, the proposed scheme "secured the advantages of a Pakistan without incurring the danger inherent in the division of India."

SHORT-TERM PLAN (JUNE 1946)

The Mission had authorised the Governor General to establish an interim government with the representatives of Indian people. Accordingly, the viceroy invited 14 Indian leaders to serve as members of a government for the interim period, comprising 5 Congressmen, 5 Muslim Leaguers, 1 Sikh, 1 Indian Christian, 1 Parsi and 1 Scheduled Caste representative. In the composition of the Cabinet the Viceroy maintained parity between the Hindus including the scheduled classes and the Muslim League.

The Council for the Muslim League after considering the proposals announced (25 June, 1946) its willingness to participate in the proposed constitution making body but at the same time, it reiterated its ultimate objective of Pakistan. It also conveyed its consent to participate in the proposed Interim government. The Congress Working Committee on its part notified its acceptance of the long-term plan 16 May but it refused to join the Interim government, as it was opposed to artificial and unjust parity between the Congress and the League in the formation of a provisional government. It felt that this position was made worse than it was in June 1945 at Simla under the Wavell Plan, because then an additional seat was allowed for the scheduled caste Hinuds. Further, the Muslim seats were not reserved for the Muslim League only, as the Congress could include non-League Muslims in the allotted seats. Obviously, in view of its national character and the presence of a large number of Muslims in its membership, it insisted on the right of including a nationalist Muslim among the Congress representatives. But Jinnah was strongly opposed to it. The Congress was of the view that "conceding the demand of the League for exclusive claim to nominate all Muslim seats would have meant for the Congress denying its own past, falsifying its history and betraying its future."[26] The other two important minority groups the Sikhs and the Scheduled Castes, too, found the Plan unacceptable. The former on the ground that the Sikhs would be kept at the mercy of the Muslim majority in Group B and the latter on the ground that no seats were reserved for them. Finding that many Indian leaders were not willing to join the Interim government, Wavell formed a Caretaker government on 29 June, 1946, consisting of officials for the Interim period. Simultaneously, the Viceroy announced the schedule for constituting the Constituent Assembly.

GROUP CONTROVERSY

One of the most controversial parts in the Cabinet Mission Plan was whether grouping of provinces into three sections was optional or compulsory. While the Congress held the view that it was optional for a province to join a group or not, the Muslim League interpreted it as compulsory and the right to opt out of a group could be exercised only after ten years. The Congress President Nehru, who had just succeeded

Maulana Azad, addressed a press conference on 10 July 1946 and in reply to a question on grouping under the plan observed: "There was a big possibility that there would be no grouping." He added that "the Congress was completely unfettered by agreements and free to meet all situations as they arise." To quote V.P. Menon, Nehru declared that "What we do there (Constituent Assembly) we are entirely and absolutely free to determine."[27] These statements from no less a person than the President-elect of the Congress caused profound concern to the League. Jinnah, who had only reluctantly accepted the Cabinet Mission Plan as "a cut and dried scheme" to meet the objectives of both sides, was upset by Nehru's remarks at the press conference. He called a meeting of the Working Committee of the Muslim League and by its resolution of 29 July, 1946 the League Council decided to withdraw support to both the long term and the short term plan. A resolution was also adopted setting 16 August, 1946 as Direct Action Day, a day on which the Muslims would demonstrate their will and determination to achieve Pakistan.

While it is true that both sides had accepted the Mission Plan only with great reluctance and reservations and some future deadlocks and complications were implicit in their acquiescence, it cannot be denied that Nehru's remark of 10 July betrayed a lack of statesmanship and political sagacity. To quote Mosley, "It was most unwise, impolite and untimely."[28] Even Nehru's closest colleague, Azad, had recorded that "Nehru's statement was wrong and that it was one of the most fiery and provocative statements in his 46 years of public life." Azad also described it as "one of those unfortunate events which changed the course of history."[29] Michael Brecher, Nehru's famous biographer, also described it "a serious tactical error." Perhaps with his deep enthusiasm for freedom for an undivided India, Nehru failed to read the writings on the wall and appreciate the strength and popularity of the Muslim League and its leader as the sole spokesman of Indian Muslims by the moment. To be sure, the country was heading fast towards bifurcation. If the Muslim League was claiming for Pakistan, Sikhs had given the slogan of Khalistan, the Scheduled Castes led by Dr. Ambedkar were demanding reservations for their community, and the Indian princes were unwilling to transfer the paramountcy heitherto owed to the British Crown to the new Dominion. Some of them were clamouring for independent status after the British withdrawal. In short, the centrifugal forces were very strong and vocal all over the country. These should have sufficed to bring home to Nehru the desirability of accepting a federated India, as envisaged in the Cabinet Mission Plan. In fact, "the sovereignty of the Constituent Assembly was at the core of Nehru's statements around the beginning of July and it is difficult to understand why his press interview of 10 July has been singled out by historians as the casus belli of the League's call for Direct Action."[30] Although the Congress Working Committee subsequently did adopt a resolution (Dec. 22, '46) reiterating its adherence to the Plan in its entirety but now it was like closing the stable door long after the horse had run away, for it had already provided an easy excuse for Jinnah to wriggle out of his earlier support to the Plan. Mr. Jinnah had now fixed up his eyes on 16 August and had begun planning how to make Direct Action Day a success.

APPRAISAL OF THE CABINET MISSION PLAN

The Plan was a mixed bag of merits and demerits. As regards its merits: (1) It offered a united India with a weak centre and thereby obviated all the apprehension of the Muslim League of Hindu domination. In other words, it was a compromise between Jinnah's fully sovereign Pakistan and Congress' strong and organic Centre; (2) The Constituent Assembly was to be formed on a very equitable and fair basis; (3) It discarded all communal weightage and only two communal groups were recognised Sikhs and Muslims; (4) It recognised for the first time the right of the people of the Indian states to decide their political destinies; (5) The Interim Government was given the greatest possible freedom in running the administration of India; (6) The Constituent Assembly was made a fully sovereign body.

As regards its demerits, (1) It made the Centre weak when disintegrating forces were raising their heads; (2) The May 16 Plan was ambiguous and open to different interpretations-while section 5 of Para 15 left provinces free to form group according to Congress, the clause V of Para 19 seemed to make it compulsory, as interpreted by the League. Jinnah felt that compulsory grouping alone could guarantee him an effective say at the Centre. Thus, "the Mission failed to square the circle; the deadly geometry of India's triangle had defeated it."[31] Being of the nature of a compromise, it is understandable if it could not satisfy either of the parties completely.

Nevertheless, as Gandhiji commented, "It was the best document the British government could have produced in the circumstances." No wonder, he congratulated the Mission "for taking the first step in the act of renunciation" To quote Ayesha Jalal, "The Mission had persuaded itself that "this 3-tier wedding cake was the best way to celebrate the sanctified union of Muslims and Hindu India."[32] Wavell too had assured Nehru that "the Scheme was designed to get over a psychological difficulty, and it was not claimed to be ideal for the administrative point of view." Another writer, Shariful - Mujahid has gone to the extent of saying "Had the Congress accepted unreservedly the Cabinet Mission Plan, the Pak demand might have, in all probability, lost its force and fury." Perhaps, League's statement that complete sovereign Pakistan remained its ultimate goal made the Congress suspicious. On the other hand, M.N. Das says that "Its rejection saved India from a disastrous fate"[33]. G.L. Jain is also of the opinion that "a united India as envisaged under the Plan would have been an enlarged version of Lebanon."[34] K.K. Aziz observes: "With its complex provisions, multiple territorial units, artificial political arrangements and the rickety 3-tier federal structure, only a miracle would have made it workable."[35] On the whole, the Cabinet Mission Plan was a definite landmark in the history of our freedom movement, as it conceded the demand of complete independence and gave to the people of India the right to frame their own constitution.

DIRECT ACTION — THE GREAT CALCUTTA KILLING

The Direct Action Day was observed on 16 August, 1946, as planned in spite of Nehru's last minute efforts to persuade Jinnah to cancel it. What the League intended by Direct Action was not clear. Jinnah himself refused to comment on it by simply saying: "I am not going to discuss ethics". Although Jinnah had called upon the Muslims to conduct themselves peacefully but his counsel for moderation were not enough to quieten his followers. In fact, he had himself bid goodbye to constitution and constitutional methods when he stated: "Today we bid good bye to constitutional methods and we have forged a pistol and are in a position to use it" Shaheed Suhrawardy, the Chief Minister of Bengal, had not only declared 16 August a public holiday but was preaching the cult of violence. He observed : "Bloodshed and disorder are not necessary evils in themselves if resorted to for a noble cause like Pakistan." The Direct Action Day in Calcutta resulted in about 10,000 deaths. Hindus were massacred on a very large scale and about 7,000 persons were done to death with the police observing the holocaust passively. The C.M. called the military action only when the Hindus appeared to be taking the upper hand. The Calcutta happening had a spin off effect. Thousands left their towns to seek refuge in Bihar. The news about these ghastly events aroused among Hindus of Bihar a spirit of revenge and retaliation and the Muslims of Bihar had to meet the same fate. The province of Bihar produced the largest "butchers' bath". Some 20,000 Muslims were estimated to have lost their lives. Soon after trouble spread to other parts of the country. The Mahatma left on 6 November, 1946 for Bengal to restore communal harmony there and Nehru visited Bihar to end the week-long horrors apart from similar appeals from different quarters.

FORMATION OF INTERIM GOVERNMENT

While the League was observing Direct Action, the Viceroy was endeavouring to form a national government. In August 1946, he asked Nehru to assist him in its formation. Nehru announced that the Congress was prepared to form a government on the basis of 6-5-3 Formula (with 6 Congressmen, including 1 scheduled caste, 5 Muslim leaders and 3 other communities). Wavell asked Jinnah also to suggest the names of League's representatives. But the latter expressed regrets and declined the offer. What he now insisted on was not Hindu-Muslim parity but Muslim League and Congress parity and this cut out all the non-League Muslims. On 3 September, 1946 the Provisional National Government with twelve members, including three nationalist Muslim names was announced. Both Wavell and Nehru, however, continued their efforts to bring in the Muslim League and succeeded only on 15 October, 1946 in persuading the League to join the government. The League got five seats and the first coalition government was formed on 24 October, 1946. However, the League joined the government without any intention to cooperate but instead to prove that any collaboration between the Congress and the League was impossible. The Muslim League members worked as a separate bloc. With the support of Lord Wavell, Liaqat Ali became the Finance Minister, who introduced a budget, allegedly designed to harm the industrialists and businessmen the majority of whom were Hindus. Though the League was persuaded to join the Interim Government, it remained adamant about the boycott of Constituent Assembly. As a matter of fact, even before joining the Interim government Jinnah had declared at Lahore; "We are going into the Interim Government to get a foothold to fight for our cherished goal of Pakistan and I assure you that we will achieve Pakistan."[36]

During the closing months of 1946, the League launched a high pressure campaign for its demand for Pakistan. In a bid to heal the growing Congresss-League breach, the Attlee government invited Nehru, Patel, Jinnah, Liaqat Ali and Sardar Baldev Singh to London who conferred there from 3 to 6 December, 1946. Although the British government in its statement of 6 December, 1946 declared that the formation of the Group was compulsory but the statement was "hortative not definitive". The Leaders therefore returned without any agreement regarding grouping formula. The League members continued to pursue obstructionist tactics and its hostile attitude hardened still further in subsequent days. Moreover, the League also decided to abstain from the Constituent Assembly which opened in New Delhi on 9 December, 1946. The convening of the Constituent Assembly without even the participation of the League members caused great resentment to the League leadership. The inauguration of the Constituent assembly was greeted with Direct Action by the League. The Leaders of the League started their hectic campaign of hatred and ill-will against the Congress and the Hindus. They went from place to place inciting violence, animosity and communalism of a virulent type. They had already injected the virus of communal hatred in Bengal. Now it was the turn of Punjab. The League National Guards began to organise public parades, demonstrations and protest meetings in Punjab. Apprehending a breach of peace and danger to law and order, the Punjab government declared communal organisations illegal and a large number of Razakars were arrested. Thereupon the League launched a civil disobedience campaign against the government leading to widespread communal disturbances and danger to life and property. Thus, between November 1946 and February 1947 League's attitude to the Interim Government, its attempt to overthrow by force the Unionist Ministry in Punjab, its refusal to enter the Constituent Assembly and to accept the Cabinet Mission Plan of 16 May, all signified its intent to achieve Pakistan.

FAILURE OF CABINET MISSION PLAN

Altogether, the Cabinet Mission Plan satisfied neither the Congress nor the Muslim League although it had the support of Gandhi. As a matter of fact, both the Congress and the League must share the responsibility for its failure. The Attlee government had become desperate after the break-down of the London Talks in December 1946. It had come to the conclusion that it was no longer possible to keep India in one piece. The Mission Plan was their last prescription to keep its unity preserved. But since the Plan misfired, the government decided to divide and quit even if it meant an act of un-doing their greatest legacy of the last two centuries a unified India.

PRELUDE TO PARTITION
(NOVEMBER 1946 to FEBRUARY 1947)

By early 1947, the Attlee government found its option in making policy for India narrowing rapidly. Its main priority was to get out of India quietly. The functioning of the Interim Government and the boycott of the Constituent Assembly by the League and the failure of the London Conference in December 1946 convinced the British that they must withdraw from India by a fixed date. In view of the prevailing deadlock between the Congress and the League over the long-term plan of constitution-making, the British Prime Minister felt that the transfer of power to Indian hands might resolve the Congress-League deadlock. On

20 February, 1947, he stated on the floor of the House of Commons that "Britain intended to transfer power to responsible Indian hands not later than June 1948, that if an Indian constitution had not by that time been worked out by a fully representative Indian Constituent Assembly, His Majesty's Government would consider handing over the powers of the Central government either to some form of Central government for British-India or to existing provincial governments or in some other way as may seen reasonable and in the best interest of the Indian people." He also declared in Parliament that it was not possible to rule India because there was tremendous disaffection not only among the people but even among the Indian personnel of the armed forces. Significantly, in this announcement "the British for the first time placed a definite term upon their rule. The aim of this announcement was to encourage all persons to come to terms but the effect was dramatically different. The prospect of the Raj coming to an end within sixteen months unleashed just those forces that threatened a strong Central Government."[37]

REACTION TO ATTLEE'S STATEMENT OF 20 FEBRUARY 1947

Gandhi complemented the British government on fixing the date for surrendering power and regarded the statement as "the noblest act of the British nation." But at the same time, he shuddered at the thought of a possible division of the country, and declared: "Even if the whole of India is in flames it will not bring Pakistan." Nehru hailed the first part of the Statement, which removed any doubt about Independence. Jinnah, however, hailed the second part and construed it as conceding the demand for Pakistan. There is no doubt that it did add to the strength of Muslim separatism. Now finding that it was nearing its goal, the Muslim League instigated Hindu-Muslim riots. During the first week of March 1947 serious riots took place in Lahore, Amritsar, Multan and other cities of Punjab and the contagion caught on in the rural areas too. The Muslim League became more intransigent than before It began a mad struggle to gain power in Punjab, Frontier Province and Assam.

Wavell viewed with dismay the decision of His Majesty's Government to withdraw from India without finding a solution to the communal tangle. He was in favour of a phased withdrawal, block by block, province by province. He was of the view that the Indians must be faced with the responsibility of settling their own future and making their own peace with each other. He, therefore, drew up a plan for this purpose and dispatched it to Attlee, but his scheme (Operation Breakdown) did not appeal to the Prime Minister. To Attlee, this seemed an indication that it was time for a new policy for India and a new man to carry it out.

The hazards of staying on appeared to Attlee to be more serious than the risks involved in withdrawing. Attlee, therefore, sacked Wavell unceremoniously and his place was taken by Lord Mountbatten- the last Viceroy of India.

LORD MOUNTBATTEN AND HIS VICEROYALTY

Mountbatten was the last Viceroy as well as the last British Governor General of India. He was the great-grand son of Queen Victoria and second cousin of George VI. Lord Mountbatten possessed an extremely lively, exciting personality. His wife also possessed a flair for making friends and influencing people. Mountbatten was sent to Delhi with instructions to expedite the withdrawal and was given 'plenipotentiary powers' to his job.

Shortly after his arrival on 23 March, 1947, Mountbatten began to negotiate with the leading personalities of India. To begin with, he tried his best to revive the Cabinet Mission Plan with Jinnah in order to retain the unity of India but without success. He, therefore, applied himself to the task for which he was commissioned; to arrange for the transfer of power in the smoothest and quickest way. In view of deteriorating law and order situation and after having talks with the various leaders, Mountbatten felt convinced that there was no hope of arriving at an agreed solution on the basis of a united India. With the administrative machinery collapsing, with the knowledge that the League would not enter the Constituent Assembly, he concluded by April 1947 that partition was inevitable.

Having himself become convinced, he began to convert the Congress leadership to the idea of partition. The Congress leaders, particularly Nehru and Patel, who earlier considered the bifurcation of the nation as a great evil, were now confronted with a situation where no alternative presented itself. They began to accept the idea of partition as unavoidable. Mountbatten devised a scheme known as the Balkan Plan whereby the elected members should vote province by province whether they wished power to be transferred to a unified or divided India. But when the Plan was shown to Nehru, the latter warned Mountbatten that it would encourage disruptive tendencies everywhere and therefore it should be redrafted. At Nehru's suggestion the Plan was revised with the help of V.P. Menon. Thereafter the partition plan was taken to London by Mountbatten himself to obtain the British government approval.

On 3 June, 1947 in a broadcast Mountbatten revealed that it would not be possible for him to obtain agreement among all the communities that would preserve the unity of India and, therefore, His Majesty's

Government had decided to transfer powers to one or two governments of India, each having Dominion Status and that a bill to that effect would be introduced in Parliament in July 1947. He also announced that the proposed legislation would not impose any restriction on the power of India as a whole or of the two new states, if there was partition, to decide in the future their relationship to each other or to other members of the Commonwealth. The same day Attlee also announced new proposals for the transfer of power into Indian hands as follows: (1) Any constitution framed by the existing Constituent Assembly would not be applied to those parts of the country which were not willing to accept it; (2) The wish of the people of these areas which decided not to take part in the existing Constituent Assembly would be ascertained to determine the authority to which power should be transferred.

THE MOUNTBATTEN PLAN

The noteworthy proposals of the Mountbatten Plan were: Firstly, the provinces of the Punjab and Bengal were to be partitioned and a commission to demarcate the boundaries to be set up; Secondly, the Muslim majority areas which would not participate in the Constituent Assembly would form a separate constituent assembly of their own; Thirdly, the members of the Legislative Assemblies of Bengal, Punjab, Sind and Baluchistan were to decide whether to join Pakistan or India; Fourthly, a referendum would be held in the North West Frontier Province, Baluchistan and the Sylhet District of Assam to ascertain the wishes of the people whether they would be included in Pakistan or in India. According to the above Plan, NWFP, Sind and Sylhet voted for Pakistan. Similarly, the Western districts of the Punjab voted for India and the Eastern districts of Bengal voted in favour of Pakistan, while the Western districts voted in favour of India.

However, it is to be noted that the new plan related only to British-India and the policy towards Indian states would remain the same as envisaged in the Cabinet Mission Plan. The existing Constituent Assembly and the new Constituent Assembly, if formed, would frame constitutions for their respective territories. To give effect to the Plan the British Parliament passed the Indian Independence Act, which finally put an end to the British rule in India.

REACTIONS OF INDIAN POLITICAL ORGANISATIONS AND LEADERS TO THE PLAN OF PARTITION.

The reaction of the Indian political leaders to the plan of partition into two separate Dominions was sharp but prompt. The Muslim League was all jubilant as it got what it wanted — a sovereign Pakistan and on 9 June it resolved to accept it. The Depressed Class League endorsed it and the Sikhs expressed their satisfaction. As regards the Congress, it welcomed the principle of self-determination for those parts of India which did not desire to remain with Indian union. Jawaharlal Nehru, the Congress President, said: "It is with no joy in my heart that I commend this proposal to you though I have no doubt in my mind that this is the right choice." Gandhi observed: "The British government is not responsible for partition. If the Hindus and Muslims cannot agree on any thing else, the Viceroy was left with no choice." He, however, expressed the hope that the two parts of the country would join ultimately. Maulana Azad reluctantly agreed to it and said, "I am sure that it is going to be a short-lived partition because the division is on the map of the country and not in the hearts of the people." Subsequently, on 15 June, 1947 the AICC adopted a formal resolution accepting the Partition Plan.

The question arises as to why did the Congress accept the plan of partition. For generations the Congress had dreamt and struggled for a free, independent and a united India. The factors that ultimately led the Congress to accept it were as follows: (1) Partition was the only way to check Hindu-Muslim riots. The administration had broken down because of persistently negative attitude of the League and loss of interest on the part of the British officers. As such, the country was heading towards anarchy and chaos. The Congress felt that by accepting partition the killing of innocent citizens might be stopped. But sadly enough, what happened was just the reverse. Rather it brought even worse form of human butchery in its train (2) If the partition was delayed, independence too might be delayed, and any furtherance of the British rule would mean greater calamity to Indians; (3) Leaders like Patel felt that if Pakistan was not accepted, India might be balkanised. A small but unified and strong India, he thought, was better than a weak though nominally united India. Nehru also agreed that partition would assure an Indian union with a strong Centre which would ensure progress and help the country take their rightful place in the world. On the other hand, if the Muslim majority provinces were forced to stay in the Union no progress and planning would be possible. "In agreeing to the partition of India, the Congress leaders chose the lesser evil. Partition was bad, but the alternatives to partition were worse. Continued slavery, civil war, chaos and the fragmentation of India, these were the only alternatives to partition in 1947."[38]

Gandhi had pleaded for a transfer of power earlier than June 1948. Mountbatten too came to realise that in order to avoid some irreparable loss the transfer of power should take place at once. So it was also announced with the Plan that the government was contemplating the setting up of Independent States at a much earlier date, and that they wanted to introduce legislation during the current session of the British Parliament for the purpose.

INDIAN INDEPENDENCE ACT OF 1947

On the basis of the Mountbatten Plan the Independence Bill was passed by the British Parliament in July 1947. Incidentally, it was passed without a division and with a speed unprecedented in British history. It was given the Royal assent on 18 July, 1947. It was exceedingly simple and brief containing only 20 sections and 3 Schedules. The Act constituted two independent Dominions of India and Pakistan with effect from 15 August, 1947. The main provisions of the Act were: (1) Two independent Dominions were to be created from 15 August, 1947; (2) For demarcating the respective territories of the two Dominions in the province of Punjab and Bengal, a Boundary Commission would be set up by the Governor General consisting of two judges from each of the Dominions with Sir Cyrill Radcliff, a British Lawyer, as Chairman, with power to give his Award in case of disagreement. (3) The Constituent Assemblies of the Dominions were fully sovereign bodies and given choice to severe their connections from the British Commonwealth of Nations; (4) The Governor General of each Dominion would be appointed by the King on the advice of the Dominion Cabinet. The Governor General became constitutional head under this provision (Mountbatten for India and Jinnah for Pakistan); (5) Until the new constitution was framed, the Act of 1935 was to govern with necessary modifications. (6) The provisions of the Statute of the West-minister of 1931 were to apply to both the Dominions. The Secretary of State and India Office were to stop functioning from 15 August, 1947; and (7) All the rights of paramountcy of the British Crown over the Indian States were to lapse from 15 August and the Indian states were free to join either of the Dominions and even to declare themselves absolutely independent.

Thus at midnight of 14-15 August, 1947 the British rule in India came to an end. The British power was fully and finally transferred to the two Dominions (India and Pakistan) which officially came into existence.

Just before the historic midnight Nehru made a stirring speech in the Constituent Assembly and said interalia: "Long years ago we made a tryst with destiny and now the time comes when we shall redeem our pledge, not wholly or in full measure, but substantially. At the stroke of midnight hour when the world sleeps India will awake to life and freedom."

REVIEW OF MOUNTBATTEN'S VICEROYALTY

It was under Mountbatten's Viceroyalty that one of the most momentous transfer of power took place; Britain relinquished her power in India after trading and ruling for about 200 years. As the last representative of the British Crown, Mountbatten was charged with one mission: masterminding 'Operation Scuttle', to borrow a phrase from Churchill. He was called upon to preside over the liquidation of the British Empire on the Subcontinent of India.

Mountbatten was gifted with drive, dynamism, deftness, decisiveness and also glamour. He was a man of 'dangerous charm'. Further, he was a human dynamo with unbounded energy, optimism and courage. But at the same time, he was egoistic and impetuous. Quite often he relied on his intuitions and hunches. A man in hurry, he was bent upon executing the process of transfer with considerable speed. To quote Andrew Roberts, "After the rule of 250 years, he gave the British a mere 73 days to get out". In fact, he wanted to end his Viceroyalty in a blaze of glory. He boldly claimed credit for having accomplished, in less than two and a half months, "one of the greatest administrative operations in history." But contradicting his claim, Ayesha Jalal writes, "On behalf of the Hindus, Sikhs and Muslims who were slaughtered in their hundreds of thousands and the refugees who in their millions stumbled fearfully across the frontiers of two states, the history has a duty to challenge Mountbatten's contention and ask whether this great operation was not in fact an ignominious scuttle enabling Britain to exonerate themselves from the awkward responsibility of presiding over Indian communal madness."[39] M.J. Akbar is also of the view that "Lord Mountbatten was the prime culprit behind the holocaust of Punjab by postponing the controversial Punjab Award." According to him, "Mountbatten could have feasibly asked for a small extension. Instead, he got into a hurry that was still not been rationally explained."[40] Similarly, a recent historian, P.J.O. Taylor, argues that "Communal carnage might have been avoided by delaying it. "More recently, Andrew Roberts in his "Eminent Churchillians' castigates Mountbatten for his reckless decision to advance the independence date possibly to coincide with the Second anniversary of Japanese surrender, which resulted in a horrific massacre in Punjab. According to Roberts, "Mountbatten was anticipating a high level of communal violence and so he thought it vital to transfer power before catastrophe overtook British India altogether." Anyway, both the early date and the delay in announcing the Boundary Commission Award (both Mountbatten's decision) compounded the tragedy that took place on the eve of partition. To conclude, Lord Mountbatten was the last culprit among the guilty men of partition and largely responsible for the tragedy that accompanied it.

Thus, on 15 August, 1947 the curtain fell over a drama which had occupied the Indian stage for three quarters of a century. Partition of the country was a tragic finale to a glorious story of the freedom struggle. The contradictory nature of the reality of 15 August continues to intrigue and torment people on both sides of the border to this day. Two questions however still remain unanswered: (1) Why did Britain decide to quit so suddenly? and (2) Was partition inevitable, and whether it was a blessing or a curse ?

Notes

1. Azad, A.K. India Wins Freedom, Orient Longman, New York, 1960, pp. 187, 188.

2. Suda, J.P., op.cit., p.306

3. Aziz, K.K., Britain and Muslim India, Heinmann, London, 1963 p.143.

4. Singh, Anita Inder, The Origins of The Partition of India, Oxford University Press, New Delhi 1987, p.24.

5. Coupland Reginald, Restatement, pp.160-62.

6. Aziz, K.K., History of Partition of India, Atlantic Publishers, New Delhi, 1988, see jacket.

7. Singh, A.I., op.cit, p.56

8. Quoted in Singh, A.I., op.cit, p.57.

9. Venkatramani, M.S., and Srivastava, G.P., Quit India: The American Response To The 1942 Struggle, N.Delhi, 1979, pp.72 and 36-61.

10. Tarkunde, V.M., The Radical Humanist, Nov. 1985,

11. Chaudhary, Sandhya, Gandhi and The Partition of India, Starling Publishers, N. Delhi, 1984, p.90

12. See Chopra, P.N. (ed.), History's Judgement on Quit India Movement, Konark Publishers, New Delhi.

13. Azad, K.K., op.cit.(vol. 1) p.76

14. Quoted in Suda, J.P., op.cit., p.331

15. Quoted in Singh, A.I., op.cit, p.85

16. Jinnah quoted in Singh, A.I., Ibid., p.87

17. Quoted in Singh, A.I., Ibid., p.89

18. Das, Durga, India From Curzon To Nehru, Rupa Publication, Calcutta, 1973, pp.204-205.

19. Wolpert, Jinnah of Pakistan, OUP, 1984, p.173.

20. Chaudhary, Sandhya, op.cit, p.103.

21. Brecher, Michael, Nehru; A Political Biography O.U.P., London (1959) p.294

22. Hodson, H.V., The Great Divide, O.U.P., Bangalore, 1985, pp.124-25.

23. Das, Durga, op.cit, p.216

24. Menon, V.P., The Transfer of Power, In India Orient Longman, Hyderabad, 1985, p.73

26. Prasad, Janendra, India Divided, 1946, p.145.

27. Menon, V.P., op.cit, p.111

28. Mosley, The Last Days of the British Raj, p.27.

29. Azad, A.K., op.cit, p.181

30. Jalal, Ayesha, op.cit, p.176

31. Ibid., p.207.

32. Ibid., p.189

33. Das, Manmath Nath, Partition and Independence of India, Vision Books, N.Delhi, 1982, p.75

34. Jain, Giri Lal, Muslims After Pakistan, Times of India, 6 Dec. 1987.

35. Aziz, K.K., op.cit, (vol. 3-4) p.796

36. Quoted in Chaudhary Sandya, op.cit, p.180

37. Jalal, A., pp.cit, pp.243-44

38. Mehrotra, S.R., op.cit, p.21

39. Jalal, A., op.cit, p.293

40. Akbar, M.J., India: The Siege Within, Penguin Books Ltd., England, 1985, p.36.

Chapter 18

BRITAIN'S DECISION TO DIVIDE AND QUIT

No doubt, India's independence was a remarkable event for the whole world but for Indians it came as a pleasant surprise. Of course, the country had been fighting for long to throw away the foreign yoke. But even her top leaders did not expect or were prepared for the event to happen so soon. One may wonder as to what would have happened if Winston Churchill had won the general elections in 1945. Would he have agreed to part with power so easily? Among several assessments the most convincing answer is provided by James Callaghan, the Ex-Labour Prime Minister of Britain. In his 'Time and Choice' he writes: "With Churchill as Prime Minister perhaps post-war Britain might have involved in a long-term conflict in a vain attempt to hold down the whole continent by force. Fortunately, it fell to Clement Attlee to make the momentous decision to offer India her freedom. With his knowledge of India he had no hesitation and his "leap into the unknown" proved to be the wisest decision of the Labour government and Churchill was left to "watch the chattering down of the Britain Empire."

But apart from personal factor, there were some compelling forces which influenced the British decision to part with the brightest Jewel of the Crown so quickly, peacefully and unexpectedly. After all there cannot be any simple or singular reason behind such a momentous decision. Hence, the imperialist answer that independence was simply the fulfillment of Britain's self-appointed mission to assist the Indian people to self-government is simply fatuous. Taking almost a Whiggish position, H.V. Hodson writes: "The date chosen was within three days of the anniversary of Mr. Edwin Montagu's historic declaration of India's goal of responsible government in 1917. It has taken exactly thirty years for that policy to reach that culmination."[1] But there is no evidence to substantiate the theory that it was 'always' on the cards, especially after the introduction of Provincial self-government in 1919, for the constitutional reforms of 1919 and 1935 were aimed at preserving, not terminating the empire."[2] As a matter of fact, it was the cumulative result of several factors such as ferocious communal killings, rebellion of the Indian Navy, and a new spirit of patriotism in the armed forces, mass stirring in the wake of INA trials, weakening of British strength and prestige, problems of reconstruction at home, etc. Some of these factors are elaborated below:

COMMUNAL RIOTS: Although communal riots have been a common phenomenon and a regular feature of Indian politics during the past several decades, the barbarism perpetrated in the wake of Direct Action starting from Calcutta and engulfing the entire country stirred the conscience of the British rulers, who began to realise that their administrative structure was rapidly falling to pieces. To quote a letter that Roy Jenkins wrote to Mountbatten, "All the king's horses and all the king's men cannot prevent conflict between communities interlocked in villages over wide across of country."[3]

REVOLT IN DEFENCE FORCES: Another important factor which influenced the British decision to leave India was the loss of faith in the loyalty of the armed forces. All the three wings of Indian military were in the grip of protest, and revolt. It is well known that the armed froces were the backbone of the British hold over India but now they were in ferment. The rulers began to be haunted by the 'mutiny of 1857'. The crumbling imperial military base was signalled further by the mutinies of the Royal Indian Air Force and the Indian Royal Navy in January-February 1946. The ratings of the Royal Indian Navy stopped work on 19 February, 1946 and threatened to resign enbloc, if their demands were not met. Signs of open revolt in the Navy were visible in Bombay, Calcutta and Karachi. The RIN Mutiny is regarded as "The grand finale of our freedom struggle." Thus, the new spirit of patriotism and growing disloyalty in the armed forces conveyed the message to the foreign rulers that their main prop of hold over India was falling. Attlee himself declared in Parliament that "it was no longer possible to rule India because there was tremendous disaffection not only among the people but even among the Indian personnel of the armed forces of India. It is therefore prudent for the Britishers to withdraw from India with grace."

INA TRIALS: The tremendous nationalist stirring in the wake of trials of INA officers also greatly influenced the British decision to transfer power. The trial of Sehgal, Dhillon and Shahnawaz created a sensation in the country. Their trials ended on 31 December, 1946 and on 3 January, 1947 the Military Court pronounced them guilty of the crime of Waging War against the King Emperor and sentenced them to transportation for life. As a sequel there were mass demonstrations in support of the demand for their release. Ultimately, the Commander-in-Chief, Auchinlek, had to grant clemency to the three accused and in February 1946, 11,000 members of INA were released unconditionally and all charges against them were withdrawn.

Thus, the political condition in India was highly explosive. To quote Lord Ismay, "India at that time was like a ship in mid-ocean with a fire in the deck and ammunition in the hold." Hence the Labour government began to perceive that it was no longer possible to suppress, by force at its command, the growth of nationalist aspirations which had become very strong since the Second World War started.

WEAKENING OF BRITISH POWER AND PRESTIGE: Again, during the II World War the myth of British military superiority was shattered by Japan. Their finest ships were sunk and their prestige and influence were at a low ebb. In Europe also Britain was faced with problems. As a result of five years of fighting, her military and industrial potential was on the point of complete exhaustion, and she had been reduced to the status of a second or even third rate power. The War left England, though a nominal victor but a weakened power. Significantly, long before the War was over, M.N. Roy had predicted that Britain would be a debtor country and no debtor nation has ever continued to hold sway over a country to whom they owe money. Notably, by the end of the War Britain's sterling balances owed to India had reached a staggering total Rupees 3,375 crore. Thus, "War had brought a situation under which keeping India in bondage was no more profitable. It was for Britain economically a better proposition to have an independent and therefore friendly India than a dependent but sullen India. India had become nothing but a burden sans glory."[4] Moreover, for food and for industrial reconstruction Britain depended upon foreign resources. As things stood, America alone was in a position to assist her in economic recovery. As such she could now more effectively urge Britain to grant freedom and democracy to India, as she herself had done in the case of Philippines a year before. In the wake of this new situation even the diehard conservatives like Churchill began to come around to the view that independence may be granted to India.

BRITAIN'S INVOLVEMENT IN THE COLD WAR: Another factor influencing the Quit India decision appears to be British involvement in the Cold War. The Soviet Union, the rival power, was making more friends by championing the cause of colonial struggles sweeping Asia and Africa. In the propaganda warfare launched by the Soviet Union, the authorities in London realised that if they failed to win their goodwill, the Cold War would turn to the advantage of the opposite camp.

NEW CONCEPT OF THE COMMONWEALTH: While the above mentioned forces were conspiring to bring about the end of 'classical imperialism,' the British were devising new method of safeguarding their interests in the erstwhile colonies. The new dictum was "the Empire is dead, long live the Commonwealth." Accordingly, in July 1947 the Colonial Office was replaced by the Commonwealth Relations Office. It changed the whole concept of the Empire, as the British Commonwealth henceforth became a loose association of autonomous states of different races, colour and belief, each willing to assist and cooperate in the progress and well-being of the other and prepared to consult each other in a completely free association. If Britain could thus accommodate the growing aspirations and urges of other Dominions and derive commercial, financial, and political benefits it was not difficult for her to add just two more to the list of Dominions. That is why Attlee, while announcing the decision to Quit India, gave Indians the unfettered right of determining her future, but at the same time expressed the hope that the Indian people would choose to associate themselves with the Commonwealth and the hope was fulfilled just by deleting the word 'Britain' as a prefix.

HOPE OF A CONTINUED FOOTHOLD: Another explanation for the British withdrawal was offered by leaders like Maulana Azad and Abdul Wali Khan etc. According to them Britain decided to withdraw only after ensuring their continued foothold on the Indian subcontinent. In their opinion the British plan to partition India was the culmination of their policy of divide and rule. They argued that a state dominated by the Muslim League would offer a permanent sphere of influence to the British and with a British base in Pakistan India would have to pay far greater attention to British interests than she might otherwise do.

ABDICATION OF POWER: Since the date for transfer of power was fixed and then advanced by the British themselves, a few writers have characterised this transfer of power as the greatest example of abdication. Attlee himself had made such a claim while announcing the date of Independence. In his own words, "It was an abdication or fulfillment of British mission." B.R. Nanda is also of the view that "It was not merely the compulsion of events but a measure of idealism which inspired the British policy which Attlee introduced and carried through during years 1946-47." No doubt, it is true that a conservative government headed by a man like Churchill would have easily mustered force enough to hold India down for a number of years. But it would be wrong to treat it as a purely voluntary offer on the part of Britain, for it was actually the force of circumstances and the inscrutable march of time that brought about the end of the British rule. Therefore the fact has to be acknowledged that India's freedom was wrested not gifted.

Notes

1. Hodson, H.V., op.cit, p.321
2. Singh, A.I., op.cit, p.244
3. Ibid., p.226
4. Dhar, Niranjan, The Radical Humanist, Feb. 1986

Chapter 19

WAS PARTITION INEVITABLE ?

There are widely different views regarding the genesis of Pakistan and several explanations are given for the partition of the country. Some of these are:

BRITISH POLICY OF DIVIDE AND RULE: A commonly believed explanation is that it was the logical conclusion of the British policy of 'divide and rule,' To illustrate, from the time of Lord Minto the British government had tried its best to create rift between Hindus and Muslims. The process began with the conferment of separate electorate which culminated in the August Offer of 1940. This policy was continued and strengthened in subsequent years. They became committed to it by various statements, pledges and proposals such as the August Offer, the Cripps Offer and Attlee's Statement of 20 February, 1947. Thus after encouraging communalism and separatism over a long period of their rule it was not possible for Britain to avoid its logical implications by proposals like the Cabinet Mission Plan. However, not all writers agree with this viewpoint. To quote Rashid Beg, "It is not so much that the British divided and ruled as that we were divided and hence they could rule for such a long time." Maulana Mohd. Ali also shares the same view. Ali had once remarked: "We divided ourselves and the British ruled us." Taking a balanced view, H.V. Hodson in his 'The Great Divide' argues that Britain was not solely responsible for the division of the country. "Given the basic and rival objectives of the great participants in the struggle-of the British, stable government; of the Congress, national independence; of the League, Muslim Security from 'Hindu Raj'- all three share in responsibility for bringing about the situation that confronted all concerned in 1947."[1] In the event , all the three sides in the triangle lost. However, the Congress was the biggest loser, for its leaders paid most dearly in sacrifice of their ideals. Nevertheless, in August 1947, the Muslim League was the only party to achieve most of what it wanted.

COMMUNAL DIVIDE: According to another explanation it was the age-old Hindu-Muslim divide which made partition inevitable. This theory is based on Whiggish interpretation of partition of India. It maintains that partition was rooted in their last few century of Indian history ridden with communal conflicts, But disagreeing with this interpretation, Anita Inder Singh writes:" "Although a sense of social division in religious terms was pervasive in Indian society, Hindus and Muslims belonging to the same class or locality often had more in common with one another than with their co-religionist in other sections of society. The religious distinction existed along with, and cut across tribal, class and caste distinctions."[2] The real question to be confronted, however, is when and how religious feeling could come to be politicised to the point when partition became inevitable.

ACCIDENT OF GEOGRAPHY AND DEMOGRAPHY: Actually, it was not only history but the facts of geography and demography that made the idea of Pakistan a reality. Perhaps geography was the most potent objective factor which made partition a practical proposition. Accidentally, the area covered under the land of Pakistan was predominantly Muslim populated though it constituted only 40 percent of Muslim India. Hence, it was not altogether impossible to detach this area to constitute another state. To quote Prof. S.R. Mahrotra, "But for this accident of geography, the idea of Pakistan-even if it were born would never have materialised. He, however, adds that even the existence of well-defined and easily separable Muslim majority provinces would not necessarily have led to the partition of India. In fact, it was the alliance of Muslim. separatism with the Muslim will to power which proved decisive.. It was the determination of A.I.M.L. to dominate the Muslim majority provinces which led directly and inevitably to the partition of India and the creation of Pakistan."[3] Incidentally, it is interesting to note that the genesis of the idea of Pakistan did not spring from Muslim majority provinces but from those areas in which they were in a minority. Actually, it was a case of powerful artificial insemination in the political sphere, the idea being fertilised in one place and subsequently grafted in another. In this it owed much to the skill, courage and determination of Mohd. Ali Jinnah.

EMERGENCE OF THE MUSLIM LEAGUE: The genesis of Pakistan was implicit in the feeling of separatism which had been inculcated in the minds of the Muslim masses by the Muslim League since its birth. But the answer to the question as to how partition became unavoidable is to be sought not only in the emergence of the Muslim League with its demand for a sovereign Pakistan since March 1940 but also in British and Congress tactics which contributed to the rise of the Muslim League and the solidification of its communal support.

SEPARATE ELECTORATE: The process of separatism got a fillip with the conferment of separate electorate in the Act of 1909. Indeed, the separate electorate was a very pernicious principle. But it is to be noted that if the League demanded it, Britain conceded it, and the Congress acquiesced in it. However, once it was conceded in the Congress-League scheme it became impossible to wriggle out of it. The incipient Muslim individuality was thus reinforced by the Lucknow Pact of 1916. Not surprisingly, the Nehru Report (1928) which tried to do away with the communal electorate was outrightly rejected by the League. Thus separate electorate ultimately led to the demand for separation.

FAILURE OF NEGOTIATIONS FOR CONGRESS-LEAGUE COALITION

Yet another explanation traces back the roots of Partition to the Congress refusal to admit Muslim League representatives to share in ministerial power in U.P. in 1937. But it is to be noted that the failure of negotiation in 1937 though embittered the provincial Muslim leaders, it never turned them into supporter of a sovereign Pakistan, for there is little evidence about political unification of Muslims before the War. Actually, it was the fear that the British would introduce the scheme of federation, as provided in the Act of 1935, and again the fact that given the weakness of the League in the Muslim majority provinces, it would have been left high and dry at the all-India level if federation had been implemented which led Mr. Jinnah and the League to think of a separate homeland.

However, it was the outbreak of the War that came to help the cause of the League. Jinnah set out to exploit the British need for the support of the Indian parties for the war effort. The League declared in several resolutions in September-October 1939 that India was not a national state and soon after proclaimed the demand for Pakistan (March 1940). These resolutions helped the Viceroy to reject Congress demand for a promise of independence in return for its cooperation with the war effort. The League thus provided the British with a pretext to tell the Congress that the demand for independence must be weighed against the objections of the minorities. Subsequently, the Cripps Offer of 1942 gave plausibility to the Lahore Resolution and strengthened the popular appeal of the Muslim League in the Muslim majority provinces. It was, however, at the Simla Conference (1945) that the British consolidated Jinnah's monopoly of Muslim representation at the Centre in allowing his demand to nominate all Muslims to the Executive Council, and thereby let the conference break up instead of going ahead without him.

GENERAL ELECTION RESULTS: Perhaps no other factor strengthened the bargaining position of the Muslim League and made

Pakistan "inevitable" as the election results of 1945-46. The League leader, Mr. Jinnah, succeeded in establishing its claim to be the sole spokesman of the Muslims as the League had secured 76 percent of Muslim votes, winning 429 out of 492 seats. However, it may be pointed out that the Muslim League's claim was a statistical illusion. The elections were not only based on limited franchise-hardly ten percent of the voting population, the percentage of actual voters was also only about five percent of the Muslim population of undivided India. And of these who voted, 30 percent did not vote for the Muslim League. Hence, it is wrong to assume that the League had secured more than 70 percent of Muslim support, for only 3.7 percent of the Muslims of India had voted for the Muslim League, some of whom at least had not voted for Pakistan. Anyway, the growing gains of the League clearly represented in turning of many Muslims from essentially provincial concerns to rally behind the only Muslim party which could take care of their interest at the all-India level in the bargaining for the spoils of the transfer of power. "The League's success at the hustings also represented a solidification and politicisation of the Muslim religious community, a rallying to "Pakistan". Yet the extent of the this political unification need not be exaggerated into a communal mandate for a sovereign Pakistan. For Pakistan still meant all things to all men. It is perhaps the effects of peace, bringing the British departure into close prospect that rallied a majority of the Muslim community to the League."[4]

It is to be noted that until 1945 the British had worked on the assumption that the Empire must survive and the demand for Pakistan had been a useful counterpoise to the Congress demand for independence. Even the Cabinet Mission preferred to transfer power to a united India.

COMMUNAL HOLOCAUST: The communal frenzy that was let loose by Jinnah's Direct Action call on 29 July, 1946 was another reason behind the decision for partition. Jinnah for the first time advocated Direct Action to achieve his goal and adopted the cult of gun, grenade and goons. Direct Action in Calcutta and Noakhali (August 1946) provided the spark which lit the fires of civil war. Rumours of rape, forced marriages, conversions spread like wild fire arousing the deepest hatred and the fiercest desire for revenge. These stirred into waging the most bloody and brutal venegeance on Muslims in Bihar and U.P. Atrocities committed on a mass scale could not be forgotten on either side and further contributed to the feelings for partition.

With an administration that was both inadequate and to some extent unreliable and unable to suppress communal violence except with military help, with increasing awareness that the administration was weak, with communal passion rising as news spread of atrocities committed on both the communities, partition appeared inevitable by the end of 1946. Developments on the constitutional front also confirmed this assumption.

FAILURE OF INTERIM GOVERNMENT (1946-47): Before joining with the Muslim League the Interim Government led by Nehru worked as a team but dissension arose soon thereafter. The League worked as a separate block and would not recognise Nehru as the leader of the government. Thus the agonising experience of the Congress leaders in the Interim Government compelled them to think on the line of a separation as a solution, far no power sharing could be made possible with the Muslim League. Having experienced the attitude and hostile stance of the League in the Interim Government the Congress leaders by February 1947 lost all hopes of achieving an independent united India.

THE CONGRESS RESPONSIBILITY FOR PARTITION: Although the Congress stood for a united India, it cannot be absolved of all responsibility for the creation of Pakistan. By accepting the Congress-League scheme (1916), by snubbing the Muslim League on the question of composite government in UP (1937), by recognising the principle of self-determination in 1942 and 1944 (thereby giving substance to the demand for Pakistan), by resigning the Congress ministry (1939) and launching the Quit India movement in 1942 (thereby losing its position of leverage with the British authorities), the Congress unwittingly and indirectly aided and abetted in the creation of Pakistan.

MUSLIM ELITE AND PARTITION: Pakistan was not created by the Muslim masses. It owed its birth to a handful of Muslim leaders, mostly belonging to the titled gentry, nawabs, landlords, big business and professional class. It is these leaders who were not content with constitutional 'guarantee' of security and demanded a separate homeland. "Muslim masses never showed any support for the Muslim League until madness seized the subcontinent in 1946-47 when Pakistan idea began to sell fast with the Muslim community, for it had all the romance of a battle cry, all the potentiality of a crusade." "The League did win Muslim support in 1946 but only after the country had begun spinning in the vortex of a great storm whose force was blinding."[5] Moin Shakir holds the opinion that "Pakistan was the end product of Muslim (upper class) anxiety at first to attain cultural and political autonomy within the framework of a federal India and later of their bold assertion that Muslims being a separate nation, must have a sovereign state."[6] Mani Shanker Aiyer in his 'Pakistan Papers' almost sharing the same view writes: "It was not the Muslim masses who brought Pakistan into being— it was the electoral politics of British India, based on separate electorates and restricted to the propertied few, that resulted in Pakistan." Aiyer further adds: "Muslim elites might have voted for Pakistan with their hands but the Muslim masses voted with their feet to stay where they were. A recent writer, Mushtaq Naqvi also agrees with Aiyer. The gravement of his argument in his book, 'Pakistan: The Real Story' is that "the Muslims of India did not opt for partition- for the good reason that they were never, in fact, really asked." In the opinion of Asghar Ali Engineer, "It was the Urdu-speaking elite (not the masses) from North India which was mainly responsible for the creation of Pakistan; and it is important to note that this elite created Pakistan not for religious reasons, as is commonly believed, but for secular reasons. In fact, it was the 'majority (Hindu) phobia' that led the Muslim elite to think that their secular interests will be better protected in Pakistan where Muslims be in majority. It is noteworthy that the Muslim religious leaders were completely opposed to the very concept of Pakistan and believed in composite nationalism."[7] Holding almost a similar opinion, Giri Lal Jain says, "Partition was in no small way the result of self-perception and activities of a class who regarded themselves as legatees of the Mughal Empire by virtue of their foreign descent, real or imaginary, and the status of their forefathers under Muslim rule and the distinct culture, though the leadership was provided by Mr. Jinnah who came from a very different background."

CRUCIAL ROLE OF JINNAH: Without doubt, Jinnah was the chief architect of Pakistan. He "achieved the sovereign Pakistan partly because he knew where he was going, while the muddling through tactics of the British and the Congress were no match for his melange of obduracy, dialectical skill and deliberate, dogged negation of everything less than a sovereign Pakistan."[8] It is true that without such qualities as Jinnah had Pakistan might never have become a reality. On the other hand, always underestimating the seriousness of the call for a sovereign Pakistan, neither the British nor the Congress formulated a strategy to challenge or to resist.

Fairly speaking, "the major blame for partition may lie with the Muslim League for demanding a separate homeland (Pakistan) but almost equal blame lies with the revivalist Hindus and the Congress for creating conditions over a long period which led to such a fantasy becoming a tangible reality. While the official creed of the Congress was secular, section of its leadership was equally revivalist, conceiving nationalism in terms of Hindu glory, reinforcing thus Muslim separatism." Thus India paid a heavy price for the achievement of freedom, a consequence of the fact that communal forces were not defeated, nor unity totally achieved.

All told, partition was the result of a highly complex political situation that had developed in India and cannot be attributed to one single factor, or to one single person or to a particular policy, action, statement or decision. As Azad says: "It (partition) cannot be explained in individual terms but in terms of historical forces at work. Individuals do make difference but sometimes individuals are only symbols of forces at work." Hence, it would be nothing short of sheer naivete to believe that United India would have been possible had Nehru been more accommodative to the Muslim League in U.P. in the year 1937, or had the Congress accepted the Cabinet Mission Plan or had a treacherous doctor (A.J.L. Patel) not acted professionally by keeping Jinnah's state of health a secret.

WAS PARTITION AVOIDABLE ?

It is true that there did emerge certain forces and factors in 1946-47 that made partition unavoidable. To quote prof. Cyril Henry Philip, "There was nothing inevitable about partition. It was not delivered from the womb of time but had its start and early course between 1937 and 1942 in the policies and decisions of men who might have chosen differently." It was the result of inconsideration on both sides, not of intransigence of one and the timorousness of the other. By accommodating the Muslim League in the UP cabinet in 1937 the Congress could have stolen the thunder of 'Hindu Raj' that became the battle cry of the League two years after. The Congress could have also avoided it if it had accepted the August Offer of 1940 or the Cripps Offer of 1942. But by 1945 it was too late to change the course of history. To quote C.H. Philip once again, "By 1945 it was a movement of ideas, ambitions, greed and rumour (both public and personal), a river in full flow; by 1946 it had become a roaring torrents, tearing great holes in the fabric of society and administration, and no man or group of men could then have stopped it. All of the major parties — the British, the National Congress, the Muslim League — bear a heavy responsibility for what was on any reckoning short or long term, a disaster, a reckless squandering of the fruits of the hard won British Raj and pax-Britannica."[9]

Probably, the proponents of partition were all men in a hurry. If Mountbatten wanted to end his Viceroyalty in a blaze of glory, Nehru was eager to keep his tryst with destiny as independent India's first Prime Minister, and Jinnah was anxious to lead a new nation. The plan to concede Pakistan, in Nehru's own admission, was a fatal solution. Yet he and his colleagues agreed to it because they were unwilling to fight Jinnah's communal programme at a political level. Their answer to communalism was to concede to it. Thus, once all the three main players the Congress, the League and the British had agreed upon the scheme of partition, there was no going back. However, there was only one extra-constitutional authority which probably could have got it undone if he so wished, and that was Gandhi. But at that time why did the Mahatma not do this is still a puzzle. Had he not declared earlier that "India would be partitioned over his dead body"? Perhaps he did not like the idea of crossing the way of Congress leadership at the final round, because launching of a movement against partition tantamonted to challenge the leadership of men like Patel and Nehru who were so dear and near to him. As he said: "It would be wrong to weaken the present leadership under the circumstances. I must therefore swallow the bitter pill." However, it was a great political renunciation, of self-effacement and of self-control. Thus partition was not unavoidable. It had become so because of the acts of omission and commission of the leadership of the League and the Congress as well as British statesmen and bureaucrats.

PARTITION — A DISASTER OR A BLESSING ?

The last pertinent question is whether partition was a wrong decision? Even today it is too early to pass any final judgement about the wisdom of vivisection. There are many defenders and detractors of this decision. For instance, Sardar Patel, while expressing his feelings on this decision, said : "I felt that if we did not accept it, India would be split into many bits and could be completely ruined." He justified it as a sort of surgical operation that had become necessary to save the motherland from further bloodshed and anarchy prevailing since August 1946. Following him, Nehru also said that "by cutting of the head we shall get rid of headache." Ramaswami Mudaliar in his 'Pakistan Without Tears' even congratulated the decision makers of Partition. According to M.V. Kamath, "Partition was not only inevitable but unrgently necessary." Sharing the same view, Giri Lal Jain in his 'The Hindu Phenomenon', writes: "Partition was an unintended blessing for India and that without it the country would have been engulfed by permanent civil war." He argues that partition ended the parity between the Hindus and the Muslims in both political and cultural civilisational terms. According to him, "had there been no partition India would have become an enlarged version of present day Lebanon. Pakistan was the best thing that could have happened to Hindus." However, he adds that "for the Muslims of the subcontinent partition was one of the greatest tragedies in the history of Islam and India." But it is worth mentioning here that not many Pakistani and Bangaladeshi intellectuals think so. Writers like Akbar Ahmed (Pak) and Farzana Sheikh (Bangladesh) consider partition to have been the fulfillment of the collective wish of the Muslims of the subcontinent for their own homelands.

On the other hand, there are several writers who have strongly denounced the decision of partition. According to S.K. Majumdar, "Partition was an unmitigated evil for all concerned." W. Brown in his

'US, India And Pakistan' says: "It was a subcontinental disaster." Edward D'Cruz in his "Indian Quest for Nationhood' writes: "It was a monumental folly." Choudhary Khaliquzzaman, once a champion of Partiion, ultimately agreed that the two-nation theory "proved positively injurious to the Muslims of India, and on the long run basis for Muslims everywhere."[10] Even Jinnah recognised the folly and in his speech on the occasion of Idul Fitter message on 27 August, 1948 said: "The bloodbath is a problem of unmitigated magnitude." In the opinion of T.N. Madan, "The partition of subcontinent resulted from, represents and keeps alive the communal divide. It did not end Hindu-Muslim discord, but provided one more mode of expression for it — namely inter-state conflict. Communal riots now have an analogue in the Indo-Pak wars that have been fought and continue to threaten the subcontinent from time to time."[11] The trauma of partition is still haunting the subcontinent, as is evident from the events in Kashmir on the one hand and Karachi on the other.

Notes

1. Hodson, H.V., op.cit, p.527.

2. Singh, A.I., op.cit, p.236

3. Mehrotra, S.R., op.cit, pp. 197-98

4. Singh, A.I., op.cit, p.140

5. Akbar, M.J., op.cit, p.29.

6. Shakir Moin, Khilafat to Partition, Kalamkar Prakashan New Delhi 1970, p.194

7. Engineer, Asghar Ali, "Ethnic and Communal conflicts in Pakistan," mainstream 16 Sept, 1995 p.13

8. Singh, A.I., op.cit, p.251

9. C.H. Philip quoted in Das, M.N., op.cit, p.65.

10. Hasan, Mushirul, 'Partition Was Not Inevitable', The Sunday Times of India, 13 August, 1995

11. Madan, T.N., Pakistan Revisited, Times of India, 19 Nov. 1994.

PART-II

COMMUNALISM
IN MODERN INDIA
CAUSES AND CONSEQUENCES

Chapter 20

MEANING OF COMMUNALISM

Communalism is the most unfortunate legacy of the Indian Freedom Movement. In fact, the supreme tragedy of partition was the logical outcome of communalism. Apart from being the root cause of India's division, it remains as the most intractable, persistent and ubiquitous problem of modern India. "In contemporary India, it is a socio-political phenomenon of dangerously negative significance with immense potential to destablise its young nationhood, weaken its basic foundation and misdirect its limited resources and energies as well as public attention and national concern on a dangerously slippery path downwards."[1] Communalism has become the enemy of progress, revolution, democracy and of nation-building on rational and scientific lines.

NATURE OF COMMUNALISM

Simply put, communalism is political mobilisation of people on the basis of religious affiliation. According to Wilfred Smith, "Communalism is an attitude of mind which regards the followers of each religious group as an exclusive social and political unit with distinct and sometimes even antagonistic interests to those of others." The authors of 'Punjab Crisis' have defined communalism "as the political, economic and social assertiveness of an organised aggregation of individuals identifying themselves with a particular group."[2] In other words, it is the antagonistic assertiveness of one religious group against another. According to them, members of each of these group have the perception that they have common cultural norms and beliefs. "Though religious differences are crucial elements of communal ideology and politics but by themselves they don't cause communalism."[3] According to Rasheeduddin Khan, "Communalism is a specific political ideology of using and exploiting both the ascriptive religious identity of the people as well as secular democratic opportunities of the citizen."[4] In other words, communalism is basically an ideology of political allegiance to religious community as a primary group in the polity, and for political action. Prof. Bipan Chandra in his outstanding publication, 'Communalism in Modern India' has made an exhaustive study of this phenomenon. According to him, "Communal ideology consists of three elements, one succeeding the other: first, that people of the same religion have common secular interest — political, social and cultural. It is the first bedrock of communal ideology; second, that secular interests, of the followers of the same religion are different from that of the followers of other religion; third, that their secular interests are not only different but mutually incompatible, antagonistic and hostile."[5]

WHAT IS NOT COMMUNALISM

Clarifying the concept of communalism still further Prof. Rasheeduddin Khan says that adherence to religion and religious system is not communalism but exploiting of religion is communalism. He further says that attachment to a religion or religiosity is not communalism but using a religious community against other communities and against the nation is communalism. Similarly, affiliation to any social, cultural and service organisation of a religious community may not be communalism, but restricting one's sympathy, help, social obligations and range of services as citizens of a secular republic just only to the community of one's birth can be communalism. Likewise, affiliation to ritualism, superstition, obscurantism, magic, charm and occult practices like astrology is not communalism. Even commitment to conservative values in social life and conservative orientation in politics is not communalism. However, Prof. Khan recognises that all these aspects can be inputs into the development of communal consciousness and the same can easily convert religiosity into political bellicosity and thus become communalism."[6] Thus, "to believe or to propagate that some economic and political interests of one religious group, caste or an ascriptive group are dissimilar, divergent or antagonistic to those of another is communalism."[7] Further, communalism should not be confused with 'fundamentalism' — a current coin these days. In fact, both the terms are now being used synonymously. But the two are quite distinct and different, thought they can become correlated and have many ideological and political elements in common. For instance, while the fundamentalists seriously urge the actual revival of the pristine past, the gaze of the communalists is clearly fixed on the modern world. Moreover, unlike the former, the latter do not favour complete theocracy."[8]

ROOTS OF COMMUNALISM

Communalism is essentially a political phenomenon. Its genesis is in politics not religion, although it draws its sustenance from religion.

To quote Asghar Ali Engineer, "While communalism germinates in politics it is watered by religious sectarianism. It flowers in an environment of unreason and orthodoxy." The root of communalism is in political demands made by different communities by exaggerating cultural and religious differences. It is commonly observed that increased religio-cultural consciousness transforms itself into political assertiveness. According to Gary Marx, "The conflict of interest- both political and economic is transformed into the conflict of ideas, based on communal ideology."

THEORIES OF COMMUNALISM

All social phenomena are complex and defy any easy explanatory framework. This is so with communalism as well. The phenomenon of communalism has been explained differently by different writers.

Various studies on communalism have been made in the last few years under three overall perspectives,[9] which are thoroughly discussed by M.S. Dhami in his article 'Punjab And Communalism':[9]

(1) The left oriented perspective, represented by Bipan Chandra (Communalism in Modern India), P.C. Joshi (Economic Background of Communalism In India), and Asghar Ali Engineer ('A Theory Of Communal Riots' and 'Socio Economic Bases Of Communalism') assign primacy to economic determinants.

(2) The second perspective includes the studies of Louis Dumont ('Nationalism And Communalism'), Satish Sabharwal, Francis Robinson and Ratna Naidu. Their approach may be characterised as cultural-historical. However, Ratna Naidu explains communalism both in terms of politico-economic and cultural factors.

(3) Thirdly, a few important studies of Paul R. Brass and Joseph Rothschild '(Ethno Politics — A Conceptual Framework') who treat the phenomenon of ethnic identities and ethnic conflict from a political perspective, assigning primacy to political determinants, that is to political elites/entrepreneurs in mobilising communal/ ethnic consciousness among the competing groups.

Bipan Chandra, who represents the first perspective, traces the growth of communal ideology and politics to the social framework, provided by the communal economy and polity. He argues that colonial underdevelopment and the crisis of the colonial economy resulted in widespread unemployment, which led to widespread scramble for jobs among the middle class. This helped communalism acquire its real mass base. He further adds that struggle between economic classes, when these happen to belong to different communities, assume communal dimension. Bipan Chandra's panacea for these distortions is that the national struggle during the colonial period should have been in terms of economic classes and this would have kept the religious consciousness in check.

For Bipan Chandra, communalism was the 'false consciousness' of the historical process of the last 150 years. He maintains that objectively no real conflict between the interests of Hindus and Muslims existed. According to him, the objective contradiction during the colonial period between the Indian people and colonialism was the efficient (or real) cause of the national movement but the Hindu-Muslim contradiction, having no basis in reality, was not an efficient (or real) cause of communalism. He means to say that it was not a religious differentiation that led to communalism but communal politics and ideological practices which transformed religious differentiations into communal cleavage." Even K.K. Aziz, who has interpreted modern Indian history from a communal point of view, in his 'The Making of Pakistan' admits: "In the final analysis, the idea of Muslim nationalism was more subjective than territorial, more psychological than political, while Indian nationalism was more territorial than cultural, more historical than religious."

Prof. Bipan Chandra favours a two pronged struggle to fight communalism: the first calls for politico-ideological education of the people for promoting secular consciousness, treating communal consciousness as "false consciousness" or something engineered by the exploiting classes to subserve their own interests; the second relates to changing the social reality or in other words, a fundamental reordering of social structure." But, as M.S. Dhami points out, Prof. Chandra in his analysis has brushed aside the reality of community-based interest altogether.

P.C. Joshi while discussing the causes which led to Muslim separatism utilises the model of "cumulative causation". For the Indian Muslims, the British colonial impact led to a setback in the economic and political sphere vis-a-vis the majority community and this engendered in them the feeling of deprivation, which ultimately prepared the grounds for secessionist demands. Joshi, however, underplays pre-existing antipathy between the two major communities.

Another leftist writer, Asghar Ali Engineer, has written extensively on communalism and communal riots Though on the whole, he views the subject of communalism from the Marxist perspective, he rightly recognises the great mobilizatory potential of religion.

Louis Dumont's cultural-historical perspective, however, provides useful insight into the Hindu-Muslim communal problem. He laments that the more or less peaceful coexistence of the two communities after the Muslim conquest could not produce any general ideological synthesis. Hence lack of ideological synthesis created "lasting social heterogeneity" of the two communities. The British rule in the modern period led to the growth of revivalist movements among the two major communities which further reaffirmed the traditional values. Subsequent growth of political parties too failed to transcend the traditional social structure and the associated value system. In the matter of injecting religion into politics, Dumont treats both the Congress and the League complementary to each other. Dumont's sociological view of the Congress provides a more balanced picture regarding its secular and national character. At the level of principles and in its overt activities "the Congress appears essentially as a purely national movement, but at the level of socio-logical reality, one can wonder whether the Congress did or did not mirror a tendency to identify the Indian nation with the domination of high caste Hindus." Dumont concludes: "It is true that Gandhi did not oppose a separate electorate for the Muslims. But the Congress as a whole was opposed to it and it was tinged with communal motives." He further argues that "the failure of the Congress to forestall partition was due to the fact that its leaders disregarded the feeling of the Muslims being treated as socially distinct. And for a long intervening period the unity could have been built on the recognition of their very separatedness."

Satish Sabharwal in his perspective analysis of communalism in India eleborates Dumont's views regarding the key role of ideas and traditions. He takes serious account of religious beliefs and institutions. While not belittling the role of national interests, he argues that "even when these interests are involved, religious symbols come to the fore by virtue of merely their mobilisational potential." He also establishes the linkage of religious ideas and symbols to the social structure. For him, the genesis of the Hindu-Muslim communalism during the colonial period should perhaps be seen in relation to the long standing separatedness of the religious network, the actual social distance expressing a high level of social antagonism between Hindus and Muslims and the growth of communally homogeneous neighbourhood in the Metropolitan cities.

Ratna Naidu, being more sensitive to the sociological reality of Indian society prefers "enlightened secularism to straitjacket secularism." She argues "where communal groups have distinct economic interest political choices are also communally based. The Indian leadership, unlike that of Malaysia, has always refused to concede the reality of communal interests.

Having discussed the above mentioned theories of communalism, M.S. Dhami concludes that "ethnicity based on religion and/or other cultural markers have become a global phenomenon. Hence, he believes that a straitjacket secularism and one-dimensional national identity decries regional and other cultural identities."[10] M.N. Srinivas, a well known sociologist of India, describes those who disclaim any loyalty to their religion as phonies." The ethical/communal groups not only provide emotional sustenance, personal identification to their members but also help them in the competitive arena for material benefit, status and power.

Notes

1. Raza, Moonis, 'Communalism in Contemporary India', Mainstream, 29 Jan. 1994, p.22.

2. Kumar, Pramod and others, (eds.), Punjab Crisis: Context And Trends, Centre for Research of Rural and Industrial Development, Chandigarh, 1984, p.23.

3. Ibid., p.24

4. Khan, Rasheeduddin, 'Fundamentalism and Communalism', World Focus, Nov-Dec., 1993, p.23

5. See Chandra, Bipan, Communalism In Modern India (Chapter -1) Vani Educational Publishers, 1984, pp. 1-3

6. Khan, Rasheeduddin, 'Secularism And Social Transformation In India', Mainstream, 1 May, 1993, p.19.

7. Ziaullah, Syed, Democratic World, 28 Sep. 1986.

8. See Chandra, Bipan, 'Fundamentalism and Communalism', World Focus, Feb-March, 1995, pp. 3-6

9. For details, see Dhami, M.S., Punjab and Communalism, Seminar, (No. 314), Oct. 1985.

10. Ibid.,

Chapter 21

BIRTH AND GROWTH OF COMMUNALISM IN INDIA

In his preface to 'Communalism In Modern India,' Prof. Bipan Chandra rejects the notion that communalism was the logical and inevitable product of Indian historical development. He points out that communalism is incapable of being explained historically and was not a mere historical accident or product of a diabolical conspiracy. Nor was its success ensured before hand. He believes that it could have been curbed and controlled and even eradicated if certain social, political and ideological conditions had been met. In his opinion, communalism is not the remnant of the past — a hangover from the medieval period or a language of the past. Medieval politics, according to him, was not communal, though religious suppression and offences did take place. He says that "communal view was not present in our tradition; it was not a primordial feeling. It was not a problem inherited from the past. In his opinion, it was not medieval history which bequeathed communalism to modern India but a particular view of Medieval history which was itself communal ideology as also a product of this ideology."[1] It is worth pointing out here that Prof. Bipan Chandra, while examining the pre-British period, has ignored some bitter historical memories shared by the two communities against each other. Regarding the historical roots of communalism Prof. Amrik Singh seems to be more realistic when he states: "Aware as they were of past glory and their sense of separate identity, the Muslims felt acutely threatened by the spectre of so called "Hindu Raj" after the introduction of participatory democracy. Hindus, on the other hand, have not been able to come to terms with the hurt and humiliation of having been governed and persecuted for close a thousand years by the Muslim rulers. Although there is no solid and substantial evidence of persecution, this feeling is dinned into their consciousness by Hindu Communalists.[2]"

But the real question is not why but how did communalism grow, spread and thrive and what were the causes or factors in Indian society responsible for its growth and for the enlargement of its social base. Prof. Bipan Chandra dos not deny the fact that differences based on caste, language and province or region were there just as religious differences were there and could be seen as the origins of communalism. Yet he is of the view that "communalism was not inherent or inevitable in the same way in which nationalism or class struggles were, nor it was a mere conspiracy by clever, power hungry politicians and administrators either. There was something in the social, political and economic situation of colonial India which favoured its emergence and growth. It did not arise from nowhere; nor did it hang in a void. It had socio-economic, historical and political, that is, structural roots. It responded to some urges of the people, and to some features in their life situation."[3] He therefore maintains that communalism is a modern phenomenon that arose as a result of British colonial impact and the response of different social classes, strata and groups. Communalism thus is a modern ideology that incorporated some aspects and elements of past ideologies and institutions and historical background to form a new ideological and political intercourse or mix.

Elaborating his thesis Prof. Bipan Chandra further says: "Basically, communalism was one of the by-products of colonialism, of the colonial character of the Indian economy, of colonial under development, and in recent years,' of the failure and incapacity of capitalism to develop the economy and society."[4] As a result, there was a keen competition for a share of the shrinking national cake. The struggle for economic opportunities was now internalised, and any means were found good enough in this struggle to save one's class position and identity. While communalism was able to draw supporters from all classes of people, its main social base was to be found in the middle classes or the petty bourgeoisie. Nehru had rightly remarked: "Communalism was an inherent weakness of a national movement largely based on the middle classes."[5] Communalism enabled them to disguise their own privileged interests in the garb of communal ideology and religious identity. For instance, with regard to Muslim Communalism, Moin Shakir says: "Muslim communalism became the nationalist ideology adopted by the emergent and precarious Muslim middle class in its struggle against domination within India by the more developed Hindu middle class. In a way, the demand for the partition of the country was a middle class affair."[6]

GROWTH OF MUSLIM COMMUNALISM

The rise of nationalism and the introduction of democratic institutions in the nineteenth century was accompanied by the emergence of communalism as a political phenomenon. The politicisation of community feeling in India was thus, in part a consequence of introduction of representative institutions and also introduction of group/community representation adopted by the British rulers. When Indian nationalism became self-conscious and assertive, the British tried to checkmate it by countering one community against the other. For decades, communalism served as the second line of defence of both imperialism and the reactionary social forces.

However, with the greater weight of Jagirdari-feudal and bureaucratic elements among the Muslim upper classes and intelligentsia, Muslims communalism, from the beginning, adopted openly pro-communal politics. Sir Syed Ahmed Khan, a towering Muslim leader in late nineteenth century, made it a point to support the colonial regime and preach loyalty to it. For instance, he welcomed Lord Lytton's repressive Vernacular Press Act as a liberal measure. He even asked Muslims not to agitate for the Ilbert Bill. Throughout he preached that the British rulers were the best guardians of Muslim interest. Further, Sir Syed's thinking was that not only were the interests of both Hindus and Muslims divergent but also actually hostile, and, therefore, they could not live side by side. Since the Muslim communalists took up basically loyalist position, the colonial authorities, in turn, actively encouraged and fostered these elements.

It is to be noted that it was not religion which divided Hindus and Muslims politically but the government jobs. However, according to Ram Gopal, in the beginning nothing alienated the two communities towards each other as did the Hindi-Urdu controversy of 1883, but in the ultimate analysis, jobs were the cause of differences over languages and scripts etc.

After the partition of Bengal and Swadeshi agitation and the Morley-Minto Reforms, when it became impossible to keep Muslims totally passive politically, the Muslim League was founded in 1906 by a group of landed magnates, ex-bureaucrats and other upper class Muslims as a loyalist and conservative political organisation. Practically it was a "government party". To start with, the Muslim League raised the slogan of special Muslim interests, specially in government services and legislatures "The Agha Khan led Muslim deputation's Memorandum to Lord Minto in 1906 emphasized the need to adapt democratic representative institutions to Indian social, religious and political conditions, otherwise their adoption was likely to place Muslim interests at the mercy of an unsympathetic majority. The logic of this position was to lead inexorably to separatism or secessionism, for if self-government and democracy led to permanent Hindu domination and perpetual maltreatment of Muslims, the only viable denouement could be dependence on British power and its perpetuations to protect the minorities or creation of two religion based separate homelands."[7] But the latter being out of question at the turn of the century the Muslim communalists of the time preferred and supported the British rule. However, by 1911, the Muslim League increasingly came under the influence of younger men oriented towards nationalism and Congress, who were opposed to the loyalist and slavish mentality obtaining in the organisation.

In 1916 came the Lucknow Pact which brought the Congress and the League closer to each other. Some young Muslim nationalists also joined the Congress and condemned the Montford Reforms of 1918.

The years between 1918 and 1922 were years of Hindu-Muslim unity and, therefore, intense national struggle was launched during this period. The Muslim League was overshadowed by the Khilafat Committee, the vanguard of Muslim community at that time, which was associated with the Non-coopertion Movement.

But after the withdrawal of the Non-cooperation Movement in 1922 the people found themselves "all dressed up and nowhere to go," and thus a favourable condition was created for the rise of communal forces. The Muslim League was revived. But now it was cleansed of nationalist elements, and the upper class leadership again came to the fore. In late 1920s the League was split on the question of boycott of the Simon Commission. But subsequently, all Muslim communalists opposed the Civil Disobedience Movement of 1930-31. Later on, they fully cooperated with the British government during the Round Table Conference in early 1930s. At the Second Round Table Conference they joined hands with reactionary sections of the British ruling class and foiled all attempts by Gandhi to solve the communal problem. During the Third Round Table Conference, the Agha Khan, the poet Iqbal and the historian Shafaat Ahmed Khan stressed "the inherent impossibility of securing any merger of Hindu-Muslim political or indeed social interests."

By 1935 the Muslim League had sunk into relative insignificance because of the death of some of its stalwarts. As a result most of the young Muslim intellectuals were attracted by the Congress, the Congress Socialist Party or the Communist Party. But the League was revived with the return of Mr. M.A. Jinnah, who reorganised the Party. In 1936, it tried to widen its social base among the lower-middle classes and the youth. As a strategic measure, however, the communalists had to adopt a more independent stance vis-a-vis colonialism. Nevertheless, the policy of collaboration with colonial authorities continued in more indirect forms. As a matter of fact, the edge of communal politics was now directed entirely against the Congress. Jinnah and the League carried on a large scale vilification campaign against the Congress and tried to identify it as a Hindu organisation.

With the advent of the Second World War, when the end of British rule became inevitable, the Muslim communalists were driven to adopt the idea of Pakistan and the two-nation theory in its support. Thus the League provided the British with their main, and in the end the only, justification for staying on in India. The colonial authorities held that they could not discuss the question of independence till the Congress and the League came to an agreement.

During the Second World War, when the Congress came into confrontation with the government, the League leadership permitted its members to support the War efforts. Jinnah hinted to the Viceroy that "a firm hand with the Congress would receive his support."

In 1940s, while the Congress was demanding an immediate declaration of independence, the League put forward the demand that no declaration regarding constitutional advance be made without the prior approval of the two major communities. Later on, it made the acceptance of Pakistan as a pre-condition for any constitutional advancement. Thus "the League enabled the British government to escape the dilemma by hiding behind the facade of communal disagreement."[8] At the same time the Muslim League denounced the Quit India Movement (1942) as being directed not so much against the British as against Muslims. The League also took support of the colonial rulers to install League ministries in Bengal, Sind and the North Western Frontier Province.

Throughout the period 1937-47 its only political movement was organised on 16 August 1946 when it observed Direct Action Day to achieve its ultimate goal — Pakistan. In fact, it was a sort of declaration of a Civil War, a development whose denouement was the division of the country.

Tracing the growth of Muslim communalism, Ram Gopal writes in metaphorical terms: "As a river is small at its source and swells on its journey towards its destination with its tributaries, so did Muslim communal politics, starting from a humble beginning, develop into a turbulent stream. Its tributaries were the use of Muslim communalism by the British rulers as a shield against rising nationalism and the counter-communalism of Hindus."[9]

GROWTH OF HINDU COMMUNALISM

Like Muslim communalism, Hindu communalism, too, was loyalist from the beginning. Its proponents too advocated cooperation with the colonial regime with a view to get concessions for the Hindus. Of course, it was less open and more circumspect in its loyalist instance.

Hindu communalism made an indirect beginning in the 1880s and 1890s with a vigorous cow protection movement, which was really directed against the Muslims. The pro-colonial and anti-Congress line of Hindu communal politics was laid down in 1909 by one of the first theoreticians of Hindu communalism. Founder of the Punjab Hindu Sabha, (1909) Rai Bahadur Lal Chand, attacked the Congress in his booklet 'Self Abnegation In Politics'. He described the Congress as the "self-inflicted misfortune". His main charge against the Congress was that it appeased Muslims and refused to protect Hindu interests.[10]

But Hindu communalism failed to consolidate itself before 1918, suffered a setback during 1918-22, and took off in an organised form only in 1923 when an all-India session of the Hindu Maha Sabha was held for the first time. For a long time the Hindu Maha Sabha was the chief communal organisation of the Hindus. It was a counterpart of the Muslim League and stood for the Hindu community. It was set up in 1923 with the object of uniting the Hindus of India on a common platform for the protection and promotion of their culture. The factors behind the emergence of the Hindu Maha Sabha were : Firstly, it was realised that the proselytising activities of the Muslims and Christians were having a largely adverse effect on the political power of the Hindus. Secondly, the Hindus suffered more losses in property and human lives than other communities in riots that followed the suspension of the Non-Cooperation Movement. It became therefore necessary to organise the Hindus for self-defence. Shudhi and Sangthan became the watchword of the Hindu Maha Sabha. Thirdly, the Muslim League was putting forth more and more aggressive demands and they were receiving the support of the British authorities. Since the Indian National Congress could not take up a strong attitude against such demands Hindus decided to organise themselves. But it never achieved the same backing of Hindu masses as the League did of the Muslims.

The advent of V.D. Savarkar wrought a great change in the character of the Maha Sabha. It developed a political programme and began to give a lead to the Hindus on political questions. Himself a theist and a rationalist, Savarkar became the High priest and theoretician of the Hindu community. He preached the doctrine of Hindu ascendancy and asserted that the politics of India must be Hindu politics. He told the Muslims that they must be content with the status of a minority community in a democratic state which orders life on the principle of majority rule. To quote Nehru, "After 1936 the Maha Sabha became as aggressively communal as the League but tried to cover up its extreme narrowness of outlook by using some kind of national terminology. The Maha Sabha was opposed to the Congress ideal of India to be a secular state and stood for Hindu Rashtra. Its aim was the maintenance, protection and promotion of the Hindu race, Hindu culture and Hindu civilisation and the advancement of the glory of Hindu Rashtra. As against the League demand for Pakistan, it gave the slogan of Akhand Bharat.

The Hindu Maha Sabha was one important factor which was responsible to a very large extent for the emergence of the idea of partition of India on communal lines. Interestingly, it was V.D. Savarkar who first propounded the two-nation theory in 1923 in his book, 'Hindutva' and reiterated it in his presidential address in 1937. Jinnah first propounded it in an article in 'Time and Tide' of March 9, 1940, and exactly a fortnight later came the League's Pak Resolution.

Like the Hindu Maha Sabha, another communal body, the Rashtriya Swayam Sevak Sangh, was founded by Baliram Hedgewar in 1925. In a few years it began to emerge as a major communal force. Its chief, Guru M.S. Golwalkar, wrote a book entitled 'We — Our Nation Defined'. It was based on Rashtra Mimansha by Baba Rao Savarkar and was published in 1939. In this book, Guru Golwalkar writes: "Hindustan is the land of the Hindus and is the terra firma for the Hindu Nation alone to flourish upon." He further adds that "minorities must live by the grace of the majority, only a Hindu could be a true Indian, those whose faith did not originate in the subcontinent were foreigners. The foreign races in Hindustan (Muslims, Christians, Jews and Parsis) would have to adopt the Hindu culture and language, must learn to respect and hold in reverence Hindu religion, must entertain no idea but the glorification of the Hindu race and culture, as of the Hindu nation, and must lose their separate existence to merge in the Hindu race, or may stay in the country, wholly subordinated to the Hindu nation, claiming nothing, deserving no privileges, far less any preferential treatment not even citizens' rights."[11] In this country Hindus alone are the nation, and the Muslims and others if not actively anti-national, are at least outside the body of the nation. However, such Hindu fundamentalism, long the thrust of a section of the middle class, has never got much response. Though their communalism could masquerade as nationalism, these Hindu communal organisations remained basically within the loyalist at least non-national framework. For instance, Savarkar made an appeal to Hindus, like Mr. Jinnah, to participate in all war efforts of the British government.

Undoubtedly, once the two communalisms developed, they promoted each other in geometrical progression. To quote Mehta and Patwardhan,

"Each has provided the raison detre and the stimulus needed for the other."[12] Their exploitation of each other had a snow ball effect. A special case of this mutual communal reaction was the two-nation theory. After 1936, Both Savarkar and Jinnah asserted that Hindus and Muslims were two separate nations. The two assertions reinforced each-other and created conditions for the emergence of separatism. Although, it is wrong to say that either communalism arose as a reaction to the other, the existence of Hindu communalism and its aggressive propaganda, along with the Hindu tinge in much of the national movement were contributory factors in the failure of the national movement to overcome Muslim communalism.[13]

While making the assessment of the two communalisms Prof. Rasheeduddin Khan observes "While all communalism is bad, majority communalism is worse." Quoting Nehru he says that "it is more dangerous than the minority communalism," for it is the majority community that determines the ethos of a nationalism. Communalism of the majority can pass off as nationalism itself, because it is pervasive, dominant and with deeper historical roots and a greater range of commonalties. It is capable of focussing on the many symbols of the past, of drawing sustenance from the basic structure of traditions, customs, conventions, festivities etc."[14] Prof. Bipan Chandra goes a step further when he writes ('World Focus'— Feb-March 1995): "While Muslim Communalism is rampant and is dangerous to both Muslims and the Indian polity, it is Hindu Communalism which poses the main danger, the fascist danger, to the people."

ROLE OF MAJOR FACTORS IN THE GROWTH OF COMMUNALISM

ROLE OF IDEOLOGICAL, SOCIAL AND CULTURAL ELEMENTS: According to Bipan Chandra, a large number of ideological, social and cultural elements contributed to the rise and growth of communalism in India. They were often in the nature of mechanisms and supportive conditions which promoted it.. Some of them also served as instruments and channels for the spread of communalisms. Some were basic constituents of communal ideology. However, Communal consciousness or its different constituents do not explain communalism; they are not its causes. But to argue that these ideological, social and cultural factors are not causative in nature is not to suggest that they do not play an important role in the rise and growth of communalism. All that is meant is that in the absence of social causation they could not have brought communalism into being.[15]

A major factor in the growth of communal consciousness was the slow rate at which the national consciousness developed and spread in the country. There were certain weaknesses in the anti-colonial political, economic, social and cultural programme evolved by the Indian leadership. More particular and concrete was the failure to organise and politically educate the Muslim lower-middle classes and masses by showing them through concrete programmes that the communal identity was false one while the national and class identities were real. In general, the nationalists did not organise an active political and ideological struggle against communalism. Thus "communalism in India was a sort of punishment for the failure to wage a correct and consistent ideological and political struggle for the spread of national and class consciousness."[16]

Furthermore, the spread of modern secular culture and scientific outlook had to be based on an active effort. For it could not occur automatically — 'in course of time' — as was believed by certain mechanical materialists. Communal ideology, once initiated, would develop on is own steam unless actively opposed. Once developed it could not be appeased, it had to be opposed. In fact, "Congress failed to evolve a viable and effective strategy to combat communalism at the ideological and cultural level."[17]

Besides, the economic and social insecurity bred among several sections of Indian society by colonialism and capitalism was conducive to the growth of irrational ideology. These feelings of uncertainty and insecurity were deepened in the 1930s and 1940s because of Great Depression (1929-32), World War-II, runaway inflation, and political uncertainty. The communal outfits naturally exploited these feelings to promote their cause of separatism.

"The strong Hindu tinge in much of the nationalist thought, propaganda and agitation and their permeation through ideas associated with Hindu religion, in spite of the basically secular approach and programme of the Congress, tended to repel and alienate Muslims instinctively."[18] This was particularly true of the strong Hindu religious element in the Extremists thought and propaganda from 1905 to 1909. Many of the Extremists identified nationalism with the revival of Hinduism, talked of Indian culture in terms of ancient Indian culture to the exclusion of medieval Indian (composite) culture and of the unity of India in terms of the unity of Hindus and saw nationalism as a religion-Hinduism. In other words, they tried to provide a Hindu ideological underpinning to Indian nationalism or at least a Hindu idiom to its political agitation.

Leaders like Arubindo Ghosh, Bipin Chandra Pal, Lala Lajpat Rai, etc. used Hindu symbols, idioms and myths in their political speeches and writings. B.G. Tilak, also, encouraged the growth of the Hindu tinge in Indian nationalism with his propagation of Ganesh Puja and Shivaji Festival with their Hindu religious overtones. India was often referred to by these leaders as Mother Goddess or compared with Kali, Durga, etc. Even early revolutionary terrorists swore by the Gita and Kali. Naturally, "this Hindu tinge", as Abid Hussain observes, "created general unrest, panic and doubt and an atmosphere of fear and suspicion." Highlighting this feeling on the part of Muslims, Maulana Mohd. Ali wrote in 'Comrade' (1912): "With the loss of empire the conservative Muslim felt as if he were to lose his self-respect as well. "The 'communal patriots' amongst the Hindus treated him as a prisoner in the dock, and loudly complained of him as an impossible factor in the scheme of India's future."[19] One result of the Hindu tinge was that a large number of educated Muslims remained aloof from the national movement or became hostile to it.

Gandhi's use of religious terms and symbols made its own contribution in this respect. Though he was secular, his political thought was couched in the language of religiosity. His motives of "spiritualising politics" and "inner voice" also tended to create a religious aura around politics. His secularism, in fact, came to represent the confluence of several religiosities or what Mohd. Ali described as "federation of religions". Gandhi's approach was paralleled, for example, by Maulana Azad who, in his early years, simultaneously promoted nationalism and religious fervour among Muslims. Perhaps they failed to understand that religion as understood by the common man could never become a unifying force or influence.

Unlike Italy and Greece, India is a multi-religious and multi-cultural country. Hence here "nationalism had to be projected as a new historical phenomenon, not the concept of the restoration of a past nationhood but that of the development of the new nation in the making had to be stressed and propagated."[20]

In India therefore simultaneously with modern mass politics, it was necessary and urgent to have a cultural revolution (as M.N. Roy suggested in the late forties) or complete modernisation which would incorporate the humanist and rational elements of the traditional culture. This was also necessary in order to strike at the popular roots of revivalism, communalism and obscurantism.

Here, of course, a sharp distinction has to be made between religious consciousness and communalism. The use of religious myths, symbols, idioms, etc. was not communalism though, yet it created space, or kept an opening, for communalism and weakened defences against it.

Although other factors were equally responsible for the growth of communalism, the intrusion of religious consciousness into nationalism, immensely contributed to the growth of communalism in India. Therefore, it must be admitted that the very strength of Indian nationalism; that is, its heavy reliance on Hindu culture and Hindu symbolism, proved its greatest weakness. Indian nationalism was often mistaken for Hindu nationalism and hence failed to integrate and pacify Muslim community.

ROLE OF RELIGION: It is generally believed that since many religions exist in India the underlying cause or reason for the rise of communalism can be attributed to religion. According to a recent writer, Gopal Krishna, "The proposition that the root of political polarisation in India was the religious antipathy between Hindus and Muslims command greater acceptance today." Almost in a similar vein, Prof. Rasheeduddin Khan also maintains that communalism was and is inevitable in a plural society marked by the existence of different religions. He means to say that a plural society cannot escape from communalism. "In a plural society there are deep cleavages, communities adhere to different pasts and pursue different destinies. They struggle continuously to carve out sphere of autonomy, to restrict the role of the state, to build contractual relationships with the state and other communities, and to acquire an effective share for themselves in the power structures."[21] But Prof. Bipan Chandra does not agree with such thought, According to him, while religious differences were real, they were not as such the cause of communal division. Communalism in modern times was not inspired by religion nor was religion the end or object of communal politics.[22]

It is necessary in this respect to distinguish between religion as an ideology or a belief system (which is not communalism) and the ideology of religious identity (which is communalism). According to Bipan Chandra "Religion was neither the cause nor the end of communalism, it was only its vehicle."[23] Another writer of leftist leaning, Prof. P.C. Joshi, also maintains that in order "to understand communalism one must go outside the sphere of religion and explore the spheres of economics and politics."[24]

Apart from the ideology of religious identity, the Hindus' tendency towards social exclusiveness made its own contribution towards the growth of communalism. The relative social gap or lack of social contact among urban Hindus and Muslims contributed to the spread of communalism.

ROLE OF HISTORY: "A communal and distorted unscientific view of Indian history, specially of its ancient and medieval periods, was both a major instrument for the spread of communal consciousness and also a basic constituent of communal ideology as also its product."[25] In fact, it would be no exaggeration to suggest that communal interpretation of history has been the main ideology of communalism in India. This interpretation has put history to political use. Both Hindu as well as Muslim communalists used the communal interpretation of history to create an atmosphere of fear, passion, propaganda and hatred. The Hindu communalists created the myth of Muslim tyranny among Hindus. To illustrate, Golwalkar wrote in his 'Bunch of Thoughts "The history of the past one thousand two hundred years is full of incidents of destruction, depredation and all sorts of barbaric atrocities." Similarly, the Muslim communalists harked back to the Golden Age of Islamic achievement in West Asia and appealed to its heroes, myths and cultural traditions. They also evoked their own version of the 'fall' theory. Likewise, the Hindu communalists tried to locate the 'golden period' of Indian history in the ancient past and attributed its decline to the advent of Islam in India. If Muslims of India were always aware of their past glory, Hindus too could not forget or overcome their sense of hurt and humiliation of having been governed by Muslim rulers for about a millennium. In both the cases the past remained a constant companion to their perception of the present. To quote Mohd. Ali, "The past had flung out its dead hands to paralyse the present." Prof. K.K. Aziz, in this context, observes: "Soon after the revolt of 1857 two sentiments began to agitate the Muslim mind. There was a fear of Hindu rule whom they ruled for several centuries and a feeling of separatedness from other Indians."[26] Moin Shakir has also emphasized that "Muslims in general have consistently been conscious of their separate identity because of historical reasons."[27]

Prof. Bipan Chandra, however, refutes the theory of 'historical antagonism' between Hindus and Muslims put forth by these writers. Of course, he accepts the fact that some ill-will did exist between Hindus and Muslims in the beginning of the Muslim rule in India. But at the same time, as he maintains, it is also a fact that the two communities had evolved an attractive pattern of cooperation, not unmixed naturally with occasional notes of discord.

ROLE OF BRITISH RULERS: Our nationalist writers have generally maintained that communalism was essentially a product of British policy and that Britain deliberately created division in society for their own imperial purposes. According to Mahatma Gandhi, "Hindu-Muslim quarrel is coeval with the British advent, and he believed, though naively, that the "iceberg of communal differences will melt under the warmth of the sun of freedom." But, on the other hand, his own grandson, Raj Mohan Gandhi, maintains: "Our study does not show that the Raj created the Hindu-Muslim divide. Though often acting wrongly, Britain was not the author of India's division."[28] According to Maulana Mohd. Ali, "The truth was that we divide and they rule." Though both the views have some element of truth, it cannot be denied that the British were quite apprehensive about the combined strength of Hindus and Muslims. Hence, "British imperialism from the very beginning operationalised its 'divide and rule' policy by compartmentalising all important aspects in Indian life along communal lines; for example, election through communal electorate, denominational institutions and communal reservation, etc."[29]

The British perception that Hindus and Muslims were two mutually antagonistic monoliths, a notion not rooted in facts, became an important basis for distribution of shares in power and resources. Lord Dufferin was one of the first Viceroys to encourage Muslims to regard themselves as a distinct political entity in India. Colonial administration increasingly saw India as "a country of unintegrated communities" or a congregation of different communities. The next Viceroy to adopt this divisive strategy was Lord Curzon. "In 1904 he told the Muslims that he would help them create a centre of power in Dacca which would invest them in eastern Bengal with a unity not enjoyed since the days of the old Muslim Viceroys and Kings."[30] No wonder in 1905, Curzon partitioned the province of Bengal to create a division between the two communities. Lord Minto also referred to the Muslim Deputationists "as the descendants of a conquering and ruling race." "If the deputation was not a 'command performance' it was guaranteed box office success in advance."[31] The manner in which communal electorate and the League came into existence highlighted the working of the British policy of counterpoise and its method of setting one community against the other. Lord Minto apprehended that a joint electorate would bring into the Legislature younger Muslims of advanced views and not the conservative, upper class Muslims. No doubt, the system of separate electorate was powerful instrument for the development of communal politics in India. Similarly, the system of reservation and weightage in representation to minority also generated communalism. To be sure, separate electorate had a disastrous effect on the process of national integration. In fact, the natural corollary to separate electorate was separate homeland.

Like Minto, Morley also entertained the same view about the two communities. Speaking in the House of Lords (1909) he said: "The differences between Muslims and Hindus is not a mere difference of articles of religious faith it is a difference in life, in tradition, in history in all the social things as well as articles of belief that constitute a community."

In 1926, Lord Irwin also referred to "Hindus and Muslims as two distinct and highly organised societies."

In 1930, the Report of the Simon Commission referred to this basic opposition between the two communities. At the Round Table Conference where the Report was presented the entire discussion was organised within the ambit of communal digits thereby making any solution of the basic problem of political advance impossible. The Joints Select Committee on Indian Constitution (1934) went even further: "Hindus and Muslims may be said indeed to represent two distinct separate civilisations." British officials also constantly egged on the Muslim community to stick to the track and run the full course. The logic of the pledge of August Offer (1940) was taken to its conclusion in March 1942, when the Cripps proposal implicitly conceded the demand for Pakistan on the basis of two-nation theory.

Thus, British rule and British policy are not in anyway less responsible for the growth of communalism in modern India. The British encouraged it and helped it reach the monstrous proportions that it ultimately did in 1946-47 leading to partition.[32] Ofcourse, British imperialism did not create Muslim communalism but it did accentuate and utilise it in pursuance of its divide and rule strategy with a view to perpetuate its domination over India. However, the policy of divide and rule was complex and subtle. British administration did not support a particular community or communalism for the love of that community. The official support to Muslim communalism was a part not of an anti-Hindu policy but of an anti-nationalist policy. The effect of this policy first became manifest in the reorganisation of the Indian army effected after the Rebellion of 1857. Outside the army, effect was given to the policy of divide and rule encouraging the one and suppressing the other community by turn.

The British fostered communalism in three ways: (1) By official policies of divide et impera; (2) By legislating separate electorate; and (3) By introducing Western values leading to cultural resurgence and revivalism in both communities. After 1937, the British shifted from balanced to uncontrolled communalism, encouraged total division, gave opens support to the Muslim League, and after 1939 allowed it a virtual veto on the constitutional advance. After the 1937 elections the communal card alone was available for playing against the national movement, and the rulers declared to use it to the limit. But the commitment to Muslim communalism became total only after 1939. Muslim leaders who opposed the nationalist claim to speak for all were courted as political allies.

The British also encouraged communalism through non-action against it. For instance, the period from 1923 to 1926 marked the worst years of communal violence before the horrible holocaust of 1946, but because of its policy of 'masterly inactivity' it refused to curb those activities which promoted discord and breach of peace through legislation, as was proposed by some Central Assembly members.

The same differential policy was followed in the sensitive area of writing and teaching of History. For instance, historians with imperial and communal outlook were encouraged while those with nationalist outlook had to suffer in every way.

In the end, communalism served as the chief social prop of colonial rule. It was one of the major political and ideological media through which mutual dependence and interaction between colonialism and those classes and strata who gained out of it, were established.

However, the genesis of communalism cannot be explained by the British policy of "divide and rule" alone. Many other factors like nature of democratic politics, capitalist economy, shift from feudal to colonial structure of power and society among others. On the basis of above discussion, it can be elicited that religious rigidity, cultural identity, political desire for power, minority consciousness, economic competition, historical events, the role of colonial power played a significant role in creating communal cleavage in the country.

ROLE OF NATIONAL MOVEMENT: The greatest misfortune of the Indian national movement was that it miserably failed to meet the challenge of communalism. It utterly failed to evolve a viable, effective strategy to combat communalism. Its approach to the problem of communalism suffered from several drawbacks:[33] Firstly, a vigorous political and ideological struggle against communalism and its feeders — religiosity, caste, social distance, the Hindu tinge in nationalist thought, the communal interpretation of history, obscurantism, etc. was not carried out. The Congress leaders, though sturdy secularists, were not able to take an effective and vigorous line of action to oppose the rising tide of communal forces or to protect their own rank from penetration by elements of communal ideology. Despite their commitment to secularism and despite Gandhi's constant emphasis on Hindu-Muslim unity and even his willingness to stake his life for its promotion and despite Nehru's brilliant analysis of the socio-economic roots of communalism, the Indian nationalists failed to wage a mass ideological-political struggle against all forms of communalism. No mass campaign of the type carried out against colonialism was organised against communalism, even at the purely political level. The need was to direct the debate with the communalist into hard, rational, analytical channels, so that the latter were forced to fight on the terrain of reason and science and not of emotion and bias. Furthermore, the "unity at the top" strategy contained another built-in mechanism to promote community-wise thinking among the political leaders invited in Hindu-Muslim talks. By negotiating with communal leaders, the Congress legitimised their politics and invested the communalist with greater importance and prestige. Even the Muslim mass contact programme under the initiative of Nehru was ill-planned and ill-organised and never sincerely implemented.

Secondly, the Congress leaders in general and Nehru and the left in particular, suffered from a certain mechanical and simplistic approach and an economistic and deterministic bias in their treatment of the problem. They began to neglect the fight against communalism at the ideological plane. But ideological struggle was as important as national or economic. The ideological-educational work leading to change in the thinking and culture of the people was never taken in right earnest.

Thirdly, they ignored he fact that India was not yet a fully structured nation. There was nothing like deep national consciousness among the people. They failed to realise that in a plural society like India there are deep cleavages and communities adhere to different pasts and pursue different destinies.

Fourthly, there was no deep comprehension of communalism in all its complexity and opacity- its ideology, its sources and roots, its social base, reasons for its growth. Even Gandhi's understanding of communalism was shallow and superficial. The unity of the Indian people would be the result of the efforts of two simultaneous phenomena: common struggle of the people for their common real interests and aims based in part on a common outlook and the evolution of a common understanding of their social condition, based in part on common struggle.

Since communalism was a petty bourgeois phenomenon par excellence, the real answer lay in all-out opposition to communalism in arenas — ideological, cultural, social and political — and in a greater shift from the national movement's social and ideological base from the petty bourgeoisie to the masses of peasants and workers. A significant change in the orientation of the ideology and politics of the middle class would therefore have had an immediate and compounded impact on politics as a whole.

Retrospectively speaking, the way out of the communal morass lay in the long term political struggle and ideological strategy and not in an instant solution at any particular political juncture. Certainly no such solution existed at the moment of partition. As a matter of fact, there is never any instant solution to a social problem like communalism. To look for such an instant solution while ignoring the past, the present interconnections is to indulge in false comfort, vain hope and futile romanticism.

To summarise, communalism and its growth were products of Indian social, economic and political developments and conditions during the 19th and 20th centuries. Economic backwardness, interests of the semi-feudal, jagirdar classes and strata, the precarious condition of the middle class, social cleavage within Indian society, its heterogenous and multifaceted cultural character and the ideological — political weakness of the nationalist force all combined to promote communalism or to weaken the struggle against it. Consequently, a multisided, multicausal understanding of the complex Indian reality and the struggle to change it were needed.

But, above all, the social framework for the growth of communalism was provided by the colonial economy and polity. Colonialism was the foundation of the social structure which generated and then propelled forward communal ideology and politics. While many other aspects of the Indian social condition helped the growth of communalism, it was the logic of the economic, political, cultural and ideological system structured by colonialism that created the space for the growth of communalism. This logic was of course supplemented by colonial policy, which in turn fully exploited the conditions produced by colonialism itself as also other weaknesses of Indian society.[34] Therefore, no real or long term success in the struggle against communalism was possible without economic, political, social and cultural transformation and development. Since communalism was based on a false consciousness, on a wrong understanding of reality, changing the reality was an essential part of the struggle against all forms of false consciousness, including communalism.

FORMS AND PHASES OF COMMUNALISM IN INDIA

There was hardly any communalism in India before the last quarter of the 19th century. As is well known, Hindus and Muslims fought shoulder to shoulder in the Revolt of 1857. But from 1870, a section of Hindu zamindars, money lenders and middle class professionals began to arouse anti-Muslim sentiments. They talked of the tyrannical Muslim rule and liberating role of the Britishers. Subsequently, the rise of nationalism and the resultant introduction of democratic institutions in India in the last quarter of the 19th century was accompanied by the emergence of communalism as a political phenomenon. About democratic elections, Sir Syed Ahmed said: "It would be like a game of dice in which one man had four dice and the other only one, and he began to speak of Muslims being a separate race." This was the beginning of Muslim communalism in India.

Indian communalism passed through three different stages or took three forms:[35] (1) Communal or Sectarian Nationalism (2) Liberal Communalism and (3) Extreme Communalism.

COMMUNAL NATIONALISM: In the first stage communal or Sectarian nationalists were persons who saw themselves as nationalist Hindus, nationalist Muslims, nationalist Sikhs and not as simple nationalists. In fact, communalism of this phase was no communalism at all. It was represented by Mohd. Ali Jinnah, Maulana Hussain Ahmed Madani, Mazharul Haq, Maulana Mohd. Ali, Hakim Ajmal Khan, Lala Lajpat Rai, Madan Mohan Malviya, Sardar Kharak Singh, etc.

LIBERAL COMMUNALISM: Communalism entered a second stage in the beginning of the twentieth century, when communalism proper made an appearance. These communalists may be described as Liberal Communalists. Liberal communalists believed that different communal interests could be accommodated and brought into harmony within the overall developing national interest, and India built as a nation. They demanded separate communal rights, safeguards, reservations, etc. within the broad conception of one Indian nation in the making. It was represented by Altaf Hussain Hali, Ali Brothers, Mohd. Ali Jinnah, M.M. Malviya, Lala Lajpat Rai and N.C. Kelkar. Most of the communalists remained at the second liberal stage till 1937 when it started taking virulent extremist form.

EXTREME COMMUNALISM: Communalists of the third stage argued that the secular interests of different communities were not only different but mutually antagonistic. Moreover, communalism of this stage was based on fear and hatred, declaring that their culture was in danger. Extreme communalists believed in separatism and two-nation theory. Savarkar and Jinnah belong to this category.

Though the three stages of communalism were different from one-another, they also interacted and provided a certain continuance. For instance, M.A. Jinnah's political career spanned all the three phases, and he actually hoped to revert to the liberal phase, as indicated by his 11 August, 1947 speech.

COMMUNAL PROBLEM IN POST-INDEPENDENCE INDIA

Communalism and communal type movements and ideology are still very much with us even today, partition of the country notwithstanding. Indian society continues to provide objective social, economic and political bases as also ideological and cultural soil for the rise and growth of such movements. Since the late 1950's the country has been repeatedly raked by a spate of communal, regional, linguistic and caste riots. Moreover, communal and caste approaches are being increasingly used on a large scale for electoral as well as non-electoral political mobilisation of the people.[36]

The problem of communalism, however, is a long term problem which requires an intense and complex struggle on the political front and in the realm of ideas. The need to develop a powerful ideological movement against communalism, casteism, linguism and regionalism remains as urgent as ever. But there is no reason to despair, for the secular, rational, liberal, democratic and humanitarian elements are not weak in India. Yet they have to be brought together on a common platform and made effective. But unless social reality is changed and intense and wide ranging political and ideological struggle waged against communal and communal type parties, movements and ideologies, the divisive forces will continue to impede the process of national integration and unity.

India still requires a vigorous effort for national integration. That India is a full fledged nation should not be taken for granted. A genuine "national integration is possible only by practising what is called "honest secularism", not "permissive communalism", by a due recognition of the plural nature of the Indian society and by a nuanced management of inter-community relations."[37]

To conclude, though communalism may be contained by adopting several safeguards and measures, as suggested in the preceding pages, it can be effectively countered only by a correlated cultural process which would imply a firm rejection of obscurantist and orthodox tenets which act as fetters to the development of a modern, scientific and rational outlook. In short, Communalism should be fought on three fronts - ideological, cultural and political.

Notes

1. See Chandra, Bipan, Preface to Communalism In Modern India, op. cit,
2. singh, Amrik, Mainstream, 19 May, 1987.
3. Chandra, Bipan, op.cit, p. 29
4. Ibid., p.34
5. Nehru's Presidential Address, 1936.
6. Shakir, Moin, op. cit, p. 272
7. Chandra, Bipan, op.cit, p.92
8. Ibid., p.109
9. Gopal, Ram, op.cit, preface, p.VIII
10. Chandra, Bipan, op.cit, pp.111-12
11. Golwalkar, M.S., We or Our Nation Defined, (1939) pp. 47-48.
12. Mehta, A. and Patwardhan, A., The Communal Triangle In India, p.181
13. Chandra, Bipan, op.cit, p.208

14. Khan, Rasheeduddin, 'Fundamentalism And Communalism,', World Focus, Nov-Dec., 1993, p.25.

15. Chandra, Bipan, op.cit, 122.

16. Ibid., p.125

17. Ibid., p.130

18. Ibid., p.141

19. Ali, Mohd., Selected writings and Speeches, pp.66-67.

20. Chandra, Bipan, op.cit, p.152.

21. Krishna, Gopal, National Integration- Nehru's Failure 1988

22. Chandra, Bipan, op.cit, p.159.

23. Ibid., p.160

24. Joshi, P.C., The Economic Background of Communalism in India — A Model of Analyis, p.171

25. Chandra, Bipan, op.cit, p.209.

26. Aziz, K.K., op.cit, Prologue, pp.1-4

27. Shakir, Moin, op.cit, p.272

28. Gandhi, Ram Mohan, Eight Great Lives, Roli Books Pvt.Ltd. 1986, N. Delhi, p. 315

29. Raza, Moonis, Communalism In Contemporary India, Mainstream, 29 Jan. 1994.

30. Quoted in Gopal, Sarvapalli, British Policy In India, (1858-1905), p.271.

31. Peter, Hardy, quoted in Chandra, Bipan, op.cit, p.266

32. Chandra, Bipan, op.cit, p.237

33. Ibid., pp. 296-306.

34. Ibid. p.292.

35. Ibid. (Appendix) pp. 321-41.

36. Ibid., (Prospect) p.310

37. Krishna, Gopal, 'National Integration Not a Lost Cause', Times of India, Dec. 1988.

PART-III

ARCHITECTS OF
INDIA'S FREEDOM

ARCHITECTS OF
INDIA'S FREEDOM AND
GUILTY MEN OF PARTITION

AN INTRODUCTION

The story of India's freedom struggle is studded with a galaxy of outstanding leaders, and laced with a large number of legendary or larger-than-life personalities. Perhaps, no other nation can boast of having such an array of towering titans in its freedom struggle thus making the story of India's freedom struggle read like an epic.

History, as we know, requires repeated rereading from generation to generation, for distance lends detachment and perspective. The present moment offers us an opportunity to be more objective not only because it is nearly fifty years since independence but also because many of the ideological shibboleths and slogans that determined the era of freedom struggle have become redundant. Now it is possible to take a more dispassionate view of events and ideas.

This part of the book, therefore, is an attempt to make a reassessment of our freedom fighters and to reexamine their role and contributions, both positive and negative, in the light of new researches and writings and also with the advantage of hindsight wisdom.

Our study begins with Raja Ram Mohan Roy (even though he died long before the birth of the Indian National Congress), who is acknowledged as the vanguard of our freedom struggle and who is also credited with laying the foundations of modern life of India, and ends with M.N. Roy, another great leader from Bengal, who (although he survived the freedom movement) is yet to find a place among the celebrated pantheon of great patriots of India, although both as a man of thought as well as of action, his contribution is next to none and who has contributed immensely to the political scenario of India's freedom struggle.

Chapter 22

RAJA RAM MOHAN ROY
—THE FATHER OF INDIAN
RENAISSANCE (1772-1883)

By the end of the eighteenth century and the beginning of the nineteenth century India was emerging from the medieval period of the Mughal rule into a modern nation. There was a wave of cultural and social revival, influenced by Western thought which was being initiated by men of modern outlook though still rooted in Indian tradition.[1] The pioneer among them was the great religious and social reformer, Raj Ram Mohan Roy.

Ram Mohan Roy has been rightly regarded as the pioneer of. the modern age in Indian history, and the father of Indian renaissance. Ram Mohan was gifted with a critical mind and a towering intellect. A refined intellectual, a genius and versatile, he was keen to remove such social, cultural and material obstacles which stood in the way of human progress and self-expression.

He took up first the task of religious reform. He began his mission with a study of comparative religions. As a result of the experiences of his early life spent in the midst of orthodox Hindu traditions, the study of Hindu Shastras at Benaras, the study of Islamic and Christian theology, he developed a cosmopolitan outlook and came to visualise the necessity of an Universal Religion. In 1803, he wrote, Tuhfat-ul Muwahidin' (A Gift To Monotheists), Through this work he suggested a rational approach and outlook to religion, and religious experiences and theology. He insisted on weighing every religious dogma on the scales of reason. He started a movement against misunderstood and misinterpreted scriptual and sacredotal authority in religion. He was bold enough to say that "falsehood is common to all religions without distinction", thus demolishing the dogmatic structure of all religions. He was equally critical of Hindus' polytheism, Christians' belief in the Trinity and Muslims' distrust of nonbelievers or "Kafirs." In short, he was an iconoclast. As such, he opposed all types of religious rituals, dogmas and beliefs in miracles. Being a cosmopolitan religious thinker, he stressed on the synthesis of all religions — a combination of Vedic cosmic awareness, the Islamic concept of Allah as Universe — the one who sustains all, and Buddhist and Christian compassion.

As a Hindu reformist, Roy tried to bring Hindus back to the purity of ancient Hinduism by making them familiar with the sublime truths of the Upanishads and the Vedanta. He repudiated idol worship, so common among Hindus, and preached religious toleration and catholicity. He wanted a regeneration of old values not for its own shake but to revive self-confidence among the people who, he felt, had lost their cultural roots.

In the social sphere, he advocated the emancipation of women from all sorts of social inequality and preached against early marriage, enforced widowhood and Sati. It was because of his efforts that "Sati Pratha" was abolished by Lord William Bentinck in 1829. He also championed the right of Hindu females to inherit property. He carried on a relentless crusade against polygamy and concubinage, and also worked for the removal of untouchability and the vagaries of the caste system.

Raja Ram Mohan Roy was in the forefront of those who espoused the cause of Western education in India, particularly Science, as against scholastic learning. He was a staunch critic of the old system of education, which was mostly confined to religious scriptures, and instead advocated the western system. He was instrumental for imparting English education to his countrymen. In 1816, he founded the first English School in Calcutta. Again, it was under his inspiration that the Hindu College was established by 1822. He was in favour of promoting a more liberal, enlightened system of instruction that would inculcate a truly scientific spirit among the people. Besides, he was a great supporter of education for women. Being an ardent advocate of freedom for the press, and of liberty of thought and expression, he became a pioneer in journalism by starting the vernacular journal 'Samvad Kaumud'. in 1821.

In the political and administrative fields, he was the forerunner of the Moderates who belonged to the early phase of the Congress (1885-1905). The Brahamo Samaj that he founded in 1828 was the first organised expression of national awakening in India. To quote A.R. Desai, "it inaugurated a new era for the Indian people by proclaiming the principles of individual freedom, national unity, solidarity and collectivism and the democratisation of all social institutions and social relations."[2] Of course, "the Brahamo Samaj was not a political movement, but its rationalism, its universalism, its concept of the 'religion of humanity' and its ideology of the synthesis of the East and the West, prepared the intellectual foundation for future national movement."[3]

However, Raja Ram Mohan Roy was not a "prophet of Swaraj". His writings revealed that in the beginning he disliked the British rule in India but towards the later stage he began to appreciate it. He believed that British rule could lead to the amelioration of the Indian masses. Even though he deplored the draining of India's resources by the British he fully and frankly appreciated the benefits of British rule in India which he regarded as a "divine dispensation". But at the same time, while deposing before the Select Committee of the House of Commons, he pleaded for increasing association of Indians with policy making and participation at the higher level of the administration. His other specific recommendations were the appointment of Indian assessors in the civil courts, appointment of Indian judges, codification of civil and criminal laws, separation of executive from judiciary, reduction in government's expenditure, abolition of the standing army and its replacement by the militia composed of mostly peasants. His ideas of economic reforms included freezing of rents payable to landlords.

ESTIMATE OF RAM MOHAN ROY

Ram Mohan Roy was a remarkable figure with foresight and vision. He was a modern man of his times and symbolised the renascent spirit of new India. As the father of religious and spiritual renaissance, he paved the way for political and national awakening, thus being first to deliver the message of political freedom to India.

Raja Ram Mohan Roy belonged to no sect, as he was a protagonist of universal religion. As a prophet of universalism and cosmopolitanism, he stood for human brotherhood and independence. Indeed, he could be considered as the first world citizen from India. Though not a socialist, he always championed the cause of the downtrodden and the peasantry.

Ram Mohan Roy was the first oriental-occidentalist of modern India. He sought to blend the best of the Indian culture with the best of the European culture. He worked as a bridge between the East and the West. To quote Collet, his biographer, "Ram Mohan Roy stands in history as the living bridge over which India marches from her unmeasured past to her incalculable future." His greatness lies in the fact that he was the first Indian to grasp and appreciate the interdependence of social, religious, educational and political reforms.

Notes

1. Chaturvedi, Badrinath, Times of India, 22 May, 1993

2. Desai, A.R., op.cit, p.290

3. Verma, V.P., op.cit, p.25

Chapter 23

SWAMI DAYANAND SARASWATI
—THE PATRIOT SWAMI (1824-83)

Swami Dayanand, was a Gujarati Brahmin, originally named Mool Shanker. He was born at Morvi in Kathiawar. Initiated into religious traditions by his father, Dayanand, he was made to pursue a vigorous scholastic life from early childhood learning the Upanishads and the various samhitas and commentaries written by the great scholars.

What Raja Ram Mohan Roy and the Brahmo Samaj did for Bengal, Swami Dayanand and the Arya Samaj did for the North West of India. Like Raja Ram Mohan Roy, Dayanand also belonged to a period when Hinduism was under the onslaught of Christianity and Islam. The Hindu resurgence to this challenge was two-fold-internal reform and a reassertion of religious identity. Dayanand played a vital role in the resurgence of Hinduism. However, he was not a political thinker like Raja Ram Mohan Roy and questions of religious and social reforms engaged his attention more intimately than political issues.

Swami was a Vedic scholar, a dialectician and a social reformer. He was an uncompromising monotheist, and denounced polytheism pantheism and idolatry. He did not establish any new religion, but only chopped off the deadwood and cleared the overgrowth that the original Vedic religion was overlaid with. Romain Rolland has called him, "The Martin Luther of India" and the greatest reformer since Shankracharya."

Swami Dayanand's record as a social reformer is most impressive. He was against early marriage, enforced widowhood, and subordinate position of women and held that these were entirely unvedic. He was an ardent champion of the cause of the "untouchables" and opened the door of the Arya Samaj to them. He was also against the Parda system and the custom of 'dowry.'

Dayanand worked not merely for religious revival but also for a national revival. He was the first Indian to preach the gospel of Swadeshi and "India for Indians". He led the revolt against the blind acceptance of Western ideas and ideals. The Arya Samaj founded by him in 1875 became a potent factor in the political awakening of India.

Significantly, Dayanand held the defects in Indian character to be mainly responsible for India's decline. He frankly stated that the British rulers had superior social efficiency, better social institutions, self-sacrifice, public spirit, enterprise, obedience to authority and, above all, patriotism. He urged the Indians towards valour, self-reliance, self-sacrifice, moral integrity and righteousness. According to him, purity of character was the indispensable basis for social and national regenerations and emancipation.[1]

Dayanand was a great promoter of education. The Arya Samaj organised a network of schools and colleges in the country both for boys and girls where education was imparted in the mother tongue. Dayanand Anglo-Vedic College was first founded as early as 1886.

Unlike the Brahmo Samaj, the Arya Samaj was a mass movement which generated a new life and spirit among its followers. But it had a more revivalist character, and was more than a reform movement. It stood for the consolidation of the Hindus, "but it had a negative and critical attitude towards Islam. Thereby it provoked Muslims to mobilise on a corresponding communal basis"[2].

As regards his political beliefs, Dayanand was liberal but not a radical. Significantly, as against democracy on West-minister model, he favoured an "enlightened monarchy" which was thoroughly rooted in obedience to Dharma. Furthermore, he did not challenge the differentiated non-egalitarian social order which was the very basis of Hinduism, because the Varana Vyavastha were sanctified by the Vedas themselves. Thus his thought had two aspects, one progressive, the other reactionary. It was progressive when it attacked superstitions and denounced polytheism and promoted mass education, but it also represented a conservative and reactionary force when it tired to bring back the forgotten past. Swami believed that the Vedas contained eternal, pure and pristine knowledge given to humanity at the primordial hour of creation. For him, Vedas were infallible, a treasure-house of knowledge, past, present and future. But his claims abut the 'infallibility of the Vedas is open to question, though, Swami Dayanand championed the cause of rationalism and freedom in theological and social matters, he could not emancipate human intellect from the chains of theology and Vedaism. Therefore, unlike Raja Ram Mohan Rai, he failed to appreciate the truths contained in the writings of Western social and political philosophers.

ESTIMATE AND CONTRIBUTIONS OF DAYANAND

Dayanand propounded a theory of nationalism based on spiritualism. He laid stress on moral and mental improvement rather than on material prosperity. He prepared the moral and intellectual foundations of Independence. He sang the glories of 'Swaraj' in the days when British imperialism was firmly entrenched in the country. His cult of 'Swadeshi', had tremendous political implications and his message of Swaraj and Swadeshi became part of India's national consciousness. Under its impact Indians started taking pride in the cultural and intellectual heritage of India. Dayanand's Arya Samaj movement gave to the nation great patriots like Lala Lajpat Rai and Swami Shradhanand.

Notes

1. Verma, V.P., op.cit, p.39
2. Desai, A.R., op.cit, p.292

Chapter 24

SWAMI VIVEKANAND
—THE PROPHET OF RESURGENT
HINDUISM (1863-1902)

Throughout the nineteenth century Hinduism had been on the defensive believing itself to be beleaguered by erosion from within and assaults from without. A spectacular demonstration of India's dignity and honour was necessary for enabling her people to get over their sense of inferiority. This was achieved by no one better than by Swami Vivekanand. More than Raja Ram Mohan Roy and Swami Dayanand, Vivekanand made Indians feel proud of their ancient heritage. He urged his countrymen to arise, awaken and not to stop till they conquer the world with their spirituality.

Vivekanand, whose real name was Narendra Nath Dutt, was born in an aristocratic Kshatriya family of Calcutta. As a student, he made his mark in many fields. "A strong athlete, a Herculean figure having broad face spotted with large eyes and vast forehead, he bore in himself a storehouse of power and strength, granite faith and rock of self-confidence, immeasurable passion of a warrior and the Napoleonic ambition for a world conquest."[1]

Vivekanand's intellect was phenomenal. He is said to have gone through all the existing volumes of Encyclopaedia Britannica. He was inspired by Western science and literature and studied the works of Kant, Hegel, Spencer, J.S. Mill, and other luminaries.

In 1888, at the age of eighteen he came into contact with the sage, Ram Krishna Paramhansa. This was the turning point of his life. Soon he became the most favourite disciple of the sage. After the death of his guru he adopted a monastic life and made extensive tour of the country. Impressed by the life and teachings of Buddha he adopted a life of renunciation.

Vivekanand considered Hinduism to be 'the mother of all religions' and he thought that this could be demonstrated historically. He espoused that the ancient Vedic religion influenced Buddhisms and the latter influenced Christianity. West Asia had also come under the influence of ancient Indian though. Hinduism for Vivekanand was a universal gospel of ethical humanism and spiritual idealism. The victorious march of Vivekanand in the American continent and Europe demonstrated to the people that Hinduism was in the process of resurgence. It was because of his propaganda that Hinduism was placed on the world map of religion. 'The Life of Vivekanand', Romain Rolland described Vivekanand "the Hindu Napolean". According to M.N. Roy, "Vivekanand called upon Young India to believe in the spiritual mission of India.... His romantic vision of conquering the world by spiritual superiority electrified the young intellectuals, whose desperate economic position made them restive. In Roy's opinions, his nationalism was a sort of "spiritual imperialism."[2]

Though a strong protagonist of Hinduism, Vivekanand, however, was a broad-minded Hindu. Like Swami Rama Krishna, he had appreciation for Christianity and Islam. Although in his Address to the Parliament of Religions at Chicago (1893), Vivekanand flaunted Hinduism and his rhetoric-ridden speech did have a ring of arrogance, it ended on a note of universal tolerance. With all his Vedantic convictions, he did not present Vedanta as the only religion for the world. He spoke not only of the fact of religious diversity but also of the need for it. "Difference, he said is the first sign of life and diversity is the sign of living." Vivekanand was against religious conversion. He believed in the unity and equality of all the religions. He not only attributed the highest importance to the unity of all religions but also favoured the fusion of all religions into one universal religion. In other words, he conceived the idea of a universal religion based on the synthesis of the virtues taught by different religions. As such, he wanted to harmonise the Vedas, the Bible and the Quran.. He tried to combine Indian spiritualism with Western materialism in order to produce a synthetic culture suited to the needs of modern man. Similarly, he was positively concerned with promoting good relations between Hinduism and Islam. Unlike Swami Dayanand, who maintained a negative attitude towards Islam Vivekanand wanted "Hinduism to have an Islamic body with a Vedantic heart." In his letter to Mohd. Surfaraz Hussain, he wrote "I am firmly persuaded that without the help of practical Islam, the theories of Vedantism are entirely valueless to the vast mass of mankind."[3]

Vivekanand was of the firm opinion that all individuals and nations were parts of the Universal Existence. According to him, Upanishads preached the solidarity of this universal fraternity of man. His concept of universalism was a world order based on equality of all nations. He affirmed international unity and brotherhood through national diversities and religious and cultural varieties.

Although basically a religious preacher, he had a deep love for the masses. Like Buddha, he emphasized the importance of removing misery instead of trying to discuss the nature of Truth. He held that the highest worship of God is through the service of man. To him altruistic service was the only true religion and all other ceremonial practices were sheer madness.

With regard to social change he adopted a moderate position. Though he favoured reform but in place of cataclysmic or radical changes he advocated evolutionary and organic reform. According to him, social customs are the result of the arrangement for self preservation, and Hinduism has maintained its vitality through its ability for absorption. Being a captive of the past like Dayanand, he also had a streak of conservativism in his outlook. To quote J.N. Farquahr: "Vivekanand personified a conservative and reactionary force trying to bring back the vanquished past."

ESTIMATE OF VIVEKANAND

Vivekanand was an ardent patriot and had immense love for the country and its culture. He was the embodiment of emotional patriotism, and a spiritual precursor of the Indian freedom movement. A great nationalist of India, he sought to revitalise the nation through the vitality of religion. In other words, he tried to build a religious theory of nationalism, for he felt that religion had to be made the backbone of national life. He tried to combine Vedant with a muscular nationalism. He believed that no political upliftment was possible without rousing the masses. Valentine Chirol in his 'Indian Unrest' observes.: "Vivekanand's teachings were one of the major causes of the terrorist movement in India." Undoubtedly he left a tremendous influence on Aurobindo Ghosh and Subhash Chandra Bose. In the end, Vivekanand placed before his countrymen the splendid and invigorating message of the Vedanta, which combined the spirituality of the East with the spirit of social service and organisational capacity of the West.

Notes

1. Gupta, R.C., 'Great political Thinkers: East & West, Laxmi Narain Agarwal Educational Publishers, Agra, 1986, p.78

2. Roy, M.N., India In Transition, 1921 op.cit, p. 193.

3. Das, H.H. and Patro, P.S.N., Indian Political Traditions, Sterling Publishers, N. Delhi, 1989, p.86

Chapter 25

DADABHAI NAOROJI — THE GRAND OLD MAN OF INDIA (1825-1917)

Dadabhai Naoroji was one of the foremost patriarchs of Indian nationalism. According to Dr. Pattabhi Sitaramayya, the official historian of the Congress, the first name in the list of patriarchs is that of Dadabhai Naoroji who, "beginning his connection with the Congress from its very outset, continued to serve it till the evening of his life, and took it through the whole gamut of evolution, from the humble position of being a people's organisation, seeking redress of administrative grievances, to that of a national assembly working for the definite object of attaining Swaraj. He presided over the Congress thrice, in 1886, 1893 and 1906 and throughout his association with it, he held aloft the Congress banner before India and England."[1] In the opinion of C.Y. Chintamani, "there was none in the galaxy of brilliant intellectuals and selfless patriots who adorned the public life of those days who could be compared to Dadabahi."[2] Mr. Gokhale said of him: "If ever there is the divine in man, it is in Dadabhai."[3] His power of intellect was combined with roburst idealism and an abiding concern for the predicament of Indian masses.

Naoroji was born in a Parsi family. After completing his study at Elphinston Institute in Bombay he served the Elphinston College as a Professor of Mathematics and Natural Philosophy until 1855. Thereafter he left for England to manage the business of Cama and Co. a famous Parsi firm, as its partner.

Naoroji was the first Indian to be elected to the British House of Commons (1892) from a British constituency, and did much useful work in that capacity in educating public opinion in England in favour of India. He founded the British-Indian Society in England to espouse the cause of his country. When the First World War broke out, he appealed to his countrymen to stand by the British government and in return asked for the right of self-government within the British Empire. Again in 1897, he appeared on behalf of the Indian National Congress before the Welby

Commission on Indian expenditure. While in India, Dadabhai had founded
no less than thirty institutions. Most of them had for their aim the political
advancement of the country, but some were meant for social advancement,
particularly for the education and emancipation of women. Also, he was
associated with the establishment of the Bombay Association which was
the first political organisation in the Bombay Presidency, He also founded
a newspaper (fortnightly), 'Rast Guftar', to voice the feelings of the
enlightened section of the people of India.

POLITICAL IDEAS OF NAOROJI

In his political philosophy, Naoroji was both a Liberal and a Moderate.
He was fully conscious of the benefits India had derived from the British
rule and advocated the continuation of British connection with India. Like
other Moderates, he had full faith in the sense of justice and fair play
of the British people. Nonetheless, he was opposed to imperialism and
demanded (1906) "Swaraj" for India though as an integral part of the
British Empire. Being a liberal he believed that the way to "Swaraj" lay
through constitutional methods and agitation. He intensely hated violence,
and the told his people to abjure violence in thought, word and deed.
He always fought his battles with arguments buttressed with hard facts.

Like other protagonists of liberalism, he advocated the concept of
moral foundations of political authorities. The political structures, according
to him, are based on justice, generosity and humanity. It is wrong to
presume that political power rests on brute force.

ECONOMIC IDEAS OF NAOROJI

Naoroji was a pioneer not only in the political awakening of the Indian
masses, but in other respect too. He was the first to formulate an economic
interpretation of Indian politics. He was also the first to build up the
theory of the economic foundations of Indian nationalism. Dadabhai was
an economist with a deep grasp of public finance, foreign trade, and
national income. He was the first Indian politician to draw attention of
his countrymen and of the British public to the drain of India's wealth
to Great Britain and to the resulting poverty of her people. His 'Economic
Drain' theory is contained in his monumental work 'Poverty and Un-
British rule in India'. This theory pointed out that Indian economy was
subjected to a heavy drain which retarded the growth of capital formation
in the country. According to his thesis, India was being made economically
destitute on account of constant draining of her revenues to the alien
coffers. He proved, with facts and figures, that not less than 50 crore
rupees were taken away from India by the British every year.

The evils of foreign rule, according to him, involved the triple loss of wealth, wisdom and work-financial extortion and administrative experience and monopolisation of prize posts. Apart from analysing the causes of Indian poverty, Naoroji offered concrete suggestions to avoid 'drain' for effecting improvements in the condition of the Indian masses. He also stressed the concept of the right to employment and representation.

PLEA FOR SELF-GOVERNMENT

Though an admirer of the British rule in the initial stages, Dadabhai later realised that self-government was the only lasting panacea of the economic and political ills of India. The reactionary policies of the British, especially the partition of Bengal and the fact of the economic drain prompted him to change his position from a proclaimed loyalty to British rule to the demand for self-government. It is interesting to note that while it was Tilak who raised the slogan: "Swaraj is my birthright and I shall have it" the credit of demanding 'Swaraj' from the Congress platform for the first time belongs to Dadabhai. In fact, 'Swaraj' was the keynote of his Presidential Address at the Calcutta session (1906). This Address began the second era in the history of the Congress.

ESTIMATE OF DADABHAI NAOROJI

Dadabhai Naoroji was undoubtedly one of the early patriots and architects of modern India. Gokhale portrayed 'Dada' as "one of the most perfect examples of highest type of patriotism." According to V.P. Verma, "Naoroji made two distinctive contributions to Indian social sciences, viz, the economic interpretation of the Indian politics and, emphasis on the concept of natural rights. Dr. Verma has rightly described him "a phenomenon in modern Indian history."[4]

Noes

1. Sitaramaya, Pattabhi, History of Indian National Congress, Vol.I p.82

2. Quoted in Suda, J.P., op.cit, p.92

3. Ibid., p.92

4. Verma, V.P., op.cit, p.129.

Chapter 26

MAHADEV GOVIND RANADE
— THE PROPHET OF LIBERALISM
(1842 - 1901)

According to C.Y. Chintamani, "Ranade was second only to Dadabhai among our patriarchs". He was a distinguished jurist, economist, historian, social reformer and educationist. He was a great scholar, thinker, patriot and unselfish worker. Ranade was a mighty intellect, a man of prodigious industry and of vast and varied learning, a profound thinker and ardent patriot."[1] Ranade was the first Indian Fellow of the Bombay University. He started his public carrier in 1862 as an editor of the English column of 'Indu Prakash'. Before being appointed as a judge by Bombay government, he was a professor of English and History at Elphinston. In 1885, he was a member of the Bombay Legislative Council. He was one of seventy two public men who attended the first Congress session in 1885.

Though not an active politician or a formal member of the Indian National Congress (because of holding the high office of the Bombay High Court judge, since 1893), he was a great source of inspiration to the Congress movement. He managed to keep in touch with the Congress since its inception by holding sessions of the Social Reform Conference which he organised along with the annual sessions of the Congress.

Ranade espoused numerous public causes and established many organisations to further them. One of them was the Deccan Educational Society, which started a school at Poona, and which later developed into the famous Ferguson College. Later on, it established the William College at Sangli. Also, Ranade was the guiding spirit behind the Poona Sarvajanik Sabha.

SOCIAL THOUGHT OF RANADE

Ranade wanted a total renaissance in society, in literature, in religion and in politics. He was a champion of social reform, and boldly supported widows' remarriage. He regarded social advancement as the necessary prelude to political emancipation. According to M.N. Roy, "Ranade was a reformer and not a crusader. Yet the patriotism of Ranade and his co-workers was revolutionary, in as much as it recognised the banefulness of old religious corruption and social customs and boldly declared war on them."[2]

POLITICAL VIEWS OF RANADE

In his outlook Ranade was a moderate. With all his love for the country, like other Moderates, he regarded the British rule as a part of beneficient divine dispensation.

ECONOMIC THOUGHT OF RANADE — ECONOMIC NATIONALISM

Ranade was the first Indian thinker to have a comprehensive view of Indian economic development. A seminal idea that Ranade tried to project was that national development in a broad sense is the basis of sound national economy. "Growth", he argued, "was either many sided or non existent". He believed that growth, in the economic sense, was not possible without social mobility, urbanisation, freedom of thought and enterprise. He emphasised that industrialisation was the essence of economic development; it was the key to the removal of India's mass poverty and economic progress. But he believed that without active state aid and protection, industrial development could not gain any worthwhile momentum. Indeed, he was the first economist to perceive that India needed protection. Although he favoured private property and free initiative but at the same time he gave due importance to the development-promoting role of the State. As such, he suggested state intervention to protect workers and tenants from exploitation. In the opinion of Prof. P.C. Joshi, "The father of 'economic nationalism and the state-led industrialisation was not J.L. Nehru but M.G. Ranade". Besides, Ranade disagreed with the views of "FDrain" theorists that economic drain was the sole cause of Indian poverty. According to him, non-industrilisation and non-modernisation of agriculture were the main reasons for the poverty of the country and both were interdependent.

ESTIMATE OF RANADE

According to S.R. Mehrotra, "Ranade was probably the greatest name in the history of India in the last quarter of the 19th century." As a prophet of liberalism, he inculcated the ideals of social emancipation, economic progress, cultural growth and national unity. "In place of constraint, credulity, authority, bigotry and fatalism, Ranade espoused the necessity of freedom, faith, reason, tolerance and the sense of human dignity."[3] Besides, Ranade was a path finder in Indian economic thought. He made major and original contributions to the emergence of the theoretical and scientific critique of colonial economy.

Notes

1. Chintamani, C.Y., Indian Politics Since The Mutiny, p.37
2. Roy, M.N., India In Transition, op.cit, p.177
3. Verma, V.P., op.cit, p.135

Chapter 27

GOPAL KRISHNA GOKHALE
— THE DIAMOND OF INDIA
(1866-1915)

"Gokhale was perhaps the greatest man if not the greatest leader that India has ever produced."[1] He was one of the most revered Indian statesmen. His unimpeachable patriotism, his nobility of soul and selfless devotion to the cause of the motherland endeared him to his fellow countrymen and won him many admirers abroad.

The latter half of the nineteenth century saw a renaissance in Maharashtra and the growth of a liberal school as in Bengal. The liberal school was represented by stalwarts like R.S. Bhandarkar, K.T. Telang, M.G. Ranade. G.K. Gokhale, who was a distinguished disciple of Ranade, imbibed the spirit of the master and never wavered from the path of moderation and sweet reasonableness laid down by him. It was Ranade who initiated Gokhale in the principles of a humane, liberal and scientific nationalism, besides giving him a thorough guidance in Indian politics and economics. To quote Dr. Zacharia, "Never had a guru a more apt pupil than Ranade in Gokhale." But if Ranade was his intellectual father, Dadabhai Naoroji was his intellectual grandfather. Gokhale often used to say "I am an intellectual grandson of Naoroji." Apart from these two gems of Maharashtra, he was also tremendously influenced by Pherozeshah Mehta about whom Gokhale said: "I would rather be wrong with Phirozeshah rather than be right without him."

Gokhale started life without the advantages of birth or fortune. He owed his rise primarily to his own outstanding ability, industry and public spirit. After graduation in 1884 in the midst of poverty, Gokhale decided to dedicate himself to the service of the country and joined the Deccan Educational Society founded by his Guru, Ranade.

Gokhale began his career as a school teacher, and taught History and Economics, but soon became the principal of the Ferguson College.

Later, in 1887, he became the editor of the Quarterly Journal of the Poona Sarvjanik Sabha, and subsequently became the Honorary Secretary of the Deccan Sabha. In 1897, he was selected along with Mr. Dinshah Wacha to proceed to England and give evidence before the Welby Commission on Indian expenditure. In 1900, he was elected a member of the Bombay Legislative Council. In 1902, he was elected to represent Bombay in the Supreme Legislative Council and continued to be there till his death. Thus, just at the early age of 36 years he forged his way to the forefront of Indian politics.

Gokhale's first speech on the budget in the Central Legislature was a revelation to the public, and since then his speeches on the budget were looked forward to with great interest, and are even now considered as classics. He had the knack of saying the hardest things in the gentlest language. Even Lord Curzon (who rarely said a good word for Indians) acknowledged his merits in these words: "I have never met a man of any nationality more gifted with parliamentary capacity, Mr. Gokhale would have obtained a position of distinction in any parliament in the world... I only wish India produced more such public men." According to Lord Minto, "his eloquence was seldom witnessed in the British Parliament." British Members of the Viceroy's Executive Council compared Gokhale's mastery over facts and figures with that of Gladstone. But while pleasant in speech and criticism, he never minced matters. In the Council Chamber he acted as the champion of the poor and the oppressed and pleaded for the abolition of the Salt Tax, the adoption of compulsory primary education, equal treatment to Indians as regards recruitment, and the removal of British control over Indian finance.

Great as was his work as a member of the Supreme Legislative Council, greater was his contribution to the nation in the shape of the famous Servants of India Society, which he established in 1905. During his political career he visited Great Britain seven times, twice as a Congress representative. He also visited South Africa and rendered great help to Gandhi in his campaign of passive resistance against the government of that country.

POLITICAL THOUGHT OF GOKHALE

Temperamentally Gokhale was a spiritualist and a convinced idealist, and lived on an elevated moral plane. Long before Gandhi, his mission as a public leader was 'spiritualisation of politics'. Yet he was not an utopian idealist. In politics, Gokhale was a true liberal. He had learnt from his Guru the desirability and necessity of moderation and sweet reasonableness, not only of manners but of aim as well, and had moulded his life on this principle. As a true moderate, he accepted the concept of negotiation, moderation and compromise. He put forward the creed of constitutional agitation. In his own words, "Constitutional agitation is agitation by methods of which we are entitled to adopt to bring about the change we desire through the action of constitutional authorities."[2] It ranged from petitions, representations and pressure of opinion at one extreme, to the non-payment of taxes on the other.

As a Moderate, "he was opposed to extremist measures and theatrical outbursts of popular frenzy."[3] He warned the people about the futility of the method of force and violence to drive out the British from India. He firmly believed that the regeneration of his country could not be achieved "amid a hurricane of political excitement", but only step by step. Like Edmund Burke, he believed in caution, gradual growth and rational progress. In such a gradual process it was of the essence of the solution of the problem to enlist the support of the British by appeals to their better nature.

Gokhale sincerely believed that with its multifarious diversities and divisions on the grounds of caste, religion, language, culture and religion and the lack of proper training to manage their own administration, India would plunge into chaos and confusion if the British ever left it in Indian hands. He therefore appealed to the Indians to first deserve and then demand self-rule. No wonder, in reply to Lord Hardinge, who once asked Gokhale's reaction if the British troops decided to leave India, his remark was : "Before you had reached Aden, we would be telegraphing you to return."

ECONOMIC THOUGHT OF GOKHALE

As a professor of Economics, he was interested in studying the economic foundations of politics. Along with Naoroji and Ranade, he laid the foundation of Indian economic thought. But he had a moral approach to political economy. He was the founder of the framework of the basic concepts of the welfare state in India. He was an ardent advocate of industrialisation through a judicious policy of protection of the infant industry and public support for home made goods.

ESTIMATE OF GOKHALE

Gokhale was much misunderstood by some of his contemporaries who described him as a faint-hearted politician and a British loyalist. As a politician, Gokhale had to suffer from the defect of his virtues. His personal polish and politeness was mistaken for cowardice and cravenness. But such an estimate of him is quite wrong. Gokhale lacked neither manliness nor courage, but he subordinated politics to ethics, and never wanted to depart from the path of moderation and sweet reasonableness. To quote Wolpert, "Gokhale's response to British rule was one of loyal acquiescence but it was by no means supine surrender of a sycophant or a mendicant."

. Gokhale was the ablest spokesman of the 'old guard'. He was the 'prince of the Moderates.' As a philosopher of moderation, he imparted greater clarity, coherence and sophistication to the ideology of the early Congress. However, he was no defender of the status quo. India's poverty and subjection were matters of constant concern to him. His consuming interest in politics stemmed from his passionate patriotism. He tolerated foreign rule not for the love of it but because it provided political stability to the country. Unlike other leaders, he would not blame all the ills from which India suffered on the British. He wanted her to shake off the shackles of social and economic backwardness as well as political subjection. He wanted to turn the encounter with the British Raj into an opportunity for building a secular, modern and democratic society. He correctly diagnosed the illness of public life. In his opinion, "Our public life is weak because our public spirit is weak." According to his biographer, T.V. Parvate, "He was in larger sense a reconciler between Eastern and Western cultures, a great master of the possible, of grasping what was immediately at hand even while yielding to none in high idealism." As a true Moderate, he wanted to reform, convince and achieve, but not destroy.

B.N. Ganguli draws our attention, in his 'Indian Economic Thought', to the surprisingly modern character of Gokhale's thinking and analysis. He, however, did not simplify the task of political and economic reconstruction. He visualised an India "of expanding industry, of awakened faculties and increasing prosperity and more widely distributed comfort and wealth."[4]

In the opinion of B.R. Nanda, "He had a rational, secular and almost scientific approach to politics and economics. He was completely free from sectarian prejudices. His belief in the disinterested principles of economics and constitutional democracy was remarkable. Across three quarter of a century, we still feel the magnetism of a man, who was the disciple of Ranade, the colleague and rival of Tilak, the hero of Sarojini Naidu, Moti Lal Nehru and M.A. Jinnah, and the political mentor of Gandhi, who mourned his death by walking barefoot for a year."[5]

Paying his tributes to Gokhale in glowing terms, Gandhi observed: "Gokhale was pure as crystal, gentle as a lamb, brave as a lion and chivalrous to a fault, an ideal political worker. He was and remains for me the most perfect man in the political field." It was because of his deep spiritual nature and adherence to rectitudes that Gandhi decided to make him his political guru on his return to India. Similarly, Tagore paid tributes in glowing terms and said "For a man like you to live in itself is a service to your country, for your life is not merely useful, but it is light to others." Gokhale's incomparable contribution was recognised by Mr. Jinnah, who himself wanted to become a Muslim Gokhale. Paying his tributes to Gokhale, Jinnah observed: "Gokhale was a great political 'rishi', a master of the finance of India and greatest champion of education and sanitation."

Regrettably for India, Gokhale overworked himself to an early death in 1915 at the age of 49. When he died, Tilak, his political rival, paid him a handsome tribute by describing him as the diamond of India, the "jewel of Maharashtra" and the "prince of workers." Lala Lajpat Rai described him "as the noblest and best of Congress workers and said that his patriotism was of the highest and purest type. According to V.P. Verma his contribution to India politics may be summed up in two propositions: one, he stood for the introduction of moral values in politics, and two, he advocated moderation, reason and compromise as political technique."[6]

Notes

1. Nanda, B.R., 'Gopal To Gokhale', Times of India, 5 Feb. 1992.
2. Gokhale quoted in Bhagwan, Vishnu, Indian Political Thinkers, Atma Ram & Sons, Delhi, 1983, p.96
3. Verma, V.P.; op.cit, p.165
4. B.N. Ganguli quoted in Nanda, B.R., Times of India, 5 Feb. 1992.
5. Ibid.,
6. Verma, V.P., op.cit, p.172

Chapter 28

BAL GANGADHAR TILAK
— THE PROPHET OF SWARAJ
(1856-1920)

Maharashtra gave to the nation not only Naoroji, Mehta, Ranade and Gokhale but also B.G. Tilak. Tilak was an "uncrowned king" of Maharashtra. He was also one of the greatest figures in the political history of modern India. He was a rock of strength in the struggle for Swaraj. He was a great politician, a renowned mathematician, a profound scholar, a powerful writer and a bold and intrepid leader.

Tilak, reverentially known as Lokmanya, was born at Ratnagiri in a Chitpawan Brahmin family. The family produced leaders like Baji Rao Peshwa, Nana Phadnavis, Gopal Krishna Gokhale etc. Thus he was heir to the glorious martial tradition. Soon after taking his first class bachelor's degree from the Deccan College, Poona and Law degree from Bombay University in 1879 he came into contact with Mr. Agarkar, and the two together matured a plan for the establishment of a school and college for imparting cheap education. The Poona New School came into existence in 1890. He was also associated with the formation of the Deccan Educational Society and the establishment of the Ferguson College. Later on, he became the proprietor of two papers 'the Kesari' and 'the Maharatta' and used them to good purpose in stimulating political consciousness among the masses. He founded the Anti-Cow Killing Society in 1893. He also demanded the lifting of the ban on the playing of music by Hindu processions in front of mosques and thereby acquired popularity as the champion of the Hindus. He also organised two national festivals, the Shivaji Festival and the Ganapati Festival, which brought him into close contact with the masses who soon began to love and admire him. His work in the famine, which visited that part of the country in 1896, and in the plague epidemic which spread in the following year won him great popularity with the masses. He was twice elected to the Bombay

Legislative Council and was also a member of the Municipal Board of Poona.

Tilak was among the first Congress leaders to suffer several terms of imprisonment at the hands of the British government. He was first tried and sentenced to four months' imprisonment for having criticised, in strong language, the treatment accorded to the Maharaja of Kolhapur. Then he was tried for having instigated the murder of Mr. W.C. Rand and Lt. Ayerst in 1897 through his articles in the 'Kesari' and sentenced to eighteen months' imprisonment, without leave to appeal. Again in 1908, he was tried for Sedition and sent to Mandalay for six years. During this period of incarceration he wrote his famous 'Gita Rahasya' and the 'Arctic Home of The Vedas'. On his release he became a national hero and organised the Home Rule League in 1916. He supplemented the activities of the Congress by the propaganda work of the Home Rule League. From the Lucknow Congress of 1916 (where he took a leading part in bringing about the Lucknow Pact along with Jinnah) to the Amritsar Congress of 1919 he was the greatest figure in the Congress and played a decisive role in its activities.

POLITICAL IDEAS OF TILAK

In his politics and method of work he differed radically from the Moderates. Whereas Ranade and Gokhale believed in moderation and sweet reasonableness, Tilak was a great advocate of agitation and ceaseless agitation. He believed that the three ps-Prayer, Pleas and Protest would not do unless backed by solid force. "Philanthropy plays no part in politics," he stated repeatedly. He poured ridicule over the method of representation and prayer, and tried to induce the Congress to adopt a more self-reliant method. His method was called "passive resistance.".

Tilak was a philosopher of aggressive nationalism. He introduced extremism in the policy of the Congress, and along with Lala Lajpat Rai and Bipin Chandra Pal, he organised the Extremist bloc inside the Congress — a development that led to the split in the Congress ranks at Surat in 1907.

Since Tilak rejected the method of political mendicancy, many foreign critics regard him as a violent revolutionary. Valentine Chirol called him "the Father of Indian Unrest" In his opinion, Tilak has been "the first to create an atmosphere which breeds murder." Similarly, John S. Hoyland said that "Tilak has been coquetting with the doctrine of physical force."[1] But it is to be noted that Tilak never advocated violence. Though he admired the Chapekar brothers and the patriotic fervour of the Bengal revolutionaries, he never preached political murder. Tilak was a political realist, though not in the Machiavellian sense. He recognised that "the military strength of the government was enormous and a single machine gun showering hundreds of bullets per minute will be quite sufficient for our largest public meetings." He felt that violence and political murder would give scope to the British bureaucrats to crush the national movement which was still in the early stage. His contention was that the Swaraj would be achieved by the united action of the people based on passive resistance and democratic means. Thus he did not sanction revolutionary methods on the grounds of policy and effectiveness However, he did not denounce them on moral grounds, as Gandhiji did, for Tilak never accepted non-violence as a creed. For him, non-violence (Ahimsa) could only be a policy, not a matter of absolute faith, as was the case with Gandhiji.

TILAK'S VIEWS ABOUT RELIGION IN POLITICS

Tilak was a devotee of Hindu religion, attached to Hinduism and to the Hindu community. Though not an orthodox religionist, he believed in the reality of mystic experiences gained by seers and yogis and in the theory of incarnation. He thought that Hindu religion provides a moral as well as a social tie. Aware of the fact that the Hindu community was a divided house, he wanted the different sections of Hindus to unite into a mighty nation. He said: "Let the stream of Hindu religion flow through one channel with mighty, consolidated and concerted force."

Tilak wanted to enlighten the people about the message of the Vedas and the Gita for providing spiritual energy and moral zeal to the nation. His religion had a political message and he was not against using religion as a political tool. His primary motive in organising Ganesh Puja and Shivaji Festival was to find opportunities for collecting and speaking to the masses. Tilak's basic propaganda and agitations were organised around political and economic issues, and contained little appeal to Hinduism as such. Prof Bipin Chandra also maintains that "Tilak's politics, ideology and agitational methods were not communal."[2] Regarding glorification of Shivaji, Tilak himself once remarked: Had I been in Northern India I would have adopted Akbar instead of Shivaji as the common hero of Hindus and Muslims."[3] Thus his political ideology and agitational methods were not communal. He always stood for Hindu-Muslim unity. It is well known that he was instrumental in the formulation of the Congress-League Scheme (1916). But he did not like to blend religious and political questions, and opposed Gandhiji for including the issue of 'Khilafat' in the Non-Cooperation Movement that he launched.

TILAK AND SOCIAL REFORM

Tilak was a reluctant social reformer, and believed in the gradual evolution of the social consciousness. He did not want to disrupt the cohesiveness of the society as evolving organism by creating sections and factions on the question of social reform."[4] He observed: "A true nationalist desires to build on old foundations. Reforms based on utter disrespect for the old does not appeal to me as constructive work. We do not want to anglicise our institutions and so denationalise them in the name of social and political reforms."[5]

Tilak wanted reform with due respect for Indian traditions. He said, "All reforms grow from within and unless people are sufficiently prepared by the assimilation of liberal ideas, it is useless to march ahead."[6] He did not entertain any blind imitation.. He objected to social reformism of Ranade, Gokhale, Bhandarkar, Agarkar, etc. In short, he accepted an organic, evolutionary and spontaneous concept of social change brought about by progressive education and growing enlightenment.

However, Tilak was not a social reactionary. He favoured foreign travel, praised the remarriage of widows, advocated female eduction, opposed untouchability and hated discrimination on the basis of caste and creed. Nevertheless, it can be argued that he did not adapt to the changing situation. For instance, he did not openly support intercaste marriages or widow remarriages. He was opposed to the Age of Consent Bill in 1891 and the Hindu Marriage Bill in 1918. Thus Tilak was not a social reformer in the sense in which Raja Ram Mohan Roy was considered.

ESTIMATE AND CONTRIBUTION OF TILAK

Tilak was a profound scholar, a refined Hindu, an ardent nationalist and an arch-patriot. He was the proponent of aggressive nationalism. The mission of his life was to rouse patriotic consciousness among Indians. As a leader, he had personal magnetism, almost charismatic in character. There was a a deep admiration for him in the minds of Indian youth. His profound erudition exalted his personal magnetism. As an Indologist, Tilak had three great works to his credit. 'The Orion', 'The Archtic Home of The Vedas' and, 'The Unfinished Chronology And Vedantic Jyotisha'.

His achievement as a social and moral philosopher is far more solid and permanent. His monumental treatise on the Gita is not a mere interpretation but is a synthesis of Eastern and Western ethics and metaphysical systems. On Tilak's death Gandhi gave his tributes in glowing terms: "His patriotism was a passion with him. His life was an open book. It was spotlessly clean. No man preached the gospel of Swaraj with the consistency and insistence of Lokmanya."[7] In recognition of the services rendered by him to the nation, the Tilak Memorial Swaraj Fund of about a crore of rupees was raised by the National Congress.

Tilak's contribution to the national movement was two-fold. Firstly, he was one of the great trio' (Lal-Bal-Pal) responsible for the emergence of Extremism in Indian politics. In the second place, he tried to make the Congress a mass movement. In this respect, he was a fore-runner of Gandhiji.

GOKHALE AND TILAK- A COMPARISON[8]

Gokhale and Tilak represent two schools of thought — Moderate and Extremist, respectively. Hence the study of their ideological conflict will enable us to have a peep into the nature of the social and political thinking of their times. Both Gokhale and Tilak were contemporaries and both were Chitapawan Brahmin. Both had extraordinary gift of intellect and character. Both were teachers in their early life. But they were poles apart in their outlook and method of action. While Gokhale was an admirer of the West and considered the British rule as a blessing in disguise, Tilak viewed the British as a predatory incubus rather than a blessing. Tilak was proud of the Indian past and did not consider the British as saviours of Indian society. As regards their temperamental differences, If Gokhale was persuasive, conciliatory and constructive, Tilak was provocative, combative and confrontationist.

As such, in their political methods they differed considerably. While Gokhale asked for concessions, Tilak demanded his rights. Gokhale made requests while Tilak made demands. If Tilak stood for direct action, Gokhale stood for constitutional agitation. Tilak advocated a three-fold political programme boycott, Swadeshi and national education. Gokhale favoured Swadeshi and national education but justified the boycott only as a weapon of last resort. In other words, Gokhale believed in passive resistance only as a measure of defence rather than attack.

Gandhi has compared Gokhale and Tilak in metaphorical terms: "Sir Pheroze Mehta had been to me like the Himalayas-unshakeable, the Lokmanya like the Ocean and one could not easily launch forth on the sea. But Gokhale was the Ganges- it invited one to its bosom." In the words of Stanley Wolpert, "Gokhale was an optimist and an idealist. He believed in the perfectability of all mankind through the agencies of education, accentuated dissemination of information and material amelioration. He was eminently practical, moderate and constructive. His leadership was evolutionary and international in approach and inspiration.

Tilak was less concerned with equality than with liberty. He showed neither Gokhale's catholic aspirations nor his evolutionary inclination. He saw the moat rather than the bridge between his world and that of the West. While Gokhale was syncretic, Tilak was chauvinistic. In rallying support Tilak did not scruple against appealing to prejudice or mass anxiety. He was neither squeamish nor doctrinaire about the methods he employed so long as they helped further his ends. He adhered to no dogmatic revolutionary theory. He outlined no long term programme of action or social reorganisation. But the ultimate explanation for the differing response of Gokhale and Tilak must remain shrouded in the hidden well springs of their personalities and their unrecorded potent influences of heredity and early environment."[9] According to Dhananjay Keer's comparison, "Gokhale was Ranade's political heir and like his mentor, he welcomed the British rule as a divine dispensation. Tilak was self-luminous and self-made. Gokhale criticised the government in a parliamentary vein, whereas Tilak agitated against it. The motto of one was love and service, that of the other was action and suffering. The goal of Gokhale was self-government for India within the British Empire whereas that of Tilak was Swaraj (full independence)." As per Dr. Sitaramya's comparison, "Both Tilak and Gokhale were patriots of the first order. Both have made heavy sacrifices in life. But their temperaments were widely different from each other. Gokhale's aim was to improve the existing constitution. Tilak's aim was to reconstruct it. Gokhale stood for cooperation whenever possible and opposition when necessary, Tilak was inclined towards a policy of obstruction. Gokhale's ideal was love and sacrifice, Tilak's ideal was service and suffering. Gokhale's method sought to win the foreigner, Tilak's was to replace him. Gokhale depended upon other's help. Tilak upon self-help. Gokhale appealed to the intelligentsia, Tilak to the masses and the millions. Gokhale's arena was the Council Chamber, Tilak's forum was the village mandap. Gokhale's objective was self-government for which the people had to fit themselves by answering tests prescribed by the English, Tilak's objective was Swaraj which is the birthright of every Indian. Gokhale was on a level with his age, Tilak was in advance of his times."

In the end, "it is notable that in many respects Indian society has evolved and will continue to evolve along lines of an uneasy compromise between the dreams of Tilak and Gokhale. Militancy, resurgent Hinduism, regional and communal sensitivity, caste consciousness, and social conservatism can be something of the heritage of Tilak and strong ties of fraternity with England and the Sterling bloc through her membership of the Commonwealth, and progressive Westernisation along liberal lines of constitutional development may be pointed to as part of the living Gokhale tradition."[10]

Notes

1. Quoted in Das and Patro, op.cit, p.135.
2. Chandra, Bipan, Communalism In Modern India, op.cit, p.144
3. Gopal, Ram, A Political History of Indian Muslims, op.cit, p.88
4. Verma, V.P., op.cit p. 183
5. Quoted in Das and Patro, op.cit, p. 125
6. Ibid., p.123
7. Quoted in Bhagwan, Vishnu, op.cit, p.67
8. For detailed comparison between Gokhale & Tilak see Ahluwalia, Architects of The Swaraj, Intellectual Publishing House, New Delhi (1982) pp. 38-42.
9. Wolpert, Stanley, A., Tilak And Gokhale- Revolution And Reform In the Making of Modern India, Surjit Publication 1982, pp. 299-301
10. Ibid. p.305

BIPIN CHANDRA PAL — THE CHIEF EXPONENT OF NATIONALISM AND EXTREMISM IN BENGAL (1858-1932)

Bipin Chandra Pal was a fiery orator, keen and intrepid patriot, inspired educationist, journalist and writer. He was the prophet of a strong, self-reliant, vigorous nationalism in India. He was a philosophical analyst of Indian nationalism and its development.

B.C. Pal began his life as a teacher and a principal. He flourished at a time when Bengal had been undergoing the ferment of an intellectual, literary and moral renaissance. He was influenced by Bankim Chandra, S.N. Bannerjea and Bijoy Krishana Goswami. In 1876, Pal joined the Brahmo Samaj. But later on, he subscribed to the traditional creed, philosophy and theology of Hinduism. Ultimately, he became a Vaishnava in his later years.

Pal first attended the Congress session in 1887 at Madras and delivered an inspired lecture in support of the repeal of the Arms Act. In 1900, he visited England and the USA. In 1901, he started his paper 'New India' and very soon he found himself in the vortex of politics, and acquired political leadership in the Congress. The partition of Bengal aroused his deeply sensitive soul, and he began to preach the gospel of a pure and self-assertive nationalism. He delivered eloquent speeches on Swaraj and passive resistance. As leader of the Extremist school, he advocated self-reliance, self-help and self-determination. He vehemently opposed the policy of begging for crumbs of self-government. He was in the forefront of Swadeshi agitation. In 1907, he was arrested but was released in 1908. In 1916, he joined the Home Rule League started by Tilak. In 1918, he accompanied Tilak to England as a member of the Home Rule League deputation. But at the Amritsar Congress (1919) he did not support whole-heartedly Tilak's slogan of Responsive Cooperation. He was also opposed to the Non-cooperation Movement launched by

Gandhi. Since 1920 Pal started losing touch with the realities of Indian politics. Gradually, he retired to the periphery from the centre of the national movement. Though he never became a Liberal in politics, he faded lout of active politics in the second phase of his political life (1920-23). Interestingly, in 1923, he pleaded for Tilak's Responsive Cooperation. Thus, "a nationalist of the first magnitude and a staunch critic of Moderate nationalists became himself a Moderate of Moderates."[1]

BIPIN CHANDRA PAL'S PHILOSOPHY OF HISTORY

As a political philosopher, Pal accepted divine determinism in history. The Absolute or Brahman is the regulative idea in cosmic evolution. His philosophy was that history is the manifestation of a divine teleology and there is an immanent meaning and supreme purpose in history. "Against Darwinian evolutionism, Spencerian agnosticism and human scepticism, Pal stood up as the prophet of the Vedic and Puranic doctrine that history is the field of habitation or the play ground of the divine being."[2] In his book, the Soul of India' and "Sri Krishna', he declared Krishna to be the soul of India. He further says that "social and civic institutions are instruments and vehicles for the "progressive revelation and realisation of God in and through man."[3]

PAL'S THEORY OF NATIONALISM

The conception of society and nation as an organism has appealed to several Indian thinkers and philosophers. Pal also accepted the organic theory of the nation. "A nation, according to him, is not the artificial agglomeration of separate individuals coming into existence through a mechanical contract. It is an organism and is informed with an all-pervasive intelligence and moral bond. Nation is the magnified and extended self of man. It is the externalisation of the 'Virat Purush'."[4] Hence Pal accepted the necessity for sacrifice for the sake of this greater self. The nation as a spiritual and moral organism expresses itself in an abiding continuity of persistent historical memories and future purposes. In an article, 'Bande Matram' (July 6, 1906) he declared: "In a nation, the individuals composing it stand in an organic relation to one another, and to the whole of which they are limbs and organs. An organism is logically prior to the organs. Organs evolve, organs change, but the organism remains itself all the same. Individuals are born, individuals die but the nation lives forever."[5]

Pal differentiated between European and Indian nationalism. The former laid stress on territorial unity whereas the latter emphasized the cultural unity. Pal was also a champion of spiritual nationalism and he described the national movement in India as a spiritual movement. The recognition of a spiritual frame of reference makes politics part of the larger religion of the nationalist, and politics becomes a department of the science of salvation. Behind his conception of nationalism in India stands the old Vedantism of the Hindus. According to him, "the separation of the secular and the spiritual is alien to Hinduism."[6]

But, in his paper 'New India', Pal expounded his concept of composite patriotism. "The New India is neither Hindu-though the Hindu unquestionably forms the original stock and staple of it, nor Mohammedan — though they have made very material contribution to it, — nor even British, — though they are politically the master of the country now, but is made up of the varied and valuable materials supplied in successive stages of its evolution, by the three great world civilisations, which the three great sections of the present Indian community represent."[7]

Ultimately, Pal stood for secularism. He believed that the modern state must be absolutely secular. According to him, religion must be kept strictly apart from politics. As such, he was opposed to Pan-Islamic movement. Pal found two aspects of Pan-Islamic movement — one cultural and the other political. He was not opposed to its cultural aspect with its emphasis on fostering fraternity among the Muslims. What worried him was the political aspect of Pan-Islamism, represented by people like Syed Ameer Ali and the Muslim League, which was trying to inject a sense of separatedness among the Muslim masses by mixing its religious and cultural aspect with Indian politics.

PAL'S CONCEPT OF IMPERIAL FEDERATION

Before his visit to England in 1908, Pal was an exponent of extreme nationalism but slowly there comes a transition in his views. In 1910, Pal visualised in his writings the necessity of a higher imperial synthesis. In 1911, he sponsored the concept of 'imperial federation.' It would be composed of great Britain, Ireland, India and other Dominions, each absolutely autonomous internally but combined for the purpose of progress and protection. It would be knit by organic relation. In his opinion, what was essential was "the moral unity of the human race." The building up of a federal empire would be the prelude to universal humanity which is the end of all social evolution. He thus considered imperialism a step towards internationalism. Strangely, Pal found no contradiction between his earlier extreme nationalism and the new theory of imperial federation.

POLITICAL PHILOSOPHY OF PAL

Pal advocated the theory of natural rights, which are primarily human rights inherent in every individual being. God bestowed such rights upon the individuals. Besides, Pal formulated the inspired concept of 'divine democracy'. His theory of 'divine democracy' has its roots in the Vedantic concept of the unity of existence. Further, Pal was also allured by the idea of federation. He was opposed to unitary or centralised government for a country like India. In his opinion, "The higher ideal of a pan-Indian Federation, the United States of India, is the only form of Swaraj in consonance with out past evolution and the eternal spirit of our philosophy of life. The sky-scraper of federation portrayed by him is as follows: "The district government shall be built upon a federation of village communities. The provincial government shall be similarly built upon a federation of the District governments; and the Central Government of India shall be built upon a federation of the various Indian provinces, reconstituted on a linguistic basis.[8]

ECONOMIC IDEAS OF PAL

Pal condemned the spirit of competitive capitalism as prevalent in the economic systems of Europe and the USA. He was not only opposed to industrial exploitation but also industrialisation itself, and pleaded for the revival of our old village life. Soon after the First World War, he wrote 'The New Economic Menace To India'. He exposed the hollowness of "imperial preference' which aimed at economic exploitation of India. He pleaded for expropriation of all excess profits by the State, a radical proposal indeed for his time.

ESTIMATE OF B.C. PAL

Pal's emphasis on federation, decentralisation, referendum and recall constitute a rich legacy worth admiring and worth adopting. Similarly, his emphasis on humanism as fundamental philosophy of race equality are noteworthy. His books on "Indian Nationalism" and 'Nationality and Empire' are inspired by great political insight.

Notes

1. Bhagwan, Vishnu, op.cit, p.69
2. Verma, V.P., op.cit, p.231
3. Ibid., p.231
4. Ibid., p.232
5. Ibid., p.232
6. Pal, Bipin Chandra, The Spirit Of Indian Nationalism, p.47
7. B.C. Pal quoted in Verma, V.P., op.cit, p.233
8. Pal, B.C., Swaraj- The Goal And The Way, pp. 65-66

Chapter 30

LALA LAJPAT RAI
— THE LION OF PUNJAB
(1865-1928)

Lajpat Rai was decidedly the greatest man produced by Punjab after Maharaja Ranjit Singh[1] and one of the top ranking leaders that India has produced. As a staunch nationalist, as a social reformer and a fearless fighter for Swaraj he was loved and admired by the whole country. Before joining politics he occupied a prominent position in the legal profession in the Punjab. He was immensely influenced by Mazzini and Garibaldi of Italy. He was a leading member of the Arya Samaj with a fighting spirit and pride in his country and its civilisation.

Lajpat Rai was a great educationist and was one of the founders of the D.A.V. College at Lahore, established in 1886. He was a prolific writer, a forceful journalist and an effective orator. He founded and edited several papers like 'Bande Matram" (Urdu daily) and the English weekly 'People'. His writings include 'Arya Samaj'. 'Young India.' 'Unhappy India' (a crushing rejoinder to Miss Mayo's 'Mother India'). 'The Political Future of India,' 'English Debt To India' etc.

Lajpat Rai was one of the founders of the trade union movement in India and became the first president of the Indian Trade Union Congress. He also led the Kisan Movement with Sardar Ajit Singh. He was the first to represent Indian workers at International Labour Organisation meet.

In politics, Lajpat Rai was inclined towards Extremism. In 1905, he was deputed to visit England along with Gokhale, but on his return he told his people not to be content to be mere beggars. He believed in winning freedom and not begging for it. He supported the four-fold demands of the Nationalist Party — Swaraj, Swadeshi, Boycott and National Education. In 1907, he was deported alongwith Sardar Ajit Singh to Mandalay where he remained for six months, and was released in

September 1907. In 1914, he again went to England along with Mr. Jinnah and others. In 1916, he went to USA from England. During the First World War, he was practically in exile in the USA, where he did much to educate public opinion in regard to India. He wrote an Open Letter to Lloyed George demanding self-determination for India. After a protracted stay (five years) in America he returned to Lahore in July 1920. He presided over the special session of Congress held at Calcutta (1920) to discuss the proposal of Non-cooperation. At first he was not in favour of non-cooperation movement. But later on, he plunged himself whole-heartedly into the struggle.

After the withdrawal of the Non-Cooperation Movement, he joined the Swaraj Party and did effective work as Deputy Leader of the Party in the Central Legislature. It was under his leadership that the boycott of Simon Commission was organised in the Punjab. While leading a procession in this connection, he was made a target of a British sergeant and he succumbed to injuries after a few weeks. He died a martyr's death.

LAJPAT RAI AND HINDU IDEOLOGY

Lajpat Rai was a great admirer of Hindu culture and civilistion. In his book, 'Arya Samaj' he pleaded that the Samaj should adopt a more universalistic and tolerant approach. He had his moorings in the traditions and historic sentiments of ancient India. He believed in conserving those old values which still had a meaning and significance. He wrote: "To attempt to divorce Dharma from life is a very very risky affair." Being a staunch nationalist, he was opposed to communal representation with separate electorates, for it could not be reconciled with the claims of Muslims that they believed in nationalism and unity. At he Unity Conference in 1925 at Delhi and at the presidential speech at the Calcutta Hindu Maha Sabha he expressed strong opposition to communal electorates. He was greatly disturbed by successive communal riots in Malabar, Multan, Amritsar and Kohat and became very protective of the Hindu community. In late 1920s, in a fit of exasperation Lalaji even suggested that the Punjab be partitioned into two sectors on communal lines-Muslims governed West Punjab and Hindus and Sikhs governed East Punjab."[2] It is worth noting that even before Iqbal, Rahmat Ali and Lord Mountbatten, Lalaji passionately pleaded through a series of articles in the "Tribune", in 1924 for the division of Bengal and Punjab. The bitter irony was that his suggestion, though made in a huff, became a reality.

But Lajpat Rai at no stage was a communalist. He never subscribed to any kind of work that could injure the cause of national unity. He always believed in cooperation and rapport between Hindus and Muslims.

As late as 1928, in an article published in 'Modern Review', he wrote: "In my judgement the cry of a Hindu or Muslim Raj is purely mischievous. The correct thing for us to do is to strive for a democratic Raj in which the Hindus and the Muslims and other communities may participate as Indians and not as followers of any particular religion." Thus he remained a nationalist till he breathed his last.

POLITICAL IDEAS OF LAJPAT RAI

Lajpat Rai was a staunch nationalist though not a violent revolutionary. He was of the view that every nation possessed the fundamental right to cherish some ideals and any interference with this right was unnatural and unjust. He believed in John Locke's theory of 'Consent of the governed' for running the government.

ECONOMIC IDEAS OF LAJPAT RAI

Like Dadabhai Naoroji and Ramesh Chandra Dutt, he also tried to unravel the story of the ceaseless exploitation of India. According to him, "The story of the British extension of mastery over India was a long process of military and economic exhaustion, a sort of killing by inches which took a century to complete."[3] The economic drain manifested itself in diverse ways — in the form of mounting cost of public services and in the shape of increasing expenditure on the army.

After his return from America he took some part in the popularisation of socialist ideas. His 'Arya Samaj' (with preface by Sydney Webb) contains his views on socialism. But his was no doctrinaire socialism. He wanted that Indian labour and capital should meet on equal ground and cooperate for the development of industries.

Lajpat Rai believed in the all round advancement of the nation. He stressed the necessity of the educational, social and economic uplift of the masses. He wanted India to cultivate a high sense of public duty and a high standard of public morality.

ESTIMATE OF LAJPAT RAI

To conclude, Lajpat Rai was a veteran nationalist and one of the foremost leaders of modern India, whose life was a record of selfless suffering, persecution and prosecution for the sake of the nation. He rendered great social and humanitarian service through the Arya Samaj and the Servants of People Society founded by himself."[4] Because of his long sojourn abroad and his deep and wide study Lajpat Rai was well aware of the dominant trends in international politics and economics. He was one of the first few leaders of India who viewed the problem of India's freedom with international perspective.

Notes

1. Verma, V.P., op.cit, p.237
2. Quoted in Saiyid, Mohd. Ali Jinnah, p.329
3. Quoted in Verma, V.P., op.cit, p. 241
4. Ibid., p.245

Chapter 31

AUROBINDO GHOSH
— THE POET OF PATRIOTISM
(1872-1950)

Aurobindo Ghosh was one of the major figures in the History of the Indian Renaissance and Indian National Movement. He was the philosopher of revolution who thought not only of political freedom for India but also of the moral and spiritual reawakening of Indians. Perhaps, he was the first to give the inspiring ideology of full independence. Besides, he was one of the most systematic and learned of all modern Indian thinkers and philosophers. "He was indeed a veritable genius — a great poet, a notable metaphysician, a profound seer, an ardent patriot and a lover of humanity."[1] Ghosh was greatly influenced by the preachings of the Upanishads and Gita and Vednatic synthesis of Rama Krishna and Vivekanand. His early patriotism also bears the mark of influence of Mazzini and the Irish patriotic movement.

In 1879, at the age of 7 he was sent to England, along with his two other brothers by his father. He returned to India after a long gap of 14 years, and after having qualified for the ICS in 1893. But during his long physical separation from India, his emotional and cultural ties with her remained intact. Throughout his sojourn abroad he was attracted towards Indian politics, and this attraction was strengthened when at Cambridge he came in contact with the Indian Majlis, founded in 1891. He also joined a Secret Society called the 'Lotus and Dagger' formed by some young Indians at Cambridge in 1892.

Like S.N. Banerjea, Ghosh was also disqualified from the ICS on a flimsy ground — his failure in the horse riding test. But he showed no regret for this dismissal, for he had no liking for the Indian Civil Services. For him public service was more rewarding than the service of the government.

To begin with, he joined the Baroda State Service and later on became the Principal of the Baroda College (1905). While in Baroda, he took great interest in the study of Indian languages, culture, history and religion, probably to compensate for the loss of contact with India while he was abroad. In 1905, he resigned from the principalship of the Baroda College to become president of the National Council of Education, formed during the anti-partition agitation in Bengal.

From 1905 to 1910, Ghosh pursued a political career as a leader in the national movement in Bengal. He entered into Indian politics when the Congress was seeking, to use his own words, "soiled crumbs". Like other Extremists, he also declared that Swaraj was the birthright of Indians. He also believed in the successful use of Swadeshi, Boycott and Passive Resistance as effective methods to fight against repressive British imperialism. He attacked the Congress as a "a middle class organisation," and wanted it to be transformed into a mass movement. Remarkably, he believed in the total emancipation of India at a time when the Congress had not dared to pronounce such a political programme in clear cut terms.

His political ideas covered in its sweep not only the doctrine of passive resistance but also the cult of revolution. Ghosh was closely associated with the revolutionary movement in Bengal. He was arrested in connection with the discovery of a bomb factory in Manicktolla but was acquitted, as a prosecution failed to prove his complicity in this case, known as the 'Alipore Bomb Conspiracy Case' (1908). Besides, Ghosh edited two dailies- Bande Matram and Yugantar, which became the mouth piece of the revolutionaries and the most effective voice of nationalist Extremism." He also wrote a booklet, 'Bhawani Mandir', in which he stated: "The one thing which we must strive to acquire before all others is strenght — strength physical, strength mental but, above all, strength spiritual. The idea of Bhawani Mandir Scheme was to set up an Ashram where youths would be so trained that they would have physical courage, intellectual sharpness and an idealistic outlook on life. The idea was to develop a band of Karm Yogis.

But all of a sudden, in 1910, Ghosh decided to retire from politics and proceeded to pondichery (then under French rule) to avoid arrest in future and to spend the rest of life there in meditation and reflection. In retreat at Pondichery (1910-1950), he wrote his main books- 'The Life Divine', 'Essays On The Gita', 'The Synthesis Of Yoga, Savitri (poem), etc. His writings reveal a mind thoroughly at home in both secret literature of the East and metaphysics of the West.

Though his most dynamic period of political activity was confined to a brief span of time, he left a great mark on the subsequent history of the freedom struggle. If as a leader of anti-partition agitation of Bengal he revolutionised our action, as a seer and sage of Pondichery, he revolutionised our thought.

METAPHYSICS OF AUROBINDO GHOSH

At the philosophical level, Ghosh claimed to have reconciled the divergent trends of Indian transcendental idealism and Western secularistic materialism. He recognised that due to its inevitability to transform terrestrial life in the image and pattern of the spirit, Indian spirituality, in its later days, generated an attitude of renunciation of the world. The result was the emergence of the philosophy of Mayabad and the cult of Nirvana. But, on the other hand, in the West, the full efflorescence of the scientific methodology had led to a tremendous growth of materialism and secularism. This scientific rationalism led to a phenomenal increase in man's knowledge about natural and social evolution, popularised the growth of democracy and socialism, gave impetus to humanism and humanitarianism and in general led to triumph of man as a creative subject. But still it did result in the negation of the life of the spirit. A deep realisation of divine life was not possible in such an atmosphere. He was of the view that both Indian spiritualism and European secularism and materialism had gone to extremes. He, however, hoped that Indian spiritualism and European secularism and materialism could be reconciled and felt that this was possible only by the creation of a philosophy which gives equal importance to the claims of both spirit and matter. For Ghosh, there was no contradiction between spirit and matter. Matter is only a veiled spirit. That is, matter is spirit unrevealed. Spirit has to manifest itself in matter during the process of evolution.[2] In other words, evolution is the progressive self-manifestation of the spirit in a material world. Spirit is the source of creation and evolution and also the final end of naturalism "In his theory of evolution, Ghosh tried to integrate intellectual cosmic outlook of the West with the spiritualist and idealistic stand point of India."[3]

Thus, Aurobindo's metaphysics grows out of the fusion of the Eastern and Western ideas. Interestingly, Ghosh avoided his alignment with any of the schools of Indian philosophy, as they all advocated either escapism or individual salvation — no attempt made to clean the earth in order to make a fuller place for human being.

AUROBINDO'S PHILOSOPHY OF HISTORY AND CULTURE

As a political philosopher, Ghosh accepts spiritual determinism in history. History, according to him, is the manifestation and progressive self revelation of Brahman, the Absolute.

The distinction between culture and civilisation is very significant in modern social science and philosophy. Anthropologists like Malinvosky have adopted their own criterion for distinguishing between them. They equate culture with totality of material instrumentalities and valuational ethics. Culture is a broader concept than civilisation. Culture represents the totality of man's activities, while civilisation is restricted to some highly sophisticated aspects of a collective existence. Nicolos Berdyaey believes that "culture is concerned with values and civilisation with the organisation of life." Generally, in Western philosophy of history, culture is equated with the advance in art, aesthetics, religion and metaphysics and civilisation with the growth of technology and economics. Ghosh adopted from Western thought the conceptual distinction between culture and civilisation but reinterpreted it in the framework of the Upnishadic philosophy. He wanted to go beyond culture and favoured the enshrinement of a supra-rational beauty and a supra-rational good.[4]

IDEALISM OF AUROBINDO GHOSH

Like many other freedom fighters of India, he was also an idealist and gave top priority to spiritual and yogic life, which was perfected at the Ashram established by him at Pondichery after his retirement from politics. As a matter of fact, his spiritual ideas had started taking shape gradually during the period of his political career. He laid stress on the use of spiritual power of a Yogi for the all round development of the material plane. He visualised the spiritual regeneration of the world in which India was to take the lead. The super structure of his political theory is therefore based upon his theory of 'Intense Idealism'.

POLITICAL PHILOSOPHY OF AUROBINDO GHOSH

In propounding his political philosophy, he starts with the concept of the spiritual man. According to him, "Man is a spiritual being with a soul and embodies the self-expression of the Universal and Transcendental Reality." Ghosh did not propound a systematic theory of state and Government. However, he was opposed to concentration of power in the hands of the government. According to him, "The state is not an organism; it is a machinery, and it works like a machine, without tact, taste, delicacy or intuition." He was opposed to the interference of the state in the sphere of education, culture and religion. Nevertheless, he believed that the state should secure for all "a just and equal chance of self-development and satisfaction to the extent of his powers and on the line of his nature."[5] Ghosh criticised the Western model of representative democracy for its short-comings and unethical nature. He also criticised Benthamite utilitarianism as an unethical political philosophy, He believed that as a spiritual being the individual should direct his efforts towards the realisation of the good of all human beings.

ECONOMIC IDEAS OF AUROBINDO GHOSH

Aurobindo was a critic of both capitalism as well as socialism. According to him, if one leads to exploitation, the other leads to authoritarian regimentation. He pointed out the flaws of the capitalist system of economy and severely criticised authoritarianism, concentration of power and increasing control of bureaucracy. However, he accepted the egalitarian philosophy of socialism.

AUROBINDO'S THEORY OF NATIONALISM AND HUMAN UNITY AND WORLD GOVERNMENT

Aurobindo was a pioneer of neo-nationalism in India. For him, nationalism is not a mere political programme. It is a religion through which we strive to recognise the presence of God in the nation and in our fellow countrymen. He believed in the divinity of the motherland. India is a divine power and is a spiritual and not geographical entity. But his creed of nationalism was not narrow and fanatical. It was of a cosmopolitan character. Aurobindo was a great visionary, and also saw the vision of a world government. Though he was conscious of discouraging features and dangerous possibilities existing in the world — ideological divisions, the cold war, the arms race and nuclear rivalry, yet he thought that some kind of world union was inevitable. He attributed this to the drive of nature, the compulsions of circumstances and the present and future needs of mankind. In other words, the economic and political necessity, common sustenance and survival in the struggle for existence are some of the binding forces of world unity. But a merely political, economic and administrative union does not create a psychological unity. For creating a psychological unity Ghosh stresses on what he calls a religion of humanity in order to draw people beyond the bounds of their narrow nationalistic religions and for that every individual must be made to entertain the single soul of humanity in his thought and life" He stated in his 'The Ideal Of World Unity': "A world state will evolve naturally as man is imbued with the desire to unify himself with the others of his species." He hoped that common interest and common sentiments would in due course lead to the creation of a world state. But such a world state should be a sort of federation of free nationalities where perfect equality will prevail. He however emphasized that the world union would be based on spiritual religion of humanity.[6]

Thus nationalism, according to Aurobindo, was not a political ideology but Dharma — a way of life which would bring about a moral resurgence of the people of India. Aurobindo hoped that "the Sun of India's destiny would rise and fill all India with its light and overflow India, overflow Asia, and overflow the world."[7]

ESTIMATE OF AUROBINDO GHOSH

Aurobindo's teachings were directed towards the ideal of divinising the whole humanity by transforming mind, life and matter. His theory of evolution, his integral Yoga and his conception of human unity and international peace were all directed toward that very ideal. "His metaphysics, his philosophy of history and culture and his conception of nationalism and spiritualised collectivism represent the synthesis of Eastern and Western concepts."[8] His moral, intellectual and spiritual accomplishments have cast a deep influence on the minds of the Indian intelligentsia. In the opinion of Tagore, "Aurobindo Ghosh was a Messiah of Indian culture and civilisation." In the words of Dr. Radha Krishnan, "Ghosh was the most accomplished of modern Indian thinkers." Admiring his clairvoyance, his well known biographer, K.R. Srinivas Iyenger wrote in his, 'Aurobindo: A Biography and A History; "For all his self-imposed silence, his perspective on world events was uncanny. For instance, his support of the Allied cause during the Second World War was vindicated by history. Nearer home, he advised the Congress to accept the Cripps Proposal. This might have prevented partition of the country."

On the whole, Aurobindo's political philosophy was too esoteric and at places even mystifying. It was full of foggy abstractions. Moreover, his recurring reference to terms like 'Spirit', 'Supermind' 'Divinity', and 'Absolute' makes much of his thought hard to subscribe to.

Notes

1. Verma, V.p., op.cit, p. 247
2. Ibid., p. 248
3. Bali, Devraj, Modern Indian Thought, Sterling Publishers, New Delhi, 1980, p.145
4. Verma, V.P., op.cit, pp. 250-51
5. Das and Patro, op.cit, p. 148
6. Bhagwan, Vishnu, op.cit, pp. 155-56
7. Pradhan, G.P., India's Freedom Struggle, Popular Prakashan Bombay, 1990, p.55
8. Verma, V.P., op.cit, p.257

Chapter 32

ANNIE BESANT
— THE REBEL REFORMER
(1847-1933)

Born in England, Dr. Annie Besant was an Irish by birth but subsequently became an Indian by adoption. She had a sustained and deep love for India and gave 40 years of her life to her adopted motherland. Perhaps, no foreigner has served India more faithfully and loyally than Annie Besant.

In the beginning, she was a socialist by conviction. Her name was linked with Charles Bradlaugh, Sydney Webb, G.B. Shaw, Oscar Wilde, G.K. Chesterton, etc. As such, she began life as an agnostic. But in 1889 she came into contact with Madam H.P. Blavatsky, the founder of the Theosophical Society. Inspired by her work 'The Secret Doctrine', Annie Besant joined it, and as result she became a deeply religious personality. Interestingly, from an atheist and a free thinker she found solace in the ancient scriptures and philosophy. As a theosophist, she found God in man as the crown of creation. Man is the final image of the Supreme on earth. True religions must be rooted in man not in God. At 18 she married Frank Besant, a clergyman. But she deserted her husband at 25 after the birth of two children.

Annie Besant was endowed not only with great learning and a penetrating intellect, but was also gifted by nature with an indomitable will and undaunted courage. She was one of the greatest orators of her time. She was the most sought after woman speaker and could be counted upon to keep large audiences hypnotised by her spellbinding oratory. She wrote two major books 'India, A Nation' and 'How India Wrought Her Freedom'. She also edited two journals, 'New India' and 'Commonwealth.' To her credit, she became the first president of Women's Association. Annie Besant entered into Indian politics in 1913 and soon left many of the old leaders far behind her. From 1913 to 1919 she struggled hard for bringing about a reconciliation between the Moderates and the

Extremists, and brought Extremists into the Congress. In 1916, she started her Home Rule League and under its auspices established organisations throughout the country. She strove hard for getting the Home Rule for India. In recognition to her services, she was selected as President of the Congress in 1917.

ANNIE BESANT ON NATIONALISM

Annie Besant repudiated the materialist approach to nationalism and instead advocated the religious approach to nationalism. The nation, according to her, is a spiritual entity pulsating with a deep inner life. It is unique revelation of God. "Like Hegel, Aurobindo Ghosh, B.C. Pal, Annie Besant also regards the nation as the unfoldment of the Supreme Divine, and like Vivekanand and Ghosh, she believed that India had a spiritual mission for the world."[1]

POLITICAL IDEAS OF ANNIE BESANT

In politics, Besant was neither a Moderate nor an Extremist. But she was more advanced than the Moderates, and was not willing to accept anything less than complete Home Rule. Accordingly, she declared: "The Montford Reforms were ungenerous of England to offer and unworthy of India to accept." Annie Besant favoured Swadeshi but not as a political weapon. She was stoutly opposed to all ideas of severing connection with Great Britain, as was desired by the Extremists. She was also opposed to the Non-Cooperation Movement and therefore left the Congress when the Movement was launched by Gandhi. She levelled three charges against the Non-Coopertion Movement. In her opinion; It was anarchical and revolutionary; It promoted racial antipathy; and It was an anti-social force. Annie Besant greatly favoured national education, and started the Central Hindu High School and College at Benaras, which subsequently developed into the great Benaras Hindu University. From 1919 Annie Besant began to isolate herself from the mainstream of politics. As such she became the butt of attack from a few Marxists. In the opinion of M.N. Roy, "In reality, she was a masked defender of the interest of imperialist bourgeoisie and she had always been a champion of the British Empire."[2] According to another leftist, "She was an unarmed imperialist working out subtler ways of holding on to the White man's burden." But these views do not stand deeper scrutiny.

ESTIMATE OF ANNIE BESANT

Dr. Annie Besant was a great personality of international fame. She was the champion of socialism, trade unionism, theosophy and

Commonwealth of India Bill. "She taught the ideals of synthesis, tolerance and universal harmony. She preached eradication of religious hatred and sectarian dogmatism. She believed in the coming together of the East and the West."[3]

Notes

1. Verma, V.P., op.cit, p. 56
2. Roy, M.N., India in Transition, op.cit, p. 216
3. Verma, V.P., op.cit, p. 61

Chapter 33

SURENDRA NATH BANERJEA
— THE INDIAN BURKE (1848-1925)

In the early phase of the Indian freedom struggle Bengal was politically the most advanced province in India and gave birth to a number of eminent personalities in the domain of politics, such as W.C. Banerjea, Manmohan Ghosh, Lal Mohan Ghosh, Ramesh Chandra Dutta, Surendra Nath Banerjea, Anand Mohan Bose, Bipin Chandra Pal, and A.C. Majumdar. Of them the leading personality was S.N. Banerjea.

After graduating in 1869, S.N. Banerjea went to London for further studies. He successfully competed the ICS examination in 1869, but he was disqualified on account of some technical discrepancy. On reference of his case to the Queen's Bench Division he was reinstated in the ICS, and was posted as Assistant Magistrate of Syllhet in 1871. But soon after he was dismissed on certain fabricated charges. After dismissal, he became a professor of English at the Metropolitan Institute in 1876. In 1882, he established a school of his own.

S.N. Banerjea went to England for a second time to qualify for the Bar. During his sojourn in England he imbibed the liberal teachings of English political philosophers like Burke, Macaulay, J.S. Mill and Spencer. He admired Burke's constitutionalism and romanticism and praised the eloquence of Fox, Pit and Sheridan. He was also inspired by the career of Joseph Mazzini (Italy). At the same time, he had a deep love for the past grandeur and magnificent achievements of India in the domains of science, art, literature and philosophy. He had great admiration for the contributions of Valmiki, Vyas, Buddha, Shankara, Panini and Patanjali.[1]

The first thing that Banerjea did on his return from England was to start the Indian Association (1876), which was designed to be a political association to represent the educated middle class. Lord Salisbury, the Secretary of State, gave the Association an opportunity to realise some of its objectives by reducing the maximum age limit for the ICS examination. On behalf of the Association, Banerjea toured Northern India creating a middle class political opinion against the reduction of age limit from 21 to 19. In 1883, he started a movement for the creation of a National Fund as a counterpoise to the European Defence Association, which was organised on the issue of the Ilbert Bill. That same year he was imprisoned for two months on a charge of contempt of court. After his release he made a triumphal tour of Northern India. In 1876, he was elected to the Calcutta Corporation and continued there for 23 years, till 1889.

Banerjea played a notable role in the establishment of the Indian National Congress. The letter inviting leading citizens of the country to attend the inaugural session of the Indian Union was issued under the joint signatures of S.N. Banerjea and A.O. Hume. Although Banerjea could not be present at its first session yet he never missed any Congress sessions afterwards. Not only he was one of the founders of the Indian National Congress, his voice resounded from the Congress platform for about 40 years. In 1890, he went to England as a member of Congress delegation to create public opinion predisposed to constitutional reform in India. He also returned to the Bengal Legislative Council four times. In 1910, he represented India in the Imperial Press Conference. He was one of the pillars of the Congress in its earlier days, and in recognition of his services to the national cause he was twice elected president of the Congress, once in 1895 at Poona and again in 1902 at Ahmedabad. However, Banerjea left the Congress in 1918 alongwith B.C. Pal, Jinnah and Annie Besant. In 1919, he gave evidence before the Joint Select Committee which discussed the Government Of India Bill of 1919. He supported the Act of 1919, and was elected to the Bengal Legislative Council, and became a minister in the Bengal Government.

POLITICAL IDEAS OF S.N. BANERJEA

In his political views, he was inspired by Vivekanand, Aurobindo Ghosh and Gandhiji. Like them, he also stressed that moral renaissance is the charter for political emancipation. "Like Cicero and Burke, he stressed the moral foundations of political power. Like Naoroji, Ranade and Mehta, he also believed that the British connection with India was divinely ordained. He regarded the British rule as providential, as one of the dispensations of the God of History."[2] Although a proponent of Indo-British connection, he never desisted from exposing the machination of the ruling bureaucracy. He fearlessly resisted the partition of the Bengal and thereby earned the title of 'Surrender Not Banerjea'. Like other Moderates, he was quite conscious of the economic roots of politics. and supported the Swadeshi Movement.

By training as well as by temperament he was a constitutionalist and not a revolutionary. In his 'A nation in Making', he pointed out that what was essential was to cultivate strength, and not to indulge in violent activities. He was a consistent advocate of the constitutional method. He was one of the pioneers in India's quest for freedom and self-government. "Self-government", according to him "is the noblest school for the cultivation of human faculties. It is the will of Divine Providence."[3]

ESTIMATE OF S.N. BANERJEA

S.N. Banerjea was one of the foremost makers of modern Bengal and of the modern Indian nation. He occupies a prominent place among the Indian leaders by virtue of his long and distinguished record of public service. He always supported an elevated moral stand in politics. In powerful voice and oratory he was hardly equalled, muchless surpassed. In V.P. Verma's words, "What Demosthemes was to Greece, and Cicero to Italy" and Burke to Britain, Baherjea was to India.[4]

Notes

1. Verma, V.P., op.cit, pp. 155-56
2. Ibid., p. 158
3. Ibid., p. 162
4. Suda, J.P., op. cit, op.cit, p. 103

DESHBANDHU CHITRANJAN DAS — THE FIRST VOTARY OF NON-COOPERATION FROM WITHIN (1870-1925)

C.R. Das was a poet, lawyer, devotee of God, freedom fighter and one of the greatest political leaders of India. While a student in London (1890-92), he had taken part in the election campaign of Dadabhai Naoroji. After his return to India he got public attention by his magnificent defence of Aurobindo Ghosh in 1908 in the Alipur Bomb Conspiracy Case. He played a notable role in the Indian freedom struggle in its earlier phase. Though his active public life covered but a few years, yet during that period he dominated the political life of Bengal and emerged as one of the top ranking leaders on an all-India level.

Das first attended the session of the Congress in Bombay in 1918, and spoke in opposition to the Montford Scheme. In 1919, he was one of the members of Enquiry Committee set up by the Congress on the Jallianwala Bagh massacre. At the Amritsar Congress (1919) he was opposed to the acceptance of the Indian Act of 1919. At the Calcutta Congress (September 1920) he opposed the Gandhian programme He eventually supported it at the Nagpur session and plunged himself wholeheartedly into the Non-Cooperation Movement. He renounced his roaring practice at the Bar, and gave up a life of ease, comfort and luxury. In 1922, he was elected the president of the Congress session at Gaya. He was very disappointed when the negotiations for the withdrawal of the Non-cooperation Movement broke down on the issue of the release of the Ali Brothers.

When Das found that the abrupt suspension of the Movement in February 1922 left India in the grip of frustration, he placed before the country the programme of 'Council Entry', and ultimately succeeded in getting the Congress, approval for it. In 1923, he founded the all-India Swaraj Party with himself as President and Motilal Nehru as Secretary of the Party. As a member of the Central Legislative Council, he defeated several government proposals by dint of his persuasive and highly emotional oratory. In 1924, he was elected as the first Mayor of Calcutta Corporation.

ECONOMIC IDEAS OF C.R. DAS

Das was a champion of agrarian resuscitation. He was an opponent of India's industrialisation on the European pattern. He equally fought for the interests of the workers and the peasants. He presided over the All-India Trade Union Congress during 1923-24.

POLITICAL IDEAS OF C.R. DAS

"Like Bankim Chandra Chatterji, B.C. Pal and Aurobindo Ghosh, Das also believed in the divinity of the Indian nation. The Vedantic conception of nationalism advocated by Das was in line with the theory of spiritual nationalism advocated by Vivekanand, Pal and Ghosh."[1] Das had a deep and fervent attachment to the concept of Swaraj. But he did not sanction revolutionary violence and anarchic technique for its attainment.

Das was a votary of democratic decentralisation. He pleaded for increasing autonomy to local authorities. He had an elaborate scheme of village Panchayats in the country.

C.R. Das died suddenly in June 1925 leaving the country, particularly Bengal, much poorer by his passing away. At the time of his death he was wearing the tripple crown of leadership of the Swaraj Party, President of Bengal Provincial Congress Committee and Mayor of the Calcutta Corporation.

ESTIMATE OF C.R. DAS

C.R. Das was a passionate nationalist with a fervour of a Vaishnava. "Though rooted in the tradition of the country, he had also grasp of world politics and had a prophetic vision regarding Asiatic Federation and the Federation of Humanity."[2] Das was not just a bourgeois leader, although some communist writers levelled charge of "bourgeois parliamentarianism" against him. In fact, he was a champion of the masses. In 1922, in a speech at Dehradun he had declared: "Swaraj must be for the masses and must be won by the masses." On the whole, the political philosophy of C.R. Das shows a synthesis of different streams of thought.

Notes

1. Verma, V.P., op.cit, p.396
2. Ibid., p.399

Chapter 35

MOTILAL NEHRU
— THE FIRST CONSTITUTIONAL
ARCHITECT OF MODERN INDIA
(1861-1931)

Like C.R. Das, Motilal Nehru had attained great success at the bar, and was used to an aristocratic and luxurious life style until he came under the influence of the Mahatma. He first attended the Congress session at Calcutta in 1906. He joined the group of Moderates and was a bitter critic of the Extremists, led by Tilak. He was present in Surat at the time of the historic split in the Congress (1907). In 1907, he became the first president of the UP Provincial Congress at Allahabad. He had also been the President of the UP Provincial Congress Committee for 7 years. Since 1910 he was a member of the UP Legislative Council. He joined the Indian Home Rule League when Mrs. Annie Besant was interned in June 1917. But Motilal Nehru came into prominence only in 1919 when he was appointed the Chairman of the Committee, along with Gandhi, Malviya and C.R. Das, to investigate the Jallianwala Bagh tragedy. Twice he became the President of the Indian National Congress, in 1919 and in 1928. At the Amritsar Congress he supported the acceptance of the Government of India Act of 1919. He also started a paper called 'Independent' in 1919 from Allahabad. He joined the Non-cooperation movement launched by Gandhi, renouncing the pleasures of life, and plunged into the whirlwind of Congress politics.

In 1923, Motilal Nehru helped C.R. Das in founding the Swaraj Party and became its General Secretary. He was the leader of the Swarajist opposition in the Central Legislative Assembly from 1924 to 1930. In several respects Motilal Nehru was a counterpart of C.R. Das in UP. Like Das, he also dominated the politics of his province. Both Nehru and Das held similar views in politics, but Motilal differed from Das in one respect. For a long time he was a moderate like Das, but a change came over him after he was 55 when he travelled far in the direction of Extremism. The differential treatment accorded to the European members of the defence forces, the internment of Mrs. Besant and the Punjab wrongs led him away from Moderate politics towards Extremism in later years.[1] Moreover, the influence of Gandhi and his own son (Jawahar Lal Nehru) were also an important contributory factor to this change.

CONTRIBUTIONS OF MOTILAL NEHRU

Nehru's work as a leader of the Swaraj Party was of a very high order and revealed his great organising capacity. With the help of Independent votes he was able to inflict defeat on the government on several occasions, and the Governor General had to use his power of certification. In 1924, he moved a resolution for convening a Round Table Conference to recommend a programme for installing full responsible government in India. In 1925, he served on the Skeen Commission which enquired into the possibility of Indianisation of the Army. His most important contribution, however, was the preparation of the memorable document known as the Nehru Report. Furthermore, he was one of the earliest political leaders who postulated and practised the secularist approach to Indian politics. He felt that the realisation of common good and national harmony was not possible in the country until the domains of religion and politics were kept separate from each-other. Perhaps, he was the first political leader so far who showed no deep attachment or love for the ancient Hindu culture. In 1907, he said that "religion as practised today is the greatest separatist force." Therefore, complete divorce between religion and politics was the only remedy that he suggested. In fact, his approach to problem of politics was juridical and secular rather than religious or transcendental."[2] In his presidential address to the Amritsar Congress (1919) he declared: "In free India there would be no privileged classes or communities, no caste system or women bondage, where education is free and open to all."

Motilal Nehru was a champion of human rights and fundamental freedom. With an urgent quest for freedom he had been an ardent advocate of a Declaration of Rights. He lamented the omission of a Charter of Rights in the Act of 1919. For him, "constitutional reform without free citizenship is like rich attire on a dead body. Better to breathe God's free air in rags than be a corpse in the finest raiment."[3]

ESTIMATE OF MOTILAL NEHRU

Motilal Nehru was one of the prominent political personalities of Indian politics from 1919 to 1931. As the leader of the opposition in the Indian Legislative Assembly, he displayed rare parliamentary gifts. His intellectual powers and his firm perseverance made him the terror for the official benches. The political ideas of Motilal Nehru show a remarkable orientation to realism and secularism. Being some what an agnostic, it was easy for him to substantiate secularism in his politics. It is indeed creditable that the Nehru Report that he prepared in 1928 found an important place in the Constitution of Free India in 1950.

Notes

1. Chintamani, C.Y., Indian Politics Since Mutiny, op.cit, p.152
2. Quoted in Verma, V.P., op.cit, p.388
3. Ibid. P. 390

Chapter 36

SARDAR BHAGAT SINGH
— THE PRINCE AMONG MARTYRS
(1907-1931)

Bhagat Singh was the most famous and popular freedom fighter of his time. He was born in 1907 and was just a school boy at the time of the Jallianwala Bagh massacre. He was tall, robust, fair and handsome. He was very popular among students because of his fearless, daredevil attitude and his warm, generous temperament. He belonged to a family which had a tradition for social and political work. His uncle, Sardar Ajit Singh, was one of the leaders of the agitation of peasants in Punjab. For his agitational activities he was arrested in June 1907 and deported to Mandalay.

During the Non-cooperation Movement, Bhagat Singh and his classmates collected clothes made of foreign cloth and made a bonfire of them at public places. After the withdrawal of the Gandhian movement, Bhagat Singh joined the National College at Lahore in 1922.

Sachindra Nath Sanyal was the famous revolutionary of the earlier generation, whose sacrifice, sincerity and, above all, revolutionary fervour cast a spell on so many students of early 1920s. In 1922, Sanyal gave a talk to a group of students at Lahore. Bhagat Singh was one of them. Influenced by his talks, Bhagat Singh joined the Hindustan Republican Association formed by Sachindra Sanyal along with Sukhdev, Bhagwati Charan, etc.

Bhagat Singh had wide intellectual interests and read the writings of Rousseau, the Memoirs of Prince Kropotkin, lives of Mazzini and Garibaldi, 'The Indian War of Independence, 1857' by Savarkar and some of the writings of Bakunin. He also read Maxim Gorki's 'Mother' and books on the French revolution. He was greatly influenced by Leonid's novel, 'Seven Who Were Hanged.'

One day when he came to know that his father wanted him to marry and was negotiating a proposal, Bhagat Singh left his home and went to Kanpur. There he met Jogesh Chatterjea, Vijay Kumar Sinha and Batukeshwar Dutt. He started working in a journal which was edited by Ganesh Shankar Vidyarthi. A voracious reader, Bhagat Singh started writing under the pen-name, Balwant Singh. He translated Don Brin's novel, 'My Fight For Irish Freedom' in Hindi. After a year he returned to Lahore. He now wrote in various journals such as 'Akali' and 'Kirti', the magazines edited by Sohan Singh Josh. Bhagat Singh and Bhagwati Charan decided to start an organisation called Naujawan Bharat Sabha which stood for complete independence.

By 1920 a number of groups of revolutionaries were functioning at different places and were preparing for a revolution. All of them believed that India's freedom could be won only through armed struggle. These revolutionaries keenly felt the need for setting up an all-India organisation with its branches in different parts in India. To coordinate their work, Bhagat Singh from Lahore and Chandra Shekhar Azad from Benaras met, and they together contacted other revolutionaries, and undertook the work of building a well-knit and efficient secret organisation. While carefully chalking out the details of the future revolutionary activity, Bhagat Singh (who had read Marxist literature by then) also made a fervent plea for the ideological orientation of the group. Consequently on 9 September 1928, at the instance of Bhagat Singh, a new organisation named as Hindustan Socialist Republic Association was formed. The idea of this secret organisation was "to overthrow by force the government in India and to establish a Federated Republic Government instead".[1] Chandra Shekhar Azad was chosen as the Chief of active wing of this Organisation known as Hindustan Socialist Republican Army. Thus the religious basis of the revolutionary faith of Bengal revolutionaries of 1905 was substituted by a modern, progressive ideology.

Hindustan Socialist Republican Association was entirely a secular organisation. This is indicated by the fact that Bhagat Singh, who was a Sikh, removed his traditional hair style and beard. The members of this organisation were serious students of politics and were watching the political developments carefully. The Hindustan Socialist Republican Army had taken a lead in staging the anti-Simon Commission demonstration.

The death of Lala Lajpat Rai, who had succumbed to a head injury that he received during demonstration against the Simon Commission, infuriated the members of the Hindustan Socialist Republican Army. Bhagat Singh, Azad and Rajguru decided to Kill Scott, the S.P. of Lahore, who had hit Lala Lajpat Rai on the chest. The action was fixed on 15 December, 1928, a day on which the leaders of Kakori Conspiracy Case were hanged. But Scott did not come to office on that day, and the action was postponed till 17th December. Eventually, instead of Scott, the Dy. Superintendent of Police, Sanders, who was mistaken for Scott, was killed.

In order to curb revolutionary activities and trade union activities, the British government moved in the Central Assembly, the Public Safety Bill and the Trade Disputes Bill. The Bills empowered the government to destroy all civil liberties and to crush the possible uprising of the workers in the mills. On 20 March, 1929 many trade unionists and communists were arrested in different parts of India and were hauled up for hatching a conspiracy to overthrow the British government. This case came to be known as the Meerut Conspiracy Case. The Bills were being opposed by M.R. Jayakar, Motilal Nehru and Vitthalbhai Patel but the Viceroy had announced that he could use his special powers inspite of objections.

Bhagat Singh, with his political insight, told his colleagues in the HSRA that an appropriate demonstration against the government policy was the urgent need of the hour, and it was decided that a violent demonstration against the proposed repressive measures would be made by throwing bombs in the Central Assembly. The task was entrusted to Bhagat Singh and Batukeshwar Dutt. On 8 April, 1929 the two secured entry passes to the Central Assembly. At 12.30 pm. Vitthalbhai Patel (the first Indian Chairman of the Central Assembly) rose and announced: "I shall now give my verdict on the proposed Bills." As soon as these words were uttered, there was a deafening noise of a bomb explosion- Bhagat Singh had thrown the bomb. It was followed by a second bomb, thrown by Batukeshwar Dutt. Bhagat Singh fired two shots also and then both of them threw red leaflets all over. The first sentence of the statement was:" It takes a loud voice to make the deaf hear." The two men did not run away but got themselves arrested. Subsequently, the trial in the Assembly Bomb Case began on 7 May, 1929. Asif Ali, a leading lawyer of Delhi, appeared on behalf of Bhagat Singh and Batukeshwar Dutt. Both Singh and Dutt themselves made a spirited and noble statement before the judge. The following are some of the extracts from this historic statement: "We bore no malice against anyone of those who received slight injuries or against any person in the Assembly. On the contrary, we repeat that we hold human lives sacred beyond words and would sooner lay down our lives in the service of humanity than injure anyone else..... We then deliberately offered ourselves to bear the penalty for what we have done and let the imperialist exploiters know that by crushing individuals they cannot kill ideas.... Can then Ordinances and Safety Bills snuff out the flames of freedom in India?"[2] Their statements ended in the following words: "Revolution is the inalienable right of mankind. Freedom is imperishable birthright of all ... for these ideals and for this faith we shall welcome any suffering to which we may be condemned. To the altar of revolution, we have brought our youth as incense. For no sacrifice is too great for so magnificent a cause. We are content. We await the advent of revolution. Long Live Revolution."[3]

Again, in the statement, titled "The Philosophy of the Bomb', the Hindustan Socialist Republican Army had explained that: "We are sorry to admit that we, who attach so great a sanctity to human life, we, who dream of a very glorious future, when men will be enjoying perfect peace and full liberty, have been forced to shed human blood. But that sacrifice of individuals at the altar of a great revolution, which will bring freedom to all, rendering exploitation of man by man impossible, is inevitable."[4] "Bhagat Singh and his colleagues realised that 'Atankvad' was not 'Sampoorna Kranti' but they believed that 'Kranti' could not succeed without 'Atankvad'. Their vision was not only the birth of a new nation, but they also envisaged an end of the suffocating control of the exploiters who had the political power in their clutches. Though they killed and got killed they could not be called a trigger-happy lot."[5]

BHAGAT SINGH AND TERRORISM

Essentially, Bhagat Singh was a revolutionary and not a terrorist, as is commonly supposed. His actions revealed that. After throwing the bombs (which were actually powerful crackers, designed to explode with a loud noise rather than cause damage in the Assembly), he did not evade arrest, even though he knew this meant a certain death sentence for his actions. He also knew that the trial of the most famous and popular freedom fighter of the time would provide an opportunity to tell the nation some important things. A voracious reader, Bhagat Singh was always willing to rethink and revise his views. While in prison, he read a lot and this led him to renounce terrorism altogether. "In his document 'To Young Political Workers', written a month before his death he explains to the country's youth why they must enter mass work and organise the workers for decades of patient work and not expect quick results. In the same document, he also makes clear his attitude towards terrorism: "Let me announce with all the strength at my command that I am not a terrorist and I never was except perhaps at the beginning of my revolutionary career. And I am convinced that we cannot gain anything through these methods. Asked to explain what he meant by the word 'revolutionary' —

in describing his aims, Bhagat Singh says: "Revolution does not necessarily involve sanguinary strife, nor is there any place in it for individual vendetta. It is not the cult of the bomb or pistol. By revolution we mean that the present order of things, which is based on manifest injustice, must change... It is my considered opinion that bombs can't serve our purpose. Throwing bomb is not only useless but often harmful. Our chief aim is to mobilise toiling masses."[6]

BHAGAT SINGH ON GOD AND RELIGION

Bhagat Singh had a comprehensive scientific world view. In his extraordinary autobiographical essay he wrote: "I began to study.... My previous faith and convictions underwent a remarkable modification. The romance of the violent methods alone, which was so prominent among our predecessors, was replaced by serious ideas. No more mysticism, no more blind faith. Realism became our cult. The use of force is justifiable when resorted to as a matter of terrible necessity. Non-violence as a policy is indispensable for all mass movements. So much about methods. The most important thing was the clear conception of the ideal for which we were to fight... Any man who stands for progress had to criticise, disbelieve and challenge every item of the old faith... mere faith or blind faith are dangerous; they dull the brain and make a man reactionary. A man who claims to be a realist has to challenge the whole of the ancient faith. If it does not stand the onslaught of reason it crumbles down... criticism and independent thinking are the two "indispensable qualities of a revolutionary."[7]

BHAGAT SINGH ON COMMUNALISM

Bhagat Singh was one of the few freedom fighters who saw communalism as the major obstacle to the growth of the national movement. The manifesto of the Naujawan Bharat Sabha (the youth organisation founded by him and his colleagues) while drawing inspiration from Guru Gobind Singh, Shivaji and Hari Singh, comes down hard on leaders who made communal demands; "Our leaders are fighting among themselves to decide what will be the share of each community in the hoped achievement. Simply to hide their cowardice and lack of spirit of self-sacrifice, they are creating a false issue and screening the real one....we need people who are ready to fight and sacrifice. Without that spirit we shall not be able to fight the great two fold battle that lies before us-two-fold because of the internal foe, on the one hand, and a foreign enemy, on the other."[8] This political statement shows that an uncompromising opposition to all communal appeal was central to Bhagat Singh's writings.

ESTIMATE OF BHAGAT SINGH

Bhagat Singh's life was one of extraordinary integrity courage and consistency. He had emerged as the symbol of the aspiration for freedom. He left behind a compact, yet mature and comprehensive body of writings which are no less important or outstanding than his legendary deeds. The writings published by his colleagues Shiv Verma and Jagmohan Singh reveal an independent mind studying all contemporary issues and events to produce documents and essays which were far in advance of the time. The statement which he made before the Court, had a tremendous impact on Indians, particularly the Indian youth all over the country. Bhagat Singh, the prince among martyrs will have a perennial place in the annals of India's history.. He is one of the few legendary figures who commands universal respect from all sides of the ideological divide, even today.

Notes

1. Pradhan, G.P., op.cit, p. 110

2. Ibid, p.116

3. Ibid., p. 116

4. Quoted in Jain, L.C., M.N. Roy Memorial Lecture, published in the Radical Humanist, April, 1991.

5. Ibid.,

6. Quoted in Monteiro, Vivek, "Revolution Unravelled', Times of India, 21 March, 1993

7. Ibid.

8. Ibid.

Chapter 37

SUBHASH CHANDRA BOSE
— A ROMANTIC REVOLUTIONARY
(1897-1945)

Subhash Chandra Bose was born on 23 January, 1897 at Cuttack (Orissa) and is said to have died on 18 August, 1945. He was the greatest revolutionary and the most colourful figure of the Indian freedom movement.

Subhash began his life as a Vedantic mystic and roamed all over Northern India in search of a Guru. While yet a college student, he came into limelight with the Efoaten incident in which a European professor, who often denigrated Indian Culture was assaulted by him at the Presidency College. He had a brilliant educational career at Calcutta University. While studying there, he joined the university unit of the territorial army a training which proved quite useful to him afterwards. In 1919, he graduated with First Class Honours in Philosophy, and was soon sent to UK to compete for the much coveted Indian Civil Service. He successfully competed in the ICS examination in 1920 obtaining fourth position.

In 1921, Bose resigned from the Indian Civil Service to join the Non-cooperation Movement. But on Gandhi's sudden decision of withdrawal of the Non-cooperation Movement he was dejected, and his comment was: "To sound the order of retrenchment when public enthusiasm was reaching boiling point was nothing short of a national calamity."

Bose was appointed as the principal of the National College set up by C.R. Das, his mentor. In 1923, he supported the proposal of his political guru to carry on the struggle against British from within the legislatures. When C.R. Das became the Mayor of Calcutta, Subhash was appointed its Chief Executive Officer. This association with C.R. Das continued till the passing away of the latter in 1925. After Das, he was the undisputed leader of Bengal. As the Chief Executive Officer, he was arrested by the government of Bengal and deported to Mandalay in 1924. While still in detention, he was elected by his compatriots to the Bengal Legislative Council.

Subhash belonged to the left wing of the Indian National Congress. Along with Jawaharlal Nehru and Srinivas Iyenger he proposed Complete Independence as the goal of India as against Dominion Status, proposed by the Nehru Report (1928). At the Lahore Congress (1929) he pressed for a socialist programme along with a constructive programme. At the Karachi Congress (1931) he stood for a Socialist Republic and wanted both political freedom as well as economic emancipation.

Bose held almost every important post open to an Indian in the public life of the country. He was President of the All-India Trade Union Congress, the Youth Congress and other organisations. He was elected President of the Indian National Congress in 1938, and successfully fought reelection in 1939 even against the wishes of Gandhi. He sought a second term so that nationalists could take the advantage of the British preoccupation elsewhere because of the imminent War. But he had to resign the presidentship soon after, because several members of the Congress Working Committee did not agree with his method of work and ideology.

After sometime Bose organised the Forward Bloc (1939). He asked the Forward Bloc to observe from 6 to 13 April, 1940 as a national week launching a campaign of Civil Disobedience, and was arrested. But on the 6th day of a fast that he undertook in jail, he was allowed to go home. While interned at home he disappeared incognito on 16 January 1941. The story of his escape from the country is an epic of adventure. He went to Afghanistan, Italy, Germany and finally to Japan.

While feeling restless and caged abroad, Bose received an appeal from Rash Behari Bose, who had escaped to Japan and was involved in the bomb attack on Governor General Hardinge in 1912 at Delhi, to join him. Rash Behari Bose had organised an Indian National Army under the command of Mohan Singh to support Japan's war effort with the belief that Japan was to liberate India. Subhash accepted the invitation with alacrity, and arrived in Japan in June 1943. On 25 August 1943 he announced the formation of the Azad Hind Fauj and took over as Supreme Commander of the Indian National Army from Rash Behari Bose. In organising an army of about 60,000 Indian troops Subhash received great help from Japan.

Acclaimed as 'Netaji', Subhash gave the clarion call: "Give me blood and I promise you freedom". He gave the battle cry of 'March to Delhi'. On 21 October, 1943 Bose established the Provisional Government of Free India, which was recognised by China, Japan and Burma. From February

1944 to April 1945, the INA carried on a heroic campaign against the Allied Forces. Subhash led the Indian National Army through Burma, and crossed into India along with the Japanese forces. The Allies fought with tenacity and determination. Netaji moved from one battle-field to another. He often flew from Tokyo to Manila to Singapore to Rangoon. Unfortunately on one such trip to Tokyo on 18 August, 1945 Bose received fatal injuries in a plane crash in Formosa (Taiwan) and died in the evening. But there is no clear evidence of his death at the Taihaku airport. The last years of his life are charged with vivid drama and present to us a stirring and moving image of a great patriot and a 'lost hero'.

POLITICAL IDEAS OF S.C. BOSE

Bose was essentially a man of action. Though a student of Philosophy, he was not a systematic thinker. He had been tremendously inspired by the writings of Vivekanand and Aurobindo Ghosh. In Vivekanand he found the embodiment of fearless manhood. He also learnt from him: "Seek your own salvation in the welfare of humanity." Bose accepted the supremacy of a Providential Dispensation but thoroughly adhered to the conception of the reality of the world, and rejected the theory of illusion (Mayabad), as propounded by Shankaracharya.

In his ideology and method of work he had struck a line different from that of the Congress. This led to a great deal of misunderstanding between him and some important Congress leaders. He was convinced of the historic necessity of an armed uprising for achieving independence. When the War began, he argued that "British difficulties were India's opportunity", a perception not appreciated by Congress leadership.

Bose never displayed the enigmatic vagueness of the Mahatma, the Hamletian hesitancy of Jawahar Lal Nehru and the disconcerting quietetude of the Sardar. However, he was not strong in political manoeuvring. He was strong on attack but weak in defence. Subhash never appreciated the mingling of political and ethical issues. He was an extreme nationalist and believed in resorting to violent means for the liberation of the country. He was a critic of Gandhian political ideas and technique."[1]

Essentially, Subhash was a philosopher of activism, modernism, pragmatism and optimism. Patriotism was the essence of his personality and the supreme expression of his mind. In his political leanings Subhash was a leftist and supported the socialist programme. To the programme of political emancipation he added the item of thorough social and economic planning. At one time he envisaged a synthesis between communism and Fascism, but he did not work out the theoretical foundations and practical implications of this synthesis. Further, when

Subhash saw the unfolding of Hitler's Nazism he realised the unreality of his hope for synthesis between Fascism and Socialism. In an interview that he gave to the British Communist newspeak, 'Daily Worker', he was candid enough to declare that there would be no room for Fascism as providing a way out for a country like ours". Although his heroes were men like Hitler, Mussolini, DeValera, Mustafa Kamal Pasha and Lenin, he never sanctioned imperialistic expansion, nor did he subscribe to the cult of racial supremacy. Further, Subhash never allied himself with the exploiting and dominant classes. Instead, he was a recognised exponent of the interests of the masses.[3] Thus, Subhash never believed in the extreme tenets of Fascism.

ESTIMATE OF BOSE

The abiding eminence of Bose will be permanently enshrined in the history of India. For his burning patriotism, his devotion to the cause of Indian freedom and his intense suffering for the sake of his country (he was imprisoned ten times and was in jail for a period of eight years), Bose will always be hailed as a national hero.[4] His failure was that he was in a great hurry. His ultimatum to Britain at a time when the Second World War was on and resignation from the Presidency of the Congress Party were actions taken without careful considerations. So was his flight to Germany and Japan which yielded no fruit.

Above all, Subhash Chandra Bose was a great nationalist, a patriot of patriots. Apart from the memory of the INA, the lasting gift of Netaji is our national salutation, 'Jai Hind' which forms the triad of expression of, our nationalism along with 'Vande Matram' and the 'Jana Gana Mana'.

Notes

1. Verma, V.P., op.cit, p. 426
2. Chakravarty, Nikhil, 'Reflections on Subhash Bose', Mainstream, January 27, 1996, p. 16.
3. Ibid., pp. 431-32
4. Ibid., p. 434

Chapter 38

SARDAR VALLABHBHAI PATEL — THE IRON MAN OF INDIA (1875-1950)

Sardar Patel was the greatest of Indian leaders apart from Gandhi and Nehru. He was an indomitable freedom fighter, a strong administrator and a devout patriot. Though he is regarded as the 'Iron Man of India' he was intensely humane, fair minded, magnanimous and self-sacrificing.

Patel started his career as a legal practitioner with specialisation in criminal law. Out of magnanimity he accepted his brother, Vitthalbhai Patel's (the first Indian President of Central Legislative Assembly) request not to go first to England for Bar-at Law study. However, in 1913 he returned from England as a full-fledged barrister, and soon became a leading legal practitioner in Ahmedabad.

Patel made his entry into politics in 1918 when he was attracted by the personality of Gandhi in the cause of the peasants of Gujarat. In 1918, Patel acted as Gandhi's lieutenant in the Kheda district. During the days of Non-Cooperation Movement, like other leaders, Patel also gave up his roaring practice at the bar.

The Bardoli Satyagraha of 1928 was a landmark in the history of the Indian freedom movement. It projected the personality of Patel and proved his organising capacity and ability to lead people. The way he conducted the Satyagraha of the Bardoli peasants against the enhancement of land revenue earned for him the title of 'Sardar' from Gandhi. Later on, the Civil Disobedience Movement of 1930-31 catapulted him to a top ranking national leader. He was elected to preside over the famous Congress session at Karachi in 1931. Again, when the Congress decided in 1937 to accept office under the Government of India Act of 1935, Sardar Patel, while remaining out of government, controlled and directed the Congress ministries in the various provinces as the Supreme Generalissimo.

PATEL'S STAND ON PARTITION OF INDIA

As early as December 1946 or in early January 1947 Patel agreed to the proposal of V.P. Menon of having a divided India on the basis of Dominion Status. After his bitter experience of the Interim government, his comment was: "whether one liked it or not there were two nations in India."

ARCHITECT OF INDIAN INTEGRATION

Patel brought about the integration of more than five hundred princely states and redraw the map of India with a remarkable speed. In the words of Michael Brecher, "Patel was the directing genius behind the merger of princely states." He steamrolled native princes into accession to India in a remarkable manner. What none-not the great Mughal nor the British could achieve even at the point of sword, Patel won though sheer guile and subtle show of sinew. In less than a year, he wove 562 unwieldy and often unwilling, states into a composite whole bringing together about 80 million Indians under the umbrella of democracy in one stroke.

POLITICAL IDEAS OF SARDAR PATEL

Patel was a realist and a man of action. In his ideas he was a Gandhian, but he never believed in the absolute sanctity of non-violence. He accepted non-violence only as a policy and not as a philosophy of life. He had no ideological fervour and had something like a horror of theories and isms. Though a pragmatist, he was not an opportunist. He had something of both the lion and the fox in him and none understood better than him the mechanics and manipulations of Indian politics. Though not a "status-quoist", he would never like to threaten the Indian capitalists. He was the acknowledged leader of the Rightist section in the Congress, and a supporter of 'Gandhian Socialism.'[1] As such, he was opposed to large scale industrialisation and mass production which might lead to unemployment.

ESTIMATE AND ACHIEVEMENTS OF SARDAR PATEL

Patel's greatest achievement was the consolidation of the country from Kashmir to Kanyakumari, from Gujarat to Guwahati under one Central government. The liquidation of personal rule of princes in five hundred and odd states leading to the unification of the whole country has few parallels in history.[2] His achievement in the integration of states has won him a permanent place in modern Indian history. "He would rank with Bismarck and even higher in this regard", was the comment of the London Times. On his death on 15 December 1950 Rajaji remarked. "Patel was the architect of the Indian integration and solidarity of the Indian administration." His name will go down in the history of our country not only as a great captain of the national forces in the struggle for freedom, but also as a great organisor and administrator. "If Gandhiji was the father of the nation, Patel was the builder of the nation."

PATEL AND NEHRU

Patel is often juxtaposed with Nehru. It was Gandhi who created this duumvirate. The duumvirate led the Indian National Congress under the guidance of Gandhiji, and the two men ruled India during the explosive period from 1947 to 1950. The two men, however, represented divergent trends in Indian politics. This has led to label and stereotyping of the personae: Nehru was modern, Patel conservative; Nehru flexible, Patel stubborn; Nehru as radical leftist, Patel reactionary; Nehru as romantic realist, Patel realist and practical; Nehru as internationalist, Patel without any defined world view; Nehru as secular and Patel communalist.[3]

Today history offers us an opportunity to be more objective in our judgement of the two personalities. Now that socialists globalisation is overpowered by capitalist globalisation some ardent supporters of Sardar Patel believe that if Patel had been the first Prime Minister, India would not have got caught in the socialist and secularist trap. Patel never favoured the idea of a Hindu state. He never supported agitation for cow protection, because to him human protection was more important. He never considered the RSS or the Hindu Mahasabha as the custodians of Hinduism. According to him, Hinduism preached tolerance.

Patel's world view had not fundamentally altered despite his stay in England. His peasant background, age, conservative life style, traditional perspective were in total contrast to Nehru, who was universalist, socialist, rebel and modern. However, Patel has ultimately emerged the ideological victor, as the events that have taken place have been like the way he had visualised them.

It is worth noting that with all their temperamental differences, both Patel and Nehru had fundamental agreements about the most important aspects of public life. Both always admired each other. Even though they differed on several issues like Kashmir, Tibet, socialism, linguistic reorganisation of states, etc. but they never acted against each other, for Patel was too modest and Nehru too liberal. To illustrate, though Patel still commanded the Congress organisation in 1946, he allowed himself to be crossed out in favour of Nehru because Gandhi named Nehru as his successor. Patel on his part spurned the crown without any fuss. This shows his magnificent magnanimity, a rare phenomenon in politics.

Notes

1. Verma, V.P., op.cit, p. 292
2. Suda, J.P., pp. 421-22
3. Ketkar, Kumar, 'Sardar Patel, Prime Minister?', A Review Article, Times of India, 20 March, 1994.

Chapter 39

DR. RAJENDRA PRASAD
— THE GENTLEMAN OF INDIAN
POLITICS (1884-1963)

"Scholar, humanist, lawyer, writer, Rajendra Prasad was the sincerest disciple of Gandhi and a saintly figure in Indian politics."[1] He was born in a middle class family of Bihar and had a very brilliant educational career. In 1902, he stood first in the entrance examination of the Calcutta University, and obtained first class Honours in the B.A. examination. To start with, he became a lecturer at Muzaffarpur in 1908, and later on, at the City College, Calcutta. In 1911, he started practice at the bar in the Calcutta High Court and continued to do so there upto 1916. Thereafter, he shifted his practice to the Patna High Court and was regarded as a leading lawyer of the day.

It was Gandhi who inspired Rajendra Prasad to devote himself to public work, when he went to Bihar to study the conditions of the oppressed peasantry of Champaran. When the Non-cooperation Movement was started, Rajendra Prasad finally decided to give up his lucrative legal practice and devote his whole time to national work. He was imprisoned several times. The work he did for the relief of the earthquake sufferers in Bihar (1934) still remain enshrined in public memory as a splendid example of disinterested and unostentatious service. Apart from being an erudite scholar and a constitutional expert, Dr. Prasad was a true Gandhian. A silent, selfless, noble and dedicated worker, he became an acknowledged and leading exponent of Gandhian thought. He was chosen to fill the highest office of the Congress thrice, in 1934, 1939-40 and 1947-48. The esteem and regard which his compatriots had for him can be gauged from the great honour bestowed upon him. He was unanimously elected the President of the Constituent Assembly when it began functioning in 1947 and became the first President of India when she became a Republic in 1950, and he alone enjoyed two terms in this capacity, till today.

It is worth mentioning here that Dr. Prasad was not in favour of the political system that he presided over. In his 'At The Feet Of The Mahatma' (1955) he observed: "In order to be able to elect persons of proven character, the voters have got to be acquainted with them, but this is not possible in the present system, which allows constituencies of over a million voters. The solution, therefore, lies in the participatory democracy, with the village panchayat becoming the centre of gravity of the political system. With constituencies becoming unmanageable, the chances of misuse of the electoral system will be nominal. So, once Gram Panchayats are elected, these members can form the electoral college for Taluka and District Panchayats whose members, in turn, will elect legislators for the state and the Centre. We have also got to invest the power pyramid with the village panchayat being at the pinnacle and the Central government only exercising control over Currency, Defence, External Affairs, Railways, Civil Aviation and Communications. What is now the base of the pyramid should get the importance that legitimately belongs to it."

ESTIMATE OF DR. RAJENDRA PRASAD

Dr. Prasad was gentle and unassuming, simple and sincere. But "his simplicity was supported by an urbanity of the most cultured and polished type. A plebeian out and out, he was almost regal in his bearing."[2] In his tributes to Dr. Rajendra Prasad, J.P. Narayan writes: "Babu Rajendra Prasad was one of the greatest gentlemen of Indian politics. He was endowed with angelic qualities. He was a moral giant. He was a symbol of all that is good and noble in Indian culture. He was sweet and self-effacing, sensitive and demure, with an inborn aversion for anything mean or low, garish or loud. A true Gandhian as he was, high thinking and simple living came naturally to him."[3] By his training and temperament and the influence of his cultural environment, he was averse to committing any kind of offence to anybody. Prasad took Gandhism very seriously and practised Gandhian ideals in his personal life and political career. "He was a strong votary of non-violence. While non-violence was a matter of policy to Patel and others, for Prasad it was a philosophy of life."[4] After his retirement, Prasad openly declared himself in favour of the unilateral disarmament for India. Among congress leaders, who have dedicated their lives for the service of the nation and have suffered much for its sake, Prasad occupies a very high place. In the words of P.R. Menon, "Among the luminaries who adorn the political firmament of India today, Dr. Prasad is undoubtedly one of the most conspicuous."[5] In verity, there has been no one of his mien in the Indian Presidency since 1962.

Notes

1. Verma, V.P. op.cit, p. 293
2. Handa, R.L., Rajendra Prasad, Twelve Years of Triumph And Despair, Sterling Publishers, 1978, p.10
3. Jai Prakash Narayan's Foreward to Handa, op.cit,
4. Verma, V.P., op.cit, p.297
5. Menon, P.R., Eminent Indians, p.79

Chapter 40

CHAKRAVARTI RAJGOPALACHARI — AN EXEMPLARY STATESMAN (1878-1972)

Rajgopalachari was a multifaceted personality. He was a freedom fighter, statesman, scholar, thinker, humanist, and humourist. He had a reputation for unpredictable actions and for a quick and keen mind. "Strongly self-reliant, he had the courage of his conviction and was for over two decades one of the most outstanding, if not controversial, figures in Indian politics"[1] Gandhiji used to call him his 'conscience keeper'. He was Gandhi's `Southern Commander.'

After getting his degree in Law, Rajgopalachari started practice in Salem (his birth place) in 1900. Like Sardar Patel, he had the beginner's luck and his practice began to flourish. Like Dr. Rajendra Prasad, he plunged himself into politics when the Non-cooperation Movement was launched. Again, 25 days after Gandhi broke the Salt Law, CR followed in the footsteps of his master. He had a 150-mile march of 98 Satyagrahis from Trichy to Vedaranyam on 13 April 1930 to break the Salt Law. As a Congress leader, he had five spells in prison. During his regime as Premier of Madras (1937-39), Rajaji did considerable work in the fields of prohibition, removal of untouchability and in scaling down rural indebtedness.

THE ISSUE OF
C.R.'S STAND ON WORLD WAR-II

On the War issue Congress members were not one in their response to it. At one extreme stood S.C. Bose labelling it an 'imperialist war', and demanding for a Congress ultimatum to the Raj. On the opposite end was Rajgopalachari. Equidistant from C.R. and Bose was Nehru who did not see how an unfree India could join the Allies. He said: "We shall not participate as slaves." Bapu stood for unconditional support and regarded War with a 'British heart'. But does blackmail go with sympathy?, Rajaji would ask Gandhiji.[2]

To begin with, Rajaji was opposed to the resignation of Congress ministries, although he was the first Congress premier to resign, He agreed with V.P. Menon, who held that "it helped create a conviction among the Britishers that the Hindus were their irreconcilable enemies, and the Muslims took advantage of the Congress being in wilderness, supported the War effort and made British feel that they were reliable friends."[3] Again, in his book 'The Way Out' Rajaji expressed his regrets over the rejection of the Cripps Proposal. According to him, "the negotiations broke down over the interim arrangement for the War period and not over the prospects for the future." Rajaji left the Congress in 1942 when Gandhi gave the call of 'Quit India'. While opposing the Quit India call he said: "I don't agree that if Britain goes away, India will have the same scope for organising itself. Japan will fill the vacuum created by the British withdrawal."

CR'S STAND ON PAKISTAN

"Pakistan has been begotten in envy, conceived in hatred and delivered in malice." But to Rajaji "Pakistan was not so dreadful." Significantly, C.R. was the first Congress leader who accepted the demand for Pakistan in principle. He realised that an agreement with Jinnah was a necessary precursor to the establishment of a National Government at the Centre. Accordingly, in April 1944, he presented his formula to Jinnah which conceded the Muslim homeland, as demanded in the Lahore Resolution. Jinnah, however, rejected it dubbing it as "a parody and a negation of the Resolution." But it is a tribute to CR's statesmanship that Jinnah ultimately got the same Pakistan that was envisaged in the CR Formula, even though in 1944 it was outrightly rejected by Mr. Jinnah.

In the post-Independence period, Rajaji decried the government policies of heavy taxations, controls, licenses, permits through his mouth piece, 'Swaraj'. In 1959, he founded his own party, the Swatantra Party, to fight against the licence-quota Raj. Besides, he was all for retaining English and was not in favour of Hindi replacing English as a link language. In the last decade of his life Rajaji became a great pacifist. He was greatly worried about the growing arms race. In 1962, he led a 3-member mission with R.R. Diwakar and B. Shiva Rao for world peace to the USA. He strongly advocated the cause of unilateral renunciation of weapons by super powers. It is worth mentioning here that after the Goa Operation his comment was: "India has lost her moral power to raise her voice."

Apart from being a great statesman, Rajaji was a man of letters as well. He was a profound scholar and a versatile writer. He has written on varied subjects and his writings reveal depth and scholarship. Perhaps, the best service he has rendered to his countrymen as a litterateur is the writings of Ramayana and Mahabharat. Moreover, he had the knack of presenting the most abstruse philosophy or a difficult scientific theory in simple and lucid language, intelligible to the average man.

Rajaji valued his conscience much more than pelf and power. He had the courage of conviction to differ from the currently fashionable and accepted opinions even at a great sacrifice. He was a passionate lover of seemingly lost causes. Whether it was his plan to concede the demand of Pakistan or his proposals for educational reforms or unilateral disarmament, he had the courage of conviction to swim against the current.

ESTIMATE OF RAJGOPALACHARI

Rajgopalachari was a model of urbanity, good taste, friendly comment, sane advice, thoughtful reflection nothing pretentious and no preaching of sentimental humbugs. Among Congress stalwarts CR was the most level-headed person. He was never enamoured of socialistic ideas and strongly opposed controlled or command economy. For him, egalitarianism was a fallacy and a fraud. He was always in favour of economic liberalisation — a policy which has acquired universal appeal and become a new mantra at the moment.

Rajaji was in essence a warrior, a non conformist, a teacher, a rebel and a statesman. In the words of R.R. Diwakar, Rajaji was "a ruthlessly logical person and an instinct distilled hundred times."[4]. He combined in himself rare intellectual acumen, profound humanity and self - effacement. He was an exemplary statesman who upheld lofty values of life. As the Premier of Madras Presidency, the Governor of West Bengal, the first Indian Governor General, the Home Minister in the Central Cabinet and finally as the Chief Minister of the composite Madras State, he made a profound impact on the public mind by his prescience, ratiocinations, ability, sagacity and integrity.

Notes

1. Ahluwalias, op. cit, p. 96
2. Gandhi, Raj Mohan, The Rajaji Story (1937-72), Bhartiya Vidya Bhawan, Bombay, 1984, p.44
3. Ibid., p.49
4. Quoted in Chaudhary, Sandhya, Gandhi and Partition of India, Sterling Publishers, N. Delhi, 1984, p.106

Chapter 41

SIR SYED AHMED KHAN — THE PIONEER OF MUSLIM SEPARATISM (1817-98)

Undoubtedly, Sir Syed Ahmed Khan was the greatest leader of the Muslim community in the nineteenth century. He occupies a significant place as a leader of Muslim political thought. He is recognised as "the pioneer in the advancement of modern learning in the Muslim community and a great promoter of enlightenment."[1]

Sir Syed was a descendant from Hazrat Hussain, the grandson of the Prophet Mohammad in the 36th degree. He came from a noble family with long connections with the Mughal imperial rule. But instead of joining service in the Mughal Court, he preferred the services of the East India Company, and joined as a petty judicial officer in 1838. He rose to the position of a Munsif in 1841.

After the Movement of 1857 had ended, he wrote his famous book 'The Causes of The Indian Revolt' (Asbab Baghawat-e-Hind). From this Revolt he drew some lessons for his political philosophy. He deplored the absence of an effective communication between the rulers and the ruled. Therefore, he felt the necessity of friendship and sympathetic intercourse between the rulers and the ruled. According to him, the original and chief cause of the Mutiny was the exclusion of Indians from the Legislative Council.

After his retirement in 1878, he was appointed a member of the Public Service Commission by Lord Dufferin. From 1878 to 1882 he was a member of the Viceroy's Council. As a member of the Central Legislative Council, he supported the Central Province's Self-Government Bill of 1883. He expressed his satisfaction that India was getting training in the art of self-government. But at the same time, he objected to the introduction of the elective element in Indian politics, and thus remained, in the words of Mohd. Ali, "a loyalist of the loyalists". For him, British rule was the most wonderful phenomenon the world has ever seen. He declared that the Britishers were "Khilafatullah" or God's representatives on earth, who would reward Muslims for their loyalty.

AS AN EDUCATIONIST

Being sensitive to the trends and tenor of the time, Sir Syed wanted a fresh orientation of Islamic thought. He stressed the necessity of modern education. On 24 May, 1875, he founded a school in Aligarh, which soon developed into the Mohammedan Anglo Oriental College, now called the Aligarh Muslim University. His aim was to popularise the scientific and rationalistic Weltanschauung of the West for the purpose of enlightenment of the mind. But his immediate and pragmatic consideration was that the Muslim community should take to English education for obtaining necessary training for getting good jobs under the government. He wanted an educational curriculum synthesising the old and the new learning. He wanted to give place of pride both to secular modern education and to Islamic theory.

AS A SOCIAL REFORMER

Like the Hindu reformers of the 19th century, he recognised the importance of social reform among the Muslim community and pleaded for it in his periodical 'The Social Reformer'. He founded the Mohammedan Educational Conference to engender enthusiasm for social reforms, modern education, general economic and intellectual progress. Sir Syed was far from being an orthodox or a fundamentalist. He had a progressive outlook. He gave a liberal interpretation of the Quran. He tried to interpret Islamic theology with reference to contemporary rationalism and values. As such, he had a rational approach to the Shariat. No wonder, Sir Syed was dubbed "an agent of devil" by the Imam of Mecca, and became an anathema to Jamal-ud-Din Afghani, the pioneer of Pan-Islamism.

POLITICAL IDEAS OF SIR SYED — AS A NATIONALIST

In the beginning, he was inspired by patriotic sentiments. He said in a speech (27 January, 1883): "India is the motherland for both of us (that is, the Hindus and Muslims) who breathe the same air, drink the water of holy rivers of Ganges and Jamuna and consume the products of the same earth which God has given to the country and live and die together." In his opinion, "India is like a newly wedded bride whose two beautiful and luminous eyes are the Hindus and the Musalmans; if the two exist in mutual concord the bride will remain forever splendent and becoming, while if they make up their mind to see in different directions, the bride is bound to became squinted and even partially blind." Another speech by him is still more revealing of his nationalistic sentiment. In his reply to an address presented to him by Arya Samaj, he observed: "The word 'Quam' refers to the inhabitants of the country. The word 'Hindu' does not denote any religion. Every Indian can call himself a Hindu, for he who lives in India is a Hindu."

In this nationalistic phase of his career, he supported the Ilbert Bill, which sought to eliminate the discrimination against the authority of Indian judges. Again, in 1884, during his trip to Punjab, he exhorted the people of both communities to forge a united front, so as to evolve a composite nationhood. Thus, Sir Syed remained a champion of Indian nationalism and stood for territorial nationalism upto 1887.

However, after 1887 we see a marked change in Sir Syed's attitude. The tide had now turned. He now became suspicious of the national movement led by the Indian National Congress. He advised Muslims to keep aloof from the Congress organisation. Quoting Sir Syed, M.N. Roy writes: "Those of the Hindus, who inaugurated the agitation for representative government and social reforms, were intellectual bourgeoisie, whereas the Aligarh alumni belong to the landed aristocracy with social and political tendencies predominantly feudal. Elements so diverse socially could not unite in a national movement."[2] Because of anti-Congress attitude, Sir Syed opposed tooth and nail the Congress proposal to hold simultaneous examinations for recruiting best talents in the country. In addition, he took lead in the establishment of two associations meant as a counterpoise to the Indian National Congress: the United Indian Patriotic Association (1888) and the Mohammedan Anglo-Oriental Defence Organisation (1893).

SIR SYED'S VIEWS ON REPRESENTATIVE DEMOCRACY

According to Sir Syed, Islam was opposed to personal rule or monarchy. He was one of the first Indians to plead for a responsive government and representative government. But he was opposed to the system of representation by election or popular government. In fact, Sir Syed had the dread of the numerically overwhelming large Hindu community. He felt that the advance of popular government would result in stifling and even suppressing the interests of the Muslims who are in a minority. He argued that "the system of representation by election was most unsuited to India because India did not constitute a homogeneous nation. It is unsuited to India because in India "caste distinction still flourish, there is no fusion of races and religious distinctions are still violent and education in the modern sense has not made an equal or proportionate progress among all sections of the people."[3]

By 1893, Sir Syed began to emphasize that India was inhabited by different nationalities, professing different faiths, speaking different languages and having different historical traditions. Hence, the Muslims cannot be considered as part and parcel of the same nation. In short, Muslims constitute a separate nation. Now his argument was "How can the Muslims and Hindus sit at the same throne and remain equal in power. It is necessary that one of them should conquer the other and thrust it down. To hope that both will remain equal is to desire the impossible and inconceivable"[4] In another speech he remarked: "No nation could be made of a mere geographical expression such as India was, for the Hindus and the Muslims were so apart in regard to their aims and aspirations that they could not be blended into a single nation."[5] Thus, an analysis of his speeches after the 80's of the last century indicate that a nationalist Syed was replaced by a sectarian communalist. Sir Syed Ahmed was no longer the upholder of territorial nationalism.

In the light of these perceptions that Sir Syed then entertained, it is not surprising that he preferred the British rule to that of the Congress, a body dominated by the Hindu community. The question arises though, as to how Sir Syed changed from an ardent nationalist to a staunch communalist ? There are several factors[6] responsible for this metamorphosis in his outlook:

1. DIVIDE AND RULE POLICY OF THE BRITISH RULERS:

As a matter of fact, the British rulers were horrified to see the remarkable unity between the two major communities during the revolt of 1857. Hence, they adopted the policy of divide and rule. Through the good offices of Theodore Beck, the first principal of the Aligarh College, efforts were made to wean Sir Syed, the rising Muslim star, away from growing nationalism in the country. Beck had great influence on Sir Syed, and he succeeded in convincing him that Anglo-Muslim alliance alone would ameliorate the Muslim community.

2. SHORTSIGHTEDNESS OF CONGRESS LEADERS:

The founders of the Congress displayed incredible shortsightedness in not reading the mental contours of Sir Syed. No attempts were made for a reconciliation with him. Sir Syed had hoped to be at best the third president of the Congress but it went to another Muslim leader, Badruddin Tyabji. Thus, getting disillusioned with the Congress Syed hastened to fall in the communalist camp, just as Mr. Jinnah did a few years later.

3. FLATTERY OF SYED AHMED KHAN:

The British made the most of the opportunity by honouring Syed Ahmed Khan with the title Knight Commander of the Star of India in

1889. Thereafter Sir Syed made frantic efforts to prove the bonafides of Muslim loyalty to the British.

4. BRITISH HOSTILITY TO HINDUS:

Syed always aimed at raising of Muslim intelligentsia to a higher and better status. With this goal in view, he always looked to the British for support. Since the British started distancing from the Congress after 1887, Syed followed suit.

5. SYED'S KEENNESS TO UPLIFT MUSLIMS:

Although the influence of Mr. Beck on Syed was undeniable, it was not the sole factor in his conversion. Syed was unhappy about British callousness towards Muslims after the Mutiny, and he was sincerely striving for a rapproachement. He believed that Muslim interests lay in siding with the foreign rulers rather than with the Congress, which had become a pinprick in the eyes of the British. He felt that any support to the Congress would have meant antagonising the British and thereby acting as a setback to the Muslims' uplift.

ESTIMATE AND CONTRIBUTIONS OF SIR SYED

Since the beginning Sir Syed emphasized the necessity of interaction between the rulers and ruled and for this purpose he suggested inclusion of chosen Indian representatives in the Legislative Council, which was done by the Indian Council Act of 1861. He himself adorned the Council for five years (1878-82). Further, he suggested the formation of a suitable organisation that could keep in touch with the British Parliamentarians regarding the needs and aspirations of the Indian people. It resulted in the establishment of the British-Indian Association in 1866. Again, Sir Syed vehemently supported the Ilbert Bill (1883) which provided for the elimination of racial discrimination in judicial administration. He also joined Surendra Nath Banerjea for securing equal facilities and opportunities for Indians to enter the Indian Civil Service.

Sir Syed's greatest achievement, however, was that he liberalised and modernised Islam in India. "He was the greatest protagonist of modernism in Islam in India."[7] He made the first concerted efforts to reconcile Islam with rationality and Western science.

Sir Syed held liberal views on social questions. He was keen to eradicate social evils which had crept into the Muslim society. For instance, he was opposed to ritualism, polygamy and easy divorce. However, he was against sweeping changes in religious and cultural matters. To quote Moin Shakir, "Despite his rationalism in politics and radicalism in religious matters, Sir Syed was not progressive in his views on social matters. He supported the system of purdah and considered the education of men more important than that of women. Moreover, his efforts were confined to the promotion of the upper and middle classes."[8] Agreeing with him, A.G. Noorani also formed the opinion that "Sir Syed modernised the Muslim Ashraf (gentry) but made them more communal."

Summarising the political views of Sir Syed Ahmed Khan, Moin Shakir observes: "His political programme was isolationism, separatism, withdrawal and adherence to mendicancy."[9] In the opinion of A.G. Noorani, "Sir Syed's three pronged approach — loyalism, separatism and modernism — paved the way which eventually led to partition of India. "All told, Sir Syed was equally responsible for Islamic integration as well as Islamic separatism in Indian body politic. He was the first Muslim spokesman who spoke of the Muslims being a separate race. "He was the first Muslim leader to declare that both Hindus and Muslims are two different nations with separate and often conflicting economic, political and cultural interests."[10] A renowned historian, B.R. Nanda also accuses Sir Syed of "sowing seeds of Muslim separatism: He was the forerunner of separatism in India." A.G. Noorani also agrees with B.R. Nanda's observation. Another well known authority, Pendrel Moon, observes: "Sir Syed laid down the premises which led naturally, perhaps, even necessarily to the idea of Pakistan." To conclude, an embryonic vision of two-nations is implicit in Sir Syed's thinking.

Notes

1. Verma, V.P., op.cit, p. 357
2. Roy, M.N., India In Transition, op.cit, p. 223
3. Quoted in Bhagwan, Vishnu, op.cit.p. 17
4. Quoted in Bhagwan, Vishnu, op.cit.p. 18
5. Quoted in Ibid., p. 19
6. Ibid., pp. 20-22
7. Gopal, Ram, op.cit, p. 266
8. Shakir, Moin, op.cit, p. 24
9. Ibid., p. 26
10. Struggle of Independence, Official Publication of Government of Pakistan.

Chapter 42

MAULANA MOHAMMAD ALI
— THE AUTHOR OF PAN-ISLAMISM
(1878-1931)

Mohd. Ali was born at Rampur (UP) in 1878 and died in London in 1931. He studied at Aligarh and Oxford. He was truly a product of the Aligarh Movement. In 1911, he began a journalistic career and started his own paper, 'The Comrade' to enlighten the Muslim community to make their proper contribution to territorial patriotism. He also edited another paper 'Hamdard', which was started in 1914.

Mohd. Ali collaborated with the Mahatma during the Non-Cooperation Movement. In 1921, he founded the Jamia Millia Islamia at Delhi. In 1923, he presided at the Coconada Congress Session where he made an eloquent argument for Hindu-Muslim unity. In 1928, he left for Europe, never to return to India. He attended the First Round Table Conference (1930-31), ignoring the decision of the Congress to boycott it.

MOHD. ALI'S VIEWS ON RELIGION

Basically, a Muslim theologian, he had a deep faith in the doctrine of the Quran. According to him, "Islam is the last word on human civilisation." As such, he was opposed to liberal and rational interpretation of Islam. Unlike Sir Syed, Azad and Iqbal, he had a revivalist outlook.

POLITICAL IDEAS OF MOHD. ALI

Mohd. Ali was the first Muslim leader of the masses. Like Tilak, Ali also used religion to provide a mass base to Indian politics. He intensified a religious approach to politics. Ali's religiosity, however, vitiated his political philosophy. To him, "the recognition of the communal identity of the Muslim was the basis of any constructive solution of Indian problems"[1].

ALI'S VIEWS ON DEMOCRACY

Ali's ideas about democracy appear vague, immature and irrelevant and betray a lack of realistic understanding. He demonstrated a revivalist outlook on the matter.

MOHD. ALI AND THE KHILAFAT MOVEMENT

Mohd. Ali was the leading figure in the Khilafat Movement. Along with his elder brother, Maulana Shaukat Ali, he played a key role in the Khilafat agitation. For him, Khilafat was the most essential institution of the Muslim community throughout the world. The Caliphate in Islam symbolised both the temporal and the religious leadership of the Muslims. The Khilafat Movement had three aims: (1) The Khilafat would not be dismembered. The Khalifa should have sufficient temporal power.; (2) In Arabia there would be exclusive Muslim control without Mandate or Protectorate; and (3) Khalifa would be the Warden of all Holy places[2]. For Ali, the Khilafat Movement was also a means to achieve the object of Pan-Islamism. A conservative with a revivalist outlook, Pan-Islamism was the concomitant of his rigid orthodoxy. As such, he accepted the ideology of Pan-Islamism sponsored by Sultan Abdul Hamid-II of Turkey, whom he regarded as the Vicegerent of God himself. Ali went to Europe in 1920 on a Khilafat deputation. But he returned in a dejected and frustrated mood.

In this context, the comment of M.N. Roy is worth quoting here: "There was no one like Ali Abdul Razak in India to declare that the Khilafat has always been and continued to be "a misfortune of Islam and a source of evil and corruption." According to M.N. Roy, "The Muslim intellectuals of modern Indian awoke not to Indian nationalism, but the dream of extra national existence, whose realisation however has been rendered impossible by various factors outside India and beyond their control and comprehension."[3] As a matter of fact, the Khilafat agitationists were flogging a dead horse, for the institution of Khilafat was no more than a historical relic.

MOHD. ALI'S CONCEPT OF NATIONALISM

Mohd. Ali's concept of nationalism suffered fluctuations in response to the demands of contemporary communal politics. His nationalism was tempered by what he called "super nationalism." In the early years, he looked to the Pan-Islamic concept of Khilafat. He had loyalty not only to teachings of Quran but he actively sympathised with Pan-Islamism. After 1924 Ali's leanings towards the concept of Islamic brotherhood received an additional psychological impetus from the dark deeds of communal frenzy in India. Later on, at the Round Table Conference, he announced that he belonged to two non-concentric circles. In his own words, "I belong to two circles of equal size but which are non-concentric. One is India and the other is the Muslim world."[4]

He treated Islam as a super-nationalist and India as a nationalist. He said "In India the Muslims are the blood-brothers of Hindus, but outside India there are millions who share their faith."

MOHD. ALI ON HINDU-MUSLIM PROBLEM

In 1911, he wrote in 'The Comrade' "We have no faith in the cry that India is united. The problems of India are almost inter-national. We may not create today the patriotic fervour and the fine national frenzy of Japan but a concord like that of Canada is not beyond bounds of practicability.[5]". It may not be a love marriage, born of romance and poetry but a marriage of convenience honourably contracted and honourably maintained."[6]

According to K.K. Aziz, "Ali's conviction about the essential disunity of India persisted. Unless some new force other than the misleading unity of opposition united this vast continent of India, it will remain a geographical misnomer."[7] In 1912, Ali had come very near to suggesting a partition of the country. In 1913, he suggested as a solution for the Hindu-Muslim problem that "North India may be assigned to the Muslims and the rest to the Hindus."

ESTIMATE OF MAULANA MOHAMMAD ALI

Maulana Mohd. Ali was a fearless but emotional man. He was a man of sentiments, straightforward, outspoken and even blunt. He was not a gifted political philosopher but a passionate propagandist. According to him, political power is coextensive with faith. In other words, in his thoughts religious and political ideas converged.

Mohd. Ali's political thinking went through three phases: The Comrade, the Khilafat and the post-Khilafat period. According to Moin Shakir, Mohd. Ali represents a remarkable synthesis of apparently conflicting trends and currents of Muslim religious and political thought in India. "Ali was at once the advocate of supremacy of Islam and the federation of faiths. He evolved his theory of cultural federalism, "federation of faiths" in order to meet the unique situation prevailing in India. He attempted at a compromise between Pan-Islamism and Indian nationalism. True to his genius for inconsistency, he advocated the ideal of the United Faith in India."[8]

Mohd. Ali was not only the author of Pan-Islamism but also the most important spokesman of Islamic nationalism. Regrettably, "it is a sad reality that those who followed the technique and strategy of Mohd. Ali fought the battle of Pakistan and won it."[9]

Notes

1. Verma, V.P., op.cit, p. 362
2. Ibid., p. 363
3. Roy, M.N., India In Transition, op.cit, p. 224
4. Mohd. Ali quoted in Verma, V.P., op.cit, p. 364
5. Mohd. Ali quoted in Ibid., p. 363
6. Mohd. Ali quoted in Shakir Moin, op.cit, p. 84
7. Aziz, K.K., op.cit, p. 119
8. Shakir, Moin, op.cit, p. 778
9. Khaliquzzaman, Chaudhary, Path Way To Pakistan, p. 110

Chapter 43

SIR MOHAMMAD IQBAL — A CONSTRUCTIVE REVIVALIST

Dr. Iqbal was an outstanding figure, a man of letters, a teacher, a lawyer, a politician and a poet, a religious philosopher and a political ideologist. Iqbal played an important role in the history of Indian Muslims.

Iqbal was born at Sialkot (Punjab). He belonged to a middle class family. He took his Master's degree in Philosophy from the Government College, Lahore, He had been a lecturer at the Oriental College and subsequently at the Government College, Lahore. After six years of service at the Government College, Lahore, Iqbal went to Europe for higher studies. He received higher education in Philosophy, both at Munich and Cambridge Universities. From 1905 to 1908 he conducted advanced research at Cambridge under McTaggart and James Ward, who considerably influenced his philosophical views. He wrote a doctoral dissertation on "Metaphysics in Persia' at the Trinity College, Cambridge. He also did a law course at London.

After his return from Europe (1908) he resumed his post at the Government College, Lahore. At the same time, he also started practice at the Bar. Though a lecturer in Philosophy, he established himself as a rising Urdu poet, whose early poems breathed strong national fervour. In 1916, he gave up teaching and began to concentrate more on poetry along with legal practice, and soon came to be regarded as an outstanding litterateur and thinker. The government honoured him with a Knighthood in 1922.

Iqbal, however, was drawn to politics in the last phase of his life. From 1925 to 1928 he was a member of the Punjab Legislative Council. In 1930, he was elected President of the annual session of the Muslim League at Allahabad. His presidential address is considered a landmark in Indian politics. Iqbal was nominated as a delegate to the Second and Third Round Table Conference at London to discuss India's constitutional problems.

In his early life, Iqbal had been deeply influenced by the ideals of Jalaluddin Rumi (1207-73), as eloquently expressed in "Masnavi Shareef". As a religious philosopher, Iqbal attempted a reconstruction of Muslim religious thought and wrote 'Reconstruction of Religious Thought In Islam'. He attempted to achieve a harmony between the dominant trends of Islamic theology and jurisprudence and the phenomenal advance of human thought in recent centuries.

Iqbal was basically a literary genius and not a political figure or thinker. He expresses his views in his poems and articles, and in his Six Lectures on the 'Reconstruction of Religious Thought In Islam'.

METAPHYSICAL FOUNDATIONS OF IQBAL'S POLITICAL THOUGHT

(A) THE ULTIMATE EGO: Iqbal started his career as a pantheistic mystic. But under the influence of his Cambridge teachers he became a theistic pluralist and as such became hostile to the Platonic and Sufist tendency of exalting contemplation. Thereafter he found solace in the doctrine of the Quran which he interpreted as a philosophy of absolute integral Ego ever rising to multiplicity and finitude. He was a strong supporter of the theory of monotheism preached by Islam. He also interpreted the Quranic doctrine of the universe as a theory of creative evolution. He adhered to the concept of an ultimate spiritual reality, and consequently believed in the actualisation of a "larger purpose" in human history." Reality, according to Iqbal, may be regarded as eternal spiritual purposive activity.[1]

The Western civilisation had two diametrically opposite effects on Iqbal. On the one hand, the scientific attitude of mind and the exuberant initiative of Europeans, their untiring energy, the immense vitality and hectic activity of European life and the vision of tremendous possibilities before the human life seemed to impress him the most. But, on the other hand, he was disillusioned by vulgar materialism of European society which resulted in the "soul destroying frustration of most individuals and by bestial competition between fellowmen and between nation and nation."[2]

In his 'Payam-i-Mashriq' he reveals the hollowness of a materialist Weltanschauung. He denounced the European civilisation as inhuman, rapacious, predatory and decadent. He approvingly quoted writers like Nietzsche, Schopenhaur, Spengler and Karl Marx, holding conflicting views to denounce its different aspects. He, therefore, did not like his countrymen to follow the West completely but to take advantage of what was valuable in Western civilisation. He considered Islam and its tenets superior to the Western civilisation. Islam, to Iqbal, is a perfect system. He induced his Muslim brethren to imbibe in themselves the dynamism of the West and the moral values of Islam. Thus the Western influence made him challenge the attitude of resignation and quiet contentment encouraged by Sufism. It made him revolutionise the Islamic thought by repudiating the concept of a fixed and static universe presided over by a dictatorial God and substitute it by the view that the world was a dynamic thing and was being advanced by man and by God through man.[3]

Iqbal was a philosopher of the cult of the Ego. He regarded God as the supreme Ego. The finite egos are the differentiation of the absolute Ego.

(B) THE PHILOSOPHY OF TIME: The universe is an organic system of interconnected events pulsating with life and energy. It is a process of continuous origination and manifestation. It is worth noting here that Iqbal formulated his metaphysical concepts at a time when Einsteinean Relativity and Plank's Quantum Mechanics were dominating the world of science. He was aware that modern researches in physics had made obsolete the old concept of matter as hard substance projected in space and time. Iqbal maintains the objectivity of the external universe but denies its material location in space and time. He departs from the trend of the mechanistic methodology of science in attributing a teleological character to the world process. He goes a step further and like a subjectivist calls matter as "spirit in space-time reference." He accepted from modern physics and philosophy the notion of the neutralisation of the substantiality of matter.[4]

Iqbal believes in a dynamic view of the universe. To him, nature is not a static closed entity. In place of the notion of fixed futurity, he sponsors the concept of creativity almost on the lines of A.N. Whitehead. Nature, according to Iqbal, is a growing process of interconnected events. There is never-ceasing growth. As an exponent of the concept of creativity, he repudiates the Nietzschean "mystery of eternal recurrence" as mechanicistic and fatalistic. According to Iqbal, time is real and Islam sees in temporal progression a symbol of reality. He also disfavours the Greek and the Hindu view of circular movement of time. He accepts the Bergsonian distinction of serial or spatialised mathematical time and pure duration which is change without sequential succession. But he differs from the French philosopher on two main respects: First, while Bergson is a vitalist, Iqbal is a spiritualist; Second, Bergson repudiated the teleological character of reality on the consideration that teleology makes time unreal. Iqbal imparts a purposive nature to reality.[5]

(C) THE HUMAN EGO: FREEDOM AND IMMORTALITY: Iqbal accepts the Quranic views regarding the human Ego. According to the 'Jawaid Nama' of Iqbal, there are three steps in the evolution of the Ego: (1) The realisation of the creative possibilities of the Ego is the first stage. It is the stage of individuality; (2) The second stage is to see the Ego in the context of other egos. This may be called the stage of sociality. Iqbal held that self has no meaning if it does not identify itself with general objectives of society. It cannot have an independent existence; (3) The third stage is to realise God and to view the Ego in the perspective of this divine consciousness. By being steadfast before the eternal light of God one can become powerful and thus partly be like the omnipresent God. The Ego is not immortal but has the capacity for immortality. Immortality is a goal and not a possession.[6]

(D) RELIGIOUS EXPERIENCE: It is possible to attain the experience of the spiritual real through intuition. Intuition, however, is not super-rational but is of the type of cognition and volition. Intuition and rational thought complement each other because intuition is the deepening and elevation of thought. If intuition reveals the eternal nature of reality, rational thought seeks to probe into the phenomenal sphere.[7]

(E) PRAYER: ITS SOCIAL AND POLITICAL IMPLICATIONS: Cosmopolitanism is the necessary political implication from the concept of a Supreme Ego. From the unity of all-inclusive Ego, who creates and sustains all Egos follows the essential unity of mankind. According to Iqbal, "The differentiations of mankind into tribes, races, and nations are only for the pragmatic purpose of identification. There are no intrinsic and inherent ranking and gradation. Prayer has a moral purpose. It expresses the yearning of man for association with the supreme Ego. But collective prayer has wider sociological aspect too. It expresses social solidarity. The annual ceremony at Mecca expresses Islamic fraternity in concrete shape. Thus, prayer has a political purpose too.[8]

(F) THE SPIRIT OF MUSLIM CULTURE: Iqbal repudiates the concept of pure contemplation and the attitude of ignoring the factual and the concrete. He condemned the mystic minimisation of the role of intellect as a factor responsible for the decadence of the oriental nations. He wanted to revive the vigorous spirit of early Islam. He appreciated the doctrine of Karmayoga taught by Sri Krishna but he was hostile to the dialectics of Sankara.[9]

The gospel of Islam, as interpreted by Iqbal, is one of activity and strength. Action contains the pith of life. From the concept of the Ego there follows the notion of a sturdy individualism. Iqbal would not put much reliance on the sheer force of numbers. The sole sources of strength in society are self-reliant individuals or what Iqbal calls "Self-concentrated individuals".[10]

(G) THE SUPER MAN: Like Nietzsche, Iqbal is an exponent of the concept of the Superman (Insan-i-Kamil), but for him superemehood comes through self-discipline and not through conceit or self-will. The two characteristics of the Iqbalian superman are: (i) absolute self-control and (ii) Willing obedience to the ordinances of God. Even his Superman is bound by the ethics of Islam.[11]

POLITICAL IDEAS OF IQBAL

Iqbal was an Islamic revivalist. In his 'Six Lectures' he wrote "The ultimate spiritual basis of all life, as conceived by Islam, is eternal and reveals itself in variety and change. But life is not for change, pure and simple. It has within it, elements of conservatisms also. Man in his forward movement cannot help looking back to his past. The spirit of man in its forward movement is restricted by forces which seem to be working in the opposite direction. Life moves with the weight of its own past on its back. No people can afford to reject their past entirely; for it is their past that has made their personal identity."[12]

But Iqbal was never an absolute revivalist. He was rather a progressive revivalist. He did recognise the immense significance of the forces of social stability and conservatisms but he wanted the liberal school of Muslim jurisprudence to interpret the "fundamental legal principles in the light of the experiences of the jurists and in view of the changed situation of the day."[13]

Iqbal accepted a religious solution of the problems of the modern world. He was repelled by materialism, atheism and plutocracy of Western civilisation. He condemned Machiavelli as a "messenger of Satan" because he separated ethics from politics and also godlessness of Nietzsche. He pleads for the assertion of the Islamic concept of Faqr which imparts strength and provides the capacity for the conquest of evils and passions. Thus, religion is a source of progress to him. What is needed is faith in the abiding continuity of historical heritage and a culture founded upon religious principles. These ideals of social and political resurrection have to be rooted in the acceptance of a spiritual cosmology.[14]

Iqbal had a theocratic conception of political power and advocated the Islamic religious orientation. He was opposed to the modern secularist approach which considers religion to be a private affair of the individual. To quote Iqbal, "The proposition that religion is a private affair of an individual has no sanction in Quran. In Islam, God and universe, spirit and matter, church and state are organic with each other." To him, religion is to shape all phases of life. He believed that religion is the power of the utmost importance in the life of the individual as well as states. The religious ideal is organically related to the social order which it has created. He believed in the total governance of all aspects and phases of life by the law of the Shariat. In his opinion, the various aspects of a man's life-social, religious, political and economic cannot be compartmentalised. Thus, politics can be separated from religion at its own peril. In his own words, "JUDA HO DIN SIASAT SE TO RAH JATI HAI CHANGEZI" The Quran therefore considers it necessary to unite religion and state, ethics and politics in a single revelation. Unlike Christianity, there is no duality of a spiritual world and a temporal world in Islam.[15]

Iqbal believed in the conception of a human commonwealth based on the acceptance of the sovereignty of God. In place of nationalism which separates, he advocated the concept of Islamic humanism. Since nationalism was a political concept, it was not in consonance with the true spirit of Islam.

The state, according to Islam, is only an effort to realise the spiritual in a human organisation. Thus, Iqbal sponsored theocracy in the sense of exalting the spiritual principle as the basis of political governance. But he never subscribed to the cult of the ruler as the vicegerent of God. His theocracy is a neutralisation of force and domination.

The modern orientation to politics expressing itself in the concept of sovereignty of the people and the supremacy of the General Will failed to satisfy him. "The notion of democracy, for him, does not take into account the dissimilarities in the inherent capacities and endowments of the individuals. The heads are counted and not weighed."[16] In a theocratic state the sovereignty of God is to prevail, according to Iqbal. But he failed to identify the medium of expression of such a divine sovereignty in matters, political and economic.

CRITIQUE OF CAPITALISM AND SOCIALISM

Adhering to a Quranic statement he says: "God has made the earth for his creatures. God is the true owner of all wealth and, the ruler is only a trustee." Iqbal was an opponent of exploitation in all its forms. He espoused the claims of the peasants and the labourers, and even predicted a revolution against inequalities of capitalism. But he never became a socialist, nor did he have any sound grounding in the economics and sociology of socialism/marxism.

PAN-ISLAMISM OR ISLAMIC UNIVERSALISM

Prior to his visit to Europe (1905-08), Iqbal was an ardent nationalist and used to write patriotic poems. His poem "Hindustan Hamara" eulogised the greatness of India. He regarded India as the best in the whole world. In another poem, "Naya Shivala' he expressed that "every particle of the country's dust was a holy as an idol." (Khake watan Ka Mujhko Har Zarra Devta Hai.). In place of strangeness, separatism and alienation he pleaded for a genuine unity among the inhabitants of the country. But later on, he became a champion of Islamic aspirations towards Muslim fraternity and declared himself to be a Pan-Islamist. When he wrote 'Tarana Millat' he forgot all about 'Tarana-i-Hind. In place of the territorial and racialist concept of nationalism he became the heralder of an Islamic renaissance. In his 'Tarana Milli' he wrote: 'China, Arabia and India are ours. We are Muslims and the whole world is ours. From the principles of Tauhid (unity of God) he drew the implication of a world unity. In the Persian Masanavis he explained: "My real purpose is to look for a better social order and to present a universally acceptable ideal of life and action before the world. When I realised that the conception of nationalism based on the differences of race and country was beginning to overshadow the world of Islam and that the Muslims were in danger of giving up the universality of their ideal in favour of a narrow patriotism and false nationalism, I felt it my duty to recall them back to their true role in the drama of human evolution." Like modern day fundamentalists, Iqbal gave the slogan, "Back to early Islam." He emphasized the concept of the Millat as the crystallisation of Muslim fraternity. The Millat was the social and political manifestation of the concept of Tauhid which implies equality, freedom and fraternity. Kaba was to represent this solidarity as a geographical centre. But Iqbal categorically stated that Pan-Islamism never dreamed of a unification of all Muslims into one political centre. Because of this supreme belief in the significance of Pan-islamic fraternity, Iqbal ridiculed the League of Nations as a "Lean structure of European diplomacy" and as one doomed to extinction.[17]

Iqbal was an opponent of nationalism on two grounds: First, he felt that the slogan of an all-India nationalism would mean the political ascendancy of the Hindus. Secondly, Iqbal felt that the concept of nationalism would loosen the bonds of Islamic fraternity because of separate patriotic feelings, as it goes against the idea of Muslim brotherhood. Nationalism, therefore, is an anachronism and dangerous to the interest of humanity. Further, according to him nationalism, with its exclusive sovereign nation state as its political expression, is the greatest single factor militating against peace, freedom and justice in the world.

Nonetheless, he accepted Pan-Islamism as a humanitarian ideal recognising no racial or nationalistic barrier or geographical frontiers. In 1938, Iqbal, the universalist, spoke: "Only one unity is dependable, and that unity is the brotherhood of man which is above race, nationality or language."

HOW IQBAL BECAME A NATIONALIST-TURNED-COMMUNALIST

Iqbal's brief European sojourn redefined his concept of Qaum. It changed his outlook considerably. It was from here that he got the idea of national identity in civilisational terms. Probably, the European influence weaned him away from Indian nationalism. His focus now shifted from Indians to the global community of Muslims. Prior to his visit to Europe the young Iqbal was an ardent nationalist and his 'Tarana-i-Hind' became almost an Indian anthem. But after the visit he was no longer a nationalist. From his earlier assertions that "We are Indian and India is our home," he began to write: China-Arabia and India are ours. We are Muslims and the whole world is ours," to quote his 'Tarana-i-Milli'. Thus, he became a "Sectarian Nationalist,"

In his famous poem 'Shikwah Aur Jawabe Shikwah' he clearly stated: "Nation is created and sustained by religion. If religion expired there will be no nation." He condemned patriotism as a "subtle form of idolatry". As such, he started describing nationalism incompatible with the spirit of Muslim brotherhood. He feared that the sentiment of nationalism might result in loosening the bonds of Islamic fraternity and induec each Muslim country to develop the feeling of separate nationalism. In addition, he also felt that the slogan of an all-India nationalism would mean the political ascendancy of the Hindus. Hence he declared that "the Muslims from the bank of Nile to the soil of Kashghor must unite to defend the Haram, the place around the Kaba and a symbol of the unity of Islam." He had the vision of such a state which would be called Islamistan. Iqbal was now inspired by the view of a new Mecca, a world-wide, theocratic, utopian state."

IDEOLOGY OF PAKISTAN

According to Iqbal, the year 1799, (defeat of Tipu Sultan) marked the nadir of Islamic decay. However, in the nineteenth century there occurred a revival of Islam. With the activities of Sayed Ahmed Barelvi, Mufti Alam Jan in Russia and Syed Jamaluddin Afghani, there began the phase of Islamic awakening.[18] But it was Jonh Bright, a British radical statesman, who probably was the first person to have suggested the idea of division of the subcontinent in 1877. In 1913, Mohd. Ali, while discussing the Hindu-Muslim problem, also suggested that North India may be assigned to the Muslims and the rest to the Hindus. But Dr. Iqbal was probably the first important Muslim political leader to put forth the idea of a separate homeland for the Muslims on the basis of two nation theory, from the official platform of the Muslim League.

Iqbal felt that the destiny of the Muslims lay in the formation of a state for themselves. He regarded the Muslims as an all-India minority and even called them a "nation." He was opposed to the unitary Indian nation on the plea that it would mean the domination by the majority. He felt that there was no future for the Muslims in a united India. As a staunch Muslim, he was apprehensive that the Hindu dominated polity may impede the cultural and religious development of the Muslim Community. Accordingly, he supported the Communal Award.

In the early 1930s, Iqbal became an advocate of the "consolidated North Western Indian Muslim State." This proposal had been put forward before the Nehru Committee as well. Later on, as President of the Muslim League session at Allahabad on 29 December, 1930 Iqbal said: "To base a constitution on the conception of a homogeneous India or to apply to India the principles dictated by British democratic sentiment is unwittingly to prepare her for a civil war." In his opinion, the only way to peaceful India was a distribution of the country on the lines of racial, religious and linguistic affinities. According to him, India is a land of many nations. In fact, "India is Asia in miniature," and there could be no peace in the country until the constituent elements got the opportunity of developing without breaking with the past. Hence, he proposed the formation of a consolidated Muslim state, He said: "I would like to see the Punjab, the North Western Frontier Province, Sind, Baluchistan amalgamated into a single state. The North Western Indian Muslims would thus possess the full opportunities of development within the body politic of India." Thus, he supported the demand for "a Muslim India within India." Later on, in a letter to Jinnah in 1937, he wrote: "To my mind the new constitution with its idea of a single federation is completely hopeless." The enforcement of the Shariat of Islam is impossible in the country without a free Muslim state. He, therefore, suggested that "in order that Muslim India could solve her problems it would be necessary to redistribute the country and to provide one or more Muslim states with absolute majority. "At the Lucknow session of 1937 he asked:" why not the North-Western India and Bengal be considered as nations entitled to self-determination as other nations are ?" Thus, Iqbal is rightly considered to be the spiritual father of the Pakistan ideology. The ideology of Pakistan was conceived in its basic form in the speech of Iqbal at the Allahabad session of the Muslim League in 1930.

ROLE OF IQBAL IN THE CREATION OF PAKISTAN

Much has been written about the role of Iqbal in the partition of India. He is considered to be the spiritual founder of Pakistan. His speech in 1930 turned out to be the forerunner of the idea of Pakistan. But according to K.K. Aziz, Iqbal was not a protagonist of the idea of Pakistan. According to him, "It is one of the myths of Pakistan nationalism to saddle Iqbal with the parentage of Pakistan, and in no sense can he be said to have envisaged a sovereign independent Pakistan."[19] His scheme was for a Muslim India within a large federation. Another writer, Waheeduzzaman, in his "Towards Pakistan' says: "The idea of Pakistan did not originate with Iqbal. He only prepared the ground for Jinnah who finally led the Muslims to the goal of Pakistan. According to Dr. Tara Chand, "It was certainly not a scheme for partition; it was only a plan for redistribution of territories." In a letter to Edward Thomson, Iqbal wrote: "I propose to create a Muslim province within the Indian federation. Pakistan is not my scheme." To Moin Shakir, Iqbal was not in favour of partitioning the country. The state he had in mind was a Muslim India within India and not one that would severe all links.[20] Even K.K. Aziz admits, "The idea of Pakistan was not his, but the force behind its coming belonged to no one else."[21] Quoting Hafeez Malik, he writes: "Nevertheless the seeds of Pakistan can be found in Iqbal's address."[22]

CONCLUSION

Undoubtedly, Allama Iqbal was one of the greatest poets of Asia. He was decidedly the greatest Urdu poet of the present century. But as a political and metaphysical thinker he was neither deep nor original. Without developing any original system of thought he tried to put a favourable interpretation upon the old Quranic tenets in the light of modern advancement in knowledge. He tried a synthetic reconstruction of Islam. He was inspired by the scientific view of the universe as an inter-penetrating organic systems of events, in never ceasing flux. But he lacked the philosophical depth and a comprehensive theoretical structure to evolve a set of concepts and fundamental propositions to integrate these diverse elements and scientific-philosophical view points. In the end he only comes out a preacher of Islam who is trying to read the concepts of evolution, emergence and creativity in the old texts.[23]

Iqbal was inspired by the concept of spiritual freedom. He accepted that the nature of reality is spiritual, eternal purposive activity. Every movement is an original, unique, creative opportunity. His advocacy of freedom of man is remarkable in the context of his advocacy of a religious orientation, which generally is based on deterministic Weltanschauung. The concept of spiritual democracy appealed to Iqbal. He believed in the full development of individual or Khudi. But in spite of his advocacy of spiritual democracy, as a supporter of Islamic theocracy, he does not sanction the sovereignty of the people. Thus, from the concept of spiritual democracy Iqbal does not draw the implication of political democracy. The emphasis on the Shariat introduces an exaggerated degree of theological revivalism in his thought. But at the same time, he was well aware of the necessity of the liberal interpretation and reconstruction of old thought to suit the changing demands of the age, and hence he adopted Ijtihad. He wanted a balance between the eternal principles of stability and changing principles of adjustment. Instead of extending the implications of the social democracy of Islam and thus giving to the people of Muslim countries a liberating vision of the democratic ideal, Iqbal championed the reactionary and medievalist and even fascistic cult of the hero.[24]

Iqbal was a prophet of action and strength. The Nietzschean cult of "live dangerously" appealed to him. As a Muslim, he wanted to accept the logical tenets of the Quran but as a philosopher, he adhered to an absolute organic idealism. This duality of standpoints is the main reason why he does not provide a clear ontological status of the finite ego. This philosophical confusion born of duality is responsible for a political confusion as well. The concept of individuality is not accurately defined in his political thought.[25]

As a Muslim theologian, he accepts the supremacy of the Millat and the Shariat, but as a philosopher, who is familiar with modern trends of thought, he stands also for individuality or Khudi. "The fundamental failure of his political thought is that neither on the basis of the Quranic concept of theocracy nor on that of absolute idealism is it possible to assert the claims and rights and potentiality of the ego.[26]

All told, "Iqbal revolutionised Muslim thinking by his philosophy and gave a new turn to Islam by his dynamic interpretation, and inspired the Muslims with his heart lifting poetry and took Islam a very long step further towards a renaissance which had originated with Shah Walliullah, had been given a practical shape by Sayyad Ahmed Khan Barelvi, had been vouchsafed a new stance by Sir Syed Ahmed Khan and had received much impetus from Sayyed Ameer Ali".[27]

ESTIMATE OF IQBAL

Iqbal still remains an enigma despite all the researches on him. In W.C. Smith's opinion, "Iqbal becomes too contradictory and unsystematic to permit of a systematic assessment." Iqbal was a poet-philosopher. He put forth most of his philosophy in poetic form and this added to confusion in his thought.

His emphasis on theocratic state at the cost of secularism and Pan-Islamism as a substitute for early nationalism speak of Iqbal as a theological revivalist. He wrote 'Reconstruction of Religious Thought in Islam' but what he emerges with is largely a rehash of tradition, for he rejects both secularism and nationalism.

Iqbal believed that Islam is perfect and eternal as a guide for social and political life. He was however aware of the fact that the medieval spirit of Islam had rendered it useless to modern man. But he did not have sufficient courage to break with traditional Islam completely and to accept the spirit of modern science and socialism. With the result "his thought is replete with paradoxes and oscillates between modernity and antiquarianism. He failed to assimilate liberal forces and could not free himself from the mooring of tradition. His inconsistencies and contradictions make it difficult to regard him as a systematic thinker or a consistent philosopher. The story of Iqbal's thought represents the tragedy of a great genius."[28]

Notes

1. Verma, V.P., op. cit, pp.371-72

2. Smith V.C., Modern Islam In India, p.114

3. Bhagwan, Vishnu, op. cit, p.167

4. Verma, V.P., op. cit, pp. 372-73

5. Verma, V.P., op. cit, pp.373-74

6. Ibid., pp.374-75

7. Ibid., p.375

8. Ibid., p.375

9. Ibid., pp.375-76

10. Ibid., p.376

11. Ibid., p.376

12. Iqbal, Mohd., Six Lectures, p.232

13. Ibid., p.234

14. Verma, V.P., op. cit, p.377

15. Ibid., p.378

16. Shakir, Moin, op. cit, p.102

17. Verma, V.P., op. cit, p.380

18. Ibid., pp.380-81

19. Aziz, K.K., op. cit, pp.296-98
20. Shakir, Moin, op. cit, p.100
21. Aziz, K.K., op. cit, p.322
22. Ibid., p.296
23. Verma, V.P., op. cit, p.382
24. Ibid., pp.382-383
25. Ibid., pp.383-84
26. Ibid., p.384
27. Aziz, K.K., op. cit, p.781
28. Shakir, Moin, op. cit, p.123

Chapter 44

MOHAMMAD ALI JINNAH
— THE FOUNDER OF PAKISTAN
(1876-1948)

In the history of the Indian freedom movement, M.A. Jinnah occupies a significant place, particularly in its last phase wherein he was the key player.

Born in Karachi on 23 December, 1876, Jinnah died in Karachi on 10 September, 1948. Jinnah belonged to the small Khojha community. His grandfather was originally a Hindu (Bhatia) but converted to a Muslim. His father was a hide merchant. His family life had been very unhappy. At 15 he married a Khojha girl who died quite early. In his forties, Jinnah again married a Parsi girl of sixteen, Ruttie Petit, the daughter of Din Shaw Petit. But he was divorced at 49; and his only daughter left him and sought refuge with her grandparents.

After matriculation Jinnah proceeded to England for higher studies. . During 1893-96 he completed his studies in Law at Lincoln Inn, London, and returned to India as a barrister at the young age of 20. He had a roaring success at the legal profession and was regarded a legal luminary.

In politics, Jinnah was a close colleague of Pherozshah Mehta and a protege of Gokhale, whom he regarded as a great political "rishi", a "master". He joined the Indian National Congress in 1906 and worked as Private Secretary to Dadabhai Naoroji. Jinnah longed both for fame and fortune and speedily ascended the dual ladder of Indian Law and politics.

Jinnah was essentially an introvert and a narcissist with an inscrutable craze for going to the top. He was cold, pedantic, rational but mistrustful. In the words of Lord Mountbatten, Jinnah was a "mass of vanity". He also described Jinnah as "frigid, haughty and disdainful." He was domineering with vaulting ambition and king-size ego. But he was an ingenious negotiator, and because of this trait he got what he wanted.

POLITICAL CAREER OF JINNAH

Jinnah began his political career fairly in the tradition of moderate national Politics. He had won great admiration when he defended B.G. Tilak in the Sedition cases against him in 1908 and 1916. In 1910, he was elected to the Imperial Legislative Council by the Muslim electorate of Bombay, which was repeated in 1916. In the Imperial Legislative Council he made political speeches on Gokhale's Elementary Education Bill, the Transfer of Ships Restriction Bill and the Indian Criminal Law. He supported the Press Bill and also favoured the Indian Defence Force Bill.

JINNAH AND SEPARATE ELECTORATES

"Although as a liberal he would not approve of a separate electorate for the Muslims, his solicitude for public opinion led him to assert that if the Muslims are "determined to have separate electorate, no resistance should be shown to their demand."[1] In 1916, he declared that separate electorate was a matter of interest to the Muslims who by this method alone could be roused from their mental lethargy. Separate electorate, he argued, served to raise Muslims consciousness of their identity.

JINNAH AND THE MUSLIM LEAGUE

The All India Muslim League came into existence in 1906. On 22 March, 1913 the League adopted a new constitution at its Lucknow session and Jinnah was persuaded by Mohd. Ali and Syed Wazir Hussain to enrol himself as its member. Although Jinnah joined the League but without leaving the Congress. In 1914, he went to England as a member of the deputation on behalf of the Indian National congress in connection with the proposed reform of the India Council.

JINNAH AND THE HOME RULE LEAGUE

During the course of World War-I the Home Rule League was founded by Tilak and Annie Besant in 1916. Jinnah at first did not join them, because of his moderate temperament. But after the internment of Mrs. Besant, he joined the Bombay Home Rule League.

JINNAH AND HINDU-MUSLIM UNITY

In October 1916, while presiding over the Bombay Provincial Conference of the Muslim League at Ahmedabad, Jinnah pleaded for firm unity between the Hindus and the Mohammedans. He did the same from the platform of the Muslim League session at Lucknow (1916). Jinnah was one of the architects of the Congress-League scheme. At the Calcutta Congress of 1917 he supported the resolution on self-government for India.

He resigned his membership of the Central Legislative Council in protest against the Rowlatt Bills, but significantly, he made it clear that he was not interested in extra-territorial affairs like the Khilafat.

But between 1917 and 1920 many of the developments in Indian politics went against Jinnah's grain, such as Gandhi's capture of the Congress in 1920 with the help of pro-Khilafat Muslims. By declaring his support for the Khilafat, Gandhi secured the allegiance of an impressive array of Muslim Ulemas. This fusion of religious and political issues had left Jinnah cold and in the wings. Besides, believing in the constitutional method of action (until the call of Direct Action, in 1946), he opposed the Gandhian programme of non-cooperation. As such, he opposed the Nagpur Resolution in December 1920. With the beginning of the Non-Cooperation Movement and the upsurge of mass awakening, Jinnah felt that he did not belong to the Congress and he therefore left it. The Nagpur session, thus, marked the beginning of Jinnah's antagonism towards Gandhi and the Congress. Later on, "his pride had been wounded by the disdain with which the Congress and Liberal Leaders of late 1920s had treated him. But Jinnah would never submit to slight, for he was supremely a man of pride".[2]

In 1924, Jinnah was appointed a member of the Muddiman Committee, which examined the working of the Government of India Act of 1919 and proposed the termination of the Dyarchy along with Tej Bahadur Sapru and others. He was also a member of the Skeen Committee along with Motilal Nehru, which examined the problem of the Indianisation of the Army officers of India.

In 1927-28, Jinnah boycotted the Simon Commission, which he dubbed as "lily-white" Commission. Perhaps, he was expecting his name to be included in the Commission, because of his loyalty to the government. But Jinnah was opposed to the Nehru Report of 1928, although it had given more seats to the Muslims than they were entitled to on population basis. In opposition to the Nehru Report, Jinnah put forward his Fourteen Points. Differences over the Nehru Report marked parting of ways between the Muslim League and the Congress.

Interestingly, at the Round Table Conference, Jinnah declared himself a nationalist Muslim. However, after the Round Table conference he became disgusted with Indian politics and decided to give up politics, and stayed back in London. But Jinnah was eventually persuaded by the Raja of Salempur and Liaquat Ali (1934) to return and resume the leadership of the Muslim League, which had been moribund after the death of League stalwarts like Maulana Mohd. Ali, Raja of Mahmudabad and Mohd. Shafi.

Returning to India Jinnah resumed the leadership of the Muslim League with all seriousness. It was under his leadership that the Muslim League fought the elections of 1937. But to Jinnah's chagrin, the League received nominal support from the Muslim masses, securing only 25 percent of Muslim seats. The disastrous performance of the Muslim League had a "traumatic effect on Jinnah". To illustrate its electoral debacle, it won 3 seats in Sind, only one in Punjab and none in North-West Frontier Province. In Bengal, however, it won a third of the Muslim Seats. In the opinion of B.R. Nanda, "it was this electoral disaster which seems to have driven Jinnah.......to use the dynamite of religious emotion for blasting his way to political influence and power." Again, the failure to reach an accommodation with the Congress in the formation of coalition governments, further compelled him to reconsider his strategy. Besides, he was greatly alarmed by the Congress policy of Muslim mass contact formulated after the 1937 elections. Furthermore, "the difficulties he had faced since 1937 in rallying support in the Muslim majority provinces and in challenging their parliamentarianism had forced Jinnah to cast his demands in communal terms[3]". This is how his Muslim nationalism eclipsed his Indian nationalism.

Jinnah's entire strategy now was aimed at getting the Muslim League accepted as the sole representative of the Muslims of India. In 1939, he put forward the claim of the Muslim League for a fifty-fifty share of political power between Muslim India and non-Muslim India. In 1940, Jinnah formulated his thesis of two-nation, pointing out that it was impossible to establish in India that bond of homogeneity which is the foundation of Western democracy. Hence, a federal constitution of Dominion type would not suit India. Thus, by 1940 he had become a fervent advocate of the two-nation theory, though he was not its author. But Jinnah did give an ideological and religious tinge to the two-nation theory.

In 1944, in course of Gandhi-Jinnah talks, he fanatically stuck to the concept that the Muslims are a nation. In one of his letters to Gandhi, in September 1944 he wrote: "We maintain and hold that Muslims and Hindus are two major nations by any definition or test as a nation. We are a nation of a hundred million and what is more, we are a nation with our own distinct culture and civilisation, language and literature, art and architecture, names and nomenclatures, sense of value and proportion, aptitudes and ambitions. In short, we have our distinctive outlook on lif and of life. By all canons of international law we are a nation."[4] By this time, Jinnah had become absolutely uncompromising, and he insisted that Pakistan was the sole solution to Hindu-Muslim differences. In 1944 he again said: "There is only one practical realistic way of resolving Hindu-Muslim differences and this is to divide India into two sovereign parts.[5]"

But it was not until the elections of 1945-46 that he could effectively establish his claim that the vast majority of the Muslims supported his demand for Pakistan. At long last, in August 1947, Jinnah realised what appeared to him just a dream a few years back.

But Jinnah was not a theocrat or a communalist at heart. Saddled in power and responsibility, he said in his inaugural address to the Pakistan Constituent Assembly on 11 August 1947, "You are free... you may belong to any religion or caste or creed — that has nothing to do with the fundamental principle that we are all equal citizens of one state. Now, I think we should keep in front of us our ideal, and you will find that in course of time Hindus would cease to be Hindus and Muslims would cease to be Muslims, not in the religious sense, because that is the personal faith of each individual, but in the political sense as citizens of the state.[6]" Thus, he made a clear statement of the secular principle as the basis of Pakistan. It seems the embers of liberal secularism of the early Jinnah were still flickering. "It is true Jinnah resisted attempts to commit the League to an Islamic ideology. But he had to contradict himself under pressure by declaring in July 1948; "The adoption of the Western economic theory and practice will not help us in achieving our goal of creating a happy and contented people. We must work our destiny in our own way and present to the world an economic system based on the true Islamic conception of equality of mankind and social justice. We will thereby be fulfilling our mission as Muslims and giving to humanity the message of peace which alone can save it and secure the cooperation, happiness and prosperity of mankind[7]." On the basis of this statement as against that of the August, 1947 statement, Khaliquzzaman holds the view that Jinnah never said goodbye to the two-nation theory and religious nationalism. Thus Jinnah's political career justified the statement of Sarojini Naidu that "in his political career Jinnah was a sort of cross bencher."

CONVERSION OF JINNAH
FROM A NATIONALIST TO A COMMUNALIST

As we have noted in his early phase of political career, Jinnah was an ardent nationalist in the non-denominal sense of the term. In fact, he was the most secular of all Muslim leaders until 1936, and cherished the principle of nationalism, democracy, secularism and the unity of the country in this phase. To be exact, right upto mid-thirties he proudly proclaimed that he was "Indian first and a Muslim second". But how an ardent nationalist became a hard-headed communalist is a pestering question. The following reasons may be attributed to this volte face in Jinnah's outlook[8].

(1) JINNAH'S OBSESSIVE EGOISM: With Gandhi's emergence on the political scene Jinnah felt that his importance would gradually diminish in the Indian National Congress. He felt that he was cheated of destiny, for Gandhi was where he would have been.

(2) JINNAH WAS AN ANTITHESIS OF GANDHI AND NEHRU: Whereas Jinnah was pompous and believed in faultlessly tailored suits and high collars, Gandhi was an embodiment of simplicity. Again, Jinnah was a believer in practical and constitutional politics, whereas Gandhi believed in agitational politics and adopted the technique of Satyagraha, non-cooperation and civil disobedience. As such, the two could not pull on well together. Jinnah also did not like another great contemporary and a rival — Jawaharlal Nehru. To Jinnah, Nehru was a visionary, a crystal gazer and a 'Peter Pan', and Nehru almost hated and could not stand Jinnah on account of his arrogance, pomposity and lack of decency.

(3) INFLUENCE OF FATIMA JINNAH: Since the death of his wife it was Fatima Jinnah, his sister, who gave Jinnah perpetual company. But Fatima was a staunch .communalist and it is but natural if she might have coloured her brother's views to some extent.

(4) LOSS OF LEADERSHIP: When Jinnah found that he had lost the leadership of the Congress he began to seek another platform where his leadership was unassailable. He found the League a proper forum for domination to satisfy his lust for acquiring and asserting supremacy. Jinnah was a domineering man, whose reversion to Indian politics in 1934-35 made him prepared to the needs and the characteristics of his people, a community looking for a great saviour who had proposed to unify the community and bring earthy glory of Islam. There was thus a congruence between Jinnah's personal history and the Pak movement. Hence this turn-about on the part of Jinnah.

(5) INJURED EGO: His vanity was hurt when he was not chosen to represent the Muslim community at the Second and Third Round Table Conferences as he was not considered a true representative of the Muslim community. Hence, he now began to cover himself in a communal coat.

(6) IMAGE BOOSTING: Jinnah got undue importance in the last decade of the freedom struggle. His ego was given a great boost when Gandhi went to him for talks in 1944 and addressed him as" Quaid-i-Azam". The British bureaucracy also did the same by standing behind him on

all issues and by conniving at his obstinacy. All this made him intransigent and belligerent.

But it is to be noted that as late as 1936 Jinnah took a liberal communalist position. At Lahore (March 1936) he said: "My role and only object has been the welfare of my country. I assure you that India's interest is and will be sacred to me and nothing will make me budge an inch from that position." But Jinnah was greatly alarmed by the Congress policy of Muslim mass contact formulated after the 1937 elections. Further the failures to an accommodation with the Congress forced him to reconsider his strategy. Besides, the difficulties he has faced since 1937 in rallying support in the Muslim majority provinces and in challenging their Parliamentarianism had forced Jinnah to cast his demands in communal terms." By 1937 he openly adopted a communal ideology and like a new convert, became a fervent advocate of the two-nation theory, and gave an ideological and religious tinge to it. During the crucial 1946 elections the Islamic card was played to the full by him. Now he began to beat his opponents by appearing more religious and thus became an extreme communalist.

It is interesting to note that Jinnah's political career spanned all the phases of communalism: communal nationalism, liberal communalism and extreme communalism. "Once the basic digits of communal ideology are accepted the ideology takes over a person bit by bit, independent of the subjective desire of the person." This is how a person who started as an ambassador of Hindu-Muslim unity and strongly stood for national unity ended by demanding partition of the country. The logic of communalism, thus, asserted itself and transformed Jinnah into, first from a nationalist into a communal nationalist and, then into a liberal communalist. But it is worth noting that until the elections of 1937 Jinnah stuck to his semi-nationalist, liberal communalist politics. But after the elections he became an extreme communalist. However, he tried (though unsuccessfully) to revert to a liberal phase in independent Pakistan as his speech on 11 August 1947 shows.[9] But, it was too late for him to back-out from his ill-conceived notion of a two-nation.

CREATION OF PAKISTAN — JINNAH'S ROLE

Jinnah is commonly considered the creator of Pakistan. In some quarters, it is believed that had there been no Jinnah there would have been no Pakistan. Some writers even believe that Pakistan was Jinnah's off-spring. To Frank Moraes, "Pak was one man's achievement. If Jinnah had not taken upon himself to lead a crusade for an Islamic "land of the Pure," it is problematical whether Pakistan would have been established." In the opinion of Sharful Mujahid, "Jinnah's presence was necessary at least as far as the calendar date of Pakistan's emergence was concerned." Endorsing his views, Ishaq Hussain Qureshi in 'Struggle for Pakistan' says, "Though without Jinnah Pakistan would have come but it would have been delayed by decades." According to S.R. Mehrotra, "Jinnah became both the architect and the symbol of the alliance between Muslim separatism and the Muslim will to rule the Muslim majority provinces."[10] Most of the writers concur that but for his unflinching stand against all offers of concession within a united India there would have been no Pakistan.

But it appears from the above statements that undue credit has been given to Jinnah for the creation of Pakistan, for, as Hernshaw maintains. "The character of the leader and the circumstances of his time are equally crucial in the shaping of events at any given point of time." The destinies of nations are moulded by the inner-most urges and their determination to achieve their purpose. But if they fail to provide a leader of necessary ability and stamina they may be frustrated. In view of Moin Shakir, "the formation of Pakistan cannot be regarded as just the result of the ambitions and intrigues of selfish leaders like Jinnah. Such a view could leave out of account the larger impersonal forces without the aid of which the results of such magnitude would be impossible."[11] According to Akbar Ahmed, "Pakistan has been the fulfilment of the collective wish of the Muslims of the subcontinent for their own homeland. Mr. Jinnah gave expression and shape to the collective sentiment but did not create it. To see him as a pied piper who mesmerised his followers and led them to Pakistan is incorrect."[12]

Again, it is worth remembering in this context that much before Jinnah there were three others who created the necessary atmosphere for fostering separatism. Sir Syed started the Aligarh Movement, the rallying point for Islamic revivalists and Aligarh professors prepared the two-nation theory and submitted it to Jinnah. Iqbal provided theoretical justification for a separate homeland. To Rahmat Ali goes the credit for coining the word PAKISTAN, and above all there was an organised political platform the Muslim League. Nevertheless, it has to be admitted that the Muslim League minus Jinnah could not have amounted to a great deal. In fact, Muslim League became both the agent and the index of Muslim resurgence during 1937-47 because of Jinnah. The irresistible demand for Pakistan and the solidarity of the Indian Muslims behind that demand were creations of the "decade of destiny" (1937-47) alone and supremely the creation of one man-Jinnah. But it is worth noting that it was not until the elections of 1945-46 that Jinnah could effectively stake his claim that the vast majority of the Muslims supported his demand for Pakistan.

THE REAL CLAIMANTS FOR PARTITION & PAKISTAN

Much has been made in recent years of the argument that Pakistan was just a bargaining counter for Jinnah. For instance, Ayesha Jalal states: "It is Congress that was interested in partition and it was Jinnah who was against it."[13] What Jinnah was clamouring for was a way of achieving an equal say for Muslims in any all-India arrangement at the Centre.

To deal with this question it is worth recalling that in the early thirties Jinnah had disowned the idea of Pakistan as "a school boy's dream." Jinnah, in fact, wrote to Rahmat Ali that "the idea of Pakistan is foolish, false and futile." Even in subsequent years, Jinnah never defined the contours of Pakistan or portrayed its profile. Even the Lahore Resolution of 1940 makes no mention of Pakistan. Ayesha Jalal, therefore, maintains that" the Lahore Resolution should be taken as a bargaining counter. The Resolution made no mention of partition, certainly none of Pakistan. In the League's considered view, the Muslim majority provinces were to be grouped to constitute independent states in which the constituent units shall be autonomous and sovereign. "Pakistan with its connotation of partition was not the League's idea but a caricature thrust upon it by the Hindu press. "They fathered the word upon us," Jinnah emphasized at Delhi in 1943."[14] According to Sri Prakash, the Ex. Governor of Bombay, "Jinnah was not interested in the creation of a separate nation but merely used it as a trump card." In the opinion of Hodson, the author of 'The Great Divide', "Jinnah wanted confederation rather than partition, and it was obtuseness of the Congress leadership which led to the latter than to the former." Another writer Prof. Alvi, in agreement with them also maintains, "Jinnah was quite happy to accept Pakistan as a regional grouping within an Indian federal union and it is testified by his ready acceptance of the Cabinet Mission Plan. He adds: "In 1946-47, as Ayesha Jalal has shown in 'The Sole Spokesman', a confederation was within the reach of the Indian people. Jinnah was willing to accept the Cabinet Mission Plan, for this would safeguard the position of Muslims in Hindustan and would avoid the inevitable division of Punjab and Bengal in case Pakistan was to be decided upon. But the proposed confederation did not accord with the Congress vision of a strong, integral and secular democracy with socialist aspirations. Alvi therefore holds that it was the Congress which rejected the Cabinet Mission Plan, as it wanted to embark upon a planned development of India."

According to these writers, Jinnah who had fought so tenaciously for Pakistan was actually keen on a political arrangement which would involve two federations — Hindustan and Pakistan — linked by a British Crown representative who would coordinate the policies of the two federations in defence and foreign Affairs.

But Anita Inder Singh does not agree with the thesis that Pakistan was just a bargaining counter for Jinnah[15]. She writes: "It is our belief that such theses represent advocacy rather than a judicious reconstruction of the past. Like any astute negotiator Jinnah had probably more than one card up his sleeve and" the confederated India" might have been one of the solutions acceptable to him. However, there is little reason to believe that Pakistan was foisted upon an unwilling Jinnah, nor is there any reason to believe that Pakistan was other than the first choice for the Muslim leaders and rank and file of British India. The fact remains on Jinnah's insistence on sovereign Pakistan." Prof. S.R. Mehrotra maintains that with Jinnah, atleast in March 1940, the demand for Pakistan was neither a bluff nor a bargaining counter but a solemn and irrevocable decision. "Jinnah achieved Pakistan because he knew where he was going, while "muddling through" tactics of the British and the Congress were no match for his melange of obduracy, dialectical skill and deliberate, dogged negotiations of anything less than the sovereign Pakistan."[17] Prof. Moin Shakir, quoting Aziz Ahmed in this context, observes: "Jinnah's role was that of a sincere and clear-headed lawyer who could formulate and articulate in precise constitutional terms what his client really wanted."[18]

JINNAH AS A LEADER

"Few individuals significantly alter the course of history and fewer still modify the map of the world. Hardly anyone can be credited with creating a nation-state. Jinnah did all these. Pakistan was indeed his offspring. He changed the map of India and altered the course of history."[19]

Notably, Jinnah was never a theocrat or a practising Muslim. He was essentially a politician with a lust for power but who posed himself as the custodian of the Muslim community. He neither spoke their language nor believed in Muslim dress nor ever visited Mosques till he was forced by circumstances to do so. He was often reviled by the traditional Ulema. They dubbed Jinnah as the "Kafir-i-Azam". But Jinnah tried to beat his Muslim opponents by appearing more religious than even the Pope.

Jinnah had a streak of commanding personality in him. He was a domineering man whose reverses in life made him imprudent, prepossessed and egomaniac. He craved for power and had insatiable lust for authority. His early nationalistic fervour was made a sacrifice at the altar of supreme leadership he had been craving to attain. But how he could delude his co-religionists in Hindu majority provinces into believing that Pakistan was good for them is one of the most astonishing phenomena of our times.

Jinnah's political genius lay precisely in his ability to orchestrate a loose, volatile and unpredictable coalition of forces. "His consummate political skill lay in the manner in which he harnessed these forces under his personal direction for the achievement of personal glory and the establishment of a political identity for the (Muslim) community."[20] According to Lord Mountbatten, "The secret of Jinnah's success was his permanently negative attitude." All the same, Jinnah was for Pakistan what Gandhi and Nehru combined were for India.

ESTIMATE OF JINNAH

Jinnah has been ill-served by his biographers. He remains one of the mystery men of modern history. He is one of history's most remarkable, tenacious and enigmatic figures and he still remains an endearing enigma. By all standards Jinnah was a paradox. A European of Europeans, he played a unique role in the creation of a Muslim state. As a political figure, he was the product of contradictions and confusions of Indian nationalism.

According to Lord Mountbatten, "Jinnah suffered from an acute form of megalomania."[21] His personal jealousy and rivalry with Gandhi and Nehru and vaulting ambition made him an uncompromising, contentious tubercular in a hurry to sit on the throne. It is really unfortunate that orthodoxy and conservativism of the Muslim community did play a role in the intellectual make-up of Jinnah, at least in his later years. It is, indeed, ironical that one who was once hailed as an ambassador of Hindu-Muslim unity left a lasting legacy of acrimony between the two communities.

JINNAH AND GANDHI — A COMPARISON

What Gandhi is for India, Jinnah is for Pakistan. Both are regarded as "Father of the Nation" in their respective countries. Interestingly, both Jinnah and Gandhi belonged to the same home state. But if one stood for a free, united India, the other demanded its partition before freedom.

Jinnah and Gandhi were antithesis of each other; they were counter-personalities, possessing contrasting character traits and outlook. If Gandhi was a man of God and believed in moral means only, Jinnah was a firm believer of practical politics and means were of no importance to him.

Again, if Gandhi was humble, overgenerous and magnanimous, Jinnah was haughty, over-bearing and obstreperous. If Gandhi was an embodiment of simplicity and lived in voluntary poverty, Jinnah was pompous and loved a life of luxury. If Gandhi advocated 'Khadi' as a mark of Swadeshi and treated it as a "livery of freedom", Jinnah believed in sartorial perfection, packing and adorning himself in foreign outfit, with flauntingly laundered suit and high collars. If Gandhi was a picture of humility, endowed with oceanic love and caring concern for all living beings, Jinnah was a" mass of vanity", offensive and distrustful. Whereas Gandhi had no craving for office nor ever tried to seek power, Jinnah would not hesitate to throw all his creeds and convictions to the winds to grab the throne. But strangely enough, Jinnah was as successful as a leader as was Gandhi.

Notes

1. Shakir, Moin, op. cit, p. 182

2. Hodson, H.V., The Great Divide, op. cit, p. 42

3. Jalal, Ayesha, The Sole Spokesman, op. cit, pp. 241-42

4. Quoted in M.K. Gandhi To the Protagonists of Pakistan, edited by A. Hingorani Rupa & Co., Calcutta, p. 120

5. Quoted in Verma, V.P., op. cit, p. 360

6. Ibid., p. 360

7. Ibid., p. 360

8. Bhagwan, Vishnu, op. cit, pp. 179-80

9. Chandra, Bipan, India's Struggle For Independence, op. cit pp. 432-33

10. Mehrotra, S.R., op. cit, p.198

11. Shakir, Moin, op. cit, p. 203

12. Quoted in Madan, T.N., 'Pakistan Revisited', Times of India, 17 Nov. 1994.

13. Jalal, A., op. cit, p. 262

14. Ibid., p. 71

15. Singh, Anita Inder, op. cit, p. 142

16. Mehrotra, S.R., op. cit, p. 205

17. Singh, A.I., op. cit, p. 251

18. Shakir, Moin, op. cit, p. 208

19. Wolpert, Stanley A., Jinnah of Pakistan, Oxford University Press, London, 1984, preface

20. Shakir, Moin, op. cit, p. 203

21. Quoted in Jalal, A., op. cit, p. 292

Chapter 45

MAULANA ABUL KALAM AZAD — A SCHOLAR STATESMAN (1888-1958)

Abul Kalam Ghulani Mohiyuddin Ahmed, whose pen name was Azad, was born on 11 November, 1888 in the Darus-Isalam quarter of the Holy City (Medina). His father, Sheikh Mohammad Khairuddin Sahib, was a reputed scholar and an eminent Muslim divine — a practising Sufi, and his grandfather was the Mufti of Medina. When Azad was about 10 years of age, his father migrated to India and settled at Calcutta.

Azad was a precocious child. At school he was respected for his knowledge, learning and oratory. A brilliant student, he finished his final education at sixteen. At a rather young age he had mastered Arabic, Persian and the Urdu language.

Maulana Azad was a profound theologian, keen intellectual, powerful writer, prolific publicist, a persuasive and eloquent orator, and a sober politician. He ranks as one of the greatest Urdu writers and orators India has produced. His speeches are considered as masterpieces of Urdu literature. He exhibited felicity of expression with profoundity of thought and analysis.

Azad was a devout and proud Muslim, and in his knowledge of Islamic theology he was second to none. He was a profound Arabic scholar. In 1908, Azad visited the Muslim countries such as Egypt, Syria, Palestine and Iraq at the very young age of 20. However, his early writings express a romantic view of Islam, which is more akin to orthodox revivalism than to liberal reformism. Like Mohd. Ali, he was also inspired by Jamaluddin Afghani in the early phase of his career. However, he departed from religious revivalism after 1920, and began to favour a reformist and rational approach to the Quran. Although, he was an intensely religious man, he showed insight of a genius by maintaining a distinction between 'Din' and 'Shariat'. While he was interned at Ranchi, he wrote his commentary on the Quran (Tarjumane-Quran). In this work, he emphasised the spiritual and moral aspects of religion. He believed that the essence of the religion is one and that is the cultivation of moral good and surrender to God. Hence, he attached importance to the essence of religion and not to the external form. In his opinion, the unity of brotherhood, the unity of God and the unity of religions constitute the message of Quran.

Before he came under the influence of Gandhi his political activities were mainly confined to writing articles for his paper, 'Al Hilal' (Crescent), which he started in 1912 and for, 'Hamdard' and 'Hamdam'. Through these papers Azad challenged the political philosophy of Sir Syed Ahmed Khan and the Aligarh School. When his another paper 'Al Balagh' was banned in 1916, he began to edit a magazine Al Nadva in 1918.

EVOLUTION OF AZAD'S POLITICAL IDEAS

In his political life Azad travelled on three paths on different times: the path of exclusive patriotism and Pan Islamism (1906-20); the path of reconciling Muslim patriotism and Indian nationalism (1920-23); and the path of thoroughgoing secularist-democratic nationalism (1923-58).

In the beginning, Azad was inclined towards Extremist politics during the Swadeshi movement, and he followed Aurobindo Ghosh, Shyam Sunder Chakravarty and Ajit Singh in this phase of his political career.

But, soon after his release from Ranchi jail, he met Gandhi on 18 January 1920. This meeting became a watershed in his life, as it marked his involvement with a movement based on the philosophy of non-violence. When the Noncooperation Movement was launched he threw himself whole-heartedly in it and gave the Khilafat question his full support. Khilafat, to him, meant representation, and the authority of the Khilafat was a kind of representative authority. Azad brought Jamait-ul Ulema-i-Hind, of which he was the President, into active participation in this movement. Azad declared: "Liberty is the natural right of man given by God and no power on earth can deny this. Political liberation, therefore, was not only a political duty but a religious act." Within three years he had the distinction of becoming the youngest president of the Congress in 1923 at 34. Incidentally, he set another record — that of the longest term, as he was the President of the Indian National Congress from 1940 to 46. As such, he negotiated on behalf of the Congress with the Cripps Mission in 1942, at the Simla Conference in 1945 and with the Cabinet Mission in 1946". The cool, collected and dignified way in which he conducted these delicate negotiations reflect highly on his personality and character."[1] While in Congress he underwent various terms of imprisonment, totalling almost eleven years.

AZAD ON HINDU-MUSLIM UNITY

Azad was one of the greatest champions of unity between the Hindus and the Muslims. In fact, it is not Jinnah but Azad who should be regarded as the real "ambassador of Hindu-Muslim unity." He was a consistent champion of communal peace and amity. He wanted his own co-religionists to follow a policy of give and take and not to be rigid.

While addressing the Congress in 1923 Azad spoke: "If Swaraj is delayed, it will be a loss for India but if Hindu-Muslim unity is lost, it will be a loss for the whole of mankind." He further added: "If an angel descends from the heaven today, and proclaims from the Qutub Minar that India can attain Swaraj within 24 hours provided I relinquish my demand for Hindu-Muslim unity, I shall retort to it. Not my friend, I shall give up Swaraj but not Hindu-Muslim unity."[2] Again in 1940, he proclaimed: "I am a Muslim and proud of the fact; Islam's splendid tradition of 1300 years are my inheritance. I am part of the indivisible unity that is Indian nationality. Everything bears the stamp of our joint endeavour. Our language was different but we grew to use a common language (Hindustani); our manners and customs were different, dissimilar but they produced a new synthesis. No fantasy or artificial scheming to separate and divide can break this unity."[3] As a student of History, he pointed out that the ancestors of the Hindus and Musalmans were common and they have been living together for nearly a thousand years.

AZAD ON NATIONALISM

Azad was one with Gandhi on the question of relating politics with religion and he did not favour separation between the two. He said: "There will be nothing left with us, if one separates politics from religion." "Religious to the core though he was, he would not countenance nationalism based on religion, specially in the Indian context of multiplicity, as it would be a force for division rather than unity in the wider sense."[4] On another occasion he said: " It is a fraud on the people to suggest that religion can unite areas which are economically, culturally and linguistically different." He was, therefore, opposed to sectarian nationalism preached by the Muslim League. He challenged the concept of Islamic nationality in the Indian context, as propounded by Sir Syed and the Aligarh School.

AZAD ON NON-VIOLENCE

Regarding the technique of revolution, Azad was guided by Islam and not Gandhi. Though Islam did sanction the meeting of violence with violence but taking in view the political situation of the day, Azad declared that he was committed to non-violence as the only course available. Non-violence, for Azad, was not a creed but a policy. He believed that "means should be appropriate and effective not necessarily non-violent."[5]

AZAD ON DEMOCRACY

As regards his views on the political system, he did not take inspiration from Islam alone but also from the West. He said: "Ours is essentially a democratic age and the spirit of equality, fraternity and liberty is sweeping over all the peoples of the world." In his broad spirit of synthesis Azad could even reconcile the seemingly opposed concepts of aristocracy and democracy. He argued that aristocracy of merit and talent may not supplant democracy but may enrich it with the richness and grace of a cultivated minority. Aristocracy may serve democracy by supplying the cultural deficiencies of a broad-based power structure. Democracy is not opposed to aristocracy if the latter serves "as an adjunct to democracy and seeks to fulfil its purposes." According to Azad, "Aristocracy develops a width of vision and a far reaching imagination and thus enriches democracy."[6]

AZAD ON PARTITION OF INDIA

Azad was a staunch opponent of the idea of partition or Pakistan. According to him, "The scheme of partition is harmful not only for India as a whole, but also for Muslims in particular, and in fact it creates more problems than it solves."[7] As President of the Congress, Azad had warned against partition. He had pinpointed and forewarned that partition would be a bitter pill which would keep the two countries at loggerheads and the condition of the minorities would be miserable. The subsequent large scale massacre on the subcontinent on the eve of partition vindicated Azad's statement that the scheme of partition creates more problems than it solves. What is more, the creation of Pakistan has given it (Hindu-Muslim enmity) a constitutional form and made it more difficult for solution.

However, even after the partition, Azad wistfully thought that the two countries would be united once again. He said: "The division is only on the map of the country and not in the hearts of the people, and I am sure it is going to be a short-lived partition."[8]

AZAD AS A HISTORIAN

Azad has given his reminiscences and reaction to the Indian freedom movement in his controversial book 'India Wins Freedom' (1958), whose full version was published in 1988. As a historian, Azad pursued a personal and subjectivist interpretation of the freedom movement. He tried to interpret historical events in terms of personal idiosyncrasies and predilections and thereby ignored the sociological and economic foundations of communal politics in India. To illustrate, it is a mistake to interpret the events during the years of 1946 and 47 as governed by the personal prejudices of Nehru, Patel and Jinnah. In a subjective mood Azad has placed the entire blame on Patel and Nehru for having accepted the partition of the country.[9]

Azad somewhat naively saw the arrangement worked out by the Cabinet Mission as the only solution to the problem within the framework of a united India, and called its acceptance by both League and Congress a glorious event. To him, compulsory grouping was worth settling for. Unlike Nehru and Patel, he was wary of an all powerful Centre. As its President, he wanted the Congress to declare publicly for a federal constitution and a weaker Centre, which commanded only a few all India subjects. He was ready to concede parity for Muslims at the Centre but was unwilling to give parity to the Muslim League.

Unlike other Indians, who have laid the blame for partition entirely on the Muslim League and British machinations, the Maulana was candid enough and courageous enough to place some of the blame on the Congress leaders, particularly Jawahar Lal Nehru, his closest colleague. Azad in his 'Prelude to Partition', a chapter added to 'India Wins Freedom' in 1988, blamed Nehru for partition of the country. He writes: "I have to say with deepest of regrets that a large part of the responsibility for the development rests with J.L. Nehru. His unfortunate statement (of 10 July 1946) that "the Congress would be free to modify the Cabinet Mission Plan" reopened the whole question of political and communal settlement to which both the parties were agreed. Mr. Jinnah took full advantage of his mistake and withdrew from the League's early acceptance of the Cabinet Mission Plan.[10] It was on the basis of distribution of power among the Centre, the provinces and the groups that the League had accepted the Plan. Congress was neither wise nor right in raising doubts. It should have accepted the Plan unequivocally, as it stood for the unity of India. Vacillation would give Jinnah opportunity to divide India, who was already under pressure to wriggle out. But Raj Mohan Gandhi, in his 'India Wins Errors' takes Azad to task for not having stood up against the partition resolution, for the only person who dissented was J.B. Kriplani and not Azad at the Congress Working Committee meeting on 8 March 1947. To quote R.M. Gandhi, "India Wins Freedom" is not a story of how India won freedom but of how Azad lost his spine."[11]

About Nehru's statement of 10 July, 1946, Prof. Mushirul Hasan of Jamia Millia says that Nehru's remarks did give handle to back out of the Plan-the last chance for preventing it (partition), but Nehru's mistake, committed as late as July 1946, even if he retracted later, would not have halted the process of partition, for partition had already been agreed to before Mountbatten's arrival. Further, it is wrong to say "Nehru succumbed to the influence of Mountbattens." According to Prof. Hassan, Azad's own failure in preventing partition was not less significant, for "he did not rally round a lot of like minded persons and forged a common front to neutralise Muslim communal forces." Prof. Hassan doubts that "by that stage even if Jinnah had wanted to retract from his demand for a separate state he would have been able to, because by then the kind of forces that had been unleashed had generated a ground swell that had made possible partition inevitable."

Azad was right in pointing out at partial culpability of Congress leaders, but where he was wrong was in asserting that the last chance in averting the creation of Pakistan was lost in 1946. As a matter of fact, it was lost eight years earlier at the time of the formation of the Congress Ministry. About this event Azad writes: "Nehru committed an almost equal blunder in 1937. This was a most unfortunate development. If the League's offer of cooperation had been accepted the Muslim League would for all practical purposes merged with the Congress. But Jawahar Lal Nehru's action (in refusing the offer) gave the Muslim League a new lease of life. Jinnah took full advantage of the situation and started an offensive which ultimately led to Pakistan."[12] No doubt, "it was one of the most disturbing features in the political history of India; it gave strength to the belief held by some adventurous Muslim leaders that the Muslims should have a separate homeland." Writing in 'India Wins Freedom' Azad says that he was in favour of conceding the demand of the Muslim League (2 Seats) even if the strength of the Ministry had to be raised to nine in order to raise the Muslim share to three. But it appears that Azad, becoming wiser after the event, shifts the blame on Jawahar Lal Nehru, who, he suggests, was not prepared to allot more than one seat to the League."[13]

AZAD AS A LEADER

To quote Dr. Zacharias, "Azad was not a politician in the commonly accepted sense. "He was first and last a humanist and educator but his gentle voice could not prevail against rabble rousers who promised heaven as a reward for making life on earth a hell." To be sure, Azad was not politically ambitious. In a way, he spurned the crown — the leadership of the Muslim community. To quote Raj Mohan Gandhi, "The Qaum leadership would have been in his palm, if to his remarkable assets- link with Mecca, his ancestry, his scholarship and his flair as a writer and orator, he had added but one more ingredient, support for separation."[14] To sum up, three passions dominated his life — love of learning, Hindu-Muslim unity and freedom of India.

ESTIMATE AND CONTRIBUTIONS OF AZAD

According to V.N. Dutta, "Azad's was a complex personality. Taciturn and reserved, he was a staunchly private person who would not easily reveal his thoughts. He was aloof, cold and detached like his arch rival, Jinnah. He was rather "a curious silent bird, "to quote Wavell."[15]

Maulana Azad was an apostle of national unity and communal harmony. He was a symbol of Hindu-Muslim unity and "composite culture". He stood like a rock for a united India. Like Gandhiji, Frontier Gandhi, Azad refused to concede the break up of India until the end. The best epitaph for Azad was written by himself: "I am proud of being an Indian; I am part of the indivisible unity that is Indian nationality and without me this splendid structure of India is incomplete." Among Muslim thinkers, he alone was successful in erecting the edifice of progressive and modern religious and political philosophy. Azad will have a place in the history of political thought in India, because he challenged the assumptions of the Aligarh School of political thought in the early twenties.

Azad was an outstanding Muslim intellectual of modern India. The range of his mind was encyclopaedic. He was a great literary artist. He never gave up scholarship and literature for politics. To the last, he was faithful to his first love. His 'Ghubar Khatir' is the tour de force of a literary craftsman. He was not only one of the great scholars of the Quran in modern times, but due to his command over Arabic and Persian, he was held in high esteem as a Quranic interpreter in the countries of the Middle-East and Africa. As such, he also helped in the formulation of India's foreign policy with regard to these countries.[16]

Azad did commendable work as Minister of Education and Research. As an Education Minister, Azad showed theoretical wisdom and he sponsored the writing of a two volume-treatise on the history of Eastern and Western philosophy, and wrote its introduction. He was also responsible for the publication of an authoritative history of the freedom struggle compiled for the national archives under the direction of Dr. Tara Chand. He was instrumental in appointing the University Education Commission in 1948 and the Secondary Education Commission in 1952 and various institutions and commissions; e.g., Kharagpur Institute Of Higher Technology, The University Grant Commission and three National Academies — The Department of Archaeology, Archives and Anthropology were developed and the Indian Council Of Cultural Relations to foster goodwill between India and Pakistan and for communal harmony. He founded with Nehru the India Council Of Scientific and Industrial Research.

Azad had a many-sided personality. He was a literary giant and possessed excellent taste and rare aesthetic sensibility. He was an embodiment of synthesis of the East and the West. According to Jawahar Lal Nehru, "He was a strange mixture of medieval scholasticism, eighteen century rationalism and the modern outlook. His 'Quran' is described as "exegetical eclecticism." The fluency in Azad's pen and tongue matched the fire of his faith. He had in him the ability to move millions by his voice and pen." In the opinion of T.V. Parvate "A more colourful personality than that of Azad has rarely walked across the stage of modern Indian history."[17]

To conclude, no Muslim thinker in India can be described as a political theorist; and none of them succeeded in making any striking contribution to political thought; they never succeeded in overthrowing the yoke of Islamic religion and tradition. The nature and character of their thought was determined by the rigid and orthodox interpretation of Islam. Their political thought moved on a very low plane. The only exception was Maulana Azad, who alone was progressive and modern in outlook and thinking.[18]

Notes

1. Suda, J.P., op. cit, p. 423

2. Quoted in Gandhi, Raj Mohan, India Wins Errors, Radiant Publishers, N. Delhi, 1989. p. 96

3. Quoted in Ibid., p. 96

4. Shakir, Moin, op. cit, p. 152

5. Ibid., p. 155

6. Ibid., p. 162

7. Ibid., p. 154

8. Quoted in Mehrotra, S.R., op. cit, p. 222

9. Verma, V.P., op. cit, p. 370

10. Azad, A.K., India Wins Freedom, Oriental Longman, Madras 1988, p. 170

11. Gandhi, Raj Mohan, India Wins Errors, op. cit, p. 92

12. Azad, A.K., India Wins Freedom, Oriental Longman, Madras 1988, pp. 170-71

13. Gopal, Ram, op, cit*, p. 247-48

14. Gandhi, Raj Mohan, Eight Lives-A study Of Hindu-Muslim Encounter, Roli Books, Pvt. Ltd., N. Delhi, 1986, p. 250

15. Dutta, V.N., Maulana Azad, Manohar, New Delhi, 1990 Preface pp-VIII - IX

16. Verma, V.P., op. cit, p. 370

17. Parvate, T.V., Modern Indian Thought, p. 97

18. Shakir, Moin, Khilafat To Partition, Kalamkar Prakashan, New Delhi, 1970, p. XI (Introduction.

Chapter 46

KHAN ABDUL GHAFFAR KHAN
— THE FRONTIER GANDHI
(1890-1987)

Khan Abdul Ghaffar Khan was born in Ashtanagar in 1890 and passed away at the ripe old age of 97 on 21 January, 1987. He was the fourth child of the Chief Khan of Utmanzai village in Peshawar district (now in Pakistan)[1]. "Straight in body and mind, sincere and simple, kindly and gentle, fearless, faithful and true, a towering personality with a finely chiselled face and a character built up in the fire of suffering and painful ordeal for the liberation of India."[2] His early life was a series of false starts. He had to give up the study of engineering at Aligarh University in favour of his elder brother, Dr. Khan Sahib. Again, he had to refuse the King's Commission in the British-Indian army because of his involvement in the freedom movement. At the age of 20 Khan founded the Darul-ulum to popularise education and other national schools in subsequent years in the North-Western Frontier Province. He refused to join the Muslim League despite several attempts to allure him. In 1929, he founded a political organisation known as Khudai Khidmatgar. He took a leading part in the Civil Disobedience Movement.

Unlike the Congress, Khan refused to acknowledge the legitimacy of partition of India. In fact, he cried at the time when the partition resolution (1947) was passed by the Congress Working Committee and even accused the Congress of betrayal. He remarked: "You are throwing us to the wolves." He was quite prophetic in his remarks, for in the next four decades he had the tortured life of an exile in his own land (North Western Frontier Province). However, he never regretted to stay in Pakistan, although he had to suffer a lot because of it. For his unrelenting views against the Pakistan rulers, he was in jail for 16 out of 20 years in Pakistan.

ESTIMATE OF KHAN ABDUL GHAFFAR KHAN

Badshah Khan's life was one long saga of indomitable courage, sacrifice and suffering. He was one of the surviving greats of the Indian freedom movement and the longest lasting titan of the freedom struggle. It was in recognition to his great services to the country and its people that India bestowed on him the: International Law Award for International Understanding, and the Bharat Ratna (1987) — the highest honour in India.

Badshah Khan was an outstanding son of subcontinental Islam, the Badshah of the Pathans, a leader of great moral and personal courage and inexhaustible stamina, a true Satyagrahi who had an unshakeable faith in non-violence like the Mahatma. He is rightly called the 'Frontier Gandhi.' In the words of Dr. Zakir Hussain, "Badshah Khan epitomises all that is great and good in human endeavour". Gandhi hailed him a "a man of God."

Notes

1. Tendulkar, D.G., Abdul Ghaffar Khan, Popular Prakashan Bombay, 1967, p. 13
2. Ibid., p. 1

Chapter 47

VINAYAK DAMODAR SAVARKAR — THE PIONEER AMONG REVOLUTIONARIES (1883-1966)

The brightest star in the galaxy of Indian revolutionaries was V.D. Savarkar. An ardent nationalist, a heroic revolutionary, a renowned terrorist, Veer Savarkar had inspired almost all the leading revolutionaries in the early decade of the 20th century. Vinayak was a visionary, a thinker, a poet, a writer, an organiser and always eager to make supreme sacrifice for the liberation of his motherland. He had a sharp intellect, and was a voracious reader even during his school days. During his impressionable days he came under the spell of the writings of Mazzini. In 1904, he and his elder brother Ganesh Damodar Savarkar, alias Baba, formed an organisation known as Abhinav Bharat, similar to Mazzini's young Italy. This was a revolutionary organisation.

After his graduation, Savarkar went to Bombay to study law. But in the meantime, on the recommendation of Tilak, he received the Shivaji scholarship from Shyamji Krishna Verma, the leading Indian revolutionary in Europe. Hence, he proceeded to England for further study. He took his lodgings in the India House founded by Shyamji Krishna Verma. From 1906 to 1910 he studied in England. He wanted to become a Bar-at-Law and was admitted to Gray's Inn of the Court, London.

"His spirited style, erudition, the force of his argument and his passionate sincerity soon enabled him to carry the youthful and impressionable student world with him. The Indian students at Cambridge, Oxford, Edinburgh, Manchester and other places were rapidly brought under the influence of the revolutionary tenets."[1] Besides, Savarkar also managed to do scholarly work of first class magnitude writing two voluminous historical works. These two works were: A Marathi translation of Mazzini's autobiography and 'Indian War of Independence' — a work throwing new light on the uprising of 1857.

Savarkar had among his associates a number of dynamic, intelligent and brave youngmen, including Bhai Parmanand, Lala Hardayal, P.M. Bapat, Virendra Chattopadhyaya Gyan Chand Verma and M.P.T. Acharya. Particularly close to Savarkar were Madan Lal Dhingra (who assassinated Curzon Wyllie, A.D.C. to the Secretary of State for India) and V.V.S. Aiyer (who was one of the translators of 'Indian War of Independence')[2]. Abhinav Bharat declared: "The liberation of the motherland was to be achieved by a preparation of war which included: one, Swadeshi, boycott and national education; two, purchase of weapons in foreign countries and smuggling them to India; three, adopting guerilla tactics wherever possible; four, making anti-British propaganda in the ranks of the Indian military forces; and five, waiting for a favourable opportunity to rise in revolt."[3] Some of the members of Abhinav Bharat tried to make bombs in the back-room of India House. The firearms as well as the bomb manual were smuggled to India packed inside bulky books and false bottoms of boxes.

After the Nasik Conspiracy Case (on account of the murder of Jackson, the DM of Nasik), the Government of India started harassing Savarkar's family and friends. His elder brother, Baba Rao Savarkar, was already sent to Andaman island. V.D.. Savarkar thought of fighting on behalf of the accused in India from London. But as soon as he got down on the platform in London he was taken into custody (13 March, 1910). The Trial Magistrate gave the decision (12 May, 1910) that Savarkar should be sent to India and should stand trial there. A writ of Habeas Corpus was moved against this decision but the earlier decision was upheld by the Chief Justice.

On 1 July, 1910 S.S. Morea sailed off, carrying Savarkar under heavy security guards. On 6 July the vessel berthed at Marseilles (France) because of some engine trouble. In the early hours of the morning Savarkar thought of a swift escape. He squeezed himself out of the porthole and jumped into the sea and reached the harbour of Marseilles. However, he was stopped by a French policeman, who handed him over to the British guard. The French newspapers declared that the arrest on the French soil was an international scandal. To be sure, it was a violation of the right of political asylum. Shyamji Krishna Verma, S.R. Rana and Madam Cama contacted the French authorities in this connection. In the meanwhile, he was taken to India on 22 July, 1910 and was put in Yervada Jail. Finally, his arrest on French soil was referred to an Arbitration Tribunal at the Hague. The Tribunal gave a decision in favour of Britain. In India, too, a Special Tribunal was appointed to try Savarkar. The Tribunal sentenced him to transportation for life. He was awarded fifty years of hard labour in the notorious Andaman cellular jail. Savarkar spent many years in the Andaman island. In 1923, he was brought from the Andaman and interned in Ratnagiri jail. He was released from the internment on 10 May 1937. After coming out of jail, Savarkar joined the Hindu Maha Sabha and became its president in 1937.

SAVARKAR'S INTERPRETATION OF INDIAN HISTORY

In his 'Hindu-pad-padshahi' Savarkar has given a nationalistic interpretation of the rise of the Maratha power. In this book he reveals that the successful assumption by the Marathas of political power was a national counterpoise to the policy of conquest, aggression, hatred and fanatical intolerance of the Muslims. However, some Marxists offered a different explanation for the rise of the Marathas. For instance, M.N. Roy said "The rise of the Marathas, like that of Rajputs and Sikhs, was the revindication of native feudalism against the state feudalism of the Mughals"[4] Savarkar significantly, justified the actions of the leaders and heroes who had adopted violence for the vindication of justice. For instance, he justified the sword of Brutus, the Baghnakha of Shivaji, the bloodshed in Italian Revolution and the beheading of Charles-I.

SAVARKAR'S THEORY OF HINDUTVA

Savarkar had immense love and admiration for the cultural and philosophical achievements of the Hindus. He firmly believed in the cultural superiority of Hinduism. He wanted to infuse in the Hindu community his revolutionary fervour and his heroic will. His main ideal was Hindu resurrection. Savarkar strongly believed that "the Hindus are a nation, bound by a common culture, a common history, a common language, a common country and a common religion." He wrote a book 'Hindutva' (published in 1923). In this book, "he defined a Hindu thus: "A Hindu means a person who regards this land of Bharatvarsh, from the Indus to the seas, as his fatherland as well as his Holyland, that is, the cradle-land of his religion." According to him, "there are three fundamental criteria for being included under Hindutva: Firstly, the territorial bond, attachment to the geographical region; Secondly, the blood bond or the jati; Thirdly, the criterion of being a Hindu is culture or Sanskriti. A Hindu is one who feels pride in the Hindu culture and civilisation represented in common historical memories of achievements and failures, in common artistic, literary and juristic creations and in common rituals or festivals and other media of collective expression. Thus, Muslims and Christians who have been converts from Hinduism cannot claim to be Hindus because they do not subscribe to Hindu culture. In short, the three bonds of Hindutva are Rashtra, Jati and Sanskriti."[5]

However, his concept of Hindutva is broader and more comprehensive than Hinduism. While Hinduism is a religious and theological category, Hindutva is a political concept and comprehends social, educational, economic, political and cultural matters as well. But this subtlety of distinction between Hinduism and Hindutva could impress only those Hindus with a communal outlook, but it could not convince secular minded people, and particularly the non-Hindus.

Savarkar did not believe in the policy of appeasement or minorityism. He thought that Swaraj could be won even without the collaboration of the Muslims. He said to Muslims: "If you come, with you; if you don't, without you; if you oppose, in spite of you, the Hindus will continue to fight for their national freedom as best as they can."[6]

For Savarkar, there was no conflict between Hindutva and nationalism. Hindutva, as interpreted by Savarkar, is not only a concept of organic socio-political unity, it comprehends also the essential elements of nationalism. Moreover his concept of Hindutva is not a narrow creed; it is not opposed to humanism and universalism. In a letter to Guy A. Alfred (editor of 'The World'), he wrote: "I hold that although mankind must march on through nationalism and federalism, yet the goal was not nationalism. The ideal of all political science and art must be a Human State. The earth is our Motherland, mankind our Nation and a Human Government based on equality of rights and duties is or ought to be our ultimate political goal."[7]

SAVARKAR AND COMMUNALISM

It is to be noted that Savarkar had been brought up in his early youth as not only a fearless revolutionist but also as a staunch Hindu who brought about solidarity among Hindus. In spite of his immense love for the country he continued to view things from the Hindu standpoint. To understand an apparent change in his outlook, his political life can be divided into two distinct phases- the one before he went to the Andaman and later. Earlier he was all praise, for the role of Muslims in the 1857 Uprising. At the time when he wrote Indian War of Independence, he was a Hindu nationalist. But then came a change in Savarkar's outlook which, according to Y.D. Phadke, can partly be attributed to the experience he went through at the hands of the Muslims in jail, and as a result, he turned to be a Hindu communalist.

Paradoxically enough, himself an atheist and a rationalist, Savarkar became the high priest and theoretician of the Hindu community. He was a great champion of Hindu solidarity. He preached the doctrine of Hindu ascendency and asserted that the politics of India must be Hindu politics.

He clearly told Muslims to be content with the status of a minority community. It is noteworthy that it was Savarkar who first propounded the two-nation theory in his book 'Hindutva' as early as 1923, and reiterated it in his Presidential Address to Hindu Maha Sabha in 1937. In this address, he gave his own version of the two-nation theory which is not much different from that of Jinnah. He spoke: "But the solid fact is that the so called communal questions are but a legacy handed down to us by centuries of cultural, religious and national antagonism between the Hindus and the Muslims. When the time comes we can solve them. It is safer to diagnose and treat the deep-seated disease than to ignore it. Let us bravely face the unpleasant facts as they are. India cannot be assumed today to be a Unitarian and homogeneous nation, but on the contrary, there are two-nations the Hindu and the Muslim."[8] Savarkar reiterated at Nagpur (Aug. 15, 1943, I have no quarrel with Jinnah's two-nation theory. It is an historical fact that Hindus and Muslims are two nations."[9]

ESTIMATE AND CONTRIBUTIONS OF SAVARKAR

Undoubtedly, Savarkar's contribution to Indian freedom struggle in its early phase is second to none. But by 1923 Savarkar was no longer a Hindu nationalist and turned to be an extreme communalist. He became an aggressive protagonist of the Hindu community, and his ideal became the resurrection and solidarity of the Hindu community rather the freedom of the country. To bring about this solidarity among Hindus, he repudiated caste system, religious rituals and conventional ideas about God.

However, Savarkar's conception that Hindus are a homogeneous race does not stand the criteria of historical accuracy, for now homogeneity of race is an exploded ethnological conception- a discarded myth.[10]

In the end, it cannot be denied that Savarkar made a negative contribution to Indian polity by propounding a theory of 'Hindutva'. It is significant that his 'Hindutva', though published in 1923, is still widely acknowledged a book on Hindu political ideology.

It is interesting to note that both Jinnah and Savarkar began their political career as staunch nationalists but ended up as extreme communalists. Rightly speaking, both jointly share the dubious honour of fathering a theory (two-nation) that eventually led to partition of India. As such, among the guilty men of partition, they may be dubbed as the main culprits.

Notes

1.   Rajgopalachari quoted in Pradhan G.P., India's Freedom Struggle, Popular Prakashan, Bombay, 1990, p. 49

2. Ibid., p. 50

3. Ibid., p. 51

4. Roy, M.N., India In Transition, op. cit, pp. 151-52

5. Quoted in Verma, V.P., op. cit, pp. 317-18

6. Ibid., p. 318

7. Quoted in Ibid., p. 318

8. Gopal, Ram, A Political History Of Muslims, op. cit, p. 264

9. Indian Annual Register, 1943 Vol. II p. 10

10. Verma, V.P., op. cit, p. 319

Chapter 48

BHIMRAO RAMJEE AMBEDKAR — A SOCIAL REVOLUTIONARY (1891-1956)

Dr. Ambedkar was one of the greatest jurists, lawyers and political leaders of modern India.

At a time when Indians were awakening from their plight and struggle for freedom, the ripples of renascent spirit touched the depressed-classes too. The stir found the instrument of reformation in Bhimrao. Responding to the call, he strode forward defiantly fighting for a better deal for the depressed classes, displaying rare crusading spirit, achieving in the process the right to be given a place among the builders of India,[1]

Bhimrao was the youngest of fourteen children. His father Ramjee, retired as Subedar Major and settled in Ratnagiri district. As a student, Ambedkar had experienced agony, anguish, frustration and humiliation because of being born in the Mahar (low) caste of Maharashtra. In school; for instance, he was forced to offer Persian instead of Sanskrit (supposedly a higher caste subject) as the second language.

Bhimrao was married to Rambai when he was only 14 and studying in the V standard. After her death he married a lady of the Sarasvat Brahmin caste.

While studying at Elphinston College he used to receive a monthly scholarship of Rupees twenty five from Maharaja Sayaji Rao Gaekwad of Baroda. As a student Bhimrao was average in his studies. But he was very respectful to his teacher and as a mark of regard and respect to his Guru he began to call himself Ambedkar, the name of his teacher. He passed B.A. in 1913, and in the same year he joined Columbia University (New York), as a Gaekwad scholar. While in America Ambedkar attracted the attention of Lala Lajpat Rai, who was living there in exile at that time. Bhimrao obtained his M.A. degree for his thesis 'Ancient Indian Commerce'. He read a paper on 'The Castes in India'.

In this paper (published in 1917) he pointed out that endogamy is the essence of castes. "A caste is an enchained class and it existed even before Manu", Ambedkar maintained. In June 1916, he submitted his thesis for his Ph.D. entitled 'National Dividend for India' which was published in 1924 under the title 'The Evolution of Provincial Finance. In British India', with introduction by prof. S.A. Seligman. In 1916, he joined the London School of Economics. In 1918, he published a brochure, 'Small Holdings in India and Their Remedies'. On his return to India, he started a weekly, 'Mook Nayak', to champion the cause of the depressed, and a paper entitled 'Bahishkrit Bharat' to voice their grievances.

Apart from having an outstanding academic achievements to his credit, Ambedkar was a prolific writer. His writings include 'Who were the Sudras?' (1946) The Untouchable Castes in India'; 'Thoughts on Linguistic States' (1955), 'Riddle of Rama And Krishna' (proscribed), 'The Buddha and His Dhamma', Pakistan or the Partition of India' (1940) etc.

In politics, Ambedkar was a ruthless critic of Gandhi and seldom agreed with the policy of the Congress led by him. As against the Congress stance, Ambedkar welcomed and cooperated with the Simon Commission (1928-29). His stand at the First Round Table Conference earned him the wrath of the Congressmen who upbraided him as a stooge of the British. At the Second Round Table Conference he not only challenged Gandhi's claim to be the leader of the untouchables but also demanded, to Gandhi's discomfiture, separate electorate for the scheduled castes,. His demand was, however, conceded by Ramsay Macdonald in his Communal Award (1932). But when Gandhi went on an indefinite fast on the declaration of the Communal Award, Ambedkar yielded to Malviyajis pressure and thereby saved Gandhi's life by signing the Poona pact. But later on, Ambedkar described the Poona Pact as a "mean deal", and never forgave Gandhi for coercing him into signing the pact. Again, when the Second World War began he supported the war efforts as War Advisory Committee Member, and described the Quit India Movement (1942) as 'irresponsible and insane'! For him, it was an 'open rebellion'.

AMBEDKAR'S STAND ON THE PARTITION OF INDIA

Ambedkar was as much interested in burying the Hindu Raj as Jinnah was in avoiding it. But he was in favour of forming a non-communal party (mixed party of Hindus and Muslims) to fight against the Hindu Raj. But later on, when he found that the Muslims were bent upon having Pakistan he began to support their demand. He felt that if their was no other alternative Pakistan had to be accepted. In his book "Pakistan or the Partition of India' (1940) he wrote "once it becomes certain that Muslims want Pakistan there can be not doubt that the wise course would be to concede the principle of it."[2] He "realistically" pointed out that "Pakistan would liberate both the Hindus and Muslims from the fear of enslavement and encroachment."[3] While surveying the relations of the Hindu-Muslims relations down the ages, he found that in Islam there is no room for "territorial nationalism." At one time in his paper 'Bahiskrit Bharat' he put forward the proposition that "Hindus and Muslims constituted two different nations."

AMBEDKAR AND INDIAN DEMOCRACY

Ambedkar was a true and sincere democrat. For him, political democracy without social and economic democracy was a double deception. He warned that as long as there was inequality on the social and economic plane there can be no political democracy, except in name or form. Unlike most of the Indian leaders, he never indulged in unnecessary glorification of the Indian civilisation. He frankly pointed out to the several weaknesses that the Indian society suffered from. He honestly contended that "democracy was a top dressing on the Indian soil which is essentially undemocratic." He believed that constitutional morality is not a national sentiment and it has to be cultivated. He recommended three things to cultivate it: (1) Adherence to constitutional method; (2) To make our political democracy a social democracy; and (3) Rejection of personality cult. For him hero-worship obtaining in India is a sure road to degeneration and to eventual dictatorship. Again, according to him, the unit of society is the individual, never the caste or the village. He never glorified the village organisation of the past, as Gandhi did. In his opinion, "these village republics have been the ruination of India. What is the village but a sink of localism, a den of ignorance, narrow mindedness and communalism."

AMBEDKAR AND THE INDIAN CONSTITUTION

Ambedkar was one of the very few Indian statesmen in politics who actively participated in the discussions on constitutional matters from the Montford Reforms to the Cabinet Mission Proposals. It was in recognition of his expertise on constitutional matters that the Nehru government appointed him the Chairman of the Drafting Committee when the new constitution was to be framed. This Committee included legal luminaries like N. Gopalaswamy Iyenger, Alladi Krishnaswamy Iyyer, K.M. Munshi, Sayied Mohd. Saadulla, N. Mathavi Rau, D.P. Kaithan. In the Making of the new constitution of India. Dr. Ambedkar played the role of the "Indian Jefferson". He brought to bear upon his task a vast array of qualities — erudition, scholarship, imagination, logic, eloquence and experience. According to M.V. Pylee, "Ambedekar espoused the cause of strong union with autonomous states."[4] Apart from being the chief architect of the constitution of free India, he was the last word on its interpretation.

AMBEDKAR'S VIEWS ON RELIGION

For a long time, Ambedkar was a follower of Kabir, as Kabir was against the caste system. but ultimately he found solace in the teachings of Buddha, another great crusader against the caste system. He regarded Buddhism as a moral and tolerant alternative to Marxism. His followers pride in glorifying him as a Bodhisattva. However, Ambedkar reinterpreted Buddhism. His 'The Buddha and His Dharma' is virtually his new Testament of Buddhism. For him, Buddhism was the most rational religion of all, integrating a materialistic view of life with a religious morality compatible with modern rational thinking. Indeed, he was of view that Buddhism was the religion of the modern era, and would eventually be embraced by the whole world.

AMBEDKAR'S VIEWS ON THE INDIAN CASTE SYSTEM

As a sociological historian, he did not accept the hypothesis of an Aryan invasion of India. He forcefully put forward the view that the Sudras were not dark-skinned aboriginals enslaved by the Aryan invaders, but they were also Aryans who belonged to the Kshatriya solar dynasty. The subordinate status of the Sudras was brought about by a violent battle between the Sudras, the Sudra King and Vashishta. Due to social vicissitudes and changes of fortune, they became degraded from their Kashtriya status. In his opinion, the Brahmins were responsible for the degradation of the Sudras.[5]

According to Dr. Ambedkar, Chaturvarna has been the parent of the caste system as well as untouchability. He believed that the problem of the untouchables could not be solved by mere tinkering and palliatives He said: "White-washing does not save a dilapidated house; you must pull it down and build anew." He demanded a radical social revolution. He was not satisfied with the constitutional provisions for them in the constitution. He demanded that there should be more members of the untouchable community in the higher bureaucracy.

THE CURSE OF UNTOUCHABILITY
— AMBEDKAR & GANDHI

Both Ambedkar and Gandhi were heroic and the very embodiment and symbols of revolt against the unjust social order obtaining in India.

Both were great champions of the underdog, great emancipators and humanists. But while Gandhi was a reformer, Ambedkar was a social revolutionary and an iconoclast. In the opinion of Prof. Bipan Chandra, "Both share in common total opposition to caste oppression and caste discrimination and commitment to transform the social, economic and cultural conditions of Harijans".[6] Untouchability, Gandhi said, "poisons Hinduism as a drop of arsenic poisons milk." The vital interests of the untouchables he would not sell even for the sake of winning freedom of India. As a matter of fact, Gandhi was the greater and more total revolutionary in this respect, for he worked for the ending of the caste system itself which was responsible for socio-economics disabilities of the untouchables. It is worth mentioning here that in the beginning Gandhi believed that untouchability was an excrescence, a pathological growth that had nothing to do with the essential nature of the caste system which was a frame work for the division of labour, and as such he simply advocated a purified varnashrana dharma. But in 1935, Gandhi declared that caste system had to go and admitted that Varna Vyawastha that he idealised earlier was today non-existent in practice. Hinduism, he asserted, had to become casteless if it was to survive, and he looked for the most effective, quickest and most unobtrusive way to destroy caste system.

In a speech on June 14, 1947 the reaffirmed that distinction between avarna and savarna must go. He believed that mere political upliftment would not eradicate the caste system. In his later years he attacked one of its major pillars, that is endogamy, and advocated intercaste marriages. But at the same time Gandhi was vehemently opposed to separate electorate for the scheduled castes, as demanded by Dr. Ambedkar, for he felt that it will ensure their bondage in perpetuity.

Ambedkar too was an enemy of the caste system, particularly of Brahmanism which buttressed it, and he too stood for its total liquidation. He believed that caste system would have to go if untouchability was to be done away with. Nothing could emancipate the outcaste except the destruction of caste.

Although the goals that both pursued were almost the same, their strategies differed. While Ambedkar worked for self-regeneration and struggle on their own by the scheduled castes, Gandhi never emphasized the autonomous activity of the untouchables as crucial to their emancipation. He, on the other hand, felt that their emancipation would come about unobtrusively through cooperation with the higher castes. In fact, Gandhi wanted to absorb the Harijans into the Hindu fold by fusing their identity with Hinduism. Therefore, he advocated cooperation in place of confrontation. But Ambedkar found in Gandhi's approach a sort of paternalism which he was not willing to accept. What is more, while forcefully rejecting it, Ambedkar repudiated Hinduism altogether. Thus, while Gandhi tried to resurrect Hinduism, Ambedkar revolted against the Hindu community as such.

However, Gandhi's approach appears to be most sound and realistic. His approach was based on four pillars: First, there was the primacy of the ongoing struggle against imperialism which called for class and caste cooperation. But for Ambedkar, on the contrary, the British presence was a check on the caste Hindu oppression; Second, Gandhi thought that the people subjected to suppression for centuries could seldom be mobilised for a militant struggle. Moreover, he was convinced that a violent approach without preparing the masses would inevitably plunge the society in turmoil. In this respect Gandhi was right as history would bear him out. It is a fact that Ambedkar did fail to mobilise the Harijans except among the Mahars — his own subcaste; Third, since caste Hindus constituted the overwhelming majority, no social change could occur by confronting the majority; Lastly, Gandhi believed that the upliftment and welfare of Harijans were linked to the overall development of the Indian society as a whole. Dr. Ambedkar too accepted these arguments at significant moments. Did he not marry a Brahmin lady though he was opposed to Brahmanism ? Again, his joining the Nehru Cabinet of independent India and performance of heroic labour in the making of the Indian constitution was based on his belief that the Harijans would develop and promote their interests only in cooperation with caste Hindus.

Thus we see that despite differences in their approaches to the problem of untouchability Gandhi and Ambedkar both began to admire each other at the fag end of their life. To substantiate, it was at Gandhi's instance that the Nehru government appointed Dr. Ambedkar as Chairman of the Drafting Committee which was set up for drafting the Indian constitution, although Nehru's own preference was either for Ivor Jennings or Granville Austin. Though belatedly, Ambedkar duly recognised Gandhi's contribution and acknowledged that the Dalits had been "nearest and dearest" to Gandhi.

ESTIMATE OF DR. AMBEDKAR

Dr. Ambedkar was a social revolutionary. He vehemently denounced the inequalities which Brahminacal Hinduism has heaped upon the untouchables. Though the movement for the liberation of the backward classes was started by another great Maharashtrian- Jatirao Phule, Dr. Ambedkar was the most renowned and the most militant champion of the untouchables. Through his scholarly writings, speeches, leadership and constructive work, he made significant awareness of the political, economic and social problems of the untouchable community. Though provoking and provocative, his life is highly instructive to everyone who yearns for human dignity and equality in social relations. More than any other Indian it is he who fought for the cause of social equality. His ultimate achievement lay in ushering in a silent social revolution in Indian society. He stood for the social liberation, economic emancipation and political advancement of the downtrodden.

Ambedkar's other major contribution to Indian progress was his faith in constitutional order. Though he believed in change, but stood for change through constitutional method only. The civil-disobedience methodology could be a dominance of anarchy, he thought. His contribution as a parliamentarian, scholar, statesman and a reformer was outstanding. Notably, the Chief Architect of the Indian Constitution he also drafted and introduced the Hindu Code Bill to end the complexities of the marriage system in India.

Notes

1.   Ahluwalia, Architects Of The Swaraj, op. cit, p. 148

2.   Ambedkar, B.R., Pakistan Or Partition Of India, 1940, p. 365

3.   Ibid., p. 238

4.   Pylee, M.V., Constitution and Government Of India, p. 138

5.   Verma, V.P., op. cit, p. 512

6.   Chandra, Bipan, Gandhi Versus Ambedkar, - Caste System and Untouchability, Times Of India, 13 April, 1994

Chapter 49

ACHARYA NARENDRA DEVA — AN ETHICAL SOCIALIST (1889-1956)

Born at Sitapur (UP), Narendra Dev was educated in Faizabad, Varanasi and Allahabad (where he changed his name from Ashirvadi Lal to Narendra Dev). Narendra Deva was a magnificent orator and a great writer in Hindi and English. He was an outstanding socialist intellectual. His writings are characterised by force and clarity.

Narendra Deva began his political career as an Extremist under the influence of Tilak and Aurobindo. Starting out as a Tilakite, he became a Marxist by the early twenties and remained so till his death in 1956. He joined the Non-Cooperation Movement led by Gandhi. For over two decades, he was associated with the Kashi Vidyapith.

Narendra Deva was one of the founders of Congress-Socialist Party. He presided over the inaugural meeting of the All-India Congress-Socialist Conference in 1934. Keenly interested in the peasant movement in India, he was one of the founders of the All India Kisan Sabha and was twice elected is president. For several years he remained a member of the Working Committee of the All India Congress Committee. He reluctantly agreed to breaking of Socialists from the Congress organisation in 1948. He endorsed the merger of the Congress-Socialist Party and the Krishak-Mazdoor Praja Party led by Acharya J.B. Kriplani, which took place at Bombay in September 1952, and thus the Praja Socialist Party was formed.

PHILOSOPHICAL FOUNDATIONS OF NARENDRA DEVA'S THOUGHT

Acharya Narendra Dev was a profound scholar of Buddhist philosophy. A great linguist, he knew several languages and had good command over Sanskrit and Pali. His most famous philosophical work was "Buddh Dharma Darshan" He was attracted to Buddhism because of its anti-transcendentalistic orientation. In his opinion, "It was not theism but the acceptance of the moral governance of the world which was the essence of Indian culture."[1]

Like Jaya Prakash Narayan, Acharyji too professed Marxist ideology and "adopted dialectical methodology to comprehend the reality in its entirety and complicated structure."[2] But one wonders whether he accepted the entire philosophy of Marxism, for, like J.P., he kept close touch with Gandhi and was sufficiently inspired by his thought as well. Following Marx, he claimed to be a scientific socialist but actually he was "an ethical socialist." He had firm faith in the primacy of moral values. His studies in Hindu and Buddhist thought had strengthened his conviction in the sanctity of human values. He was therefore called a "Marxist suiting to the genius of India."[3]

As a Marxist, Acharya believed in the materialistic interpretation of history. He also felt that capitalism had exhausted its creative possibilities on the Marxist line of thinking. But he disagreed with Hegel who denied the reality of the world of experience and only recognised one absolute Idea. According to Acharyaji, Marx has always held that what was originally derivative had the power of becoming an independent cause. An idea, according to Marx, can influence the course of history when it realises itself in fact. Thus it is wrong to say that Marx recognised only one single cause of historical evolution. He did accept the influence of non-economic factors upon the structure of the productive system.[4]

Acharya was equally influenced by Bukharin's famous book 'Historical Materialism', which recognised more than two classes. However, unlike Gandhi, he supported the theory of class struggle and had no faith in class conversion or trusteeship theory. He attempted to view the social and economic problems of India in terms of the sociology of class struggle. He pleaded for an alliance between the lower middle classes and the masses. He wanted to broaden the basis of the Indian freedom struggle for a united front of the industrial workers, the peasants and the petty bourgeois intellectuals.

Narendra Deva was inspired simultaneously by the twin ideologies of nationalism and Marxism. He was an exponent of socialist nationalism. Besides, he was a sturdy secularist. He thought that theological considerations should not cloud the attempt at rational, social planning. For him it was essential that an atmosphere of secular democracy must pervade the country.

Acharyaji emphasized the humanist foundations of socialism. He agreed with Franz Mehring in regarding Marx as a Prometheus of modern history, who was inspired by the humanist zeal of suffering for the redemption of exploited and tormented humanity.[5]

ACHARYA NARENDRA DEVA'S CONCEPT OF
A NEW POLITICAL SYSTEM AND
HIS TECHNIQUE OF REVOLUTION

"As a socialist politician Narendra Deva was more influenced by the Marxist ideology of class struggle than by the Leninist creed of capturing power by an armed party."[6] The acceptance of class struggle idea also took him away from Gandhian thinking of "class conversion." But being a revolutionary he was not satisfied with constitutional methods alone. Fully conscious of two opposing forces — communism and capitalism — competing with each other he envisaged the ushering in of the era of democratic socialism.

Acharya Narendra Deva put forth his thesis of democratic socialism at the second Annual conference of the PSP at Gaya (1953). His 'democratic socialism' is antithetical to totalitarianism and bureaucratism. It favours decentralisation of power and responsibility. Narendra Deva suggested that a network of local democratic centres should be set up and functional associations be organised on democratic lines. He believed that decentralisation in administrative and economic sphere alone well save the state from totalitarianism. He believed that for the maximisation of production of wealth and human welfare socialisation of industries and planned economy is indispensable. In his opinion, cooperatives are an essential factor in socialism. Co-operative farming and multi-purpose cooperative societies should be organised for marketing, irrigation and He supply of better seeds, manure and implements. Thus he wanted to establish an industrial democracy in the country.

Narendra Deva stood for social ownership and opposed trusteeship idea, as advocated by Gandhi, He believed that property rights should be in consonance with national interests. But, in order to end exploitation and oppression of the working classes he favoured Gandhian technique — Satyagrha and strike. He was not in favour of violent revolution, and advocated democratic, peaceful and non-violent means only. He also suggested class co-operation between peasants, industrial workers, and other working classes. In his opinion, only those who have a firm faith in democracy and socialism can be the vanguard of the new movement for world peace.

ESTIMATE OF ACHARYA NARENDRA DEVA

"Narendra Deva was a Marxist and democratic socialist with an emphasis on human values and cultural heritage."[7] He was a man who never believed in compromising ideals for immediate political gains. Besides being a respected teacher and a gifted orator, Narendra Deva was a front rank intellectual and writer. His captivating manners, his unassuming but towering scholarship, his sterling character and massive intellect, endeared him to all those who came in his contact. It was in recognition of his intellectual stature that he was called to act as Vice-Chancellor of Lucknow University and the BHU when these Universities were facing some trouble in the early fiftes.

Acharya Narendra Deva attempted to give the Indian Freedom Movement a socialistic orientation. His emphasis on economic programme for mobilising mass action enabled him to combine the nationalist freedom struggle with the agitation for emancipating the working class and peasants. He made valiant efforts to bring the toiling masses into the national mainstream during the liberation movement so as to make them feel the utility of political and economic emancipation.[8]

Notes

1.   Verma, V.P., op. cit, p. 463
2.   Ibid., p. 463
3.   Bhagwan, Vishnu, op. cit, p. 208
4.   Deva Narendra, Socialism and National Revolution, pp. 20-21
5.   Verma, V.P., op. cit, p. 467
6.   Ibid., p. 467
7.   Dixit, Chandroday Democratic Socialism in India, (1971) p. 7
8.   Bhagwan, Vishnu, op. cit, p. 215

Chapter 50

DR. RAM MANOHAR LOHIA — THE STORMY PETREL OF INDIAN POLITICS (1910-67)

Dr. Ram Manohar Lohia was one of the front rank leaders of the Indian national movement. He played a notable role in the Quit India Movement. He was a great socialist intellectual who had done vigorous thinking on Indian problems.

Lohia was born on 23 March, 1910 at Akbarpur (UP). As a student in Calcutta, he started taking an active part in the freedom movement. In 1928, he led the college students to boycott the Simon Commission. In 1929, he left for Berlin for higher studies and returned to India in 1933 after having earned a Ph.D. degree in Economics.

Along with JP and Narendra Deva he played a vital role in the formation of the Congress-Socialist Party. In 1934, he was entrusted with the task of propagating socialist ideology as editor of the weekly, 'The Congress Socialist'. He proved himself as a fiery propagandist of socialist thought in India. In 1936, he was made the Secretary of the Foreign Department of the Congress on the recommendation of Nehru, who was very much impressed by his razor-sharp mind and intellect, In 1938, he was included in the Executive Committee of the Congress-Socialist Party. In 1947, the Congress Socialist Party held a session at Kanpur under the Chairmanship of Dr. Lohia. It was at this session that the word 'Congress' was dropped from its name. In 1952, there was a merger of the Socialist Party with the Krishak Mazdoor Praja Party, and the Praja Socialist Party was formed. In 1952, as President of CSP, Lohia had pleaded for a greater incorporation of Gandhian ideas in socialist thought. In 1953, as General Secretary of the PSP, he advocated the significance of a decentralised economy based upon the resuscitation of cottage industries. He was not in favour of over-mechanisation and preferred small machines which could utilise maximum labour power with small capital investments. Lohia was therefore, opposed to both capitalism as well as communism because of their emphasis being on heavy machines. While Ashok Mehta (another socialist stalwart) pleaded in 1953 for greater cooperation between the Congress and the PSP on the ground of "compulsions of backward economy," Lohia offered his equidistant theory and described Mehta's socialism as "paralysed socialism". With his growing Gandhian leanings, Lohia felt that the Socialists were almost equidistant from the communist and the Congress. While still a leader of the PSP, Lohia was mainly responsible for convening the Asiatic Socialist Conference in 1953. In 1954, however, a serious crisis occurred in the PSP leadership when Lohia demanded the resignation of the PSP government of P.T. Pillai, as it had ordered police firing upon agitators demanding a linguistic state in Travancore Cochin. When the PSP government refused to resign, there came a split in the PSP and a new socialist party under Lohia's leadership was formed in 1955.

POLITICAL AND SOCIOLOGICAL IDEAS OF DR. LOHIA

Lohia's political and sociological ideas are contained in his numerous writings such as 'Wheel of History' (1950), 'Marx, Gandhi And Socialism' (1963), 'Aspects of Socialist Policy' (1952), 'Problems of Asian Socialism', 'Will To Power', 'Guilty Men of Partition', etc.

As regards interpretation of history, Lohia dismissed both Hegelian and Marxian interpretation of history. History, according to Lohia, moves in a cyclical, inexorable way. He repudiated the notion of straight linear historical advance or unilinear progress. In the course of cyclical movement, a country may attain to the heights of civilisation and may go down to the nadir, to rise, perhaps, again. In this he was in agreement with Aristotle, Spenglar, Northrop, Toynsee and Sorokin, etc. But Lohia rates Sorokin higher than Oswald Spenglar and Northrop.[2]

As a Marxist, Lohia accepted the theory of dialectical materialism but attributes greater significance to consciousness than orthodox Marxism. "He advocates the creation of an intellectual tool that could combine spirit and matter into an autonomous relationship."[3]

Lohia did not accept the Marxian theory of class war. For him it was "inadequate and substantially wrong." He believed that in human history there is a tussle between crystallised castes and loosely cohesive classes. The internal ocillation between class and castes is a prime factor of historical dynamics. Castes represent conservative forces of stagnation, inertia and prescriptive rights. Classes represent a dynamic force of social mobilisation. In his opinion, "class was but ossified caste." According to him, all human history uptill this time has been an internal movement between castes and classes — castes loosen into classes and classes crystallise into castes.[4] This slow swing between class and caste has so far been a law of human history. According to V.P. Varma, "Lohia's concept of the struggle between classes and castes is only a popular form of Pareto's theory of the struggle between the landed interests of rentiers who represent "residues of persistence" of aggregate and the monied interest who represent "residues of combination"[5].

LOHIA'S THEORY OF STATE

Unlike anarchists and syndicalists, Lohia did not advocate for the abolition of the state, nor did he glorify it, like the idealists. Unlike Marx, he also did not believe in the "withering away of the state." Recognising the importance of the state, Lohia wanted it to cater to the welfare of the people rather than be an instrument of coercion. He cold not stand the concentration of power in the hands of a few. Like pluralists, he was opposed to the concept of a monolithic state which concentrates all authorities at the centre. He believed in the diffusion of authority. Like Prof. Laski, he espoused pluralism to safeguard individual liberty. In his own words, "Any recognition of popular sovereignty would be fictitious that does not simultaneously provide for the sharing of the state power at various levels and direct participation in administration." Following the line of Bertrand Russell, Laski, Webbs, Huxley, he advocated decentralisation of power, as concentration of power leads to authoritarianism.[6]

LOHIA'S CONCEPT OF FOUR PILLAR STATE

Lohia envisaged a four pillar state structure. In this scheme, an attempt is made to synthesise the opposed concepts of centralisation and decentralisation. In this structure, the village, the mandal (district), the province and the central government all retain their importance and are integrated in a system of functional federation. To quote N.C. Mehrotra, "The scheme of four pillar state incorporates the principle of mass participation and decentralisation so as to impart dynamics into local units and to work for integrated society."[7] In this scheme the cohesive bond is provided by the performance of functions.

WORLD UNION: THE FIFTH PILLAR

In addition to the four pillar state, Lohia also felt the necessity of creating a fifth pillar in the form of a world government, as it was necessary for bringing about peace in the world. Lohia urged all the socialist parties of the world to think in terms of an effective world union through the world government. He said: "No true internationalism can arrive unless its votaries realise that the present crisis of foreign policy is a crisis of human civilisation and that it can be overcome only by the union of minds all over the world that cut across national frontiers and interests and is prepared to hold general principle even when they operate against one's own system of national or world alliances."[8] Lohia had been an outspoken critic of India's foreign policy. Criticising India's foreign policy, Lohia remarked that it was more a glittering quilt of imaginary international achievements to cover up the poverty and misery at home than a genuine effort to create new world forces."[=9] He did not subscribe to non-aligned philosophy of Nehru, and believed in having solid friendly nations abroad. He advised India to build up a third system, which adheres to the principle of equal irrelevance as regards the two Camps and to refuse to put itself in alternative service of either. In other words, Lohia favoured genuine non-alignment.

LOHIA'S CONCEPT OF 'NEW SOCIALISM'

Lohia stated that orthodox socialism was "a dead doctrine." Hence he made a plea for 'New Socialism'. Lohia was an exponent of decentralised socialism. He states that equality, democracy, nonviolence, decentralisation and socialism are the five supreme principles. He thought that 'New Socialism' must aim at the attainment of these principles, and for this he outlined a six-point plan for realising it, as under: (1) Maximum attainable equality towards which nationalisation of economy may be one necessary step ; (2) A decent standard of living throughout the world; (3) A world parliament elected on adult franchise, leading to world government; (4) Collective and individual practice of civil disobedience; (5) Freedom of the individual — freedom of speech and association and freedom to private life over which no authority may exercise control; and (6) Evolution of technology consistent with these aims and processes.[10]

Lohia stood for an equalitarian society- equality between sexes, equality between classes and every other kind of equality was dear to him. Moreover, he wanted to clothe the abstract principle of equality with certain concrete terms so that the equalitarian objective may not remain a myth. This he called the 'principle of immediacy,' that is, the maximum and immediate attainability relevant to the current situation in relationship to the ideal. Lohia vehmently opposed the caste system of Indian society. According to him, caste represents restricted opportunity, restricted opportunity constricts ability and constricted ability further restricts opportunity. When caste prevails, opportunity and ability are restricted to ever narrowing circles of the people. According to him, "caste turns a country into the arid desert of intellectual inadequacy. Lohia was extremely critical in his denunciation of caste oppression. He believed that Indian political future was doomed without the uplift of the shudras, harijans, the tribal population and other backward classes. He advocated preferential treatment for the downtrodden to enable them to act at par with the rest. Lohia also considered the mixing of dogmatic religion and political consideration a bane of Asian politics, because it leads to development of communal outlook.

ESTIMATE OF DR. RAM MANOHAR LOHIA

Dr. Lohia was an ebullient and arresting personality. He stands up as a lone and inveterate prophet of social justice, unrelenting before the highest odds and the greatest threats. He always stood for all kinds of liberties, economic equality and upliftment of the downtrodden. As a political leader and astute strategist, he had some original ideas to contribute to Indian politics. It was he who introduced the politics of 'anti-Congressism' in the post-Independence period. He was mainly responsible for formulating the philosophy as well as the platform of non-Congress political forces. As such he turned out to be a quintessential opposition politico. The General Elections of 1967 and the subsequent political developments vindicated his political strategy of anti-Congressism. Again, Lohia was the godfather of caste calculus in the electoral politics of India. It was he who took the initiative in mobilising all depressed and backward people on a common platform. As such he may be regarded as the progenitor of 'Mandalism' in Indian politics.

Another notable political idea of Lohia was that there should be a confederation of India and Pakistan — the 'two distant neighbours'. His contention was that Pakistan was created because the ailing and old Indian leaders were anxious to assume political power. According to him, Pakistan could be created because the British diplomacy wanted to drive a permanent wedge in the subcontinent. Another fundamental basis of Pakistan movement, according to him, was the suspicion of the Muslims of Bihar and UP of being dominated by the Hindu majority. Lohia also felt that Gandhi should not have yielded to the demand for Pakistan.

Lohia was a great protagonist of Hindi as official language of India. For him, English was the symbol of exploitation and domination by a slender minority. It was Lohia who initiated the movement for independence of Goa as early as June 1946. He also initiated the movement against the Ranas of Nepal. Lohia inspired the Indian socialists to develop Asian outlook towards the problems of the day. Internationalist in outlook, Lohia aspired for a true international society.

Lohia was an inveterate foe of all dogmas. His socialism by and large was based on humanistic foundations which sacrificed the interests neither of the individual nor of the society, neither of the country nor of the world.

In the words of late Madhu Limaya, "Lohia was an original thinker, a unique leader and a rebel but he was not an ivory tower philosopher. He was essentially a man of action and a great political strategist." To be sure, Lohia was a passionate, fearless and reckless fighter for freedom in all its aspects.

To conclude, the Indian socialist thinkers — Narendra Dev, J.P. and Lohia — were advocates of the synthesis of political liberty and economic reconstruction. They believed in parliamentary method for achieving power. Under the influence of Gandhism, they eschewed violence as a technique of revolution and, like Gandhi, they were attached to the concept of decentralisation.[11] Lohia was one of those great leaders who not only advocated the need for a fundamental reordering of our social relations but also provided an ideological basis for such a revolutionary transformation. He called this radical transformation seven revolutions or Saptakranti,[12] It is significant that like J.P. Narayan, he also talked of Seven Revolutions. against injustice and tyranny and their various manifestations, and they are: (1) Revolution to achieve equality between men and women, (2) revolution against the tyranny of colour, (3) revolution against caste; (4) revolution against foreign rule (5) revolution of economic equality; (6) revolution to protect individual's entity against collective encroachment, and (7) revolution against arms and weapons.

Notes

1. Bhagwan, Vishnu, op.cit, p.349

2. Verma, V.P., op. cit, p.472

3. Lohia, Ram Manoher, Wheel of History, p.37

4. Ibid., p.51

5. Verma, V.P., op.cit, p.472

6. Bhagwan, Vishnu, op.cit, pp.354-55

7. Mehrotra, N.C.(ed.) Lohia A study, 1978, p.101

8. Gupta, R.C., Great Political Thinkers, op.cit, pp. 186-87

9. Ibid., p. 187

10. Bhagwan, Vishnu, op.cit, p.354

11. Verma, op.cit, p. 475

12. Chopra Rakhi, "Lohia and his Movement for Social Equality, Mainstream, March 30, 1996, p.32

Chapter 51

JAYA PRAKASH NARAYAN
— A RELUCTANT MESSIAH
(1902-79)

Jaya Prakash Narayan remains one of the most tantalising characters in Indian politics. He has been the foremost leader, propagandist and spokesman of Indian socialism.

Born in a middle class family, he was the fourth child of his parents. He was tall and strikingly handsome. He was educated partially in India and partially in USA. He had an eventful life in school at Patna. He came into contact with national activities through his association with Saraswati Bhawan, which was a centre of national leaders at Patna.

The period between 1914 and 1922 proved to be particularly significant in the life of J.P. He was attracted towards Gandhi because of his simplicity, and his non-violent technique of civil disobedience and non-cooperation. He got married to Prabhawati Devi at the age of 18. His father-in-law, Brij Kishore Babu, was an established Congress leader of Bihar. Through him J.P. came in contact with other important leaders of the province. Inspired by Gandhi's call he left studies to take part in the Non-Cooperation Movement.

Although J.P. had walked out of the Patna College as a gesture of non-cooperation with the government, he continued to cherish a strong desire for higher studies in Science. In 1922, he sailed for the USA for higher studies, where he stayed for seven years, studying at the Universities of California, (Wisconsin) and Ohio. Here he came in contact with East European intellectuals and became a Marxist. In his own words: "It was at Madison Wisconsin that I drank deep at the fountain of Marxism."[1] Simultaneously, he was influenced by the pungent writings of M.N. Roy which almost completed his conversion to Marxism. He was particularly impressed by the Marxian philosophy of revolution. He said; "The Marxian cult of revolution seemed to me as a surer and quicker method to attain independence than the civil disobedience and non-cooperation."[2] He was thrilled by the triumph of Lenin in Russia. But soon he began to feel that knowledge of social science was essential to deal with Indian Socio-economic problems. Hence he joined the Ohio University to study Social Sciences. He did his M.A. in Sociology and wrote a thesis on 'social variations.'

Though a professed Marxist, he never became an apologist of Russian communism. In fact, he was shocked at the atrocious deeds of the Russian Bolshevik Party, and soon developed a deep moral revulsion against Russian communism.

On return to India (November 1929) he found the country in the midst of a new nationalist upsurge. So instead of joining the Benares Hindu University, where he was offered a post of professor, he joined the Congress and became its General Secretary in 1932. In the 1930s he favoured the idea of forging a united front with the Communist Party of India. But since the Communists took no part in the Civil Disobedience Movement he gave up the idea.

During the Civil Disobedience Movement J.P. too was put under arrest. He came out of the prison with an idea, a purpose and a vision and out of that was born the Congress Socialist Party. In 1934, the CSP was launched with the help of like-minded persons and J.P. became its first General Secretary. For sometime JP was the chief organisor as well as the chief ideologue of this organisation. In his book 'Towards Struggle' (1946) he claimed "The Congress Socialist Party played a notable part in giving shape to the socio-economic content of the Congress Party and a keener edge to the struggle for freedom."[3]

The sad experience of working with communists in the thirties had a lasting impact on his mind. He noted that Indian communists were not free agents but a tool of Moscow. Moreover, the doubts on the soundness of the Soviet system raised by numerous trials and purges of the Communist leaders in the 1930s loosened the hold of Marxism on his mind. After re-examining the basic postulates of Marxism and their practical application, he began to question Marxism-Leninism as safeguard to social revolution or to socialism. The evil ends that had resulted from the evil means in Soviet Russia, particularly the foul means that were used to perpetuate the staggering crimes during the purges, made J.P. revolt against the "revolutionary ethics" of Marxism and forced him to question if good ends could ever be achieved by bad means.

Gradually, J.P. began to feel that Marxism was not an appropriate solution for India's problems. This made him change his ideology in favour of Democratic Socialism. However, this shift from Marxism to Democratic Socialism took a number of years to complete.

As soon as the Second World War broke out he saw it as a great opportunity for hastening India's march to freedom. His heroic activities during the War years mark him out as one of the heroes of India's liberation struggle. He deprecated all efforts at a compromise with the British. In 1940, he was imprisoned, but he kept track of the onward march of the struggle from his cell in Hazari Bagh Central Jail, in Bihar.

The news of the famous Quit India Revolution adopted by the AICC on 8 August, 1942 exhilarated him, but the equally widespread demoralisation and depression in the wake of the suppression of the uprising made him equally worried. To an intrepid freedom fighter like him, it appeared galling to sit idle in prison while such a momentous struggle was going on in the country. With the help of some of his trusted comrades he, together with five other prisoners, managed to scale the prison walls on Diwali night (8 November 1942). This daring and death defying feat at once made him a hero in the eyes of the people. Indeed, this was his finest hour as a freedom fighter. On coming out of jail he soon established contact with other freedom fighters and infused a new life into their efforts. The ideology of the Congress Socialist Party now emerged as the ideology of the 1942 movement. He now boldly asserted that recourse to violence was unavoidable in the next phase of struggle. He observed: "I should not allow cowardice clothed in shastric subtleties to block the development of this revolution and lead to its failure". He also organised a guerilla force which he named as "Azad Dasta". But on 19 September, 1943 he was arrested in a running train from Delhi to Rawalpindi, and he was kept in Lahore Fort along with Dr. Lohia as a "State prisoner". He remained in jail from 1943 to 1946. On his release he again began to think in terms of a mass revolution. As such, he was not willing to consider the Cabinet Mission Plan, which was strongly condemned by him.

While actively engaged in the struggle during 1940-47, he gave due attention to the type of society required to build up in future India. During the jail period he was impressed by James Burnham's 'The Managerial Revolution' (1941) and Eric Fromm's 'the Fear of Freedom' (1942). He developed a dislike for Marxism and came out as a convinced social democrat. Although he did not challenge the theory of violence as a "midwife for revolution", it became clear to him (a) that in a society when it was possible for the people by democratic means to bring about social change, it would be counter-revolution to resort to it and (b) that socialism could not exist nor be created in the absence of democratic freedom. As a logical corollary he rejected the theory of Dictatorship of the Proletariat. This did not, however, mean total abandonment of Marxism but its synthesis with some of the basic teachings of Gandhi and the values of Western democracy. The combination of Marxism, Gandhism and Western democracy comes out best in his two articles: (1) 'My Picture of Socialism' (1946) and (2) 'The Transition to Socialism' (1947). JP's picture of socialism is a picture of an economic and political democracy. In this democracy, he asserts, "man will be neither slave to capitalism nor to party or the state. Man will be free."

In the succeeding years, however, the Gandhian component in JP's political philosophy went on increasing till a state arrived when he disavowed his faith in dialectical materialism and proclaimed his adherence to Gandhian philosophy of Sarvodaya, describing it as a higher form of socialism. But his transition from Socialism to Sarvodaya cannot be described as abandonment of socialism but the enrichment of its contents. For J.P. the greatest teaching of Gandhi was that means and ends are correlated, that evil means can never lead to good ends and that fair ends require fair means. JP found Gandhi as a social revolutionary of an exceptionally original kind and was fascinated by three aspects of Gandhism: (a) Its stress on moral and ethical value; (b) Its great contribution to revolutionary technique in the form of civil disobedience and Satyagraha; and (c) its insistence on political and economic decentralisation. Besides, by now J.P. had disavowed the philosophy of materialism as well. In his from "Socialism to Sarvodaya" J.P. wrote: "Materialism as a philosophical outlook could not provide any basis for ethical conduct." In his opinion, "In a material civilisation, there is not rational incentive to be good."

Disillusioned by the defeat of the Socialist Party in the General Elections of 1952 and also because of growing disenchantment with Marxism, JP joined the Bhoodan Movement led by Vinoba Bhave. He resigned from the National Executive of the PSP in 1954 and offered himself as a 'jeevan dan' to the Sarvodaya. Thereafter J.P. became actively engaged in the work of Sarvodaya for about two decades.

Significantly, even in the midst of his hectic programme in connection with the Bhoodan movement, J.P. found time to think in depth about an ideal political system for India, and put down his thesis in 1959 in a tract entitled 'A Plea for Reconstruction of Indian Polity'. This is one of the most significant works on political systems written by an Indian in modern times. In this work, J.P. pleaded for a replacement of parliamentary democracy by a new kind of polity consistent with India's own tradition as well as with the true nature of man and community.

This he called 'communitarian democracy' or partlyless democracy'. He wrote; "The surest foundation of democracy in India would be self-governing village units in which there is bound to be lesser difference of opinion and greater hope for realising the concept of participatory democracy. The problems of the transition from the old polity to the new are dealt with more fully in 'Swaraj for The People' (1961).

During 1954-74 J.P. had withdrawn from party or power politics and was engaged in the work of social reconstruction. But the general moral degradation in Indian social and political life made him very upset, and hence after twenty years of wilderness in Sarvodaya, J.P. again took to active politics. In 1973, he launched a movement against corruption, unemployment, high prices and misrule. He thought of organising the people, especially the youth, to save democracy and for a 'total revolution'. He saw great strength in the uncommitted youth of the country. He was impressed by the student agitations in Gujarat, which forced the dissolution of the State Assembly. Encouraged by this development, the students of Bihar also started an agitation in March 1974. J.P. took the opportunity to turn it into a people's movement for complete social change. Gradually, it developed into a massive mass movement. J.P toured the whole country and made it clear that he was leading the movement for what he called the 'total revolution'.

By 1975, the movement led by J.P. began to gather momentum. Soon after, when Indira Gandhi's election was invalidated by the Allahabad High Court, she became panicky and out of desperation she imposed 'internal emergency' on 26 June, 1975, resulting in the arrest of all opposition political leaders, including J.P. However, J.P. was released in 1976 on parole on grounds of health. Coming out of Jail, J.P. called upon the political leaders of the opposition parties to create a sound basis for 'total revolution' in the country. As a result the opposition parties combined and a new party called the Janata Party was formed, which emerged victorious in the 1977 General Elections. Now J.P. was acclaimed as the Lok Nayak by the people. But the Janata Party did not survive for long due to inner contradictions, ego clashes, individual ambitions and angularities, and personal antipathies. The country slipped back into the old order of political infighting once again. Thus the dream of J.P. remained unfulfilled despite his life-long struggle, and he died a disillusioned man on 8 October, 1979.

J.P. AND THE CONCEPT OF TOTAL REVOLUTION

The idea of 'total revolution' took its birth in JP's mind when he was staying at Paunar Ashram in the last months of 1973. It was strengthened by the events of Gujarat and Bihar. But it was elucidated in jail during emergency when J.P. wrote his 'Prison Diary,' (published in 1977).

In this diary, J.P. wrote: "The struggle for freedom was not fought simply for national independence" Because the spirit of the constitution was much abused and real democracy seemed to be in great danger, particularly during the past four years in India, the call for 'total revolution' was given to the nation. The idea of 'total revolution' aims at bringing about a complete change in the present structure and system of Indian society. It is not only a system of social and economic reconstruction of the Indian society but it is also a philosophy of moral and spiritual rebirth of the Indian people. Brahmanand, in his book "Towards Total Revolution', writes: "Total revolution is not a dogma but an attitude to life. It is not a revolution in the sense of a sudden change but it is a deep, comprehensive change in individual and society. It is different both in its methodology and objectives. Its methodology is non-violent and peaceful. It is essentially a people's movement and not a partisan's movement, aiming at a thorough social transformation in every activity of man, economics, politics, education, culture, social relations. It visualises setting up of a real and effective people's power for the upliftment of all."[4] In short, J.P.'s 'total revolution' is a blend of seven revolutions-civil, economic, political, cultural, ideological intellectual, educational and spiritual.[5]

J.P. ON INTERNATIONAL ISSUES

Though rooted to Indian soil, J.P.'s vision was not confined to India only. It encompassed the whole world. Like Nehru, Lohia and M.N. Roy, J.P. always kept himself aware of international events and developments. But his foreign policy outlook, just as his political outlook in general, was shaped by pure idealism unhampered by practical considerations. No wonder, his stand on certain foreign policy issues made him quite unpopular with the elite and the people. However, his stand on several international issues were laudable and were often vindicated by subsequent events.

Generally speaking, J.P. supported the policy of Non-alignment. But when he felt that the policy was deviating from the path he came out with scathing indictment of the conduct of India's foreign policy. To illustrate, he was critical of Nehru's policy towards the Soviet action in Hungary (1956) and Chinese action in Tibet (1959). He wrote: "It was political myopia induced by ideological prejudices which prevented a timely appraisal of Hungary that made us acquiesce in the rape of Tibet."

J.P. was also critical of the Goa operation in 1961. His comment was: "It was the military action for the liberation of Goa which cost us international regard, particularly in the West, and tarnished India's image as a peace loving country." Significantly, his was one of the earliest voices in favour of recognition of Bangladesh. It is worth mentioning that in Nagaland, normalcy could be restored by 1964 only on the lines suggested by J.P. No wonder, he won the prestigious Ramon Magsaysay Award in 1965 as a mark of recognition for his services to the people. On the Kashmir issue he suggested a confederation of Pakistan, India and Independent Kashmir as a way out to end the prevailing tension in Indo-Pak relations. Since, in his opinion, partition had been a complete failure, J.P. suggested for a South-Asian community to rectify it. He founded the Indo-Pak Conciliatory Group in 1962.

ESTIMATE OF JAYA PRAKASH NARAYAN

Jaya Prakash Narayan was an enigma to many, perhaps even to himself. He had travelled many roads but almost every time he had hit upon a blind alley- from Marxism to Democratic Socialism to Sarvodaya. He had journeyed through a tortuous course. As a matter of fact, J.P. was no stickler for consistency and changed paths several times in his life. To illustrate, in the sixties he stood for partyless democracy but in the seventies he himself brought into existence the Janata Party and thereafter he gave up again the idea of partyless democracy. A strange dissenter with a maverick's touch, he had a queer penchant for championing lost causes. But despite different political labels, his underlying concern for freedom and liberty was consistent. To be sure, two facets in his character stand out: (1) His total devotion to the service of man without personal reservation; and (2) The pragmatic pursuit of his idealism. But at the same time, there were two negative traits in his character — escapism and romanticism. To illustrate his escapism, it is known that he refused Congress leadership that Nehru offered to him after his retirement. As regards the romantic streak in his character, there can be no better illustration than his advice to students to overthrow the corrupt government, and to suspend their studies for the purpose without realising its dangerous consequences. Similarly, his advice to armed forces to disobey orders of the government was nothing short of a romantic illusion. All the same, J.P. was not only the last flicker of idealism in the politics of India but also the last of the legends to leave the land.

Among the Indian socialists, J.P. was the most well-known; he was a recognised personality in the history of the Indian socialist movement. His socialism was not only a philosophy of social and economic revolution of Indian society but also a philosophy of moral and spiritual rebirth of life. The idea of participatory democracy conceived by him is a valuable contribution that he made to political thought of India.[6]

J.P. AS A LEADER

Writing in his 'Gandhi, Nehru and JP — Studies in Leadership' (1985), Prof. Bimal Prasad says: "While Gandhi led India to freedom and Nehru laid the foundations of a modern democratic state, it was left to J.P. to go on a struggle for the establishment of a just social order. J.P.'s single-minded devotion to the cause of a social revolution, untrammeled by any lure for office or power is bound to inspire succeeding generations of social revolution in India." Like Nehru, J.P. has left behind the outline of a valuable political philosophy based on Marxism, Gandhism and Western democracy. Though equal to Gandhi and Nehru in idealism, dedication, courage and capacity for sacrifice, he, however, lacked shrewdness, practical wisdom and was often led astray by his romanticism and unrealistic dreams. The existence of a certain romantic streak in his personality always militated against hard-headed realism, which was amply shown when he allowed the Communist Party's leaders to capture the key position in the Congress Socialist Party organisation.

Like Nehru, J.P. too failed to build up a second level of leadership, a team of youngmen. He lacked Gandhi's charisma, political flair and skill in building a team. But like Gandhi, he belonged to the same genre of leadership who devoted their whole lives to political activities and brought about major changes in politics without ever aspiring to hold state power in their own hands.

While J.P. played a notable part in the struggle for freedom, his most important contribution lay in laying the foundations of a new India after independence. He played a notable role after the achievement of freedom as a leader of the Congress Socialist Party, and later on, when he walked out of the field of power politics, he contributed in building the power of the people rather than capturing the power of the state. Thus, his whole life was marked by the quest for a revolution which might usher in a new society. To be sure, J.P. has an assured place among the great political thinkers of modern India.

J.P. AND M.N. ROY — A COMPARATIVE ASSESSMENT

It is well-known that J.P. was considerably influenced by M.N. Roy. In JP's own words, "In the states I was drawn towards him (M.N. Roy), as a disciple to the master. I am one of the followers of Roy." Again, while expounding his own philosophy of Bhoodan and also in his 'Swaraj For the People (1961) J.P. refers to "significant and seminal contribution of the late M.N. Roy to the body of thought with which I am dealing."

But although J.P. and Roy were related to each other as guru and chela in more than one way, but heir relationship was in the tradition of Plato and Aristotle.

INTELLECTUAL ODYSSEY OF J.P. AND ROY

Both J.P. and M.N. Roy began by analysing the Indian society from the Marxist viewpoint and both were impressed by the Marxist technique of revolution. If Roy was the founder of communist movement in India, JP too was the pioneer of socialist movement in the country. But ultimately both disowned their Marxian past. Interestingly, if Roy journeyed from nationalism to Marxism to Radical Humanism, JP's journey was from nationalism to Marxism to Sarvodaya. However, while Roy criticised each and every aspect of Marxist philosophy before producing his own philosophy and his critique of Marxism was more systematic and comprehensive, JP's main concern was with the practice of Marxism in Soviet Russia. In comparison, J.P.'s critique of Marxism was sporadic, piecemeal and less comprehensive.[8]

Another difference between the two thinkers was regarding their philosophical outlook. Whereas Roy was free from mystical approach and maintained rational and scientific outlook at all levels of his thought in the reconstruction of Indian polity, J.P. was drawn towards the concept of Dharma and spirituality under the impact of Gandhism. While Roy, a revolutionary and a philosopher, was rationalist to the core, J.P. had acquired spiritualist learnings. J.P. was not satisfied with materialistic metaphysics. He often argued. "In a material civilisation man has no rational incentive to be good."

SIMILARITIES IN POLITICAL IDEAS OF J.P. AND ROY

Nevertheless, both J.P. and Roy gave the central place to the individual in their respective political philosophies and criticised all systems which eroded his liberty. Again, for both of them, the state was a means to an end and the end was individual freedom and unfoldment of his personality. Further, both were advocates of diffusion of power to the lowest and of giving the least responsibilities to the state. Again, both were critical of the nation-state and stood for a world state. Like Roy, J.P. also dreamed that "a day might come when the national communities might federate together to form the world community." Moreover, both stood against imperialism, fascism, interventionism, power blocks and arms race.

But despite these similarities there were some basic differences between the two. Whereas Roy gave a full account of the origin of the state and its distinction from the government, J.P. was mainly concerned with the state as it was in existence. Although both were advocates of diffusion of power to the lowest level, there was a difference between the two over the retention of the state. Roy in his Marxist phase subscribed to the Marxian theory of state particularly the conception of 'withering away of the state'. But after experiencing the role of the communist state in Soviet Russia he changed his views. He stated: "The ideal of Stateless society is obviously an absurd utopia."[9] He believed that in organised democracy "the state will be coincident with the entire society and consequently will be under a standing democratic control." He, therefore, rejected the idea of abolishing the state altogether.

J.P.'s concept of the state however remained fluid and shifting in consonance to his phases of political evolution. During his Marxian phase he considered the state as a powerful organisation of society and attributed to the state a progressive role and recognised its continued necessity. But after coming under the spell of Gandhism he began to plead for a stateless society. Although his ultimate aim was to do without the state, he was realistic enough to concede that "a fully stateless society was beyond the reach of the individual and the whole of human endeavour could only be to reduce the powers and scope of the state to the minimum."[10] It is worth mentioning here that he did not suggest statelessness in his communitarian concept of Indian polity but he says that "it exists only for a case of emergency, which is like the chain bell of the railway train of which the passengers are not even aware."[11]

Regarding political organisations, both J.P. and Roy were critical of the evils of parliamentary system and power politics. Both were disillusioned with party politics and favoured partyless democracy. J.P. maintained: "If the state is to melt away, to wither away, the party also must wither away."[12]

Regarding economic reorganisation, in the post-independence period J.P., on the lines of Roy, advocated setting up of cooperatives and community-owned industries in place of state or capitalists-owned industries to avoid totalitarianism and exploitation.

Regarding technique of revolution, both J.P. and Roy were inclined towards Marxian theory of revolution in their Marxian phases. But later on, both rejected the violent and insurrectionary method of capturing state power, and stressed on peaceful and moral means. For both, revolution meant an all round change in all aspects of man as well as his institutions. Revolution, for both of them, was a long term process of social change and not an event. Both regarded revolution as a means and not as an end in itself. Although both believed in social engineering but they favoured social change through persuasion and education only. To Roy, however, philosophical revolution was a precondition for a successful democratic revolution in India. According to him, cultural backwardness of India was the reason for its decline and for the imposition of British rule. The spiritual heritage of India, which was upheld and even applauded by J.P., was regarded by Roy as the cause of cultural decay. J.P. strongly differed with Roy on this point. Moreover, unlike J.P., Roy gave an unconditional support to the War efforts against Fascism. With the result, J.P. became the hero of the Quit India Movement and Roy, on the contrary, became a "traitor," because he characterised it as a "sabotage movement" in the light of his stand on the issue of World War-II.

At the end of their intellectual odyssey, because of his rational and logical approach, M.N. Roy turned out to be a system builder and an original thinker but J.P., because of sentimental and romantic approach, remained an intellectual philanderer or just an interpreter.[13]

Notes

1. Quoted in Bhagwan, Vishnu, op.cit, p.317

2. Narayan, J.P., From Socialism to Sarvodaya, 1959, p.

3. Narayan, J.P., Towards Struggle, 1946, p.65

4. Brahmanand, Towards Total Revolution, (4 Vols.), Extract from a note on the jacket of the book.

5. Narayan, J.P., Prison Diary, Popular Prakashan, Bombay 1978, p.87

6. Das and Patro, op.cit, p.294

7. Goswami, Subir, Review Article on 'The Political Ideas of M.N. Roy & J.P.- A Comparative Study, by Bhola Singh, (1985), The Radical Humanist, July, 1986.

8. Ibid.,

9. Roy, M.N., Politics power and Parties, Ajanta Publications, 1981, p.73

10. Singh, Bhola, "The State-Roy & JP', The Radical Humanist, April, 1994, p.40

11. Narayan, JP, A Plea For Reconstruction of Indian Polity; Sarva Seva Sangh Prakashan, p.63.

12. Ibid., p.29

13. Goswami, Subir, op.cit,

Chapter 52

JAWAHARLAL NEHRU
— THE JEWEL OF MODERN INDIA
(1889-1964)

Next to Mahatma Gandhi, Nehru was the tallest figure in the Indian freedom movment who left lasting impress on the history of modern India. Nehru was India's man of destiny, the maker of modern India, an apostle of world peace, a world statesman with vision and idealism, who lifted the plane of politics to a higher artistic sphere. He was one of those who pioneered the concepts of complete independence, socialism, and Indian constituent assembly. He was one of the front rank fighters who brought India's freedom struggle to a successful termination.

Born in a lap of luxury (the only male child of Moti Lal Nehru), educated at Harrow and Cambridge, Nehru chose to cast his lot with a hard task master like Gandhi, and spent quite a large part of his life in jail, sometimes under trying conditions. Nehru had so completely identified himself with the fight for Indian freedom that if there is any Indian other than Gandhi about whom it can be said that the history of his life is the history of the Indian struggle, it is Jawaharlal Nehru. No wonder, Nehru became the father figure for India after the death of the Mahatma.

During his seven years' stay in England, Nehru imbibed the traditions of British humanist liberalism whose protagonists were J.S. Mill, G.B. Shaw, Bertrand Russell and J.M. Keynes, etc. On his return from England (1912), Nehru joined the Allahabad High Court as a barrister, but soon he lost interest in the legal profession.

Nehru began his political activities by his association with the Home Rule Movement. He met Gandhi in December 1916 at the Lucknow Congress and thus began one of the most memorable political partnerships of our time. If Motilal Nehru was his biological father, Gandhi became his political father. Nehru plunged himself in the Non-Cooperation Movement (1920-22) under the leadership of Gandhi and, like other leaders, was also incarcerated. in 1923, he was appointed general secretary of the Congress and held this post for seven years. Nehru's main contribution in the late twenties was that he stood for the ideal of complete independence for India, like S.C. Bose and Srinivas Iyer, although his father favoured Dominion Status.

With Gandhi's blessings and also because of his father's wish, Nehru became the President of the Indian National Congress at the Lahore Congress and it was under his presidentship that the Congress declared Complete Independence for India as its goal in the midnight of 31 December, 1929. He again became the president of the Congress in 1936-37 and in 1946- both crucial occasions. He graced this post twice in the post-independence period as well. Thus, Nehru alone had the distinction of presiding over the Congress five times, whereas no other leader had the honour more than thrice. Nehru played a leading role in the various movements of civil disobedience during 1930-34. Like other leaders, he also suffered imprisonment for nearly three years in the 1942 movement.

After his release from prison in 1945 Nehru became the leading spokesman of the Indian National Congress in the several negotiations with the British. In 1946, he formed the first Indian (Interim) Government of India and after Independence he remained the Prime Minister of India for seventeen years (till his death on 27 May, 1964) the longest term so far.

Nehru was an author of established repute. His 'Glimpses of World History,' 'Autobiography' and 'The Discovery of India' are notable contributions to the realm of learning in Indian history and Indian political thought. His letters, speeches and addresses are an eloquent testimony to his mighty intellect. As a writer, he was effective, inspiring and full of literary flourishes.

PHILOSOPHICAL FOUNDATIONS OF NEHRU'S POLITICAL THOUGHT

Nehru was not a political philosopher in the academic sense, yet he was a man of ideas and convictions. Essentially a man of action, he had also the capacity for political detachment. Like his father he was an agnostic. Besides, he was a rationalist and a realist. In his own words, "Essentially, I am interested in this world, in this life, not in some other world, or future life." In spite of over three decades of deep contact with a devout and prophetic personality like Gandhi, Nehru continued to be agnostic. Though not a dogmatic materialist, he was not a spiritualist either. As a thinking introvert, he had been tormented by doubt and question.

Nehru's early philosophy of life was partly cyrenaic. He was influenced in his impressionable years by the writing of Pater and Oscar Wilde. But his philosophy of life was not solely formed by intellectual studies or metaphysical argumentations; it had also proceeded mainly from reflections on his own experiences. Besides, Buddhist influence is also clearly marked in his philosophical outlook. Significantly, he used the Buddhist concept of 'Panch Sheel' in a secular context to vindicate the principles of coexistence in a divided world. He was particularly influenced by the rational-ethical doctrine of the eight-fold path, compassion, serene vitality and exalted nobility epitomised in the personality of Gautam Buddha.[1]

NEHRU'S PHILOSOPHY OF HISTORY

Nehru was a keen student of history and had a thorough historical perspective. He was deeply interested in the historical evolution of civilisations. His historical approach had been reinforced by his studies of Marxist sociology. His 'Glimpses of World History' presented panoramas of the evolution of civilisations. This book is an attempt at the construction of historical sociology. Like Marxists, Nehru analyses the situational context amidst which social and political events take place. He would not regard history just as the biography of great men. He would rather stress the primacy of objective forces in history. But at the same time he would not ignore the tremendous role of heroes in history. Keeping in mind the role of men like Lenin and Gandhi, he stated that the will of one man can alter the lives of millions.[2]

NEHRU AND MARXISM

The watershed in Nehru's political thinking dates from 1926 when he revisited Europe. During this trip he came into contact with the main currents of radical thought and movements there. He attended in 1927 the Congress of the League of Oppressed People at Brussels as the representative of the Congress. Later on, he made a short visit to Soviet Russia in November 1927 and attended the 10th anniversary of the Russian Revolution. This visit revealed to him the great achievements of that country in the field of education, female emancipation and the betterment of the conditions of peasants. He recorded his impressions in his 'Soviet Russia' (1928). After his return from Europe he began to popularise the ideas of socialism.

Nehru was inspired by the Marxist approach to the cosmos and history. In his 'Autobiography' he confessed that the Marxist philosophy of life gave him comfort and hope. Its freedom from religious dogmas won the intellectual appreciation of the agnostic Nehru. This theoretical appeal derived from the acceptance of order in history was reinforced in Nehru's mind by the lesson of the Great economic Depression (1929-32). Besides, the Marxian stress on the role of technological-economic "forces" which march with an inevitable finality to the promised goal of a classless society appealed to Nehru. In his 'Autobiography', Nehru wrote: "The theory and philosophy of Marxism lightened up many a dark corner of my mind. History came to have a new meaning for me." He agreed with the contention of Marx that the British rule brought about a social revolution in Indian society. But unlike Marx, Nehru believed that far from liberating the Indian society from its age-old decadence, the British arrested the normal development of India in its political, social and industrial aspects.

But Nehru never became a thoroughly convinced Marxist, although there is clear evidence of deep Marxist-Leninist influence on Nehru in the thirties. Nehru's concept of socialist economy differed from the Marxian concept. For instance, he showed little interest in the labour theory of value or the theory of surplus value. He was also not willing to accept the philosophy of Dialectical Materialism. The concept of matter-in-motion as the ultimate reality did not satisfy him. The pervasive mystery of the cosmos would frequently haunt him. Moreover, he refused to ascribe a purely class character to ethical propositions. He was disillusioned with the Soviet aggression in Finland (1939) and purges and blood liquidations of Stalinism. Nehru also thought that the advances in human thought in the field of liberal and social sciences made Marxism somewhat outdated. In 1952, he drove the communists almost mad with fury when he made the declaration that "hundred years of development in the field of philosophy, social sciences, and economic thought has rendered Marxism out of date."[3] Significantly, a few years later he made some prophetic remarks with regard to the future of communism. In his 'Basic Approach' articles (published in AICC Economic Review 1958), Nehru wrote: "There is much talk in communism of the contradictions of capitalist society and there is truth in that analysis but we see the growing contradictions within the rigid framework of communism itself. Its suppression of individual freedom brings about powerful reaction. Its contempt for what might be called the moral and spiritual side of life not only ignores something that is basic in man, but also deprives human behaviour of standards and values. Its unfortunate association with violence encourages a certain evil tendency in human beings... communism had definitely allied itself to the approach of violence... its thought is violent and it does not seek to change by persuasion or peaceful democratic processes but by coercion and indeed by destruction and extermination....

I find this approach wholly unscientific, unreasonable and uncivilised. Whatever we may think about it, we have arrived at a stage in the modern world when an attempt at forcible imposition of ideas on any large section of people is bound ultimately to fail." These remarks provide a measure of his vision and foresight as they have been vindicated by the course of events.

ECONOMIC IDEAS OF NEHRU: HIS SOCIALISM

While a student in London (1905-12) Nehru became attracted to the ideas of Fabian socialism of Shaw and the Webbs, but in a vague and humanitarian way. But during 1926-27 he was again in Europe and there he imbibed more radical ideas of social and economic emancipation. Back in India, he presided at the annual conference of the Indian Trade Union Congress in 1929, and from the presidential platform of the Lahore Congress he categorically enunciated his commitment to socialism and republicanism.

By now Nehru was fully dedicated to the ethical, sentimental and emotional aspects of socialism as a philosophy of compassion for the suppressed classes and nationalities. But till 1932 his socialism remained rather vague and ambiguous. Between the years 1933 to 1936, however, Nehru bent more and more in the direction of Marxian Socialism. In 'Wither India' (published in 1933) he recognised the conflict between the old nationalist ideology and the new economic ideology" making its appearance on the Indian scene, and pleaded for combining the national struggle with the struggle for economic emancipation. It was, however, in his Presidential Address to the Lucknow Congress on April 12, 1936 that Nehru's socialism acquired a distinct Marxian colour. But since 1936, Nehru gradually drifted away from Marxism and went back to his old socialistic ideals which were nearer to a diluted form of Fabianism. His occasional Marxist tone after 1936 was largely a matter of habit, not of conviction. Thus we may safely conclude that socialism for Nehru was largely a matter of economic strategy rather than an economic doctrine.

Not surprisingly, therefore, the Lucknow Congress of 1936 is not only considered as the high watermark of Nehru's radicalism but also regarded as the "Swan Song" of his socialism by the ultra leftists. After 1936 his socialism revolved round planning and the public sector. But planning to him was neither a dogma nor a doctrine. Though he felt the need of an expert-controlled economy, he did not believe in an autonomous sphere of economies beyond the realm of politics. Anyway, by the end of 1938 a National Planning Committee headed by Nehru was set up. But the development model that he put forth envisaged the simultaneous participation of both the private and public sector. Primacy, of course, was given to the public sector as it was considered to be the chief agency of development and modernisation.

In the post-independence period, the Indian National Congress accepted the ideal of a "socialistic pattern of society" at the Avadi (Andhra Pradesh) session in January 1955. The socialistic pattern connotes social ownership or control of the principal means of production, acceleration of national production and the equitable distribution of the wealth of nation. In a Lok Sabha speech, he pointed out that "equality, removal of disparities and the possibility of everyone to live a good life constitute a socialist pattern of society." In Nehru's scheme, the public sector in the field of heavy and basic industries was to be the dominant phase of the economic advance of the country. But for the advance of production private sector was also to be encouraged. In a way, he now subscribed to the ideas of a welfare state rather than a socialist state. Besides, cooperative farming had been recognised since the Nagpur Congress of 1958 to be one of the dominant techniques for the realisation of a welfare society. This shows that Nehru was committed to the theory and practices of mixed economy. All the same, Nehru took the lead in putting socialism as a concrete social and economic objective before the Congress and the country.

POLITICAL IDEAS OF NEHRU

NATIONALISM: Though a great nationalist leader, Nehru did not develop any theory of nationalism as such. Nevertheless, he defined the meaning and content of Indian nationalism. In his 'UNITY OF INDIA', there is indication that he believed in the objectivity of the fundamental unity of India nurtured on cultural foundations, "which were not religious in the narrow sense of the term." He defined nationalism as essentially a collective memory of past achievements, traditions and experiences. Briefly speaking, Nehru's theory and practice of nationalism had three foundations. First, Nehru was against the racial arrogance of the British rulers. The second source of his nationalism was economic in nature. He blamed the British for the rampant poverty and ruthless exploitation of the country. The third foundation of his nationalism was political and administrative. The foreign rulers had the monopoly of decision making. They cleverly followed the policy of 'divide and rule' and tried to disrupt the unity of the country.[4] To Nehru, nationalism is, indeed, a noble phase of self-magnification. In his view, nationalism has also solid social, political and economic foundations as well as material advantages to offer.[5] Nehru had been a firm believer in the concept of self-determination.

SECULARISM: An agnostic, Nehru had been a secularist in his approach since the beginning. In his secular outlook he was greatly influenced by the family environment and the personality of his father, who himself was an agnostic. In his own words, "Of religion I had very hazy notion; for me it seemed to be a woman's affair."[6] The Anand Bhawan, the ancestral home of Nehru, was free from religious atmosphere. Here, There were three cultural strands — Hindu, Muslim and Christian. This influence of mixed culture turned Nehru broad-minded and ultimately a secularist. According to Chester Bowles, the US Ambassador, "One of Nehru's greatest achievements is the creation of a secular state. By proclaiming Indian democracy neutral in matters of religion, he laid down the foundations of a secular state and saved the country from falling prey to religious fanaticism and chauvinism." In the words of Ashok Mehta, "A distinctive contribution to Indian political life was Nehru's insistence on secularism." As a secularist in the Western sense, Nehru believed in keeping the state neutral in religious matters.

HINDU-MUSLIM PROBLEM: According to Nehru, "It would be patently wrong to assert that the Hindu Muslim problem in India was created by the British government." But at the same time, he drew attention to the continuous British efforts to keep that problem alive. As a social realist, Nehru was not satisfied with the generally prevalent religious explanation of Hindu-Muslim tensions. As a Marxist, he offered an economic analysis of this phenomenon. But being unaware of Hindu-Muslim hostility at the grass roots level, he could not go beyond a simplistic class analysis of the whole issue.

PARTITION OF INDIA: Regarding Nehru's responsibility for the partition of India, historians are still divided. His critics and detractors hold him responsible for the partition of India on two grounds: (1) The bungling committed by the Congress, led by him in forming ministries in the provinces, particularly UP; (2) His statement of 10 July 1946. As regards the first charge, it is not sustainable, even though alleged by such an eminent person as Maulana Azad, who writes: "The talks for a Congress-League Coalition Ministry failed because of Nehru's insistence on the appointment of only one member from the League, while the latter demanded two of its representatives to be taken in." Agreeing with Azad, H.M. Seervai in his 'Partition of India — Legend and Reality' (1989) says, "After resounding victory, Nehru showed no magnanimity towards the Muslim League. League's offer of coalition was treated with disdain." Nehru's detractors hold him personally responsible for it. They charge that Nehru, as Congress President, spurned the offer and demanded League's virtual liquidation in return for accepting the coalition with the

League. But according to S. Gopal, "It is a wrong contention that it turned the mind of League leaders to turn towards Pakistan." All the same, it is generally admitted that it did lead to unfortunate consequences. It is the consequent feeling of frustration which enabled the League to emerge as a really powerful organisation within two years. But the defender of Nehru, S. Gopal maintains: "The League leaders were determined from the very beginning to maintain their separate political/cultural identity. They wanted for them a substantial share in power not necessarily limited to the proportion of their population in the country but commensurate with their supposed historical and political importance."

Again, in 1946, when the country stood on the brink of partition and there was a slight chance that it might turn back, Nehru's uncompromising position on the issue of the grouping of provinces and the power of the Central government contributed in a significant way towards wrecking that chance, though of course, several other developments contributed to it. In his statement of 10 July 1946, Nehru had stated that "after the transfer of power the Congress would be free to change the political arrangement." The Muslim League professed to be offended by this statement and passed a resolution withdrawing its acceptance of the Cabinet Mission's Scheme. But the apologists of Nehru argue that the League's original acceptance had not been unqualified. It had agreed to cooperate with the Cabinet Mission Scheme with the hope that it would ultimately result in the establishment of a sovereign Pakistan. For the League, the Plan was a prelude to partition. The charge against Nehru in person is not just, because the entire leadership of the Congress was opposed to compulsory grouping of provinces and favoured a strong centre. Anyway Nehru's decision and statement did provide handle to those who wanted to accelerate the process of Partition.

However, Nehru was not happy with the decision of partition and remained convinced that "somehow partition would be reversed, the absurdity of it all was simply too difficult to absorb."[7]

DEMOCRACY: Nehru firmly believed in the theory and practice of Parliamentary democracy. He detested authoritarianism and dictatorship of any variety. He was always repelled by the crudities and vulgarities associated with fascism, Nazism and totalitarianism.[8] He was a passionate and genuine defender of freedom — civil, political and economic. He deplored the absence of a strong opposition in Indian polity, which is essential for the success of Parliamentary democracy. Regarding press freedom, another pillar of democracy, Nehru's famous remark was: "I would rather have a completely free press, with all the dangers involved in the wrong use of that freedom, than a suppressed or regulated press."

INTERNATIONALISM: A great patriot, Nehru was no narrow nationalist. Intensely proud of his country, he felt it a great honour to be called a "citizen of the world". To him, the whole of humanity was one and the whole world was the stage in which he wanted India to play her part. Nehru was one of the leading spokesmen of Asian and African aspirations for absolute political and economic freedom.

It was Nehru who broadened the outlook of the Indian National Congress and made it take keen interest in international affairs. He made Congress realise that the Indian struggle for freedom was a part of global struggle, and it could be made to succeed if it is geared in the international context. He visited Spain and China (1936-37) to express India's sympathy with the freedom fighters in pre-independence period.

After independence, the credit for India's key role in arranging cease-fire in Korea, in the ending of hostilities in Indo-China, in advocating the ending of Anglo-French military action in Suez, and for sending Indian peace-keeping troops to Gaza Strip and Congo goes to Nehru.

He was fully aware of the growing interdependence among nations. He stated: "The world had become internationalised, production is international, markets are international and transport is international. Only men's ideas continue to be governed by a dogma which has no real meaning today. No nation is really independent."[9]

He was a firm believer in the ideals of the United Nations. He was opposed to the bipolarisation of world politics and persistently refused to join any power bloc, and instead adopted the policy of Non-alignment. But he sponsored a dynamic concept of Non-alignment and not a passive one of neutrality. In 1949, he declared: "Where freedom is threatened, where justice is menaced and where aggression takes place, we cannot and shall not be neutral." Nehru was the architect of the Indian foreign policy. The foundations of his foreign policy were: non-alignment with power blocs, active pursuit of peace and freedom, opposition to imperialism and racialism, interest in developing close relationship with Asian countries, and a deep concern with the plight of the people of Africa.

Further, Nehru was the exponent of the Panch Sheel or the five cardinal tenets of international amity and accord: (1) Maintaining respect for each other's territorial integrity and sovereignty; (2) Non-aggression; (3) Non-interference in each other's internal affairs; (4) Peaceful coexistence an; (5) Equality and mutual benefit.

Nehru adhered to the ideal of a world state. But he did not imply the extinction of the nation-state. He wanted some sort of fusion between nationalism and internationalism. He pleaded that the world must have a world police force and advocated disarmament for realising the ideal of world peace.[10]

LEGACY AND CONTRIBUTIONS OF NEHRU
TO INDIAN POLITICS AND POLITICAL THOUGHT

To quote Michael Brecher, "Few statesmen in the twentieth century have attained the stature of Jawaharlal Nehru. As a leader he bears comparison with Lenin, Mao and Roosevelt." Nehru was one of the greatest figures of our generation, an outstanding statesman, and an interested fighter for freedom. As the maker of modern India, his services are unparalleled. More than any other leader, Nehru represented more fully and authentically the new enlightened generation of modern India, Nehru was responsible for drawing the intelligentsia to the National Movement just as Gandhi was instrumental in mesmerising the masses. Nehru was undoubtedly the bridge between the generations, the link between nationalism of the past and the new post-War Asian resurgence. He was instrumental in procuring an honourable place for his country in the comity of nations and thereby inculcating in her a new sense of self-respect.

Nehru's contribution to the realm of Indian political philosophy lies in his attempt at sociological understanding of Indian history. He tried to make retrospective reflection on India's past. But unlike Dayanand and Savarkar, he did not glamourise India's heritage, although he showed an abiding loyalty to the historical heritage of this ancient land. He tried to discover the secret of the enduring vitality of India's historical evolution and marvelled at her capacity for rejuvenation, and that is why Nehru wrote 'Discovery of India'. The best epitaph for Nehru would be: "He mastered history, he wrote history and he made history."[11]

Although, there is not much of philosophical depth or theoretical originality in Nehru's sociological and historical writings, there is a solid realism in them, which proceeds from his immense grasp of human group psychology and political dynamics.

Nehru always believed that political revolution must be accompanied by economic revolution. He visualised a synthesis of political and economic democracy. Although the synthesis of political freedom and economic justice was not his original thesis but he was certainly a leading exponent of this idea in India. It was more due to his efforts than that of any other leader that socialism became a vital issue of Indian politics.

Nehru detested revivalism and was a sworn enemy of communalism. He did not have metaphysical leanings, nor did he favour the clothing of political and economic ideas in the language of religious mysticism.

He wanted to bring the scientific orientation to viewing things social and political. The quest for scientificity and modernism may be regarded as a contribution of Nehru to the empirical side of Indian political and social thinking."[12]

Nehru had a good grasp of the dominant currents of international politics. As the chief architect of the Indian foreign policy, Nehru laid its foundations. It goes to his credit that his foreign policy framework remained sound and valid, until very recently. His main contribution to the making of Indian foreign policy was his attempt to reconcile high-minded idealism with hard-headed realism. Nehru sought to synthesise geopolitical compulsions with Indian ethos. The policy of Non-alignment was his unique contribution not only to Indian foreign policy but to the theory and practice of international relations. Undoubtedly, in the Nehru period, India came to enjoy a prestige and exercise an influence out of all proportions to her conventional power. He raised India to an important position among the comity of nations, where its voice was listened to with attention and respect. To sum up, Nehru wanted and worked for the development of representative institutions, Parliamentary democracy, planned social and economic change, socialism and internationalism.

Nehru's personality, however, was so complex and made up of so many facets that none can comprehend all his great qualities. To quote Norman Cousins, Nehru's famous biographer, "Nehru was not one man but a procession of men."[13] He was a philosopher, writer, historian, political thinker, all harmoniously integrated into one."

Naturally, such a complex personality is bound to have his admirers as well as critics, his defenders as well as detractors.

According to Dr. Radha Krishnan, "Nehru was an enfranchised human being and a great emancipator, a man of deep humanity, who had led a consecrated life and built modern India as a monument for himself."

In the opinion of S. Gopal (Nehru's political biographer and the son of Dr. Radha Krishanan), "Nehru made certain objectives so much a part of the general consciousness of India that they can today be taken for granted, even if they have not been as yet fully obtained — unity, democracy, secularism, a scientific and international outlook, planning to realise the vision of socialism." In the views of Dr. Rasheeduddin Khan, "Nehru was not a mere individual. He had a rare intellectual ability to subsume in his style of articulation, political formulation and projection of national goals — Gokhale's parliamentarianism, Tilak's vision of Swaraj, Gandhi's mass appeal and Swadeshi, the patriotic fervour of revolutionary and militants, and the call of Marxist revolutionaries for land reforms and radicalism."[14]

To quote Dr. Rasheeduddin Khan, again, "In his life and work Nehru reflected the great synthesis between the three dominant trends of what may be called the heritage of enlightened man. These may be identified as the Vedantic vision imbued with a sense of toleration and respect for many paths to truth, the composite culture of India incorporating the elegance and ethos of the Indian Muslim, the passion of the tribal, the cosmopolitanism of the urban-cultural streams and the vibrant propositions of liberty, nationalism, secular polity and democratic socialism that had governed the modernisation process of contemporary civilisation. His acute sense of history, his mystic communion with the Indian people, his ever present concern for the relevant, the rational and the progressive, and the incessant longing for the transformation of the traditional society into a modern polity committed him to a life long mission for the completion of the gigantic socio-economic revolution in India."

Critically appreciating Nehru, Ajit Bhattacharjea writes: "Nehru stood as post-independence Indian titan, her most charismatic leader, venerated, idolised darling of the masses and the intelligentsia alike. But was his sensivity a sophisticated veneer merely masking an all too easily malleable personality with a penchant for the dramatics? His handsome, contemplative looks and energetic bearing helped him stand out in any gathering. But he was wanting in the essential quality of leadership, namely, the capacity to make decisions and face unpopularity."

Regarding the legacies of Nehru, Michael Brecher identified then with political stability, democracy, planning, secularism, social change, together with the growth of inefficiency, corruption and neglect of land reform. According to prof. Bimal Prasad, "A major component of Nehru's legacy consists in the foundation of India's economic development on modern liens under his leadership. Mixed economy was part of that legacy." In his opinion, "the record of achievement of Nehru both before and after independence is certainly a mixed one. Nehru as Prime Minister contributed significantly to the strengthening of the foundations of national unity, secularism and democracy. He laid the base for a modern industrial society in our midst, scientific in temper, socialist in content, democratic in spirit and secular in its ethos. He also launched India on the path of planned development. But the actual targets achieved fall short of expectation. The socialist faith of Nehru, abiding commitment to secularism as an essential part of his vision of India of the future constitutes his most valuable legacy to the Indian people. He made economic planning an integral part of our political system. The development of modern science in India is another field in which he played a pivotal role. He did his best to nourish the plant of political democracy in India-through both example as well as precept."[15] According to B.R. Nanda ('Jawaharlal Nehru — Rebel and Statesman'), "Nehru's basic contribution was the establishment of democracy in a backward and largely illiterate country." But in the opinion of Prof. Bipan Chandra, "Nehru was neither a party builder and organisor nor a political strategist but an ideologue, an inspirer and an agitator. He did not know how to transform the party (Congress) into a viable modern political party with a strong institutional structure."[16]

REAPPRAISAL OF NEHRU

Despite the fact that Jawaharlal Nehru was devoted to the cause of India's independence for more than a quarter of a century, and for the next seventeen years guided the destiny of the infant Indian democracy with unflinching loyalty and selfless devotion, he was a victim of perennial shafts of criticism, and, in the last few years, was subjected to serious attacks from all sides. Nehru has also been described as a romanticist, an impractical spinner of ideas which were idealistic and unrealistic in the prevailing conditions. His concepts of secularism, socialism, planning and Non-alignment have become the main targets of attack.

In short, Nehru is no longer in vogue. His brand of socialism and centralised planning are no longer approved and appreciated. Today, when socialism worldwide has suffered a serious setback on account of the collapse of "socialist" experiments in Eastern Europe and the former Soviet Union, the free marketeers are up in arms against the so-called Nehruvian economics. Today, leftists have gone out of fashion. Nationalisation is no longer the panacea for industrial ills. Public sector enterprises, the hallmark of Nehruvian economics, are no longer models of the future but considered as wasteful examples of bureaucratic sloth and incompetence. Today, private sector represents modernity, competence and progress, and free enterprise or market economy has become a buzz word, a new magic mantra. Besides, the policy of non-alignment, Nehru's most distinctive contribution to international politics, too, has become an anachronism in the post-Cold War or post-bipolar world.

All told, "Nehru played a decisive role in the history of the twentieth century— as a leader of the Indian people, as a representative of the new mood of Asia and as a spokesman of the international conscience."[17]

NEHRU AND GANDHI — A COMPARATIVE ASSESSMENT

Both Gandhi and Nehru dominated the Indian political scene for about a generation and were equally linked and loved by the people of India.

If the period between 1919 and 1947 can be described as the age of Gandhi, that between 1917 and 1964, with equal justification, can be regarded as the Nehru era.

On the face of it there seems little in common between the agnostic, socialistically oriented westernised Nehru and the devout God-fearing oriental Gandhi. Yet, Nehru always had a profound emotional attachment to the Mahatma. Nehru came under Gandhi's spell in 1920 and thus began one of the most memorable or rather historic partnerships of our time. With the advance of years that bond of affection, attachment and loyalty deepened, and after the death of Motilal Nehru, Gandhi became a fatherly figure (Bapu) in the Nehru family.[18] It is rightly said that if Motilal was Nehru's biological father, Gandhi was his political father.

Nehru had been greatly influenced by Gandhi's tremendous earnestness and devotion to work. He also admired the harmonious poise and emotional integration that characterised the personality of Gandhi.[19]

According to V.P. Verma, "Nehru was drawn to Gandhi for three reasons: (1) He admired the heroism and the spirit of defiance of all odds and terrors by Gandhi. From Gandhi he learnt that fearlessness is the indispensable moral preparation for ending the enveloping gloom and tragedy of modern man. Nehru may have lost his temper easily but he never lost his nerves. Secondly, Nehru found that Gandhi's leadership and political action brought important results. Being a comprehensive personality, Gandhi acted as a bridge between the past traditional ideals and the future modernising aspirations of India. He was also a link between the minority of Westernised Indians at the top and the vast masses below. Gandhi's methods of action also appealed to Nehru, because they brought success. Gandhi had the extraordinary capacity to sense the public mood and had a fine grasp of the problems of India. Nehru found Gandhi to be the greatest revolutionary of recent times in India, despite his ideology, Thirdly, Nehru had also been influenced by Gandhi's moral approach to politics with its inculcation of non-violence and peace. Gandhi advocated the purity not only of ends but also of means. However, Nehru accepted nonviolence only as a policy and never as an absolute creed. Gandhi too was equally drawn towards Nehru. Thus, both appreciated each other's worth and significant role in the freedom struggle. If the Father of the Nation described Nehru as his political heir, the latter reverently called the former as Bapu.

But it is to be noted that the link between Nehru and Gandhi was more emotional or sentimental than intellectual. On intellectual and ideological plane there was a good deal of difference between the two. As a matter of fact, Nehru had very settled views against the proclaimed convictions of Gandhi. While Gandhi stood for Ram Rajya and Gram Rajya, Nehru clearly told his mentor that he did not regard Ram Rajya something great in the past nor did he want it back. Again, Gandhi regarded Western civilisation and industrialisation as subjects for resistance, but Nehru was clear that Western civilisation and industrialisation were bound to conquer India. Nehru was greatly enamoured of the progress made by the West in the field of science and technology. He firmly believed that rapid industrialisation of India was the crying need of the hour. He was of the opinion that if free India is to mean a nation of intellectually free people, scientific approach and technology has to be accepted. Nurtured in the West, Nehru was eager to rejuvenate the structure of the Indian Society in the light of the progress achieved by the West. Gandhi was against urbanisation and commended a village-oriented life for India, but Nehru openly said that villages are more prone to untruth and violence, and he gave a thrust to urbanisation. Further, Gandhi was against parliamentary democracy and favoured Panchayat Raj system without elections, while Nehru was for parliamentary democracy and relegated Panchayats to the unenforceable Directive Principles of the Constitution.

While Gandhi was a deeply religious man, and for him religion was as necessity to politics, Nehru was an agnostic and did not entertain any religious belief (he, however, recognised that religion had supplied some deeply felt inner need of human nature and the vast majority of people cannot live without it). Although, both stood for secularism but Nehru's concept of secularism was radically different from that of Gandhi. While Gandhi stood for equal respect for all religions — Sarva Dharma Sama Bhava, Nehru, being closer to Western views of secularism, wanted to keep the state strictly neutral in religious matters. That is, he favoured separation between religion and politics.

According to Prof. J.D. Sethi, "Nehru and Gandhi were antithetical to one another in the field of economics, science and technology, education and health and political organisation. Gandhi did not believe in technological determinism. He was against want-driven technologies and disapproved self-alienating modern modes of production. He stood for production by the masses and not for the masses. He was against massive mechanisation. Moreover, he pleaded for decentralisation rather than centralisation. He favoured popular participation rather than representative political system."[19]

Finally, as a leader, Gandhi was far ahead of Nehru. Gandhi not only made men out of clay but always put the right person at the right place. Nehru, on the other hand, was indulgent towards second rate persons whom he appointed. Unlike Gandhi, Nehru failed to build up a second line of leadership, a team of youngmen. He also failed to make him dispensable, which is the hallmark of a good leadership. On the contrary, he stood like a "banyan tree" under which no plant could grow.

To sum up, despite differences of thought, temperament and style, Gandhi and Nehru stood together for more than a quarter of a century. However, the political equation between them was not static. Nehru's passion for clarity and logic often clashed with the Mahatma's intuitive and pragmatic approach. But Nehru realised the indispensability of Gandhi's leadership and felt certain that the Mahatma was leading the country in the right direction. As regards their impact at the moment, interestingly and ironically enough, while the image of the "back to the village" of Gandhi seems to be growing, that of the creator of modern India with its "new temples" has started fading.

Notes

1. Verma, V.P., op.cit, p. 403
2. Ibid., p. 404
3. Ibid. p. 407
4. Das add Patro, op.cit, p.209
5. Verma, V.P., op.cit, p.412
6. Quoted in Ahluwalias, op.cit, pp. 131-32
7. Akbar, M.J., Nehru- The Making of India, Viking, 1988, New Delhi, p.415
8. Verma, V.P., op.cit, p.415
9. Quoted in Bhagwan, Vishnu, op.cit, p-255
10. Verma, V.P., op.cit, p. 417
11. Gupta, R.C., op.cit, p. 156
12. Verma, V.P., op.cit, p. 419
13. Quoted in Das and Patro, op.cit, p. 216
14. Khan, Rasheeduddin, Centenary Special, Mainstream, Dec. 1985.
15. Prasad, Bimal, op.cit, R.7
16. Chandra, Bipan, Sunday, 29 Sept. 1986.
17.
18. Gopal, Sarvepalli, Jawahar Lal Nehru. - An autobiography, Volume (1889 - 1947) Oxford University Press (1975)
19. Verma, V.p., op.cit, pp.410-11.
20. Sethi, J.D., 'Gandhi and Nehru', Illustrated Weekly, 12 June, 1988.

Chapter 53

MOHANDAS KARAMCHAND GANDHI — THE FATHER OF THE NATION (1869-1948)

Of all the leaders of the Indian freedom movement certainly the most towering was Mahatma Gandhi. "More than any single individual, Gandhi brought about the fall of the British Empire," to quote a British historian. But Gandhi was much more than the greatest leader of modern India; essentially and fundamentally, he was a world leader with a message for humanity. A pride of history though he was, Gandhi was, indeed, a figure out of history. He was a quintessential 'outsider'.

At school Mohandas Gandhi was a mediocre student. After matriculation he was sent to England for higher studies. He returned from there in 1891 after completing his law degree. As a lawyer he had a poor start. But he got an assignment from Dada Abdullah & Co., a rich Gujarati merchant to assist their Counsel in a law suit. It was a Godsend gift for Gandhi, and so he went to South Africa to conduct this case.

Gandhi's political career passed through three phases. The first phase of his public life began outside India. In South Africa, he was shocked to see the ill-treatment meted out to the Indian settlers. Colour prejudice, apartheid and humiliation by Europeans tormented young Gandhi's soul and led him to enter politics. Himself a victim of racial humiliation, he launched Satyagraha in South Africa a number of times between 1904 and 1914, and eventually succeeded in his mission to a large extent. He left South Africa in July 1914 and thus the first phase of his life came to an end.

The second phase of Gandhi's political career began in India when he returned to the country. In 1915, Gandhi came on the Indian political scene at a very critical period of the Indian national movement. The Moderate leaders were rejected and the Extremists and terrorists were equally frustrated and leaderless. With most of the Extremists behind bars, the remaining ones were avoiding active politics. At this juncture "Young

India" needed a new leadership and new programme. Gandhi fulfilled that requirement, because in him there was a harmonious blending of the best elements of political moderation and extremism. Like the Moderates, he had great faith in the sense of justice and fair play of the British government. But at the same time, the knew that the Moderate methods of prayers, petitions and protests would no longer be effective. Gandhi talked with a strength and determination unknown to the Extremists. While talking softly, he struck terror in the hearts of the foreign masters. He tried to rid the Indian people of the pervasive, perpetual and paralysing fears with which they were seized since 1857. Gandhi offered a practical alternative to the futility of verbal violence and scareful folly of political revolutionaries and militants. He presented to his countrymen a practical alterative to speech making and bomb throwing between which Indian politics had so far oscillated. As a result, Gandhi became a favourite of the Indian people within a short span of time. His meteoric rise on the Indian political scene was also facilitated by some accidents of history, such as the death of three stalwarts — Gokhale, Mehta and Tilak.

It so happened that with the passage of time, Gandhi became increasingly disillusioned with the British government. During the First World War he had asked Indians to support the British government with the hope that the government would be obliged to take progressive steps in the direction of realisation of the Swaraj. But the Government of India Act of 1919 gave him the first cause of disappointment. Even then Gandhi was willing to work out the Reforms Act (Montford Scheme), although in his own words, "it was inadequate, unsatisfactory and disappointing."

As a matter of fact, the first jolt came in the shape of the Rowlatt Bill. Later on, his bitterness against the British government increased manifold after the Jallianwala Bagh tragedy, the proclamation of Martial Law in the Punjab and the findings of the Hunter Committee. Eventually, he lost all faith in the good sense and fair play of the rulers and decided to start the non-violent, non-cooperation movement. Thus, the process of transition from a loyalist to rebel was completed in 1920, although, it had begun much earlier with his experiences in Champaran, Ahmedabad and Kheda (Gujarat).

It is worth noting that by 1920 Gandhi, like a tornado, transformed the political landscape of India. With his advent, Indian politics in general and the national movement in particular assumed a kind of dynamism which was not known before. Under his leadership the Congress for the first time decided to launch a nationwide movement in 1920-22. In fact, this was the first experiment of direct action in Indian politics, for this movement the whole nation was involved. As a result of this movement, the people of India acquired a feeling of self-reliance and the courage to challenge the might of the British government. To quote S.R. Mehrotra. "The Non-cooperation Movement proved beyond doubt that "Gandhi was a great organisor and institution builder. He transformed the character of the Congress by giving it a new direction, a new constitution, a new technique of agitation, a new leadership and a new programme of action."[1]

From 1920 to 1947 Gandhi dominated the Indian national movement in a manner which had few parallels in the history of the world. The leading events and landmarks in the second phase of Gandhi's public life may be summarised as under: The establishment of Ashram on the banks of Sabarmati (the political power house of the freedom movement) on 25 May, 1915, his joining the Indian National Congress in 1916, his launching of Satyagraha against the Rowlatt Act and leading the Non-cooperation Movement in 1921 as a sequel to Jallianwala Bagh Tragedy, launching of the Civil Disobedience Movement (1930-31), attending the Second Round Table Conference as the sole representative of the Congress (September 1931), the revival of civil disobedience movement in 1932 after the failure of the Conference, the sponsoring of the famous Quit India Movement (1942), followed by the declaration of independence and the partition of India (1947) — the last event, however, symbolised both the victory and defeat of Gandhian leadership.

The third phase of his public life commenced after 1947. As his wont, he could not remain a silent spectator to the drama of barbarism and carnage following India's partition. Gandhi toured the riot affected areas as a "one man boundary force." and resorted to fast in order to restore communal harmony. He made a vibrant appeal for Hindu-Muslim unity, restoration of mosques converted into temples, and the payment of Rupees 55 Crore which was due to Pakistan by way of division of assets. All this infuriated the orthodox and narrow-minded Hindus and Gandhi was shot dead by Godse, a Hindu fanatic on 30 January, 1948. It is indeed ironic that the apostle of non-violence had to meet a violent death.

INFLUENCES ON GANDHI'S THOUGHT

The first influence on Gandhi was that of his mother. It was a religious minded mother who made Gandhi a deeply religious person. As far as academic influence is concerned, Gandhi was not a great scholar. As such, he was not familiar with the major tracts of political philosophy. His knowledge was confined mainly to religious literature and a few utopian thoughts. But whatever he read he assimilated perfectly. Besides, his mind was a mine of ideas. He read the Bhagwad Gita and gave it a novel interpretation. Gita was the main source of inspiration for him. It became a dictionary of duty and an infallible code of conduct. He learnt about truth and nonviolence from this book. This faith was reinforced by Buddhist and Jain literature. He was also influenced by Patanjali's 'Yoga Sutra', the Ramayana and the Mahabharata. From the Upanishads, he got the inspiration for his faith in non-possession. He read the new Testament of the Bible and was greatly influenced by the Sermon on the Mount, which taught him: "Overcome evil by good and love your enemies." He was also influenced by the teachings of Lao Tse and Confucius. The studies of Buddha's life and the Gita, and his contacts with Ray Chand Bhai strengthened his moral convictions.

Apart from religious literature, some Western Utopian thinkers like Thoreau, Ruskin, Emerson and Tolstoy also influenced the moral and political philosophy of Gandhi. In fact, Gandhian thought has been influenced more by occidental thinkers rather than by Indian saints and philosophers. If Thoreau taught him the technique of civil disobedience, non-payment of taxes and the idea of minimum government, Emerson gave him the idea of 'self rule', Ruskin's Unto This Last' instilled in him the dignity of labour and Tolstoy's masterpiece, 'The Kingdom of God is Within You', inspired him to think in terms of philosophical anarchism. It was under the influence of Tolstoy and other Western thinkers that Gandhi became a carping critic of modern civilisation based on force and exploitation. Like Tolstoy, Gandhi also laid stress on the reform of individual- a first step towards social regeneration and on purity of means, and advocated ascetic morality and preached extreme simplicity of life, labour and virtual celibacy as essentials for the moral growth of the individual. Yet, Gandhi being more practical, differed from Tolstoy, the utopian. While for Tolstoy non-violence meant avoidance of violence in all forms, Gandhi laid emphasis on the motive and justified, in certain cases, even killing as 'ahimsa'. In the opinion of Dr. G.N. Dhawan, "Due to this vital difference Gandhi excels Tolstoy in devising ways to remove social evils which Tolstoy so brilliantly exposes and passionately denounces."[2] Under the total impact of these influences, Gandhi achieved a calmness of spirit and an integration of personality which are reserved for the blessed few.

METAPHYSICAL IDEALISM

The fundamental basis of Gandhism is the conception of God or an omnipresent fundamental spiritual reality. For Gandhi, the entire universe is permeated by God. He believed that, in the ultimate analysis, God or Truth is the final reality. But according to him, the spiritual truth was not to be realised by dialectical skill or conceptual cognition but by spiritual experience. For him, "Reason is a poor thing in the midst of

temptations — Faith that transcends reason is our only Rock of Ages."
Gandhi's faith in "fundamental truth was not born out of arguments and
external observations but out of spiritual apprehension and intuition.[3]

GANDHIAN PHILOSOPHY OF HISTORY

Gandhi was not a philosopher of history. But if we reconstruct his
scattered ideas into a philosophy of history, we find that he accepts
theological determinism. Nothing can happen but by His will. For Gandhi,
God signifies an unchanging and living law. He is the supreme
determinant of things and movements in the world. But determinism in
Gandhism applied only to the final explanation of things. It never
degenerated into fatalism, because Gandhi was a strong advocate of the
strenuous activism and energism of the Gita. His own life was full of
ceaseless actions.[4]

ETHICAL ABSOLUTISM

A metaphysical idealist, Gandhi believed in the supremacy of ethical
values and Sarvodaya (the goodness of all). His philosophy of Sarvodaya
is based on the Vedic concept of unity of existence. It has its roots in
the mantra of the Yajurveda, which says that the entire universe is
permeated by the supreme God. This idealistic philosophy necessarily
inculcates the values of eternal truth and justice. It teaches universal love
as the only law of life. It refuses to be satisfied with the progress and
well-being of a class or a nation but advocates the emancipation and
realisation of the good of all living beings.

The Gandhian theory of ethical absolutism can be traced to the Vedic
concept of the Gita — the doctrine that there are moral ordinances which
govern both men and gods. Buddha also had faith in the existence of
a moral order. Gandhi's own experience in life completely convinced him
of the superior efficacy of the moral norm.

Gandhi interpreted history in terms of the progressive vindication of
superiority of ahimsa. He believed in teleology. "It is my faith that man
is by nature going higher", he wrote. He believed that the world is moving
towards perfection. According to him, human history is the history of
this urge to achieve perfection and salvation. The world has been created
by God to achieve this goal. This 'orderliness of the universe' is a sure
proof of God who is willing for the victory of non-violence, the fixed
goal of the world. He considered truth and non-violence to be absolutely
binding. He said: "Non-violence is the first article of my faith. It is also
the last article of my creed." For Gandhi, it was the imperative duty of
the Satyagrahi to make endless endeavours for the realisation of truth
through non-violence.[5]

GANDHIAN PHILOSOPHY OF NON-VIOLENCE

To Gandhi, non-violence was a total philosophy of life. Ahimsa means avoiding injury to anything on earth in thought, word and deed. Of course, Gandhi was not the originator of the idea of non-violence. Ahimsa has been part of Indian religious traditions for centuries. Though not its originator, Gandhi refined, adapted and implanted the philosophy of non-violence in his public life and struggle for freedom. Apart from being the greatest exponent of the doctrine of Ahimsa, he was the first to use it on a mass scale and in the field of politics. To quote B.R. Nanda, "It was his genius which transformed what has been an individual ethics into a tool of social and political action."[6]

Gandhi was of the view that the highest violence can be met by the highest non-violence. Hence, non-violence is the 'bravery of the Soul', an 'adventure in love'. For him, non-violence did not mean weak submission to one's enemy, passivity or pacifism. It does not mean submission to the will of the evil doer. Rather, "it is a matchless weapon of potency". It is positive, dynamic and constructive.

Like Gokhale, Gandhi stood for spiritualisation of politics. But his attachment to the concept of non-violence was far deeper and more extensive than that of Gokhale.

Closely connected with his insistence on non-violence was Gandhi's emphasis on the requirement that our means must be moral. He was of the view that immoral means can never lead to truth and justice. According to him, "as the means, so the end." He firmly rejected any dichotomy between ends and means. Relating means to ends is the greatest contribution of Gandhi to political theory. G.N. Dhawan is of the view that "Gandhi's effort to give concrete expression in the form of Satyagraha to his principle of moral approximation of the end and the means is perhaps the most unique contribution of our times to the philosophy and technique of revolution."[7] Gandhi was one of the few thinkers who stood against the common belief that moral considerations apply to ends only and not to means, as ends have a moral priority.

SATYAGRAHA — HOLDING ON TO TRUTH

Satyagraha is the heart and soul of Gandhism. The idea and practice of Satyagraha is, in fact, his unique contribution to political thought.

Dr. G.N. Dhawan describes Satyagraha as "the relentless pursuit to truthful ends by non-violent means." It is the weapon of the non-violent struggle. It inculcates 'agraha' or moral pressure for the sake of truth. It means resistance to evil with all the moral and spiritual force that a person can command. According to Dr. Pyare Lal, "The starting point

of Gandhian technique was that non-violence is the strength of the weak."
"Satyagraha is an inherent birthright of a person. It is not only a sacred
right but it can also be a sacred duty." From family to the state, wherever
one meets injustice and untruth one can resort to satyagraha. But truth
must be the basic principle of Satyagraha. Thus, non-violence is a struggle
for truth; it is a fight for righteousness. The Satyagrahi, who wages non-
violent struggle, must see that the cause for which he fights is absolutely
true. According to Gandhi, Truth brings the Satyagrahi nearer to God.
He takes his order from him. For Gandhi, Truth and God are identical
because he defines Truth as God.

Gandhi believed that there is something of God in every man and
that the Satyagrahi can appeal to this divine element in man through
love and conscious self-suffering. If truth is the basic principle of non-
violence, love is the means by which it is realised. Satyagraha, thus, is
"an adventure in love." Non-violence, according to Gandhi, can melt even
the stoniest heart. It was also his conviction that man could hate the
evil without hating the evil doer.

According to Gandhi, a Satyagrahi should adopt poverty, observe
chastity, follow truth (both in words and thoughts) and cultivate
fearlessness. Fearlessness is the first requisite of spirituality, for cowards
can never be moral. He believed that non-attachment and renunciation
will give the required inner purity and character to the Satyagrahi. He
also suggested that a Satyagrahi, while resisting the laws of the state,
should see that social structure is not subverted, and it should never be
resorted for personal gain.

DIFFERENT TECHNIQUES OF SATYAGRAHA

There are different forms of Satyagraha such as (a) Non-cooperation
(in the form of Hartal, social ostracism, etc.), (b) Civil-Disobedience- there
can be individual as well as mass civil disobedience. (c) Fasting, (d)
Hijarat, (e) Peaceful picketing, (f) Strike, and (g) Peace Brigade.

DIFFERENCE BETWEEN SATYAGRAHA
AND PASSIVE RESISTANCE

Satyagraha is different from passive resistance. It contemplates action
in resistance of injustice. But there is no internal violence towards the
enemy. Again, while passive resistance is mainly contemplated at a
political level, Satyagraha can be practised at all levels — domestic, social
and political. Satyagraha condemns violence on moral grounds but passive
resistance is not completely non-violent. For instance, Tilak and Aurobindo
Ghosh, the advocates of passive resistance, did not condemn violence on
moral grounds. While passive resistance means use of compulsion,

Satyagraha believes in infliction of self-suffering, It aims at the change of heart and is actuated by the principle of love and charity. Satyagraha is the weapon of the brave and it is a moral weapon and not a weapon of political expediency.' According to Stanley Jones, "The concept of Satyagraha is one of the greatest contributions of Gandhi to the world."[8]

RELIGION AS A FACTOR IN HISTORY AND POLITICS

Gandhi accepted the creative force of religion in human history. To him, religion signifies belief in the ordered moral governance of the world. He accepted the spiritual and moral essence of Hinduism which was the essence of all good religions of mankind, such as Judaism, Christianity, Islam and Zoroastrianism. True religion implied an emphasis on the moral values. All religions were founded on the same moral law. "My ethical religion is made up of laws which bind all men all over the world," he wrote. Religion provided the dynamic impetus to his actions and life.

Gandhi was a Karmayogi. Karmayoga means disinterested pursuit of one's obligations and duties. It was this concept of Karmayoga, as dynamic altruism, that Gandhi wanted to make the basis of transformed social and political action.

But Gandhi's religion is not to be identified with any credal, dogmatic theology. In fact, Gandhi did not believe in any particular religion, and his religion was the service of the whole community. He took religion in the sense of philanthropy, forbearance, justice and fraternity, peace and all embracing love.[9] By religion he understood an inner spiritual life or belief in the superior virtues of life.

Gandhi wanted to assimilate religion with politics and public life. In his opinion, "those who hold that religion had nothing to do with politics do not know what religion is. For him, "there is no politics devoid of religion." He states: "For me politics bereft of religion are absolute dirt, ever to be shunned." In his view, "Politics bereft of religion was a death trap, because they kill the soul." Therefore, "religion was as necessary to politics as nose was to breathing." According to Gandhi, religion and politics cannot be separated, because both pursue the same ideal — the service of humanity. However, his religion as basis of politics did not mean political exploitation of religion. His support to the Khilafat agitation (1920-22) was more out of humanitarianism rather than bargaining consideration. He stood for employing only moral means for the attainment of political ends. He believed that a good end cannot be achieved by immoral means. In fact, for Gandhi religion and morality were the same. Religion was more of an ethical code than a formal dogma. The essence of religion was morality and ethics. For him, religion and morality are interwoven. "True religion and true morality are inseparably bound up with each other. Religion is to morality what water is to seed that is sown in the soil."

Though Gandhi was born a Hindu but his interpretation of Hinduism was his own. Gandhi said, "I reject any religious doctrine that does not appeal to reason and is in conflict with morality." In his opinion, "Every formula of any religion has in this age of reason to submit to the acid test of reason and universal assent. If the Vedas or Manusmriti sanction untouchability we have to change the Vedas or the Manusmriti."

GANDHI AND SECULARISM

Gandhi was a staunch secularist, but in his own way. Earlier his secularism represented respect to all religions or what Mohd. Ali called "federation of all religions." But in view of growing politicisation of religion, he began to preach separation of religion from politics. His religious mindedness, thus, could not detract from his concept of secularism. He never believed in state or "official" religion. Any state interference in religious matters was unwelcome to him. To quote Prof. Bipan Chandra, "Gandhi said in 1942; "Religion is a personal matter which should have no place in politics." Again, in 1947, he said; "Religion is the personal affair of each individual and it must not be mixed up in politics or national affairs."[10]

ECONOMIC IDEAS OF GANDHI

Gandhi challenged the foundations of modern civilisation. The sophisticated, technological, aggressive and lustful aspects of modern Western civilisation repelled him. Even earlier than Oswald Spangler, he predicted the decline and demise of Western civilisation. True civilisation, according to him, consists not in the accumulation of commodities but in the deliberate and voluntary reduction of wants. He condemned the monster god of materialism. In his "Hind Swaraj', he attacked large scale industrialisation and massive mechanisation, and condemned Western commercialism, imperialism and consumerism. Gandhi preached a return to simplicity and plainness of nature.

Gandhi was basically a ruralist. He saw that India lived in villages. Hence, his slogan was "back to the villages." In fact, he wanted to revitalise the village economy.

Gandhi was a critic of capitalism and its underlying doctrine of laissez faire. He favoured equal distribution of wealth. He said: "My ideal is equal distribution, but so far as I can see, it is not to be realised. I, therefore, work for equitable distribution." To realise the concept of economic equality he suggested that all persons should be supplied with the basic necessities to satisfy their natural needs. The constituent elements of economic equality were a balanced diet, a decent house, medical relief and educational facilities.

In matters of economics and politics, Gandhi wanted India to become a network of self-governing and self-sustaining village republics, each one of them leading an autonomous existence. Decentralisation in both politics and economics was the key-word for Gandhi. He believed that greater industrialisation may provide more goods but does not necessarily lead to moral progress. In the words of Schumacher, "Gandhi believed that the poor of the world cannot be helped by mass production but production by the masses."

TRUSTEESHIP SYSTEM

Gandhi believed in the dignity of man. It is from this deep feeling of spirituality of man that Gandhi derived his ethico-economic theory of trusteeship. For him, everything belongs to God and comes from God. When an individual had more than his proportionate portion he became a trustee of that portion of God's property. The rich should utilise the surplus wealth for the benefit of society at large. Gandhi claims that trusteeship is a peaceful way of liquidating class conflict. However, it is not a theory of class collaboration but one of class liquidation in a slow process and without violence.

FEATURES OF TRUSTEESHIP SYSTEM

(1) Trusteeship system provides a means of transforming the capitalist order of society into an egalitarian one. It gives the capitalists a chance of reforming themselves; (2) It does not recognise any right of private ownership of property except in as much as is permitted by society for its own welfare; (3) It does not exclude legislative regulation of ownership and use of wealth; (4) An individual is not to hold wealth for selfish satisfaction or in disregard of the interest of the society; (5) Not only a decent minimum living wage is to be fixed but also a limit to be fixed for the maximum income. The difference between the minimum and maximum is to be reasonable and equitable and variable from time to time; (6) The character of production will be determined by social necessity and not by personal greed or whim.[11] According to J.D. Sethi, the idea of trusteeship system is the most original contribution of Gandhi to economic thought. In 'Gandhi Today,' he writes: "Of all Gandhi's ideas and concepts trusteeship was the most original as it was also the most tentative",[12] since the had no time either to define it precisely or to' spell out its full implications, what to say of experimenting with it on a grand scale.

PHILOSOPHY OF SARVODAYA

"The Gandhian concept of Sarvodaya is the most original contemporary attempt at an Indian contribution to political thought."[13] The idea of Sarvodaya is the apex of Gandhian socialism. Sarvodaya does not mean that majority alone is enough; the growth and upliftment of everyone is vitally necessary. Gandhian socialism advocates the concept of organic unity where all individuals have equal importance and the rise of every one is dependent on the rise of every other. It suggests development of people's capacity to man their affairs with minimum governmental control and assistance.

GANDHIAN POLITICAL PHILOSOPHY — PHILOSOPHICAL ANARCHISM

Gandhi is called a philosophical anarchist. Like anarchists, Gandhi was opposed to the institution of state and government. He did not consider it natural or necessary institution. He believed in the essential goodness of man and had unshakeable faith in God. For him, human nature is never beyond redemption, for man can develop his spiritual and moral personality.

Gandhi rejected the state on ethical, historical and economic grounds. In his opinion, "The state is rooted in violence; it is an organisation of force. It represents violence in a concentrated and organised form. While the individual has a soul, the state is a soulless machine. The state exploits and oppresses the poor. Further, the excessive interference of the state kills individual initiative and action. As a coercive authority, it is destructive of individual freedom and personality. Since the state originated in an essentially violent society, in a non-violent society it becomes superfluous, unnecessary and dysfunctional. According to Gandhi, "Voluntary cooperation and decentralisation will be the two essential marks of a non-violent society."

In his introduction to Thoreau's 'Essay On Civil Disobedience', Gandhi writes: "I heartily accept the motto. "that government is the best which governs the least." I also believe in the maxim: "that government is the best which governs not at all."

Gandhi's Ramrajya was a state of enlightened anarchy. In the words of Abid Hussain, "His Ramrajya is a perfect anarchy, a stateless society which is governed by no other law except the moral law implicit in human nature, by no other force except the force of love."[14] The ideal society envisaged by Gandhi is a stateless democracy. About this state, he wrote in his "Young India': "In such a state everyone is his own ruler, he rules himself in such a manner that he would never be a hindrance to his neighbour. In the ideal state there is no political power because there is no state. Although an ideal society would be a stateless society consisting of self-sufficing, self-regulating and self-securing village communities joined together in a voluntary federation, Gandhi realised that the tension of such a federation may require the need of a government as an umpire. Thus, Gandhi was realistic enough to realise that the goal of a stateless and classless non-violent society was not easily attainable and the government was not altogether unnecessary.

Writing in "Harijan' (28 July, 1946), Gandhi envisages a new state structure thus: "In this structure composed of innumerable villages, there will be ever widening, never ascending circles. Life will not be a pyramid with the apex sustained by the bottom. But it will be an oceanic circle whose centre will be the individual, always ready to perish for the village, the latter ready to perish for the circle of villages, till at last the whole becomes one life composed of individuals, never aggressive in their arrogance, but ever sharing the majesty of the oceanic circle of which they are integral units... the outer most circumference will not wield power to crush the inner circle but will give strength to all within and derive its own strength from it."

GANDHISM AND MARXISM — A COMPARISON

K.G. Mashruwala in his "Gandhi and Marx" (1956) described Gandhism as "Marxism minus violence". Of course, there are certain similarities between Gandhism and Marxism to substantiate this statement. But some fundamental differences take them poles apart from each other. No doubt, both Marx and Gandhi were harbingers of hope for the toiling millions and suppressed sections of humanity. Similarly, both stood for a stateless and classless society. But while Marx stood for class conflict, Gandhi stood for class collaboration. Unlike Marx, Gandhi never contemplated the deliberate destruction of the state machinery. Of course, both were opposed to capitalism and private property. But unlike Gandhi, Marx stood for a class struggle to remove the system of capitalism. He also envisaged a transitional phase of proletarian dictatorship, which in reality, instead of abolishing the state has perpetuated it. Again, both Gandhi and Marx stood for social change. But Gandhi wanted social change to be brought about by non-violent methods. He never contemplated any violent revolution, like Marx. The spiritual socialism, which Gandhi wanted, was to begin with the moral regeneration of man, although he was not unmindful of changes in the political, economic and social structure. But, the emphasis of Marx was confined to structural change only. Finally and more importantly, Gandhi was a philosophical idealist, whereas Marx was a dialectical materialist. For Marx religion was the opium of the people, but for Gandhi it was the warp and woof of life. Whereas Gandhi believed in the purity of means and his contention was "As the means so the end,," but for Marx the end justified the means.

GANDHI AND INTERNATIONALISM

Though Gandhi was mainly engrossed in the Indian freedom struggle and the problem of poverty in the country, he was equally concerned with the miseries of the downtrodden and exploited people all over the world. Though he was intensely attached to his country, he was international in outlook. According to him, the concept of nationalism did not mark the climax of political evolution. It was only a stage to internationalism. To a French paper, Gandhi wrote: "My nationalism is intense internationalism". He once stated: "I want the freedom of my country so that the resources of my country might be utilised for the benefit of mankind. My mission is not merely freedom of India but through its realisation I hope to realise and carry on the mission of brotherhood of man."[15] George Marshall rightly remarked: "Gandhi is the spokesman for the conscience of all mankind."[16]

GANDHI AS A SOCIAL PHYSICIAN

Gandhi is known as a great social physician. As early as 1925, he came to the conclusion that the Indian society was sick and sinful. He summed up the evils of Indian society in what he called the Seven Sins': "Politics without principles, wealth without work, pleasure without conscience, knowledge without character, commerce without morality, science without humanity, worship without sacrifice." However, his diagnosis was correct about symptoms of the disease only not the disease itself. That is why, Gandhi was a physician who failed. His patients refused to respond to what he recommended by way of prescription. With the result, his impact on Indian society remained negligible and ultimately he became just a cult figure, who is venerated periodically but constantly ignored. Gandhi failed because he could not go to the root of the problem. Indian public life is vitiated because the Indian people lack the sense of public duty; they lack social discipline and sense of social obligation. Gandhi was right when he said that the Indian society was rotten, but because of his religious mode of thinking, he remained blind to the reality that the rot was rooted in the religious tradition itself, whose emphasis was on life negation — self salvation not social salvation, escaping not changing the world, neglecting life not levelling it up. However, Gandhi himself remained unaffected by this negative aspect of Indian Weltanschauung, because he was essentially an "outsider". He was Indian in appearance but basically Western in outlook. That is how he and Nehru could flow on the same wave length and Gandhi could speak with such a good deal of assurance that "Nehru will speak his language after him."

GANDHI AS A LEADER

For about three decades Gandhi remained the colossus on the Indian scene. It was a period when the country was gifted with a galaxy of great leaders. It is a measure of his greatness that Gandhi could attract to his movement, personalities and intellectuals as diverse as Nehru, Patel, Bose, Azad, Rajaji, Rajendra Prasad and J.P. to name a few.

It is interesting to note that Gandhi entered the portals of politics with great reluctance. But he took no time to realise the importance and evils of political power in a modern state. In his own words, "Politics encircles us today like the coil of a snake from which one cannot get out, no matter how much one tries." Gandhi was not a politician in the normal sense. Essentially, he was a religious man but got dragged into politics because of his great concern for his fellow beings. He believed that politics, if purified, is the finest art and the most creative profession. Gandhi never lost touch with his spirituality even in the moments of his great political engagements. What made him different from and greater than the other leaders was the synthesis of the politician and the saint in him. Significantly, Gandhi was an ascetic who did not flee from the world but stayed to·serve the people.

Gandhi was a superb judge and leader of men. "He had in him the marvellous spiritual power to turn ordinary men around him into heroes and martyrs."[17] He could make heroes out of clay. He knew how to spot, train and harness talented men and women for public causes. He also knew how to build up a solid, coherent team. His flair for spotting talented persons, providing them with suitable training as well as opportunities for leadership was an important aspect of his organising ability. To quote S.R. Mehrotra, "One of his greatest contributions to the national movement in India was that he provided it with able leadership at various levels and ultimately made himself dispensable."[18] The real credit lay in the fact that he created a credible second line of leadership before he left the scene.

To quote Dr. Rasheeduddin Khan, "Gandhi stood the test of true leadership. He passed creditably the most crucial test of institutional leadership- of making oneself dispensable, of enabling smooth succession, of building structures that just not survive but keep rejuvenating with new talent and creativity."

One of the keys to the continuance as well as emergence of his leadership was his supreme sense of tactics. He knew better than any body when to start and when to stop or suspend a movement. With his fingers firmly on the pulse of the country, he was able to assess the people's mood accurately. To illustrate, he suspended the Non-cooperation Movement (1922) when he found that the "Movement was petering out." The Chauri Chaura was simply the last straw and not the main reason for it.

One of the characteristic features of Gandhi's leadership was his preparedness to accommodate his colleagues to the maximum extent possible without giving up his fundamental position on any given point. To substantiate, the Congress had prepared itself for partition by March 1947 in spite of Gandhi's warning, so when the 'partition' was declared he only said: "My life work seems to be over. I hope God will spare me further humiliation." The secret of his power over his colleagues lay in his power of persuasion, flair for salesmanship and, above all, his fatherly love for them.

Another distinctive mark of his leadership was his extraordinary organising ability. He knew that the vitality of an organisation depended not on structure but on the persons who manned it. He paid a good deal of attention to the selection of leaders and assigned to them roles for which they were ideally suited. To quote Prof. Bimal Prasad, "With all his awareness of the moral dimension of politics, one of the distinctive features of his leadership and its success was his mastery of nuances of power, his ability to maintain himself as repository of the Congress power for decades, without of course tempering with its democratic character. Gandhi tolerated dissent until it became a challenge to his leadership. He alone could debar Subhash Chandra Bose for three years from holding an active office, and significantly, he himself had drafted the resolution to this effect. Since Bose did not bend he had to go. But Nehru was treated in a different way because he was ready to bend. It is worth recalling here that on the 1942- Resolution (Nehru was earlier opposed to it) even he was served a notice that he was not indispensable."[19]

GANDHI AS A COMMUNICATOR

Apart from being a great leader Gandhi was also a great communicator. In fact, he was a public relations phenomenon. "He left out no measures, no technique to rouse the consciousness of the people and instil in them the importance of their actual participation in the national movement. He not only broadened the base of the freedom movement but also used the weapon of public relations to raise public consciousness. Gandhi tried to activate all the diverse sectors of the national spectrum. From the affluent classes to the impoverished, from the intelligentsia to the unlettered, nobody was left out. And for this purpose he took up a wide range of activities pertaining to all sections of the people from education to village welfare, from the spinning wheel to cattle protection. His effort at total identification with the village poor made him design his personal attire and way of living."[20]

For instance, to draw the masses in the movement, the defiance of Salt Law was taken up as the initial item of the Civil Disobedience Movement (1930-32). As a result, the whole nation was electrified by the new form of mass action. Gandhi often used religious idioms as the best means of arousing the rural masses so familiar with religious lore. In short, it was his simplicity, earnestness and directness that made ready appeal to the masses.

FAILINGS OF GANDHIAN LEADERSHIP

GANDHI AND PARTITION OF INDIA: It is well known that Gandhi was one of the staunchest opponents of partition. His famous comment was "India will be partitioned over my dead body." Even as late as 31 May 1947 he publicly opposed the partition proposal and remarked at a prayer meeting. "Even if the whole world burns we shall not concede Pakistan even if the Muslims demand it at the point of the sword."

But Michael Brecher and Dr. R.C. Majumdar put him in the dock on the question of partition. According to them, "The Quit India Movement, started by Gandhi, paved the way for the creation of Pakistan. This movement not only accentuated the differences between the Congress and the British, an aspect about which Gandhi was cautioned by Sir Tej Bahadur Sapru, Azad and Dr. Radha Krishanan, but the political vacuum created by the arrest of Congress leaders for about three years provided an opportunity to the Muslim League to consolidate Muslims under its banner."[21]

Again, "the talks with Jinnah" (September 1944), in Brecher's view, "placed Jinnah on a footing of virtual equality with Gandhi."[22] Gandhi's readiness for a dialogue on the basis of "Pakistan' vitiated his stand against the vivisection of the country and added a feather to Jinnah's cap. Of course, during the talks Gandhi did maintain all through that "Hindus and Muslims of India are not two nations and those whom God has made one, man will never be able to divide."[23]

In the opinion of Lord Wavell, "It was Gandhi who wrecked the Cabinet Mission Plan, which might have saved a united India and prevented all the massacres. I do not believe that he really worked for understanding with the Muslims when his influence might have secured it."[24]

Nevertheless, partition was a tragic event in the history of India. The very thought of it turned Gandhi's soul and made him to say just two days before the announcement of the 3rd June Plan. "Let it not be said that Gandhi was party to India's vivisection. But everybody is today impatient for independence. Therefore, there is no other help."[25]

When the partition plan was announced on 3 June, 1947, Gandhi kept silent. His silence was the riddle of the time. Perhaps his leadership had slipped out of hand by then. However, Gandhi created an enigmatic situation for one studying his life and leadership, the baffling question arising; why did he not oppose the decision of the Congress Working Committee and appeal to the nation to reject it, when he was so intensely disturbed at the partition decision? Gandhi felt that by overruling the decision of his colleagues, he might have prevented partition but he would have paid a high price for that in terms of disruption of the Congress and weakening of the non-violent struggle and which could mean "curing the patient at the cost of his life.[26] Besides, he was not unaware of the fact that leadership of the Congress that had accepted the partition could not be easily dislodged. He confessed: "I did not have the strength to take over the reign of the Congress and the government, otherwise I would have declared rebellion single-handed."[27] Quoting Gandhi, J.B. Kriplani writes: "The Congress has signed on your behalf. You can disown them. But you can do so if you can start a long revolution. I don't think you can do it. I can't challenge the present leadership. I have not the time to build up such an alternative. I must therefore swallow the bitter pill."[28]

It can however be safely said in defence of Gandhi that no one did more to prevent the division of India and to mitigate the consequences than Gandhi. Even after the 'partition' "Gandhi was sure that Pakistan was shortlived and he believed that a time would come when the division would be undone and India would be once again a united country."[29]

GANDHI AND HINDU-MUSLIM UNITY: Gandhi was an ardent votary of Hindu-Muslim unity and the unity of India. Throughout his life he championed the cause of amity between the two communities. Indeed, it became a mission of his life. But sadly enough, his mission failed, even though he did his best to bring the two communities closer to each other. Perhaps, it was with this end in view that he supported even the Khilafat agitation, which was a lost cause and thereby invited severe criticism from both secularists as well as communalists, including Jinnah. As a matter of fact, "his failure lay not so much in supporting the cause of caliph in order to cash on Muslim religious sentiments, but in letting the Hindu-Muslim entente crumble after the suspension of the non-cooperation movement and the abolition of the Caliphate."[30] Gandhi felt that communal harmony could be built on the concept of "federation of religions", but as it turned out, this policy led to communal strife rather than communal harmony. "Gandhi's major failure was in his inability to perceive the Muslim elites' deep nostalgia and longing for lost power and in making no serious attempt to provide reasonable assurance for its satisfaction.[31]. Further, though a great communicator, he failed to establish communication link with the Muslim masses. Perhaps, he felt that the "iceberg of Hindu-Muslim difference will melt under the warmth of the sun of freedom." However it is to be acknowledged that even after realising his dream of securing India's freedom in his life time he said: "I would not allow the Muslims to crawl on the streets in India, they must walk with self-respect." Thus he never gave up the mission of Hindu-Muslim unity till be died. Ultimately, only his martyrdom could achieve what he could not achieve in his life. His sacrifice went a long way to convert the hearts of the people, who realised the futility of fanatic fratricide. Here too, his life was his message but the message was most pithily expressed in his death.

CONTRIBUTIONS OF GANDHI AND GANDHISM

Undoubtedly, Gandhi was the greatest architect of India's freedom. "More than any other single individual Gandhi brought about the fall of the British Empire." Of course, in this he was amply aided by objective factors as well. To quote B.R. Nanda, "The final consummation (1947), the transfer of power, was due to the interaction of numerous national and world forces but there is no doubt that the timing and method of British withdrawal was largely influenced by what Gandhi has said and done for a quarter of a century."[32] In the opinion of S.R. Mehrotra, "It is true that India would have been free sooner or later even if Gandhi had never lived but without Gandhi's leadership the national movement in India would have been deprived of its poetry, his drama, moral elevation and spiritual enthusiasm."[33]

Gandhi's great contribution to politics in particular and life in general was his interpretation of non-violence and its applicability in the modern age of incessant wars and bloody conflicts. "In the 20th century, as K.P. Karunakarna says "no one else has taken the task of curbing the spirit of violence in the minds of men as Gandhi has done."[34] Gandhi was an apostle of peace and his dictum was: "There is no way to peace; peace is the way."

Gandhi was a revolutionary extraordinary, though his life style was traditional and his message was couched in religious idioms. To quote B.R. Nanda, "Despite his traditional idioms Gandhi was a tremendous force for modernisation, with his advocacy of secularism, abolition of untouchability, equal rights for women and concern for the millions at the bottom of the social pyramid." Besides, Gandhi was one of the pioneers to realise that mega-technology in itself contains the germs of dehumanisation and environmental disaster.

ESTIMATE OF GANDHI AS A THINKER

Among Indian thinkers Gandhi is the most fascinating subject for study. Although, his is the most documented life ever of any human historical figure, even today, the interest in Gandhi continues unabated.

Gandhi is acknowledged as the greatest leader of our age. According to B.R. Nanda, "Few men in their life time aroused stronger emotion or touched deeper chords of humanity than Gandhi did." Human history provides few parallels, for leaders like him are born after ages.

Gandhi was not a system builder or a metaphysician in the academic sense. The philosophical foundations of Gandhism are full of contradictions, confusions and illogicalities. One would look in vain to find any profoundity and originality in his thought. He was essentially a man of action and not of contemplation. He did not have either the requisite time or philosophical comprehension to work out mature academic expositions of his sociological, economic and political ideas and precepts. His ideas, in fact, are discrete responses to his personal and political experiences and obviously, they are original. Some of his moral, sociological and political insights are remarkable and significant for all times to come.[35] Gandhi was essentially a path finder towards definite social and individual goals.

However, it is difficult to categorise Gandhism and cage it in the parameter of any particular 'ism'. To quote Horace Alexander, "Gandhi was a conglomeration of a conservative, a liberal, a socialist, a radical, a communist and an anarchist."[36] Nehru has rightly remarked: "It is impossible to judge Gandhi by the usual standards and even to apply the ordinary canons of logic."[37]

Gandhi may not be an original thinker but he was a great teacher. What Gandhism lacks in the shape of a well-unified, coherent and consistent social philosophy, or a systematic major treatise on political philosophy, is more than compensated by the majestic life of the man. His life itself was his greatest message. "He demonstrated the seriousness of his teachings by the sanctification of his own life and conduct, a work which no other speculative thinker has done so far."[38] In the opinion of Bhiku Parekh, "Gandhi's own existential theory of truth required that he should be read through the text of his action and not through the footnotes of his abstract utterances."[39]

Admittedly, no other leader has so consistently practised what he preached. No one better epitomises the unity of precepts and practices, as Gandhi. The unity of knowing, being and doing was the hallmark of his personality. If he identified himself with the least, the lowest and the last, it corresponded to his convictions. To quote George Orwell, "There is a characteristic clear smell about Gandhi's entire life."

ASSESSMENT OF GANDHI BY HIS ADMIRERS AND DETRACTORS

As early as 1909 Gokhale (Gandhi's Guru) observed: "A purer, a braver and a more exalted spirit has never moved on this earth. Gandhi had in him the marvellous spiritual power to turn ordinary men around him into heroes and martyrs"[40]

According to Tagore, "Gandhi became great because of his goodness. Great as he was as a politician, as an organiser, as a leader of men, as a moral reformer, he is greater than all these as a man, because none of these aspects and activities limit his humanity."[41] Gandhi is immortalised because of his moral example. As a leader he can be classed with Buddha, Socrates and Christ." Dr. Rajendra Prasad remarked: "Gandhi is dead but Gandhism will live till the stars shine and oceans roll on."

In Nehru's opinion, "The essence of Gandhi's teachings was fearlessness and truth and action allied to these, always keeping the welfare of the masses in view."[42]

In the view of Jaya Prakash Narayan, "Far from being reactionary, Gandhi was an exceptionally original social revolutionary, and he had made contributions to social thought and the methodology of social change that are indispensable." Arnold Toynbee's remark about him was: "Gandhi was as much a benefactor of British as of his own country. He made it impossible for us to go on ruling India, but at the same time he made it possible for us to abdicate without rancour and without dishonour."

But the best epitaph on the noblest man of our age was written by the greatest scientist of this century — Einstein wrote about Gandhi: "Generations to come will scarcely believe that such a one as this, ever in flesh and blood, walked upon the earth."

Notwithstanding his countless admirers and adulators, there is no dearth of Gandhi's detractors and denigrators. His critics have generally dismissed him as a mythical figure and treat Gandhism as nothing but "sanctimonious humbug." Bu interestingly, many of them who came to scoff stayed to pray. To illustrate, M.N. Roy in his earlier assessment of Gandhi had dismissed him as a leader fit for the medieval age. But at the fag end of his life he recognised the worth of Gandhi as a political awakener and a great communicator. He duly acknowledged that his message has a moral, humanist and cosmopolitan appeal, and even expressed regret for having failed to detect his secular approach beneath his religious idioms.

Michael Edward, in his 'Myth of the Mahatma' also failed to make a proper assessment of Gandhi when he adjudged him as double-faced hypocrite. For him, "the theatre of the Mahatma's life is a theatre of masks."[43] For Lord Wavell, "Gandhi was a malevolent old politician." In Mountbatten's assessment, "Gandhi may be a saint but he is also disciple of Trotsky."

But the most damaging denigration of Gandhi was made by T.K. Madhevan when he remarked: "I found Gandhi the greatest disaster that overtook modern India."

In 'Gandhian Discourse; Bhiku Parekh's analysis of Gandhian religio-political discourses reveals "A man of intuition who, while offering novel perceptions and interpretations of Hinduism, failed to provide a workable foundation on which a modern society in India could be built." In his opinion, Gandhi's analysis of modern age was faulty; he was an outsider to modern civilisation, missing its positive aspects. Further, his blue-print of self-sufficient communities, hereditary caste system (Varna Vyavastha), intense moralism, sexual abstinence and anti-intellectualism leave the modern generation cold and puzzled." No wonder, the ourtowrd respect shown to the Mahatma by the new generation is accompanied by inner indifference; he is deified yet discarded. Similarly, in the opinion of another critic, R.H. Evelin, "Gandhi's metaphysical politics (which identifies Truth with God, exalts faith and intuition above reason and confuses religion with ethics) has been in effect an unconscious agent of reaction." In the opinion of this author, the greatest drawback of Gandhi was his confusion of religion with morality. His statement that "religion has to guide politics lest politics turn immoral" had a negative impact on Indian politics. He utterly failed to realise that religion to the majority of Indians is more a matter of custom, tradition, rite and ritual rather than morals. Moreover, one fails to understand how could he ignore the acknowledged fact of history that the unsavoury mix of politics with religion has caused some of the greatest tragedies in the world.

Notes

1.   Mehrotra, S.R., op.cit, p. 154

2. Bhagwan, Vihsnu, op.cit, pp. 106-07

3. Verma, V.P., op.cit, pp. 274-75

4. Ibid., p.275

5. Ibid., pp. 275-76

6. Nanda, B.R., Grammar of Gandhi, Times of India, 3 Oct. 1994.

7. Quoted in Bhagwan, Vishnu, op.cit, p. 125

8. Jones, Stanley, Mahatma Gandhi, p.108

9. Verma, V.P., op.cit, pp.276-77

10. Gandhi, M.K., Harijan, 16 March, 1947.

11. Bhagwan, Vishnu, op.cit, p.132

12. Sethi, J.D., Gandhi Today, Viaks Publishers, N.Delhi, 1979 p.156

13. Appadorai quoted in Bhagwan, Vishnu, op.cit, p.142

14. Abid Hussain, quoted in Bhagwan Vishnu, op.cit, p.126

15. Ibid., p.142

16. Das and Patro, op.cit, p.192

17. Gokhale quoted in Mehrotra, S.R., op.cit, p.156.

18. Ibid., p.156

19. Prasad, Bimal, op.cit, p.58

20. Chakravartty, Nikhil, 'Gandhi-Great Communicator' Mainstream, 8 April, 1995 pp. 26-28

21. Chaudhary, Sandhya, Gandhi and The Partition of India, op.cit, pp. 101-02

22. Brecher, Michael, Nehru- A Political Biography, OUP, London, 1959, p. 294

23. Mehrotra, S.R., op.cit, p. 207

24. Wavell, Viceroy's Journal, p.439

25. Dr. Pyare Lal, Mahatma Gandhi- Last Phase, Vol. II, p. 211

26. Chaudhary, Sandhya, op. cit, pp. 204-05

27. Dr. Pyare Lal, Mahatma Gandhi, The Last Phase, Vol. 2, p. 252

28. Gandhi, Raj Mohan, India Wins Errors, op.cit, p.82

29. Chaudhary, Sandhya, op.cit, p. 206

30. Prasad, Bimal, op.ict, p. 76

31. Ibid., p. 76

32. Nanda, B.R., 'The Man who Turned History Around Gently' Indian, Express, 2 Oct. 1994.

33. Mehrotra, S.R., pp. 156-57

34. Karunakarn, K.P, 'Gandhiana Interpretations', p.68

35. Verma, V.P., op.cit, p. 287

36. Horace, Alexander, Gandhi Through Western Eyes, p. 179

37. Nehru, Autobiography, p.365

38. Verma, V.P., op.cit, p. 287

39. See Parekh Bhiku, Gandhian Discourses.

40. Gokhale's speech at Bombay on 14 Dec. 1912. Reproduced in Collected Works, Vol, XI, p.579

41. Quoted in Suda, J.P., op.cit, p. 434

42. Nehru, Discovery of India, 1961, p.

43. Edwards, Michael, The Myth of The Mahatma Gandhi. Constable Company Ltd., London, 1986, p.179.

Chapter 54

MANABENDRA NATH ROY
— A THINKING REBEL (1887-1954)

Amongst the leading personalities of the Indian freedom movement, M.N. Roy was undoubtedly the most colourful and the most controversial. An intellectual of international eminence, Roy was also an active participant in a large number of major struggles for social and political emancipation of the present century. But at the same time, M.N. Roy is the most misunderstood, misrepresented and maligned man of his time.

Truly speaking, M.N. Roy lacked all those qualities which usually generates mass appeal in an Indian leader. Some of these can be enumerated as follows: cant of spiritualism, cultural narcissism, an exaggerated sense of pride in the heritage of the country, willingness to come to terms with the temper of times, keeping pace with the mainstream, identification with the lowest common denominator among the people, viving with the mass psychosis, populistic gimmickry, et al. Unlike other thinkers of modern India, Roy was never a captive of the past. On the contrary, he was incorrigibly rebellious, nonconformist, fiercely independent in outlook, firm in conviction, ruthless in logical analysis, unyielding on questions of principle. Moreover, in a religion-ridden country Roy was a thorough-going materialist and a confirmed atheist. He would never hesitate to lock horns with the highest and the mightiest in case of disagreement. He would never stoop to mortgage his mind to anyone on earth. Throughout his life "he was a lie hunter, a demolisher of myth and an iconoclast in the land of idols."[1]

Naturally, with these personality traits he could hardly be acceptable either to establishment or to the common people, and as such he could never become part of the political pantheon. "He rather remained isolated and obscure figure working on the periphery of Indian politics."[2]

EARLY LIFE OF M.N. ROY

Manabendra Nath Roy (his original name was Narendra Nath

Bhattacharya) was born on 21 March, 1887 in 24-Parganas district of Bengal which was known as home of the Indian revolution.

Roy received his early education from his father. Later, he managed to go to Calcutta for higher studies. There he came under the influence of the revolutionary secret societies. As a school boy, he was an ardent admirer of the famous revolutionary, V.D. Savarkar. He was also attracted by the reform movement led by Swami Ram Tirth, Swami Dayanand and Swamy Vivekanand. He drew his revolutionary inspiration from Bankim Chandra Chatterjee's 'Anand Math'. At the age of 14 he left school and joined Aurobindo's National College. However, he could not complete his studies.

Being young, sensitive and adventurous, he was gradually drawn into the movement in which he was to play an important role. He was caught in the revolutionary upsurge that shook Bengal and was started in protest against the partition of Bengal. Roy was a leading member of Anushilan Samiti, founded by Prannath Mitra on the model of 'Anand Math'. He also developed intimacy with Jatin Mukherjee, the famous "Bagha" and worked in close cooperation with the Yugantar Group, founded by Barindra Ghosh.

Roy distinguished himself in the Bengal Movement while still in his teens. He was prosecuted for political dacoity in 1907. This was the first political trial in the country after 'Tilak Case.' He was also involved in the Howrah Conspiracy Case in 1910 and the Garden Reach Dacoity in 1914. In all these activities, his guide was Jatin Mukherjee of Balasore.

ROY IN SEARCH OF 'THE GOLDEN FLEECE'

"More than a quarter of a century before India finally attained freedom, the tempting vision of an earlier possibility of India's liberation with foreign money had beckoned a generation of Indian youth to fruitless adventure." On the outbreak of the First World War (1914) Indian revolutionaries in exile looked towards Germany (British rival) as the land of hope and rushed there full of expectations.

By the end of that year, news reached the revolutionaries in India that the Indian Revolutionary Committee in Berlin had obtained from the German government the promise of arms and money for initial expenditure. The task for brining arms and money was entrusted to Roy, according to the plan made by the terrorist organisation of Bengal, which was led by Jatin Mukherjee. The Dutch East-Indies was chosen by this organisation as the suitable place to deliver arms and money. Before the end of 1914, Roy left for Java. This was his first trip abroad. He returned within two months with some money, but, as regards arms, (which he ironically called "the coveted cargo of golden fleece"), it was a wild-goose chase. But his youthful enthusiasm, thoughtless optimism and, above all, still lingering faith in the liberation mission of Germany were not to be easily daunted. A new plan was made under which Roy left India for the second time early in 1915 in search of foreign assistance. This time he did not return until 1930. Roy, however, did manage to extract a fairly large sum of money from the Germans and remitted it to India.

Thereafter, he went to Japan to meet Rash Behari Bose, whose mission was to free India with the help of Japan. He also met Sun Yat Sen, who had then taken refuge in Japan. On his advice, Roy went to China to meet the German ambassador. But the German Minister — in-charge at Peking pleaded inability to advance any funds. Roy saw through the German ploy of using Indian revolutionaries for their purpose. Incidentally, Roy was the first revolutionary who realised this.

For several months, Roy wandered through Malaya, Indonesia, Indo-China, the Philippines, Japan, Korea and China and on 15 June, 1916 he landed at San Francisco, as Father C.A. Martin with a copy of the Holy Bible. In America, he happened to meet Dhan Gopal Mukerjee (a contact person for Bengali revolutionaries) at the University of Stanford, who advised him to wipe out the past and begin as anew and thus was born Manabendra Nath Roy in the University campus.[3] Here, he also met Evelyn Trent, a Stanford graduate, who later became his first wife and worked with him till their separation in 1926. "Evelyn, too, played an important role in shaping the life and thought of M.N. Roy in the early stages"[4]

ROY IN THE USA

Roy had gone to North America as the emissary of revolutionary nationalism, actively in alliance with Germany, in the fight against British imperialism. "Walking in the foot-steps of the future Netaji nearly a quarter of a century ahead of time, he was on the way to Germany."[4]

While in New York, Roy frequented the New York Public Library and undertook a thorough study of the various branches of natural and social sciences. He was very impressed by the writings of Marx, and it was not long before he accepted Marxism minus its materialist philosophy. He also wrote an essay, 'A Critique of Pacifism' — his first literary work.[5] The Article appealed to American radicals with whose contact Roy got over his original limited outlook of a nationalist. The road from revolutionary nationalism to communism was short. Roy had thought that America was a safe place for arranging help from Germany. But when the US joined the War, there was anti-German feeling all over the country. Hence, Roy had to go underground to escape arrest. During this period he wrote an open letter to President Wilson under the title 'The Way to Durable World Peace'. While in America, he also worked in collaboration with Lala Lajpat Rai for sometime. However, Roy could not stay in America for long. He chose Mexico as a land of escape for various reasons. Firstly, Mexico was under a state of social revolution and so it appeared to him a "land of promise". Then there was also, as Roy writes in his Memorise, "a patriotic belief that in the pre-historic days India had colonised Mexico." That made his longing irresistible and he left for Mexico in 1917.

ROY IN MEXICO

When Roy reached Mexico (15 June, 1917) he found the country in the throes of a revolution, led by Obregon and Caranza. The Bolsheviks had just captured power in Russia and a faint echo of the revolution had reached across the Atlantic also. In 1915, Roy had left India in search of arms with naive ideas about revolution and international relations but his experience in the Mexican social revolution destroyed many of his illusions. He now learned that revolutions took place out of necessity, and discovered that India needed a social revolution and not mere national independence. He realised that old revolutionary methods were not leading anywhere. In short, the Mexican concept of revolution attracted his attention. In Mexico, he met Ignazio-Santibanez, a great Marxist of his time. With his contact Roy's wavering faith in the historical role and the invincible power of world proletariat was enlivened and reinforced. He also translated into Spanish his work 'The Way to Durable Peace' with a chapter on the Monroe Doctrine added to it. In this book, Roy revealed that the conflict of imperialist ambition and its scramble for colonies was the root cause of the Great War. The chapter on the Monroe Doctrine attracted attention of the President of Mexico, Venustiano Caranza, and both became friends. Roy also wrote a book in Spanish entitled 'India's Past, Present And Future'. In this book, Roy made his first attempt to apply Marxism to the study of Indian history. The ongoing Mexican social revolutionary movement gave Roy his first experience of practical politics. The first conference of the Socialist Party of Mexico met in December 1918 and Roy was elected its first General Secretary.

As the General Secretary of the Mexican Socialist Party, Roy came in contact with Michael Borodin, who was sent to Mexico as the first emissary of the newly founded Communist International (1919). It was Borodin who initiated Roy in the intricacies of Hegelian dialectics and its materialist version as the key to Marxism Roy now became a materialist in his philosophical thought. His lingering faith in the cultural superiority in India also faded when he learned from Borodin the history of European culture. A special conference of the Socialist Party and associated organisations was convened on Roy's suggestion, and as a result the first communist party outside Russia was founded. Roy's exploits in Mexico soon drew the attention of Lenin who invited him to attend the Second World Congress of the Communist International. The attraction of going to Russia, the land of socialist revolution and the Mecca of World communism, forced him to leave Mexico. About this Roy wrote: "I left the land of my rebirth (Mexico) as an intellectually free man, though with a new faith. I no longer believed in political freedom without the content of economic liberation and social justice and I also had realised that intellectual freedom from the bondage of all traditions and authority was the condition for any effective struggle for emancipation."[6].

Roy crossed the Atlantic armed with a Mexican diplomatic passport and after visiting Spain and Geneva reached Berlin. Though he had started for Berlin four years ago, he could reach there only at the end of 1919, but no longer in search of arms. By this time Roy had come to realise that freedom could not be won on borrowed strength.

While in Germany, Roy came in contact with the leaders of the German revolutionary working class movement. His experience in the United States and Mexico and Germany having revolutionised his ideas about revolution, he lost the incentive to return to India in the near future. Now he believed that revolutions were brought about by the operations of social forces.

His perspective of the process of revolutionary development in India, opened up by the new faith of Marxism, was indicated in his 'India In Transition' which was written in 1921, as soon as sufficient statistical material was available to him in Moscow. In this work, he gives a critical analysis of Indian society and a clear perspective of the development of the Indian national movement. It was his first serious effort to make a sociological study of contemporary India. In this work he condemned the contemporary schools of political thought. As a Marxist he stated that "the task of winning the freedom of India would have to be shouldered by the workers and peasants consciously organised and fighting on the grounds of class struggle."[7] For a long time this work remained the standard book of reference for communist in colonial countries until the official change of line adopted at the Sixth World Congress of the Communist International (1928).

ROY IN SOVIET RUSSIA

By the time Roy arrived in Moscow (early in 1920), the Soviet revolution had come out triumphant. Historic changes were taking place. Lenin was translating the revolutionary principles of Marxism into practice.

The Second World Congress met in Moscow in July-August 1920. This Congress set out to formulate a policy on what was known as the 'National and Colonial Question'. Roy attended this Congress as an Indian delegate. On 21 July, 1920 the Congress appointed a commission to consider the colonial question and draft a report. The report was presented to the Congress for discussion and Roy took part in it. Talking about this report, E.H. Carr writes: "It was the first time the Indian delegate (M.N. Roy) remarked that he had ever been able to take part seriously in a discussion of the colonial question at a Congress of the Revolutionary Proletariat."[8]

The Commission found itself confronted with two sets of theses on the question presented respectively by Lenin and Roy.. In this controversy with Lenin, Roy distinguished himself as an original and bold thinker. Lenin advanced the thesis that the masses should obtain the cooperation of the bourgeoisie to overthrow their imperialistic yoke. Its implication was that the bourgeoisie would play a progressive role in colonial revolutions. Roy, on the other hand, in his thesis, anticipated that the relationship of the mother country to its colony would change eventually from one of imperialist tyranny to one of mutual cooperation, because the national bourgeoisie may compromise with imperialism in return for some political and economic concessions to their class. Hence, according to Roy, the bourgeoisie would not play a progressive role. He, therefore, wanted colonial communist parties to lead the proletariat, peasantry and petty bourgeoisie against both foreign and domestic capitalism. Lenin was large hearted enough to call upon the Congress to adopt Roy's thesis also as supplementary to the thesis drafted by him.

After this Congress Roy became very popular in the Communist International. His striking personality and organisational ability soon won for him an important place among the members of the Communist International. Roy rose very rapidly to occupy almost all the important positions in the Communist International — a membership of the Executive, the Presidium, the Secretariat, the Educational Board, Chairmanship of the Eastern Commission and membership of the Chinese Commission. Besides, Roy also edited 'Vanguard', 'The Masses', and 'Advanced Guard' from 1922 to 1928. On behalf of the Comintern he visited several countries. Meanwhile, he had made a deep study of the philosophy of Karl Marx and rubbed shoulders with some of the greatest Marxists of the contemporary period as the Executive member of the Communist International. Further, he had opportunities to study and observe Marxism both in theory and practice.

ROY'S VISIT TO CENTRAL ASIA

In 1920, Roy went to Central Asia to carry through the revolution in the Central Asian provinces of the fallen Czarist Empire and consolidate the New Regime. From Moscow he carried a considerable quantity of military equipment meant to be sent to North-Western Frontier of India where a liberation army was to be organised. He also helped to form the Tashkent Military Training Centre for Asiatic revolutionaries. This Military School was joined by a number of Muslim youths who had marched out of India in defence of holy places like Mecca and Medina against the contemplated British aggression. In Central Asia, Roy acquired the experience of leading a backward colonial people in a revolutionary struggle.

At the Third World Congress (1921) Roy criticised the policy of the Comintern because the Eastern Question was almost neglected. The Fourth Congress, however, took up the Eastern Question in November 1922, and "Roy speaking about India argued that two years' experience has shown that the anti-imperialist front could not be left in the hands of wavering bourgeoisie and the foundation of the whole movement must be its most revolutionary social element."[9]

Towards the end of 1922 Roy published a book entitled 'India's Problems and its solutions'. In this book written in a Marxian Vein, he was particularly critical of the medievalism and conservatism of Gandhian social idealism and dismissed Gandhism as petty bourgeois humanitarianism.' He characterised the proceedings of the Ahmedabad Congress of 1921 as a betrayal by the bourgeois leadership of the revolutionary forces. He also expressed his displeasure at the constructive programme of revolution adopted at Baroda on February 12, 1922. In its place he argued for the creation of a revolutionary mass party. Instead of civil disobedience which was the programme of the Congress Party, Roy advocated militant action of the masses. He also advised mass strikes led by a class conscious vanguard. In 1922, he sent a programme to the Indian National Congress on the eve of the Gaya Congress. This programme of national freedom and reconstruction pleaded for complete national independence for India, universal suffrage and the creation of a federal republic.[10] Besides, it contained an elaborate social and economic programme. In these documents the fundamental principles of leftism in

India were formulated for the first time along with the demand of Complete Independence.

In his book, 'One Year of Non-Cooperation' (1923), he presented a critical estimate of Gandhian thought. While comparing him with medieval thinkers he however acknowledged his significance in mobilising mass action. But he pointed out several short-comings of Gandhism, such as: (1) Gandhism lacked an economic programme for the masses; (2) It failed to unite different classes into one movement; (3) By injecting religion and metaphysics into politics it sacrificed political dynamism at the altar of subjective consideration of conscience; and (4) The economics of the Charkha was dubbed as reactionary. Roy summed up that Gandhism was not a revolutionary philosophy but a 'weak and watery' reformism.[11]

In 1926, Roy wrote 'The Future of Indian Politics'. In this work, he dealt with the significance of 'People's party' After the collapse of the Swarajist movement, the only alternative for Roy was a democratic party of the people bringing together the petty bourgeoisie, peasantry and proletariat with a programme which included: (a) complete independence; (b) establishment of a republican government; (c) radical agrarian reforms and (d) advanced social legislation.

ROY IN CHINA

China was the next scene of Roy's activities. The success of the Russian revolution had affected the Chinese National Revolutionary Movement. Soon, the situation in China demanded reorganisation of the Kuo Min Tang on the basis of a well formulated programme of national revolution. In compliance with the decision of the Second World Congress, the Communist International directed the Chinese Communist Party to effect a united front with Kuo Min Tang. The central point of the policy suggested by the Communist International in November 1926 was that the Chinese Revolution from that time developed as an agrarian revolution. But the leadership of the Chinese Communist Party as well as the representative of the Communist International were of a different view. They still maintained that the nationalist bourgeoisie should be helped to lead the Revolution and the class struggle should not be accentuated for the sake of national unity. Roy was alone to advocate a different point of view; namely, that the Chinese revolution had reached a critical moment in which it must strike out a new course and a fetish should not be made of the alliance with the Quo Min Tang."[12] He advised the Chinese Communist Party to adopt an alternative plan of agrarian revolution in order to extend their social base. The Comintern Executive adopted his point of view. Immediately, Roy was sent to China as the head of a new delegation of the Communist International.

Roy succeeded in persuading the Fifth Congress of the Communist Party of China to endorse the new line in spite of the opposition of practically all the leaders of the party. In a book, 'Chinese Revolution,' published officially in Moscow in 1932, the author, Mif wrote: "It was Roy who gave the young Chinese Communist Party for the first time a real Leninist prognosis of the events taking place. From Roy the party heard for the first time a thoroughly thought out perspective of the movement and received directions on a series of cardinal questions. Roy gave the young Chinese Communist Party the experience of World Bolshevism."[13]

"The Fifth Congress of the Communist Party of China met under the spiritual guidance of the Indian communist delegate. It is therefore quite possible that its resolutions partially reflected Roy's views which were at that time somewhat to the left of the official communist line as enforced by Borodin."[14] It is to be noted that Roy had deviated a little from the official viewpoint in so far as he advocated a new line of action as against the policy of alliance with the Wuhan government, recommended by the Communist International and the Communist Party of China. Roy's stand at that time however was controversial. But be that as it may, China marks a turning point in his political career.[15]

THE 'RED PURISM' POLICY OF THE COMMUNIST INTERNATIONAL

Roy returned to Moscow in 1927 just in time to witness the climax of the historic struggle for power between Stalin and Trotsky with the Comintern policy in China as one of the central issues. In October, 1927 Trotsky and Zinoviev were expelled from the Communist Party of the Soviet Union. To outmanoeuvre his opponents and to establish his control on the Communist Party of the Soviet Union and the Communist International, Stalin now had, on the one hand, to win over the various powerful but vacillating groups in the two organisations, and, on the other hand, to sacrificing, if necessary, some of his friends who would be less useful in his game of power politics. It was in this background that the Communist International abandoned the tactics of "United Front" and adopted a new policy as a result of the failure of the Chinese Revolution at the Sixth Congress in 1928, which was held in an atmosphere of defeatism. In pursuance of this policy the Congress passed a resolution advising the Indian Communists to leave the Indian National Congress, which was roundly condemned as counter-revolutionary organisation of the nationalist bourgeoisie. The proletariat was regarded as the only revolutionary class and the anti-imperialist struggle was to be organised under its leadership. But Roy categorically rejected this line. He deplored the failure on the part of the Communist International to appreciate the revolutionary significance of the lower middle class and intelligentsia. He recommended the programme of a multi-class democratic movement against the developing alliance of imperialism and the colonial bourgeoisie.

Here, it is worth mentioning M.N. Roy's theory of 'decolonisation' which led him to differ from the Official line. At the time of the Sixth World Congress Roy advocated his 'decolonisation theory.' Decolonisation' signified the growing exhaustion of British imperialist finance and the partial transfer of its benefits to the Indian bourgeoisie. 'The decolonisation thesis' stressed the growing exhaustion of the exportable capital of the Home countries, necessitating a joint partnership with the native bourgeoisie. He prophesised that in the long run the depreciating value of imperialism would compel the foreign capitalists to part with power.

But owing to illness Roy could not be present at the Sixth World Congress (1928). He disagreed with the entire ultra-left policy or the extremist policy of 'red purism' inaugurated by the Sixth Congress. He warned that the ultra left slogan was in utter disregard to the realities of the situation. He pointed out to the growing menace of Fascism and advocated a democratic front to face it.

ROY'S EXPULSION FROM
THE COMMUNIST INTERNATIONAL

In 1938, Roy wrote 'Our Differences' for the purpose of narrating the history of the controversy about his expulsion from the Communist International. In its preface he writes: "But for the sake of discipline I kept quiet. I was the victim of internal intrigue, the desire of the British Communist Party to establish its protectorate over its Indian counterpart, and an internal struggle in the Russian Communist Party had a good deal to do with it. For the first time in the history of the Communist International an Indian delegation was called with the object of denouncing me obviously with a previously laid plan. This mysterious delegation informed the Congress that I was a person unknown in India having no connection whatsoever with revolutionary movement. During the discussion of the Indian question utterly unfounded charges were made against me. The underlying object was to give some plausible excuse for my removal from the leadership of the Communist International. I could not permit the theoretical criticism (though I ignored intrigues against me personally) levelled against me to go unchallenged, and I submitted to the Executive of the Communist International a comprehensive statement of my views to disprove the utterly unfounded charges. But no notice was ever taken of that document. On the contrary, a year later (1929), in a plenary (tenth) session of the Executive Committee of the Communist International, it was decided that I had put myself outside the Communist International on the charge of having written some article criticising certain adventurist action of the German Communist Party (while under-treatment of my illness). However, I was expelled from the Communist International as "a right wing deviationist" and as 'a lackey of imperialism."[16] But North and Eudin in 'Roy's Mission to China' (1963) maintain that Roy was sacrificed as a scapegoat for the China debacle.

Anyway, Roy was forced to severe his connections with the Communist International in 1929 as he had now serious differences with the Comintern on various issues. But it should be noted that Roy's opposition and criticism of the Comintern at first did not mean a rejection of theoretical communism as such, but merely as a complaint against the above mentioned policies of the Communist International.

RETURN TO INDIA

Europe at that time appeared to him divided between futile conventionalism and anti-libertarianism. Thus, after a lapse of fifteen years, the prodigal son of Mother India returned to her lap not with any smuggled arms but with new ideas and a world-wide experience. It is worth noting here that even when he was away from India he never lost touch with the events in India. Since he was being wanted and hunted by the British Indian police, he had to live and move incognito after his return to India. As such, he attended the annual session of the Indian National Congress at Karachi (March 1931) impersonating as Dr. Mahmud. According to secret police records, he was one of the authors of the resolution on fundamental rights and economic policy adopted at the Karachi Congress.

But the price of his return to India that Roy had to pay was a sentence of twelve years of rigorous imprisonment on the charge of being the principal accused in the Kanpur Conspiracy Case (1924) On appeal the sentence was reduced and he was released after six years.

While in Jail Roy read vigorously and wrote extensively. His major philosophical works like 'Materialism' Science and Philosophy,' 'Philosophical Consequences of Modern Science' were written during this period.

ROY'S WORK WITHIN THE CONGRESS

After six years in jail Roy came out to resume his life-long rebellious fight for freedom. He entered actively into Indian political life. Incidentally, in 1937, he married Ellen Gottschalk (his second wife, who had also actively participated in revolutionary activities in Germany and other European countries). Now Roy began to work inside the Congress. He was of the opinion that as a movement the Congress was of great significance because it commanded the confidence of the oppressed and exploited masses. It could not be looked upon just as a political party of the bourgeoisie. He held that there could not be a proletarian revolution without the proletariat, and in India the modern proletariat, conscious of its historical mission, was still in its infancy.

While in the Congress, Roy made a serious effort to activise the primary Congress committees with his famous slogan," Power to the people". Although Roy never subscribed to Congress ideology. But the Congress being a mass movement, he continued to work inside the Congress, though in his own way, till the beginning of the Second World War.

THE ISSUE OF WORLD WAR-II — ROY'S DIFFERENCES WITH THE CONGRESS AND THE COMMUNISTS

It was on the issue of War that differences of a grave nature arose between Roy and his followers, on the one hand, and the Indian nationalists and orthodox communists on the other. When the Second World War against the Nazi Germany broke out, the Congress leaders thought that India was not to gain anything by supporting the British. Roy, on the other hand, was in favour of unconditional support to the British. Consequently, he broke with the Congress. Internationalist as he was, Roy viewed every problem not merely from the Indian point of views but in the international context. In fact, he thought in terms which applied first to the world as a whole and then he would apply them to India with the necessary modifications. This fact obviously annoyed many nationalists who thought first of India. As a matter of fact, Roy had little enthusiasm for nationalism. In a book, 'Nationalism' (1942) Roy held that "nationalism was a reactionary and antiquated cult".

At the very beginning of the War Roy held that India being a part of the world was inextricably involved in an anti-Fascist War prevailing all over the world. Roy regarded the War as neither an imperialist war (like the communists) nor just a war between nations. For him, "It was a cataclysmic upheaval marking a historical turning point; it was an international civil war. The real enemy therefore was not a state but a rampant ideology — Fascism."[17] Notably, Roy was the first virulent critic of Fascism in India and wrote a whole book, 'Freedom or Fascism 1942).

In his analysis of the Second World War, Roy was also guided by his 'decolonisation thesis' that he had propounded in 1928. As such, when Churchill became the British Prime Minister in 1940, Roy saw that the consummation he had predicted about the imperialist parting with power could take place any time, if only the Congress would adopt a responsible attitude to the War. He believed that the Congress opposition to the War and the Quit India Movement was not based on principle but was against the eventuality of an Axis victory. It was this conviction which led Roy to regard the 1942- Movement as a "sabotage movement" and condemned it as the mischief of whipping up forces which undermine the Indian home front."[18] and as a result, he had to suffer a great deal in terms of popularity. In a way, it sealed Roy's fate as a political figure in India. But he was firm in his stand that in the circumstances it was not merely permissible but obligatory for a sincere opponent of Fascism to support the War and the British which he did.

During the War years, he thoroughly alienated Indian public opinion because of his open support to Britain and the Allies. However, Roy's analysis of the War was vindicated by later events, and he was proved as a man with prophetic vision and clairvoyance. However, he was too harsh on the Congress and its leadership. For instance, his interpretation of the Congress refusal to participate in the War as fascistic was quite baseless and unwarranted.

FOUNDING OF THE RADICAL DEMOCRATIC PARTY

In view of the above mentioned divergence of opinion on the issue of War, Roy and his handful of followers, distanced themselves from the Indian nationalists as well as the communists and founded the Radical Democratic Party in 1940. The same year he also founded the Indian Federation of Labour. Although this sharp break took place immediately on the issue of the War, the differences on both sides were fundamental, involving philosophical and ethical questions of political theory and practice.

The War period gave Roy much food for thought. The problem of nationalism and democracy was in the melting pot during the War. Now, he began to question the practice of the Soviet pattern of democracy, for it was not leading mankind towards freedom but tending to become a new Leviathan — a mighty Octopus. Parliamentary democracy was already discredited in many parts of the world. Roy, therefore, drew up a Draft Constitution of Free India and a People's Plan and began to advocate Radical Democracy and Cooperative Economy for free India three years before independence (1944).

NEW ORIENTATION IN ROY'S VIEWS

By the end of the Second World War, after reviewing the international situation and examining the various trends of thought, Roy came to the conclusion that a new orientation as regards political practice and economic reconstruction was urgently needed to meet the requirements of the contemporary world. He felt that humanity was experiencing a crisis of culture which called for a new attitude to life as a whole — a new ideology, a new philosophy. In 1946, an important meeting of the Executive of the Radical Democratic Party was held at Dehradun. On this occasion the Party also held a political study camp from 8th to 18th may, 1946. Here, the fundamental principles of political theories and practice were discussed. At the end of 1946 an All-India conference of the Radical Democratic Party endorsed a document formulating the principles of Radical Democracy. Though this was stated as the principles of theory and practice of a particular party, it covered not only the entire field of human activity but also man's relation to the physical universe, and the philosophy thus developed was called New (Scientific) Humanism or Radical Humanism.

NEW HUMANISM

A manifesto incorporating the fundamental principles of New Humanism which had been developing ever since the foundation of the RDP was published on 15 August, 1947. But on the whole, the philosophical principles, social doctrines, political theories had been developed over a number of years by a group of critical Marxists and former communists. It is pertinent to note here that although, as early as 1939, Roy had felt the necessity of modifying Marxism yet he did not disown Marxism till the end of the Second World War. But by the end of the War when he reviewed his own heretical past, he found that although he was basically a philosophical materialist, he could not call himself any longer a Marxist. New Humanism marked the culmination of his manifold heresies into a full fledged system of thought. He further elaborated his philosophy in a book, 'Beyond Communism' in 1947. It is remarkable that Roy was not only the first communist but also the first ex-communist of India.

Broadly speaking, Roy's life and ideas fall in three principal phases. In the first phase, he was a revolutionary nationalist anarchist. In the second phase, he was an active Marxist but not an orthodox one. In the third phase, he went beyond communism and developed his own philosophy of Radical Humanism. Although it may be convenient to divide his political life into three different phases but it is somewhat misleading, for if he was a nationalist in the first stage he was so with a difference.

Similarly, if he was a Marxist in the second stage he was never an orthodox Marxist. From the very beginning he had a cosmopolitan outlook. Hints of his world view and his concept of revolution from below can be seen in his early writings. It is worth noting that the quest for freedom was the running thread in the chequered career of his life. In his own words, "My whole political life has been nothing but a tormented soul's urge and search for freedom," Taken as a whole, the story of Roy's political life reads like an epic tale, the concluding chapter of which constitutes a philosophy of life.

DISSOLUTION OF THE RADICAL DEMOCRATIC PARTY

When it became clear to him that India was going to achieve the status of an independent nation after the War, Roy began to devote himself entirely to serious writing work. Some began to speculate that he had retired from politics but that was not quite correct. Of course, he was no longer associated with any party, having withdrawn from party politics since 1948 when the RDP was transformed into the Radical Humanist Movement. The latter adopted a programme which constitutes a challenge to the very concept of conventional politics.

FOUNDATION OF THE INDIAN RENAISSANCE INSTITUTE

Having given politics a new content he tried new means to achieve his aim of social revolution. For this purpose he started what he called 'The Indian Renaissance Movement.' He believed that such a movement must precede any social change. His wish was to develops the Indian Renaissance Institute into some kind of twentieth century Nalanda University.

Roy was not merely an active revolutionary but virtually a veritable genius of international eminence. In spite of the fact that he had been an active and front rank participant in a number of major struggles for social emancipation, he was a profound scholar of modern science in most of its branches. To trace the evolution of his thought one has to go through at least fifty volumes of his writings big and small, in addition to numerous articles in several weeklies and monthly journals, The Radical Humanist (formerly 'Independent India 1937-49) and a quarterly Journal devoted to enquiry and learning called 'The Humanist Way' (formerly 'The Marxian Way'). Roy himself used to edit both 'The Radical Humanist' and 'The Humanist Way.' Thus, Roy had a rare combination of political activism and intellectual pursuit.

However, Roy could not live a full life. In June 1952 Roy met with a serious accident at Mussoorie. Before he could recover, he had several attacks of cerebral thrombosis. The last one proved fatal and ended his life on 25 January, 1954. Thus, ended a peripatetic life, a chequered career — "a figure in three Revolutions" (John Gunther), a rebel thinker and a colourful personality.

The purpose of dwelling at length on his life and career is two-fold. First, to remove the lingering misunderstandings about his political persona and, second, to highlight his positive role in the Indian freedom movement through his writings and activities both in India and abroad.

Roy was certainly a man of vision and action. He was not merely an intrepid freedom fighter and a constructive revolutionary of modern India but also a great scholar as well as a prolific writer. Unlike most of the Indian leaders, Roy had a real taste for things academic. The outstanding works to his credit are:

1) India in Transition (1922)

2) Revolution and Counter Revolution in China (1930)

3) The Russian Revolution (1930)

4) Heresies of the Twentieth Century (1939)

5) Materialism (1940)

6) Science and Philosophy (1947)

7) Scientific Politics (1947)

8) New Orientation (1947)

9) Beyond Communism (1947)

10) New Humanism (1947)

11) Reason, Romanticism And Revolution (two volumes) (1952)

12) Politics, Power & Parties (1960)

13) India's Message (1982)

Abundantly enriched both by world-wide experience and still wider learning, M.N. Roy was able to evolve in the course of his crowded life of thought and action a new political philosophy which is termed as Radical Humanism or New humanism. It is radical in the sense that it penetrates through all abstractions to reach the root of society — the individual human being. It is humanist in its dedication to those human values which preserve the integrity of the individual — freedom and truth. Roy has taken the abiding values of Renaissance Humanism and reinforced them in the light of recent knowledge. Consequently, the ideas of reason, freedom and morality acquire a new meaning in his system. To quote Hiranmay Karlekar, "Continuing the philosophical lineage descending from the Greek sophist like Protagoras, the Dutch Erasmus of Renaissance

Europe, Roy enriched humanism and gave it a new dimension by incorporating the scientific advance."[19]

In formulating his philosophy Roy begins with the analysis of the present day crisis, which he characterises as a moral crisis. Since he thought that the existing ideologies were historically exhausted and had lost their exhilarating qualities, he argued that a new philosophy should be built up to satisfy the requirements and aspirations of mankind. His analysis is now largely vindicated. The last few years have witnessed some historic changes on the world scene. The most dramatic developments however are the collapse of communism, the consignment of the Soviet Union, and as a corollary, the end of the Cold War. Although, the leading industrially advanced countries based on capitalist system are gloating over the failure of the command economy and are celebrating the triumph of economic neo-liberalism or market-friendly economy, but the facts indicate otherwise. The so-called developed countries are facing unabated recession, economic stagnation, galloping inflation and mounting unemployment along with political instability. No one can ignore the reality of periodic boom and depression. Moreover, with the globalisation of the economy the recurring crisis in the capitalist system may now affect not only a particular nation which has this system but the entire world. In addition, the so called democratic system in these countries is not free from "suitcase" politics and recurring scams and scandals.

One needs to recall that more than forty years ago, M.N. Roy, with his philosophical insight and profundity, could foresee the failings of the capitalist and the communist system as well as the short-comings of parliamentary democracy. But being a constructive thinker, he not only anticipated the recent developments but offered an alternative system of thought. Though his philosophy bears certain similarities to other systems of thought in some of its aspects, it is also different from them. This difference gives it a character and individuality of its own.

M.N. ROY'S MATERIALISTIC METAPHYSICS

M.N. Roy was a Marxist and as such a Dialectical Materialist for about two decades. But then came a phase in the development of his thought when he rejected Marxism together with its Dialectical materialism. However, Roy continued to remain materialist, for he never denied matter as the ultimate reality. "The ultimate reality of the universe was a physical substance," he used to maintain. So philosophically he remained a full-blooded materialist.

It is worth noting that Roy was never enamoured of India's spiritualism which was raised to mystical heights by Dayanand, Vivekanand,

Aurobindo Ghosh and many others. He denounced Vedantic idealism and never accepted India's claim to spiritual superiority over the West. He wrote: "I am a confirmed, unmitigated materialist philosophically. I am of the opinion that materialism is the only philosophy possible, and any other philosophy, in the last analysis, takes us outside the physical universe into the wilderness of a mystic metaphysics over which presides God."[20]

However, Roy makes a distinction between the orthodox concept of materialism and the materialism of his concept, because the classical concept of matter is unacceptable in view of the modern knowledge discovered by the New Physics. The New Physics has shown that matter is not an indivisible unit, as was held by classical Physics. But he maintains that it does not prove that the ultimate reality, as known today, is immaterial. He contends that if there had been a revolution in the notion of substance, it is only in the perceptual sense and not in the conceptual sense.[21]

Roy wrote 'Science and philosophy' (1947) wherein he tried to interpret the researches of Albert Einstein (Relativity Theory), Max Planck (the principle of Inderminacy) Schrodinger, Dirco Niels Bohr (Theory of the Atom), D.E. Broglie (Theory of Light) in a materialistic way.

Roy was a robust rationalist. He was opposed to the creative evolutionism of Bergson and the voluntaristic philosophy of Schopenhauer and Hartmann. He also tried to interpret the Vaisheska and Nyaya philosophy in a materialistic way in his book, 'Materialism' (1940). Although the philosophical implication of New Physics is no rejection of materialism as such, Roy renamed materialism as 'Physical Realism' in view of certain confusion associated with the term 'materialism',. He asserts that modern science does not destroy the conception of the existence of some external objective basis as the substratum of all our experiences. In his opinion, New Physics has rather freed materialism of some vulnerable features by discarding the indefinable concepts of space, time, force, substance, etc. and established materialist philosophy on a firmer foundation of empirically acquired knowledge.

Materialism, according to Roy, is the explanation of the world without the assumption of any supernatural force of power. "Efforts made throughout the ages for such an explanation have established a monistic view of the universe and revealed the substratum of every thing — body, mind — as a material substance, a physical entity, largely known and progressively knowable. Existence precedes thought; things, ideas; matter spirit."[22] As a materialist, Roy asserts that there is nothing sacrosanct, nothing permanent, nothing eternal. To change is the nature of everything. "Change is the only thing permanent," as Heraclitus held. To Roy, Materialism is the philosophy of revolution, and materialist philosophy is the necessity in all ages.[23] It inspires man to change the world and himself in the process. Materialism also shows the way to reconstruct the world and this ideal of transforming the world is the highest form of practical idealism.

It was Hegel, who learning from Heraclitus, declared "Change itself to be a reality. Hegel said: "Everything that is, is real or real is rational." He viewed history as the process of continuous change. But he himself made logically a wrong inference from this view, because, as Roy says, the ideal changes are no less real than the material changes. Roy argues that Hegel's own dialectics destroys his "Absolute Idealism,"[24] for if change is the law of nature then how ideals can ever be perfect or absolute.

Marx and Engels also took over the idea that everything is in a state of constant flux from Hegel's philosophy as the "algebra of revolution". Roy states that "modern materialism triumphed as the inevitable outcome of the entire process of intellectual development ever since the dawn of human history. It is the greatest human heritage."[25] But Roy points out that this solid foundation of materialism was, however, weakened when it was associated with the Hegelian dialectics by Marx and Engels. The concept of dialectics has created a confusion in the philosophy of materialism, because dialectics was considered both a system of enquiry as well as a system of metaphysics under Marxism. But what is actually a system of logic should not be supposed to be a description of natural processes. Roy observes: "The basic error in the philosophical thinking of the propounders of dialectical materialism was to confound logic with ontology. In the Marxist system, dialectics is the fundamental law of thought and it is also a description of the process of nature. animate as well as inanimate. Since in Marxian philosophy, logic as well as ontology bear the identical label of dialectic confusion is inevitable."[26] Roy therefore rejects dialectical materialism. But at the same time, he points out that there is no necessary connection between dialectics and materialism.

Roy denounced dialectical materialism for another reason also. Dialectics implies that change in the process of nature takes place through contradiction. that is, "movement is contradiction". He says that the proposition that "movement is contradiction" is absurd. The absurdity becomes evident when we ask: "Contradiction of what ? Movement is the contradiction of the absolute being, which alone can be conceived as entirely motionless but absolute being is non-being, because being without motion is inconceivable (there is no motion apart from moving bodies). If movement is the basic reality and if it is the contradiction of non-being, then, according to dialectical materialism, the world originates in something coming out of nothing."[27] Thus, Roy shows that the concept of dialectical materialism contradicts the philosophy of materialism which starts with matter as the ultimate cause of everything and which, in the light of new knowledge shown by Physics, holds that motion is the inherent property of matter and is not the result of contradiction.

Side by side, historical determinism of Marx, which is a derivative of dialectical materialism, is also rejected by Roy as a teleological concept. Roy says that "historical necessity" has essentially a teleological implication." The very concept of "force" which is implicit in the idea of economic determinism has turned out to be metaphysical. "The conceptual picture of physical universe no longer makes any room for the hypothetical category of 'force',"[28] Roy maintains.

According to Roy, the purpose of applying dialectics to history is to prove that everything is permissible for bringing about revolutionary changes. "Dialectics divorces political practice from morality, denies the existence of human values, makes of revolution a teleologically predetermined outburst of violence and destructive frenzy beyond any control by the will of man."[29] The purpose of the theoretical system of Marx was to prove that revolutions took place of necessity and as such were inevitable. As against this, Roy holds that neither revolutions are inevitable nor are the events of history and social progress predetermined. Man's creative power, his struggle for existence, the biological urge for the unfolding of his potentialities are the motive force of social evolution and history. As a matter of fact, historical events and social transformations are brought about by a variety of causes. But the belief in dialectics preclude the scientific attempt to discover those actual causes. That is why, Marxism regards history and social evolution as predetermined and disregards the realities of history. Thus Roy rejects dialectical materialism altogether because "it is no materialism at all. It is simply dialectics."[30]

M.N. ROY'S THEORY OF KNOWLEDGE

The problem of ontology is very intimately connected with that of epistemology. As we have seen, Roy holds that the ultimate reality is matter. Now the problem arises whether it is possible to know the ultimate reality. Most of the earlier philosophies were based on this very issue. Today, this controversial issue has been reduced to the question of perception and to the question as to how far our knowledge corresponds with objective reality.

THE PROBLEM OF PERCEPTION

Roy takes up the problem of perception first and shows that this problem can now be solved. He says that the result of modern physical research, supplemented by the latest contributions of biological science enables us to free the empirical theory of Bacon, Hobbes and Locke from the fallacy and ambiguity, which opened it to the attacks of Berkeley, and as such led to subjectivism. The old theory of knowledge held that sense perceptions were the only source of knowledge and that senses gave true representation of outside objects. But the causal theory of John Locke confounded sensation with perception. Locke's theory reduced the mind to the position of a passive observer of pictures presented to it without any active function. But modern analysis of sensation shows that perception is not caused by external agencies; external stimuli cause sensations which are perceived by the mind. "Mind is a complicated state of consciousness which itself originates as the reaction to sensation,"[31] and, therefore, it requires no proof how the states of mind are caused by external agencies. Now it can be said that ideas do represent the reality but ideas should not be identified with sensation, for ideas are products of interaction between mind and the physical world; that is, they are the results of mental activity. Roy points out that ideas are representation of realities in as much as they are derived from experience. They are mental pictures representing the knowledge of things, but not the things themselves. And knowledge results from perception which is organic reaction to physical contacts. So, knowledge is not composed of ideas; on the contrary, ideas are derivatives of knowledge. As the knowledge of the world changes, ideas also change. Thus the representative character of ideas with regard to objective reality is proportional to the extent and accuracy of knowledge.

Roy further maintains that ideas correspond with objects and not with things. Roy differentiates objects from things. An object is a thing perceived but things are not always objects of perception. It means that things have their existence independent of our knowledge of them. They do not exist because we know them, and thus reality exists even we do not know it. If this were not so then it would mean that America did not exist before Columbus discovered it.

Roy further states that knowledge of a thing may be incomplete, yet it is objective. "Scientific knowledge is always objective, although ideas resulting from it may change from time to time. Being based on objective knowledge all scientific ideas are representation realities"[32] We acquire our knowledge, because our mind, being highly developed, extremely complicated state of consciousness, can react to external stimuli. In other words, knowledge is possible because there is causal connection between mind and matter. The greatest defect in the old theory of knowledge was that they did not accept the objective reality of both mind and the external world. Modern biology, however, has shown that mind is an objective reality; it is a characteristic of matter at a higher stage of its development. Its findings also reveal that matter has capacity to organise itself into complex, conscious, knowing, thinking beings. In short, mind is an emergent property of biological beings. Thus, all our knowing faculties are interwoven with the process of external world. Even the most intimate act of mind such as introspection or self-contemplation has some objective reference. It is on the grounds of this fact that Roy says that the very term "external world" is misleading, as the world is not external to us; we are its integral parts." Thus, biology cuts at the very root of centuries-old mind-matter problem. That is, it leads to disappearance of what is called the psycho-physical problem. Bertrand Russell also points out: "The dualism of mind and matter is out of date."

Roy further points out that knowing is an act of mind and as a mental act it is subjective, but knowledge is not identical with mind. Knowledge increases the thinking faculty of the mind. The greater the knowledge, the sharper the faculty.

Roy further adds that "although experience is the foundation of knowledge, yet knowing is not purely empirical process. On the contrary, it is selecting, interpreting systematising, coordinating of empirical materials in a rational coherent explanation of perceptual facts."[33] According to him, "Sense perception, human experience, gained not in passive contemplation, but in active functioning of the human organism and having for their source the material world existing objectively outside our consciousness, independent of it, are the points of departure of knowledge."[34] There is nothing as perfect knowledge or absolute truth or truth with the capital T (which Gandhi identified with God). Even objective truth is not absolute. Even science does not entertain the illusion of knowing the whole truth. Roy therefore believes only in search for truth. In view of this observation, "idealism has no legs to stand on, as it is now established that the knowledge of the objective world is possible." But it is not to be denied that since the process of knowing the objective realities sometimes involves abstractions, it may contain a large subjective element also.

Although the theories of atomic physics appeared to be mental constructions, nevertheless, they are derived from observation and experiment as any other scientific theory. According to Roy, "Physical research is leading to a point where the line of demarcation between the subjective and the objective disappears."[35] Both biological science and physical science have now established that our knowledge is both subjective and objective at the same time. Roy maintains that modern sciences, by proving the objective reality of mind and its possibility of knowing the objective world and by accepting the subjective element in our knowledge, have given a final blow to idealism and put materialism on a surer ground.

ROY'S EPISTEMOLOGICAL FORMULATIONS

After discussing Roy's theory of knowledge it is proposed to deal with his epistemological formulations. Einstein's Relativity Physics has thrown new light on the question of scientific method. The theory of Relativity states that the continuum appears different from every point event and this creates the problem of illusion. Roy solves it by suggesting to include into our scientific method three further considerations revealed by the researches of Physics, Biology and Psychology. They are the law of approximation, the law of probability and the law of epistemological progress. The law of approximation suggests that there is no moment in history when absolute knowledge may be reached. The validity of our knowledge increases when more and more data are included into the ranges of apprehension of individual point events and the achievement of greater and greater coherence among the categories reached through the incorporation of new data."[36]

Now coming to the application of the concept of probability, Roy observes that at no moment can one point event comprehend consciously the entire continuum and therefore the categories of knowledge need constantly to be modified in the light of new aspects of continuum that may be subsequently known. "The conscious correlation of the total point event pattern in the continuum being inadequate, the perspective of determinist relation between the causal pattern and the effect pattern ceases to be scientifically valid."[37] The relation that actually exists between these patterns of events is that of multifold probabilities of development of which some may be predominant in the light of available knowledge. This proves the uniform dimensional relation of cause and effect between one pattern of events and another, as found in Plato's idealism and Marx's economic determinism, as inadequate. But this principle of probability should not lead one to scepticism in so far as our knowledge is concerned. All that it means is greater approximation to the objective pattern of change through incorporation of the element of probability.

The last element, which should be made use of in the process of knowing, is the law of epistemological progress. This law suggests that an allowance for the probable alternatives of adjustment must be made while incorporating new data. According to this law, knowledge should be visualised as an endless historical process and the idea of absolute wisdom (which Dayanand found in the Vedas) be rejected once and for all.

It is noteworthy that Roy adopted the latest scientific method in the development of his philosophy of Radical Humanism. He made full use of recent findings of scientific knowledge in his methodology to arrive at the basic formulations of his system of thought.

To conclude, Radical Humanism is not only different from subjective and objective idealism but also from empiricism or mechanical materialism. To Roy, truth can be arrived at through scientific methods only and not through meditation, tapasya, divagyan (IIham) or Yoga.

THE PROBLEM OF ETHICS

The question of morality has been an eternal problem since the beginning of human society. Almost all philosophers have made attempts to solve it but without complete success. The liberal school of thought; for instance, believed that with political and economic reforms through laws an ideal order would be produced and the aim of establishing public morality in life would be achieved. No doubt, it did start with the elevating principle that the individual was a moral entity and as such he should be regarded as sovereign. But the religious faith in man's moral essence subordinates him to some transcendental power and thereby limits his sovereignty.[38] Not satisfied with this moral theory of early liberals, the later liberal thinkers like Bentham and J.S. Mill advanced the utility principle of morality. But it made no improvement on the older concept, for if the former was a metaphysical concept, the latter rendered moral values devoid of any objective moral standard.

Subsequently, in opposition to the reformism of liberals, socialists and communists believed that economic reconstruction on the basis of common ownership was the ideal order for moral development. But actually the results of such reconstruction has been the eclipse of the individual by collectivities, either group, class, state, nation or party, and the rise of totalitarianism in political practice as a corollary to it.

In his system of thought Roy takes up the problem of social morality and gives a very high place to ethics, particularly in the political sphere, because in our public life dishonesty, corruption, demagogy and unscrupulous scramble for power are found to be rampant. But his approach to ethical problems is based on the implications of modern sciences. He is not one of those thinkers who believe that science, by undermining the influence of religion, has made us morally irresponsible. He rather maintains that social thought and political practice can be harmonised with moral values only by abolishing the boundary line between science and philosophy.

Until recently ethics was a part of speculative philosophy and as such it was thought that no causal relation could be established between moral values and the world of science. No doubt, some of the earlier thinkers like Hobbes, Grotius, Helvetius, Kant, etc. tried to secularise ethics, but since rationalism in man, the source of morality was itself shrouded in mystery, their philosophy of ethics had a very weak foundation. Hence Roy argues that religion, in the last analysis, remained the only sanction of morality in practice. But the advancement of science has undermined the faith in supernatural power (God), hitherto supposed to be the guardian or overseer of morality. The result is the religion no longer dictates the norms of social behaviour. Roy believes that with the integration of science with philosophy the roots of the problem of social and individual life can now be traced down to the whole process of biological and physical evolution and this will enable to solve the intractable problem of our life, including that of morality.

THE SANCTION OF MORALITY

Roy is of the opinion that the vexed question of morality can be solved in the light of modern scientific knowledge. The central problem of ethics is that of the sanction of morality, and in order to get at the root of the problem, Roy says, it is necessary to dig deep into the subsoil of human existence. Modern biology has solved the mystery of man to a very large extent. It has now established that man is the outcome of biological evolution. He says that in order to find the sanction of morality in man himself and avoid at the same time the morass of mysticism, the roots of what is called conscience or moral sense must be traced in the biological functions articulated as instincts and intuitions. "Biological evolution takes place in the context of the physical universe, its mechanism being a part of the cosmic mechanism. Life grows out of the background of inanimate nature. The descent of man therefore can be traced to the physical universe governed by the laws of nature. Man's rationality and moral sense, which are causally connected, are the expression of cosmic harmony. Therefore, it is in the nature of man, as a biological organism, to be rational and as such he is capable of living with others in peace and harmony."[39]

Although this attempt to establish a logical connection between ethics and the physical world seems to be farfetched and a doubtful proposition, but Roy tries to explain it. He says that the universe is a physical system and the man who grows out of that background is also a physical system.

However, he points out to a great difference that lies between the two systems. The physical universe is law governed, the laws being inherent in itself whereas man possesses will and can choose. Between the world of man and the world of inanimate nature there lies a world of biological evolution. Conscience appears at a much later stage. It is at this stage that the mechanism of evolution ceases to be blind or amoral. Therefore, human will cannot be directly related to the laws of the physical universe. It is rooted in the intervening biological world. Thus, it is wrong to say that human will is an antithesis to the law governedness of the physical universe. Reason harmonises the two and it results from the consciousness of man's being an integral part of the law-governed physical universe. It is the expression of the orderliness of nature or an echo of the harmony of the universe. Man, with his mind, intelligence and will, is a part of the physical universe, with the result, his being and becoming, his emotions and ideas are also determined; for example, the laws and necessities of psychological life determine man's mind. But although his intelligence, desire and will are inherited from nature, man is free to the extent that his life is self-determined.[40] According to Rossi, "Man is free because he is bound by his own laws."[41] But the mere fact that the universe is harmonious does not imply that it is moral, or has any ethical sense, because morality is based on will, feeling and consciousness. Only human individual, because he can feel, can know and make choice, is capable of becoming a moral agent, and only rationally conscious man can have the sense of moral obligation. In the course of historical development as Morris Ginsberg argues, "Man is slowly rationalised and that man is moralised in proportion as he becomes more rational."

Thus, according to Roy, Morality must be referred back to man's innate rationality. Only then man can be moral spontaneously and voluntarily. Reason is thus the only sanction of morality, which is an appeal to conscience, and the latter, in the last analysis, is nothing mystic or mysterious; it is a biological function on the level of consciousness. Ethics is the product of the function of rationality to satisfy the social urge of life. Since, it is established that the sanction of morality is embedded in human nature itself, Roy contends that the innate rationality of man is the only guarantee of a harmonious social order. "Since, as biological beings, all men are similarly constructed they are likely to react more or less in a similar way under similar circumstances provided a minimum background of knowledge is there. In other words, the universality of reason demands from all rational beings the same behaviour in the same circumstances."[42] Thus, according to Roy, "a Secular rationalist system of ethics could be biologically deduced from materialist cosmology."

Roy's biological foundation of Axiology thus rescues rationalism and ethics from the devastating consequences of scepticism. Moral values are placed on a firm foundation when they are referred back to the innate rationality of man and the spring of moral conduct is to be found in human nature itself.

Thus, Roy's approach to the problem of ethics is also materialistic. He states "I believe that not only a materialistic ethics is possible, but that materialistic morality is the noblest form of morality, because it enables man to be moral without debasing himself before an imaginary super human power."[43] Since morality is an appeal to conscience and the latter is conceived by Roy as awareness of social responsibility, the sense of social responsibility does not necessarily run counter to individual freedom. On the other hand, it results from the eternal urge for freedom found in all human beings.

Roy further points out if we do not trace ethical sense to the rationality of man the moral values become dogmatic propositions. It seems as if somebody dictates them to us. It is this moral dogmatism which leads to the rise of the relativist ethics. "The relativist attitude to morality," according to Roy, "is nothing but the natural reaction to the dogmatic irrational coercive ethics and moral relativity is immorality."[44] A relativistic ethics having no common criterion of moral values is no ethics at all. In this system of ethics end will justify the means.

THE RELATION BETWEEN MEANS AND ENDS

Most political thinkers have been concerned only with the attainable and desirable goals of a political system and the question of means to achieve the same has been a study in expediency for them. In their view the ends have a moral priority over means. In other words, they have accepted a dichotomy between ends and means. Writers from Machiavelli to Marx have argued in favour of the maxim that 'end justifies the means.' Even Plato in his 'Republic had exempted the philosopher rulers from the conventional code of morality and justified this maxim in their case. But means cannot be justified by motives only; it must be judged by consequences as well. We should estimate impartially the total consequences of means, including possible deleterious effects on the end desired. But since in most of the cases it is difficult to estimate the possible consequences it is better to reject the proposition that end justifies the means. The ethics of a simple society is naturally preoccupied with the question of ends in the sense motive inspiring an action. But, in the world at large, grown incomparably more complicated than it was ever before, this is clearly a wrong approach to problem of ethics. But the Marxian approach, too, followed this approach. Since Marx held that struggle between the capitalists and the proletariat will eventually lead to a classless society whatever hastens this ultimate end was good. Lenin's oft quoted statement was: "Our morality is wholly subordinate to the interests of the class struggle." Likewise, Engels observes: "As society has hitherto moved in class antagonisms, morality was always class morality, and adds "We therefore reject every attempt to impose on us any moral dogma whatsoever as an eternal, ultimate and forever immutable moral law."[45] According to Roy, "It was Hegel from whom Marx inherited a preference for casting moral ideals in the guise of the inevitable. Hegelian influence is also responsible for inducing Marx to reject the individualist approach to moral problem. According to Roy, "While the ethical realtivism of the utilitarians was rational, because of its individualist approach to morality, Marxian relativism, notwithstanding its appearance, is dogmatic, being a projection in the future of the Hegelian moral positivism."[46]. If for Hegel, what exists is rational and therefore good, for Marx, the future resulting inevitably from the present will also be rational and good. Marxian ethics thus is nothing but an application of the Hegelian cosmic ethics."[47] Therefore, Roy concludes that this is nothing but moral nihilism.

Lewis Mumford points out: "Like any futurist utopia, Marxism denied the values that lie in the process of achievement. But the process by which a goal is achieved is part of that achievement."[48] But unlike Marx, Roy believes that both ends and means are identical and equally important. According to him, the relation between means and ends is logical and therefore moral ends cannot be promoted through immoral means. Thus like Tolstoy, Gandhi, Alduous Huxley and others, Roy also insists on the purity of means. He pleads for the recognition of the supreme importance of moral values in public life.

Roy further contends that moral values are universal. He says, "If we want at all an ethics we shall have to start from the proposition that there are such things as human values and they are eternal in so far as humanity is eternal."[49] What he means to say is that ethical concepts and moral values have originated with human species. He concludes that the only possible ethics, an ethics which could not violate the spiritual dignity of the modern man must be logical, anthropological, social and psychological. Thus, Radical Humanism recognises that there are universal ethical values which transcend the limits of ethnicity, nationality or cultural identity. It provides a set of ethical standards for the global community.

CRITERION OF VALUE

The problem of morality is intimately connected with the criterion of value. Roy also provides a test of value. In his system of thought. Roy's value criterion is the synthesis of a two-fold considerations. The first is "Maximum distinctiveness for individuals" and the second is "maximum harmonisation between individuals." Both of these may in their respective concrete aspects be described as freedom and progress. To Roy, "Freedom means an opportunity of the distinct to make experiments in its response to the situational pattern. It implies conscious choice between alternative ways of responding to environment. By progress he means the diminishing chance of an individual's experimentation obstructing the freedom of another. Freedom is looked upon as a value from the individual point of view and progress is justified from the social point of view. According to Roy, the degree of freedom is the barometer to measure any progress. So whatever institution or code of behaviour conduces to produce greater individual freedom and social progress is valuable. In short, Roy's criterion may be described as the harmonisation of distincts in some institutional or organised form. Whatever personal or social function goes to obviate difficulties in the way of individuation and cooperation becomes a value. Thus, Roy's ethics does have objective standards.

Roy's axiology deduces all other values from the supreme value of freedom, because the urge for freedom is the essence of human existence. Of course, man was not born free, as Rousseau imagined, but certainly man was born to be free. Ever since its appearance on earth the human species had to undertake a struggle first against the environment for physical survival and then for other achievements, and since the whole universe is environment, the urge for survival is also eternal. Freedom, thus is an undying urge. Freedom is not only progressive elimination of all restrictions on the unfoldment of human personality but it is also the basic incentive to acquire knowledge and conquer environment by knowing them. In course of these struggles man discovers truth which is the content of knowledge. "The hierarchy of humanist axiology, thus, is freedom, knowledge and truth. However, these values are not autonomous but logically as well as ontologically interrelated,"[50] for knowledge endows man with the power to carry on the never ending struggle for greater and greater freedom and search for truth.

Radical Humanism, thus, proclaims the sovereignty of man on the authority of modern science which has dispelled all mystery about the essence of man. It maintains that a rational and moral society is possible because man is essentially rational and potentially moral.

However, few will totally agree with M.N. Roy that a secular rationalist system of ethics can be logically deduced from the mechanistic cosmology of the materialist philosophy. In the opinion of G.P. Bhattacharjea, "Any attempt to establish a logical connection between ethics and the physical world is far-fetched. To him, "Roy's pan-rationalism is not a sufficiently strong basis of the system of secular morality,"[51] for the ethical progress requires not only development of the reasoning power but also training of the emotion. Prof. M.K. Haldar also finds "the weakest link in Roy's approach to morality in his endeavour to derive man's moral sense from his rationality."[52]

ROY ON HUMAN NATURE

The consideration of human nature is a cardinal point in all social philosophies. In fact, it is the cornerstone on which the edifice of a social philosophy is erected, and hence no philosopher can afford to ignore it. Every political philosophy, in the last analysis, is based explicitly or implicitly upon the concept of human nature. Roy, too, took up this aspect of social philosophy and tried to analyse and understand it in order to provide a solid basis to his system of philosophy.

THE NATURE OF HUMAN NATURE

Roy studied human nature from various angles — the biological, the anthropological and the psychological. Strangely enough, the knowledge of human nature is extremely scanty in comparison with the knowledge of physical nature. This fact makes Roy's study of human nature more significant.

As far as his biological approach is concerned, Roy observes that since the appearance of man on earth is nothing more than the origin of a new biological species, the laws of development of the human race cannot be essentially different from the general laws of organic evolution. That is, the laws of the latter apply to human nature as well.[53] According to Roy, "Man, with all his emotional and spiritual make up, being an integral part of the physical universe, human nature is changeable as all other aspects of nature."[54] The logical inference therefore is that since human nature is also governed by an evolutionary process, it cannot be an immutable category. Though several writers like Pareto, Garham Wallas, etc. believe that "centuries roll by and human nature remains the same", but, according to Roy, the modern view based on the researches in Anthropology should be: "to change is human nature." As a matter of fact, the whole of social history proves the progressive change of human nature, otherwise there is no sense in regarding the history of civilisation as an evolutionary process.

THE MARXIAN VIEW OF HUMAN NATURE

Marx and Engels also contend that human nature is essentially subject to change. "It is basic to the whole Marxian concept of society that man changes history and is thereby himself changed and that in this sense all history is really nothing but a continual transformation of human nature."[55] Although Marx maintains that human nature changes but he recognises only economic factor as the primary cause of change and considers other factors of secondary significance. Roy, on the other hand, insists that a number of factors like cultural, political, ideological, religious, besides economic factor are involved in it.

In dealing with the concept of human nature, Roy first takes up the question of origin of humanness. The origin of species, according to Roy, is preceded by the origin of humanness. In fact, the residue of humanness is the biological heritage of reason. Reason is a biological property of higher organisms, for in a rudimentary form it can be traced in higher animals as well. Roy regards human rationality as a continuation of reason in nature. He defines man's rationality as the microcosmic echo of the macrocosm. In other words, the reason in man is an echo of the harmony of the universe.[56]

Roy further maintains that human nature is not to believe but to enquire and search for truth. Even the search which led to man's inventing the gods of natural religion for explaining natural phenomenon was an expression of his innate rationality. The natural religions were simply theoretical systems devised by human reason without supernatural aid or revelation. In short, natural religions were nothing but 'primitive rationalism."

Roy further asserts that man is moral by nature. The latest researches in the field of Anthropology and Sociology have now proved that even savages have the sense of good or bad. Therefore, according to Roy, "the law of jungle only betrays human conceit." Hobbes was wrong when he said that man is fundamentally wicked.[57] As we find, even higher animals have their rules of conduct. These rules go into the composition of human instinct and being part of man's biological heritage they are the constant of human nature. In man they expressed themselves as the sense of morality. One knows from experience what is good or bad for him.[58] Thus, it is rational inference of experience rather than religion which is the sanction of morality. According to this analysis, the moral principles must accord with the natural impulse rather than with theology. "Moral principles that exalt themselves by degrading human impulse are in effect committing suicide. The badness of the good people is the revenge taken by human nature for the injuries heaped upon it in the name of morality."[59]

Morals cut-off from positive roots in man's nature are bound to be mainly negative.

Roy enumerates some of the more important elements in human nature, namely, quest for freedom, search for truth, urge for progress and, above all, instinct of self-preservation or of self-interest. However, he regards freedom as the basic human value. "Freedom is the supreme value of life because the urge for freedom is the essence of human existence."[60] There is nothing more divine than freedom. But "freedom is nothing but the continuation of struggle for existence on the level of intelligence".

According to Roy, "The search for knowledge and truth is ultimately associated with the quest for freedom as the essence of human nature. Truth is neither a mystic- metaphysical category nor an abstract value. It is a matter of experience and not the result of revelation, as claimed by different theologies. It is correspondence with objective reality. In one word, "it is the content of knowledge."

Roy also examines another element of human nature which is said to be the most predominant in man- the instinct of self-preservation. According to him, "It is also inherited by the homosapiens from their biological ancestry and is essentially rationalist. It is this instinct which persuaded man to live in herds."[61] "Man's gregarious tendency led him to form groups and communities for mutual aid and protection."[62] As a matter of fact, human society originated in the interest of self-preservation which is best guaranteed by collective efforts. Therefore, "it is quite legitimate to say that self-interest being the governing instinct man is selfish by nature."[63] But Roy suggests that no narrow meaning should be given to the term. Broadly conceived, self-interest is conducive to social welfare. When the individual becomes socialised, his self-merges in the community and becomes the expression of social life, and since the individual interest is promoted by collective interest, individual selfishness becomes enlightened selfishness or collective selfishness. In other words, when rationality extends man's selfishness to a wider field it becomes a social virtue. Thus there is no necessary conflict between the true interest of the individual and the society at large. "At bottom individual and general welfare are not contradictory and the antithesis between social and personal well-being is only on the surface."[64]

Roy also examines the element of urge for progress in human nature. He writes: "Soon after human society originated in the instinct of self-preservation, the original instinct was reinforced by a new instinct — the instinct of progress.[65]" But Roy takes the term progress in its scientific connotation. It is the conquest of nature by man. In fact, he uses the term 'nature' in a very wide sense. To the extent man conquers nature, to that extent he progresses.

Rejecting the traditional notion of human nature, Roy says that it is neither evil nor divine as some old philosophers like Hobbes and Rousseau held. To Roy, man is inherently rational and, given the opportunity, every human being is capable of thinking for himself, judging right and wrong and acting properly. Like Bertrand Russell, Roy believes that reason and education can transform human nature and society. However, it may be pointed out that Roy takes too optimistic a view with regard to the role of reason and education in changing our society. To borrow the words of Graham Wallas, Roy seems to suffer from "the tendency to exaggerate the intellectuality of mankind." He seems to forget that people, by and large, are swayed more by emotions than by reason, more by propaganda than by education. We cannot deny the fact that human will and emotion sometimes tend to go against rational consideration. Human thought and conduct are often determined by appetite, passion, prejudices, and reflexes, etc. By asserting that man is essentially rational Roy over-simplified the problem of human nature.

ROY'S PHILOSOPHY OF HISTORY

In evolving a philosophy of life no thinker can ignore the question of historiology. Without a philosophy of history, neither the past can be understood, nor the present can be explained, nor trends of the future can be indicated. History has been hitherto interpreted from various angles but the generally accepted view is that history is an evolutionary process and that man is the maker of history. "Man," as Marx said, "is the root of mankind." This statement of Marx implies that society, culture, science, religion, morals, economics, etc. are all the results of human endeavour.

The evolutionary view of history, which is generally accepted today, owes its origin to Aristotle. Thereafter this evolutionary concept of history was developed by a galaxy of luminaries in the firmament of the world of thought. Later on, Hegel formulated it as the key to the history of civilisation. Roy on his part was very impressed by Vico's view of history that he presented in 'New Science' (1725). Vico asserts that "humanity is its own creation." That is, the social world is certainly the work of man. Roy observes that the humanist philosophy of history founded by Vico on the basis of Epicurean tradition and the pioneering works of Bacon, Hobbes, Grotius, Helvetius, Condorcet, Michelet and others must be revived. According to Roy, Vico interprets the origin of society and its subsequent development as causally determined and, therefore, he must be recognised as the founder of historicism which was elaborated in grossly one-sided manner by Marx, more than a hundred years after Vico's death, as the dialectics of history or historical materialism."[66] When the Darwinian doctrine revealed the animal origin of the human species, the evolutionary view of history was established empirically also. Marx and Engles hailed Darwin's idea of "struggle for existence" as an essential ingredient of dialectical materialism.

Under the impact of Vico's philosophy Marx evolved his doctrine of economic interpretation of history. While Hegel had said that history of ideas or of philosophy was the history of the world, Marx believed that he had corrected the Master when he declared that "the history of civilisation was the history of class struggle." But in the opinion of Roy, he had only converted dialectical idealism into dialectical materialism.

Criticising Marxian theory of class struggle Roy observed: "Undoubtedly society was always divided into classes and had conflicting class interests, but, at the same time, there was a cohesive tendency which held society together, otherwise it would have disintegrated time and again and there would be no social evolution."[67] Linked with this theory of social cohesiveness was Roy's emphasis on the progressive role of the middle class in modern society. Again, whereas in the Marxian class theory, the working class had a special place, in Roy's formulation the middle class has a special status. In addition, Roy gives place of pride to the middle class intelligentsia and not to the proletariat, whom he characterised as the "most backward stratum of society."

Marx believed that existence determines consciousness. Roy acknowledged that this formulation of Marx was essentially correct. But for Marx, the basic influence was economic and therefore he stated that social evolution proceeds under the stress of economic forces Although at one stage Marx admitted that political relations, science, etc., once produced, operate as causes of subsequent events and can modify the operation of economic forces, but later on, this qualification was also relegated to background to defend all comprehensive character of economic determinism. This over-stress on economic determinism made a teleology out of his essentially scientific view of history. With this impersonal concept of the forces of production it introduced teleology in history thereby crassly contradicting his own belief that man is the maker of history.

In economic determinism, as Roy points out, the forces of production are taken to be an autonomous process of development. But it is wrong to suppose that material relations are the basis of all relations. Marx assumed that economic institutions are slef-begotten and all social changes are the by-product of that automatic technological development. In other words, he believed that material conditions and technological inventions are self-executed entities existing in and by themselves but the productive forces cannot be viewed as a fundamental category, as their devising itself presupposes existence of human mind. Logically following this notion of self-developing system of productive forces, Marx contended that all social changes take place on account of historically conditioned necessities. In a sense, Marx translated Hegelian fatalism into economic terms. "Is it not a sort of secularised Messianism" to borrow the words of Martin Buber. But "the notion that society advances with iron necessity towards an inevitable goal belongs to the realm of religion or fate rather than to that of science of history."[68] In the opinion of Rudolf Rocker, "It is nothing but a new belief in fali (fate) springing from Hegel's spectral world except that in this case (of Marx) condition of production has assumed the role of the absolute spirit."[69] It was dialectics again which led Marx to false simplification of highly complex situation and formulation of a teleological concept of history. Thus, "Marx was wrong to hold that "socialism is the inevitable next stage irrespective of human volition or desirability,"[70] as the phoenix may fail to rise from the ashes.

Though Marx had stressed the role of knowledge in human development but not having the knowledge of modern psychology and sociology he failed to grasp the nature of that creativeness fully and thereby allotted a subsidiary role to ideas. His over emphasis on the economic factor at the cost of proper appreciation of the role of ideas in human history may be a recoil from the idealism of Hegel.

ROY'S CRITICISM OF MARXIAN INTERPRETATION OF HISTORY

Marxian theory of surplus value and its appropriation by the property-owning class (exploiting class) provided the theoretical foundation of the class struggle, and Marx traced it throughout history backwards until the dawn of civilisation, and thus for him economic determinism became the only clue to explain all historical events. But economic determinism can be established neither logically nor empirically. His theory of class struggle in its turn led him to predict that this struggle will culminate in establishing a classless society. But Roy would ask: will not the classless society be stagnant since class struggle is the lever of all progress, according to Marx himself."? This theory therefore passes a death sentence for mankind. "This teleological character of economic determinism seems to be a throwback to the doctrine of predestination."[71] Coming from a protagonist of a new revolution it is not surprising if "Marxian philosophy of history fuses logic of analysis with the poetry of passion."[72] In practice also, economic determinism becomes a negation of the Marxist utopia. It is now an established fact that the fact that the state does not wither away under communism; instead it swells to totality.

The Marxist approach to history, Roy says, is inadequate because it is derived from a lack of sensitiveness to the dynamics of social progress. Materialistic interpretation accords no place to intelligence in the process of social evolution."[73] It makes the process of history external to human choice and plan."[74] In short, this interpretation allows a slender roll to mental activity in the social process.

As a matter of fact, social change moves along an extremely complicated pattern and it would be a mistake to look to a single set of events for the full explanation of social conditions. The chain of historical causation is too variable and often too obscure to be reduced to formula, as was done by Marxism. Besides, the means of production, political power, climate, the physical structure of the inhabitants are also material forces in social revolution.

ROY'S 'HUMANIST' APPROACH TO HISTORY

According to Roy, social pattern is a very complicated phenomenon. He points out that "often interpersonal logic of institutional relationships has been overemphasised at the cost of active influence and importance of the very individuals who are responsible for establishing such interpersonal relationship."[75] Of course, it was to the credit of Marx and Hegel who recognised laws of institutional relationship, but both of them under the influence of the law of dialectics committed the mistake of assuming that human institutions have an irreversible logic, and therefore the only choice open to individuals is to act voluntarily to its dictates.

The humanist approach of Roy, however, rejects both the purely romantic interpretation of history and the purely environmental or institutional interpretation of history, as the latter introduces dictatorial politics, positivist morality and a concealed religious attitude to life.[76]

His approach does not commit the mistake of finding a single cause for all events. In fact, there is rather an element of eclecticism in his philosophy of history. Roy says: "The equation of science of history must embrace all determining factors." This approach believes that all social phenomena are the result of a series of causes, in most cases so inwardly related that it is quite impossible to separate one from the other. Roy, therefore, puts stress on the multiplicity of causes of social change. His interpretation takes into account all these factors of history and considers social evolution as an integral process. It points out that this integral logic indicates probability of human influence ultimately deciding the whole pattern of social development. It thus "reconciles the positive elements of both romantic and materialistic interpretation of history."[77]

Roy, therefore, must be said to have constructed a more comprehensive and objective interpretation of history than Marx because, in his interpretation economy and ideology are not related as foundation and superstructure but as mutually interacting elements, each organically correlated to the other to result in the concrete complex of social phenomenon. However, in his interpretation, Roy does not minimise the important contribution of economic factors and the mode of production in influencing the pattern of social development. But he does point out that with social evolution, ideological and cultural factors tend to have more and more decisive influence. Therefore, it is wrong to hold that cultural and ideal influences are only superstructures, for often it happens that the ideas and philosophies evolve in direct reaction to previous ideas without being influenced by economic factors. To substantiate, "the appearance of a Galileo or an Einstein is not the result of some economic crisis but as the response of some accidental genius to a basic cultural crisis."[78] Similarly, one cannot explain Marx in terms merely of his economic context. Roy, therefore, argues that historical determinism should not be considered as purely economic.

Roy rejects economic determinism also because it is a dualistic concept, whereas the quintessence of materialist philosophy is monism. Economic determinism is dualistic in the sense that by its implication it makes any reconciliation between idealism and materialism impossible. It is so because for Marx an acceptance of materialism meant the denial of the realities of ideas. It is this dualism which explains the basic and superstructure in the Marxian interpretation of history. Roy's philosophy, of history however, has resolved this dualism. It is to be noted that in spite of conceding the objective reality to ideas, Roy remains essentially a materialist, for the origin of ideas is discovered inside the physical universe. Radical Humanism traces the double process, mental and physical, of the biological world, including the social evolution to a common origin. Origin of ideas can be traced in the context of prehuman biological evolution, the latter in its turn takes place in the context of physical universe. While tracing it Roy exposes the fallacy of economic determinism, because he shows that ideas are not mere by-product of economic conditions but they precede any change in the means of production.

IDEAS PRECEDED THE FIRST MEANS OF PRODUCTION

Roy holds that "man's brain is also a means of production. It produces ideas which are the most iconoclastic of commodities."[79] He says that the march of events is not predetermined either by divine or transcendental power or inexorable economic laws. As a matter of fact, revolution in society presupposes iconoclastic ideas.

Now, in order to understand the precedence of ideas over means of production, Roy gives an imaginary illustration to hammer home his point. He writes: "The creation of the original means of production can be imagined as the first ape breaking a branch of a tree to prolong his arm with it, and plucking fruit with its help without having to climb to the top of the tree. That would have been the greatest step in the struggle for existence. But this creation took place in the monkey's brain out of its urge to be free of necessity of growing longer arms."[80] Thus, the first extra-organic means of production was created by the ancestor of man in continuation of the struggle for existence, which was the basic impulse of the pre-human biological evolution. The development of the biological organ, the brain, preceded that event. The creation of the first extra-organic means of production was a deed done by an animal with a highly developed brain capable of thought. An idea thus preceded the creation of the first means of production. As economic determinism cannot be traced beyond the stage at which the foundation of economic life was just being laid, the origin of ideas is to be discovered outside the economic process, for it was the physical urge of survival which led to the creation of the first means of production.[81] An explanation of the origin of ideas is thus put forward by tracing it in pre-human biological impulses.

Roy further points out that economic determinism should not be confused with physical determinism. Marx did make the mistake of identifying economic determinism with physical determinism, and it was because of this mistake that he concluded that the origin of society and subsequent human developments were economically motivated. It is no wonder if Marx gave an economic interpretation of history when the point of departure of his historiography was the blunder of confounding physical urge with economic motive.

Roy says that ideas are therefore biologically determined, priority belonging to the physical being. But once the biologically determined process of ideas is complete; that is, once ideas are formed they continue to have an autonomous existence and an evolutionary process of their own, and they are governed by their own laws. "After the generation of ideas, the single basic current of physical events bifurcates, so to say; the biological world on the higher level of evolution is composed of a double process- the dynamics of ideas and succession of physical facts."[82] Roy's theory of parallelism of ideas and the texture of the objective society implies that no direct specific correlation is possible between a system of ideas and a set of events. The two parallel processes, ideal and physical, compose history and both are determined by their logic or dynamic. At the same time they are mutually influenced, the one by the other. That is how history becomes an organic process.

According to Roy's philosophy of history the rational order of nature and history is determined and it must run its course. The rationalist view apparently seems to exclude revolution. But it is not actually so, because human will is also a part of nature; it grows out of a rational order. Man's desires and endeavours in pursuance thereof are also determined; therefore revolutions take place of necessity; they are historically determined. By tracing will, emotion and intelligence to the common biological origin, Roy reconciles the romantic doctrine that man makes history with the rationalist notion of orderly social progress. "History being the record of human endeavour and man being an integral part of the law-governed universe, history is not a chaotic conglomeration of fortuitous events."[83] Of course, social evolution is a determined process but it is determined by various factors and human will is one of them, and the latter indeed, is the most powerful factor. Of course, will is also determined but man is free to act as he wills. Determinism therefore does not rob him of the freedom of action, and that is how revolutions in a rationally determined process of social revolution are possible. But Roy maintains that human will as well as ideas can seldom be referred directly to economic incentives. That is, ideologies cannot be directly related with the materialist condition of life. The logical development of ideas and the generation of new social forces take place simultaneously together providing the motive force of history, But in any given period they cannot be causally connected, except in the sense that action is motivated by ideas. In as much as action is motivated by ideas, determinism in history is primarily ideal.[84]

Roy, therefore, pleads that materialism must be restated so as to recognise explicitly the decisive importance of the dynamics of ideas in history — social, political and cultural. He states that "the monocausal approach either idealist (in the Hegelian sense) or materialist (in the Marxian sense) is bound to give partial view of history. History must be studied as the process of integral human evolution — material, intellectual and social. "We must trace the parallel currents of ideal and physical events. By connecting new ideas causally to established economic relations we put things on their head. A new system of ideas grow out of older system. The relation between the growth of a new ideology and the rise of a new class is not causal either way, it is accidental."[85] Ideas have their own history — past, present and future. For example, from the fact that the European Renaissance approximately synchronised with the rise of the trading class it is deduced by Marxists that individualism and humanism — the legacy of the Renaissance movement were principles of the ideology of the bourgeoisie. But historically that is not true, for the Renaissance was a humanist revival. In fact, the Renaissance was inspired more by the humanist, rationalist and scientific ideas of the ancient Greek civilisation than by the economic interest and political ambition of the medieval trading class. The Renaissance declared the dignity and sovereignty of man on the authority of Sophists, Epicureans, Stoics and also of early Christianity. The heroes of the Renaissance like Leonardo, Copernicus, Galileo, etc. had no connection with the rising bourgeoisie.[86] Similarly, the eighteenth century materialism was not the philosophy of the rising bourgeogise nor was the Enlightenment a bourgeois ideological movement. Roy also rejects the view that the French revolution was a bourgeois revolution. Marx wrongly interpreted liberal democracy as an ideology peculiar to the middle class. In fact, liberalism can be traced all the way back to Greek rationalism. Liberalism as a philosophy developed independently according to the logic of the evolution of thought. Modern liberalism which is called bourgeois philosophy rose before the establishment of capitalism. Further, basic principles of parliamentary democracy (the so-called bourgeois democracy) were expounded by Marsilio of Padua at a time when the bourgeoisie were hardly out of the swaddling cloth. Actually, the philosophical foundation of liberalism was laid by Hobbes much before the rise of the middle class. Likewise, Fascism was neither a class ideology nor it was economically determined. Its basis was emotional.

Marxism asserted that causal relations between movement of ideas and historical or social events can be established. Roy admits it when he says, "yes, but in a reverse direction not in the Marxian sense."[87] Roy, therefore, rejects economic determinism as a causative force, and maintains that ideologies are not superstructures but structures standing by themselves. His contention is supported by Nadezhda Mendelstam, who in his 'Hope Against Hope' states: "The real stuff of history is ideas, the prime mover of history is not the economic force." He further adds that "it is ideas that shape the minds of whole generations, winning adherents, creating new forces of government and Society, rising triumphantly, then slowly dying away disappointing." Marx may have put Hegel on his feet but he had certainly placed himself on the head."[88] Roy rightly claims to have set both of them right by his own interpretation of history, which maintains: "The dynamics of ideas and the dialectics of economic development are parallel processes, both growing out of the original urge of man for freedom."[89] In the opinion of the author this formulation of

Roy is perhaps his most distinctive contribution to the philosophy of history.

THE TELEOS OF HISTORY

The general acceptance of the evolutionary view of history proves that the dynamics of ideas, being manifestations of natural law through human intelligence, unfolds itself independently of sequence of the physical events of history. The autonomy of thought is the foundation of spiritual freedom — the highest ideal of human existence. The ideal of freedom is, therefore, teleos of Radical Humanist historiography. For, according to Roy, "the history of all hitherto existing societies is the history of expanding freedom."

To sum up Roy's philosophy of history, "History is not a mere chronicle of events, not only the story of kings and battles and wars waged, won or lost, nor it is the history of the conflict of classes or the evolution of the forces of production. History is all that, but in addition, history is also the history of the dynamics of ideas."[90] To quote E.P. Thompson. "History is a determinate, not random process; it is made by real flesh and blood people acting in groups, social classes under constraints but nevertheless acting in the exercise of their wills, shaped by perceptions, beliefs, ideas, experiences of the world." Thus, Roy's philosophy of history harmonises humanism with naturalism, freedom with determinism, will with reason and romanticism with rationalism."

STATE ORGANISATION — ROY'S THEORY OF STATE

Significantly, of all the modern Indian political thinkers it was only M.N. Roy who could develop a full-blooded theory of state. He discussed the institution of state in all its aspects — its origin, nature, development, purpose and functions. Besides, he worked out his own scheme of political order. While working out his scheme of political organisation he first of all took up the question of relationship between the state and the individual.

RELATION BETWEEN THE STATE AND THE INDIVIDUAL

The relation between the state and the individual has always been the most obstinate and challenging issue of political philosophy. "The idea of individual liberty and social cohesion, it seems, are in a state of conflict and uneasy compromise. But the proposition that there is essentially a conflict between political organisation and individual liberty is as unsound as it is dangerous, because once it is assumed that the restriction on individual liberty is unavoidable for the sake of collective welfare it follows logically that the absence of one may mean the fullest attainment of the other."[91] The result is that the fundamental principle of political practice of our time is collectivism of one form or other. In this way, the perennial and persistent problem of reconciling individual freedom with the necessity of political organisation remains unsolved. So if collectivism and individualism are supposed to be mutually exclusive principles, the idea of a democratic state is self-contradictory; rather the very notion of democracy is unrealisable. According to Roy, it is on the ground of this unrealistic nature of democratic state that Marx came to the conclusion that the state is nothing but an engine of coercion and that it must be replaced by the dictatorship of the proletariat, although the latter in practice sets individual liberty at naught.

Roy says that "the modern conception of democracy has come to grief because of the contradiction is inherent in its origin. Rousseau, the father of modern democracy, in his notion of General Will, which is the metaphysics of democratic political philosophy, himself provided the sanction and theoretical justification of totalitarianism, though he might not have meant it." His 'Social Contract' (1762) implied complete alienation of individual rights and interests and their sacrifice at the altar of the General Will. "Parliamentary democracy, fascist totalitarianism, proletarian dictatorship all can be referred back to this false notion about the relation between the state and the individual, which is the common point of departure of modern political philosophy. It is this basic fallacy of modern political philosophy which gave rise to totalitarianism whether nationalist and communist, on the one hand, and anarchism, on the other."[92] This also explains why, on the one hand, collectivists like socialists, communists and fascists considered the individual as a mere cog in the wheel of social mechanism while, on the other, the anarchists advocated for the total disappearance of the state.

According to Roy, the effort to rehabilitate democracy must begin with a new approach to the old problem of the relation between the state and the individual. Indeed, for posing the problem properly, it is necessary to go a step further back and begin with an enquiry into the original relation between man and society. Roy clearly states that society is a creation of man. This idea emanates from the scientific theory about the descent of man. "It logically follows from the theory of evolution that mankind at a lower level of development existed before society and state came into being, and that these are human creations. The logical deduction is corroborated empirically by the existence even today of primitive tribes living almost like animal herds."[93] Roy is of the view that man created society in order to conduct his struggle for existence and satisfy his urge for society. He observes: "Society is a creation of man in quest of freedom.

Cooperative social relationships were established originally with the purpose of reinforcing the struggle for existence which the primitive man had undertaken as individual."[94]

Roy states: "Like society, the state is also a human creation. It is the political organisation of human community and its relation with the individual is a continuation of the relation between man and society." Recent anthropological findings have established that man has created society so that his struggle might be more effective in leading society to better survival. Thus, society originated as a voluntary association of individuals. The relation between the state and the individuals logically follows from that empirical fact and therefore the state is also a creation of man. And given this relationship, it is absurd to hold that state can claim subordination of the individuals without revising the relation between the creator and creation.[95] The state is built for man and not man for the state. Here it may be added that, Roy did not envisage any contradiction between the fullest freedom of the individual and a harmonious social order. A social organisation impeding the free development of human personality is opposed to the original purpose for which society was created. "He considered national prosperity and social progress as frauds if they did not aim at progress, prosperity, welfare and freedom of the individuals- the only criterion of measuring social progress."[96]

According to Roy, the individual is both logically and ethically prior to the state. Here it may be pointed out that although in order to defend democracy and freedom Roy very rightly considered individual freedom as ethically prior to social organisation, but he has given no solid evidence to substantiate his view that historically also individual is prior to the society. Roy's view about the origin of society and its relation to the individual appears to be over simplistic, for the accepted view of Sociology is that social life arose out of the extension of the family life or the tribal life. But Roy never explained how the primitive tribes were dissolved into individuals, though he did accept the existence of primitive tribes.[97]

ORIGIN OF THE STATE

Roy further asserts that the primitive state was founded neither as a result of social contract nor as a deliberately created instrument for the domination of society by some individuals or particular classes. It was a spontaneous process promoted almost mechanically by the common realisation of the necessity of cooperation for the security of all concerned. State came into existence in order to fulfil two necessities: (a) the administration of public affairs and the maintenance of law and order;

and (b) the coordination of various departments of social life. The fact that in course of time, the physically stronger and mentally more advanced members assumed the control and leadership of the community does not affect this view about the origin of political organisation and its relation with the individual.[98]

Roy regards man (the individual) as the archetype of society and, like Aristotle, he believes that potentiality of evolving entire social pattern is inherent in every human being and that he can therefore establish a social set up in which he will not have to surrender his individual liberty for the sake of society.

THE CONCEPT OF SOVEREIGNTY

Since the function of social and political organisation was to help the growth of human personality, the state must be organised on the principle that sovereignty belongs to the people, and since the people is composed of individual human beings, therefore, in the last analysis, sovereignty belongs to the individual components of society. According to M.N. Roy, "sovereignty of the individual is the essence of democracy." Although Roy belongs to the category of individualists, his individualism is not to be equated with egocentrism, as his concept of individual freedom is not incompatible with social responsibilities.

Roy critically examined how the concept of people's sovereignty became a constitutional fiction — a pious wish in actual practice. Theoretically, the concept was a promising start but in practice it became a mere formality because human essence of the democratic political philosophy was from the beginning eclipsed by the stark reality of actual life.

The undeniable and inexorable fact of a greatly uneven intellectual and cultural development of the community and of growing population of modern states justified the practice of the delegation of sovereignty by the people at large to a few qualified persons to administer public affairs. These privileged few thus formed the ruling class, and for all practical purposes deprived the rest of the community of their sovereign right to rule themselves. Thus, according to Roy, "From its very birth modern democracy was haunted by the ghost of Rousseau's totalitarianism. The apparently unavoidable, and therefore, plausible, practice of delegation of sovereignty amounted to total alienation of particular interests to the General will, as advocated thoughtlessly by the romantic prophet of an ill-fated democracy."[99]

According to Roy, another fact which brought democratic practice to the present undesirable level is the rise of the nation state. The misalliance with nationalism put into the concept of democracy a collective connotation. The nation is conceived as a metaphysical concept and is considered greater than the sum total of its component units. Here can be located for democracy the point of departure from its humanist tradition. It is because of this that economic human beings were counted as so many hands and political human beings, so many heads to be coerced and cajoled at the time of election. A return to the humanist approach to the fundamental problem of political philosophy, indeed, a revival of the humanist view of life as a whole, therefore, is the condition for the rehabilitation of democracy and for making it a reality.[100]

THE IDEAL OF EQUALITY

The ideal of equality of men, Roy believes, need no longer be a mere make believe by formal declaration in the constitution. "It can be attained in increasing degree of approximation because human being, as biological units, are endowed with equal potentialities of development in every respect."[101] To help the free unfolding of these human potentialities is the function of social organisation.

THE PURPOSE OF STATE

The purpose of state, according to Roy, is to regulate political organisation in such a manner as to promote general welfare without any prejudice to the freedom of the individual. The state is meant "to create conditions in which the individual can enjoy widening measure of freedom, to maintain harmony in social relations and to coordinate the activities of diverse and autonomous institutions. "Since social cooperation regulated by democratic laws facilitates the unfolding of the potentialities of human existence, freedom of the individual cannot be inconsistent with social organisation."[102] Thus, according to Roy, democracy is not a far cry, if the humanist philosophy is accepted; it is a practicable proposition and not merely an idealistic belief. His philosophy considers that man is rational as well as creative, and therefore, it hopes that the ideal of democracy is within the reach of practical possibility. Roy proposes that the state should be so organised that democracy may cease to be just a mass of passive voters, manipulated and swayed by political parties scrambling for power. This can be achieved by reintroducing the system of direct democracy. Roy maintains that even in the large political units and highly complex social organisation, as obtaining today, direct democracy is possible in the form of a network of cooperative commonwealths, which will replace the helpless atomised voters of formal parliamentary democracy. The new structure of the state will prevent the recent tendency of centralisation of power, as the latter amounts to negation of democracy.

PARTY SYSTEM AND DEMOCRATIC GOVERNMENT

Since Roy advocates a decentralised political and economic structure in order to safeguard individual freedom, a system which leads to concentration of power can find no place in this set up. As such, political parties will have to go in this set up, because the primary aim of all parties is to capture power and to entrench it by centralising the whole machinery of the state.

But political parties are generally considered to be indispensable in modern times. According to Bryce, "Party organisation is a natural and probably an inevitable incident of democratic government."[103] Specially in the contemporary world, politics has been so associated with the party system that we cannot think of carrying on political administration with out parties. Roy, however, rejects this popular notion and conceives the possibility of politics without parties.

Democracy demands rule of the people or people's government. But according to Roy, "From the very birth modern democratic government in reality came to be government for the people instead of being of the people and by the people. The people thus shorn of their sovereignty were condemned to the position of the ruled."[104]

REPRESENTATIVE GOVERNMENT AND POLITICAL PARTIES

According to Roy, the concept of representative government is a negation of popular sovereignty, as it necessarily entails the delegation of power to popular representatives. But this delegation of power in essence becomes abdication of power. It is this system of representative government that gave rise to the growth of political parties. Under this system the sovereignty of the people, in actual practice, is transferred to a group of politicians who run the government machinery. But the representative government strikes at the very root of democracy, a the latter postulates individual sovereignty. "A representative government, really speaking, represents only the party which controls it, and the membership of even the largest party is only a fraction of the people"[105], and thus by no stretch of imagination it is the rule of the people. It is at best the rule of a minority.

Roy asserts that it is absurd to associate democracy with the party system, because this notion ignores the fact that political parties are relatively recent institutions. Political parties, as we know them today, are a development only of the nineteenth century. Although the fundamental principle of democracy is that the sovereign power belongs to the people, the people are no where in this scramble for power to which politics has been debased by the party system. The essence of democracy is diffusion of power which means its decentralization. Concentration of power, on the contrary, leads to dictatorship or authoritarianism. This may not be apparent on account of formalities but this smoke-screen does not last long in actual practice. The electorate delegates its sovereign power to a party and only a few members of the party are represented in parliament. Here also fewer still actually compose the government and wield actual power. So at best parliamentary democracy can only be 'benevolent despotism'.

EVILS OF PARTY SYSTEM

The evils of party system are well-known and quite apparent. But in the opinion of Roy, it has two main defects: Firstly, the primary aim of every party, irrespective of description, is to capture power whether through a revolution or through constitutional means. Secondly, the delegation of power by the people necessarily leads to a scramble for power among the contending political parties, and the success in this struggle goes to the party which makes the most skillful use of people's weaknesses. Narrow nationalism, parochialism, ethnic, community and caste prejudices, etc., being the weakness of most of the people, political parties become the champion of such prejudices in order to capture power. Though political parties are formed professing certain doctrines with the object of introducing specific socio-economic programme for the good of the people, yet every party thinks that it should be in office and control the reins of government in order to put its programme into practice. But once it is assumed that nothing can be done for the good of the community without first attaining power by a party, the evils of the party system necessarily follow. The capture of government being a precondition for doing anything everything must be done to capture power. Thus the means become the end, and the end is forgotten. Politics is divorced from morality, and the end justifies the means.[106] The party system has a corrupting influence on the party members due to other reasons as well. The term of holding office being limited, the first and primary concern for politicians in power is to have a second or more terms, and in order to do that they indulge in all sorts of demagogy, giving populist slogans and presenting a rosy picture of days ahead. This breeds dishonesty and to compete dishonest persons in a dishonest system one must come down to their level if one wants to succeed. No one who is involved in such affairs can go uncontaminated by the corrupting atmosphere around. Even the best of men suffer moral degradation under the influence of party politics. It is therefore not accidental that mediocrity, political careerism, rank opportunism, sycophancy and demagogy are rampant within all parties without exception. The politician all over the world has become a "non-person", to use Vaclav Havel's apt expression. The elimination of party system therefore becomes a precondition for purifying politics. As long as there are political parties, politics cannot be immune to evil practices like casteism, communalism, criminality and corruption.

But mere disgust with power politics or disenchantment with politics and politicians will produce no results, for politics is a social necessity and society cannot do away with political organisations. The state must be there and government must be carried on: Since in the present system of representative government party system is unavoidable, Roy thought of reorganising the whole existing structure of the state, and came to the conclusion that "a constitutional structure based on an even distribution of power can alone purify politics and such a democratic order is possible if the individual is restored to his place of primacy."[107] Roy therefore devised a new type of state structure so that under it power may remain with the people who will directly control the state and have participation in the government. The state, according to this scheme, will be based on the foundation of a network of locally organised democracies. Sovereignty will belong to the entire people, and sovereign power shall express itself through local people's committees in villages, towns and cities. He further visualised that in course of time political parties will be eliminated and replaced by a network of people's committees at the grass roots level. These people's committees would remain vested with a great deal of effective power, and such power as may have to be exercised at higher centres would be in the hands of persons elected as representatives of the people's committees, These representatives would remain answerable to people's committees and the people's sovereignty over them may, when necessary, be exercised by suitable methods such as those of recall and referendum. This, according to Roy, would be a real participatory democracy. To Roy, such a state alone will be a truly democratic state — the political organisation of a free society.

Roy believed that a decentralised state of local republics must come into existence to safeguard the interest of democracy. Being reared upon a broad foundation of direct democracies the state will really become democratic and thus a pluralistic modern society can be built up at the same time doing away with centralisation of power in politics and economics.

FUNCTIONS OF THE RADICAL DEMOCRATIC STATE

This decentralisation of power will mean that the state power will be minimised and its functions will be limited. Roy believes that it is not difficult to conceive of a time when he state will again revert to its previous position instead of becoming a leviathan. But, according to him, it will not necessarily be a stateless society without any public administration. He suggests that we shall have to search for the ways and means to reduce the functions of the state to the minimum; in other words, restore it to its native functions of coordinating the various functions of different autonomous social institutions. But here it may be pointed out that the various institutions, economic, political, cultural and educational, etc. are so inter-related that to coordinate them would mean substantially to control them.

The means to bring about such a democratic order, Roy thinks, is not by capturing power but by making the people conscious of the desirability of such a state, and to enable them to perform these functions. The programme of the capture of power is thus replaced by a programme of the education of the people. Roy believed that the spread of education (not in the academic sense) is the precondition for the successful working of democracy.

ECONOMIC REORGANISATION — ROY'S ECONOMIC IDEAS

Radical democracy presupposes economic reorganisation of society so as to eliminate the possibility of exploitation of man by man. Progressive satisfaction of material necessities is the precondition for the individual members of society unfolding their intellectual and other finer human potentialities. Economic liberation of the masses is the essential condition for the advance towards the goal of freedom.[108]

It is now universally recognised that man is a social being or a community-building animal and that it is not possible for man to exist by himself. The diverse needs make the individual mutually dependent, and if such interdependence is developed intelligently it creates a congenial atmosphere for the development of each individual. Roy holds that man, being rational, will take an enlightened view of his needs as well as those of others.

Roy's approach to all social phenomena, including economic, is based on the maxim that "man is the measure of all things." This approach is applied to the problem of economic reorganisation as well. Since the individual alone possesses the capacity to feel wants and their satisfaction, the idea of economic welfare means nothing but the satisfaction of an increasing range of wants of the individual. Thus, the actual welfare enjoyed by the individual consistent with the ideal of freedom is the true measure of economic progress and the acid test of the efficiency of the economic system. Therefore, any economic reorganisation must be guided by the requirements of the individual. "The concept of national prosperity and social progress that ignores individual welfare and freedom is rather a kind of fraud and delusion."[109] But Roy points out that economic welfare is not an end itself, and therefore, the moral values and human needs should not be disregarded, in the name of economic welfare.

The approach of all other major schools of economic thought was however different. For instance, the classical school of economic thought believed that self-interest, free competition and profit motive governed the economic life of the individual. Naturally, for them to maintain this idea of competition as far as possible was the only way of promoting economic progress. Since their concept of man was an economic man, their study of economic phenomenon made on the basis of this concept was bound to be fallacious because the economic practices (under laissez faire economy) sanctified by this concept came in conflict with the non-economic needs of mankind.

Later on, the Marxist school of economic thought condemned the laissez faire economy and instead advocated the socialist system of economy. But actually, this was only a special version of the concept of "economic man," the only difference being that economic competition was between classes rather than between individuals, as was the case in the classical economic theory. Thus, we see that the competitive theory of human nature in one form or the other remained common to both. The two major economic systems hitherto obtaining, namely, capitalism and socialism have the same roots in this respect. But such a theory of human nature regarding man as a selfish animal guided essentially by his narrow self-interest and not by enlightened self-interest and urge for freedom, as determined by his rationality, is bound to subordinate the individual to some abstraction and to deny his claim to freedom.

Modern knowledge of man has definitely demonstrated that homosapiens are more comprehensive and complex than the homo-economicus, which is the point of departure of almost all schools of economic thought and that economic activity is only a part of total activities of man. "The obvious error of these economic philosophies was to confuse the totality of man with one of his facets and to reduce the multi-fold potentialities of homosapiens to one of its more obvious expressions."[110] Economic activity, however, is in no way more important than other activities.

Roy points out that economic progress is largely dependent upon the progress of human knowledge and culture. He believes that the rational in man makes him seek harmony and moral good. Therefore economic activity should not be divorced from moral values.

ROY'S VIEWS ON SHORT-COMINGS OF CAPITALISM

The evils of capitalism are well-known to be recounted here. It is a matter of common knowledge that capitalistic system goes through ups and downs, and recurring depressions and recessions cause immense loss to the community as a whole. Besides, it is also marked by gross inequality, monopolistic control of production and limitations of production by actual purchasing power, under-consumption, mass unemployment and rampant scams and scandals.

Another vice of the capitalist economy is the lack of good planning and efficient allocation of resources. The experience of its working has shown that it can offer no solution to modern economic crisis whatever modifications may be made in this system.

In order to overcome the inherent contradictions of capitalism, socialism has proposed a socialistic mode of production by instituting state ownership of means of production and distribution. As a natural corollary to it, a centralised economic planning is advocated in place of private enterprise.

But to Roy, state ownership and planned economy do not necessarily lead to an equal distribution of wealth. The only difference is that in the capitalist system the exploiter is some private owner, whereas under socialism it is the state which plays the same role. Roy believes that capitalism and communism are not fundamentally opposed to each other but are born from the same root. According to him, capitalism and communism "being variants of the same theme, the conflict between them is a blood feud and not a contest between two antithetical philosophies of life."

While disapproving the Marxian economy Roy also rejects the Marxian theory of surplus value. He observes: "The theory that production of surplus value is the specific feature of capitalism and represents the exploitation of the working class is the fundamental fallacy of the Marxist economics,"[111] for under socialism also the producer is not given the full value of his labour. Then again, to Roy there is nothing wrong with the social surplus as such, and he points out that without this social surplus social progress would not have been possible in history. Ancient civilisations have disappeared from history owing to inadequacy or shrinkage of social surplus.[112.]

Roy further points out that planned economy on the basis of socialised (nationalised) industries presupposes a powerful political machinery. Democratic control of that machinery alone can guarantee freedom under the new order. State control of the economic as well as other aspects of social life means so much concentration of power that it rules out the possibility of democratic freedom. Further, it is an unfounded assumption that state planning necessarily leads to economic democracy and social justice. "Economic democracy is no more possible in the absence of political democracy than the latter is in the absence of the former."[113]

The experience of he last few decades has now shown that the socialist system has proved a miserable failure. The collapse of the Soviet Union within 75 years of its establishment has conclusively established that the Marxian method of establishing socialism on the basis of dictatorship, denial of freedom of the individual, and controlled state-planned economy is not at all a reliable method for attaining the laudable objectives of socialism; viz, an egalitarian society. The Soviet system has utterly failed to usher in freedom of individuals, equality and economic prosperity of the people.

Thus, while free competition or monopolies of capitalism lead to waste, misery, chaos, socialism of all varieties leads to regimentation, bureaucratisation, exploitation, corruption and encroachment on liberty. According to Roy, since each leads to an impasse, there is nothing to choose between the two systems.

Roy, therefore, rejects both capitalism as well socialism. But while rejecting them Roy makes full use of some positive elements found in them for economic reorganisation. From capitalism he borrows the idea that every individual should be assured the conditions of self-maintenance. For this, he must have access to the means of production but without the scope of exploitation. From socialism Roy takes its moral appeal and its proposal to organise economic activity with the purpose of meeting human demand; that is, production for use and not for profit. So if economic activity is to have moral sanction it ought to be conducted in a rational cooperative manner. The idea of planning resulted from this very consideration and so had its appeal for Roy. But Roy rejects the negative side of both the systems. For him, the important requirements of a sound economic system is the mutual adjustment between freedom and planning. Both freedom and planning represent organisational ideals which are admitted to be essential to human progress. Economic activities should be planned for producing more wealth, for giving greater scope to the initiative, capacity and freedom of the individual. Therefore, he says that a new economic system has to be devised.

The economy of the new society will, on the one hand, eliminate production for profit and, on the other hand, avoid unnecessary concentration of control. It will not allow individual freedom to be jeopardised by considerations of technological efficiency. As such, the economy will be neither capitalist nor socialist but cooperative. It will consist of a network of consumers' and producers' cooperatives. The cooperative economy shall take full advantage of modern science and technology and effect equitable distribution of social surplus through universal social utility services.

PLANNED COOPERATIVE SYSTEM OF ECONOMY

The rational essence of planning, according to Roy, is intelligent coordination which presupposes cooperation. As such, planning must be the result of voluntary cooperation and not imposition by some central authority. Again, planning will develop from the bottom upwards. Under this kind of planning production is to be planned not with the object of increasing the purchasing power of the people but with that of supplying their requirements. The object is not to create effective demand but to estimate human demand and to equate production with it.[114]

As regards the problem of ownership, cooperative ownership and cooperative operation of means of production, and cooperative enterprise and direction of economic activities are to be the fundamental features of such a system. In the cooperative sector, surplus will be held jointly and allotted locally or regionally according to a broad plan which may be formulated by consultation among representatives of cooperatives, assisted by expert from time to time. Such a procedure will avoid concentration of economic power, exploitation of man by man, wastage of resources and labours and ensure a balanced development of economic activities as well as economic efficiency.[115]

Another important issue of economic life is that of incentive. Under capitalism it is the profit motive which governs entire economic system. Under the cooperative system production will be for use and not for profit. Therefore, under this system incentive can be effective only if the narrow incentive of selfishness is replaced by rational common sense and sound incentive of benevolence and cooperation, which alone can contribute to the genuine self-development.[116]

THE PROBLEM OF ORGANISING PRODUCTION

Modern economic organisations suffer from tendency towards centralisation and this is due primarily to the technological development. Collective ownership and command economy necessarily lead to centralisation. But due to modern technology and methods of splitting up of the process of production on an intensive division of labour, it is now possible to decentralise industry without reverting to the primitive or medieval economy. Unlike Gandhi, Roy is not against modernisation of industries. He believes that it is possible to avoid the evils of industrialisation as well as the backwardness of medieval economic organisation. In an economy which makes use of developed technology, problem of size of the production unit assumes great significance. Roy warns: "If the size is too big the individual initiative, personal stake and feelings of direct interest are lost and actual producer is turned into a mere cog in the complex machine."[117] Cooperative ownership and enterprise will be an appropriate way of solving this difficulty. A genuine economic democracy can function in such cooperatives endeavours, because in it the desires and needs of the people will get full expression and satisfaction. The local and regional cooperatives will be able to give more attention to the rational adjustments of the demands of each group and to the relative magnitude of economic resources which are to be devoted to consumption and capital formation respectively.

ADVANTAGES OF COOPERATIVE ECONOMY

A great advantage of cooperative economy is that under it decentralised production, through local economic organisation, makes allocation of resources more perfect than in the case of production under centralised economy. This is so, because local or regional cooperatives are in a position to have more knowledge of their own geographic and economic resources than any central administrative apparatus. Similarly, the needs of economy will be expressed through consumer cooperatives. Most of the prime necessities of life will be satisfied by local production and consumption and the surplus will be transported to and fro by cooperative trade channels.

Roy suggests that economic reconstruction must begin from the bottom. The direct producers themselves should be encouraged to build up local economic organisations entirely relying on their own resources; capital investment will be raised locally through cooperative societies. Cooperative societies will be the basic units of a truly democratic state. "The capitalistic system may not be able to hold its own against a truly democratic order."[118] But it is to be noted that these cooperative communes should not be like the self-sufficient village economy of the old. As the constituent units of national economy, they will be interdependent. integrated in a larger cooperative community. "The archaic system will break down because of the impossibility to compete with a non-profit making economy sustained by the cooperative efforts of practically the entire society."[119]

The functions of the cooperatives will cover diverse aspects of economic activities. There will be multipurpose cooperative societies which will perform all essential functions of an economic unit and will be directly controlled and managed by its members. The multipurpose cooperatives as units of the economic order will be autonomous institutions mutually adjusting and accommodating their activities through regional and central boards as well as conferences and consultations.

ECONOMIC ROLE OF THE STATE

Under the new economic order "the role of the state in economic affairs would be confined to public finance. It will raise and spend funds for its purely political functions."[120] Thus we see that in this system of economy, "the state is deprived of direction, control, superintendence, regulation, interference and ownership in economic matters." But it is to be noted that some state interference in economic affairs is unavoidable. The state will have to intervene not only to avoid inflation and industrial stagnation, but to grant relief against the increasing scale of unemployment. In developing countries, state interference is essential for increasing employment opportunities and relieving poverty.

To conclude, it is noticed that M.N. Roy only lays down some fundamentals of economics and leaves ample scope for necessary institutional modifications in his economic framework. However, it becomes clear from the examination of Roy's system of economy that Roy is actuated by a strong desire in propounding a scheme of economic reorganisation which would eradicate the evils which he finds inherent in the contemporary economy systems. But realistically speaking, it seems that his scheme of economic decentralisation and local planning by local people can be practised only to a very limited extent. To talk about cooperative economy in the modern world which is globalising at a rapid rate on the basis of a market friendly economy is not a realistic proposition. In the light of recent trends towards economic organisation on global scale and the growth of multinational corporations, his scheme will have few takers. But at the same time, it is also being increasingly realised that contemporary capitalism cannot be given free rein to exploit the consumers in developed countries and the peoples of the developing world.

TECHNIQUE OF REVOLUTION AND RECONSTRUCTION

It has been noticed that the aim of Roy's political philosophy is to reconstruct a new society. Broadly speaking, there are two ways of reconstruction: One is by evolution and the other is by revolution. Roy, however, adopts the method of revolution for the reconstruction of new society. But his concept and technique of revolution is different from the orthodox one.

THE NATURE OF REVOLUTION

Social convulsions take place when old forms exhaust all possibility of peacefully adjusting themselves to the pressure of new forces and fail to resolve their internal conflicting tendencies by outgrowing their inadequacies. So when the course of social evolution is somehow held up, social explosions become imperative. To put it differently, "the slowness of evolution is the cause of revolution"

According to Roy, there are two factors which go to make a revolution: The first is the complete exhaustion of existing forms; outgrown institutional framework and anachronistic technical systems and side by side, there is accumulation of new forces so developed as to be able to force a break-up of inhibitions and obstructions found in the old forms. Besides, a general mass discontent is also required to develop simultaneously with the emergence of the new social group representing the new force. Simultaneously, with it there is another factor which is distinct but not dualistic development and unless this development takes place no revolution is possible. It begins with a number of individuals, inspired by the ideal of freedom and social good, strongly sensitive to their absence in the existing order, highly rational and morally integrated, who understand the deficiencies of the present order, formulate the pattern of the next stage of social development and who then begin their work of systematic propaganda, or launch their movement in an organised way.

Similarly, the factors that become an obstacle in the way of social progress can be divided mainly under two heads. On the one hand, there is the factor of the biological inertia which is inherent in the organism of the people which takes the form of what Erich Fromme calls "fear of freedom" and preference for fixed grooves. On the other hand, there is institutional inertia which takes the form of vested interests. The first obstacle, according to Roy, can be removed only through social and philosophical renaissance and irradiation of knowledge and, the second one through technological development and equitable distribution of power. Thus, any scheme of social revolution must incorporate the task of cultural renaissance, technological development and politico-economic democratisation of power and control.[121]

However, unlike Marx, Roy does not believe that every social change is for progress. A convulsion takes a revolutionary significance only when the leadership of the subversive force is consciously oriented by the incentive of greater freedom and better social harmonisation. Roy further adds that although in a social change having a progressive significance, the decisive influence is that of reason, science and individuality, yet the structural setting for such social emergence is also influenced by the existing technology and social institutions.

Roy also differs fundamentally from Marx as regards the human composition of the forces of revolution. For Roy, the revolutionary force is not confined to any particular section or class. He believes that the revolutionary organisation in order to achieve real success must include all people except the few who have vested interest in the status quo. Roy further contends that revolution is a social phenomenon and takes place out of necessity. But the revolution must have for its success programmes which promise to the common people greater freedom and social good. Roy is of the view that the ideological initiative of the revolution can come only from such people who have outgrown, in their character, the influence of mass inertia and who have outgrown their class limitations and can therefore think in terms of the good of human society as a whole. He emphasises this because his contention is that the necessity for the change of the established social relations and political institutions is consciously felt only by a comparatively few. He seems to be very impressed by the role of this classless intellectual aristocracy in the history of revolutions that he goes so far as to say that "a revolution is acceleration of tempo of the evolutionary process brought about by the will of a minority."[122] He reiterates that the classless intelligentsia has the most decisive importance in social history, because it consists of persons who are the most freedom loving and socially minded section of the society. Its members are capable of rational thinking and choice. It is through them that the dynamism of ideas operates. The whole history shows that it was the members of the intelligentsia that fought and shed their blood against obsolete social institutions since Vedic times. The reason why they always become the spearhead or vanguard of any revolutionary struggle can be ascribed to the advanced knowledge and reasoning power which enables them to understand earlier than others the contradictions involved in the decadent system and visualise the probable alternative to it. "They embody the essential qualities of a revolutionary which are rationality, understanding, creative imagination, moral idealism, sensitiveness and integrity. The harbingers of revolution can only be such people who are highly developed both morally as well as intellectually"[123] The pioneers of revolution can only be those who have creative thought, and creative thought is conceived by the creative mind and not by the community, though conditions favouring its reception, spread and persistence are also necessary for the success of a revolution.

But no social revolution is ever automatic or inevitable as some revolutionary teleologists or dialectical materialists believe. Social change is not a necessary consequence of causal logic. "It agent-principle is rational choice and organised endeavour by the human constituents of social life."[124] A mechanically caused structural change may have little revolutionary or progressive significance. Take the case of the Russian revolution, the failure of which is now universally acknowledged after the collapse of the Soviet Union.

EXISTING TECHNIQUES OF REVOLUTION

Political thinkers generally prescribe two ways of effecting a revolution — one is insurrectionary and the other is constitutional. The former means forcible capture of power, and this method is strongly advocated by the communists and the fascists. The latter implies utilisation of the formal opportunities offered by existent law of the state to bring about change in the state machinery. That is, the first is the path of organised violence resorted to by a small band of disciplined revolutionaries and the second is the path of loosely organised gradualists who prefer to pay in terms of time what they imagine to gain in economy of human resources. But to Roy, "the insurrectionary method is inadequate as a technique for the capture of power, because the vastly increased might and coercive strength of the modern state renders the idea of a minority insurrection impractical and out of date. "Modern states are possessed of such a formidable armed forces that any attempt of a minority to capture power by armed insurrection is bound to be crushed."[125] Further, the insurrectionary method, even if practicable, is a risky and chaotic process, and is more prone to bring into being a new group of political vested interests than of making the social order more liberal and democratic. In this context, Roy refers to the French Revolution which gave birth to a "Reign of Terror" and later to Napoleanism. So was the case with the Bolshevik Revolution. Thus, revolution brought about by the insurrectionary method results in the emergence of personal or group or party dictatorship which, after suppressing all the opposite forces, becomes reactionary. It only creates a new system of political domination, cultural regimentation and economic enslavement. Roy was opposed to cataclysmic way of revolution particularly for two reasons: "Firstly, his historicism taught him that history has not been marked by periods of total break. Nowhere there has been such a thing that an entire old order has been abolished or something entirely new had come into its place. He emphasised that we should give up the idea that there can be no change unless whatever exists is first destroyed, for it is possible to create something good in the midst of an established order, and secondly, this way compels us too often to use those means that do not lead to good ends."

The constitutional method, on the other hand, possess little potentiality or strength by itself, and has been found utterly ineffective when employed against a militant state machinery.

In the light of his own long and wide experience in so many revolutions, Roy ruled out both the techniques of revolution. The proper method of revolution in our time, Roy felt, must be something novel, incorporating some of the merits of both these techniques. He, therefore, offers a new method of revolution. It is new in the sense that it is democratic not only in its incentive and object but also in its means and methods. It learns from insurrection the value of organisation and militant action and from constitutionalism the importance and desirability of utilising all the formal or dejure potentialities of the existing social structure effectively. Thus, Roy's technique of revolution is a sort of synthesis of the positive achievements of both the methods.

The bearings of Roy's philosophy on the method of achieving social change are probably the most important and significant, and constitute a major departure from most of the views concerning it. His philosophy is an activist or better a creativist one and so implies creative action. But the action which it implies is very different from those employed by other techniques of social reconstruction. The commonly adopted method of social reconstruction in our time is first to bring about changes in laws and institutions of society, and to bring about these changes it is believed that a political party wedded to a revolutionary programme must come to power by any means fair or foul. In this strategy, the capture of political power is made sinequanon for realising justice in social relations and institutions.

But such a technique of social change is inconsistent with the ideals Roy stands for. According to him, to start social change from changes in institutions and laws is to start from a wrong end, because it ignores the fact that behind these institutions are men and ideas. Alterations of institutions and laws may bring about certain superficial and outward changes but they cannot usher in new life. Changes in state structure and economic system by themselves do not lead to a higher civilisation. The danger of the external method of transformation consists in the fact that it only outwardly changes without really transforming men.

Therefore, the method and programme of social revolution, Roy argues, must be based on a reassertion of the basic principles of social progress — freedom, reason and social harmony.

Broadly speaking, the method of revolution which Roy suggests falls into two parts. The first is that of socio-cultural renaissance which can only come through determined and wide-spread endeavour to educate the people in the principles of freedom and rational cooperative living. Roy therefore pleads for a cultural movement as the first step. This movement is meant for strengthening the foundations of democracy among the people — the values of liberty, equality and fraternity — and for promoting humanist values like rationalism, secularism and scientific outlook.

Concurrently with it there is the necessity of organising people into effective democratic bodies, on the one hand, and to build up socio-political foundations of post-revolutionary order, on he other. So the political struggle for social emancipation will be synchronously supplemented by a countrywide renaissance movement and the latter will go hand in hand with the process of politico-economic organisation of the people on democratic lines. That is, simultaneously with the broad cultural movement, democratic institutions based on the participation of more and more people in the administration of social affairs shall have to be built up. These institutions, which will be known as people's committees, shall be the effective centres of organised democracy bridging in the process of the growth and development the existing gap between the state and society.

Thus, Radical Humanist way of revolution implies constant and relentless struggle against the existent versed interests; it means increasing participation of the people in the struggle; it works by building up the foundations of an organised democratic society in the course of the struggle.

Here it is necessary to mention the relationship of the new renaissance men with the people's committees. The first task of the leaders of the movement will be to educate the common people in the fundamental task of running their social life themselves. It will bring them the opportunity of training themselves about their affairs. It will give them guidance in effecting a social renaissance without which democracy can never be achieved. They will teach the people to think for themselves to resist the easy temptation of relying on political leadership. The next task of the movement will be to develop a sufficiently large cadre from the common people who consider freedom and social progress to be the greatest values of life and also through their integrity, rationalism and organisation will form a strong bulwark against the opposition of the vested interests. "An increasing large number of men, conscious of their creative power, motivated by the indomitable will to remake the world, moved by the adventure of ideas, and fired with the idea of a free society of free men can create the conditions under which real democracy will be possible."[126]

Here it is worth noting that Roy has given to the idea of Plato's "philosopher king" a place of honour in his political thought. The task of these philosophers will be an approximately correct formulation of a scientific philosophy in the contemporary context. They will have to bring about a renaissance of the creative spirit in the entire humanity. In other words, the philosophy of revolution must spread among the common people, must go to orient their whole outlook of life, must permeate the whole pattern of interpersonal relationship. In short, they must revolutionise the whole outlook of the people. This revolution in outlook, according to Roy, will mean a romantic confidence in man's creative ability, democratic aliveness to personal responsibility, scientific mentality of coherent thinking, moral acceptance of personal happiness and growth as the criterion of good and of consistency between knowledge and conduct as essential to that growth, and finally a rational recognition of the need of a free moral society to secure a happy normal life for the individual himself. This permeation of social ethics by the ideas of a revolutionary philosophy is what Roy describes as a social renaissance or a philosophical revolution. It is a well known fact that almost all great social changes are preceded by a philosophical revolution. To illustrate, the ground for the French Revolution was prepared long before 1789 and this preparation was the work of the Philosophies of the Encyclopaedists. Similarly, the Russian Revolution (1917) was the result of the revolutionary ideas of communism which was evolved in the latter part of the nineteenth century by Marx and Engels.

To sum up, Roy adopts the method of revolution to realise his aim of reconstructing the present society. However, it is worth noting that his technique of revolution does not preach violence at any stage. His criterion of a revolution is that it aims at greater freedom for a significant part of society sufficiently large to make the whole society freer than it was before. Of course, according to this criterion, Roy's technique of social change is revolutionary in essence. But if revolution simply means a sudden or cataclysmic change, his technique becomes evolutionary, for it implies a long term process of social change. This approach of Roy makes him a reformist rather than a revolutionary though he has been an advocate of radical change. Agreeing with Roshwald, Roy believed that "The most successful revolutions are achieved by evolutionary means". However, it may be pointed out that there is little inspiration or excitement for the common man in the strategy of action suggested by M.N. Roy.

PEACE AND INTERNATIONALISM

Today, mankind has reached a point when events or forces originating at any one place on the globe are bound to affect the lives of men and policies of states everywhere. The time is past when any national unit could be self-sufficient and function prosperously and securely from the rest of mankind. It is no more possible for men and nations to live in isolation. Globalism has become the order of the day. The world has shrunk so as to become a "global village".

Strikingly, nearly fifty years back Roy was fully conscious of this trend in human thought and took due note of it while dealing with the problem of international peace in his scheme of thought. He observed that humanity having learned through centuries of bitter experience, was now beginning to realise the necessity of forgetting differences and emphasising affinities in order to come closer to one another with the object of inheriting the achievements of the evolution of human race, which are the common heritage of all. He stated: "in this period of history a growing number of people are beginning to realise that there is common bond of humanity among the various members of human race and the idea of internationalism or the idea of making the human race into one fraternity, is gaining ground in place of the old parochial, selfish, narrow-minded nationalism, which has caused so much misfortune and misery to the world"[127] Almost everywhere the feeling is growing that beyond all questions of national self-interest people have a moral obligation to humanity as a whole.

The present situation of mankind is characterised by the desire for a world organisation; some sort of global order has become imperative in our time. It is imperative mainly for two reasons. Firstly, to resolve the conflict of national interests and secondly, the continuous internationalisation of our life, specially in matters of economic development, international trade, protection of human rights, the development of education and culture and many others, require concerted attention on an international scale. To these reasons may be added the whole existing paraphernalia of mass destruction which has made it a matter of stark necessity, if mankind is to survive.

But Roy did not fail to observe that beneath the superficial unity of industrial civilisation of our time lie ancient interests, habits and passions which divide peoples and perpetuate conflicts. For all its material progress the world is still divided by innumerable differences of language, religion, race, tradition and economic condition. It is these forces which make the task of international cooperation infinitely harder than the task of cooperation within a national community.

According to Roy, the two fundamental notions governing international relations being those of nationalism and power, cooperation between nations is a self-contradictory concept, as they divide mankind and undermine the faith in common humanity. Both nationalism and power are essentially divisive and disintegrating forces and therefore they are against the interest of humanity.

THE NOTION OF NATIONALISM

Regarding nationalism, Roy observes that so long as it implied only an aspiration of a certain people or a nation to be free from the control of any foreign power it had no dangerous significance. It was rather an elevating concept, a revolutionary and liberal creed, but today nationalism does not connote any such idea, It has now become a sort of cultural ideal. But how did this concept come to acquire this new meaning? Roy says that it is the logical development of the idea of the nation-state. The idea of nation-state necessarily involves the idea of national sovereignty. The theorists of the French Revolution supported the idea of popular sovereignty which was deduced from the theory of General Will of Rousseau. The French Revolution also linked the idea of sovereign nation with the idea of popular sovereignty, and thus popular sovereignty came to mean national sovereignty in due course of time. In this way, the idea of national sovereignty is the logical consequence of the idea of nation-state. Nation being a collectivist concept the claims of "fatherhood" or "motherhood" are attributed to it, with the result the idea of people as such has gone by the board. Nations are treated like parents and this personification of the nation-state is strengthened by the use of symbols like the national flag., the national anthem and the Head of the nation-state. Though aware of the progressive role played by nationalism in the past, Roy cautioned against its aggressive aspect. In this context Roy holds that of all nationalisms, cultural nationalism is the worst, because it shuts the society into a shell and makes it not only narrow but also aggressive. It eventually leads to militarism and fundamentalism.

It is notable that of all the Indian leaders it was Roy who came out boldly and strongly against cultural nationalism. But now the relevance of his views is being appreciated. It was in this context that Roy described nationalism as an anachronism, "a reactionary" or "antiquated cult." In his view, nationalism and cosmopolitanism work at cross purpose with each other.

But since even now the political unit of international organisation is the sovereign nation-state, the idea of sovereignty as a basic notion in international organisation is bound to introduce irresponsibility, collective selfishness and aggressiveness in international dealings. For once the idea of national sovereignty is theoretically granted in international organisation and international relationship, the seed of discord is sown with all its consequences. The interests of the individual and the claims of humanity alike are disregarded in the face of absolute claims of nation. Therefore, the ideal of peace is incompatible with the idea of national sovereignty and nationalism. So the most difficult barrier in the way of world community is the rigidity of state communities. Thus the foundation of a realistic approach to international politics is a recognition of a fact that the principle of national sovereignty is fatal to all prospects of peace.

THE NOTION OF POWER

The second governing principle of international relations is power. According to Schwarzenberger, "Power politics has been a constant feature of international relations throughout the ages."[128] The cult of power is a concept related with nationalism, because the greatness or prestige of a nation is measured in terms of power, and the power of a nation is generally supposed to consist in its armed strength, its economic hold over others. or of feeding its war machine or its manpower with reference to its ability and intensity of desire to sacrifice itself for the greatness or glory of the nation. That is, in the comity of nations the prestige of a nation depends upon its power content. Naturally, guided by this notion each nation aspires to be great by any means and often at the cost of others, and there is no limit to this aspiration. As a result, power politics on an international scale is let loose and with it the chances of war. So the accumulation of power becomes the primary, though by no means exclusive, end of foreign policy, for which every other consideration in the realm of international relations is subordinated.

Thus, it is clear that in the field of internationalism what exists in reality is the nation-state. Here people, deal not with men but with nations and geographical entities. The underlying basic human relations between countries; namely, that each nation is composed of living human beings who are in essence one and the same is forgotten. Therefore, in order to develop international cooperation, Roy suggests to reject the disintegrating concept of nationalism and power, because it give us the ambition of collectively becoming great, while as individuals we actually find ourselves increasingly helpless and powerless. We mistake the greatness and powerfulness of the state for the greatness of the people.

NEW WORLD ORDER

In view of the failure of internationalism, Roy suggests a new world order. In working out the scheme of a new world order, Roy goes at the root of the problem concerning organisation. First, he questions the aim of any social organisation, and says that cooperation between men is necessary for their mutual progress. The need for cooperation arises from the recognition of individuals as real entities and their need for self-development. But once this principle is admitted it knows no bounds till the entire mankind is enveloped by the practical application of this idea of cooperation as a means to progress. Nationalism, like religion, is essentially a divisive force which generally thrives on hatred or enmity and therefore should find no place in the idea of progress. Any organisation being a means to an end, the ideal, according to Roy, should be to strive for a cosmopolitan-universal society composed of men who are recognised as individuals and not merely as nationals.

Further, Roy stands for a federal type of world state. He believes that only a federal set up can reconcile local variety, general uniformity, and can harmonise world authority and local individuality, power and freedom, unity and multiplicity. But the idea of one world or a world government is not compatible with continuation of nation-states. The one makes of the other a pious desire or wishful thinking."[129] According to Roy, the federal relationship is not incompatible with the widest extension of local self-government, with cultural autonomy and with all that is essential for the advancement of local groups. Under the world federation, as envisaged by Roy, all peoples as cooperative communities will live on terms of equality, freedom and friendship and will not interfere with the legitimate and peaceful aspirations of one another. However, Roy does not offer a detailed scheme of such an organisation and confines himself to suggesting only a few guiding principles.

ROY AND THE PROBLEM OF PEACE

Since any practical and constructive scheme of world unity depends on the elimination of interstate conflicts, the foremost problem is the problem of peace.

Taking into consideration the fact that "wars begin in the minds of men, it is in the minds of men that the defences of peace should be constructed. Roy, therefore, urges that a vigorous movement for peace must be launched. The fact that no country wants another world war will help this movement for peace. Roy, however, is of the opinion that the leadership of the movement which is needed is moral and idealistic rather than political and pragmatic. Detached individuals who are apprehensive of traditionally cherished values being destroyed in the scramble for power to rule and dominate the world, must come forward as the bold defenders of freedom and culture. Thus, the movement for defence and peace must be organised non-officially. The initiative can be taken by the non-officials in each single country. They must roundly condemn war waged on any pretext or even with the most plausible justification as a relic of barbarism."[130] The task is to build a clear and articulate sentiment against war and launch what Roy called "an aggression for peace" among over increasing number of men and women. It should be brought home to the minds of the people that wars in our days can possibly serve no other purpose than the destruction of life and liberty, moral degradation and cultural brutalisation. Our hope lies in the fact that the world is gradually getting immune to the insanity of the belief that wars can solve the problems of today.

The corollary to this movement is a powerful opposition to the mad race for military preparation through propaganda in the defence of peace. People should be convinced of the enormity of the cost of war in terms of material loss and human suffering. They should be made aware that war as an instrument of national policy has become an obsolete weapon and is considered unviable.

Roy believed that "a cosmopolitan commonwealth of free men and women is a distinct possibility. It will be a spiritual community not limited by the boundaries of national states which will gradually disappear under the impact of cosmopolitan humanism." "That is the Radical perspective of the future of mankind."[131]

CONCLUSION — CONTRIBUTIONS OF M.N. ROY

Having examined Roy's analysis and understanding of the modern crisis in human affairs one can only be impressed by his serious attempt in developing a philosophy of life to overcome that crisis. The belief in the possibility of a secular rational morality, which Roy particularly emphasised upon, opens up a new perspective before the modern world. It makes the time honoured concepts of men's dignity, personality, sovereignty and creativeness full of meaning and makes this self-realisation restore man's confidence in himself. This, perhaps, is one of the most important contributions of Roy to social thought.

Another notable contribution of Roy lies in his attempt to make a synthesis between history of material progress and dynamics of ideas. Roy maintains that both run on parallel lines and are continually influencing each other, new ideas leading to new material developments, and material developments giving rise to new ideas. Thus, Roy's historiography offers a comprehensive theory of social change in which both economic forces and dynamics of ideas find their due recognition, and this is a definite improvement on the historiography of both Hegel and Marx.

Since the object of social philosophy and of political and economic theories, according to Roy, is to facilitate the creation of a society of free, rational and moral men and women, the appropriate political and economic institutions that he suggests are 'organised democracy' and 'cooperative economy'. Radical democracy that Roy advocates aspires to bridge the gulf between the state and society by drawing the entire society in the administration of state affairs so as to make both coterminus.

According to Roy's scheme, the state is organised from below, like a pyramidal structure based on local people's committees so that people may actively participate in the day to day affairs of the government.

Furthermore, Roy's plan of organised democracy without political parties is a definite contribution to the art and technique of government. Perhaps, Roy was the first political thinker who conceived and developed the idea of a partyless democracy and suggested a political system in which political parties could be dispensed with.

Further, Roy believed that a truly democratic order can be built largely around the principle of cooperation, where the workers will also be the owners of particular units. He suggests a cooperative system of economy as the most suitable institution for solving the economic problems of our time.

Moreover, rejecting both parliamentary democracy and competitive or market-friendly economy, on the one hand, and political dictatorship and centralised planning, on the other, Radical Humanism offers a concrete programme for the construction of a new political and economic order which attaches supreme importance to the freedom and initiative of the individual.

Roy further insists that appropriate democratic institutions can be created only when the spirit of democracy permeates the people. He rejects the dogma that cultural improvement will automatically follow institutional changes. Therefore he suggests that a philosophical revolution must precede any political and economic revolution, just as thought precedes action. Besides, he also pleads for the development of a cosmopolitan society of free men and women. He thinks that his cosmopolitan philosophy can be realised only in a world state, in a universal brotherhood, in a cooperative commonwealth, embracing the whole human race. Radical Humanism, thus, is a supranational pan-human philosophy of universal relevance; it is the philosophical counterpart of planetary patriotism and cosmopolitan concern.

But it is to be noted that no closed system of thought is presented by M.N. Roy, His philosophy is scientific and dynamic in character. It does not lay down any horoscope for humanity, like Marx. It knows no dogma and respects no authority — supernatural, scriptural or human. It is prepared to enrich its contents with the advancement of human knowledge. Though there is nothing altogether new in his philosophy but by summing up the current trends of thought, Roy constructed a philosophical system which has acquired a character of its own. His system of thought tries to bring to a common focus the element of rationalist renaissance, physical-realist cosmology, humanistic ethics and a passionate quest for freedom. One finds in his political philosophy a glimpse of the boldness and profoundity of Plato, the dedication to learning and the search for truth of Aristotle, the compassion for the common man and the comprehensive canvas of Karl Marx and consistency and logical coherence of Hobbes. In short, it is a synthetic philosophy exhibiting the influence of thinkers from Thales to Marx.

But not philosophy is perfect, absolute or infallible, and Roy's philosophy is no exception. It does suffer from certain short-comings which the author has already pinpointed topic-wise in the preceding chapters. Admittedly, some of his ideas do appear as utopian at the first instance. Though a visionary, Roy was aware of this fact, but believed that human progress consists only in realising one utopian idea after another. Is it not a fact that the utopia of today is only a reality of tomorrow ? Roy believed that what is theoretically sound and logically correct is bound to become real one day.

ESTIMATE OF M.N. ROY — AS A MAN OF POLITICS AND POLITICAL THOUGHT

Inspite of his remarkable intellectual power, strong personality and almost legendary career, Roy failed to capture the imagination of Indian people. Roy eventually failed in the game of politics. But at the same time, he was eminently successful in the realm of ideas. As a matter of fact, Roy looked upon politics not as art of the possible but as a search for truth. For Roy, the politician, this search for truth proved to be disastrous, but for Roy, the philosopher, it was his great strength and achievement. However, the greatness of a human being is not to be measured in the end by his success during his life time but by the grandeur of his endeavour. "Even if Roy was a failure, his failures, whatever their nature, were not due so much to either his being wrong in his crucial judgements, or to his being out of touch with realities, as has been often alleged, but to the fact that he was far, far ahead of his times, of his surroundings and of this contemporaries."[132]

Writing about Roy, V.M. Tarkunde states, "he was a prophet of a new order, he could not be leader of the old,"[133] and this is the reason why the relevance of his thought is gaining more and more acceptance at the present moment. He is bound to be heard more and more as history moves forward towards the 'third revolution'.

MESSAGE OF M.N. ROY

Unlike other thinkers of modern India, Roy was never a captive of the past, He believed that a captive of the past can never conquer the future. In India's Message' he wrote: "A critical examination of what is characterised as India's cultural heritage will enable the Indian people to cast off the chilly grip of a dead past. It will embolden them to face the ugly realities of a living present and to look forward to a better, brighter and pleasanter future."[134] In the opinion of this author, this is a very noteworthy message of Roy.

To conclude, "in the diversity and enrichness of his revolutionary experience, Roy had few peers in this century and that his more influential and well-known contemporaries — Lenin, Mao, Gandhi and Nehru did not have quite the sweep of trans-continental range of his direct political praxis."[135] To be sure, M.N. Roy was the most learned, the most original and the most prolific (as a writer) among the political thinkers of the modern India and also the most colourful and fascinating among our freedom fighters. He occupies a secure place among the seminal thinkers of the twentieth century.

M.N. ROY AND GANDHI — A COMPARATIVE ASSESSMENT

Perhaps, no two thinkers of modern India were alike as well as unlike each other as were Roy and Gandhi. Paradoxically, despite adopting different approaches and having divergent premises and perceptions, the conclusions they arrived at were almost the same.

For a long time Roy had been aggressively critical of Gandhi. Particularly in the early phase of his political career, Roy was a devastating detractor of Gandhi. His instant disapproval of the Mahatma might have been an emotional hangover of his nationalist-revolutionary phase which was reinforced in the Marxian phase that followed it. In his Marxian interpretation, Gandhism seemed to Roy to be restraining the politically revolutionary movement by a reactionary ideology. But by late thirties there was a perceptible change in Roy's attitude towards Gandhi. In 1938, Roy discovered the greatness of Gandhi in is role as a political awakener of the Indian masses. Again, in 1948, while paying tributes in his obituary article, 'The Message of the Mahatma', Roy pin-pointed four messages of Gandhi that impressed him most: (1) Rejection of the intolerant collective ego; (2) The relevance of morality in politics. (3) Ends and Means relationship; and (4) Cosmopolitan humanism.[136]

Interestingly, both Gandhi and Roy were initiated in practical politics not in India but abroad. "Roy was a master strategist but Gandhi had an edge over him as a master tactician. The Mahatma was a shrewd compromiser (on non-essentials), but Roy was an utter non-compromiser."[137] However, both looked upon politics not as art of the possible but as a search for truth. Both rejected amoral politics and believed in valuational foundation of politics. With Gandhi, Roy came to share the view that the means are as important as the ends. Because of their bold thinking and courage of conviction, both had to swim incessantly against the current and popular sentiment, and because of their non-conformism if one had to live in wilderness most of the time, the other had to meet his end at the hands of an assassin. To be sure, both had exceptional qualities of courage and commitment which enabled them to play the role they did; both were genuine individuals, outstanding in their fearlessness. They followed their own convictions as the only lode-star and maintained intellectual integrity throughout their life. In fact, intellectual integrity was the hallmark of their personalities. But in the final analyses, both emerged as lonely .souls, towering yet alone, admired yet followed by few.

On political and economic matters, Roy and Gandhi showed as much agreement as disagreement. While for Gandhi. "The state by its very nature, is an instrument of coercion and violence. It was rooted in violence, as it originated in an essentially violent society. Hence in an ideal nonviolent society it will become unnecessary. But for Roy, on the other hand, the state is a political organisation of society;" it is an essential and purposeful institution; its purpose is to protect the people from the violence of power and anarchy, and to create foundations of their progress; it plays a significant role of an umpire and coordinator. Hence, "the ideal of a stateless society is obviously an absurd utopia,"[138] according to Roy. Yet, both Roy and Gandhi argued that the state should have limited power. Both were against concentration of power and favoured decentralisation in every field, political, economic and social.

Similarly, both Gandhi and Roy were dissatisfied with parliamentary democracy or representative system of government and were critical of its defects — its formalism its atomisation of the individual, etc. and favoured participatory democracy in its place. Both wanted the organisation of the local community to be the real seats of all authority. If Gandhi pleaded for "Gram Swaraj', Roy was for 'People's Committees'. Both considered political parties unnecessary and even harmful.

In the economic sphere, both Gandhi and Roy rejected the concept of a laissez faire economy as well as state socialism. But the alternative system of economy that they suggested had nothing in common. While Roy stood for cooperative economy, Gandhi was for trustee-capitalism.

No doubt, there were many similarities between the philosophies of Gandhi and Roy, but the differences were also significant and apparent. For instance, in their metaphysical views Gandhi and Roy, were antithesis of each other. If Roy was a thorough-going materialist and a confirmed atheist, Gandhi was an out and out spiritualist and a highly religious person, with abiding faith in God. If Roy believed in reason and science and had a modern outlook, Gandhi placed faith above reason and gave preference to intuition or "inner voice" over science and logic. While for Gandhi, religion was a unifying force, and it was believed to play a purifying role in politics, for Roy, religion was a divisive force and was most likely to communalise politics. Again, Roy was a secularist in the Western sense, but, according to him, "Secularism is not a political institution, it is a cultural atmosphere and it cannot be created by the proclamation of individuals or by constitutional provisions." Further, in the opinion of Roy, the state had nothing to do with religion, but in the view of Gandhi, the concept of secularism means Sarva Dharma Samabhava. Although, Gandhi's secularism was given a fair trial and it came to grief in the end, Roy's secularism is yet to be given a trial. Philosophically a materialist, Roy outrightly rejects metaphysical and religious basis of Gandhism.

Furthermore, while Gandhi was opposed to massive mechanisation and large scale industrialisation, and even gave the slogan of back to the village economy of the old, Roy, on the contrary, appreciated the advancement of the scientific knowledge and technology. He even advocated that the economy should take full advantage of modern science and technology and effect an equitable distribution of social surplus through universal social utility services.

In the technique of reconstruction, Gandhi and Roy, had a common approach. Both believed that unless man is changed any social structure cannot bring any good. Hence, both suggested that the remaking of man must precede the remaking of society. Thus, "they had much in common both in their criticism of modern societies and trends and their proposed alternatives."

To conclude, Roy and Gandhi were the two greatest thinkers of modern India. If Roy, with his brilliant mind, was an intellectual giant, Gandhi, with his deep feelings, was an emotional colossus, If Roy was gifted with an amazing power of analysis and clairvoyance, Gandhi was endowed with deep and holistic insight and prophetic vision. If Roy's mind always moved on the right track, Gandhi's heart was always on the right place. If Roy was logically sound, Gandhi was instinctively correct. "If Gandhi's appeal was to the heart, Roy's appeal was to the mind. If Gandhi was the spiritual conscience of India, Roy was certainly its intellectual conscience."[139] Eventually, what brought them to a common point, despite their diverse paths, was their common commitment to man, one rationally and the other from some deep emotional convictions. Thus, "we find that inspite of their diametrically opposite premises, the gulf between Roy and Gandhi is not unbridgeable, and their approach to social and political issues are rather amazingly similar. Individual freedom and the sovereignty of man were equally dear to them. Both advocated maximum decentralisation of power and organised democracy and establishment of a moral order. Both swear by humanism, had faith in the unbounded capacity of human beings, in the unfoldment of human personality, and in the dignity of mankind."[140] Indeed, it was a great misfortune for India, that Roy and Gandhi could not join hands and share a common platform in the freedom struggle for India's independence.

Notes

1. Karklekar, Hiranmay, "A Rebel Thinker', Indian Express, 23 March, 1987

2. Mitra, P.C., Illustrated Weekly, 8 March 1977

3. Roy's, M.N., 'Memoirs' The Radical Humanist Weekly, 1 Feb. 1953

4. Innaiah, N., "Evelyn Leonora Trent,' Radical Humanist, June 1995

5. Roy; s M.N. 'Memoirs,' The Radical Humansit Weekly, 1 Feb. 1953

6. Roy's M.N. 'Memoirs,' The Radical Humanist, Weekly, 30 August, 1953.

7. Roy, M.N., India In Transition, op.cit, p.241.

8. Caarr, E.H., Bolshevik Revolution, Vol, 3, p. 252.

9. Ibid., p.480

10. Verma, V.P., op.cit., p.437

11. Ibid., p. 438

12. Roy, M.N., Revolution And Counter Revolution In China, 1946, p. 538

13. Ibid., p. 538

14. Brandt And Others, A Documentary History of Chinese Communism, 1952, p.92

15. Snow, Edgar, Red Star Over China, 1937, p. 161

16. Roy, M.N., Our Differences, 1938, Preface page III

17. Roy, M.N., War and Revolution, 1942, p. 20

18. Roy, M.N., Freedom Or Fascism, 1942, p. 105

19. Karlekar, Hiranmay, A Rebel Thinker, Indian Express, 23 March, 1987

20. Roy, M.N., and Spratt, Philip, Beyond Communism, Renaissance Publishers, Calcuta, 1947, p. 58

21. Roy, M.N., 'The Concept of Causality 'In Modern Science' The Humanist Way, Vol. IV, (1949-50), p. 162

22. Roy, M.N., Materialism, 1951, p.148

23. Ibid., p. 233

24. Ibid., p. 163

25. Ibid., p. 163

26. Roy, M.N., Editorial Notes, The Marxian Way, Vol. II, No. 4, (1946-47), pp. 356-57

27. Ibid. p. 359

28. Ibid., p. 362

29. ibid., p. 362

30. Ibd., p. 361

31. Roy, M.N., Science And Philosophy, 1947, p. 195

32. Ibid., p. 198

33. Ibid., pp. 205-206

34. Roy, M.N., Materialism, op.cit, p. 204.

35. Roy, M.N., Science And Philosophy, op.cit, p. 70

36. Roy, S.N., Radicalism, 1946, pp. 75-76

37. Ibid., p. 77

38. Roy, M.N., Radical Humanism, published by Economics Pamphlets Editor, E.P.W. daCosta (1952). p.9

39. Ibid., p. 16

40. Ibid., pp. 16-17

41. Rossi, Mario, A Plea For Man, 1956, p. 135

42. Roy, M.N., 'The Humanist Way', The Radical Humansit weekly, 29 May 1949

43. Roy and Spratt, Beyond Communism, op.cit, p.70

44. Ibid., p. 73

45. Engels, Frederick, Anti Duhring (Translated by Emile Burns) Vol. I, 1934, p. 108

46. Roy, M.N., New Humanism: A Manifesto, Renaissance Publisher, Calcutta (1947), p. 28

47. Ibid, p. 28

48. Mumford, Lewis, The Conduct of Man, 1944, p. 338

49. Roy & Spratt, Beyond Communist, op. cit, p. 73

50. Roy, M.N., Radical Humanism, op.cit, p. 18

51. See Bhattacharjee, G.P., Evolution of Political Philosophy of M.N. Roy, Minvarva Publication, Calcutta, 1971

52. Haldar, M.K., The Radical Humanist, 17 Nov. 1971, p. 46

53. Roy, M.N., 'Human Nature; The Marxian Way, Vol. III No. I 1947-48, p. 49

54. Roy, M.N., Heresies of The Twentieth Century, 1939, p. 166

55. Venable, Human Natue; Marxian View, 1946, p. 33

56. Roy, M.N., Human Nature, op.cit, 50

57. Ibid., p. 59

58. Ibid., p. 59

59. Dewey, John, Human Nature And Conduct, 1930, p.2

60. Roy, M.N., Radical Humanism, op.cit, p. 17

61. Roy, M.N. (ed.), Man and Nature, 1940, p. 8 (Introduction)

62. Ridley, G.N., Man: The Verdict of Science, (1946), p. 89

63. Roy, M.N. (ed.), Man and Nature, op.cit, p. 8

64. Cohen, Chapman, A Grammar of Free Thought, 1921, p. 185

65. Roy, M.N. (ed.) Man and Nature, op.cit, p. 9

66. Roy, M.N., Reason, Romanticism And Revolution, Vol. I, Renaissance Publishers, 1952, p.212

67. Roy, M.N., New Humanism, Renaissance Publishers, Calcutta Second Edition, 1953, p.26

68. Sabine, A History of Political Theory, 1948, p. 591

69. Rocker, Rudolf, Nationalism And Culture, 1937, p.195

70. Schumpeter Joseph A., Capitalism, Socialism And Democracy, George Attenand Unwin Ltd. London (1952) p. 56

71. Roy, M.N., Radical Humanism, op.cit, p.2

72. Hook, Sidney, from Hegel To Marx, 1936, p. 141

73. Roy, M.N., Reason, Romanticism And Revolution, op.cit, p. 10

74. Mumford, Lewis, The Conduct Of Life, 1952, p.225

75. Roy, Ellen And Ray, S.N., In Men's Own Image, 1948, p. 120

76. Ibid., pp. 121-22

77. Ibid., pp. 122-23

78. Ray, S.N., Radicalism, op.cit, p. 49

79. Roy, M.N., Beyond Communism, op.cit, p. 146

80. Ibid., p.147

81. Ibid., p.148

82. Ibid., p. 149.

83. Roy, M.N,, 'Our Creed, 'Radical Humanist, Weekly, I Feb. 1953

84. Roy, M.N., 'Philosophy of History,' The Marxian Way, vol.II, 1946-47, p. 256

85. Roy, M.N., Beyond Communism, op.cit. pp.51-52

86. Roy, M.N,., Reason Romanticism And Revolution, op.cit, p.-3

87. Roy & Spratt, Beyond Communism, op.cit, p. 57.

88. Ibid., p.111

89. Ibid., p. 150

90. Roy, M.N., 'New Humanism', The Radical Humanist, Weekly 8 April, 1956.

91. Roy, M.N. 'Radical Humanism; op.cit. p.20

92. Ibid., pp.21-22

93. M.N.Roy qutoed in Bhagwan Vishnu, op.cit, p.196

94. Roy, M.N., Reason, Romanticims And Revolution, Vol. II, op.cit, p.277

95. Roy, M.N, Radical Humanism, op.cit, pp.22-23

96. Roy, M.N., New Humanism, op.cit, p.29

97. Bhattacharjee, G.P., op.cit, pp. 182-83

98. Roy, M.N., Radical Humanism, op.cit, p.23

99. Ibid., p.24

100. Ibid., p.25

101. Ibid., p. 25

102. Ibid., pp.25-26

103. Bryce, Modern Democracies, Vol.II, 1921, p.28

104. Roy, M.N., Radical Humanism, op.cit, pp.29-30

105. Ibid., p.30

106. Ibid., p.33

107. Ibid., p.40

108. Thesis-17 of Twenty Two Theses of Radical Humanism adopted by the Radical Democratic Party, Dec. 1946

109. Mukharjee, Nirmal, M.N. Roy's Quest For Morality in Politics and Social Life', Radical Humanist, April 1994 p. 21

110. Roy, Ellen And Ray, S.N., In Man's own Image, op.cit, pp.205-06

111. Roy, M.N., New Humanism, op.cit, p.31

112. Ibid., p.32

113. Thesis-10 of Twenty Theses of Radical Humanism, op.cit.

114. Roy, M.N., Foreward To People's plan, 1944.

115. Dalvi, G.R., 'An Essay On Cooperative Economy, Humanist Way, Vol. IV No. IV, pp. 49-50

116. Dalvi, G.R., New Economic Orientation, The Radical Humanist, Weekly, 7 May 1950. p.330

117. Ibid. p.333

118. Roy, M.N., 'Cooperative Economy,' The Radical Humanist Weekly, 30 Dec., 1950.

119. Roy, M.N., Radical Humanism, op.cit, p. 54

120. Dalvi, G.R., 'New Economic Orientation,' op.cit, p. 336

121. Ray, S.N., Philosophy of Radicalism, The Marxian Way, Vol. II, 1946-47, pp. 142-43.

122. Roy, M.N., 'Our Creed', op.cit, The Radical Humanist Weekly, 1 Feb. 1953.

123. Ray, S.N., Philosophy of Radicalism, op.cit, p. 145.

124. Ibid., p.146

125. Roy, M.N., Humanist, Politics, The Radical Humanist weekly, 12 Feb. 1956,

126. Thesis-15, op.cit.

127. Roy, M.N., Nationalism, 1942, p.VII

128. Schwarzenberger, George, Power Politics, 1951, p.17

129. Roy, M.N., New Humanism, op.cit, p.50

130. Roy, M.N., Aggression For Peace, Thought, Delhi weekly 10 Nov. 1950

131. Roy, M.N., New Humanism, op.cit., p. 50

132. Introduction, A. Souvenir on M.N. Roy's Birth Centenary 1987

133. Tarkunde, V.M., Introduction to souvenir, op.cit,

134. Roy. M.N., India's Message, Ajanta Publication (1982) Jacket of The Book.

135. Ray, S.N., Selected Works of M.N.Roy, Vol. I. 1987, p. 3

136. Kundu, Rama, Roy and Gandhi, The Radical Humanist, Monthly, June 1988.

137. Wadia, J.B.S., M.N.Roy: The man, Popular Prakashan, Bombay, (1983), p.108

138. Roy, M.N., Politics, Power and Parties, op.cit, p.73

139. Wadia, J.B.S., op.cit, p.114

140. Saxena, Kiran, Modern Indian Political Thought, Chiki Publication, 1978, Preface p.VI

INDEX